WAR

WHAT IS IT GOOD FOR?

THE ROLE OF CONFLICT
IN CIVILISATION, FROM
PRIMATES TO ROBOTS

IAN MORRIS

IAN MORRIS is Willard Professor of Classics and a fellow of the Archaeology Centre at Stanford University. He has appeared on a number of television networks, including the History Network and PBS and has directed excavations in Greece and Italy. His first trade book *Why the West Rules— For Now* was published to critical acclaim and won a number of prizes including a PEN USA Literary Award. Morris's second book *The Measure of Civilisation*, a companion volume to his first, was praised as a "treasure trove of information about social development".

CONTENTS

ILLUSTRATIONS

WAR

WHAT IS IT GOOD FOR?

INTRODUCTION: FRIEND TO
THE UNDERTAKER

I was twenty-three when I almost died in battle.

It was September 26, 1983, around 9:30 in the evening. I was hunched over a manual typewriter in a rented room in Cambridge, England, pounding out the first chapter of my PhD thesis in archaeology. I had just come back from four months of fieldwork in the Greek islands. My work was going well. I was in love. Life was good.

I had no idea that two thousand miles away, Stanislav Petrov was deciding whether to kill me.

Petrov was the deputy chief for combat algorithms at Serpukhov-15, the nerve center of the Soviet Union's early-warning system. He was a methodical man, an engineer, a writer of computer code—and not, fortunately for me, a man given to panic. But when the siren went off a little after midnight (Moscow time), even Petrov leaped out of his chair. A red bulb blinked into life on the giant map of the Northern Hemisphere that filled one wall of the control room. It signaled that a missile had been launched from Montana.

Above the map, red letters came to life, spelling out the worst word Petrov knew: "LAUNCH."

Computers checked and double-checked their data. Again the red lights flashed, this time with more certainty: "LAUNCH—HIGH RELIABILITY."

In a way, Petrov had been expecting this day to come. Six months earlier, Ronald Reagan had denounced Mother Russia as an evil empire. He had threatened that the Americans would build a space-based antimissile shield, ending the mutual balance of terror that had kept the peace for nearly forty years. And then he had announced that he would speed up the deployment of new missiles, able to hit Moscow with just a five-minute flight. Next, as if to mock the Soviet Union's vulnerability, a South Korean airliner had strayed over Siberia, apparently lost. It took the Soviet air force several hours to find it, and then, as the plane was finally making its way back to neutral airspace, a fighter shot it down. Everyone on board died—including a U.S. congressman. Now, the screen was saying, the imperialists had taken the final step.

And yet . . . Petrov knew that this was not what World War III should look like. An American first strike ought to involve a thousand Minuteman missiles roaring over the North Pole. It should mean an incoming inferno of fire and radiation, a frenzied, all-out effort to destroy the Soviet missiles as they sat in their silos, leaving Moscow with no way to respond. Launching a single missile was insane.

Petrov's job was to follow the rules, to run all the mandated tests for malfunctions, but there was no time for any of that. He had to decide whether the world was about to end.

He picked up the phone. "I am reporting to you," he said to the duty officer on the other end. He tried to sound matter-of-fact. "This is a false alarm."

The duty officer asked no questions, betrayed no anxiety. "Got it."

A moment later, the siren was turned off. Petrov's staff began to relax. The technicians turned to their prescribed routines, systematically searching the circuits for errors. But then—

"LAUNCH."

The red word was back. A second light appeared on the map; another missile was on its way.

And then another bulb lit up. And another, and another, until the entire map seemed to be burning red. The algorithms that Petrov had helped to write now took over. For a moment, the panel above the map went dark. Then it flashed back into life with a new warning. It was announcing the apocalypse.

"MISSILE ATTACK."

The Soviet Union's biggest supercomputer automatically sent this message up the chain of command. Every second now counted. The aging, ailing Yuri Andropov, General Secretary of the Communist Party of the Soviet Union, was about to be asked to make the most important decision of all time.

You may not be very interested in war, Trotsky is supposed to have said, but war is very interested in you. Cambridge was—and still is—a sleepy university town, far from the seats of power. In 1983, though, it was ringed by air force bases, high on Moscow's list of targets. If the Soviet General Staff had believed Petrov's algorithms, I would have been dead within fifteen minutes, vaporized in a fireball hotter than the surface of the sun. King's College and its choir, the cows grazing as punts drifted by, the scholars in their gowns passing the port at High Table—all would have been blasted into radioactive dust.

If the Soviets had launched only the missiles that they were pointing at military targets (what strategists called a counterforce attack), and if the United States had responded in kind, I would have been one of roughly a hundred million people blown apart, burned up, and poisoned on the first day of the war. But that is probably not what would have happened. Just three months before Petrov's moment of truth, the U.S. Strategic Concepts Development Center had run a war game to see how the opening stages of a nuclear exchange might go. They found that no player managed to draw the line at counterforce attacks. In every case, they escalated to countervalue attacks, firing on cities as well as silos. And when that happened, the first few days' death toll rose to around half a billion, with fallout, starvation, and further fighting killing another half billion in the weeks and months that followed.

Back in the real world, however, Petrov did draw a line. He later admitted to having been so scared that his legs gave way under him, but he still trusted his instincts over his algorithms. Going with his gut, he told the duty officer that this too was a false alarm. The missile attack message was stopped before it worked its way up the chain of command. Twelve thousand Soviet warheads stayed in their silos; a billion of us lived to fight another day.

Petrov's reward for saving the world, however, was not a chestful of medals. It was an official reprimand for submitting messy paperwork and failing to follow protocols (it was the General Secretary's job to decide whether to destroy the planet, not his). He was shuffled sideways to a less sensitive position. From there he took early retirement, had a nervous breakdown, and sank into grim poverty as the Soviet Union fell to pieces and stopped paying its old-age pensioners.*

---

*In 2004 the San Francisco–based Association of World Citizens awarded Petrov a redwood plaque thanking him for saving the world and gave him a check for $1,000, and in 2013 he also won Germany's Dresden Prize, which comes with €25,000. Further contributions can be made at www.brightstarsound.com.

A world like this—in which Armageddon hung on shoddy engineering and the snap judgments of computer programmers—had surely gone mad. Plenty of people at the time thought so. Within the American alliance, where people were free to do such things, millions marched to ban the bomb, or protested against their governments' aggression, or voted for politicians who promised unilateral disarmament. On the Soviet side, where people were not free to do such things, a few more dissidents than usual took a stand and were betrayed to the secret police.

But none of it made much difference. Western leaders were returned to office with increased majorities and bought even more advanced weapons; Soviet leaders built even more missiles. In 1986 the world's stockpile of nuclear warheads reached its all-time high of more than seventy thousand, and the meltdown of the Soviet nuclear reactor at Chernobyl gave a tiny taste of what might be in store.

People cried out for answers, and on both sides of the Iron Curtain the young turned away from aging, compromised politicians toward louder voices. Speaking for a new post-baby-boom generation, Bruce Springsteen took the greatest of the Vietnam-era protest songs—Edwin Starr's Motown classic "War"—and sent a supercharged cover version back into the top ten:

> *War!*
> *Huh, good God.*
> *What is it good for?*
> *Absolutely nothing.*
> *Say it, say it, say it . . .*
>
> *Oooh, war! I despise*
> *Because it means destruction*
> *Of innocent lives*
> *War means tears*
> *To thousands of mothers' eyes*
> *When their sons go to fight*
> *And lose their lives . . .*
>
> *War!*
> *It ain't nothing but a heartbreaker.*
> *War!*
> *Friend only to the undertaker . . .*

*Peace for Our Time**

In this book, I want to disagree. Up to a point, anyway.

War, I will suggest, has not been a friend to the undertaker. War is mass murder, and yet, in perhaps the greatest paradox in history, war has nevertheless been the undertaker's worst enemy. Contrary to what the song says, war *has* been good for something: over the long run, it has made humanity safer and richer. War is hell, but—again, over the long run—the alternatives would have been worse.

This will be a controversial claim, so let me explain what I mean.

There are four parts to the case I will make. The first is that by fighting wars, people have created larger, more organized societies that have reduced the risk that their members will die violently.

This observation rests on one of the major findings of archaeologists and anthropologists over the last century, that Stone Age societies were typically tiny. Chiefly because of the challenges of finding food, people lived in bands of a few dozen, villages of a few hundred, or (very occasionally) towns of a few thousand members. These communities did not need much in the way of internal organization and tended to live on terms of suspicion or even hostility with outsiders.

People generally worked out their differences peacefully, but if someone decided to use force, there were far fewer constraints on him—or, occasionally, her—than the citizens of modern states are used to. Most of the killing was on a small scale, in vendettas and incessant raiding, although once in a while violence might disrupt an entire band or village so badly that disease and starvation wiped all its members out. But because populations were also small, the steady drip of low-level violence took an appalling toll. By most estimates, 10 to 20 percent of all the people who lived in Stone Age societies died at the hands of other humans.

The twentieth century forms a sharp contrast. It saw two world wars, a string of genocides, and multiple government-induced famines, killing a staggering total of somewhere between 100 million and 200 million people. The atomic bombs dropped on Hiroshima and Nagasaki killed more than 150,000 people—probably more people than had lived in the entire world

---

*It is the kind of detail that only a professor could care about, but peace *for* our time— not peace *in* our time—is what Neville Chamberlain actually said he was bringing home from Munich in 1938.

in 50,000 B.C. But in 1945, there were about 2.5 billion people on earth, and over the course of the twentieth century roughly 10 billion lives were lived—meaning that the century's 100–200 million war-related deaths added up to just 1 to 2 percent of our planet's population. If you were lucky enough to be born in the industrialized twentieth century, you were on average ten times *less* likely to die violently (or from violence's consequences) than if you were born in a Stone Age society.

This may be a surprising statistic, but the explanation for it is more surprising still. What has made the world so much safer is war itself. The way this worked, I will try to show in Chapters 1–5, was that beginning about ten thousand years ago in some parts of the world, then spreading across the planet, the winners of wars incorporated the losers into larger societies. The only way to make these larger societies work was for their rulers to develop stronger governments, and one of the first things these governments had to do, if they wanted to stay in power, was suppress violence within the society.

The men who ran these governments hardly ever pursued policies of peacemaking purely out of the goodness of their hearts. They cracked down on killing because well-behaved subjects were easier to govern and tax than angry, murderous ones. The unintended consequence, though, was that rates of violent death fell by 90 percent between Stone Age times and the twentieth century.

The process was not pretty. Whether it was the Romans in Britain or the British in India, pacifiers could be just as brutal as the savagery they stamped out. Nor was the process smooth: for short periods in particular places, violent death could spike back up to Stone Age levels. Between 1914 and 1918, for instance, nearly one Serb in six died from violence, disease, or starvation. And, of course, not all governments were equally good at delivering peace. Democracies may be messy, but they rarely devour their children; dictatorships get things done, but they tend to shoot, starve, and gas a lot of people. And yet despite all the variations, qualifications, and exceptions, over the ten-thousand-year-long run, war made governments, and governments made peace.

My second claim is that while war is the worst imaginable way to create larger, more peaceful societies, it is pretty much the only way humans have found. "Lord knows, there's got to be a better way," Edwin Starr sang, but apparently there isn't. If the Roman Empire could have been created without killing millions of Gauls and Greeks, if the United States could have been built without killing millions of Native Americans—in these cases and countless others, if conflicts could have been resolved by discussion instead of force, humanity could have had the benefits of larger societies without paying such a high cost. But that did not happen. It is a depressing thought, but the evidence again seems clear. People hardly ever give up their freedom, including their rights to kill and impoverish each other, unless forced to do so, and virtually the only force strong enough to bring this about has been defeat in war or fear that such a defeat is imminent.

If I am right that governments have made us safer and that war is pretty much the only way we have discovered to make governments, then we have to conclude that war really has been good for something. My third conclusion, though, goes further still. As well as making people safer, I will suggest, the larger societies created by war have also—again, over the long run—made us richer. Peace created the conditions for economic growth and rising living standards. This process too has been messy and uneven: the winners of wars regularly go on rampages of rape and plunder, selling thousands of survivors into slavery and stealing their land. The losers may be left impoverished for generations. It is a terrible, ugly business. And yet, with the passage of time—maybe decades, maybe centuries—the creation of a bigger society tends to make *everyone*, the descendants of victors and vanquished alike, better-off. The long-term pattern is again unmistakable. By creating larger societies, stronger governments, and greater security, war has enriched the world.

When we put these three claims together, only one conclusion is possible. War has produced bigger societies, ruled by stronger governments, which have imposed peace and created the preconditions for prosperity. Ten thousand years ago, there were only about six million people on earth. On average they lived about thirty years and supported themselves on the equivalent of less than two modern American dollars per day. Now there are more than a thousand times as many of us (seven billion, in fact), living more than twice as long (the global average is sixty-seven years) and earning more than a dozen times as much (today the global average is $25 per day).

War, then, has been good for something—so good, in fact, that my fourth argument is that war is now putting itself out of business. For millennia, war (over the long run) has created peace, and destruction has created wealth, but in our own age humanity has gotten so good at fighting—our weapons so destructive, our organizations so efficient—that war is beginning to make further war of this kind impossible. Had events gone differently that night in 1983—had Petrov panicked, had the General Secretary actually pushed the button, and had a billion of us been killed over the next few weeks—the twentieth century's rate of violent death would have soared back into Stone Age territory, and had the toxic legacy of all those warheads been as terrible as some scientists feared, by now there might have been no humans left at all.

The good news is not just that this didn't happen but also that it was frankly never very likely to happen. I will return to the reasons why in Chapter 6, but the basic point is that we humans have proved remarkably good at adapting to our changing environment. We fought countless wars in the past because fighting paid off, but in the twentieth century, as the returns to violence declined, we found ways to solve our problems without bringing on Armageddon. There are no guarantees, of course, but in the final chapter of this book I will suggest that there are nevertheless grounds for hope that we will continue avoiding this outcome. The twenty-first century is going to see astounding changes in everything, including the role of violence. The age-old dream of a world without war may yet come to pass—although what that world will look like is another matter altogether.

Stating these arguments so baldly has probably set off all kinds of warning bells. What, you might well wonder, do I mean by "wars," and how can I know how many people died in them? What am I counting as a "society," and how can I tell when one is getting bigger? And what, for that matter, constitutes a "government," and how do we measure how strong one is? These are all good questions, and as my story unfolds, I will try to answer them.

It is my central argument, however, that war has made the world safer, which will probably raise most eyebrows. This book is being published in 2014, exactly a hundred years since World War I broke out in 1914 and seventy-five since World War II erupted in 1939. The two conflicts left 100 million dead—surely enough to make marking their anniversaries with a book saying that war has made us safer seem like a sick joke. But 2014 is also the twenty-fifth anniversary of the end of the Cold War in 1989, which freed the world from reruns of Petrov's nightmare. I shall argue in this book that the whole ten-thousand-year-long story of war since the end of the last ice age is in fact a single narrative leading up to this point, in which war has been the major actor in making today's world safer and richer than ever before.

If this sounds like a paradox, that is because *everything* about war is paradoxical. The strategist Edward Luttwak sums the issue up nicely. In everyday life, he observes, "a noncontradictory linear logic rules, whose essence is mere common sense. Within the sphere of strategy, however, . . . another and quite different logic is at work and routinely violates ordinary linear logic." War "tends to reward paradoxical conduct while defeating straightforwardly logical action, yielding results that are ironical."

In war, paradox goes all the way down. According to Basil Liddell Hart, one of the founding fathers of twentieth-century tank tactics, the bottom line is that "war is always a matter of doing evil in the hope that good may come of it." Out of war comes peace; out of loss, gain. War takes us through the looking glass, into a topsy-turvy world where nothing is quite what it seems. The argument of this book is a lesser-evil proposition, one of the classic forms of paradox. It is easy to list all the things that war is bad for, with killing coming at the top of the table. And yet war remains the lesser evil, because history shows that it has not been as bad as the alternative—constant, Stone Age–type everyday violence, bleeding away lives and leaving us in poverty.

The obvious objection to lesser-evil arguments is that they have a decidedly mixed record. Ideologues love them: one extremist after another has assured his followers that if they just burn these witches, gas these Jews, or dismember these Tutsi, they will make the world pure and perfect. And yet these vicious claims can also be turned around. If you could go back in time and strangle Adolf Hitler in his cradle, would you do it? If you embrace the lesser evil, a little killing now might prevent a lot of killing later. The lesser evil makes for uncomfortable choices.

Moral philosophers are particularly interested in the complexities of lesser-evil arguments. Imagine, I have heard a colleague in my university's philosophy department ask a crowded lecture hall, that you have captured a terrorist. He has planted a bomb but won't say where it is. If you torture him, maybe he'll tell you, saving dozens of lives. Will you pull out his fingernails? If the students hesitate, the philosopher ups the stakes. Your family, he says, will be among the dead. Now will you reach for the pliers? And if he still refuses to talk, will you torture *his* family?

These uncomfortable questions raise very serious points. In the real world, we make lesser-evil decisions all the time. These can be wrenching, and in the last few years psychologists have begun to learn just what the dilemmas do to us. If an experimenter were to strap you down, slide you into a magnetic resonance imaging machine, and then ask you morally challenging questions, your brain would behave in startling ways. As you imagined torturing a terrorist, your orbital cortex would light up on the machine's display as blood rushed into the circuits of your brain that handle unpleasant thoughts. But as you calculated the number of lives you would save, your dorsolateral cortex would follow suit as a new set of circuits activated. You would experience these conflicting emotional and intellectual urges as intense inner struggles, which would fire up your anterior cingulate cortex too.

Because lesser-evil arguments make us so uncomfortable, this book might be a disturbing read. After all, war is mass murder. What sort of person says something good can come from that? The sort of person, I would now answer, who has been astonished by the findings of his own research. If anyone had told me even ten years ago that I would one day write this book, I don't think I would have believed him or her. But I have learned that the evidence of history (and archaeology, and anthropology) is unambiguous. Uncomfortable as the fact is, in the long run war has made the world safer and richer.

I am hardly the first person to have realized this. Three-quarters of a century ago, the German sociologist Norbert Elias wrote a densely theoretical two-volume treatise called *The Civilizing Process*, arguing that Europe had become a much more peaceful place over the five centuries leading up to his own day. Since the Middle Ages, he suggested, upper-class European men (who had been responsible for the lion's share of brutality) had gradually renounced the use of force, and the overall level of violence had declined.

The evidence Elias pointed to had been lying around in plain sight for a very long time. Like a lot of other people, I encountered some of it for myself the first time I was told (in high-school English, back in 1974) to crack the spine of one of Shakespeare's plays. What got my attention was not the beauty of the Bard's language but how touchy all his characters were. At the drop of a hat they flew into rages and started stabbing each other. There were certainly people like that in 1970s Britain, but they tended to end up in jail and/or therapy—unlike Shakespeare's thugs, who were more often praised than blamed for cutting first and asking questions later.

But could Elias really be right that our own world is more peaceful than that of earlier centuries? That, as Shakespeare put it, is the question, and Elias's answer was that by the 1590s, when Shakespeare wrote *Romeo and Juliet*, his murderous Montagues and Capulets were already anachronisms. Restraint was replacing rage as the emotion that defined an honorable man.

This was the sort of theory that ought to have made news, but—as publishers always tell authors—timing is everything. Elias's timing was simply tragic. *The Civilizing Process* came out in 1939, just as Europeans began a six-year orgy of violence that left more than fifty million of them dead (Elias's mother among them, at Auschwitz). By 1945, no one was in the mood to be told that Europeans were getting more civilized and peaceful.

Elias was not vindicated until the 1980s, when he was well into retirement. By then, decades of painstaking labor by social historians, working through archives of crumbling court records, had begun yielding statistics suggesting that Elias had been right all along. Around 1250, they found, roughly one western European in a hundred could expect to be a victim of homicide. By Shakespeare's day, that had fallen to one in three hundred, and by 1950, to one in three thousand. And, as Elias insisted, the upper classes led the way in getting along.*

In the 1990s, the plot thickened further. In his book *War Before Civilization*, as remarkable in its way as Elias's *Civilizing Process*, the anthropologist Lawrence Keeley marshaled rafts of statistics to show that the Stone Age societies that still existed in the twentieth century were shockingly violent. Feuding and raiding typically carried off one person in ten or even one person in five. If Keeley was right, this would mean that Stone Age societies were ten to twenty times as violent as the tumultuous world of medieval Europe and three hundred to six hundred times as bad as mid-twentieth-century Europe.

It is harder to calculate rates of violent death in the Stone Age societies of prehistory, but when Keeley looked at the evidence for murder, massacre, and general mayhem in the distant past, our early ancestors seemed at least as homicidal as the contemporary groups studied by anthropologists. The silent testimony of stone arrowheads lodged between ribs, skulls smashed by blunt instruments, and weapons piled in graves reveals the civilizing process as a longer, slower, and more uneven business than Elias realized.

Not even the world wars, Keeley recognized, had made modern times as dangerous as the Stone Age, and a third body of scholarship has now reinforced his point. This began taking shape back in 1960, with the publication of another remarkable (albeit almost unreadable) book. This was

---

*Criminologists usually express rates of violent death in terms of deaths per 100,000 people per year. Personally, I always have a little difficulty envisaging what that means in real-life terms, so I will usually couch the numbers as percentages of the population dying violently (calculated by multiplying the death rate by thirty [the number of years in a generation] and dividing by one thousand to reach a percentage) or as the odds that any individual would die violently.

Statistics of Deadly Quarrels, by the eccentric mathematician, pacifist, and (until he abandoned his career after realizing how much it helped the air force) meteorologist Lewis Fry Richardson.

Richardson spent the last twenty-odd years of his life seeking statistical patterns behind the apparent chaos of killing. Taking a sample of three hundred wars fought between 1820 and 1949, including such bloodbaths as the American Civil War, Europe's colonial conquests, and World Wars I and II, he found—to his evident surprise—that "the losses in life from fatal quarrels, varying in magnitude from murders to world wars, were about 1.6 per cent of all deaths in this period." If we add the modern world's wars to its homicides, then, it seems that just one person in 62.5 died violently between 1820 and 1949—about one-tenth the rate found among Stone Age hunter-gatherers.

And there was more. "The increase in world population from 1820 to 1949," Richardson discovered, "seems not to have been accompanied by a proportionate increase in the frequency of, and losses of life from, war, as would have been the expectation if belligerency had been constant." The implication: "Mankind has become less warlike since A.D. 1820."

More than fifty years on from Richardson's book, building databases of death has grown into a minor academic industry. The new versions are more sophisticated than Richardson's and more ambitious, extending back to 1500 and forward beyond 2000. Like all academic industries, this one is full of controversy, and even in the best-documented war in history, the American-led occupation of Afghanistan since 2001, there are multiple ways of counting how many people have died. But despite all these issues, Richardson's core findings remain intact. As the world's population has grown, the number of people being killed has not been able to keep up. The result: the likelihood that any one of us will die violently has fallen by an order of magnitude.

The new intellectual edifice got its capstone in 2006 with the publication of Azar Gat's monumental *War in Human Civilization*. Drawing on an astonishing range of academic fields (and, presumably, on his own experience as a major in the Israel Defense Forces), Gat pulled the new arguments together into a single, compelling story of how humanity had tamed its own violence across thousands of years. No one can nowadays think seriously about war without engaging with Gat's ideas, and anyone who has read his book will see its influence on every page of mine.

Thinking on war has gone through an intellectual sea change. Just a generation ago, the decline-in-violence hypothesis was still the wild speculation of an aging sociologist, not even worth mentioning to schoolchildren baffled by Shakespeare. And it still has its opponents: in 2010, for instance, Christopher Ryan and Cacilda Jethá's book *Sex at Dawn*, strenuously denying that early human societies were violent, became a bestseller; in 2012, after several years of making similar arguments in the pages of *Scientific American* magazine, John Horgan pulled them together in his book *The End of War*; and in 2013, the anthropologist Douglas Fry assembled essays by thirty-one academics in his volume *War, Peace, and Human Nature* questioning whether rates of violent death really have fallen across the long term. But though all of these books are interesting, full of information, and well worth reading, all seem to me (as will become clear in the chapters that follow) to use the evidence rather selectively, and all have been overtaken by a tidal wave of broader studies reinforcing the key insights of Elias, Keeley, Richardson, and Gat. While I was writing the first version of this introduction, not one but two major works on the decline in violence appeared in the space of a single month: the political scientist Joshua Goldstein's *Winning the War on War* and the psychologist Steven Pinker's *Better Angels of Our Nature*. A year later, the Pulitzer Prize–winning geographer Jared Diamond devoted the longest section of his book *The World Until Yesterday* to the same point. Arguments continue to rage, but on the basic issue, that rates of violent death really have declined, there is growing agreement.

Until, that is, we ask *why* violence declined.

War Makes the State, and the State Makes Peace

On this question, the divisions are deep, heated, and very, very old. They go back, in fact, to the 1640s, a time when hardly anyone thought there was a decline in violence to explain. The very bloodiness of this decade in Europe and Asia was in fact what prompted the philosopher Thomas Hobbes to put the key question on the table. Hobbes had fled England for Paris when it became clear that his homeland was descending into civil war, and the subsequent slaughter of a hundred thousand of his countrymen convinced him of one big thing: that left to their own devices, people will stop at nothing—including violence—to get what they want.

If so many had died when England's central government collapsed, Hobbes asked himself, how much worse must things have been in prehistoric times, before humans had even invented government? He answered the question in *Leviathan*, one of the classics of political philosophy.

Before the invention of government, Hobbes reasoned, life must have been a war of all against all. "In such condition," he famously mused, "there is no place for industry; because the fruit thereof is uncertain: and consequently no culture of the earth; no navigation, nor use of the commodities that may be imported by sea; no commodious building; no instruments of moving, and removing, such things as require much force; no knowledge of the face of the earth; no account of time; no arts; no letters; no society; and which is worst of all, continual fear, and danger of violent death; and the life of man, solitary, poor, nasty, brutish, and short."

As Hobbes saw it, murder, poverty, and ignorance would always be the order of the day unless there was strong government—government as awesome, he suggested, as Leviathan, the Godzilla-like monster that so alarmed Job in the Bible. ("On earth there is nothing like him," said Job. "He beholds every high *thing*; he *is* king over all the children of pride.") Such a government might be a king ruling alone or an assembly of decision makers, but either way Leviathan must intimidate its subjects so thoroughly that they would choose submission to its laws over killing and robbing each other.

How, though, had unruly humans managed to create Leviathan and escape from violent anarchy? In the 1640s there was little anthropology and less archaeology to inform discussion, but that did not stop Hobbes from holding strong views. "Savage people in many places in America" illustrated his thesis, Hobbes claimed, but he was always more interested in abstract speculation than in evidence. "The attaining to this sovereign power is by two ways," he reasoned. "One [is] by natural force: as when a man maketh his children, to submit themselves, and their children to his government, as being able to destroy them if they refuse; or by war subdueth his enemies to his will, giving them their lives on that condition. The other, is when men agree amongst themselves, to submit to some man, or assembly of men, voluntarily." The violent path to Leviathan, Hobbes called "commonwealth by *acquisition*"; the peaceful, "commonwealth by *institution*." But either way, Hobbes concluded, what makes us safe and rich is government.

This really set the cat among the pigeons. *Leviathan* was so unpopular among the Parisians who had given Hobbes shelter that he had to flee back to England. Once there, he faced a storm of criticism. By the 1660s, to call an idea "Hobbist" was to imply that any decent person should dismiss it; in

1666, only the intervention of the recently restored king saved Hobbes from prosecution for heresy.

Not content with getting rid of Hobbes, Parisian intellectuals soon set about disproving his depressing claims. From the 1690s onward, one French thinker after another announced that the Englishman had had things completely back to front, and seventy-five years after Hobbes was safely dead, the Swiss philosopher Jean-Jacques Rousseau pulled the critiques together. Government could not be the answer, Rousseau concluded, because in the state of nature man was "an equal stranger to war and every social connection, without standing in any shape in need of his fellows, as well as without any desire of hurting them." Leviathan had not tamed our warlike spirits; rather, it had corrupted our simplicity.

Rousseau, however, proved even less popular than Hobbes. He had to flee French Switzerland for the German part, only for a mob to stone his house when he got there. He next fled to England, which he did not like, before sneaking back into Paris, even though he had been officially exiled from France. But despite this stormy reception, Rousseau gave Hobbes a run for his money. In the later eighteenth century, Rousseau's optimism about mankind's innate goodness made many readers consider Hobbes reactionary. In the later nineteenth century Hobbes bounced back as Darwin's evolutionary ideas made his dog-eat-dog vision seem more in accordance with nature, but in the twentieth he lost ground once again. For reasons we will return to in Chapter 1, the idealism of Edwin Starr's "War" swept the field. By the 1980s, Hobbes's stern vision of strong government as a force for good was in full retreat.

Hobbes's critics spanned the ideological spectrum. "Government," Ronald Reagan assured Americans in his first inaugural address, "is not the solution to our problem; government *is* the problem." But Reagan's great fear—that bloated government would stifle individual freedom—also shows just how far the modern debate over the merits of big and small government has taken us from the kinds of horrors that worried Hobbes. To people in any age before our own, our current arguments would have made no sense; for them, the only argument that mattered was between extremely small government and no government at all. Extremely small government meant that there was at least some law and order; no government at all, that there was not.

Reagan once joked that "the ten most terrifying words in the English language are 'Hi, I'm from the government, and I'm here to help,'" but in reality the ten scariest words are "There is no government, and I'm here to kill you." And I suspect that Reagan might have agreed; on another occasion he said, "One legislator accused me of having a nineteenth-century attitude on law and order. That is a totally false charge. I have an eighteenth-century attitude . . . [T]he Founding Fathers made it clear that the safety of law-abiding citizens should be one of the government's primary concerns."

In 1975, just a few years before Reagan's first inaugural address, the sociologist Charles Tilly had suggested that out of all the muddle of dates and details that clog up European history, we could draw out a single big story, that "war made the state, and the state made war." Fighting, he observed, drove the rise of strong governments, and governments then used their strength to fight even more. I am a great fan of Tilly's work, but here, I think, he missed the real headline. The plain fact, as Hobbes had understood, is that over the past ten thousand years war made the state, and the state made peace.

In the thirty-odd years since Reagan's speech, scholarly opinion has moved back toward Hobbes, in a sense going beyond Reagan to embrace a seventeenth-century attitude on law and order. Most of the recent books identifying a decline in violence cite Hobbes approvingly. "Hobbes was closer to the truth," says Gat in his *War in Human Civilization*, than the "Rousseauite Garden of Eden."

However, Hobbes's new champions rarely seem entirely at ease with his bleak thesis that the power of government is what makes us safe and prosperous. Keeley, the anthropologist, clearly prefers Hobbes to Rousseau but feels that "if Rousseau's primitive golden age is imaginary, Hobbes's perpetual donnybrook is impossible." Stone Age peoples do not really wage a war of all against all, Keeley concluded, and the rise of government has brought as much pain as peace.

Elias, the sociologist, took a different tack. He never actually mentioned Hobbes in *The Civilizing Process*, although he shared the philosopher's hunch that government was crucial in curbing violence. But where Hobbes made Leviathan the active party, overawing its subjects, Elias put the subjects in the driver's seat, suggesting that they lost their taste for violence because they adopted gentler manners to fit in better at elegant royal courts. And in contrast to Hobbes's guess that the great pacification took place in the distant past, Elias dated it to the years since 1500.

Pinker, the psychologist, put things bluntly in his 2002 book, *The Blank Slate*. "Hobbes was right, Rousseau was wrong," he announced. But in his more recent work *The Better Angels of Our Nature*, Pinker steps back a little, diluting the Leviathan thesis. The story of the decline of violence, Pinker argues, is not just about Leviathan. It "is a tale of six trends, five inner demons, and five historical forces." To understand it properly, says Pinker, we need to break the story down into multiple phases—a Civilizing Process, a Humanitarian Revolution, a Long Peace, and a New Peace—and to recognize that each has its own causes, some going back millennia, some operating only since 1945 (or even 1989).

Goldstein, the political scientist, goes further still. The important changes, he argues, are all postwar (post–World War II, that is), and to understand them, we have to out-Hobbes Hobbes. The greatest blow to violence, Goldstein argues, was not the rise of government, as Hobbes suggested. It was the rise of an über-government, in the form of the United Nations.

Clearly, the experts disagree deeply over the roles of war and government in making the world safer and richer. What that kind of disagreement usually means, in my experience, is that we have been looking at the question in the wrong way and therefore finding only partial and contradictory answers. We need a different perspective.

War Pig

In some ways, I am the least likely person to be able to offer such a perspective. My brush with Petrov aside, I have never fought in a war or even seen the carnage close-up. The nearest I've come was in Tel Aviv in 2001, when a suicide bomber blew up a disco a few hundred yards from where I was staying, dismembering twenty-one teenagers. I think I heard the blast, though it's hard to be sure; I was sitting in the hotel bar, where a high-school graduation party, crowded with luckier students, was in full swing. No one could fail to hear the ambulances, though.

Nor do I come from a distinguished military family. My parents, both born in England in 1929, were too young for World War II, and by going down the mines, my father also missed out on Korea. Coal mining had killed his own father before World War II broke out, while my mother's father was kept back from the fighting because he was a steelworker. (He was a communist too, although that became less of an issue after Germany attacked the Soviet Union in 1941.) My mother's uncle Fred did serve with Monty in North Africa but never fired his rifle or even saw a German. By his account, war consisted of jumping into trucks to chase unseen enemies through the desert, then jumping into other trucks to be chased back to the starting point. His closest brush with danger, he always said, was when he lost his false teeth in a sandstorm.

Instead of serving my country, I misspent my youth in rock bands. I was perhaps a bit less peace-and-love than many of my 1970s contemporaries, but my inarticulate instincts were still largely on the side of the song "War." The first guitar part I ever mastered, in fact, was the crashing riff to Black Sabbath's epic "War Pigs," with its immortally heavy-handed opening lines:

> *Generals gathered in their masses*
> *Just like witches at black masses.*

Eventually, after several diverting but not very lucrative years of grinding out songs that sounded suspiciously like "War Pigs," I discovered that being a historian and archaeologist came more naturally to me than being a heavy metal guitarist.

The founding fathers of history writing, Herodotus and Thucydides in ancient Greece and Sima Qian in ancient China, made war their central topic, and if you were to judge solely by the documentaries airing on the History Channel or what you see for sale on airport book stands, you could be forgiven for thinking that historians have been following their lead ever since. But in fact—for reasons I will come back to in Chapter 1—professional historians and archaeologists have largely turned their backs on war in the last fifty years.

For my first couple of decades in their ranks (I got my PhD in 1986), I largely followed my elders' example, and it was only while I was writing my book *Why the West Rules—for Now: The Patterns of History, and What They Reveal About the Future* that I finally got a sense of what war has been good for. My wife, normally more a consumer of modern fiction than of history books, had been reading each chapter as I drafted it, but when I gave her one particularly big chunk of text, she finally confessed, "Well . . . I did like it . . . but there's a lot of war."

Up to that moment it really hadn't occurred to me that there was a lot of war in the book. If anything, I'd thought I was keeping the war stories in the background. But once Kathy pointed it out, I realized that she was right. There was a lot of war.

As I obsessed about this—Should I cut out the wars? Should I go into a long explanation of why there was so much fighting in the story? Or had I in fact got the story wrong?—I realized that this was the way it had to be, because war really is central to history. And by the time I finished writing the book, I'd come to see that war will be as central to our future as it has been to our past. Far from writing too much about war, I had barely scratched the surface.

That was when I realized my next book had to be about war.

Almost immediately, I began to get cold feet. "O for a Muse of fire," Shakespeare wished when it came time to write about war, and I soon saw what he meant. If even he despaired of bringing forth so great an object on his unworthy scaffold, what hope had I?

Part of the problem is the sheer amount of thinking and writing about war that has already been done. Despite the professional historians' retreat from the subject, millions of books, essays, poems, plays, and songs have been written about war. According to Keeley, by the mid-1990s there were already more than fifty thousand books on the American Civil War alone. No one can possibly master this flood.

It seems to me, though, that the outpouring of words actually breaks down into just four main ways of thinking about war. The first, and in recent years the most widespread, is what I would call the personal approach. It evokes the individual experience of war—what it feels like to stand in the battle line, suffer or inflict rape and torture, grieve for the fallen, live with wounds, or just put up with the petty privations of life behind the lines. The best of it, whether it comes in the form of journalism, poetry, songs, diaries, novels, films, or just stories told over a drink, is visceral and immediate. It shocks, excites, breaks the heart, and inspires, often all at the same time.

The personal approach tries to tell us what war feels like, and here, as I have already confessed, I have nothing to add to the voices of those who have actually experienced the violence. The personal approach, however, does not tell us everything we need to know about war and in the end only answers part of the question of what war is good for. War is about more than what it feels like to live through it, and the second broad way of thinking about war, what I loosely call military history, addresses this gap.

The boundary between personal accounts and military history can be blurry. At least since 1976, when John Keegan's pathbreaking book *The Face of Battle* appeared, the individual experience of soldiers in past wars has been one of military history's enduring areas of interest. But military historians also tell bigger stories, of entire battles, campaigns, and conflicts. The fog of war is famously thick, and no one person ever sees the whole of what is going on or understands the full implications of events.

To solve this problem, historians draw on official statistics, officers' after-action reports, visits to battlefields, and countless other sources in addition to the personal experiences of fighters and civilians, all to reach for an overview that transcends any individual.

The military-history approach regularly bleeds into a third perspective on war, which we might call technical studies. For thousands of years, professional soldiers, diplomats, and strategists—usually drawing deeply on both their own experiences and their readings in history—have abstracted principles of war from its practice, trying to explain when force should be used to resolve disputes and how it can be applied most effectively. The technical approach is almost the opposite of the personal approach: where the personal approach looks at violence from the bottom up and generally sees no point to it, the technical looks from the top down and often sees a great deal of point to it.

The fourth approach, however, takes us even further from the personal, looking at war as part of the broader pattern of evolution. Biologists have long recognized that violence is one tool among many available to living things in their struggles for resources and reproduction. The obvious implication, many archaeologists, anthropologists, historians, and political scientists conclude, is that we can only explain human violence if we identify its evolutionary functions. By comparing patterns of human behavior with patterns found in other species, they hope to identify the logic behind war.

No one has ever mastered all four ways of thinking about war, and perhaps no one ever will. After spending several years now reading books and talking to professionals, I am painfully aware of the gaps in my own background. But that said, I would also like to think that the thirty years I've spent in dusty libraries and on even dustier archaeological excavations has given me at least some basis for bringing the four approaches together to try to explain what war is good for. You will have to judge for yourself whether I am right, but as I see it, we make most sense of war by starting from a global, long-term perspective and then zooming in at key points to scrutinize the details. It seems to me that looking at war is like looking at any other enormous object: if you stand too close, you cannot see the forest for the trees, but if you stand too far away, it fades over the horizon. Most personal accounts and many military histories, I think, stand too close to war to see the big picture, while most evolutionary treatments and many technical studies stand too far away to see the violent details.

This back-and-forth movement shows us just how different long-term results can be from the short-term actions that cause them. "In the long run," the economist John Maynard Keynes famously observed, "we are all dead"; and in the short run—the run we actually live in—war just makes us dead quicker. And yet the cumulative effect of the last ten thousand years of fighting has been to make people live longer. As I suggested earlier, in war, paradox goes all the way down.

Keynes spent much of his career trying to finance Britain's part in the world wars, but could still write in 1917 that "I work for a Government I despise for ends I think criminal." He understood, perhaps better than most, that many governments *are* criminal. And yet the paradox remains: the cumulative effect of ten thousand years of Leviathans has been to create societies that are more peaceful and prosperous. We might call this the what-about-Hitler (or Stalin, or Mao, or Idi Amin . . . take your pick) problem. The Nazi regime was an abomination, as interested in murdering its subjects as in protecting them—so how can anyone argue that the overall effect of government has been to make us safer and richer? Hitler, it is tempting to conclude, trumps Hobbes.

But the what-about-Hitler problem has a problem of its own. Hobbes's is not the only argument apparently trumped by Hitler; as I mentioned earlier, it seemed for decades that Hitler also trumped Elias—until it became clear that he didn't. Between 1933 and mid-1945, the Nazi Leviathan devoured its young and drove rates of violent death up to horrendous levels. But if we take just a slightly longer perspective, by the summer of 1945 this monster had of course been defeated by other Leviathans, and the downward trend in rates of violent death resumed.

I will return to the what-about-Hitler question in more detail in Chapter 5, but right now I just want to say that the reason Hitler does not trump Hobbes is that picking out extreme cases of vile or virtuous rulers will never prove or disprove a bigger theory about what war is good for. The reality is that no two governments are the same (indeed, given the inglorious history of political U-turns, no one government remains the same for very long), and we can only make sense of Leviathan's impact by looking at government, as well as war, over the longest possible run.

Table 1, designed by the historian Niall Ferguson, is a handy tool for thinking about this. "The table should be read as a menu rather than a grid," Ferguson explains; each society makes one or more selections from each column, mixing and matching as it chooses. There are tens of thousands of possible combinations. Hitler's Germany, for instance, was run as a tyranny. Its objectives included security, raw materials, treasure, and above all land (the notorious *Lebensraum*). The public goods it provided are less obvious but probably included health. Its rule was mainly military, its economic system planned (albeit badly), the main beneficiaries a ruling elite, and its social character decidedly genocidal.

No two societies make quite the same choices. Two thousand years before Hitler, the Roman Republic was governed by an aristocracy, which was interested above all in extracting military manpower. The major public goods it provided were probably trade and law, and it ruled chiefly by delegation to local elites, benefited most of its inhabitants, and shifted over time from a hierarchical to an assimilative character.

For history buffs, slotting different societies into Ferguson's menu can be a lot of fun, but there are weightier points to be made too. Across the five thousand years for which we have written evidence, some governments have acted more like Hobbes's Leviathan and others more like Hitler's Third Reich, but the overall trend, I argue in this book, has been toward Hobbes's end of the spectrum, and this is why rates of violent death have declined so much.

The only way to see this pattern—and the method I will pursue throughout this book—is to step back from the details to look over the long run at what actually happened, rather than at what theorists and self-proclaimed great men said was (or ought to be) happening. On the whole, for reasons I

Metropolitan system	Self-interested objectives	Public goods	Methods of rule	Economic system	Who benefits?	Social character
Tyranny	Security	Peace	Military	Plantation	Ruling elite	Genocidal
Aristocracy	Communications	Trade	Bureaucracy	Feudal	Metropolitan populace	Hierarchical
Oligarchy	Land	Investment	Settlement	Mercantilist	Settlers	Converting
Democracy	Raw materials	Law	NGOs	Market	Local elites	Assimilative
	Treasure	Governance	Firms	Mixed	All inhabitants	
	Manpower	Education	Delegation to local elites	Planned		
	Rents	Conversion				
	Taxation	Health				

Table 1. So many ways to do things: the historian Niall Ferguson's "menu" of forms of government

will come back to in Chapter 6, governments pursue what they perceive as their best interests, not blueprints laid out for them by philosophers. Hitler did not need pseudoscientists to convince him to make war on Europe and exterminate what he called *Untermenschen* ("subhumans"); rather, he decided on war and then looked for pseudoscientists to justify it. Europe's chattering classes were scandalized when Hitler and Stalin signed a pact proclaiming friendship between fascism and communism in 1939—"All the isms have become wasms," some wit in the British Foreign Office quipped—but they should not have been. The truth of the matter is that the isms have *always* been wasms. The hard, paradoxical logic of strategy has always trumped everything else.

Consequently, I spend a lot of time in this book talking about ordinary people—workers, soldiers, managers—and much less about thinkers or ideologues. As we will see, the grand ideas for which men and women laid down their lives or slaughtered the innocent turn out to have been like foam on the surface of waves, driven by much deeper forces. Only when we understand this can we see what war has been good for—and how that will change.

The Plan of Attack

The first five chapters of this book tell the story of war, moving from the violent, impoverished world of prehistoric hunter-gatherer bands to the age of Petrov. It is a messy story, as history always is when we burrow into the details, but it reveals a powerful trend. Under certain circumstances—which I examine in Chapters 1 and 2—war can be a productive force, in the sense that it produces Leviathans, which make people safer and richer. Under other circumstances—which I examine in Chapter 3—it can turn downright counterproductive, breaking the bigger, richer, and safer societies back down into smaller, poorer, and more violent ones. But under other circumstances still—which I examine in Chapters 4 and 5—war can turn more productive than ever, producing not just Leviathans but globocops. These bestride the world like colossuses, transforming life in ways that would have seemed like magic in any earlier age, but they also wield so much destructive power that they could potentially wipe life out altogether.

In Chapter 6, I break the narrative to try to make sense of this story by setting it in its broader evolutionary context, before turning in Chapter 7 to ask what it all tells us about where the world might be heading in the twenty-first century. The answer, I argue, is both alarming and uplifting—alarming because the next forty years are going to be the most dangerous in history, but uplifting because there is reason to think that rather than just surviving them, we will triumph in them. The long story of war is approaching its extraordinary culminating point, but to understand what is happening, we must begin—as I will now do—by looking back deep into our violent past.

THE WASTELAND? WAR AND PEACE
IN ANCIENT ROME

The Battle at the Edge of the World

For the first time in memory, the tribes had made peace—Vacomagi with Taexali, Decantae with Lugi, and Caereni with Carnonacae—and every man who could hold a sword was streaming toward the Graupian Mountain. This, the chiefs agreed, was the way the Romans would come. And here, where the highlands dropped down toward the cold North Sea (Figure 1.1), the Caledonians would make a stand that would live in song forever.

We will never know what praise the long-haired Celtic bards heaped on the heroes who fought that day; all their epics are long forgotten. Only a single account of what happened now survives, written by Tacitus, one of the greatest of ancient Rome's historians. Tacitus did not follow the army to the Graupian Mountain, but he did marry the general's daughter, and when we put his description of the fighting together with archaeologists' finds and other Roman writings, we get two things—not only a pretty good idea of what happened when the armies clashed nearly two thousand years ago,* but also a stark statement of the problem that this book tries to solve.

"Men of the North!"

Calgacus was shouting at the top of his lungs, trying to be heard over

---

*Making sense of ancient battle descriptions is a notoriously thorny problem for historians. I discuss the (many) issues of interpretation in the "Notes" and "Further Reading" sections at the end of this book.

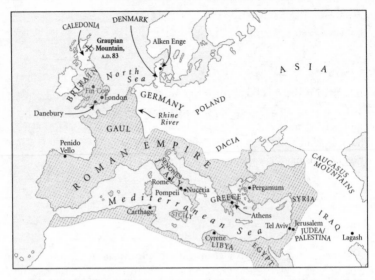

Figure 1.1. The wasteland? The Roman Empire at the time of the battle at the Graupian Mountain, A.D. 83

the chanting of war bands, the braying of copper horns, and the clattering of chariots in the valley below. In front of him were thirty thousand jostling, disorderly men, more than anyone had ever seen in these northern wilds. He raised his arms for quiet but got none.

"Men! Listen to me!" For a moment, the din got even louder as men started chanting Calgacus's name, but then it dipped slightly, in respect for the great warrior, the fiercest of the dozens of Caledonian chieftains.

"Men of the North! This is the dawn of freedom for Britain! We're going to fight, all of us in it together. It's a day for heroes—and even if you're a coward, fighting's going to be the safest thing now!" For a moment, the pale sun broke through the leaden northern sky, and cheering interrupted Calgacus again. He threw back his head and roared defiance.

"Listen to me! We live at the end of the world. We're the last free men on earth. There's no one else behind us—there's nothing there except rocks and waves, and even those are full of Romans. There's no escaping them. They've robbed the world, and now that they've stolen everything on land, they're even looting the sea. If they think you've got money, they attack you out of greed; if they think you've got nothing, they attack you out of arrogance. They've robbed the whole of the East and the whole of the West, but they're still not satisfied. They're the only people on earth who want to rob rich and poor alike. They call stealing, killing, and rape by the lying name of government! They make a wasteland and call it peace!"

A groundswell of hoarse shouting, stamping feet, and swords clashing on shields swallowed the rest of Calgacus's words. Without anyone giving orders, the war bands started moving forward. Some were in groups of a hundred or more behind a chief, while other men charged forward on their own, dancing with excitement. Calgacus pulled on a chain-mail shirt and ran after his men. The battle was on.

Half a mile away, the Romans were waiting. For six summers, their general Agricola had been looking for a fight, pushing farther and farther north, burning the Britons' homes and crops to goad them into taking a stand. And now, in A.D. 83, as autumn closed in, he had finally got what he wanted: a battle. His men were outnumbered, far from their forts, and at the limits of their supply lines, but it was a battle all the same. He was delighted.

Agricola had drawn his men up in two lines, running straight as rulers without regard for the dips and folds of the land. Out in front were the auxiliaries, fighting for the money (which was good), the hope of plunder (which was better), and the promise of Roman citizenship after twenty-five years of service. On this campaign, most were Germans, hired along the banks of the Rhine. Some were on horseback, covering the wings, but most were on foot. These were no broadsword-swinging tribesmen: standing almost shoulder to shoulder, they carried javelins and short stabbing swords, sweating under thirty-pound loads of chain mail, iron helmets, and shields (Figure 1.2).

In the second line were the even more heavily armed elite citizen legionaries, the best soldiers in the world. Sending away his horse, Agricola took a place with the standard-bearers in front of them.

Just as Agricola had expected, the fight did not take long. The Caledonians surged into the valley, running as close to the Romans as they dared before throwing their spears and scrambling back to safety. Agricola's men were falling here and there, wounded in their unarmored thighs or sometimes killed outright, but the general waited. Only when he judged that enough of the enemy had crowded into the valley to make maneuver difficult did he order the auxiliaries forward.

Some of the Caledonians turned and ran right away. Others stood,

Figure 1.2. In the service of the empire: a first-century-A.D. German auxiliary fighting for Rome

trying to find room to swing their two-handed broadswords in huge arcs that smashed through armor, flesh, and bone, chopping men in two. But the auxiliaries steadily came on, rank upon rank in heavy metal armor, pushing in too near for the scattered highlanders to use their unwieldy weapons. Intimately close, Romans smashed iron-rimmed shields into noses and teeth, drove their short swords through ribs and throats, and trampled their victims in the wet grass. Eruptions of blood clotted thickly on their chain mail and visors, but they kept moving, leaving those in the rear to finish off the dazed and injured.

No plan survives contact with the enemy, the saying goes, and as the Roman auxiliaries pushed uphill, the orderly ranks that had so far made them unstoppable began breaking up. Exhausted, soaked now in sweat as much as blood, they slowed and then stopped. In twos and threes, Caledonian swordsmen turned and stood their ground among boulders and trees. For minutes that felt as long as hours, they shouted abuse at the Romans and threw stones and any remaining spears; then, as their line grew firmer, the bravest edged closer to the invaders. More and more fighters came running back down the slopes, emboldened, and spilled around the Romans' flanks. The auxiliaries' advance ground to a halt. As they felt the tide turning, Caledonian cavalry on mud-spattered ponies came pushing behind the Germans, spearing them in their legs and hemming them in so tightly that they could not fight back.

Across the valley, Agricola still had not moved, but now he gave a signal, and a trumpet blew a new command. His auxiliary cavalry jingled and clattered forward. Neatly, as if on a parade ground, their deep column unfolded into a wide line. The trumpet blew again, and the men lowered their spears. A third time it blew, and the riders kicked their horses into a gallop. Gripping the horses' bellies with their knees (this was five centuries before the coming of stirrups), they leaned into the wind, blood pounding and the thunder of hooves filling their world as they shrieked out their rage.

Here and there knots of Caledonians turned to fight as Roman riders fell on them from behind. There was frantic stabbing, spear against spear, as the Romans rushed past. In a few places, horses crashed straight into each other, spilling riders and steeds to the ground in screaming tumbles of broken legs and backs. But for the most part, the northerners fled, unreasoning panic blacking out every thought but escape. And as the men around them melted away, the fury drained out of those few who had kept their ground. Throwing down their weapons, they ran too.

An army becomes a mob in moments. There were still enough Caledonians to smother the Romans, but with all order gone, hope departed too. Through gorse and stream, across the slopes of the Graupian Mountain, Roman riders speared everything that moved and trampled anything that did not. When trees provided cover, Caledonians would cluster in their shadow, hoping to wait out the Roman storm, but the Roman riders, methodical in the midst of chaos, dismounted, flushed the enemy back into the open, and then resumed the chase.

The Romans kept killing till night fell. By their best guess, they butchered about 10,000 Caledonians. Calgacus was probably among them, since his name never crops up in our sources again. Agricola, by contrast, had not a scratch on him. Just 360 Roman auxiliaries had died, and not even one legionary.

In the darkness, the historian Tacitus tells us, "the Britons scattered, men and women wailing together, carrying off their wounded or calling to survivors. Some fled their homes, and in a frenzy, even set fire to them. Others chose hiding places, only to abandon them straightaway. At one moment they started forming plans, only to stop and break up their conference. Sometimes the sight of their loved ones broke their hearts; more often it goaded them to fury. We found clear signs that some of them had even laid hands on their wives and children in pity—of a kind."

By the time the sun came up, Tacitus continues, "an awful silence had settled everywhere. The hills were deserted, houses were smoking in the distance, and our scouts met no one." Calgacus had been right: Rome had made a wasteland and called it peace.

Pax Romana

Winter was coming. With his enemies broken and his army stretched thin, Agricola left the Caledonians to their suffering and led his troops back toward their bases.

The farther south they marched, deeper into territory Rome had held for decades, the less it looked like a wasteland. There were no burned-out ruins, no starving refugees; rather, the Romans saw well-tended fields, bustling towns, and merchants eager to sell to them. Prosperous farmers were drinking Italian wine from fine imported cups, and Britain's formerly wild warlords had exchanged their hillforts for luxurious villas. They sported togas over their tattoos and sent their sons to learn Latin.

Here was a paradox that might have troubled Calgacus, had he been alive to see it. To most people on the Roman side of the frontier, though, the explanation for why the Roman Empire was *not* a wasteland was obvious. The orator Marcus Tullius Cicero put it best a century and a half earlier, in a letter to his brother Quintus, who was then governing the wealthy Greek province of Asia (roughly the western quarter of modern Turkey). This was an excellent posting, but Quintus had temper problems, and the provincials under him had been complaining.

After a few pages of stern elder-sibling advice, Marcus's tone changed. The fault, he concluded, was not all on Quintus's side. The Greeks needed to face facts. "Let Asia think on this," he pointed out. "Were she not under our government, there's no calamity of foreign war and civil strife that she'd escape. And since there's no way to provide government without taxes, Asia should be happy to purchase perpetual peace at the price of a few of her products."

Calgacus or Cicero; wasteland or wonderland? These two competing views of the consequences of war, formulated so sharply two thousand years ago, will dominate this book.

In an ideal world, we could settle the debate by just running the numbers. If violent deaths fell and prosperity rose after the Roman conquests, we could conclude that Cicero was right; war was good for something. If the results came out the other way, then obviously Calgacus understood his age better, and war made only wastelands. We could then rerun the test on later periods of history in Chapters 2–5, coming to an overall conclusion about what—if anything—war has been good for.

But reality is rarely that convenient. I mentioned in the introduction that building databases of deaths in battle has grown into a minor academic industry, but few reliable statistics go back past A.D. 1500, even in Europe. Only one kind of evidence—the physical remains of our bodies, which often carry telltale traces of lethal violence—has the potential to span every period, going back to the origins of humanity itself. One day we can expect to have reliable statistics from this source, but right now the problem is that not many scholars have made large-scale studies of this complicated, technically challenging material, and even when they have, the picture remains rather unclear.

One study (published in 2012) of skulls in collections at Tel Aviv University, for instance, found precious few differences in levels of violence across the last six thousand years. A 2013 analysis of skeletons from Peru, however, found spikes in violence in periods when bigger states were being formed (roughly 400 B.C.–A.D. 100 and A.D. 1000–1400)—which is roughly consistent with this book's arguments. Until we have far more of this evidence, all we will be able to do for periods before A.D. 1500 (and in some parts of the world, even into our own century) is bundle together all kinds of evidence, including archaeology, literary anecdotes, and anthropological comparisons, with—once in a while—some actual numbers.

This is a messy business, made even messier by the sheer scale of the Roman Empire. By Calgacus's day it sprawled across an area half the size of the continental United States and contained about sixty million people. Roughly forty million (Greeks, Syrians, Jews, Egyptians) lived in the complex, urban societies of its eastern half, with another twenty million (Celts and Germans) in the simpler rural and tribal societies of the west.

We have already heard Cicero's views on the violence of Greek Asia before the Roman conquest, and other writers made the barbarians (as Romans dismissively called them)* of the west sound even worse. Fights, raids, and battles were everyday activities, the Romans said, and every village was fortified. While a Roman gentleman might feel underdressed without his toga, a German felt naked without his shield and spear. The barbarians, Romans insisted, worshipped severed heads, which they liked to hang outside their front doors (suitably treated with cedar oil to stop them from smelling). They sacrificed humans to their angry gods, and sometimes even burned them alive inside wickerwork statues. Tacitus was blunt: "Germans have no taste for peace."

Small wonder, then, that Cicero and his peers thought Rome was doing its neighbors a favor by conquering them. And it is equally unsurprising, some historians suggest, that when modern classical scholarship took shape in the eighteenth century, most of its towering intellects agreed with the Romans. Europeans liked to think that they too were doing the world a favor by conquering it, and so the Romans' arguments struck them as eminently reasonable.

On the heels of Europe's retreat from empire in the later twentieth century, however, classicists began wondering about the Romans' gory picture of the people they conquered. Ancient imperialists, some scholars suggested, might have been just as eager as the modern version to paint their victims as uncivilized, corrupt, and in general need of conquest. Cicero wanted to

---

*Romans borrowed this condescending catchall label for foreigners from Greeks, who claimed to think that other languages sounded like people saying "bar bar bar." One of the ironies, lost on no one, was that most Greeks included Romans on the list of barbarians.

justify exploiting Greeks; Caesar, to make attacking Gaul (roughly modern France) look necessary; and Tacitus, to glorify his father-in-law, Agricola.

Taking Caesar's word that the Gauls needed conquering might be as unwise as simply swallowing whole Rudyard Kipling's now-notorious claim (which I will come back to in Chapter 4) that governing new-caught, sullen peoples was the white man's burden. Fortunately, though, we do not have to take the Romans' word for anything, because plenty of other voices survive too.

In the eastern Mediterranean, literate upper-class Greeks wrote their own accounts, sometimes fawning on the Roman conquerors, sometimes fiercely anti-imperialist. The surprising thing, though, is that they all present much the same grim picture of a preconquest world full of failed states, vicious pirates and bandits, and spiraling wars, uprisings, and rebellions.

Take, for instance, an inscription carved on the base of a statue set up in honor of the otherwise unknown Philip of Pergamum in 58 B.C. (Pergamum was in the province of Asia, and 58 B.C. was just one year after Quintus Cicero's stint as governor of Asia ended; Quintus and Philip would almost certainly have known each other.) Among various good deeds, it tells us, Philip had written a history, intended as "a narrative of recent events—for all sorts of sufferings and constant mutual slaughter have gone on in our days in Asia and Europe, in the tribes of Libya, and in the cities of the islanders." Philip apparently agreed with the brothers Cicero that without the Roman presence, Asia would be a bad neighborhood.

In the West, few among the conquered could write, and virtually none of their thoughts survive for us to read, but archaeology suggests that here too the Romans knew what they were talking about. Many—perhaps most—people really did live in walled and ditched forts before the Roman conquest, and while excavations cannot show whether men habitually carried arms, mourners certainly regularly buried their fathers, brothers, husbands, and sons with weapons (and sometimes with shields, breastplates, and even complete chariots too). The way they wanted their menfolk remembered was as warriors.

Most spectacularly, Celtic and Germanic gods really did like human sacrifice. Millions of visitors to London's British Museum have seen the most famous example, a disturbingly well-preserved two-thousand-year-old corpse pulled from a bog in Cheshire in 1984 (and immediately nicknamed Pete Marsh). One day in March or April, a decade or two before the Romans arrived in Britain, this lost soul was stunned by two blows to the head, stabbed in the chest, garroted, and, just to be sure, drowned in a bog.

Analysis of his waterlogged gut produced mistletoe, which is how we know what month he died in (the year is harder to fix). Mistletoe was the sacred plant of the Druids, who—according to Tacitus and Caesar—specialized in human sacrifice, which encourages many archaeologists to think that Pete Marsh was the victim of some homicidal ritual.

Altogether, several dozen bog bodies that look as if they were sacrificed (as well as sites where people worshipped skulls) have been dug up, and in 2009 archaeologists found an astonishing two hundred corpses in a bog at Alken Enge in Denmark. Many had been hacked to pieces, and their bones were mixed with axes, spears, swords, and shields. Opinions differ on whether they were slaughtered in a battle or sacrificed after one.

Of course, we might be misinterpreting these finds. Burying weapons with the dead and sacrificing humans in bogs need not mean that war was everywhere; the excavated remains might actually mean that violence had been banished into rituals. And walls and ditches might not have been for defense at all; perhaps they were just status symbols, like the ghastly mock castles that Victorian gentlefolk liked to build on their country estates.

But none of this is very convincing. The reason that people poured thousands of hours into digging ditches and building walls was clearly that their lives depended on it. At the most fully excavated fort, Danebury in southern England, the great wooden gates and parts of the village were burned down twice, and after the second conflagration, around 100 B.C., about a hundred bodies—many bearing telltale wounds from metal weapons—were dumped in pits.

Nor was Danebury unique. Grisly new finds keep turning up. In 2011, British archaeologists reported on a massacre site at Fin Cop in Derbyshire, where nine bodies (one of them a pregnant woman) were found in a short stretch of ditch, buried at the same time around 400 B.C. under the fort's collapsed wall. The excavators speculate that dozens—perhaps hundreds—more victims remain to be found.

Cicero was surely right that the pre-Roman world was a rough place, but Calgacus would probably not have disputed this. His point was that conquest by Rome was even worse.

No one really knows how many people were killed in Rome's wars of expansion, which began in Italy in the fifth and fourth centuries B.C., spreading to the western Mediterranean in the third century, the east in the second, and northwest Europe in the first. The Romans did not really keep count (Figure 1.3), but the total might have surpassed five million.

Figure 1.3. Counting heads: barbarian auxiliaries fighting for Rome present the emperor with a gruesome tally of the enemies they have killed during a campaign in Dacia (modern Romania) in the 110s A.D.

Even more might have been dragged off into slavery. Calgacus's claim calls for serious scrutiny.

The level of violence varied, depending on Rome's internal politics and the amount of resistance offered. In extreme cases, Roman armies would devastate enemy territory so thoroughly that no one lived there for decades after, as happened to an Italian tribe called the Senones in 283 B.C. The Greek historian Polybius, himself taken to Rome as a captive after being on the losing side in a war, says that by the end of Rome's third-century-B.C. wars with Carthage it became normal practice "to exterminate every form of life they encountered, sparing none . . . so when cities are taken by the Romans you may often see not only the corpses of human beings but also dogs cut in half, and also the dismembered limbs of other animals."

Those who submitted without too much fighting got off more lightly, but the Romans reserved their real rage for people who surrendered but then changed their minds. This happened quite often. After overrunning most of Gaul with relatively little killing in 58–56 B.C., for instance, Julius Caesar had to spend the next half-dozen years putting down revolts. Ancient authors claim that he ended up killing one million out of the three million Gallic men of fighting age and selling another million as slaves.

The worst offenders (in Roman eyes) were the Jews. According to Josephus, a Jewish general who defected to Rome early in the great Jewish revolt of A.D. 66–73, the Romans not only burned the temple in Jerusalem and stole its sacred treasures but also killed more than a million Jews and enslaved another hundred thousand. And that was just for starters: when the Jews rose up again in A.D. 132, the Romans really turned nasty. They "went on killing until their horses were submerged in blood to their nostrils," one Jewish source claimed—exaggeration, certainly, but another half million died. The province of Judea was renamed Palestina, after its ancient Philistine occupants, and the surviving Jews—banned from Jerusalem except for one day each year—scattered into exile across Europe and the Middle East.

What Cicero had in mind when he took the opposite view from Calgacus was what happened *after* the conquests. From his vantage point in Rome's ruling class, Cicero could see that after the legions moved on and the fires of revolt were quenched in blood, peace descended. Warrior graves and bloodthirsty gods faded away. The walls of ancient cities—no longer worth spending money on—decayed and fell down, and new cities, which were sprouting up everywhere, simply did without fortifications.

Cicero would probably have accepted Calgacus's point that Rome regularly made wastelands. Despite his enthusiasm for Rome's civilizing mission, Cicero knew as well as anyone that conquest was an ugly business, for the conquerors as well as their victims. Successful war generated unprecedented plunder, and between the 80s and the 30s B.C. Rome's political institutions repeatedly collapsed in civil wars over the spoils. There were years when no merchant in his right mind would travel the highways of Italy without armed guards. For months at a stretch, mobs had the run of the streets of Rome, forcing elected consuls to cower in their (fortified) mansions, terrified to step outside.

First-century-B.C. Roman aristocrats were as touchy as anyone, constantly ready to avenge any slight with violence (not for nothing did Shakespeare set so many of his plays in Rome). Cicero made his name by prosecuting a string of the worst villains before a general's henchmen sent him to an early grave. His head and hands were hacked off and nailed up in the Forum as a warning to others to think carefully before speaking or writing against the mighty.

One of Cicero's many enemies, Marcus Licinius Crassus, reputedly said around this time that "no one should count himself rich unless he can afford his own army," but in the 30s B.C. one such man—Julius Caesar's grand-nephew Octavian—showed where this logic led. Fighting his way free from the roiling mass of aristocrats, Octavian made himself Rome's first emperor. Cleverly, he defused resistance by insisting he was just a regular guy, albeit the richest such guy in the world, and also the guy who happened to be in complete control of the world's greatest army.

The only honor Octavian would accept was a new name, Augustus, literally "Most August One." Most aristocrats, however, immediately understood what was going on. "The readier men were to be slaves," Tacitus said, "the higher they were raised by wealth and promotion, so that, heads turned by revolution, they preferred the safety of the present to the dangers of the past." Noblemen stopped talking like Crassus; recognizing that only Augustus could now use lethal violence, they found quieter ways to work out their differences. Leviathan defanged the aristocracy.

In his book *The Civilizing Process*, which I mentioned in the introduction, Norbert Elias suggested that Europe became less violent after about A.D. 1500 because its turbulent aristocrats gave up on killing as a way to solve their disputes. Elias touched on Rome several times in the course of his argument but seems not to have realized that the Romans had anticipated the early-modern European pacification by a millennium and a half. Rich Romans remade themselves as men of peace and gloried in what they called the Pax Romana, the "Roman Peace," of the first two centuries A.D.

The whole empire seems to have breathed a collective sigh of relief. "The ox roams the fields in safety," the poet Horace rejoiced. "Ceres [the goddess of agriculture] and kind Prosperity nourish the land; across a pacified sea fly sailors." Educated authors showed a rare unanimity about the wonders of the age. Rome "has provided us with a great peace," gushed the slave turned Stoic philosopher Epictetus. "There are no longer any wars or battles or great bandits or pirates; at any time we can travel and journey from sunrise to sunset."

It would be easy to pile up examples of such fizzy prose—so easy, in fact, that when Edward Gibbon sat down in the 1770s to write the first properly modern history of Rome, he concluded that "if a man were called to fix the period in the history of the world, during which the condition of the human race was most happy and prosperous, he would, without hesitation, name that which elapsed from the death of Domitian to the accession of Commodus" (that is, A.D. 96–180).

Gibbon said this despite knowing that the Roman Empire remained a rough place. The first two centuries A.D. were the golden age of gladiators, when huge crowds flocked to watch men murder each other (the Colosseum alone seated fifty thousand), and the violence was not always confined to the arena. In A.D. 59, for instance, the people of Pompeii put on a big gladiatorial show, and sports fans from Nuceria, a few miles down the road, came to see the fun. "During an exchange of abuse, typical of these rowdy country towns," the urbane Tacitus tells us, "insults led to stone-throwing, and then swords were drawn." This might have struck wild Caledonians as perfectly reasonable, but what came next would not. Instead of exacting bloody revenge, the Nucerians complained to the emperor. Committees met and reports were filed; Pompeii's festival organizers were exiled, and the city was banned from holding gladiatorial shows for ten years (no small punishment, as it turned out, because Mount Vesuvius erupted and wiped Pompeii off the map another ten years after that). And there the matter ended.

When Bosnia erupted into ethnic violence in the 1990s, one Croat observed that before the breakup of Yugoslavia, "we [had] lived in peace and harmony because every hundred meters we had a policeman to make sure we loved each other very much." Yet first-century Pompeii had no such police force to impose peace; indeed, there was nothing like a modern police force anywhere in the world till London got one in 1828. So why did the killing stop?

The explanation seems to be that Rome's rulers succeeded in sending a message that only the government had the right to get violent. If Pompeians had carried on killing Nucerians in A.D. 59, more memos would have moved up the chain to the emperor, who had thirty legions to deal with people who gave him trouble by fighting without permission and killing potential taxpayers. But the paradoxical logic of violence was at work: because everyone knew that the emperor could (and, if pressed, would) send in the legions, he hardly ever had to do so.

I mentioned in the introduction that Hobbes liked to distinguish between "commonwealth by *acquisition*," or using force to compel people to be peaceful, and "commonwealth by *institution*," or using trust to get them to follow rules. In reality, however, the two go together. The Pompeians laid down their swords in A.D. 59 because centuries of war had built such a great Leviathan that they could trust it to overawe its subjects. The empire,

Gibbon pointed out, had replaced war with law. In the first two centuries A.D., using force to settle disagreements became, if not completely unthinkable, then at least highly inadvisable.

Government and laws bring their own problems, of course. "Formerly we suffered from crimes," Tacitus had one of his characters joke. "Now we suffer from laws." A government strong enough to stamp out wrongdoing, the empire's subjects learned, was also a government strong enough to do even greater wrong.

Some Roman officials exploited this to the full, but—as usual in Roman history—the worst crimes date to the first century B.C., when central government was at its weakest. Gaius Verres, who governed Sicily between 73 and 71 B.C., joked that he needed three years in the post—the first to steal enough to get rich, the second to steal enough to hire good lawyers, and the third to steal enough to bribe a judge and jury. Verres proceeded to do all three, beating, jailing, and even crucifying those who would not pay him.

All, though, for naught. Marcus Cicero made his name prosecuting Verres, who only escaped conviction by fleeing into exile. Over the next two centuries, prosecuting corrupt officials became the standard way for young lawyers in a hurry to get ahead, and even though villains with friends in high places regularly got off, new laws steadily narrowed the scope for using violent extortion.

The empire that Rome's wars created was no utopia, but the tone of the mass of surviving writings (by Romans and provincials alike) does suggest that it made its subjects safer than they would have been without it. And it also, apparently, made them richer. With pirates and bandits suppressed, trade boomed. To move its armies and fleets around, the government built state-of-the-art roads and harbors, which merchants used too. In return, Rome taxed the traders and spent most of the money it raised on the armed forces.

The army was concentrated in frontier provinces, few of which were fertile enough to feed so many men who did not work on the farm (by the first century A.D., about 350,000 of them). The army therefore spent much of its money buying food that had been shipped by merchants from the empire's more productive Mediterranean provinces to its less productive frontier ones. This generated more profits for the traders, which the government could tax, generating more money to spend on the army, creating more profits still, and so on, in a virtuous circle.

The flows of taxes and trade tied the Mediterranean economy together as never before. Each region could produce whatever it made cheapest and best, selling its goods wherever they fetched high prices. Markets and coinage spread into every nook and cranny of the empire.

Thanks to bigger markets, bigger ships became profitable; thanks to bigger ships, transport costs fell. And as they did, more and more people could afford to flock to the great cities, where the government spent most of the money that did not go to the army. In the first two centuries A.D., a million people lived in Rome—far more than had ever lived in one place before—and Antioch and Alexandria boasted perhaps half as many each.

These cities were the wonders of the world, seething, stinking, and raucous, but full of pomp, ceremony, and gleaming marble—all of which required more people, more food, and more bricks, iron nails, pots, and wine, which meant more taxes, more trade, and more growth.

Little by little, this frenetic activity increased the quantity of goods in circulation. By the best estimates, per capita consumption typically rose about 50 percent in the first two centuries after incorporation into the empire. The process disproportionately favored the already rich, who grew even richer, but every class of objects that archaeologists can count—house sizes, animal bones from feasts, coins, the height of skeletons—suggests that tens of millions of ordinary people profited too (Figure 1.4).

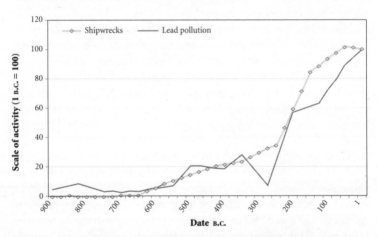

Figure 1.4. An age of plenty: parallel increases in Mediterranean shipwrecks, documenting levels of trade, and in lead pollution in the Spanish bog of Penido Vello, documenting levels of industrial activity. Numbers of wrecks and amounts of lead have been normalized so they can be compared on the same vertical scale, with the amounts of each in 1 B.C. being counted as 100.

"Who does not now recognize," the Roman geographer Pliny (most famous for getting himself killed by standing too close to Mount Vesuvius when it erupted) asked just four years before the battle at the Graupian Mountain, "that thanks to the majesty of the Roman Empire, communications have been opened between all parts of the world? Or that standards of living have made great strides? Or that all this is owed to trade, and the common enjoyment of the blessings of peace?" The Roman Empire was no wasteland.

Stationary Bandits

To Gibbon, the explanation for the empire's joy was obvious. Rome had been blessed with good rulers, who felt themselves "over-paid by the immense reward that inseparably waited on their success; by the honest pride of virtue, and by the exquisite delight of beholding the general happiness of which they were the authors."

The a-few-good-men theory has a certain appeal, above all its simplicity. If what made Rome such a success story really was just a run of great leaders, we would not need to reach the unpleasant conclusion that war was good for something in ancient times. It might simply be that an organization that has good enough bosses can survive pretty much anything. Perhaps the ancient world got safer and richer in spite of its wars, not because of them.

But the Gibbon thesis also has weaknesses. The first is that there were limits on how much ancient emperors could actually do. Rome certainly did have energetic rulers who rose before dawn and worked deep into the night answering letters, hearing lawsuits, and making decisions. But to get results, they had to work with layer upon layer of bureaucrats, lawyers, and scholars, all of whom had their own agendas. Even the most dynamic emperors—and men like Augustus were very dynamic indeed—struggled to produce change.

A second problem is that for every Augustus, the empire also had a Caligula or a Nero, men whose exquisite delight came more from fiddling while Rome burned, having sex with siblings, and appointing horses as consuls than from beholding the general happiness. According to the people who wrote the histories—that is, the bureaucrats, lawyers, and scholars— Rome had bad emperors more often than good in the first century A.D. (Tiberius, Caligula, Nero, and Domitian all got bad press and between them reigned for fifty-six years). Yet these hundred years probably saw peace and prosperity advance faster than ever before.

On balance, it does not look as if wise shepherds can take the credit for making the mass of ordinary mortals safer and richer. Most of the time, Rome's ruling elites pursued nothing more enlightened than their own self-interest. Yet in pursuing it, they found themselves wandering down paths that did leave most people better-off.

The Augustuses of this world become rulers by defeating their rivals and keep on ruling because they have more force at their disposal than anyone else. That force, however, has to be paid for. A ruler could just plunder his subjects to pay his troops (the wasteland model), but eventually there will be nothing left to steal. And in any case, as Rome's worst governors regularly learned, the wretched of the earth will probably revolt long before reaching the point at which everything has been stolen from them.

In the long run, governments only survive if their rulers learn when to stop stealing, and even learn when to give a little back. The economist Mancur Olson made the point nicely by comparing rulers with bandits. Your typical bandit, said Olson, is a rover. He comes into a community, steals everything not nailed down, and rides out again. He doesn't care how much damage he does; the only important thing is to steal as much as possible and then move on.

Rulers steal from their people too, Olson recognized, but the big difference between Leviathan and the rape-and-pillage kind of bandit is that rulers are *stationary* bandits. Instead of stealing everything and hightailing it, they stick around. Not only is it in their interest to avoid the mistake of squeezing every last drop from the community; it is also in their interest to do whatever they can to promote their subjects' prosperity so there will be more for the rulers to take later.

It is normally worth a ruler's while to spend some money to keep other potential bandits out, since anything a roving bandit steals is something the ruler cannot tax. It makes sense too to suppress violence within the community—murdered subjects cannot serve in the army or pay taxes, and fields laid waste in feuds between villages produce no crops. Even spending royal or aristocratic revenues on roads, harbors, and welfare can start to seem sensible, if the investments yield even bigger payoffs within a tolerable length of time.

Leviathan is a racket, but it may still be the best game in town. Rulers in effect use force to keep the peace and then charge their subjects for the service. The more efficiently the rulers do this, the more profits they reap. Over the generations, competitive pressures nudged the business of Roman government toward more efficient solutions. Allowing tax collectors to steal so much that their victims could not pay the next year's taxes was bad for business, so Rome stamped it out; letting potentially productive city dwellers starve was even worse, so Rome built harbors and even gave out food for free. Self-interest had the welcome side effect of making the empire's subjects safer and richer. The paradox of war was hard at work. Men who mastered violence carved out kingdoms, but to run them, they had to turn into managers.

As so often, Julius Caesar was the classic case. "Veni, vidi, vici," he famously wrote; "I came, I saw, I conquered." But he might have done better to say, "Veni, vidi, vici, administravi"; after coming, seeing, and conquering, he administered, and did it magnificently. Among his many reforms was the invention of the Julian calendar, still in use two thousand years later. July is named after him.

Ancient emperors were not Keynesian economists, sitting around calculating whether a sestertius spent now on keeping the peace would yield two sesterces in taxes down the road. Many of them, though, were hard and clever men who not only grasped the principles of the deal between Leviathan and its subjects but also saw the value of letting everyone know that they understood. One of the oldest surviving political texts in the world, dating back to the 2360s B.C., makes just this point. In it, King Uru'inimgina (also known as Urukagina; reigned ca. 2380–2360 B.C.) of Lagash, in the south of what is now Iraq, proclaimed that he had "freed the inhabitants of Lagash from usury, burdensome controls, hunger, theft, murder, and seizure. He established freedom. The widow and the orphan were no longer at the mercy of the powerful: it was for them that Uru'inimgina made his covenant with [the god] Ningirsu." Augustus could not have put it better.

Uru'inimgina is a shadowy figure, almost lost in the mists of time, but he clearly understood the value of investing in this message. In another parallel with doing business, a nontrivial portion of the art of government is really about confidence. People who suspect that their rulers are mad, corrupt, and/or idiots are likely to resist their demands, while if the management seems skilled, fair, and perhaps even loved by the gods, the attractions of plotting against it decline.

That said, the law of averages meant that the ancient world necessarily got its share of mad, corrupt, and/or incompetent rulers. The real heroes of the story—the men who actually made Leviathan work—were the bureaucrats, lawyers, and hangers-on. Pen pushers and bean counters often made it difficult for Augustus to get much done, but, more to the point, they also made it difficult for Caligula to get much done.

The surviving sources are full of stories of emperors' rages against obstructionist senators and the highly educated slaves who managed much of the court's business. On the whole, these episodes ended badly for the underlings. But in the background of these colorful accounts we can also make out thousands of men who lived less glamorous lives. On tombstones set up everywhere from Britain to Syria, men recounted with pride the offices they had held and honors they had won as they served on committees, collected taxes, and worked their way up the lower rungs of the bureaucratic ladder. "I, even I," boasted one North African who had started out working in the fields, "was enrolled among the city senators, and chosen by them to sit in the house of that body . . . I have passed through years distinguished by the merits of my career—years that an evil tongue has never hurt with accusation . . . Thus have I deserved to die as I lived, honestly."

There is no shortage of evidence that the empire's middle managers could be just as self-interested as their rulers, lining their pockets and promoting their relatives whenever the opportunity arose. But neither are we short of signs that plenty more really were earnest, industrious, and diligent. They made sure that aqueducts got built, roads were maintained, and the mail was delivered. They kept the Pax Romana going.

Catastrophic blunders could happen, and Rome went through phases of lurching from crisis to crisis. But in the long run, the pressures at work were inexorable. Warriors conquered small states, which forced them to turn into managers. Good management made states more efficient, safer, and richer, and the resulting efficient, safe, and rich states gave managers the tools they needed to compete with rival states. This, though, forced the managers to turn back into warriors who could put their rivals out of business—violently.

Can We All Get Along?

In April 1992, a jury in Simi Valley, just outside Los Angeles, reached a surprising decision. They had watched a videotape showing police landing fifty-six baton blows and six kicks on Rodney King during his arrest after a high-speed car chase. They had heard from doctors that King had suffered a facial fracture and broken ankle. They had listened while nurses reported that the police officers who brought King to the hospital had joked about his beating. And then they acquitted three of the defendants and failed to reach a verdict on the fourth.

That evening, riots broke out in Los Angeles and in the next few days spread across the United States. Fifty-three people were killed, more than two thousand were injured, and a billion dollars' worth of property was destroyed. On the third day of violence, King went on television and asked one of the most famous questions of the decade: "People, I just want to say, you know, can we all get along? Can we get along? Can we stop making it, making it horrible?"

It is a good question, which people must have asked in ancient times too. Instead of working their way toward peace through the violent, wasteland-making process of war, could they not have just sat down together, agreed to create larger organizations, drawn up rules, handed over taxes to fund enforcement, and got along?

Apparently not. "To jaw-jaw is always better than to war-war," Winston Churchill once said, but in all the archives of ancient history it is hard to find a single convincing case of people agreeing to come together in a larger society without being compelled to do so by violence, actual or feared.

Take the case of Philip of Pergamum, whose account of how war, piracy, and banditry had ruined the Greek world in the first century B.C. I mentioned a few pages ago. "With my pious hand I delivered this [history] to the Greeks," he explained, "so that . . . by observing the sufferings of others, they may live their lives in the right way." The Greeks, however, were unimpressed and went on killing each other. When they did stop, it was not because of Philip's jaw-jaw; it was because of Roman war-war.

In 67 B.C., the Roman senate sent Gnaeus Pompey (known, with some cause, as "the Great") to crush the pirates who infested Greek waters. As usual, they did this not out of benevolence but out of self-interest. The raids had gotten so bad that in 77 B.C. one band had kidnapped the young Julius Caesar (who joked with his captors that when he was ransomed, he would come back and crucify them, which, of course, he did). By the early 60s B.C., other bands were even raiding Italy's harbors.

The Greek cities had completely failed to suppress the violence, but Pompey brought Roman organization and a surprisingly modern approach to bear. In 2006, bloodied by reverses in Iraq, the U.S. Army adopted a new counterinsurgency doctrine known as "clear, hold, and build." Instead of focusing on killing or capturing troublemakers, soldiers switched to sweeping them out of an area, securing it, and reconstructing it, before moving methodically on to the next area. By 2009, violent deaths had fallen more than 80 percent. Pompey figured out the same strategy two thousand years earlier. He divided the Mediterranean into thirteen sectors and in a single summer worked through them one by one, clearing, holding, and building (Figure 1.5). Instead of crucifying the twenty thousand ex-freebooters he rounded up, Pompey imposed peace on them. "Wild animals," his biographer wrote, "often lose their fierceness and savagery when subjected to a gentler existence; so Pompey decided to move the pirates from the sea to the land and give them a taste of civilized life by making them used to living in cities and farming the soil."

The sea secured, Pompey turned to the land. In five spectacular campaigns he led Roman armies through the cities of Syria to the mountain fastnesses of the Caucasus and the borders of Egypt, crushing foreign kings, rebellious generals, and riotous Jews as he went. Again, he cleared, held, and built, drawing up law codes, installing Roman garrisons, and overhauling finances. Cracking down on corruption and extortion, he simultaneously lowered taxes and raised Roman revenues. Peace reigned; several Greek cities, Athens among them, announced that Pompey was a god in human form.

Figure 1.5. Sweeping the seas: Roman marines getting ready to board an enemy ship on a relief carving of the first century B.C.

Pompey resorted to violence not because Romans lacked the skills for jaw-jaw—the city was bursting with orators like Cicero—but because he, like a lot of other Romans, saw that jaw-jaw worked best when it followed war-war. Tacitus, for instance, tells us that after spending his first summer in Britain (A.D. 77) terrorizing the natives—"people living in isolation and ignorance, and therefore prone to fight," Tacitus called them—Agricola devoted the winter to "getting them used to a life of peace and quiet by providing amenities. He gave private encouragement and official assistance to the building of temples, public squares, and good houses."

The Britons liked it. "The result," says Tacitus, "was that instead of loathing the Latin language they became eager to speak it effectively. In the same way, our national dress came into favor and the toga was everywhere to be seen." The political scientist Joseph Nye has called such an approach "soft power," by which he means using "intangible factors such as institutions, ideas, values, culture, and the perceived legitimacy of policies" to win people over, as opposed to the coercive "hard power" of war and economics.

Tacitus understood the lure of the soft side. "The population was gradually led into the demoralizing temptations of arcades, baths, and sumptuous banquets," he observed. "The unsuspecting Britons spoke of such novelties as 'civilization,' when in fact they were only a feature of their enslavement." But he also knew that softness only worked in the wake of hard power—or, as Americans would put it in Vietnam nineteen centuries later, "Grab 'em by the balls, and their hearts and minds will follow." The Romans in Britain accomplished this much better than the Americans in Vietnam, winning hearts and minds because they had already robbed the Britons of their freedom to fight back. When Agricola came up against Britons who still had this freedom, like Calgacus, there was no talk of togas.

Archaeology largely confirms this. Roman goods, especially wine (transported in highly distinctive containers), were wildly popular far beyond the empire's frontiers. According to hearsay, Gallic chiefs would willingly sell a man into slavery in exchange for a large jar of wine, and Roman writers unanimously agreed that barbarians near the frontiers, who had gotten used to soft Roman ways, fought less fiercely than far-off barbarians, who remained as savage as ever.

The most seductive softness of all was intellectual, and in the first few centuries A.D. the Romans perfected a string of compelling systems of thought. The most successful were Stoicism and Christianity. Neither started out as a form of imperial soft power; in each case, in fact, the founding fathers of the faith were critics of the status quo, penniless Greek philosophers and a Jewish carpenter speaking truth to power from the social and geographical margins. But as the generations passed, the hard, clever men who ran the empire did what such men always do. They subverted the counterculture. Instead of fighting it, they brought its best and brightest young men into the establishment. They picked and chose among its ideas, rewarding former radicals who said things the ruling class liked while ignoring those who didn't. Little by little, they turned the critiques of empire into justifications for it. "Render therefore unto Caesar the things which are Caesar's," Jesus urged good Christians, "for," Saint Paul added, "there is no power but of God: the powers that be are ordained of God."

Stoicism and Christianity assured the empire's subjects that unauthorized violence was wicked, which was good news for Leviathan, and the empire then vigorously exported these intellectual systems to its neighbors. Yet for all the contagiousness of the new ideas, they did not by themselves persuade anyone to join the empire. Only war or the fear of war could do that. Soft power worked its magic later, binding the conquered together and giving the empire a degree of unity.

As so often, it is the apparent exceptions to the war-first principle that prove the rule. The little city-states of ancient Greece, for example, had lots of reasons to forget their differences and come together in a larger community. Within each city, Greeks generally pacified themselves very well: by 500 B.C., men no longer went about their daily business armed, and around 430 one upper-class Athenian even complained that he could no longer go around punching slaves on the street (it was, in fact, illegal). When cities were at peace, their rates of violent death must have been among the lowest in the ancient world. Most, though, went to war roughly two years in every three. According to Plato, "What most men call 'peace' is just a fiction, and in reality every city is fighting an undeclared war against every other."

No surprise, then, that dozens of squabbling Greek city-states agreed to surrender much of their sovereignty to Athens in 477 B.C. But they did not choose this course out of love of peace or even admiration for Athens; they did it because they were frightened that the Persian Empire, which had tried to conquer Greece in 480, would gobble them up if they stood alone. And when, in the 440s, the Persian tide receded, several of the cities thought better of their submission to Athens and decided to go it alone—only for the Athenians to use force to prevent them.

In the third and second centuries B.C., a new wave of city-state amalgamations swept Greece. This time, groups of cities bundled themselves into *koina* (literally "communities," but usually translated as "federal leagues"), setting up representative governments and merging their arrangements for security and finance. Once again, though, their prime motive was fear of wars they could not win by themselves—initially against the mighty Macedonian successors of Alexander the Great and then against the encroaching Romans.

The most peculiar stories may be those of Ptolemy VIII (nicknamed Fatso) and Attalus III, kings of Egypt and Pergamum, respectively. Ptolemy had been kicked out of Egypt by his brother (also named Ptolemy) in 163 B.C., and in 155 B.C. the dispossessed Ptolemy drew up a will leaving his new kingdom of Cyrene to the Roman people if he died without heirs. Attalus, though, went further; he actually did die without heirs in 133 B.C., whereupon his subjects discovered—to their astonishment—that they too had been bequeathed to the Roman Empire.

We do not know how the Romans felt about Ptolemy's will, since the overweight monarch in fact lasted another four decades and, after seducing his own stepdaughter, left rather a lot of heirs. We do know, though, that the Romans were as surprised as the Pergamenes by Attalus's bequest, and with self-interest strongly to the fore, competing factions in the senate fell into heated arguments over whether Attalus actually had the right to give his city to them.

Ptolemy and Attalus did what they did not because they loved Rome but because they feared it less than they feared war.* Lacking heirs, both men dreaded civil war. The brothers Ptolemy had already tried fratricide and gone to war even before Fatso drew up his will, and Attalus's position was worse still. A pretender to the throne, claiming to be Attalus's half brother, was stirring up revolt among the poor (and might have begun a civil war even before Attalus died), and four neighboring kings were waiting in

---

*So far as we can tell, what Ptolemy and Attalus really loved were their own womenfolk. Before seducing his stepdaughter, Ptolemy had married his sister (which meant that his stepdaughter was also his niece), while Attalus's attraction to his own mother struck even the worldly Greeks as unhealthy. (The other love of Attalus's life was growing poisonous plants, for which he apparently had a real talent.)

the wings to dismember Pergamum. No wonder a bloodless Roman take-over looked good to both kings.

This was the classical world's answer to Rodney King: No, we can't all get along. The only force strong enough to persuade people to give up the right to kill and impoverish each other was violence—or the fear that violence was imminent.

To understand why that was so, though, we must turn to another part of the world entirely.

The Beast

In a jungle clearing on a South Sea island, a boy named Simon is arguing with a dead pig's head on a stick.

"Fancy thinking the Beast was something you could hunt and kill!" says the head.

Simon does not reply. His tongue is swollen with thirst. A pulse is beating in his skull. One of his fits is coming on.

Down on the beach, his chums are dancing and singing. When these schoolboys first found themselves marooned on the island, all was fun and games: they swam, blew on conch shells, and slept under the stars. But almost imperceptibly, their little society unraveled. A shadow crept across their fellowship, haunting the forest like an evil beast.

Until today, that is. Today, a troop of teenage hunters impaled a screaming sow as she nursed her young. Whooping with excitement, the boys smeared each other with blood and planned a feast. But first, their leader recognized, there was something they had to do. He hacked the grinning head off the carcass and skewered it on the sharpened stick that they had used to kill the pig. "This head is for the beast," he shouted into the forest. "It's a gift."

And with that, the boys all set off running, dragging the flesh toward the beach—all except Simon, who crouches alone in the dappled, unreal light of the clearing.

"You knew, didn't you?" asks the pig's head. "I'm part of you? Close, close, close! I'm the reason why it's no go? Why things are what they are?"

Simon knows. His body arches and stiffens; the seizure is upon him. He falls, forward, forward, toward the pig's expanding mouth. Blood is darkening between the teeth, buzzing with flies, and there is blackness within, a blackness that spreads. Simon knows: the Beast cannot be killed. The Beast is us.

So says William Golding in his unforgettable novel *Lord of the Flies*. Cast away in the Pacific, far from schools and rules, a few dozen boys learn the dark truth: humans are compulsive killers, our psyches hardwired for violence. The Beast is us, and only a fragile crust of civilization keeps it in check. Given the slightest chance, the Beast will break loose. That, Golding tells us, is the reason why it's no go. Why Calgacus and Agricola fought, not talked.

Or is it? Another South Sea island, perhaps not so far from Golding's, seems to tell a different story. Like the novelist Golding, the young would-be anthropologist Margaret Mead suspected that in this simpler setting, where balmy breezes blew and palm fronds kissed the waves, she would see the crooked timber of humanity stripped of its veneer of civilization. But unlike Golding, who never actually visited the Pacific (although he was about to be posted there in charge of a landing craft when World War II ended), she decamped from New York City to Samoa in 1925 (Figure 1.6).

"As the dawn begins to fall," Mead wrote in her anthropological classic *Coming of Age in Samoa*, "lovers slip home from trysts beneath the palm trees or in the shadow of beached canoes, that the light may find each sleeper in his appointed place."

Pigs' heads hold no terrors on Samoa. "As the sun rises higher in the sky, the shadows deepen under thatched roofs . . . Families who will cook today are hard at work; the taro, yams and bananas have already been brought

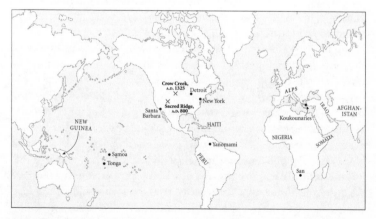

Figure 1.6. Lands of beasts and noble savages: locations outside the Roman Empire discussed in this chapter

from inland; the children are scuttling back and forth, fetching sea water, or leaves to stuff the pig." The families gather in the evening to share their feast in peace and contentment. "Sometimes sleep will not descend upon the village until long past midnight; then at last there is only the mellow thunder of the reef and the whisper of lovers, as the village rests till dawn . . .

"Samoa," Mead concluded, "is a place where no one plays for very high stakes, no one pays very heavy prices, no one suffers for his convictions or fights to the death for special ends." On Samoa, the Beast is not close at all.

Golding and Mead both saw violence as a sickness, but they disagreed on its diagnosis. As Golding saw things, violence was a genetic condition, inherited from our forebears. Civilization was the only medication, but even civilization could only suppress the symptoms, not cure the disease. Mead drew the opposite conclusion. For her, the South Seas showed that violence was just a contagion, and civilization was its source, not its cure. Calgacus and Agricola fought two thousand years ago because their warlike cultures made them do it, and people carried on fighting in the twentieth century because warlike cultures were still making them do it.

In 1940, as France fell to Hitler, bombs rained down on London, and trenches filled up with murdered Polish Jews, Mead found a new metaphor. "Warfare," she argued, "is just an invention." Certainly, she conceded, war is "an invention known to the majority of human societies," but even so, "if we despair over the way in which war seems such an ingrained habit of most of the human race, we can take comfort from the fact that a poor invention will usually give place to a better invention."

Mead was not the only champion of this view, but she rapidly became the most influential. By 1969, when she retired from her position at the American Museum of Natural History, she was the most famous social scientist in the world and had proved, to the satisfaction of millions of readers, that humans' natural state was one of peace. Swayed by the consensus, anthropologist after anthropologist came back from the field reporting that their people were peaceful too (anthropologists have a habit of calling the group among whom they do fieldwork "my people"). This was the age of "War," love-ins, and peace protesters promising to levitate the Pentagon; it was only to be expected that Rousseau would seem at long last to have won his bitter, centuries-old debate with Hobbes.

This was what Napoleon Chagnon thought, at any rate, when he swapped graduate school in Ann Arbor, Michigan, for the rain-forest borderlands of Brazil and Venezuela in 1964. He fully expected the Yanomami people,* whose marriage patterns he planned to study, to live up to what he called "the image of 'primitive man' that I had conjured up in my mind before doing fieldwork, a kind of 'Rousseauian' view." But the Yanomami had other ideas.

"The excitement of meeting my first Yanomamö was almost unbearable as I duck-waddled through the low passage [in the defensive perimeter] into the village clearing," Chagnon wrote. Slimy with sweat, his hands and face swollen from bug bites, Chagnon

> looked up and gasped when I saw a dozen burly, naked, sweaty, hideous men staring at us down the shafts of their drawn arrows! . . . [S]trands of dark-green slime dripped or hung from their nostrils—strands so long that they clung to their pectoral muscles or drizzled down their chins. We arrived at the village while the men were blowing a hallucinogenic drug up their noses . . . My next discovery was that there were a dozen or so vicious, underfed dogs snapping at my legs, circling me as if I were to be their next meal. I just stood there holding my notebook, helpless and pathetic. Then the stench of the decaying vegetation and filth hit me and I almost got sick . . .
>
> We had arrived just after a serious fight. Seven women had been abducted the day before by a neighboring group, and the local men and their guests had just that morning recovered five of them in a brutal club fight . . . I am not ashamed to admit that had there been a diplomatic way out, I would have ended my fieldwork then and there.

But he stayed and in more than twenty-five visits over the next thirty years learned that Yanomamiland was not Margaret Mead's Samoa. He witnessed, he said, "a good many incidents that expressed individual vindictiveness on the one hand and collective bellicosity on the other . . . from the ordinary incidents of wife beating and chest pounding to dueling† and orga-

*Few things get anthropologists more worked up than terminology. According to one study of the arguments over Chagnon's work, "*Yanomamö* is the term Chagnon gave the collective group, and those who refer to the group as *Yanomamö* tend to be supporters of Chagnon's work. Those who prefer *Yanomami* or *Yanomamo* tend to take a more neutral or anti-Chagnon stance." Eternally optimistic about finding middle ground, I go with Yanomami.

†Chest pounding involves two angry men taking turns to punch each other in the left breast until the pain proves too much for one of them. In a duel, two even angrier men

Figure 1.7. Not the noble savage: A Yanomami club fight over a woman, photographed in the early 1970s. The dark line down the chest and stomach of the man at center-left is blood from his head.

nized raids . . . with the intention of ambushing and killing men from enemy villages" (Figure 1.7).

Armed with statistics going back decades, Chagnon discovered that roughly a quarter of Yanomami men died violently, and two men out of every five took part in at least one homicide during their lives. Worse still, he concluded that violence paid. On average, men who killed fathered three times as many children as men who did not kill. The Beast was alive and kicking in the Orinoco headwaters.

Unlike Hobbes and Rousseau, Chagnon was never driven into exile (in fact, he spent much of his career teaching in Santa Barbara, one of the cushiest berths a professor could ask for), but his academic enemies certainly made their best efforts. The first challenges focused on how he had collected his data, largely because Chagnon was much more forthcoming than most anthropologists about the difficulties of doing fieldwork. As soon

---

hit each other over the head with wooden stakes (sometimes sharpened) until one collapses.

as he arrived in the village of Bisaasi-teri, he confessed, he had run into trouble: he found that most Yanomami considered speaking another man's name out loud to be deeply disrespectful (disrespectful enough to justify violence), which made his planned study of family trees distinctly tricky. Chagnon, undeterred, kept pushing. Offended by his rudeness, people got back at him by making up names, the sillier the better. To everyone's amusement, the foolish foreigner kept writing them down.

Five months passed before Chagnon learned the truth, when, on a visit to another village, he let slip a name he had been given in Bisaasi-teri. "A stunned silence followed," he says, "and then a villagewide roar of uncontrollable laughter, choking, gasping, and howling. It seems that I thought the Bisaasi-teri headman was called 'long dong' and his brother 'eagle shit.' The Bisaasi-teri headman had a son called 'asshole' and a daughter called 'fart breath.'"

It is always a good idea to have a Plan B when doing fieldwork, and now, his strategy in tatters, Chagnon unveiled his. Yanomami might refuse to name their own kin, but they would happily rattle off the names of their personal enemies' kin. Chagnon found that a little bribery or blackmail would usually elicit the facts he needed.

Plan B worked, but it was hardly an uplifting example of how to interact with other cultures. In fact, in 2002 the Executive Committee of the American Anthropological Association formally approved a report censuring Chagnon for his fieldwork methods—a first—only to rescind its approval (another first) after a referendum in 2005. Feelings were running high. If Chagnon could treat "his" people so dishonestly, some anthropologists asked, should scholars accept anything he said? Several who had worked in Yanomamiland simply refused to believe him, insisting that the Yanomami were not violent at all; Chagnon, they said, had falsified data to get attention.

And then things got really nasty. Some critics accused Chagnon of complicity in Brazilian plots to split Yanomamiland into tiny reservations so that gold miners could intimidate the tribes and exploit the resources more easily. In 2012, Venezuelan activists accused miners of murdering eighty Yanomami, but government inspectors found no bodies. One critic even claimed that Chagnon had helped spread a measles epidemic that killed hundreds of Yanomami.

It has been an unsavory episode in the history of scholarship, but what goes around comes around. As the attacks on Chagnon and his *Lord of the Flies* vision intensified, Margaret Mead and the *Coming of Age* thesis started getting the same treatment. In 1983, Derek Freeman, an anthropologist from New Zealand who had been working on Samoa since 1940, published a book charging that Mead had completely misunderstood the place.

Freeman learned from Mead's unpublished papers that far from "speaking their language, eating their food, sitting barefoot and cross-legged upon the pebbly floor," as she had described herself, she had actually picked up only the shakiest smattering of the local tongue, had stayed on Samoa just a few months, had misled people about who she was, had lived in a bungalow with an American pharmacist and his family, and had dined with the admiral of the U.S. Pacific Fleet. As a result of her colonialist lifestyle, Freeman concluded, Mead failed to notice what police records from 1920s Samoa make clear: that the island had higher rates of violent death than the United States (no small thing in the age of Al Capone).

Worse still, in an interview in 1987, Fa'apua'a Fa'amu (by then a great-grandmother, but back in 1926 one of Mead's main informants) confessed that she and her girlfriend Fofoa had found Mead just as comical as the Yanomami would find Chagnon, but with one big difference: Mead never realized that people were pulling her leg. Embarrassed by Mead's obsession with sex, Fa'amu said, "we just fibbed and fibbed to her." *Coming of Age in Samoa* rested on teenagers' tall tales about their sexploits.

By the 1990s, with mutual recriminations coming thick and fast, it was tempting to conclude that anthropology really had made no progress since Hobbes and Rousseau. Things got so bad that some anthropologists actually began celebrating their field's apparent inability to produce results. Fieldwork, a new generation of scholars proclaimed, is not really a method of data collection at all; it is more a kind of artistic performance, weaving creative fictions. Those who expect it to establish "the facts" are missing the point.

Fortunately, these claims are just plain wrong. Quietly, often unnoticed amid all the mudslinging and name-calling, hundreds of anthropologists have spent decades steadily getting on with the real work, slowly assembling an impressive database on violence in small-scale societies. Bringing together studies made everywhere from Africa to the Arctic, this patient work has produced the key discovery that rates of violent death in small-scale societies are usually shockingly high.

In the twentieth century, the industrialized world fought two world wars and carried out multiple genocides. Thanks to all the databases compiled since Richardson's *Statistics of Deadly Quarrels* (mentioned in the introduction), we can now say with some confidence that of the roughly

10 billion people who lived in these hundred years, somewhere between 100 million and 200 million met violent ends in wars, feuds, and
homicides—roughly 1–2 percent of the total. In the small-scale societies
that anthropologists and archaeologists were able to study, however, the
proportion of people dying violently seemed to be on average between 10
and 20 percent—*ten times as high.*

This does not mean that the Yanomami and the Samoans were like
nineteenth-century stereotypes of savages, randomly killing and maiming
from dusk to dawn. Anthropologists have also found that even the fiercest
cultures have elaborate networks of kinship, gift exchange, and feasting,
which they use to find peaceful solutions to most conflicts. But the hard
fact remains that blood is their argument appallingly often. In 2008, the
biologist and geographer Jared Diamond, traveling around highland New
Guinea doing fieldwork, was astonished to hear his driver—"a happy, enthusiastic, sociable person," says Diamond—casually chatting about his part
in a three-year cycle of killings that claimed thirty lives. (Diamond was
even more astonished when his former driver sued him for $10 million
over the story. The case was eventually dismissed.)

The reason it took anthropologists so long to notice that "their" people
regularly acted like extras from *Lord of the Flies* was simple: anthropologists rarely spent long enough looking. Take the case of Elizabeth Marshall
Thomas (nowadays best known for her book *The Hidden Life of Dogs*), who
spent her late teens with her anthropologist parents among San hunter-
gatherers in the Kalahari Desert.* She wrote a sensitive account of San life,
which she called *The Harmless People*—even though in the 1950s San were
killing one another faster than the residents of inner-city Detroit would do
at the high point of the crack cocaine epidemic.

Thomas chose the title *The Harmless People* not because she was un-
observant but because the numbers worked against her. If the rate of
violent death in a particular hunter-gatherer society ran at 10 percent, that
would mean that a band of a dozen people would have roughly one murder
every quarter of a century. Few anthropologists have the funding—or
fortitude—to spend twenty-five months in the field, let alone twenty-five
years. It takes repeated revisits, ideally incorporating multiple communities

---

*Here again, terminology can cause offense. A conference of San speakers agreed in
1996 to use "San" as a collective label instead of the older term "Bushmen," but some
consider "San" derogatory because it means "outsider" in the Nama language.

(like Chagnon's studies of the Yanomami), to reveal that an awful lot of people are meeting grisly ends.

The evidence for high levels of violence is unambiguous, but making sense of it is more complicated. If, as the *Coming of Age* theory says, war is a contagion of civilization, it might well be that the high rates of violence among the San were a disease they had caught from westerners. This idea inspired the classic 1980 comedy *The Gods Must Be Crazy*, but some of Chagnon's critics took it in a much nastier direction, blaming him personally for infecting the Yanomami with war (as well as measles) by trading them steel axes for information.

The obvious way to settle the question is to look back in time, to see whether wars were common in small-scale societies before they came into contact with more complex societies (the *Lord of the Flies* view) or whether wars began only after contact had begun (the *Coming of Age* view). But when we do this, we run into a chicken-and-egg problem: most small-scale societies had no written records until they came into contact with more complex ones.

Samoa, Margaret Mead's stomping ground, is a case in point. The earliest detailed account of the islands is by John Williams, a British missionary, and almost the first thing he saw on arriving in 1830 was the village of A'ana in flames. A "disastrous war," Williams wrote, "continued with unabated fury for nearly nine months in which many of our people fell victims so that the dead & wounded were brought over every day." It created a wasteland: "All the districts in AAna [Williams's spelling] are depopulated & in sailing along the beautiful coast for ten or twelve miles not a habitation is to be seen."

Just in case A'ana did not convince Williams that the Samoans were tough men, their chiefs showed him the preserved heads of men killed by their ancestors and regaled him with stories of the wars and massacres of the past. One village put a rock in a basket for each battle it fought: Williams counted 197.

But there is one difficulty. Williams was the first European to write much about Samoa, but he was not the first European to go there. The Dutch explorer Jakob Roggeveen had arrived in 1722, and others had followed over the next hundred years. For all we know, every single head, rock, and story that Williams encountered had accumulated since 1722 and was the fruit of contagion by civilization.

Archaeology, however, suggests otherwise. The interior of Samoa is packed with prehistoric hillforts. Some must have been built since 1722, but carbon 14 dating shows that others are between six hundred and a thousand years old. Samoans had been building forts, and probably waging war, long before Europeans showed up. Samoan traditions describe great wars against invaders from Tonga, apparently around eight hundred years ago, providing a plausible context for the fort-building, and the wooden clubs and war canoes still in use when Europeans arrived seem to have descended from Tongan prototypes of this era, suggesting a continuous tradition of using deadly force.

Even on Samoa, the *Coming of Age* theory seems not to work very well, but there are always multiple ways to interpret archaeological finds. Archaeology is a young field, and as recently as the 1950s there were still very few graduate programs training future professionals. The people who dug up the past tended to drift into it from other walks of life, and a remarkable number were former military men. Many of them, perhaps unsurprisingly, tended to see war and destruction almost everywhere they dug. But in the 1960s and '70s, a new generation of men and women colonized the field, educated in university departments of anthropology and archaeology, and often steeped in the *Coming of Age* view of prehistory. They—equally unsurprisingly—tended to see war and destruction almost nowhere.

It can be painful for the middle-aged to look back on the follies of their youth. As a graduate student in the 1980s (probably the glory days of *Coming of Age*–ism), I dug for several summers at Koukounaries, an extraordinary prehistoric Greek site on the fairy-tale-beautiful island of Paros. On our first visit to the site, the director explained that it had been destroyed by violent attack around 1125 B.C. Its fortifications had been cast down and its buildings burned. The defenders had piled slingstones by the walls, and the skeletons of several donkeys—caught in the final disaster—had been excavated in the narrow alleys on the acropolis. But I (and, I hasten to add, my graduate student peers) flatly refused to believe that any of this was evidence of war, and once we had ruled out war as impossible, whatever explanations remained—no matter how improbable—had to be true.

It was this kind of thinking that led so many archaeologists to insist, in the face of equally overwhelming evidence, that the pre-Roman hillforts of western Europe mentioned earlier in this chapter were ceremonial centers, status symbols, and basically anything except military bases. But like the anthropologists, archaeologists began realizing in the 1990s that the evidence just could not be shoehorned into a *Coming of Age* pattern anymore.

New scientific methods played a part in this shift. When hikers found the celebrated Ice Man in the Italian Alps in 1991—a deep-frozen corpse dating around 3300 B.C.—archaeologists initially assumed that he had died in a snowstorm. In 2001, scanning technology revealed an arrowhead embedded in his left armpit, but even then some archaeologists hypothesized an elaborate funeral involving his dead body being carried up into the mountains. But in 2008, new immunohistochemical methods showed that the Ice Man had been attacked at least twice. The first assault gave him a deep wound in his right hand; in the second, a couple of days later, he was hit in the back with a blunt object and shot with the arrow, which severed an artery. In 2012, a nanoscanning atomic force microscope found intact red blood cells that proved he had bled to death within hours of being hit by the arrow.

We would not know any of this were the Ice Man not so spectacularly preserved, but systematic study of large samples of skeletons can produce equally nasty and brutish results. Sometime around A.D. 1325, for instance, at least 486 people were slaughtered and their bodies tossed into a ditch at Crow Creek in South Dakota. A good 90 percent—and possibly all—of the dead had been scalped. Eyes had been gouged out, tongues sliced off, teeth shattered, and throats cut. Some were beheaded. For a few, this was not even the first time they had been scalped or shot: their bones bore the telltale marks of older, partially healed wounds.

Excavations began at Crow Creek in 1978, and since then evidence for Native American massacres has come thick and fast. The most recent example (as I write) is at Sacred Ridge in Colorado, where a village was burned down around A.D. 800 and at least thirty-five men, women, and children were tortured and killed. Their enemies used blunt weapons—clubs, or perhaps just rocks—to smash their feet and faces to pulp. The killers scalped everyone, cutting off ears and hacking some corpses into dozens of pieces. Like the Romans described by Polybius a thousand years earlier, they even killed the village dogs.

In fact, not much about Crow Creek, Sacred Ridge, or Samoa would have surprised the Romans. Cicero and Tacitus, like Hobbes and Golding, knew perfectly well that the Beast was close, close, close, and that only an even more terrifying beast—Leviathan—could cage it.

Getting to Rome

In his book *The Origins of Political Order*, the political scientist Francis Fukuyama asks a penetrating question: How do we get to Denmark?

Fukuyama asks this not because he doesn't know how to buy a plane ticket but because for social scientists Denmark has come to stand in as (in Fukuyama's words) "a mythical place that is known to have good political and economic institutions: it is stable, democratic, peaceful, prosperous, inclusive, and has extremely low levels of political corruption. Everyone would like to figure out how to transform Somalia, Haiti, Nigeria, Iraq, or Afghanistan into 'Denmark.'"

If there had been political scientists two thousand years ago, they would have asked instead how to get to Rome. The Roman Empire was not very democratic, but it certainly was peaceful and, by the standards of the day, stable, prosperous, and inclusive (corruption is a little harder to judge). The alternative to getting to Rome was to live in societies with more than a passing similarity to modern-day Somalia, Haiti, Nigeria, Iraq, or Afghanistan— but more dangerous.

I have suggested in this chapter that the explanation of how the Romans got to Rome is very much a paradox. On the one hand, Leviathan was what suppressed violence, and suppressing violence was what being Roman (or now Danish) was all about; but on the other, violence was what made Leviathan possible in the first place. All in all, war seems to be good for something. And yet . . . not all roads led to Rome. In the Mediterranean Basin, war proved to be the path to peace and prosperity, but in many other places it did not. Archaeologists have uncovered evidence of incessant fighting around the shores of the Baltic, in the deserts of Australia, and in the forests of central Africa, but none of these regions produced its own Roman Empire.

Why not? Why did the Beast not turn into a stationary bandit everywhere? War, it would seem, is only *sometimes* good for something. We need to know what makes the difference.

CAGING THE BEAST:
THE PRODUCTIVE WAY OF WAR

Not the Western Way of War

"The Greeks had a word for it," the saying goes, and one of the words they gave us is "chaos." In Greek mythology, chaos was the disordered void that existed before the gods created the cosmos; in Greek warfare, it was the kind of scene that greeted the Persian general Mardonius one August morning in 479 B.C. as the sun came up over the country town of Plataea. For a week, a dense mass of armored Greek infantrymen had lined the hills overlooking Mardonius's camp. During the previous night, they had started withdrawing but had made a monumental mess of it. Some had refused to pull back, insisting that retreat would be cowardly. Some had followed orders but gone in the wrong direction. And some had disappeared altogether.

It was Mardonius's moment. He led his best men in a charge straight at the Spartan contingent, which was cut off from the other Greeks by a steep ridge. Within moments, the rest of the Persian host had broken ranks and rushed forward too, swamping the heavily outnumbered Spartans. The fifth-century Greek historian Herodotus tells what happened next: "The Persians were as brave and strong as the Greeks, but they had no armor, no training, and nothing like the same skill as their enemies. Sometimes one at a time, sometimes in groups of ten or so, they rushed at the Spartans. But regardless of whether there were more or less of them, they were cut down.

"Wherever Mardonius was, riding round on his white horse and surrounded by his thousand crack troops, they would attack fiercely. While he was still alive, they held their own, fighting hard and killing many Spartans. But as soon as he went down, and his personal bodyguard was destroyed, then all the other Persians broke, turned, and ran." The harsh truth, Herodotus concluded, was that "the Persians . . . had many men, but few soldiers" (Figure 2.1).

This, suggests the military historian Victor Davis Hanson, is the key to a contrast in fighting styles that has shaped all subsequent history. "For the past 2,500 years," Hanson argues, "there has been a peculiar practice of Western warfare, a common foundation and continual way of fighting, that has made Europeans the most deadly soldiers in the history of civilization."

Hanson calls this peculiar practice the Western way of war. It was invented, he tells us, by Greeks, who, between about 700 and 500 B.C., began

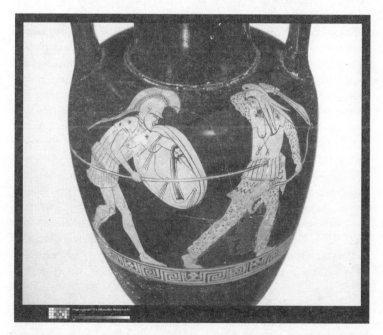

Figure 2.1. Real soldiers: a heavily armored Greek infantryman skewers an unarmored Persian soldier on an Athenian red-figured vase, painted around 470 B.C.

settling their differences with head-on charges between phalanxes of armored spearmen. "It is this Western desire for a single, magnificent collision of infantry," Hanson concludes, "for brutal killing with edged weapons on a battlefield between free men, that has baffled and terrified our adversaries from the non-Western world for more than 2,500 years."

The late John Keegan, the dean of twentieth-century military historians, took the argument further. Since Herodotus's time, Keegan suggested, there has been "a line of division between [the Western] battle tradition and the indirect, evasive, and stand-off style of combat characteristic of the steppe and the Near and Middle East: east of the steppe and south-east of the Black Sea, warriors continued to keep their distance from their enemies; west of the steppe and south-west of the Black Sea, warriors learned to abandon caution and to close to arm's length." Mardonius came from the wrong side of the line.

At the end of the last chapter, I asked how the Romans got to Rome (as it were) while so many other people in ancient times did not. If Hanson and Keegan are correct, we perhaps have the answer: building on their arguments, we might suggest that the Romans got to Rome because they inherited the Western way of war from the Greeks, and only this direct, bloody form of fighting was capable of creating Leviathan. We might then draw the further conclusion that when I say war has been good for something, what I really mean is that the Western way of war has been good for something.

The only way to find out if this is true is by broadening our perspective. We need to know first whether the way the Greeks fought at Plataea really was uniquely Western, and next whether the growth of large, safe, and prosperous societies was also a Western peculiarity.

In this chapter, I will try to show two things: first, that the answer to both these questions is no; and second, that that is precisely what makes the questions interesting. As we widen our inquiry from the Mediterranean Basin to the rest of the world, the real explanation for how the Romans got to Rome begins to emerge, and with it the key to understanding why war has been good for some things.

Age of Empires

I want to start with the second of my questions: Were large, safe, and prosperous societies a Western peculiarity?

The answer is no. We can see this just by looking at a map (Figure 2.2). In the two or three centuries after the Battle of Plataea, a band of rather

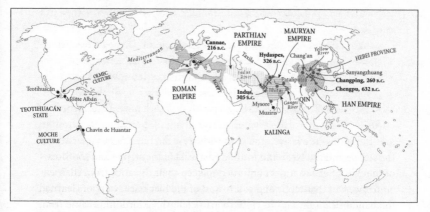

Figure 2.2. Ancient empires: the Mauryan Empire around 250 B.C.; the Roman, Parthian, and Han Empires around A.D. 100; the Moche culture around A.D. 200; and Teotihuacán around A.D. 300

similar empires grew up across the Old World from the Mediterranean to China. All were large, peaceful, stable, and prosperous. Across the oceans, smaller but still formidable states also ruled parts of Central America and the Andes.

At their height, the greatest of these empires—the Roman in the West, the Han in what we now call China, and the Mauryan in modern India and Pakistan—each covered about 1.5–2 million square miles, governed thirty to sixty million people, and beat (most of) its swords into plowshares. In each empire, rates of violent death declined sharply, and people put their plowshares to good use, prospering in a golden age of relative peace and plenty.

On the whole, we know less about the Han and Mauryan Empires than about Rome, and less still about states in the New World. In the Americas, the shortage of evidence is so acute that specialists cannot even agree on where Leviathans first appeared. Some archaeologists see the Olmec culture in Mexico (ca. 1200 B.C.) and Chavín de Huantar in Peru (ca. 1000 B.C.) as the pioneers. Mainstream opinion, however, holds that it was only a thousand years later, in the age of the Moche culture in Peru and the city-states of Monte Albán and Teotihuacán in Mexico, that America's first functioning governments put in an appearance, imposing their will over thousands of square miles and populations probably running up into a few million. They built great monuments, oversaw elaborate trade networks, and presided over rising standards of living, but remained pre-literate.

That is bad news for historians. Even when archaeology reaches the highest standards possible, there are limits to what it can tell us about Leviathan. Perhaps the human sacrifices excavated at Teotihuacán show that this was a more violent society than the Old World's ancient empires, but since Romans did flock to watch gladiators hack each other to pieces (plenty of their dismembered bodies have been dug up), perhaps not. The sixty bodies found buried in a royal tomb of the Andean kingdom of Wari around A.D. 800—long after Old World empires had given up such practices—might also point to higher levels of violence in the New World than in the Old, but when we get right down to it, the evidence is just not good enough for systematic comparisons. What we really need is a Mesoamerican Tacitus who would tell us what was going on.

Yet the fact that we do not have one, and almost certainly never will, is revealing in itself. There seems to be a general rule that the stronger a Leviathan becomes, the more evidence it leaves for historians and archaeologists, because great governments need to build a lot of things and write down even more. The absence of writing probably means that New World Leviathans were not governing at the kind of level that made writing indispensable—which probably also means that they never got anywhere near as close to Denmark as the Romans.

The Parthian Empire, centered on what are now Iran and Iraq, seems to have fallen somewhere between Rome and the New World states in its level of development. The Parthians inherited southwest Asian literary traditions stretching back millennia and certainly had rulers and bureaucrats who could read and write, but very few of their texts survive. Technical factors explain part of this. Bureaucrats shifted from writing on baked-clay tablets, which last forever, to writing on parchment and papyrus, which do not, and archaeological fieldwork slowed down massively under Iraq's Saddam Hussein and Iran's ayatollahs. But that cannot explain the whole pattern. Parthia also had rather weak government. Roman writers were amazed by Parthia's anarchic aristocrats (Norbert Elias would not have approved), who sometimes ruled virtual mini-kingdoms in their own right and regularly went to war with one another, simply ignoring their king.

China and India, however, are different matters. It is hard not to be impressed by the parallels between the empires of Rome and Han dynasty China (206 B.C.–A.D. 220). After an escalating spiral of wars that filled the fourth and third centuries B.C., the Han dynasty created a Pax Sinica to rival the Pax Romana, imposing peace across the length and breadth of the land. Warrior burials, which had still been common until the third century B.C., virtually disappeared in the second. Travelers began going around unarmed, and cities let their pounded-earth walls fall into disrepair. Law replaced war.

As in Rome, the government suppressed bandits and pirates, and officials were made to answer for excesses. The first-century-B.C. governor Yin Shang is a good example: he ended his career in a blaze of glory after stamping out violent gangs in the capital city of Chang'an, but only after being fired from an earlier posting in Hebei Province for using too much force in making the roads safe to travel.

Again like Rome, Han China was no paradise and remained much more violent than any stable modern state. Officials regularly complained that people took matters into their own hands, even hiring gangs of thugs to kill rivals. Nor were the officials themselves above reproach. No right to remain silent here: one set of official guidelines for judges investigating murder begins by demanding multiple witnesses, cross-examination, and physical evidence but ends by adding, casually, "When one has questioned pressingly to the limits of the case . . . beat with rods those whom the statutes allow to be beaten."

Compared with earlier eras, though, the Han were well on their way to Denmark. One pre-Han law code had punished even minor acts of violence with amputations of noses, ears, feet, and hands, while major acts called for holes to be bored into perpetrators' skulls, varying numbers of ribs to be removed, heads to be cut off, and bodies buried alive or chopped in two at the waist. Nor was this just talk, meant to scare people straight. Records of court decisions, found in the tombs of judges, show that these penalties really were carried out.

I have commented several times on Elias's argument in his classic book *The Civilizing Process* that the key to peace is getting the rich to calm down, and in this regard the Pax Sinica perhaps outdid the Pax Romana. As each empire made its internal provinces more peaceful, it shifted its troops to the frontiers. But while Rome continued to recruit soldiers from all over its empire, and honorable men like the geographer Pliny and the historian Tacitus shuttled back and forth between lawyering, writing, and commanding armies, China went further. It moved to staffing its armies with convicts or hired swords from outside the empire, leaving Han dynasty gentlemen to make do with just lawyering and writing. Where Romans embraced Stoicism, which taught them to live with things they did not like rather than going berserk and killing someone, the Han elite took on various forms of Confucianism, in which the man who knew how to use a pen far outranked the man who could use a sword. Even more than in Rome, the path to success ran through education and culture.

Something rather similar was going on in South Asia too, although the outlines of the Pax Indica are a little harder to pin down than the Chinese or Roman versions. Bad workmen, the saying goes, blame their tools, and bad historians regularly blame their sources, but the hard fact is that we just do not know as much about India's Mauryan Empire as about the Roman or the Han. Very few documents survive from ancient India, and the most important—the *Arthashastra*, an eight-hundred-page treatise on statecraft*—was in fact lost for many centuries. It only resurfaced in 1904, when a local scholar (whose name none of the officials bothered to note) walked into the Mysore Oriental Library in southwest India with the last surviving manuscript, written on palm leaves, tucked under his arm.

Along with pronouncements on everything from how to build a fort to how many hairdressers a king should have, the *Arthashastra* describes an elaborate judicial system, laying down the rules magistrates must follow to investigate murder and assault. Doctors who suspected foul play in a patient's death were required to file reports; so too village headmen who witnessed cruelty to animals. The law prescribed penalties for every imaginable kind of violence, distinguishing, for example, between assaults involving spitting and those involving vomiting on someone, with fines further subdivided according to whether the fluid in question struck the victim below the navel, above the navel, or on the head.

The *Arthashastra* certainly makes the Mauryans sound serious about suppressing violence, and its author, Kautilya (also known as Chanakya, and perhaps as Vishnugupta too), should have known what he was talking about. He had led the uprising that established the Mauryan dynasty around 320 B.C. and then served as prime minister to its first king, Chandragupta.

Kautilya was perfectly placed to describe Mauryan institutions, but that is where the problems begin. Scholars cannot agree on whether Kautilya was describing reality or prescribing what an ideal king ought to do, and some even question whether Kautilya wrote the *Arthashastra* at all. The

---

*Also available as a (highly) dramatized thirty-hour Hindi television series, with English subtitles (http://intellectualhinduism.blogspot.com/search/label/Chanakya).

book mentions objects (like Chinese silk) that apparently did not reach India till later, and analyses of its language suggest that it might have been compiled long after Kautilya's death from a ragbag of materials spanning centuries.

We have some other evidence to compare with the *Arthashastra*, but each piece has its own problems. Megasthenes, a Greek diplomat who spent time at the Mauryan capital Pataliputra around 300 B.C. (and would surely have met Kautilya), wrote that Indians were extremely law-abiding—so much so, he said, that when Chandragupta went to war, his troops never devastated the countryside, let alone killed farmers. However, given that Megasthenes also thought that some Indians had their feet attached back to front and that Indian dogs bit so hard that their eyeballs popped out, doubts necessarily remain about his testimony.

The most important source to set alongside the *Arthashastra* is a group of thirty-nine inscriptions erected by the later king, Ashoka, after he conquered Kalinga in the 250s B.C. In striking contrast to the kind of bombast that typically fills royal proclamations, Ashoka announced that "on conquering Kalinga, the Beloved of the Gods [that is, Ashoka] felt remorse, for, when a country is conquered, the slaughter, death, and deportation of the people is extremely grievous to the Beloved of the Gods."

Ashoka had won "victory on all his frontiers to a distance of fifteen hundred miles," but now announced that he would follow *dhamma*. There is some debate among Indologists over whether *dhamma* was a straight-forwardly Buddhist concept or was Ashoka's own idea, but the king tells us that what he meant by it was "good behavior . . . obedience . . . generosity . . . and abstention from killing living things. Father, son, brother, master, friend, acquaintance, relative, and neighbor should say, 'This is good, this we should do.'"

Ashoka set up "officers of *dhamma*" in the cities and countryside, charged with implementing a battery of new laws. He sent out inspectors to check on his officers' success and followed up with personal tours. As in Rome, what Hobbes would later call "commonwealth by acquisition" and "commonwealth by institution" apparently went together, and Ashoka learned that "legislation has been less effective, and persuasion more so." But the bottom line, he concluded, was that "since [*dhamma* had been instituted], evil among men has diminished in the world. Among those who have suffered it has disappeared, and there is joy and peace in the whole world."

Once again, what we really need is proper statistics on violent death in ancient India to set alongside these sources, and once again, none exist. Nor, in this case, is the archaeology very helpful. Few graves of any kind are known, so we cannot tell whether people went on seeing weapons as a normal part of male fashion. Fortifications spread along the Ganges Valley in the sixth century B.C., suggesting that fighting was increasing. In the Roman Empire, most cities let their walls decay once the initial wars of conquest were over, but in India fortifications remained normal throughout the life of the Mauryan Empire. Why remains an open question. Possibly the Mauryan Empire was less settled than the Roman, or possibly its brief life (created around 320 B.C., it fell apart after a coup in 185 B.C.) meant that its cities did not have time to outgrow walls that had become redundant. Without more excavations, we cannot know.

The agreements among Kautilya, Megasthenes, and Ashoka, combined with the general similarities between the rule of law in India and China, make me suspect that the Mauryan Empire, like the Han and the Roman, made its subjects safer. But while this question must for the moment remain open, there is less room for debate over the fact that all three empires made their subjects richer.

In China, texts and archaeology agree that economic life intensified as states became larger. Canals, irrigation ditches, wells, fertilizer, and oxen became common sights in the fields. Iron tools proliferated. Coinage spread from city to city, and traders shipped wheat, rice, and luxury goods to wherever they fetched the best price. Governments slashed customs duties and invested in roads and harbors. From the mighty capital of Chang'an with its half a million residents down to the humblest village, Han-era markets bustled with rich and poor, selling what they could produce cheaply and buying what they could not. Philosophers worried over whether it was right for merchants to get quite so wealthy.

Chinese archaeologists have not (yet) quantified enough data to produce a Chinese equivalent of Figure 1.4, charting rising living standards. But since 2003, excavations at the little village of Sanyangzhuang have been providing the next best thing.

One day in A.D. 11, the levees broke along the Yellow River. The rain must have been coming down in sheets for days, and floods had been reported upriver, but the farmers of Sanyangzhuang apparently kept on working the fine, fertile soil and hoping for the best. It is hard to tell, two thousand years on, what would have been the first sign of catastrophe. Perhaps it was a dull, distant roar as the dikes collapsed and billions of gallons of brown water surged through. Most likely, though, the rain pounding on their tile roofs drowned that out. Only, I suspect, when muddy water started oozing under their doors would the awful truth have dawned: this was not just a storm anymore. The unthinkable had happened. Dropping everything, the farmers ran for their lives. Their village had stood on this spot for a thousand years, but within a few hours it was gone.

Archaeology is a ghoulish profession. It has turned the tragedy of A.D. 11 into a scientific triumph, uncovering a Han village so perfectly preserved that journalists have labeled it "the Chinese Pompeii." Meticulously separating the mud carried in by the flood from the mud that fills any normal village, excavators have exposed the imprints left by bare feet and iron-shod hooves as villagers and horses fled across the plowed fields.

Gripping stuff, but archaeologists tend to get even more excited about the humdrum remains of what the farmers left behind than about the human drama. These Han villagers lived in sturdy, mud-brick houses strikingly like those found four thousand miles to the west, in the Roman Empire. The tile roofs were very similar in both empires, as was the impressive quantity and variety of iron tools and well-made pottery.

Naturally, there were differences too. Careful excavation at Sanyangzhuang has recovered impressions on mud from the mulberry leaves used to feed silkworms, a resource Romans would have loved to have had. In the 70s A.D., the learned but curmudgeonly Roman geographer Pliny grumbled that fine ladies were squandering millions of sesterces on filmy Chinese silk so they could flaunt their charms in public. But on the whole, the finds at Sanyangzhuang are remarkably like those from Roman villages, or even Pompeii itself.

Our evidence from India is again less full but again points the same way. Like the Han and Romans, the Mauryans standardized weights and measures, minted coins on a huge scale, clarified commercial law, built roads, and helped villagers clear new lands. They also promoted trade guilds, which played important parts in commercial life.

India struck the Greek ambassador Megasthenes as a prosperous place, and archaeology bears him out. The subcontinent has yielded no Pompeii or Sanyangzhuang, and the biggest samples of Mauryan housing are still those excavated at Taxila and Bhita in the days of the British Raj. But despite the deplorable standards of these digs (out-of-date even in their own era), they still produced enough information to show that third-century-B.C. houses were bigger, more comfortable, and better furnished than earlier ones. Like Han and Roman houses, they had brick walls and tile roofs, with several rooms clustered around a courtyard. Most had wells, drains, kitchens with ovens, and storerooms.

The bad news (for archaeologists) is that there were no tragedies here, and the occupants had time to clear out their houses when they left. The good news, though, is that Mauryans were messy people. They left behind enough fragments of broken pottery, kitchen implements, iron tools, and even a little jewelry to show that they were much better-off than earlier Indians.

Greek and Roman visitors to India found much to astonish them (talking parrots! boa constrictors! and, of course, elephants!), but what impressed them most was the sheer scale of the trade that grew up between the Mediterranean and the subcontinent after about 200 B.C. "In no year," Pliny wrote, "does India drain less than 550 million sesterces [enough to feed a million people for a year] out of our empire, giving back in exchange her own goods—which are sold among us for fully a hundred times what they cost!"

Pliny's arithmetic cannot be right, because his numbers would mean that a few thousand merchants realized profits of 55 billion sesterces, which was nearly three times as much as the entire Roman Empire's annual output. Many classicists therefore suspect that there has been a copying error and that Pliny originally wrote that the trade with India was worth 50 million sesterces, not 550 million. Recent discoveries suggest that 50 million sesterces, while still a staggering sum, may be about right. In 1980, the Austrian National Library acquired a papyrus scroll looted from a Roman site in Egypt, dating around A.D. 150. When studied, it turned out to describe the financial arrangements for a ship returning to Egypt from Muziris in India. The ivory, fine cloth, and perfume in the ship's hold was valued (in Roman prices) at nearly 8 million sesterces—enough to feed more than fifteen thousand people for twelve months. Rome taxed these imports at 25 percent; five hundred such shipments would have covered the entire empire's annual military budget.

We have not yet found written records at the Indian end of the chain, but in 2007 excavations began at Muziris (modern Pattanam in Kerala), and the first four seasons of digging generated more Roman wine containers than are known from any other site outside the empire. India was clearly a prosperous place.

In Rome, China, and India, then, it seems that large empires were making people safer and wealthier in the late first millennium B.C. In Parthia, there was a large but apparently rather less safe empire; in Mesoamerica and the Andes, smaller states that were perhaps less safe still; and beyond this band of latitudes, roughly 20 to 35 degrees north of the equator in the Old World and 15 degrees south to 20 degrees north in the New, were tiny societies where rates of violent death probably remained in the 10–20 percent range.

What explains this pattern? Why was it only people within these lucky latitudes who started getting to Denmark, and why did some of them get so much farther along the path than others?

The Cage

Another map will help us answer this new question. Figure 2.3 shows the same ancient empires as Figure 2.2 but with some extra details added. The areas marked in gray show the agricultural heartlands where humans first invented farming, in the years between about 10,000 and 5000 B.C. The beginning of farming was one of the two or three real turning points in human history, and I described it in some detail in my book *Why the West Rules—for Now*; I return to it here, though, because of the coincidence between the places where farming began and the places where ancient empires appeared several thousand years later. The reason that war gave birth to Leviathan in these lucky latitudes, while life outside them remained as poor, nasty, and brutish as ever, is that farming made war productive.

The story begins about nine thousand years before the Persians and Greeks fought at Plataea, when the world began warming up after the last

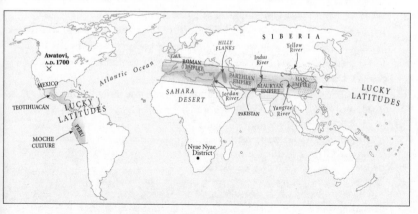

Figure 2.3. Farmers and fighters: the lucky latitudes

spasm of the Ice Age.* Plants and animals, including humans, reproduced madly. At the coldest point in the Ice Age, twenty thousand years ago, there had been barely half a million people on earth; ten thousand years later, there were ten million.

Then as now, global warming affected every part of the planet but affected some parts more than others. What made the lucky latitudes lucky was that in this part of the world, climate and ecology conspired to favor the evolution of large-grained grasses and big, meaty mammals. The hunting and gathering were better here than anywhere else on earth, and of the ten million people in the world of 8000 B.C. more than half lived in the lucky latitudes.

During the ice ages, humans had spent their time in tiny bands of foragers, but even before the Ice Age had completely finished, the pickings were so good in some parts of the lucky latitudes (particularly, it seems, the Jordan Valley) that people settled in permanent villages, feeding year-round from the newly abundant food sources. As they did so, a remarkable thing happened. By cultivating and tending plants and animals, humans unconsciously exerted selective pressures that modified these food sources' genetic structures. This process—domestication†—happened first in the lucky latitudes, because they had by far the densest concentrations of potentially domesticable plants and animals on earth.

Jared Diamond makes the point well in his classic study *Guns, Germs, and Steel*. The world, Diamond observes, has roughly 200,000 species of plants, but humans can only eat about 2,000 of these, and only about 200 have much genetic potential for domestication. Of the 56 plants with edible seeds weighing at least ten milligrams, 50 originally grew wild in the lucky latitudes, and just 6 in the whole of the rest of the planet. Of the fourteen species of mammals weighing over a hundred pounds that humans domesticated before twentieth-century science kicked in, nine were natives of the lucky latitudes.

No surprise, then, that domestication began in the lucky latitudes, nor

---

*Paleoclimatologists technically date the end of the Ice Age proper around 12,700 B.C. but regularly treat the twelve-hundred-year mini ice age known as the Younger Dryas (10,800–9600 B.C.) as the Ice Age's final phase.

†Technically, domestication means the genetic modification of one species so that it can only survive with continued intervention from another species, as happened when human intervention turned wolves into dogs, wild aurochs into cattle, and wild rice and barley into domesticated versions that depend on humans to harvest and replant them.

that within the lucky latitudes it appeared first in southwest Asia, which had the densest concentrations of potential domesticates of all. The first signs of this process (the appearance of unnaturally large seeds and animals, which archaeologists usually call "cultivation") show up in the Hilly Flanks between 9500 and 9000 B.C., and full-blown domestication is evident by 7500.

What we now call China had high concentrations of domesticable plants and animals too, but not as high as the Hilly Flanks. Between the Yellow and the Yangzi Rivers rice was being cultivated by 7500 B.C. and domesticated by 5500. Millet and pigs followed over the next millennium. In Pakistan, barley, wheat, sheep, and goats were cultivated and then domesticated on roughly the same schedule. Squash, peanuts, and teosinte (the ancestor of corn) were being cultivated in Mexico by 6500 and had been domesticated by 3250, and quinoa, llamas, and alpacas in Peru by 6500 and 2750 (Table 2.1, on page 88). The fit between the density of potential domesticates and the date at which domestication began is almost perfect.

Domestication was a long, drawn-out process, and with every passing year a little bit more of the wild was planted and a few more fields were weeded, hoed, plowed, watered, and fertilized. Farming had its costs— farmers typically worked more than foragers and ate more monotonous, less healthy diets—but it had one huge attraction: it produced much more food from an acre of land. As the food supply grew, humans in the lucky latitudes did what every animal does in such circumstances, turning the extra calories into more of themselves, and the lucky latitudes began looking more and more peculiar. In the rest of the world, wandering hunter-gatherers were spread thinly across the land, typically at densities of less than one person per square mile. By the first millennium B.C., however, some parts of the lucky latitudes had hundreds of farmers packed into every square mile.

The population explosion set off cascades of unintended consequences. One was that farming spread: as the best land in the original agricultural cores filled up, farmers boldly went where no peasant had gone before, seeking out fertile fields beyond the horizon. Within four thousand years prehistoric frontiersmen had vaulted from the westernmost core of domestication in the Hilly Flanks as far as the Atlantic coast of France, and from the easternmost core between the Yellow and Yangzi River valleys as far as Borneo.

Another unintended consequence was that as agriculture pushed up population densities, people found more reasons to fight. This was not, however, because farming itself directly caused more war; from Helen of Troy to the War of Jenkins's Ear,* men have contrived to kill each other over almost anything that can be imagined, with property, prestige, and women taking the top places on the list. But cramming more bodies into the same landscapes (rather like cramming more lab rats into the same cage) simply meant there were more people to fall out with and more to fall out over.

The consequence of crowding that matters most for the story in this book, though, was what defeat began to mean for fighting farmers. Gradually, over the course of millennia, it became clear that losing a conflict in a settled, crowded agricultural landscape was a very different proposition from losing one in a fluid, fairly empty landscape of foragers.

Take, for instance, the story of ≠Gau,† a San hunter in the Kalahari Desert. Sometime in the 1920s or '30s, ≠Gau fell out with another hunter, Debe, over bush food. ≠Gau, a hothead, speared Debe, killing him. Debe's angry family then attacked ≠Gau, but in the struggle that followed, ≠Gau killed again, shooting a man in the back with a poisoned arrow. Realizing he had gone too far, "≠Gau grabbed his people and left the area" (the words of another San, telling the story in the 1950s). A posse pursued ≠Gau, but after a skirmish that cost three more lives, the San storyteller said, "≠Gau and his group ran away." Among hunters and gatherers, when the going got tough, the tough simply got going. So long as there was room to keep moving, no one could make ≠Gau pay for his crimes. (≠Gau ultimately came to a fittingly violent end, speared through the heart by a young man from his own group.)

How different the fate of farmers who lose fights. In 58 B.C., Julius Caesar tells us, a farming tribe called the Helvetii abandoned their home in what is now Switzerland and migrated into Gaul to find better land. Gaul, as they knew, was full; all the good farmland had been settled long ago. But the Helvetii did not care. They would simply take what they wanted, beginning with the lands of the Aedui tribe.

---

*My candidate for the most peculiarly named conflict in history. The casus belli was a Spanish coast guard's decision to cut the left ear off a British merchant named Robert Jenkins in 1731. For eight years the British government did nothing about this but in 1739 decided war was the only possible response.

†The San language is full of clicks, glottal stops, and other sounds not used in English, so anthropologists' accounts are littered with names beginning with ≠, !, /, and even //.

What were the Aedui to do? One option was to sit out the storm and hope for the best, but the best was not looking good. As soon as the Helvetii arrived, Caesar says, the Aedui found "their earth scorched, their children enslaved, and their towns stormed." The fruits of doing nothing promised to be death, ruin, and bondage.

A second option was to fight back, but given that "the Helvetii exceed the other Gauls in ferocity, because they are embroiled in almost daily battles with the Germans" (Caesar's words again), many Aedui found that an alarming prospect. The necessary experience and organization, they felt, could not simply be plucked out of thin air. Others among the Aedui, though, were very keen on fighting. A certain Dumnorix ("highly audacious, extremely influential . . . and ambitious for revolution," says Caesar; he sounds like a Gallic version of ≠Gau) had raised a private force of horsemen. He planned to use the crisis to overthrow the ineffective Aeduan aristocracy and make himself king, turning the Aedui into a regional power.

A third possibility, the one the Aedui actually chose, was to put themselves under the protection of powerful friends. This, however, was anything but straightforward. To most Aeduans, the obvious friend was Caesar, the newly appointed governor of the neighboring Roman province. Dumnorix, however, was playing a double game; far from reorganizing Aeduan society to fight off the Helvetii, he actually planned to put the Aedui under Helvetian protection. The Helvetii would then help him become king, and together the two tribes would dominate Gaul and keep Rome out.

The one option the Aedui did not have was to run away and start over, like ≠Gau and his people in the Kalahari Desert. ≠Gau's band had relatively little to lose by decamping, but the Aedui would lose everything. Farmhouses, fields, and stored food would be forfeited; generations' worth of ditch-digging, well-sinking, terrace-building, and brush-clearing would be wiped away. And where, in any case, would they go? They were surrounded by other farming groups—Boii, Arverni, Allobroges—and if the Aedui moved, they would find themselves in just the same position as the Helvetii, attacking another tribe to steal its land.

The crowding that farming created in the lucky latitudes was one of the most important things that has ever happened to humans—so important, in fact, that not one but two enterprising social scientists have tried to claim ownership of the idea by thinking up a clever name for it. Back in 1970, the anthropologist Robert Carneiro wrote a paper about it in the journal

Science, calling it "circumscription," and in 1986 the sociologist Michael Mann rebranded it as "caging."

The important thing about circumscription/caging, Carneiro and Mann argued, is that the people it traps find themselves forced—regardless of what they may think about the matter—to build larger and more organized societies. Unable to run away from enemies, they either create a more effective organization so they can fight back or are absorbed into the enemy's more effective organization.

The Aedui are a perfect example. Because they had nowhere to hide, only three outcomes were really possible in 58 B.C. They could end up being dominated by the Helvetii; the Aedui and Helvetii could get together, forming a single society that would dominate Gaul; or the Aedui, the Helvetii, and everyone else in Gaul could end up dominated by the Romans (which is what happened). From the Aeduan perspective, the three outcomes had very different levels of desirability, but seen in a broader perspective, they all led to basically the same result. Someone—Dumnorix, the Helvetian aristocracy,* or Caesar—would become a stationary bandit in Gaul. A single larger society would be formed, with either a king, a clique of warriors, or a Roman governor providing stronger government than the old tribal aristocracies had. And last but not least, Leviathan—in the interests of having a nice, well-behaved population to tax—would stamp out the intertribal feuds that made Gaul such a violent place.

Mann's label, caging, strikes me as the best name for this process. Ever since humans had evolved, they had been killing each other in quarrels. In the short term men like ≠Gau might profit handsomely from fighting, but in the long term their violence was unproductive. It was just the background noise of *Lord of the Flies*. Only when climate change generated farming and sent people in the lucky latitudes down the road toward caging could war become productive, with winners incorporating losers into larger societies.

Of all the places in this book where words might cause discomfort, labeling war in the lucky latitudes "productive" and war in the rest of the world "unproductive" may be the extreme case. The labels smack of a moral judgment, that the lucky latitudes' wars have been good while everyone else's have been bad, even though there are plenty of perspectives from

---

*When the Helvetii first decided to invade, a man named Orgetorix was trying to make himself their king, much as Dumnorix was doing among the Aedui. Things came to the verge of civil war before Orgetorix abruptly (and suspiciously) died.

which that is patent nonsense. In terms of sheer numbers killed, for instance, productive war has vastly outstripped the unproductive version. Some of history's most productive wars—in the sense I use that expression, of accelerating Leviathan's growth—have been among its most dastardly. Whatever else we might say about the Yanomami, they never crucified their enemies, as the Romans regularly did.

Morally uncomfortable as it may be, though, there seems to be no escaping the facts. What kicked off the long, slow, and still ongoing process of caging the Beast within us was the rise of productive war in the lucky latitudes.

Leviathan Meets the Red Queen

At midnight on February 27, 1991, President George Bush (the Elder) announced a cease-fire in the Middle East. It had taken just a hundred hours for an American-led coalition to annihilate the Iraqi forces that had occupied Kuwait. Two hundred and forty soldiers had been killed from a coalition force of 800,000, as against 20,000 or so of the Iraqi defenders. It was the most one-sided victory in modern history.

In the avalanche of talk shows and op-ed columns that followed, policy wonks increasingly put the triumph down to something extraordinary—a revolution in military affairs. This, according to the prominent analyst Andrew Krepinevich, "is what occurs when the application of new technologies into a significant number of military systems combines with innovative operational concepts and organizational adaptation in a way that fundamentally alters the character and conduct of conflict." Such revolutions "comprise four elements: technological change, systems development, operational innovation, and organizational adaptation." And they lead to "a dramatic increase—often an order of magnitude or greater—in the combat potential and military effectiveness of armed forces."

Krepinevich identified ten such revolutions in the West in the last seven hundred years, but this is actually just the tip of the iceberg. "There is no new thing under the sun," the Good Book tells us. "Is there any thing whereof it may be said, 'See, this is new'? It hath been already of old time, which was before us." And so it is with revolutions in military affairs. The ten thousand years that it took to turn the first violent, poor farmers in the lucky latitudes into the peaceful, prosperous subjects of the Roman, Han, and Mauryan Empires were basically one long string of revolutions in military affairs. We might, in fact, see the various revolutions as merely moments of particularly rapid change within a single long-term evolution in military affairs.

One of the longest-running debates in biology is between gradualists, who argue that evolution proceeds steadily and consistently, and critics who argue that evolution consists of long periods when not much happens, punctuated by (relatively) short episodes of (relatively) rapid change. The debate will continue, no doubt, but it seems to me that the punctuated model is a very good description of this evolution of military affairs since the end of the Ice Age. On the one hand, tiny changes gradually accumulated across these ten thousand years; on the other, a handful of dramatic revolutions interrupted the story. Different archaeologists might pick out different details, but I will emphasize the coming of fortification, bronze arms and armor, military discipline, chariots, and mass (usually iron-armed) formations of shock troops.

Like the late-twentieth-century military revolution, the immediate causes of all these changes lay in the interaction of technology, organization, and logistics, but in every case the ultimate cause was caging. All the revolutions were adaptations to the new, crowded landscape, and all occurred, in the same sequence, in most parts of the Old World's lucky latitudes (although, for reasons I will come to in Chapter 3, not in the New World's). This answers both the questions I raised at the beginning of this chapter: neither the way the Greeks fought at Plataea nor the growth of large, safe societies was a uniquely Western phenomenon. There was no Western way of war.

The people who began cultivating barley and wheat in southwest Asia's Hilly Flanks back around 9500 B.C. were distinctly low-tech, disorganized fighters. Everything archaeologists have recovered from their graves and settlements suggests that they fought in much the same ways as the simplest agricultural societies observed by anthropologists in the twentieth century. Their deadliest weapons were chipped stone blades. They showed up and ran away as the mood took them. They could rarely campaign for more than a few days before running out of food.

For all these reasons, when anthropologists first encountered modern Stone Age societies, they tended to leap to much the same conclusion as Margaret Mead: that these people were no fighters. The few battles anthropologists saw in New Guinea or Amazonia were desultory affairs. Ragged lines of a few dozen men would form up. Standing just out of effective arrow range, they would taunt each other. Every so often one or two men would run forward, shoot, and then run back again.

The affair might last all day, then break for dinner, and perhaps reconvene the next morning. If someone got hurt, the fight might be abruptly called off. Sometimes, rain was enough to stop play. It all seemed consistent with *Coming of Age in Samoa*: so-called battles were rituals of masculinity, allowing young bloods to show how tough they were without (as Mead put it) playing for very high stakes.

What the anthropologists rarely saw, because few of them could stick around long enough to see it, was that the real Stone Age fighting went on between battles. Battles, after all, are dangerous; anyone who stays put when the arrows fly, let alone runs up to enemies to hit them with a stone ax, stands to get hurt. How much safer to hide, then pounce on people who are not expecting it . . . which, anthropologists found, was exactly what twentieth-century Stone Age warriors liked to do. A handful of braves would slip into enemy territory. If they caught one or two men from the rival tribe alone, they would kill them; one or two women, they would rape them and drag them home. If they encountered groups big enough to fight back, they hid.

Even better than ambushes, though, were dawn raids, grisly episodes that crop up so often in the anthropological literature that habitual readers become numb to their horror. For a raid, a dozen or more warriors must creep all the way to an enemy village. It is nerve-racking work, and most ventures are abandoned before the killers even reach their destination. But if all goes well, the raiders get to their target during darkness and attack just as the sun rises. Even then, they normally manage to kill just one or two people (often men stepping out to urinate first thing in the morning) before panicking and running away. But sometimes they hit the jackpot, as in this Hopi account of the sack of Awatovi in Arizona around A.D. 1700.

> Just as the sky turned the colors of the yellow dawn, Ta'palo rose to his feet on the kiva* roof. He waved his blanket in the air, whereupon the attackers climbed to the top of the mesa and began the assault . . . They set the wood stacks on top of the kivas aflame and threw them down through the hatches. Then they shot their arrows down on the men . . . Wherever they came across a man, no matter whether young or old, they killed him. Some they simply grabbed and cast into a kiva. Not a single man or boy did they spare.

*A room entered through a trapdoor in the roof.

Bundles of dry chili were hanging on the walls . . . the attackers pulverized them . . . and scattered the powder into the kivas, right on top of the flames. Then they closed up the kiva hatches . . . The chili caught fire, and, mixed with the smoke, burned most painfully. There was crying, screaming, and coughing. After a while the roof beams caught fire. As they flamed up, they began to collapse, one after the other. Finally, the screams died down and it became still. Eventually, the roofs caved in on the dead, burying them. Then there was silence.

Raiding suited Stone Age societies nicely. Their relatively egalitarian way of life meant that no one could enforce the kind of harsh discipline that kept Spartan soldiers standing there while Persians fired arrows at them, but on raids no one needed to expose himself to such dangers. Right up to the last minute, the raiders could run for it if detected. There was almost no risk, except for the virtual certainty that the village being raided would raid back in return—unless, of course, the raiders killed everyone.

Tit-for-tat raiding and counter-raiding were largely responsible for the appalling rates of violent death in modern Stone Age societies, and the archaeological evidence from prehistoric ones seems consistent with this pattern. Among the twentieth-century Yanomami and in great stretches of highland New Guinea, for instance, raiding got so bad that swaths of land miles wide were left as buffer zones, too dangerous to live in. Once again, there is nothing new under the sun: Caesar reported the same practice in pre-Roman Gaul and Tacitus in Germany, and archaeologists have documented it in prehistoric North America and Europe.

The buffer-zone strategy clearly worked, but it was wasteful, and people must have seen very early that there was an alternative. Instead of abandoning good land, they could build a wall big enough to keep raiders out of their villages. The problem with this, though, was that fortification requires discipline and logistics, just what Stone Age societies are weakest on. Worse still, if village A does organize itself well enough to build a serious wall, the odds are that village B will simultaneously be acquiring the discipline and logistics needed to mount a serious siege.

There is a much-loved scene in Lewis Carroll's *Through the Looking-Glass* in which the Red Queen takes Alice on a madcap race through the countryside. They run and they run, "so fast that at last they seemed to skim through the air," but then Alice discovers that they're still under the same tree that they started from. "In our country," Alice crossly tells the queen, "you'd generally get to somewhere else—if you ran very fast for a long time." Astonished, the queen explains things to Alice: "*Here*, you see, it takes all the running you can do, to keep in the same place."

Biologists have elevated this Red Queen Effect into an evolutionary principle. If foxes evolve to run faster so they can catch more rabbits, the biologists observe, then only the fastest rabbits will live long enough to reproduce, breeding a new generation of bunnies that run faster still—in which case, of course, only the fastest foxes will catch enough rabbits to thrive and pass on their genes. All the running the two species can do just keeps them in the same place.

During the Cold War, as American and Soviet scientists produced ever-more-alarming weapons of mass destruction, this Red Queen Effect was often extended into a metaphor for the madness of war. No one gets anywhere, critics of the arms race argued, but everyone ends up poorer. I will have more to say about this in Chapters 5 and 6, but for now I will just make the obvious point that it is very tempting to identify a Red Queen Effect in prehistoric times.

The invention of fortifications is a striking example, though there is some debate about when this happened. As early as 9300 B.C., people at Jericho in the Jordan Valley (Figure 2.4) built an intimidating tower, but many archaeologists doubt that this had military functions. Even if it did, it seems not to have impressed anyone, because there follows a five-millennium gap in the record before the next case of fortification, a wall dating around 4300 B.C. at Mersin in what is now Turkey.

After Mersin, fortifications come thick and fast in southwest Asia. By 3100 B.C., Uruk in Sumer (modern southern Iraq) had a wall six miles long. It is very impressive, but the evidence of settlements that were destroyed despite the walls their residents built suggests that the organization needed to storm such defenses evolved just as fast as the organization needed to erect them. We might conclude that the Sumerians, like the Red Queen, were running very fast to stay in the same place.

But that is not the full story. By running fast for a long time, farming societies in the core of the lucky latitudes *did* get somewhere else. The fortifications of the fourth millennium B.C. are the first revolutionary jump we can detect within the larger evolution of military affairs, and the fact that societies were managing to build these walls—and to storm those that their enemies built—might mean that war was already turning productive. Leviathans were flexing their muscles, making larger, more organized, and probably (although we cannot prove this until we have much more

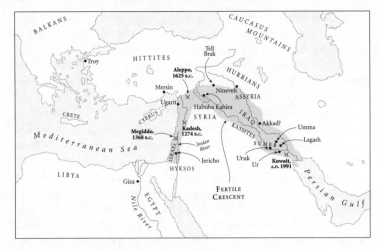

Figure 2.4. The heartland: the sites of the original revolutions in military affairs, ca. 9300–500 B.C.

skeletal evidence to study) more pacified societies, able to pull off tasks that had previously been beyond them. Wars were no longer tit-for-tat raids. Winners were swallowing up losers, creating larger societies.

It was also, however, a nasty process. A Sumerian text from the third millennium B.C., by which time writing had reached the point that poetry could be recorded, gives us a hint of the thousands of voices silenced by the brutality. "Alas!" it laments, "that day of mine, on which I was destroyed!"

> *The foe trampled with his booted feet into my chamber!*
> *That foe reached out his dirty hands toward me!*
> *. . . That foe stripped me of my robe, clothed his wife in it,*
> *That foe cut my string of gems, hung it on his child,*
> *I was to tread the walks of his abode.*

The consequence of the brutality, though, was that fewer cities came to rule over more people, and by 3100 B.C., when it built its six-mile wall, Uruk seems to have exercised some kind of control over much of Sumer. As far north as what is now Syria, some sites—especially Tell Brak, the scene of heavy fighting around 3800 B.C., and Habuba Kabira—look as if they were conquered or colonized from Uruk.

This larger Uruk society was developing more complex internal structures. It had genuine cities, with populations running into the tens of thousands, and kings who claimed descent from gods. Eventually, stationary bandits drew up law codes, commanded bureaucracies that kept written records, extracted taxes, and, they liked to say, acted as shepherds to their people.

The first Leviathans oversaw societies that were less equal than those of earlier times but richer and probably safer. In the absence of statistics, we are of course largely guessing about this, but in the highly caged Nile Valley, where deserts trapped farmers into a narrow strip of land, it seems undeniable. After several centuries of fighting, three small states emerged in the upper Nile Valley by 3300 B.C. By 3100 only one still stood, and its king, Narmer, became the first pharaoh to rule the whole of Egypt. He and his successors stamped out war in their five-hundred-mile-long kingdom and took stationary banditry to a whole new level. Where other kings of the third millennium B.C. claimed to be like gods, the pharaohs claimed to *be* gods, and where other kings built ziggurats, pharaohs built pyramids (the Great Pyramid at Giza, weighing in at a million tons, is still the heaviest building on earth).

Megalomaniacal as it now seems, divine kingship worked well to centralize power. So far as we can tell, Egypt's aristocrats began concentrating so hard on competing for royal favor that they largely gave up violent competition with one another, in more or less the same pattern that Elias saw happening in Europe forty-five centuries later. The art and literature that survive from the third millennium B.C. only allow us to form very general impressions, but the overwhelming implication is that Old Kingdom Egypt was, by ancient standards, a very peaceful place. Leviathan was outrunning the Red Queen.

Stand Your Ground

Southwest Asia and Egypt (which archaeologists usually lump together as the Fertile Crescent) led the way in bringing forth Leviathans, but over the centuries that followed, other farming societies around the lucky latitudes moved along much the same path. As we might expect, there is generally a good fit between the date when farming began and the date when cities, Leviathans, and fortifications began. The denser the availability of domesticable plants and animals at the end of the Ice Age, the sooner people took up farming, and the sooner they took up farming, the sooner caging turned their wars productive.

I find that nothing brings out patterns quite like a good chart, and I think that Table 2.1 shows nicely how the story played out across the lucky latitudes. Domestication of plants and animals typically began in a region two to three thousand years after cultivation had begun, and walled cities, godlike kings, pyramid-shaped monuments, writing, and bureaucracy typically made their appearance three to four thousand years after domestication (around 2800 B.C. in what is now Pakistan, 1900 B.C. in China, and 200 B.C. in Peru and Mexico).

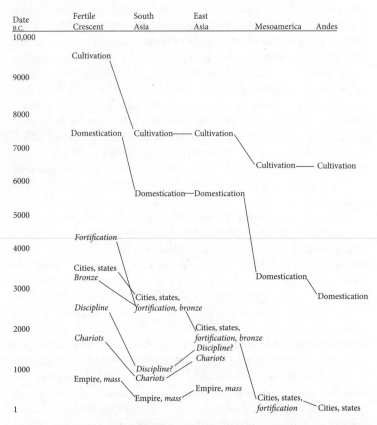

Table 2.1. Caging and the evolution of military affairs, 10,000–1 B.C. Military developments are in italics and social ones in roman type. The lines linking development are there purely to make the stages clearer, not to imply links between areas.

Table 2.1 also reveals that developments tended to cluster, showing up in packages. Within the Old World, that was very much the case with the invention of bronze arms and armor. This, the second revolutionary change within the broader evolution of military affairs, generally arrived at roughly the same time as fortifications, cities, and governments. Craftsmen in southwest Asia had begun tinkering with copper, making pretty ornaments, as early as 7000 B.C. (just five hundred years after domestication really got going), although it was not until about 3300 B.C. that they learned to make real bronze, mixing copper with tin or arsenic to produce metal hard enough to be useful for arms and armor. Bronzeworking took off in the Fertile Crescent right around the time Leviathan really got going in Uruk. There was probably a connection: bronze also appears in South and East Asia right at the same time as cities and states. (The story was rather different in the Americas, and I will come back to it in Chapter 3.)

Using metal on the battlefield seems to have led directly into a third revolution, which once again happened earliest in the Fertile Crescent. It is one thing to have a spear with a bronze point, but it is another altogether to have the intestinal fortitude to walk right up to someone and stick it in him, especially while he and hundreds of his friends are trying to stick their spears into you. Getting the most out of metal called for the invention of military discipline, the art of persuading soldiers to stand their ground and follow orders.

This was arguably the most important of all the ancient revolutions in military affairs. A disciplined army is as different from an undisciplined rabble as the Thrilla in Manila* is from two drunks mauling each other in a bar. Soldiers who will close and kill when told to or storm high walls despite boiling oil, falling rocks, and showers of arrows will usually beat those who will not. The evolution of somewhat-reliable command and control, formations that would maneuver more or less as ordered, and men who would usually do what they were told changed everything.

Unfortunately, archaeologists cannot dig discipline up. But even though actual evidence for disciplined troops only appears several centuries later, it seems logical to suspect that they in fact began appearing around the same time as centralized governments and that it was at this point (around

---

*I am showing my age, but to my mind there are few better examples of discipline in the face of violence than Muhammad Ali and Joe Frazier forcing themselves back into the ring in 1975, concussed and half-blinded, for round after round of vicious assaults. Ali described the experience as "next to death."

3300 B.C. in the Fertile Crescent, 2800 B.C. in the Indus Valley, and 1900 B.C. in China) that wars began to be settled by pitched battles as much as by raids and sieges. Persuading young men to follow orders in life-threatening situations was one of Leviathan's first great achievements—even if, thanks to the lack of hard data, just how prehistoric chiefs did it remains among the least-understood questions in archaeology.

The first tangible evidence comes from art. Stone Age cave paintings, some of them as much as ten thousand years old, regularly represent gaggles of men firing arrows and tossing spears at each other (Figure 2.5), but the Vulture Stele (Figure 2.6), a Sumerian limestone relief carved around 2450 B.C., is very different. It shows dense, apparently disciplined ranks of infantrymen with helmets, spears, and large shields, led by King Eannatum of Lagash. The men of Lagash are trampling on dead enemies, and an accompanying inscription says that Eannatum had won a pitched battle against the city of Umma, which had occupied some of Lagash's farmland. Eannatum subsequently incorporated Umma and much of the rest of Sumer into his kingdom.

Sumerians apparently instilled enough discipline and esprit de corps into their fighting men to settle wars with decisive battles, getting up close regardless of the risk, rather than raiding and running away in the time-honored tradition. In the 2330s, King Sargon of Akkad could even boast of the "5,400 men I made to eat before me each day," apparently referring to a standing army. His subjects provided food, wool, and weapons so his troops could train full-time.

Wild warriors were being turned into disciplined soldiers. Modern

Figure 2.5. Crying havoc: chaotic fighting in a prehistoric cave painting from Los Dogues rock shelter in Spain, dating between 10,000 and 5000 B.C.

Figure 2.6. The birth of discipline: this relief carving, known as the Vulture Stele and made at Lagash (in what is now Iraq) around 2450 B.C., is the oldest known representation of soldiers drawn up in regular ranks.

military professionals have elevated loyalty, honor, and duty into cardinal virtues, far removed from the humdrum selfishness of civilian life, and while the discipline of Sargon's soldiers would probably not have impressed Caesar's centurions, the kind of man who would die before disgracing his regiment probably made his first tentative appearance in third-millennium Sumer and Akkad.

The results are very clear. Akkad conquered most of what is now Iraq, winning battles against Lagash, Ur, and Umma and pulling down their walls. Sargon set up governors, fortified Syria, and campaigned as far as the Caucasus and the Mediterranean. His grandson even crossed the Persian Gulf, where, an inscription says, "the cities on the other side of the sea, thirty-two, combined for the battle. But he was victorious and conquered their cities, kill[ing] their princes."

Like Rome two thousand years later, Sargon's city of Akkad went on to grow rich trading with India, and if the Indus Valley did not have armies with some kind of discipline before 2300 B.C., it probably learned of them now. It has proved particularly difficult, though, to document the rise of such armies in third-millennium South Asia. In fact, the bottom of Table 2.1 reveals that something rather more complicated was going on here. In the third millennium B.C., the Indus Valley had been the second region in the world to come up with cities, governments, fortifications, and bronze weapons, several centuries behind the Fertile Crescent but several centuries ahead of East Asia. By the first millennium B.C., though, South Asia had fallen into third place, well behind East Asia.

In a superficial sense, we know what happened: Indus Valley civilization collapsed around 1900 B.C. Its cities were abandoned, and people turned their backs on Leviathan, shattering the apparently smooth progression in Table 2.1. Nearly a thousand years would pass before cities and governments would reappear in South Asia, this time in the plains of the Ganges rather than the Indus, and by then China, which experienced no such collapse, had pulled ahead.

What we don't know is *why* Indus civilization collapsed. We cannot (yet) read the few texts that have survived, and given the continuing challenges involved in excavating in Pakistan, the evidence remains thin. In the late 1940s, when former military men ruled the archaeological roost, it was generally agreed that Aryan invaders, described in later Indian epics, had destroyed the Indus cities. By the 1980s, at the height of *Coming of Age*-ism, the general agreement was that they had not, and new culprits— climate change, internal rebellions, economic breakdown—were fingered. In the enlightened 2010s, we have to admit that we simply do not know.

I will have a lot more to say about how Leviathans break down as this book goes on, but I do want to dwell for a moment on the Indus collapse four thousand years ago. If, instead of sitting at my desk in California in A.D. 2013, I had written this book in South Asia around 1500 B.C., I might well have concluded that war was good for absolutely nothing. All around me, I would have been able to see the lost cities of the Indus civilization decaying into mounds of mud, haunted by spirits and shepherds. Maybe war made us safer and richer for a while, I might have said, but then it stopped.

Yet if I had been writing around 500 B.C. (still in South Asia), and if I had known about the lost Indus civilization, I might have reached a very different conclusion. By 500 B.C., the rising states of the Ganges Valley were as remarkable in their own way as the Indus cities had been fifteen hundred years earlier. The obvious implication of this pattern would have seemed to be that productive war was real but cyclical. Out of chaos,

Leviathan brought order, only to set off a reaction that returned the world to anarchy. That, however, called forth another Leviathan—and on it would go, in an endless oscillation between order and chaos.

But then again, if I had been writing around 250 B.C., in Ashoka's heyday, I would surely feel (again, if I had complete knowledge of the past) that I had reached a deeper insight. Yes, I would concede to the me of a quarter of a millennium earlier, productive war is cyclical; but it works in waves, each one cresting higher than the last. Yes, I would go on, the Indus civilization was extraordinary; and yes, the collapse after 1900 B.C. was terrible. But the Mauryan Empire is more extraordinary still. Productive war works.

Armed with this understanding, if I had been reincarnated one last time another 250 years later, I would not have despaired when I looked upon Ashoka's works. The Mauryan Empire had fallen, like the Indus civilization before it, and its vast territory had been shared out among squabbling princes. But I would remain confident about the future. Leviathan had taken a step back but—just as had happened when the Mauryans filled the shoes of the fallen Indus civilization—would soon take two more steps forward.

What can we learn from this thought experiment? One tempting interpretation is that everything is relative; whether productive war exists at all, or is cyclical, or keeps moving forward depends entirely on the perspective from which we look at it. But that, I think, would be an overhasty conclusion. The real lesson of the last few millennia B.C. in South Asia is that the magic worked by productive war, making humanity safer and richer, only operates over the *very* long run. Theorizing about how war works over a timescale of millennia would surely have seemed like a cruel joke to the real people killing and being killed in ancient South Asia; once again, the moral implications of the long-term history of war are unsettling. But the evidence keeps pointing us back toward the same paradoxical hypothesis. War has made humanity safer and richer.

Chariots of Fire

South Asia was not the only place where collapses interrupted productive war. As early as 3100 B.C., in fact, something similar might have happened in Sumer. The evidence is obscure, but the control that the city of Uruk had built up now broke down. Uruk itself burned, and for centuries southwest Asia was divided into warring city-states. Around 2200 B.C., an even bigger upheaval came around, shattering both Sargon's Akkadian Empire and Old Kingdom Egypt and even sending ripples of disaster out all across the Mediterranean. There might have been similar (albeit smaller) collapses in China around the same time. The precise causes of these breakdowns are hotly debated, but matters gradually become clearer after 2000 B.C. At this point, we begin to see that revolutions in military affairs could themselves be the causes of massive destabilization.

The fourth great revolution in military affairs began not in the glittering cities of the Fertile Crescent or Indus Valley but on the arid steppes of what is now Ukraine. Hunters here had managed to domesticate wild horses back around 4000 B.C. Like the men who had domesticated cattle, sheep, and pigs in the lucky latitudes, these herders originally just wanted a more secure supply of meat. Around 3300 B.C., though, they had a bright idea. On the steppes, being able to move quickly from one watering hole to another was often a matter of life and death; by yoking their small horses to wagons, herders vastly increased their mobility and chances of survival.

Further improvements accumulated, and by 2100 B.C. herders in modern Kazakhstan had bred bigger, leggier horses and trained them to pull lighter carts. These horses were still much smaller than most modern breeds, but the light carts they pulled—chariots—were a hit. Traders and/or migrants (probably a little-known group called the Hurrians) brought them across the Caucasus Mountains into the Fertile Crescent around 1900 B.C. At first they were used just for transport, but once they had been adapted into fighting platforms—which took a century or two—they revolutionized productive war.

Despite the way they are often portrayed in sword-and-sandals epics, chariots were not tanks crashing through enemy lines. They were difficult to drive and fragile too (by the fourteenth century, they might have weighed less than a hundred pounds), and horses are in any case terrified to charge disciplined infantry who stand firm. What chariots had going for them was not mass but speed (Figure 2.7). Light chariots, carrying two or three armored men (a driver, an archer, and sometimes a shield bearer), could turn plodding foot soldiers into arrow fodder. So thick was the air with their fire, the ancient Indian epic the *Mahabharata* claimed, that "the sun disappeared behind arrows shot back and forth."

Chipped stone arrowheads found in South African caves show that people have been using bows for more than sixty thousand years. So far as we can tell, though, archers got by until nearly 2000 B.C. with what modern specialists call the self bow, a single stave of wood strung with animal gut.

Figure 2.7. Speed king: Egypt's pharaoh Ramses II, riding down his enemies at Kadesh, the biggest chariot battle in history (1274 B.C.)

Since wooden bows rarely survive for archaeologists to excavate, the details are foggy, but at some point—perhaps on the central Asian steppes—bowyers began laminating two or more strips of different woods together to increase the weapon's power. Inventiveness then accelerated, and by 1600 B.C. a new type, the composite bow, was in use in the Fertile Crescent. Instead of producing a simple stave, craftsmen now started curving the bow tips forward, allowing the archer to produce far more force. Most self bows had an effective range of less than a hundred yards, but composite bows could shoot four times as far, driving arrows hard enough to penetrate everything except metal armor.

The composite bow might also have been invented on the steppes, and it might even have entered the lucky latitudes along with the chariot. But whatever the details, the chariot-plus-composite-bow package transformed the battlefield. Initially, charioteers probably had a secondary role, firing arrows at enemy infantry to disrupt their formations before spearmen delivered the final blow, but chariots proved so effective that rulers gradually stopped deploying large masses of infantry at all. Battles came to be decided almost entirely by "the chariot fighters [who] circle each other on their chariots, loosing arrows as nimbly as clouds let go their water streams" (the *Mahabharata* again).

Battlefields had been gruesome enough before the seventeenth century B.C., with thousands of infantrymen pushing and shoving, stabbing bronze spears above enemy shields into throats and faces or below them into thighs and groins. Big battles left hundreds dead and even more hundreds dying slowly—"some swearing, some crying for a surgeon, some upon their wives left poor behind them, some upon the debts they owe, some upon their children rawly left," as Shakespeare would one day put it. "I am afeard there are few die well that die in a battle." By 1600 B.C., though, a whole new level of horror had been added. Horses were bigger targets than men and usually unarmored. The fastest ways to stop a chariot were either to shoot its horses or for men with nerves of bronze to stand firm as the vehicle thundered past and then leap out to hamstring or disembowel the horses from behind. (Skirmishers carried nasty, sickle-shaped knives specifically for this purpose.) For the next three and a half thousand years, right into the twentieth century A.D., Eurasian battlefields would be choked as much with mute, bleeding horseflesh as with shrieking, bleeding humans.*

Chariots took several centuries longer to spread from the Kazakh steppes to China but got there around 1200 B.C. and got to India (still recovering from the Indus collapse) by 600 B.C. In each part of Eurasia's lucky latitudes, chariots arrived as they had in the Fertile Crescent, brought by immigrants and traders from central Asia (from the Mediterranean to the China Sea, the design of chariots was virtually identical, indicating their shared origin). In each place, chariots answered the same military need for mobility and firepower, and in each place they had similarly chaotic consequences.

It is perhaps part of human nature that organizations that work well with one way of doing things sometimes seem reluctant to embrace a new way, and this certainly seems to be what happened with chariots. In the Fertile Crescent the early adapters were not great kingdoms like Egypt

---

*In A.D. 2004, after thirty-eight centuries of horse slaughter, a monument to all the animals killed in war was unveiled on Park Lane in London. It has a simple inscription: "They had no choice."

and Babylon; they were smaller, marginal groups such as the Kassites, Hittites, and Hyksos, who—starting around 1700 B.C.—defeated, looted, and sometimes even overthrew the rulers of richer states. Similarly, in China, the Shang dynasty was brought down in 1046 B.C. by more chariot-friendly Zhou tribes. However, it was only when the biggest, wealthiest states finally embraced chariots (around 1600 B.C. in the Fertile Crescent, 1000 B.C. in China, and 400 B.C. in India) that their real golden age began. This was because only rich states could afford to use chariots properly.

Chariots were expensive. According to the Bible, Israel's King Solomon paid 600 silver shekels for each chariot and a further 150 for each horse, at a time when slaves were valued at just 30 shekels. A fourteenth-century text from the Hittite Empire gives us some idea of what cost so much, with a day-by-day account of a seven-month training program required for chariot horses.

Chariots also worked best in bulk, with hundreds of vehicles swarming around open flanks and filling the sky with arrows. The more chariots the enemy has, the more you need yourself, and chariot forces grew exponentially. Around 1625 B.C., the Hittites attacked Aleppo with just a hundred chariots, but at the Battle of Kadesh in 1274 B.C. they mustered thirty-five hundred, along with ten times as many infantry. (Their Egyptian enemies fielded similar numbers.)

Raising, training, and feeding such hosts called for a quantum leap in the scale and skill of bureaucracies and commissariats, and controlling so many vehicles on crowded, dusty battlefields demanded even more from officers. The great military challenge in the third-millennium Fertile Crescent had been how to discipline infantry to fight face-to-face; in the second millennium it was how to get chariots going in the right direction at the right time. The answers: more hierarchy, more officers, more spending.

Stationary bandits in the chariot age hardened their hearts, taxed their subjects more heavily, and raised bigger armies to keep up with their neighbors. Those who failed, seeing their chariots smashed on the battlefield and their infantry hunted down and slaughtered, could only put hope in the strength of their walls. The scale and sophistication of walls and towers therefore leaped ahead too, which, the Red Queen Effect being what it is, only encouraged the building of better rams and digging of deeper tunnels. (Homer's *Iliad*, written down in Greece around 750 B.C., may preserve distorted memories of a ten-year siege at Troy around 1200 B.C.)

Leviathans had to become bigger and scarier in the age of chariots, their administration tighter, and their armies and civil services more professional. And yet, in the now-familiar paradox, the consequence might have been less violence. As one state swallowed up another, the number of states available to fight each other steadily shrank, and when wars did break out, there were surprisingly few big battles. So far as we can tell, the kings of the thirteenth-century-B.C. Fertile Crescent felt much the same way about their armies as rulers would do in eighteenth-century-A.D. Europe: these proud professionals cost so much, and battles destroyed them so quickly, that no one in his right mind would send them into a head-on clash unless he had to. The biggest chariot battles that we know much about—at Megiddo in 1368 B.C. and Kadesh in 1274—both involved at least one and perhaps both sides being taken by surprise.

As usual, we have no official statistics on rates of violent death, but circumstantial evidence suggests that the golden age of chariots in the lucky latitudes—1600–1200 B.C. in and around the Fertile Crescent, 1000–600 B.C. in China, and 400–100 B.C. in India—saw the overall risk of violent death declining. Over such a huge area, the patterns are of course spotty, but warrior burials often became less common, elite art tended to emphasize the arts of peace, and fortifications grew rare outside the militarized frontiers.

All the while, trade kept expanding, driving up wealth. Again the patterns are spotty, but those regions most active in commerce—for example, Ugarit on the Syrian coast or the cities of Minoan Crete—are filled with large, comfortable houses that speak of prosperous middling people. Spectacular finds from Mediterranean shipwrecks give us a glimpse of far-flung trade in metals, wine, and other little luxuries, while documents from royal palaces and traders' offices talk of timber, food, and textiles moving within and between the great kingdoms. War was being more productive than ever.

Until, all of a sudden, it wasn't. The chariot age had begun with changes on the periphery and ended the same way. This time, though, the relevant periphery was in Europe, not central Asia. Farming had spread from the Fertile Crescent across much of Europe by 4500 B.C., and over the next three millennia population there rose, steadily closing the cage. For three thousand years Europeans had fought in classic raid-and-run mode with bows and daggers, but around 1450 B.C. smiths in what is now northern Italy and Austria came up with a new answer to local warriors' needs. A thousand years earlier, when fighters in the Fertile Crescent had begun shifting from raiding to pitched battles, bronze alloys had still been quite crude, and the best weapons craftsmen could produce were heavy thrusting spears. The relatively soft bronze then available was good enough for daggers or awkward, sickle-shaped short swords that could only be used for hacking, but true swords*—long enough and hard enough for cut and thrust, reliable enough to stake a life on—were beyond any smith's capacity.

By 1450, however, bronze workers were making metal tough enough to cast long, straight-sided swords with the blade and hilt made from a single piece of metal. The handle would never come off, no matter how hard a warrior slashed at his enemy's armor. He could stab too: most swords have two shallow grooves running down the length of the blade, which archaeologists gruesomely (but probably accurately) call blood channels.

Within a couple of centuries after 1450 B.C., the new swords spread across northern and western Europe. Archaeologists usually find them in hoards or graves along with bundles of tiny spearheads (which must come from javelins, made for throwing rather than thrusting) and sometimes breastplates and shields too. This package was hardly necessary for murdering sleeping villagers in dawn raids; it surely speaks of fierce pitched battles. Small groups of armored men would hurl javelins from fifty paces or less to wound their enemies or pierce their shields to make them useless; then, when the men closed to arm's length, the gleaming bronze swords would do their deadly work.

European fighters had murderous new weapons, but the sophisticated soldiers of the Fertile Crescent seem to have been in no hurry to learn from the uncivilized North. When thousands of charioteers could blot out the sun with their arrows, they must have asked, what need was there for riffraff carrying javelins or cut-and-thrust swords?

They got their answer around 1200 B.C., when swordsmen started moving into the eastern Mediterranean. Some came as lone desperadoes or in little bandit gangs; others signed up as mercenaries in the pharaohs' armies; and others still joined mass migrations, with entire tribes taking to ships and wagons. Climate change might have played a part, with drier weather making life harder in the Balkans, Italy, and Libya. Whatever the causes, though, the consequences were spectacular.

It must have been hard, at first, for professional armies to take this

*Technically, blades less than fourteen inches long are daggers, those of fourteen to twenty inches are dirks, and anything in the twenty-to-twenty-eight-inch range is a short sword. Proper swords are over twenty-eight inches long. (The blade of the famous Roman short sword, the *gladius*, was typically twenty-four to twenty-seven inches long.)

rabble seriously, and up to a point the arrogant charioteers were clearly right. When Egypt's pharaoh Merneptah caught a migrating host moving in from the Libyan Desert in 1208 B.C., he destroyed them completely, killing 9,274 warriors (tallied by counting the penises sliced off corpses). The Egyptians also captured 9,111 swords but only twelve chariots, a strong hint that the invaders were using new tactics. To be on the safe side, Egypt then raised its own corps of swordsmen (probably hired from among the invaders) and won an even more dramatic victory in 1176 B.C. So why worry?

Because, it turned out, the invaders learned not to play by the rules. So far as we can tell, they avoided pitched battles, and a string of asymmetrical wars dragged on for decades. Diffuse, shapeless threats emerged suddenly and disappeared just as quickly. One day, chariot horses would be run ragged trying to bring raiders to battle; the next, they would find themselves suddenly surrounded. Cheap javelins brought down expensive horses; barbarian swordsmen came in for the kill.

A single mistake could bring on disaster, as when raiders burned the trading city of Ugarit while its army was away helping the Hittite Empire against another set of raiders. Between about 1220 and 1180 B.C., beginning in Greece and working their way down to Israel, the migrants got the better of one king after another, wearing down their armies and sacking their palaces. Egypt's battlefield victories saved it from this fate but could not stop a slower infiltration of migrants, who, by 1100 B.C., had effectively taken over the Nile Delta.

Bureaucracies collapsed and literacy declined all across the Fertile Crescent. No one paid their taxes anymore, and with no money coming in, governments could not pay armies. Raids went unchecked. Poverty crept up, disasters fed off each other, and population plummeted. A new dark age had come.

Getting to Chang'an (and Pataliputra)

And then things got worse. Without Leviathan's protection, long-range trade dried up; without trade, few smiths could find tin to make bronze. Unable to arm the few men they could muster, the Leviathans' woes increased. Central organization broke down still further.

By 1050 B.C., however, ingenious metalworkers on Cyprus were already finding a solution to the bronze shortage, although at first it only added to the problems Leviathans faced. Cypriot craftsmen had known for centuries how to work iron, an unattractive but abundant ore. They had rarely bothered, though, because good bronze was superior to this ugly, brittle metal in almost every way. Only when trade routes broke down and the tin ran out did they go back to iron and learn how to work carbon into it. Soon they were forging serviceable weapons and tools—not as good as the best bronze, but much cheaper. Iron was so cheap, in fact, that almost anyone could afford it. Iron swords were the ancient equivalent of AK-47s, giving every angry young man the same killing power as the representatives of law and order.

The slide into anarchy accelerated between 1050 and 1000 B.C., when new monuments and written records almost disappeared from the Fertile Crescent, but then it bottomed out. With so few rich kingdoms left to plunder, there was less incentive for raiders to strike from the deserts or across the seas, and as the security environment settled down, chieftains began rebuilding the shattered states. By 950, Solomon had created a new kingdom in Israel. This split in two around 930, but by then Assyria was building an empire in what is now northern Iraq. In 918, for the first time in nearly three centuries, an Egyptian pharaoh led a major military campaign beyond his country's borders, burning and plundering almost as far as Lebanon. Once again chariot wheels were throwing great plumes of dust into the sky above battlefields on the plains of Syria.

The early first millennium B.C. was not simply a rerun of the mid-second, however. Chariots never regained their battlefield dominance, for two reasons. The first was that the horse breeders out on the steppes had not been idle. For a thousand years, herders on the steppes had been goading teams of horses to drag heavy wagons from one watering hole to the next. As I mentioned a few pages ago, mobility was all-important for the scattered peoples on the grasslands; being able to move quickly between pastures as the grass sprouted and then withered could be a matter of life and death. The result, of course, was that big, strong horses were always in demand, and by about 900 B.C. breeders near the western end of the steppes (in modern Ukraine) were producing horses so big and strong that people could climb on their backs and ride them all day long. Confronted with this new opportunity, would-be equestrians came up with reins and bits that could control horses. Stirrups were still far in the future, but by clutching their mounts with their knees and sitting in elaborate horned wooden saddles, riders learned to fire arrows at a full gallop and even thrust with spears without shoving themselves out of their seats.

A new revolution in military affairs was beginning. As we will see in Chapter 3, another thousand years would pass before its real significance was felt in the agricultural empires, but on the steppes its importance was immediately obvious. Rideable horses cut the travel time between fertile pastures from weeks to days. So long as every man, woman, and child in a community could ride and shoot a bow, there was now nothing to stop them from trotting across the plains as fast as their flocks could go, fighting when they needed to. Ancient Greek stories about Amazons, female warriors from central Asia, probably reflect the women who fought in these great treks; archaeologists have found that in some periods fully one-fifth of the steppe graves that contained weapons belonged to women.

The rulers of southwest Asia's new Leviathans quickly saw that cavalry were cheaper, faster, and more reliable than chariots. The Assyrians began recruiting nomads to fight for them and importing horses to ride by 850 B.C. By 400 B.C., expanding states in China were doing much the same thing, and by 100 B.C. even Indian kings—shielded from the steppes by the Himalayas and the Hindu Kush—were moving the same way.

The other reason that chariots largely disappeared in the first millennium B.C. was, at first, even more important: the real advantage of iron weapons revealed itself. Iron spearheads, swords, and chain mail were so cheap that vast numbers could be bought. Cavalry cost less than chariots, but iron-armed infantrymen cost *much* less than bronze-armed ones. Assyria took the lead, raising (according to royal accounts) fifty thousand infantry in the 870s B.C. and more than a hundred thousand in 845. First-millennium-B.C. Assyrian kings regularly put more cavalry on the battlefield than second-millennium pharaohs had put chariots on theirs, but they raised such vast armies of infantry that first-millennium horsemen could hardly ever dominate the battlefield in the way that chariots had in the second millennium. The only thing that could stop these dense columns of foot soldiers was equally dense columns of the same kinds of troops.

The man who really cracked the secret of this new arms race was a usurper who seized the Assyrian throne in 744 B.C. under the name Tiglath-Pileser III. Beset by rivals, he had no choice but to be unorthodox, and he quickly saw that his one chance to survive was to build up a stronger central government than his predecessors had. Former kings, lacking the strength to create effective bureaucracies, raise taxes, and bend unruly noblemen to their will, had tried to sidestep the problem by cutting deals with their warlike aristocrats. If the local lords would raise troops from their estates, the most common version went, the kings would bring them together, lead them to victory, and then give them generous shares of the plunder. This was a cheap way to raise lots of soldiers, but Tiglath-Pileser could not rely on the fractious Assyrian lords to support him. Yet there was a way around this: he would cut the nobility out of the picture by striking a deal directly with the peasants. The meager surviving sources do not explain exactly what he did, but Tiglath-Pileser somehow gave peasants direct ownership of the land instead of holding it as clients of great lords. In return, the peasants paid the king taxes and served in his armies. With tax revenue rolling in, Tiglath-Pileser hired managers and paid salaries to his underlings—which allowed him not only to impose stricter discipline on them but also to hold on to the loot from his wars, rather than sharing it with his overmighty lords.

All this worked wonders for Leviathan. A lot of people got impaled (an Assyrian specialty) in the wars of the eighth and seventh centuries, but the booming cities hosting Assyria's high-spending governments were as famous for pleasure gardens and libraries as for barbarity. Like Egyptian noblemen before them and Renaissance courtiers after them, the cream of Assyrian society found more profit in impressing the king with their cultivation than in fighting duels in the streets of Nineveh.

As always in ancient history, no statistics survive on homicide rates or elite feuding, but the circumstantial evidence again seems strong. Tiglath-Pileser found a new way to tame the aristocracy, which, as Elias showed in his *Civilizing Process*, was just the path that early-modern Europe would take toward peace more than two thousand years later. Tiglath-Pileser and his successors also pushed Assyria's borders outward, swallowing up smaller states and preventing them from fighting each other. The Assyrian Empire expanded enormously, forcing its neighbors either to submit or to adopt similar policies of centralization.

Once the process began, there was no turning back. The rise of Assyria spawned dozens of new small states around its edges as peripheral peoples organized governments to fight back, raising taxes and training armies. When a coalition of these enemies overthrew the Assyrians in 612 B.C., a sixty-year tussle over the empire's carcass ended in the rise of the Achaemenid Persian Empire, the biggest the world had yet seen (although it has to be said that much of the area the Achaemenids ruled had almost no one in it, and its population was barely half what the Roman and Han Empires would one day have).

Persia's growth set off another phase of state formation around its periphery, and in the 330s B.C. it met the same fate as Assyria. It took just four years for Alexander the Great, ruler of what struck the Persians as a backward kingdom on their northwest frontier, to overthrow the great empire.

By then, though, still newer fringe societies were appearing, and in the third century B.C. Rome and Carthage fought the largest, fiercest wars in ancient history. By the time Carthage surrendered in 202 B.C., Rome had built the greatest war machine in the world and across the next century swallowed up the entire Mediterranean Basin. For the next thousand years, the Fertile Crescent and the Mediterranean were always to be dominated by a few huge empires, holding sway over—and imposing peace on—tens of millions of people (Figure 2.8).

This was the age, according to Hanson and Keegan, when the Western way of war was born. But when we look across the rest of Eurasia's lucky latitudes in the first millennium B.C., we see remarkably similar patterns. Thanks to their later start on farming and caging after the end of the Ice Age, China and India began down this path several centuries after the Mediterranean world, but each independently discovered the same secret of success as Assyria, Greece, and Rome, raising mass armies paid for by powerful governments and winning wars in huge, face-to-face battles settled by shock tactics. Each region added its own twists to the tale, but from the Atlantic to the Pacific the story remains recognizably the same.

Once again, this is clearest in China. After being adopted later than in the Fertile Crescent, chariots continued to dominate battlefields until the

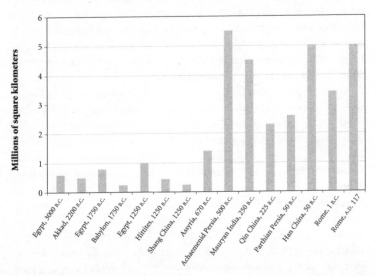

Figure 2.8. Size matters: Eurasian empires compared, 3000 B.C.–A.D. 117

sixth century B.C. (the biggest Chinese chariot battle on record, at Chengpu, was in 632 B.C.), but by 500 B.C. kings were starting to figure out the same strategy that had worked so well for Tiglath-Pileser. They cut aristocrats out of war, granted peasants rights to their land, and then taxed and conscripted them as payback.

By the time that big horses from the steppes reached China around 400 B.C., battlefields were already dominated by masses of infantry with iron swords and spears, plus—ancient China's great contribution to military technology—crossbows. A crossbow took longer to load than a composite bow and could not shoot as far, but it was simpler to use and fired iron bolts that could penetrate thicker armor, making it ideal for huge armies slugging it out at close range.

Iron reached China around 800 B.C., and by the fifth century smiths could make true steel, harder than anything in the Fertile Crescent. These iron weapons spread slowly, not replacing bronze completely until after 250 B.C., but by then there were strong similarities between ways of fighting at the two ends of Eurasia.

As in the Fertile Crescent and the Mediterranean, Leviathan kept outrunning the Red Queen, with small feuding states being combined into large pacified ones. Chinese texts tell us there were 148 separate states in the Yellow River valley in 771 B.C. These fought constantly, and by 450 B.C. just fourteen remained, but only four of them really counted. As they struggled, new states sprang up to their south and west, but in the third century B.C., one of the western states—Qin—devoured all the rest.

In western Eurasia, the climax of violence began when Rome and Carthage went to war in the 260s B.C., and eastern Eurasia followed much the same timetable. The Changping campaign of 262–260 was probably the biggest single operation in ancient times, with at least half a million men from Qin and Zhao locked in trench warfare. By day, the armies tunneled under enemy lines; by night, they infiltrated raiding parties and stormed strongpoints.

The tide finally turned when Qin spies convinced the king of Zhao that his general was too old and cautious to prosecute the war properly. Zhao sent a younger, wilder man in his place. According to our main source—the historian Sima Qian—the new general was such a poor choice that even his parents complained, and just as Qin had hoped, he promptly led a frontal assault. Thirty thousand Qin cavalry then sprang a trap, enveloping the Zhao army on both flanks. Rather like the archaeologists who call Sanyangzhuang "the Chinese Pompeii," military historians often call the

Battle of Changping "the Chinese Cannae," likening it to Hannibal's equally dramatic double envelopment of a Roman army in 216 B.C. Cut off, the Zhao troops dug in on a hill and waited for relief, but none came. After forty-six days, with their rash young general dead and their food and water gone, they surrendered. Another bad move: Qin massacred the entire force, except for the youngest 240 men, who were left alive to spread word of the disaster.

Qin had invented the body count, looking to win wars not by subtlety or maneuver but by simply killing so many people that resistance became impossible. We will never know the total numbers beheaded, dismembered, and buried alive, but it must have been several million, and over the next forty years Qin bled its rival warring states white.

When Qin's King Zheng accepted the surrender of his last enemy in 221 B.C., he renamed himself Shihuangdi, "August First Emperor." Most famous today for the eight-thousand-man Terra-Cotta Army that accompanied him into death, the First Emperor seems to have been hell-bent on proving Calgacus right about wastelands. Rather than demobilizing his armies and leaving his subjects to enjoy the fruits of peace, he dragooned them into vast construction projects, where hundreds of thousands died laboring on his roads, canals, and Great Wall. Like Rome, Qin replaced war with law, but unlike Rome, Qin managed to make law even worse than war. "At the end of ten years," the historian Sima Qian claimed, "the people were content, the hills were free of brigands, men fought resolutely in war, and villages and towns were well ruled," but in reality the costs were ruinous. When the First Emperor died in 210 B.C., his son (named, predictably, Second Emperor) was overthrown within twelve months. After a brief but brutal civil war, the Han dynasty took over the empire and began tempering the excesses of Qin state violence. Within a century, the Han were overseeing from their bustling capital of Chang'an the Pax Sinica described earlier in this chapter.

We see a similar story line in India, although the evidence is as usual messier. Iron weapons largely replaced bronze in the fifth century B.C., cavalry appeared in the fourth (although chariots hung on here for another three hundred years), and Indian kings were raising forces hundreds of thousands strong by the third. There were differences too, though. One passage of the *Arthashastra* (the great book of statecraft mentioned earlier in this chapter) rated infantry in chain mail as the best troops for battling full armies, but most Indian foot soldiers were unarmored bowmen, not the heavy spear- and swordsmen of Assyria, Greece, Rome, and China. The best-trained Indian infantry (the *maula*, a hereditary standing army) could be as disciplined and determined as anyone, but the grunts were always at the bottom of the fourfold hierarchy of Indian troops. This, however, might have been because what the Indians had in the top rank was bigger and arguably better than any kind of infantry: the elephant.*

"A king relies mainly on elephants for victory," the *Arthashastra* bluntly tells us. What it does not tell us, though, is how unreliable elephants could be. Even after years of training they remained panicky, regularly stampeding in the thick of battle. If an elephant rampaged in the wrong direction, the only way to stop it from trampling friends rather than foes was for its driver to hammer a wooden wedge into the base of its skull. The result was that even the winning side often lost most of its expensively trained elephants. But despite all these drawbacks, when elephants got moving in the right direction, few armies would stand firm. "Elephants," the *Arthashastra* calmly explains, "shall be used to: destroy the four constituents of the enemy's forces whether combined or separate; trampling the center, flanks, or wings."

An elephant charge might have been the most terrifying experience in ancient war. Each beast weighed in at three to five tons, and many carried a ton or more of armor. Hundreds or even thousands would come crashing across the plain, shaking the earth in deafening rage. The defenders would try to slash their hamstrings, castrate them with spears, and blind them with arrows; the attackers would fling down javelins, thrust with pikes, and goad their mounts to trample men underfoot, exploding their bones and organs. Horses—sensible animals—would not go near elephants.

Even Alexander the Great had to concede that armored elephants were formidable shock troops. After overthrowing the whole Persian Empire in just eight years, he reached the Hydaspes River in modern Pakistan in 326 B.C., only to find King Puru (called Porus in the Greek sources) blocking his path. Puru's hundreds of chariots proved useless against the Macedonian phalanx, but his elephants were another story altogether. To get the better of them, Alexander had to pull off the most brilliantly executed maneuver of his whole career, but on learning that Puru was actually just a second-tier king, and that the Nandas (precursors of the Mauryans) who ruled the Ganges Valley had far more elephants, Alexander decided to turn back.

---

*The second and third ranks were chariots and cavalry (in that order).

In 305 B.C., after Alexander's death, his former general Seleucus returned to the Indus River and squared off against Chandragupta (rendered in Greek as Sandrakottos), founder of the Mauryan dynasty, somewhere along its banks. This time the Macedonians could not prevail. Even more impressed by elephants than Alexander, Seleucus agreed to give Chandragupta the rich provinces of what are now Pakistan and eastern Iran in exchange for five hundred of the beasts. This sounds like a bad deal for Seleucus, but his judgment was vindicated. Four years later, after his men had herded the pachyderms twenty-five hundred miles to the shores of the Mediterranean, the beasts tipped the scale in the Battle of Ipsus, securing his kingdom in southwest Asia. These new shock weapons so impressed the monarchs of the Mediterranean that in the third century B.C., everyone who was anyone bought, begged, or borrowed his own set of elephants. The Carthaginian general Hannibal even dragged dozens of them over the Alps in 218 B.C.

The wars being fought in South Asia in these years proved just as productive as those of East Asia and western Eurasia. Dozens of small states formed in the Ganges Plain during the sixth century B.C., fighting constantly, and by 500 B.C. four big states—Magadha, Kosala, Kashi, and the Vrijji clans—had swallowed all the rest. India's great epic poem the *Mahabharata* even came up with a name for this process: "the law of the fishes." In times of drought, the poet says, the big fish eat the little ones.

As the Ganges states expanded, new small states formed around their edges in the Indus Valley and the Deccan. By 450 B.C., though, just one big fish (Magadha) survived in the Ganges, and from its great walled capital at Pataliputra three successive dynasties pushed their power deeper into India before the Mauryans outdid them all. Raising armies of hundreds of elephants, thousands of cavalry, and tens of thousands of infantry, they fought massive set-piece battles and undertook complex sieges.

The Mauryans' wars climaxed around 260 B.C., the same time as Rome's and Qin's, with the great victory of King Ashoka over Kalinga that I mentioned earlier in this chapter. "A hundred and fifty thousand people were deported, a hundred thousand were killed, and many times that number [also] perished," Ashoka recorded—only for victor's remorse to set in and the reign of *dhamma* to begin.

When we look at the big picture in the first millennium B.C., it is hard to find much sign of a unique Western way of war, with its distinction between Europeans closing to arm's length and Asians keeping their distance. From China to the Mediterranean, the first millennium B.C. saw the rise of much bigger Leviathans that taxed and controlled their swelling populations more directly than ever before. Their rulers were killers, ready to do whatever it took to stay on top. They conscripted hundreds of thousands of men, disciplined them fiercely, and sent them in search of decisive victories, which were won with bloody, face-to-face shock attacks. In Assyria, Greece, Rome, and China, the decisive blow usually came from heavy infantry. In Persia and Macedon, cavalry played a bigger part. In India, it was down to elephants. But from one end of the lucky latitudes to the other, the same basic story played out across the first millennium B.C.

In the West, this story got the Romans to Rome; in the East, it got the Chinese to Chang'an and the Indians to Pataliputra. Each, in its way, was a similar sort of place: not very democratic, but peaceful, stable, and prosperous. Caging, not culture, was the driving force, and it created a productive way of war, not a Western way.

Wider Still and Wider

Rome, Chang'an, and Pataliputra still had a long way to go to get to Denmark. Romans crucified criminals and killed gladiators for fun; Chinese and Indians flocked to public beatings and beheadings. Torture was legal everywhere and slavery widespread. These were violent places.

That said, though, the evidence we have seen in the last two chapters suggests that the ancient empires had already come a long way from Samoa. Anthropological and archaeological data suggest that roughly 10 to 20 percent of the people in Stone Age societies died violently; historical and statistical data show that just 1 to 2 percent of the twentieth-century world's population died violently. The risk of violent death in the Mauryan, Han, or Roman Empire probably lay somewhere between the modern 1–2 percent and the prehistoric 10–20 percent, and my guess (given the near-total lack of quantifiable information, it can only be that) is that it was nearer the lower than the upper end of this range.

I say this because of some numerical modeling I did in my two most recent books, *Why the West Rules—for Now* and *The Measure of Civilization*. In these I calculated a rough index of social development, measuring societies' abilities to organize themselves and get things done in the world. Social development does not correspond exactly to the strength of Leviathan, but it comes pretty close.

The scores on this index suggest that by the time of the battle at the Graupian Mountain in A.D. 83, Roman social development was at roughly the same level that western Europe would regain in the early eighteenth century A.D. Development in Han China peaked a little lower, around about where western Europe would be in the late sixteenth century, when Shakespeare was beginning to make his name. Mauryan development peaked a little lower still, perhaps around the level western Europe would reach in the fifteenth century.

The implication of these scores, I think, is that while the ancient empires did not get to Denmark, they did get to where western Europe would be between about A.D. 1450 and 1750. And if that assumption is valid, it might also be the case that rates of violent death in Roman, Han, and Mauryan times were comparable to those in fifteenth- through eighteenth-century western Europe, pointing us toward a figure above 2 but below 5 percent (Figure 2.9).

This is, of course, a very rough-and-ready estimate, with a lot of ifs piled on top of each other. At the very least, there must have been huge variations, both within and between the ancient empires. The risk of violent death might still have been closer to 5 percent than to 2 when Rome fought Carthage in the third century B.C. and might have drifted back up

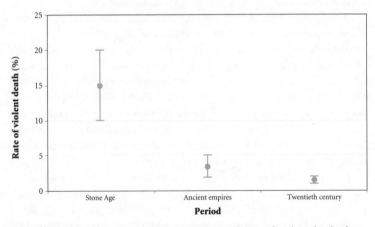

Figure 2.9. How far to Denmark? My estimates of rates of violent death, showing the range for each period (10–20 percent for Stone Age societies, 2–5 percent for ancient empires, and 1–2 percent for the twentieth-century world) and its midpoint

toward 5 percent during the tumultuous first century B.C. But in the second century A.D., which Gibbon singled out as Rome's golden age, a figure at the bottom end of the 2–5 percent range seems much more likely.

Neither the Han nor the Mauryan Empire seems to have gone quite this far, and the less well-documented Parthian Empire could well have stayed above 5 percent. But overall, the conclusion must be that by the late first millennium B.C., all the ancient empires were well on their way toward Denmark. Rates of violent death might have fallen by three-quarters since caging began in the lucky latitudes.

It was a dramatic decline, to be sure, but it took nearly ten thousand years. This might in itself explain why Cicero and Calgacus disagreed so wildly over what Rome's wars had wrought. Calgacus, a warrior in a pre-literate society, looked only at recent history and—quite reasonably—saw nothing but death, destruction, and wastelands. Cicero, an intellectual in a great empire with a long history, looked back across seven centuries of expansion and saw that it added up to a productive way of war that had gradually made everyone—conquerors and conquered alike—safer and richer.

When Agricola led his armies back to their camps at the end of A.D. 83, he was confident that he was waging productive war. He might have left a wasteland after the battle at the Graupian Mountain, but he would be back, and in his wake would come farmers, builders, and traders. They would plow up fields, lay down roads, and import Italian wine. Wider still and wider would the empire's bounds be set; farther still and farther would peace and prosperity spread.

At least, that was the plan.

3

THE BARBARIANS STRIKE BACK:
THE COUNTERPRODUCTIVE WAY
OF WAR, A.D. 1–1415

The Limits of Empire

The plan did not pan out. Instead of coming back to Caledonia, Agricola settled into retirement in the Italian sunshine. The cream of his army was redeployed to the Balkans, and the remainder pulled back into a string of forts across northern England. Their days of conquest were over.

Since 1973, archaeologists have painstakingly excavated a set of noxious garbage dumps at Vindolanda, one of these Roman fortresses. In one pit, so drenched with urine and feces that oxygen could not penetrate it, they found hundreds of soldiers' letters, written in ink on wooden boards. The earliest go back to the 90s A.D., just after Agricola's campaigns. There are a few highlights, including an invitation to a birthday party, but most exude nothing so much as boredom. Roman soldiers in first-century Britain apparently thought about much the same things as American soldiers in twenty-first-century Afghanistan: news from home, the foul weather, and the eternal quests for beer, warm socks, and tasty food. Garrison life has not changed much in the last two thousand years.

In these forts the remnants of Agricola's army stayed for the next forty years. They wrote home, they fought deadly little skirmishes with Caledonians ("there are lots of cavalry," another urine-soaked memo from Vindolanda observes), and—above all—they waited. Only in the 120s A.D. did they move on, but not to new triumphs. Rather, the emperor Hadrian set them to building the great wall across Britain that bears his name. Rome had abandoned the conquest of the North (Figure 3.1).

Figure 3.1. The limits of empire in the West: sites in western Eurasia mentioned in this chapter

As Tacitus saw it, all this came about because the emperor Domitian was jealous of Agricola's triumphs. Perhaps he was right, but it was the ruler's job to see the big picture, and in the 80s A.D. that picture was turning distinctly dark. Even before the battle at the Graupian Mountain, Domitian had been withdrawing contingents from Agricola's legions to bolster defenses along the Rhine, and when the emperor pulled the best troops out of Britain in A.D. 85, it was to plug gaps in the crumbling Danube frontier. This strategic pivot worked, and the river frontiers held. But Domitian drew a radical conclusion from it: that Rome no longer had much to gain from productive war.

Romans had been drifting toward this conclusion for nearly a century. Between 11 B.C. and A.D. 9, the emperor Augustus had methodically pursued what would—had it succeeded—have been the most productive war Rome ever fought, pushing the frontier northeast to the Elbe River to swallow up what is now the Netherlands, a slice of the Czech Republic, and almost all of Germany. But it ended in disaster: stretched out along ten miles of winding paths through dark forests, their bowstrings and armor soaked by torrential rains, the Romans were betrayed by their guides and ambushed. In the three-day running battle that followed, about twenty thousand Romans were killed, and—even more horrifying to Rome's warrior class—three legionary standards were captured. Roman armies took revenge with a decade of rape, pillage, and killing, but in the end the disaster prompted them to rethink the empire's grand strategy. Conquest seemed to be more trouble than it was worth. When Augustus died in A.D. 14, his will contained just one piece of strategic advice: "The empire should be kept within its boundaries."

Most of the men who followed him onto the throne did what he said. Claudius broke the rule by invading Britain in A.D. 43, only for Domitian to close the campaigns down in the 80s. Trajan broke it more flagrantly after 101, overrunning much of modern Romania and Iraq, but when Hadrian succeeded him in 117, abandoning many of these gains was almost his first act.

Rome's emperors were groping their way toward a profound strategic insight, which would be formalized seventeen centuries later as one of the basic maxims of war-making by Carl von Clausewitz, arguably the greatest of all military thinkers. "Even victory has a culminating point," Clausewitz observed. "Beyond that point the scale turns and the reaction follows with a force that is usually much stronger than that of the original attack." Whether Clausewitz learned this from his own career (he witnessed Napoleon's disastrous experience with culminating points in 1812 at first hand, fighting for Russia because his native Prussia had dropped out of the war) or from his deep study of Rome's wars remains unclear. It is perhaps no coincidence, though, that Edward Luttwak, the modern strategist who has looked hardest at the paradoxical nature of culminating points, has also written the best book on Roman grand strategy. "In the entire realm of strategy," Luttwak notes, "a course of action cannot persist indefinitely. It will instead tend to evolve into its opposite."

For centuries, wars of conquest had (over the long run) been productive, creating larger empires that gradually made people safer and richer. But as ancient imperialism neared its culminating point, the back-to-front logic of war threw everything into reverse. War did not just stop being productive; it turned downright counterproductive, breaking down large societies, impoverishing people, and making their lives more dangerous.

The first sign that the ancient empires were approaching their culminating points was the onset of diminishing returns to conquest. So long as the Romans stayed near the Mediterranean Sea, size was no great issue, because water transport was relatively cheap and fast. But in a world where armies moved at the pace of an oxcart, pushing inland—into Germany, Romania, and Iraq—drove costs upward. It cost almost as much to load a ton of grain onto carts and drag it ten miles overland as it did to ship it from Egypt to Italy, and despite the Romans' famous roads, by the first century A.D. the gains from war—whether measured in gold or glory—rarely seemed to justify the costs.

At the other end of Eurasia, China's rulers were wrestling with the same calculus (Figure 3.2). Between about 130 and 100 B.C., Han armies had gone on a rampage, bringing into the empire what are now the Chinese provinces of Gansu, Fujian, Zhejiang, Yunnan, and Guangdong, as well as a great chunk of central Asia, most of Korea, and a piece of Vietnam (not to mention punitive campaigns deep into Mongolia). After 100 B.C., though, the feeling grew in the court at Chang'an that the cost in blood and treasure was just not worth it. The farther the armies got from the Yellow and Yangzi Rivers, the higher the costs rose and the lower the benefits fell. There were renewed pushes into central Asia and toward Burma in the 80s and 70s B.C., then another lull, and in the aftermath of a terrible civil war in A.D. 23–25 expansion more or less ended.

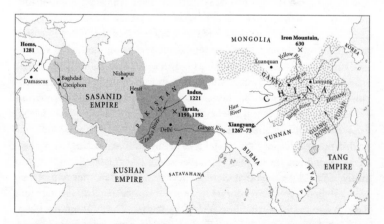

Figure 3.2. The limits of empire in Asia: sites mentioned in this chapter, and the greatest extents of the Sasanid (around A.D. 550), Kushan (around A.D. 150), and Tang (around A.D. 700) Empires

By the first century A.D., the Roman and Han Empires had conquered similar areas (around two million square miles each) and ruled similar populations (fifty to sixty million people each). The problems their emperors faced were similar too, and both sets of overlords reached the same conclusions. They recalled their ambitious generals, built walls along their increasingly rigid frontiers, and settled hundreds of thousands of soldiers in forts much like Vindolanda. Some sites on China's arid northwest frontier in fact outdo Vindolanda; since the 1990s, excavators at Xuanquan, a Han military post office, have found twenty-three thousand undelivered letters, painted on bamboo strips between 111 B.C. and A.D. 107 (many of them complaints about how unreliable the mail was).

First-century-A.D. emperors could see perfectly well that war did not pay the way it used to, but they could not see that the very success of productive war had transformed the larger environment in which it operated. To be fair to them, it is always hard to know when to stop. "If we remember how many factors contribute to the balance of forces," Clausewitz mused, "we will understand how difficult it is in some cases to determine which side has the upper hand." Over the next few centuries, however, it would become all too clear who had it.

War Horse

The ancient empires reached—and passed—their culminating points because by the first century A.D., productive war had entangled them with the horsemen of the steppes. This was a long, drawn-out process, which made it all the harder for emperors to identify what was going on. We saw in Chapter 2 that the entanglements began as early as 850 B.C., when the Assyrian Empire began buying the big new horses—strong enough to carry riders on their backs—that herders on the grasslands had succeeded in breeding. Over the centuries that followed, the empires kept expanding. Their farmers plowed up the edges of the steppes to grow grains, and their traders pushed deeper into central Asia to buy animals; and as they did so, the nomads along the ecological frontier where arid grasslands blurred into cultivated fields learned that they had new options. Often, they found, they could do better by selling horses to imperial agents than by rushing from oasis to oasis to fight other horsemen for a few mouthfuls of muddy water. Better still, they learned, when the imperialists would not pay the price they demanded, they could shoot their way into the empires and take what they wanted from the unarmed, peaceful peasants.

We first hear about an empire having trouble with steppe nomads in Assyrian sources before 700 B.C. Assyria had expanded into the Caucasus Mountains, right at the edge of the steppes (Figure 3.3). When Scythian riders began terrorizing the borderlands, Assyrian kings simply hired some nomads to fight the other nomads for them. They quickly found, though, that the skills that made Scythians attractive employees—mobility and ferocity—also made them uncontrollable. The seeds of disaster were being planted.

In the seventh century B.C., gangs of Scythians went into business for themselves, robbing anyone who came along and effectively taking over much of what we now call northern Iraq, Syria, and eastern Turkey. "Life was thrown into chaos by their aggression and violence," the Greek historian Herodotus wrote, "because they rode all over, carrying off everything." In the 610s, anti-Assyrian rebels hired Scythians of their own, and before the decade was out, the empire was in ruins. This, though, left the victorious rebels with the problem of what to do with the Scythians. They eventually solved it in the 590s (according to Herodotus, by getting the Scythian leaders drunk and murdering them).

The more Eurasia's empires grew, the more they found themselves facing a peculiarly modern problem: how to fight asymmetric wars around the edges of central Asia. In the late 1990s, when Osama bin Laden perpetrated his first massacres, the United States found no way to "neutralize"

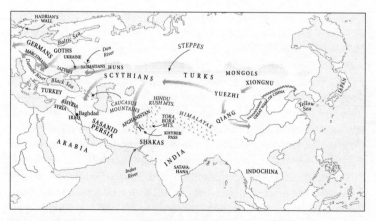

Figure 3.3. Storms on the steppes: a millennium of asymmetric wars, ca. 700 B.C.–A.D. 300

(the preferred term) him in his Afghan lair except by firing million-dollar cruise missiles at terrorists' ten-dollar tents. Ancient empires, with their vast, ponderous infantry armies, found chasing bands of horsemen around the wilderness similarly difficult.

This was a matter not of Western versus non-Western ways of war but of agrarian versus nomadic ways. From Europe to China, the rulers of wealthy empires all faced more or less the same challenges in dealing with steppe horsemen, and by the age of Agricola they had all worked through every possible permutation for waging asymmetric war. Then as now, the obvious approach was preemptive war, and Persian kings sent a series of armies onto the steppes to chase down the Scythians. But pursuing the nomads into their hiding places, the Persians learned, could be almost as problematic as doing nothing, because infantry could not force nomad cavalry to fight if they did not want to. Sometimes preemptive wars paid off quickly, as in 519 B.C., when the Persians crushed a confederation that they called the Pointy-Hatted Scythians, but often they did not. In 530 B.C., nomads had killed King Cyrus, the founder of the Persian Empire, and annihilated his army. In 514, King Darius of Persia—after chasing the Scythians around the steppes for months without being able to catch them—only avoided the same fate by scrambling back across the Danube under cover of darkness.

Assyria and Persia were the first empires to become entangled with the steppes, but by the third century B.C. China was going the same way. In 213 B.C., the Qin First Emperor launched a preemptive war, annexing a great swath of the steppes in an effort to push the Xiongnu nomads away from his frontiers. But it brought the Middle Kingdom little joy: in 200 B.C. the Xiongnu lured a Chinese army deep into the steppes and destroyed it completely.

In 134 B.C., the emperor Wudi tried preemptive war again and half a dozen times over the next fifteen years sent armies hundreds of thousands strong into the steppes. Few of his men returned, and the costs wiped out the budget surpluses his cautious predecessors had accumulated, driving the government deep into debt. But despite spending so much, Wudi—like Darius—never did get his decisive battle with the nomads.

From Athens to Chang'an, intellectuals denounced preemptive war as disastrous. But in another peculiar parallel with modern experiences, in the long run it proved surprisingly difficult to tell who had won the preemptive wars, or even when they were over. The costs in blood and treasure had been terrible, but the Scythians never again threatened Persia after 513, and Xiongnu raiding had declined sharply by 100 B.C.

The conclusion emperors eventually reached was that the hard power of expensive expeditions onto the steppes worked best when combined with softer, albeit still pricey, techniques. The most popular was containment, which usually meant building walls to keep nomads out. The most famous, the Great Wall of China, goes back to the 210s B.C.; the wall that Hadrian built in the 120s A.D., mentioned at the beginning of this chapter, was its distant cousin. Walls could not keep nomads out altogether, but they did at least channel where the horsemen came in.

The most successful (or, perhaps, least unsuccessful) strategy was bribery. Nomad raids killed a lot of people and lowered the empires' tax take, so why not just pay nomads not to raid? As long as bribes cost less than preemptive war, protection money was a win-win-win proposition—the emperors saved cash, the peasants in the borderlands saved their lives, and the nomads saved themselves a lot of trouble. Two thousand years on, bribery retains its appeal in asymmetric warfare: by handing out $70 million in cash to Afghan warlords in 2001, the CIA also saved a lot of money, lives, and trouble.

There is a saying in Chicago that an honest politician is one who, when you buy him, stays bought, but expectations are lower in asymmetric wars. The Afghan commander who took $10,000 in December 2001 to guard escape routes from the Tora Bora Mountains, only to let al-Qaeda fighters through when they offered him more, would have fit right in on the ancient steppes. Scythians and Xiongnu regularly took payoffs and then raided anyway. Bribery, it turned out, was the worst way to deal with nomads—except for all the other ways. Persian and Chinese strategists found that handouts worked best as part of a package of carrots and sticks. A stream of sweeteners combined with the occasional massive, violent, preemptive war could more or less keep the peace.

Combining all these tricks, rulers in the last few centuries B.C. learned to manage their frontiers. They turned their relationships with the steppe nomads into something resembling bad marriages, in which the partners could live neither with nor without each other. When an empire was strong, it could impose a settlement on part of the steppes and keep violence within tolerable limits; when it was weak, it had to pay more and suffer more.

The only way to keep the upper hand, every empire discovered at some point in the millennium between roughly 500 B.C. and A.D. 500, was to beat the nomads at their own game. This meant that emperors had to leaven their huge infantry armies with more and more cavalry. Historians who think there is a Western way of war rooted in ancient Greek culture often see fighting from horseback as typical of Eastern evasiveness, while fighting on foot is the hallmark of Western values. In reality, though, the great shift toward cavalry between 500 B.C. and A.D. 500 was driven by geography, not culture. Empires whose frontiers ran right up to the steppes shifted toward cavalry relatively soon after 500 B.C.; those that were shielded by mountains and forests shifted later, and less completely. But, willingly or not, all the empires in the Old World's lucky latitudes moved in the same direction.

Not surprisingly, the shift began in Persia, the empire most exposed to nomadic raids. When Darius chased the Scythians around Ukraine in 514 B.C., almost all his men were walking, but by 479, when the Persians fought the Greeks at Plataea, they relied almost as much on cavalry as on infantry. And in 334, when Alexander the Great invaded Persia, the empire looked almost entirely to riders for victory. China, the next-most-exposed empire, was also the next to move down the riding trail. Emperor Wudi raised huge mounted forces before launching his preemptive wars. In 110 B.C. he had 180,000 horsemen on his payroll, making up one-third of the army and costing twice as much to feed each year as the entire empire paid in taxes. India, largely shielded from the steppes by the Himalayas and the Hindu Kush, was less exposed, and between the fifth and the second centuries B.C. its kings felt safe sticking to what they knew. Head-on clashes of armored elephants still won battles, with horsemen doing little more than covering the elephants' flanks—until another oddly modern development shifted the ground under their feet.

In 1954, faced with mounting demands to do something about the spread of communism in Southeast Asia, President Dwight Eisenhower warned America about "what you could call the 'falling domino' principle. You have a row of dominoes set up," he explained, "you knock over the first one, and what will happen to the last one is the certainty that it will go over very quickly. So you could have a beginning of disintegration that would have the most profound influences."

Whatever its strengths or weaknesses as an analysis of 1950s Indochina, this is an excellent description of the steppes in the first century B.C. As Han China's huge cavalry armies began getting the better of the Xiongnu, many of the nomads migrated westward into lands where the Yuezhi peoples had traditionally grazed their flocks. The terrified Yuezhi then moved still farther west, which took them into Scythian territory. As the next domino fell, the Scythians (called Shakas in India) moved south through what is now Afghanistan, crossed the Khyber Pass, and descended into the Indus Valley. By 50 B.C. the Shakas had overrun much of northwest India.

A century later—after more half-forgotten cavalry wars on the steppes—the Yuezhi followed the Shakas over the Hindu Kush. Pushing the Shakas deeper into India, the Yuezhi conquered a huge domain stretching from modern Turkmenistan to the middle Ganges, known to historians as the Kushan Empire. The Kushans prospered mightily, becoming one of the great cavalry powers of the day. By the second century A.D., their fearsome mounted archers, commemorated in countless sculptures in what are now Afghanistan, Pakistan, and northern India, controlled the Silk Roads linking Rome and China. The Kushans even fought their own preemptive wars, including one against a Han expedition to Afghanistan.

India's experience revealed the hard fact that revolutions in military affairs are irresistible. As dominoes fell and agrarian empires came under pressure, the empires could either turn themselves into cavalry powers, as Persia and China did, or, like India, be overrun by nomad groups that were already cavalry powers—in which case the invaders would turn the society they conquered into a cavalry power anyway. The choices rulers made might speed up or slow down the process, but the paradoxical logic of war always won in the end.

In the same years, the Han Empire in China (which had started India's woes by setting dominoes tumbling across the steppes) learned an even harder fact—that the long story of the empires' entanglement with the steppes was now reaching its culminating point. China had been fighting Xiongnu nomads along its northern frontier since 200 B.C., but all had been quiet on its western front, which was shielded from the steppes by a hundred-mile-thick band of mountains and forests. But that changed when the Xiongnu migrated around 50 B.C. While one branch of the confederation moved west and toppled the dominoes that drove the Yuezhi and Shakas into India, a second branch moved south, plundering the Qiang farmers on China's western border.

For decades, the Qiang had shielded China by fighting bitter frontier wars against hit-and-run nomad raids, but in the first century A.D., caged between the nomads and the Han imperial frontier, the Qiang began to form their own governments. Large, well-organized groups of Qiang moved into Han territory to get away from the Xiongnu, fighting the empire's troops if they had to. The Qiang were changing from a shield into a sword, thrusting at the empire's vitals.

Chinese border officials could see where things were heading. "Recently," one observed in 33 B.C., "the Western Qiang have guarded our frontier, and thus come into regular contact with Han people"; however, his report continues, as more Qiang moved into Han territory, "minor officials and greedy commoners have robbed the Qiang of cattle, women, and children. This has provoked the Qiang's hatred, so they have risen in rebellion."

In the first century A.D., the Han lost control of their western frontier. In A.D. 94, 108, and again in 110, great rebellions/invasions (it was hard to tell the two apart) got out of hand. The borderlands spiraled down into violence. "Even women bear halberds and wield spears, clasp bows in their hands and carry arrows on their backs," an official named Gong Ye lamented.

At the far western end of Eurasia, a similar set of facts was about to end Agricola's productive war and bring Rome to the same culminating point. The Roman Empire had long been shielded from the steppes by a zone of Germanic herders and farmers that was even thicker than the Qiang zone on China's western frontier, but here, too, steppe migrations now turned the shield into a sword aimed at the empire's heart.

The motor might have been the Sarmatians, nomads living along the Don River, who began moving west in the first century A.D. They were a fierce lot: according to Herodotus, they descended from the Amazons, and no Sarmatian woman was allowed to marry until she had killed a man in battle. Be that as it may, their distinctive combination of light and heavy cavalry, with horse archers disrupting enemy lines before armored riders charged home with spears, proved devastating. It was the arrival of a Sarmatian tribe called the Iazyges on the north bank of the Danube in the early 80s A.D. that prompted Domitian to recall Agricola's troops from Britain, and the spread of other tribes across eastern Europe caused chaos for everyone whose path they crossed.

In the first two centuries A.D., warmer weather brought population growth to Europe, increasing caging among German farmers. Consequently, any tribe that tried to get out of the Sarmatians' way immediately set off desperate wars with neighbors determined to defend their fields. The Germans living nearest the steppes copied their tormentors and started fighting from horseback, and even those Germans farthest from the steppes adopted better weapons and tactics. Under the pressure of war,

chiefs turned into kings who centralized power, extracted taxes, and organized real armies.

Sometime around A.D. 150, a German people known as the Goths
abandoned their old farmlands near the Baltic Sea and began drifting south,
toward the Black Sea. Their great trek drove other tribes before them, until
in the 160s a vast federation, called Marcomanni (literally, "Border Folk")
by the Romans, started pushing across the Danube. Germans had been
drifting back and forth across Rome's frontiers for centuries, usually coming as small bands of young men looking for work or stealing what they
could, then running home again, but this time was different. Now thousands of families were on the move and planning to stay.

Confronting them was Marcus Aurelius (Figure 3.4), Rome's emperor
between A.D. 161 and 180. More than anyone else, it was this learned, literate, and humane man—perhaps the ultimate stationary bandit—whom
Gibbon had in mind when he called the second century A.D. the happiest
age of mankind. Given the choice, Marcus would have spent his days
disputing the finer points of Stoic philosophy with bearded Greek profes-
sors, but the storms on the steppes instead forced him to spend them fighting and marching through the forests beyond the Danube. By going without
sleep in the breaks from battle, he did, however, find time to write the

Figure 3.4. Warrior for the working day: bronze equestrian statue of Marcus
Aurelius (Roman emperor, A.D. 161–180)

Meditations, the classic of Stoic thought. (If any ancient emperor deserves the label "great man," it is surely Marcus.)

Like Eisenhower's successors in the 1960s, Marcus was pulled by the need to prop up dominoes into a war he never wanted, fought in ways he never anticipated. Harry Summers, an American army colonel, tells a story about being sent on a delegation to Hanoi in 1975, soon after Eisenhower's prediction had come true and the South Vietnamese domino had fallen. An English-speaking North Vietnamese officer named Colonel Tu met him at the airport, and, not surprisingly, their conversation soon drifted toward the late unpleasantness between their countries.

"You know," Summers told Tu, "you never defeated us in the field."

Tu thought for a moment. "That may be true," he finally said. "But it is also irrelevant."

Like the Americans in Vietnam, Roman armies in the 160s A.D. could usually count on beating their enemies in a straight fight,* and like the North Vietnamese the Germans therefore sought to make such fights irrelevant. As a result, Rome's proud legions were reduced to tactics all too familiar from Vietnam. With alarming honesty, the column set up to adorn Marcus Aurelius's tomb in 180 was decorated as much with scenes of Romans burning villages, stealing farm animals, and killing prisoners as with fights between armed men (Figure 3.5).

To make things worse, when the Romans did get pitched battles, they were rarely the kind they expected. The first time Roman troops ran into the Iazyges' cavalry, for instance, they got an unpleasant shock. Using classic nomad tactics, the Iazyges pretended to run away, luring a legion out onto the frozen Danube. With their pursuers slithering around on the ice, the riders doubled back, surrounded the Romans, and came in for the kill.

Only the Romans' discipline saved them. "The Romans stayed calm," the historian Cassius Dio wrote.

> They formed a square, facing all the attackers. Most of the men put their shields down and stood with one foot on them, so they wouldn't slip as much. Then they took the enemy's charge. They grabbed the riders' bridles, shields, and spears. Pulling them forward, they dragged men and horses over. If a Roman fell backwards, he pulled his enemy on top of him, then used his legs to flip him over, like a wrestler, and got on top. If he fell

---

*The opening scenes of the 2000 film *Gladiator* re-create in stirring style the last great battle of the Marcomannic War, in A.D. 180.

Figure 3.5. Destroying the village to save it: Roman troops burn huts and drag away women and children on a monument erected in Marcus Aurelius's honor in the 180s A.D.

> forward, he would bite the Sarmatian . . . The barbarians, not used to this kind of thing, and wearing lighter armor, lost heart. Only a few escaped.

On that day, Rome's infantry beat the cavalry, but over the next hundred years more and more Germans took to horseback, and more and more Sarmatians (and other nomads) raided as far as the borders. Compounding Rome's misery, an assertive new dynasty—the Sasanids—seized the Persian throne in A.D. 224 and began fielding thousands of cataphracts, superheavy cavalry with horses as well as riders encased in chain mail and steel. "All the companies were clad in metal," a Roman eyewitness wrote in the fourth century, "so well fitted that the stiff joints conformed with those of the riders' limbs. Images of faces were so skillfully fitted to their helmets that their bodies were completely armored. The only spots where arrows could lodge were the little holes left for their eyes and nostrils, which allowed them a little light and air."

Historians argue fiercely over exactly when the Romans drew the obvious conclusion that they needed more cavalry of their own, but between about A.D. 200 and 400 Rome moved down the same road as Persia, China, and India. The proportion of horsemen in Roman armies rose from about one in ten to one in three or even one in two, and by A.D. 500 the latest revolution in military affairs was complete. From the Mediterranean to the Yellow Sea, the war horse reigned supreme.

Just how each empire used cavalry varied with geography. The Han and Kushans relied on hosts of light horsemen, striking quickly across the open steppes; the Sasanid Persians, on frontal charges by armored knights with spears; and the Romans, on combined-arms tactics, raiding deep into barbarian forests to burn villages and ambush troublemakers. But each system worked well enough against its immediate enemies, and for the first few centuries A.D. it was rarely obvious that the ancient empires had horribly overshot the culminating point of their productive wars.

It took an altogether unanticipated enemy to bring that point home.

The Graveyard of Empires

Aristocrats in the ancient empires loathed nomads. For Herodotus, Scythian scalping practices said it all. "When a Scythian kills his first man, he drinks some of his blood, and brings the head back to the king," he recorded. Next, "he cuts the head in a circle around the ears, and then, taking hold of it, shakes off the skin. Then he scrapes it out with an ox's rib and works the skin in his hands till he has made it soft; and then he uses it as a napkin." A thousand years later, the Roman writer Ammianus Marcellinus was even blunter about the Huns. "They have squat bodies, strong limbs, and thick necks," he insisted, "and are so hideous and deformed that they might be two-legged beasts."

What should really have alarmed these civilized gentlemen, however, was not the nasty nomads who came riding in on horses. It was the even nastier microbes that came riding in on the nomads.

Right up to the twentieth century A.D., the biggest killer in war was always disease. By bringing together thousands of men, packing them into small spaces, feeding them badly, and leaving them to wallow in their own filth, armies acted as petri dishes in which microbes could multiply madly. In crowded, unsanitary camps, exotic viruses thrived even when they killed their human hosts, because there was always another host to leap to. Dysentery, diarrhea, typhoid, and tuberculosis: these have ever been the soldier's lot.

But in A.D. 161, the year Marcus Aurelius assumed the purple in Rome, something even worse was brewing. We hear of it first on China's northwest frontier, where, as so often, a large army was fighting the steppe nomads. Reports describe a puzzling new disease, which killed a third of the men in the camps within a few weeks. Four years later, equally awful infections raged through Roman military bases in Syria. The sickness reached the city of Rome in 167, where it killed so many people that Marcus delayed his departure for the Danube while he performed rites to protect the city. When his army did leave for the front, it took the disease with it.

Descriptions by eyewitnesses make the plague sound a bit like smallpox. Geneticists have yet to confirm this from ancient DNA, but we can be fairly sure that the cause of the simultaneous outbreaks at each end of Eurasia was the tumbling of dominoes on the steppes. For thousands of years, each of the great Eurasian civilizations had been evolving its own unique disease pool. In perfect Red Queen style, lethal pathogens and protective antibodies raced against each other, running faster and faster but getting nowhere, staying neck and neck in an unhealthy equilibrium. Between one-quarter and one-third of all babies died within a year or so of being born; few adults survived past fifty; and even when people were in what passed for the best of health, their bodies oozed with germs.

Distance had kept these disease pools separate, but the success of productive war changed that. As the empires grew, migrants moved between them, particularly across the steppes. Mobility merged the previously distinct disease pools, brewing up a vicious epidemiological cocktail that was new to everyone. Not many people were lucky enough to have been born with antibodies that could fight it, and until their robust genes spread through the pool of survivors (which could take centuries), the plagues kept coming back.

The best records come from Egypt, where the population apparently fell by a quarter between A.D. 165 and 200. Elsewhere we are forced to guess from archaeological remains, but these suggest that Egypt's experience was widely shared. With fewer people around, empires then struggled to raise soldiers for their armies and taxes to pay them. This made it harder to prop up dominoes along the edge of the steppes, and Roman and Han rulers watched in horror as their frontiers collapsed and great migrations spread diseases still faster. And as if all this were not enough, climate change also picked up its pace in just these years. From ice cores in Antarctica to peat bogs in Poland, climatologists see signs that the world was getting colder and drier. Global cooling shortened the farmers' growing season, reduced yields, and set yet more climate migrants moving across Eurasia.

Battered by migrations, disease, and declining yields, the complicated networks of tax and trade that had been built up by centuries of productive war began unraveling. In China, as tax revenues shrank and the costs of defending the frontiers grew, some second-century-A.D. civil servants started suggesting that the wisest path was simply to stop paying the troops. After all, they reasoned, the western border where Qiang rebels/invaders were doing so much damage was a long way from the capital at Luoyang; how bad could things get if the government simply left the army to fend for itself?

The answer: very bad indeed. Soldiers turned into bandits, plundering the peasants they were supposedly defending, and generals turned into warlords, obeying only those orders that suited them. "These strongest and bravest of the empire," the official Gong Ye noted, "are dreaded by the common people." In A.D. 168, with the plague raging everywhere and the army disintegrating, palace eunuchs launched a coup against the twelve-year-old emperor and the circle of friends and in-laws who controlled his policy. It was a disaster. Government broke down altogether as civil servants murdered each other by the thousands in purge and counter-purge. Law and order began collapsing too, and rebellions claimed uncounted lives through the 170s and 180s. In 189, the most terrifying of the warlords on the western frontier marched on Luoyang, torched the city, and kidnapped the latest boy-emperor (this one just eight years old).

For the next thirty years one strongman after another plundered his way across the realm, claiming to be restoring it, until in 220 the Han Empire finally split into three warring kingdoms. The frontiers dissolved, hundreds of thousands of Qiang and central Asian nomads migrated into northern China, and millions of ethnic Chinese fled from northern into southern China. Officials stopped even trying to count the dead.

Rome fared just as badly. With population, agriculture, and trade in free fall, cash-strapped emperors stinted on soldiers' pay or debased the coinage to make their limited stock of silver go further. The result, predictably, was that worthless coinage set off vicious inflation, depressing the economy even more.

Angry soldiers took matters into their own hands. In A.D. 193 and again in 218 the imperial guard sold the throne to the highest bidder, and between 218 and 222 the empire was ruled—if that is the right word—by the crazed teenager Elagabalus, who stood out even among Roman emperors for his corruption, cruelty, and incompetence. Between 235 and 284, Rome had, depending on how you count, as many as forty-three emperors. Most were military men, and all died violently except one, who was carried off by the plague. Of the other forty-two emperors, Gothic invaders killed one in battle, and the Sasanid Persians captured another, whom they threw in a cage, mocked, and tortured until they got bored and murdered him. The remaining forty were all killed by fellow Romans.

Forced to face multiple military threats, emperors had no choice but to entrust large armies to subordinate generals, even though these subordinates repeatedly repaid their rulers' confidence by launching coups (this even though hardly anyone survived promotion to the purple by more than a few months). Once a general rebelled, his army would normally abandon its post on the frontier so that it could wage civil war, leaving the empire open to anyone who wanted to enter.

The Goths built ships, sailed over the Black Sea, and looted Greece. The Franks (then based in what we now call Germany) rampaged across Gaul and into Spain. Other Germans raided Italy, while Moors overran North Africa and Sasanid Persians burned Syria's prosperous cities. Realizing that the central government could not or would not protect them, the eastern and western provinces formed their own governments, and in A.D. 260 the Roman Empire—like the Han—split into three smaller states.

The bloody breakdown of great empires was becoming the norm. India's Kushan Empire, defeated by Sasanid Persian armies and Scythian raiders, split in two in the 230s. The western kingdom was absorbed by Persia after a final defeat in 248, and in the 270s the eastern kingdom shrank to a rump after losing control of the Ganges cities. Farther south, the great second-century trading kingdom of Satavahana also struggled to handle the Scythians, and in 236 it too collapsed.

Mancur Olson, the economist from whom I borrowed the term "stationary bandit" in Chapter 1, liked to draw a contrast between these relatively benign thieves and completely malign "roving bandits." Whereas stationary bandits came, saw, conquered, and administered, roving bandits came, saw, stole, and rode off again. The empires of the first millennium B.C. flourished largely because their stationary bandits were usually strong enough to keep roving bandits out, but by the third century A.D. this was no longer the case. Almost everywhere in Eurasia, war turned counterproductive, tearing the huge, peaceful, and prosperous ancient empires apart.

Almost everywhere—but not quite everywhere. The big exception to the rule of third-century imperial collapse was Persia, where, after over-throwing the Parthians in A.D. 224, the new Sasanid dynasty went from strength to strength. It smashed Kushan and Roman armies, rolled back the steppe nomads, and centralized power. By 270, when the great conqueror Shapur I died, the Sasanid capital at Ctesiphon was one of the world's grandest cities.

But on closer inspection, the Sasanid exception turns out not to have been an exception at all, because the rule in these years was not simply one of imperial collapse. Rather, the twelve hundred years between roughly A.D. 200 and 1400 were an age of cycles of productive and counterproductive wars. As we saw in Chapters 1 and 2, the millennia leading up to A.D. 200 were an era of expanding Leviathans, rising prosperity, and falling rates of violent death, and as we shall see in Chapters 4–7, this is even truer of the centuries since 1400. But the long Middle Ages separating these two periods constituted a complicated, messy, and violent interlude.

It is a tangled story. For a while in the late third century it looked as if the Sasanid revival were actually the first example of a new trend toward imperial recovery. After half a century of anarchy, Rome had regained control over the whole Mediterranean Basin by 274, the Western Jin dynasty had reunited China into a single empire by 280, and in the 320s the Gupta dynasty had begun doing the same in India. By then, though, the recovery was already ending in other parts of Eurasia. Xiongnu nomads burned China's ancient cities, executed a string of Western Jin emperors, and massacred millions of refugees. Sixty years of fighting followed, until in 383 it looked as if a new dynasty were about to unite China once again; but its army mysteriously dissolved in panic after a minor defeat, and another cycle of slaughter engulfed East Asia.

Rome too slid back toward chaos in the late fourth century. Goths destroyed the empire's field armies at Adrianople in 378 and the frontiers began dissolving. Westward migrations of Huns (the most terrifying of all the ancient nomads) toppled more dominoes, and on New Year's Eve 406, thousands of Germans flooded across the frozen Rhine River. Western Europe spiraled down into violence and chaos, and in 476—just seventy years after the Rhine frontier failed—a Germanic king announced that the western half of the Roman Empire had ceased to exist.

In 484, it looked as if Sasanid Persia would go the same way when another branch of the Huns wiped out its army and killed its king. But the Sasanids hung on, and by this time China too was moving back toward unity. In the fifth century another new dynasty reunited the Yellow River region, and in 589 the Sui dynasty finally brought the whole of China back under a single government.

For a few giddy years, the Mediterranean also seemed to be swinging back toward unity. In the 520s, Justinian, ruler of the Byzantine Empire—as the surviving (eastern) portion of the old Roman Empire is often called—won back Italy and parts of Spain and North Africa. By 550, though, expansion had stalled, and in the later sixth century fresh invasions rolled the Byzantines back. India had an equally rough ride: after 467 the Gupta Empire started disintegrating in the face of attacks from another branch of the Huns, and despite a great victory over the nomads in 528, by 550 the empire was to all intents and purposes history. And on it went, century after chaotic century, all across Eurasia's lucky latitudes.

I have not tried to tidy up the fact that this is a confusing narrative, and I think that Figure 3.6 sums up its messiness nicely. The graph divides the lucky latitudes into four regions (Europe, the Middle East, China, and India) and charts the geographical size of the biggest empire in each across the first fourteen centuries A.D. Admittedly, there are all kinds of technical problems in simply using size as a measure of Leviathanness (by which I mean the strength of centralized government). The most obvious is the great spike in the Middle Eastern curve between A.D. 650 and 850, representing the Umayyad and Abbasid caliphates established by the Arabs. In

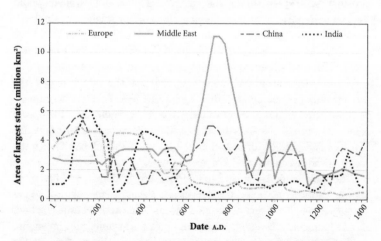

Figure 3.6. One damned thing after another? The rise and fall (and rise, and fall) of Leviathans in Eurasia's lucky latitudes, as reflected by the size of the largest state in each region, A.D. 1–1400

theory, the caliphs ruling from Damascus and Baghdad controlled 4.3 million square miles, one of the biggest empires in history, but in practice hardly anyone outside Syria and Iraq took much notice of them. The Indian spike around A.D. 150, representing the Kushan Empire, raises another problem: the Kushans ruled 2.3 million square miles, but most of these square miles had hardly anyone living in them.

But despite these (and other) issues, this tangled graph does make one big point. Between the second century and the fourteenth, there were few years when every part of the lucky latitudes was moving in the same direction. For every empire that rose, another fell. One society's golden age was another's dark age.

What does this mean? The obvious interpretation, and the one most favored by historians, is—as the brilliant polymath Arnold Toynbee put it back in the 1950s—that the past is simply "a chaos unamenable to [scientific] laws; a meaningless succession of events that a twentieth-century novelist who was also poet laureate called Odtaa, standing for 'one damned thing after another.'" On the face of it, Figure 3.6 looks like the poster child for Odtaa. Empires rise and fall, battles are won and lost, but nothing much changes. Everything is an exception to everything else.

Toynbee, however, conjured up the image of Odtaa only to dismiss it. After spending decades studying world history, he knew perfectly well that the story is full of big patterns that go beyond Odtaa, and I think he would have seen several such patterns in this graph. First, he might have observed, there is an obvious trend here, which Figure 3.7 draws out. Behind all the noise, the size of empires steadily declined across the first fourteen centuries A.D. The lucky latitudes had become the graveyard of empires.

Second, Toynbee would surely have seen that the wild swings in the size of states are not simply Odtaa: they came in a repetitive boom-and-bust pattern. Counterproductive wars that drove empire size down were followed by productive wars driving it back up, only for counterproductive war to return and break Leviathan down again. Rather than Odtaa, the lucky latitudes were trapped in a terrible cycle.

The explanation is not hard to find. Because productive war had overshot its culminating point, the steppes and the agrarian empires had become tied together. Every action now had an equal and opposite reaction. At one moment, plagues, rebellions, and invasions would bring an empire crashing down in counterproductive war, leaving millions dead; at the next, local warlords—or perhaps an invader—would wage new productive wars, exploiting the vacuum to bring forth another Leviathan. Its king,

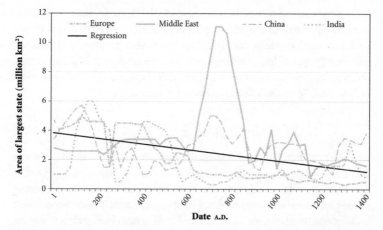

Figure 3.7. Order out of chaos: the dark line shows the falling average size of empires in the Eurasian lucky latitudes, A.D. 1–1400 (calculated by the Tukey, or median-to-median, method; $\hat{y} = 3.83 - .047x$).

enthroned in pomp and circumstance, would struggle mightily to bring back the rule of law and squeeze taxes out of his subjects, only for the wealth of the new state to draw in more raiders and rebels, setting off a new downward spiral of counterproductive war . . . and so on.

Each region in the lucky latitudes flipped back and forth between productive and counterproductive war on its own schedule, mostly because one kingdom's success in driving off raiders tended to increase the pressure on neighboring kingdoms. Some migrations off the steppes were so overwhelming that they seemed to hit everywhere at once, as when Huns plundered all the way from India to Italy in the fifth century and Mongols attacked from Japan to Germany in the thirteenth, but even then the accidents of battlefield victory and defeat randomized the results, producing the apparently chaotic outcomes we see in Figure 3.6.

There had been counterproductive wars before, but even the worst of these had been breakdowns within a larger pattern of productive war. Some of the collapses had lasted for centuries, but despite the fall of the Akkadian Empire and the Egyptian Old Kingdom around 2200 B.C., the Indus Valley cities around 1900 B.C., and the kingdoms of the eastern Mediterranean's international age around 1200 B.C., Eurasia's lucky latitudes had kept moving toward Rome, Chang'an, and Pataliputra. For every step backward, there were two or three steps forward.

Between A.D. 200 and 1400 that ceased to be the case. The power of the steppe horsemen was simply too great. One king or another might thrust back the forces of chaos, but none could permanently stop the steppe migrations. Sooner or later, the roving bandits would be back, and until someone learned how to stop them, Eurasia's lucky latitudes could not break the bloody cycle of productive and counterproductive wars.

The Counterrevolution in Military Affairs

Counterproductive wars threw all the developments described in Chapters 1 and 2 into reverse. Overwhelmed by enemies, governments failed in their basic duty of providing security. Traders stayed home, with disastrous consequences for the kings who taxed them and for the people who needed their goods. With rulers unable to pay their armies, troops made up the shortfall by plundering the peasants, and the peasants sought safety under the protection of great landlords. These worthies organized the increasingly subservient villagers into militias to fight off invaders and tax collectors and generally saw little reason to pay anything to distant monarchs.

The productive wars of the last five millennia B.C. had driven a string of revolutions in military affairs that converted disorganized rabbles into disciplined, well-led legions, but counterproductive wars now set off what we can only call a counterrevolution in military affairs. Kings, generals, and foot soldiers did not forget the advantages of mass, discipline, and regular meals—after all, what has once been invented cannot simply be uninvented—but as Eurasia's Leviathans lost their teeth, governments stopped being able to pay for these fine things.

Armies shrank, navies rotted, supply chains broke down, and command and control collapsed. Back in the eighth century B.C., Tiglath-Pileser III of Assyria had made his mark by cutting the aristocracy out of war, raising (and paying) armies loyal to him alone. A thousand years on, kings started doing exactly the opposite. Unable to squeeze the money for armies out of their wayward barons, they instead started cutting deals with them.

In the old days, kings and landlords had both taken bites from the meager incomes of their peasants, with monarchs calling their share taxes and local bosses calling theirs rent. Finding themselves too weak to collect taxes, kings now gave up their claims and handed out grandiose titles and privileges to every thug with his own armed gang. In return for leaving the aristocracy to run their estates like mini-kingdoms, the crown extracted promises that its earls, counts, and barons would turn up whenever the monarch wanted to go to war, bringing with them troops raised from their own fiefdoms.

The easiest way for noblemen to find these soldiers was by repeating the kings' strategy, passing some of their lands and laborers on to lesser knights in return for more promises to show up and fight. These knights, in turn, passed lands and laborers to still lesser personages, and so on, until webs of rights and duties bound together everyone from the king in his castle to the poor peasants who actually did the work.

For kings slithering down the slopes of counterproductive war, these arrangements had an obvious advantage: the throne no longer had to pay professional soldiers to fight or bureaucrats to raise taxes. However, organizing armies this way also had disadvantages. The first was that kings now had little leverage over their followers, who often cared more about their own fame and glory than about any larger plan, tending to plunge into battle (or to run away) as the mood took them. The most famous of all medieval battles, at Hastings in 1066, turned on just this issue. At the critical moment, the Normans attacking the right wing of King Harold's Anglo-Saxon army turned tail and ran. Forgetting orders, doctrine, and common sense, Harold's brothers Leofwyne and Gyrthe plunged down the hill after them, followed by their cheering men. At the foot of the slope the Normans rallied, turned, and cut down their disorganized pursuers. Its cohesion broken, the Anglo-Saxon line now came apart. The kingdom was lost.

According to legend, King Harold was shot through the eye by a Norman arrow, but even if he had extricated himself from the rout, Harold would have run straight into the second great problem of warfare in this age. Kings who did not win battles did not win plunder either, and despite all the oaths and talk of duty, kings who had no loot to hand out got little loyalty from their men.

The Norman leader William the Conqueror, on the other hand, could now reward his followers by sharing out England's broad acres. Yet even he and his heirs soon ran into difficulties, because the new arrangements created a third problem. As generation succeeded generation, the webs of duty and obligation binding a king and his knights grew increasingly tangled. Clever or lucky lords used inheritance, dowry, and purchase to expand their estates, but each new estate brought new obligations. All too soon, a man would find himself owing allegiance to multiple masters.

Such was the fate of Count Robert II of Flanders. In 1101, Count Robert swore fealty to King Henry I of England, pledging—as was customary—to aid his master "against all men who live and die." However, Robert added, that did not include the one man King Henry was actually worried about, King Philip of France. Robert could not promise to fight Philip, because he was already Philip's vassal. Robert assured Henry that if King Philip decided to attack England, he (Robert) would try to talk him (Philip) out of it, but if jaw-jaw failed and Philip went ahead with an invasion, Robert admitted that he would be obliged to fight on the French side—but insisted that he would only send enough troops to avoid looking unfaithful.

If, on the other hand, King Henry of England wanted Count Robert's help in a war that was not against France, Robert would gladly provide it—unless (a) Robert was unwell, (b) the king of France asked Robert to fight in a different war, or (c) the German emperor (who was another of Robert's masters) had also called on Robert. As if this were not complicated enough, Robert's final promise was that if France invaded Normandy—which would almost certainly mean war between France and England—he would send just 20 of his knights to fight on the French side and the other 980 to fight for the English.

This impossible mess of crosscutting allegiances was the outcome of centuries of decline. A few pages ago I mentioned the Byzantine emperor Justinian's attempt to reunite the Mediterranean Basin in the sixth century A.D., but after that failed, Leviathan's breakdown had begun in earnest. Starting in the 630s, Arabs bringing the new faith of Islam infiltrated out of the desert, overwhelming the tiny armies that the Byzantine Empire could now afford. In the 650s, the Arabs overthrew Persia's Sasanid rulers, and for the next half century Byzantium looked as if it were about to go the same way.

By 750, Muslim war parties had triumphed everywhere from Morocco to Pakistan, raiding deep into France and putting Constantinople under siege, but the caliphs never managed to put their Leviathan on a very firm footing. From the earliest days of Islam, caliphs had held an ambiguous position, somewhere between a divinely inspired successor to Muhammad and a conventional king. None really succeeded in converting religious authority into secular rule over more than a small part of his vast empire. By the ninth century many local sultans were effectively independent rulers, fighting each other, the caliph, and anyone else who came along.

Far to the northwest, the Germans who had overrun the western Roman Empire built up new kingdoms, which waged productive war when they had strong kings and counterproductive war when they did not. The most productive of their rulers was the Frankish king Charlemagne, who conquered much of western and central Europe between 771 and 814. Bureaucrats in the wooden halls of his capital at Aachen bullied local lords, squeezed taxes out of them, promoted literacy, and desperately tried to impose order on the king's subjects. In 800, a thoroughly cowed pope even put a crown on Charlemagne's head and proclaimed him Holy Roman emperor, but the dream of a revived Roman Empire quickly died. The immediate cause was that Charlemagne's son and grandsons got far too busy fighting each other to spare much time for keeping unruly aristocrats in line. "This caused great wars," a contemporary chronicler lamented, "not because the Franks were lacking princes who were noble, strong, and wise enough to rule their kingdoms, but because they were so equally matched in their generosity, dignity, and power that the discord increased, because no one excelled so much above the others that they would submit to his lordship."

Even before Charlemagne died, however, new raiders—Vikings coming from the north in longboats and Magyars coming from the east on horseback—had begun plundering the wealth that his productive wars had generated. Aachen was simply too far from the frontiers to respond to these hit-and-run attacks, and in a familiar story local lords stepped in to fill the security void. Not even the great Charlemagne could have held the forces of counterproductive war in check. By 885, when the much-less-great emperor Charles the Fat conspicuously failed to show up at Paris while Count Odo held off a Viking siege, the empire was effectively a dead letter.

It was every man for himself in this messy new world. The first reference in our sources to a man serving multiple masters in fact comes just a decade after Odo's defense of Paris, but across the centuries that followed, it just got more and more common. By the 1380s, five hundred years after Odo, the problem had become so bad that a French cleric proposed a one-size-fits-all solution. The overcommitted warrior, he recommended, should fight for the first lord to whom he had sworn an oath while discharging his obligations to his second (and third, and fourth, and so on) lord by hiring substitutes to fight instead.

This never caught on, perhaps because substitutes cost money. Much more common was the noble Enguerrand de Coucy's response when his master (the king of England) summoned him to war against his other master (the king of France) in 1369. Coucy declared a personal peace treaty with both kings and, rather than choose one master over the other, found himself a third master, going off to fight in the pope's army in Italy. When the papal campaigns fizzled out in 1374, Coucy took ten thousand men and waged a private war in Switzerland instead.

In the 1770s, while he was writing *The Wealth of Nations* in the safety of enlightened Edinburgh, Adam Smith contrasted his own well-ordered world with the tumultuous times of Coucy, Count Robert, and Kings Henry and Philip. That era, Smith sadly concluded, had been an age of "feudal anarchy" (so called after *feoda* or *feuda*, the Latin name for the land grants that so entangled everyone's loyalties), when "great lords continued to make war according to their own discretion, almost continually upon one another, and very frequently upon the king; and the open country still continued to be a scene of violence, rapine, and disorder" (Figure 3.8).

Since Smith's day, scholars have had a hard time deciding what significance to attach to the age of feudal anarchy. It was reading about medieval mayhem that made Norbert Elias decide in the 1930s that Europe must have subsequently gone through a civilizing process, driving down rates of violent death. But that was only half-correct. Because Elias did not take a long-term perspective, he assumed that feudal anarchy was simply the natural state of humanity, not the end point of a millennium of counterproductive wars that followed the breakdown of the ancient empires.

Figure 3.8. Feudal anarchy: the flower of Christian and Muslim chivalry hack each other to pieces at Damietta in Egypt, in 1218 (from a book dating from around 1255).

By the 1960s, though, as the spirit of *Coming of Age in Samoa* convinced more and more academics that humans were naturally peaceful, many historians began to ask whether "feudal anarchy" really was the right way to describe Coucy's world. After all, for every William the Conqueror hacking off heads, there was a Francis of Assisi ministering to the meek, and most of the time Europeans did settle their disputes without resort to force. But so, of course, did most twentieth-century Yanomami—and yet something like one-quarter of their men still died violently. What makes "feudal anarchy" such an appropriate label for fourteenth-century Europe is that many of its residents (much like Yanomami men) turned to violence with shocking casualness.

My own favorite story, out of thousands that survive, is about a knight who dropped in at a neighbor's castle for dinner. "My lord," he said by way of small talk. "This rich wine, how much did you pay for it?"

"Ah," his gracious host replied. "No living man ever asked a penny for it."

It seems to me, in fact, that "feudal anarchy" is an excellent description not just of western Europe between about 900 and 1400 but also of most of Eurasia's lucky latitudes in the same period. From England to Japan, societies staggered toward feudal anarchy as their Leviathans dismembered themselves. In third- and fourth-century northern China, documents speak of the rise of *buqu*, clients who followed warrior-landlords into battle, providing soldiers in return for shares of the plunder. In sixth-century India, rulers of the declining Gupta Empire began recognizing the virtual independence of *samantas*, local lords who provided soldiers when the imperial bureaucracy collapsed. In the ninth-century Middle East, the *iqta'*—lands granted by the caliph to local sultans who might, or might not, raise troops in return—provided what little glue still held the Arab world together. By 1000, the Byzantine Empire had moved in the same direction, with emperors making land grants called *pronoiai* in return for military service. Everywhere, the ancient empires went to their graves.

Zombie Empires

But they did not stay there; like Hollywood zombies, empires rose from the dead again and again.

Take China. When the Buddhist priest Yang Xuanzhi visited the former capital Luoyang in 547, the desolation stunned him. "The city walls had collapsed, palaces and houses were in ruins," he wrote. Just thirteen years before, a great rebellion had sacked the city, carried off its population, and split the Northern Wei kingdom that had briefly reunited this part of China into two warring states. Since then, said Yang, "beasts of the field had made their holes in the overgrown palace steps and mountain birds had nested in the courtyard trees. Wandering herdsmen loitered in the highways, and farmers planted millet between the ceremonial towers."

But just thirty years after Yang's visit, northern China had been reunited, and another twelve years later, in 589, most of China was under the rule of the Sui dynasty. China had clawed its way back up the slope in Figure 3.6.

Counterproductive wars, like productive ones, had their culminating points, and when they overshot them, men who excelled at violence found themselves (like the rulers of antiquity) spending less time killing and more time in meetings. "Understand this truth," a Persian prince told his son around 1080: "The kingdom can be held by the army, and the army by gold; and gold is acquired through agricultural development; and agricultural development through justice and equity. Therefore be just and equitable."

Conquerors who refused to learn this truth did not last long. After reuniting China in 589, the Sui dynasty kept raising bigger and bigger armies and launching them into disastrous wars in Korea. In the 610s, their subjects refused to take any more, and for a while it looked as if China were sliding back into feudal anarchy. Banditry increased, the number of households paying taxes fell by 75 percent, and much of the countryside was overrun by warlords (including thousands of militant Buddhist monks, apparently unconvinced by their own nonviolent teachings). But the winners of the civil wars, who set themselves up as the Tang dynasty, had learned the lessons of productive war well. "The ruler depends on the state," the emperor Taizong wrote, "and the state depends on its people. Oppressing the people to make them serve the ruler is like someone cutting off his own flesh to feed his stomach. The stomach is filled but the body is injured: the ruler is wealthy but the state is destroyed."

As good as their word, Tang monarchs granted amnesties, promoted talented officials regardless of their previous loyalties, and rebuilt a professional civil service. Setting the standard himself, Taizong reputedly had his bureaucrats hang memos on his bedroom walls so he could study them each night as he dozed off. He even brought the rebellious Buddhists on board, hiring those who surrendered to pray for the war dead (of both sides) in new monasteries built at the sites of his biggest battles.

Nor did the Tang rulers stop there. As descendants of invading nomads, they understood steppe politics well enough to know how to sow dissent within the Turkic tribes facing them across the Great Wall. In 630 they sent ten thousand cavalry charging out of a heavy morning mist to sweep away the Eastern Turk encampment at the battle at the Iron Mountain, and for the next half century China's frontier was secure.

But the achievement that really raised Tang rulers above feudal kings was reestablishing civilian control of the military. Being practical men, they cut deals with mighty nobles when they had to but refused to exchange land for armed service. Instead, they kept everyone on the Tang payroll and even revoked land grants made by previous dynasties. They rotated generals around the empire to prevent them from forming strong local ties. An officer who moved even ten troops without permission risked a year in jail; one who moved a regiment might be strangled.

The Tang basically did everything right, and the seventh century turned into an East Asian golden age. Peace was restored, the economy boomed, and Chinese poetry reached its peak of perfection. Tang armies overran Korea and the oases of central Asia; Chinese thought indelibly marked Japan and Southeast Asia. Yet despite these triumphs, not even the Tang could break the cycle of productive and counterproductive wars.

By the middle of the eighth century, China had grown so rich that the Turkic nomads on the steppes were forming new confederations to plunder it. To defend themselves, the Tang had to put ever-bigger armies on their frontiers, and in 755 one of their generals—a Turk who had joined the Chinese side—rebelled. The government crushed the revolt, but its methods, which involved granting enormous powers to other generals and inviting more groups of Turks into the empire to fight on its behalf against the groups of Turks that had already invaded, led to even worse disasters. There were brief intervals when hope flared anew, but overall the empire spent the next century and a half in free fall. Security broke down almost completely. Criminal gangs grew strong enough to beat the imperial army in pitched battles, and in 883 the mightiest of the outlaws (known to his friends as the Heaven-Storming Generalissimo, to his enemies as the Mad Bandit) even sacked Chang'an. Before the Mad Bandit showed up, Chang'an had been the world's biggest city, home to perhaps a million people. After, said the poet Wei Zhuang (who was there),

> Chang'an lies in silence; what's there now?
> In ruined markets and desolate streets, ears of wheat sprout . . .

The Hanyuan Hall is the haunt of foxes and hares . . .
Along the Avenue of Heaven you walk on the bones of high officials.

So many people were starving, one story says, that a thousand peasants were being killed and eaten every day in 883, with the Mad Bandit's men salting and pickling some bodies to save for later. By 907, when the last Tang emperor was deposed and China formally split into ten kingdoms, it seemed that no one would ever break the cycle of productive and counter-productive wars.

No Way Out

The revolution in military affairs that had brought mounted warfare to the lucky latitudes between 500 B.C. and A.D. 500 was different from most of the previous revolutions. These earlier revolutions—the rise of fortifications and siege warfare after 4300 B.C., bronze arms and armor after 3300, discipline sometime between then and 2450, mass iron-armed infantry forces around 900 B.C.—had generally played to the lucky latitudes' strengths, giving Leviathans tools to suppress internal strife and to conquer their neighbors, making bigger societies. Even chariots, invented on the steppes around 2000 B.C., had ultimately worked better in the hands of the empires than in those of raiders, because only empires could afford to build vehicles and train horses by the thousands.

With cavalry, though, it proved impossible to convert the lucky latitudes' wealth, organization, and numbers into victory over the nomads. The insuperable problem was that the nomads ruled lands that were perfect for horse-breeding. Most tribes had more horses than people, and they practically lived in the saddle. Even the richest and cleverest of the agrarian empires (above all, Tang China) could only win temporary advantages, which would eventually be wiped out by bad luck, bad judgment, or the rise of a particularly big nomadic federation. What the lucky latitudes needed was another revolution in military affairs to tip the balance back in their favor, but none came. For every technical improvement that worked to the lucky latitudes' advantage (such as improved ships, castles, and infrastructure), another (such as stirrups or the breeding of even stronger horses) benefited the nomads even more.

What eventually changed the equation was gunpowder, but you would have needed a very good crystal ball to have seen that coming before A.D. 1400. The earliest reference to gunpowder goes back to the ninth century, when Chinese Daoist monks searching for elixirs of immortality set fire to a mixture of sulfur and saltpeter and discovered that it burned and fizzed in marvelously entertaining ways. They quickly found two uses for the powder. The first, fireworks, did nothing to extend life, while the second, firearms, promised only to shorten it.

The oldest surviving recipe for gunpowder, dating to 1044, did not use enough saltpeter to explode. Instead of making guns, in which gunpowder blasts a ball or bullet out of a barrel, Chinese craftsmen designed weapons that sprayed burning powder out of bamboo tubes or used catapults to launch paper bags full of the "fire chemical." On the whole, gunpowder was probably more dangerous to its users than to its targets.

If anything, as late as the fourteenth century the balance of military power still seemed to be tilting toward the barbarians, largely because they proved so good at learning from their adversaries. When the Goths flooded into the Roman Empire in 378, they had found that they could win battles but not storm cities. "Keep peace with walls," their chief advised them. But just two generations later, when Attila the Hun invaded the exact same area, very different scenes unfolded. Finding his way blocked by the massive fortifications of Naissus (modern Nis in Serbia) in 442, Attila had the Huns chop down trees and build dozens of battering rams. "From the walls the defenders tumbled down wagon-sized boulders," the Roman diplomat Priscus wrote. "Some of the rams were crushed, along with the men working them, but the Romans could not hold out against the great number of machines. Then the enemy brought up scaling ladders . . . and the city was taken."

Attila used the plunder from his victories to hire the best Roman engineers, who repaid his generosity by exploiting the weaknesses of the defenses they had themselves built. As a result, says a fifth-century writer, the Huns "captured more than a hundred cities and almost brought Constantinople into danger, and most men fled from it. Even the monks wanted to run away from Jerusalem." One of the sacked cities, Nicopolis in what is now Bulgaria, has been excavated extensively, and the thoroughness of the Hunnic destruction is astonishing. No one ever rebuilt its mansions.

For centuries, the nomads got better and better at fighting the lucky latitudes, and by 1219, when Genghis Khan invaded the mighty but now largely forgotten Khwarizmian Empire in eastern Iran, his Mongol army employed a permanent corps of Chinese engineers. This corps directed prisoners of war to dig tunnels; divert rivers; build catapults, rams, and towers; and rain burning gunpowder onto defenders. According to Giovanni da Pian del Carpine, the first European to live in a Mongol khan's court, the engineers constantly refined their nasty methods. "They even take the fat of the people they kill," Carpine claimed, "and, melting it, throw it onto the houses, and wherever the fire falls on this fat it is almost inextinguishable."

Baghdad, Islam's richest city, surrendered in 1258 after Mongol catapults concentrated their fire on a single tower and brought it crashing down in just three days. After mocking the city's ruler for hoarding his wealth instead of spending it on defense, the Mongols rolled him in a carpet and crushed him to death, officially ending the caliphate.

In 1267 the Mongols capped this by besieging Xiangyang, possibly the greatest fortress on earth and certainly the strategic key to China. For six years it defied them. Nothing—not rams, not fire weapons, not scaling ladders—worked, but then the ever-adaptable nomads adapted even more, swapping their horses for ships. After sweeping the Chinese fleet off the Han River, they used new styles of catapults to blast holes in the walls of Fancheng, which guarded the bank of the Han across from Xiangyang. Once Fancheng fell, Xiangyang's position became hopeless, and once Xiangyang fell, China's position became hopeless too. In 1279, Khubilai Khan chased the last emperor of the Song dynasty into the sea and seized the celestial throne for himself.

Nomad armies proved equally adaptable in open battle. In 1191, for instance, the steppe cavalry of the Ghurid Empire fled in disorder when they first encountered elephants in India, and their commander was lucky to escape with his life. Returning the following year, however, the same commander fought the same alliance of Ganges Valley kings on the same battlefield at Tarain but used different tactics. Four wings of horse archers, each ten thousand strong, took turns harassing the Indian forces, avoiding direct contact with the terrifying elephants; and then, as night drew in, the Ghurid reserve of twelve thousand armored lancers charged home, shattering the demoralized Indian ranks.

The Ghurids' enormous army—more than fifty thousand cavalry—bears witness to the last, and most important, reason that the nomads' power grew. As well as learning how to get the better of walls, ships, and elephants, nomads learned logistics. By the thirteenth century, nomads were regularly raising and supplying armies like the Ghurids', with each rider typically bringing along three or four spare mounts. When armies from the steppes fought each other to control the lucky latitudes—as happened when Genghis Khan annihilated the Khwarizmians on the banks of the

Indus in 1221, or the Turkic Mamluks repulsed a Mongol invasion of Syria at Homs sixty years later—half a million horses might be crammed into a square mile of dust and arrows, drawing in every scrap of forage from hundreds of miles around. All this had to be organized, and the great nomad conquerors assembled huge general staffs (usually men captured from the cities they sacked) to do it for them.

The human and animal carnage of the great battles was staggering, but it paled in comparison to the massacres of civilians that followed. Some of the numbers written down by survivors—1,747,000 people plus all the cats and dogs killed by Mongols at Nishapur, says one Persian historian; 2,400,000 at Herat, says another—simply cannot be true, not least because they are so much bigger than the total populations of the cities in question. But even if we discount the wilder claims, it does seem that each time horsemen from the steppes burst into the lucky latitudes, hundreds of thousands died, and sometimes millions. Genghis Khan's head count probably reached the tens of millions, and when Tamerlane led a second wave of Mongol invasions around 1400, sacking Delhi, Damascus, and dozens of other cities, he might have come close to matching that tally. (Had he not died of fever as he was marching against China in 1405, he might even have surpassed it.)

Stunning as it is to read about these bloodbaths, we should bear in mind that the rape, pillage, slaughter, and starvation that armies spread across Eurasia was only one part of the era's violence. All the while, the background noise of casual, small-scale killing—homicides, vendettas, private wars, civil strife—rumbled on, rising in crescendos as kingdoms collapsed into feudal anarchy, dying down again as productive war temporarily worked its magic.

For the first time in history, we have semi-reliable statistics on one kind of bloodshed, in the form of western European murder trial records. These go back to the thirteenth century, and although they are difficult to interpret, riddled with gaps, and—given the incentives for lying when the stakes were so high—full of distortions, they are almost as alarming as the stories about Genghis Khan. Across England, the Low Countries, Germany, and Italy, roughly 1 person per 100 was murdered between 1200 and 1400. England was the safest place, where only 1 person in 140 met this fate; Italy, the roughest, with nearly 1 death in 60 being a homicide. (Western Europe's twentieth-century rate, by contrast, was 1 murder per 2,388 people.)

Western Europe was only a small part of Eurasia's lucky latitudes, homicide was only one form of lethal violence, and the thirteenth and fourteenth centuries were only one part of the period under review here. All of this means that extracting a single figure for the rate of violent death in Eurasian lucky latitudes between 200 and 1400 is a hazardous business. We have no way to weigh up the relative contributions of homicides, vendettas, private wars, civil strife, and interstate war, but if—for the sake of argument—we just treat each of these five forms equally, we get a total rate of 5 percent for western Europe (with England at 3.5 percent and Italy at 8.5 percent).

This figure may or may not be close to the truth (personally, I suspect it is on the low side), and whatever is true of western Europe may or may not apply to the rest of Eurasia, but it does give us a sense of the order of magnitude of the mayhem. It is also consistent with the impression provided by qualitative evidence, that the twelve-hundred-year cycle of productive and counterproductive wars between A.D. 200 and 1400 undid many of the gains made by the ancient Roman, Mauryan, and Han Empires.

The tone of the writings surviving from the most successful of the empires between A.D. 200 and 1400, such as Tang China, hints that they may have pushed the rate of death back into the 2–5 percent range that I suggested in Chapter 2 that the ancient empires were managing, while nomad invasions and feudal anarchy clearly drove it back up. However, unless the most extreme figures for nomad massacres are actually true, rates cannot have gone back up into the 10–20 percent range that anthropologists have found among Stone Age societies. If this reasoning is right, and the rate of violent death across Eurasia's lucky latitudes between 200 and 1400 was higher than that in the ancient empires but lower than that in Stone Age societies, the figure must have been somewhere in the 5–10 percent range.

What that meant for the people who lived with it is hard to extract from the medieval manuscripts. My own sense of it, I must admit, has been shaped by a very different literary genre: the detective story. Under the pen name Ellis Peters, Edith Pargeter wrote twenty novels and a book of short stories about a medieval monk turned sleuth named Brother Cadfael (played in a fine television adaptation by Derek Jacobi). Cadfael lives a quiet life, tending the herb garden in a Benedictine monastery outside the market town of Shrewsbury in England. Even so, in the eight years (1137–45) covered by the novels, by my count Cadfael runs across thirty-three murders, ninety-four men hanged after the siege of Shrewsbury, and undisclosed numbers killed in another siege and two battles (not to mention an accidental drowning and sundry assaults, whippings, and attempted rapes).

Pargeter's characters are cautious. They know how easily mistakes can prove fatal. Answering back to their betters invites a beating. Walking in the woods alone risks robbery and death. When the mead flows, old friends can suddenly turn into killers. And yet, despite a rate of violent death that must run to at least 5 percent, Pargeter's people do not live in a state of constant dread, cowering in expectation of a fatal blow. The odds, after all, are nearly twenty to one in any person's favor, but more to the point, violence was simply part and parcel of life in this brutal world. Even their entertainment was vicious. One chronicler describes how his fellows in the little town of Prato in northern Italy would nail a live cat to a post and then, with shaved scalps and hands tied behind their backs, compete to head-butt it to death, "to the sounds of trumpets." When the people of Mons in Belgium were short of something to do, they decided—having no criminals of their own on hand—to buy a robber from a neighboring town, tie a horse to each of his ankles and wrists, and then have him torn limb from limb. "At this," we are told, "the people rejoiced more than if a new holy body had risen from the dead." The only upsetting thing about the episode, said the chronicler, was that the good citizens of Mons paid too much for the man.

In a world like this, not even Cadfael could keep the Beast in its cage.

Caging the World

Despite all its hazards, twelfth-century western Europe was still safer than most of the planet. But that was beginning to change, because while the steppes and the Eurasian empires were locked in their bloody cycle, caging was spreading across the rest of the globe, driving down rates of violent death.

Plenty of parts of the world have climates and soils suitable for farming, but because the distribution of wild plants and animals that could be domesticated was so uneven, the lucky latitudes were the only part of the earth where agriculture had begun within five thousand years after the end of the Ice Age. By Cadfael's time, however, three forces had intervened to spread farming far beyond the limits of the original lucky latitudes, and in its wake caging and productive war brought Leviathans to almost every continent.

The first of the forces was migration. Agriculture drives up population, and ever since farming began, people had responded by spreading out, looking for more land. So long as frontiers remained open, early farmers could avoid most of the effects of caging, but once the best locations had filled up, caging began trapping them on the path toward productive war.

We see this best in the vast expanses of the Pacific Ocean (Figure 3.9). Stone Age farmers from what is now China had already colonized the Philippines by 1500 B.C., and over the next two thousand years their descendants made epic canoe voyages, rowing far out of sight of land to discover and settle the hundreds of uninhabited but fertile islands that make up Micronesia. They planted taro (a fibrous root that originally evolved in Southeast Asia), raised large families, and fought, and when their new island homes filled up, they sent out more canoes.

In the first millennium A.D. these argonauts of the Pacific spread across

Figure 3.9. The medieval Pacific Rim: sites in East Asia and Oceania mentioned in this chapter

Polynesia, reaching distant New Zealand by 1200. A few heroes probably paddled all the way to America's West Coast and back again (although there is no direct evidence, there is no other obvious explanation for how American sweet potatoes got to Polynesia around this time), but the three-thousand-mile trip from Hawaii to California was too far for proper migrations. This meant that by 1200 the cage was closing in the Pacific.

We know the story best from Hawaii (largely, I suspect, because archaeologists have never needed much encouragement to work there). Humans arrived between A.D. 800 and 1000, and population boomed between 1200 and 1400. Oral traditions collected in the nineteenth century and more recent excavations agree that fighting intensified, and in the fifteenth century great warriors consolidated entire islands into kingdoms.

The first of these was Ma'ilikukahi, who killed all his rivals on Oahu (probably in the 1470s) and turned into a stationary bandit. He built irrigation canals and temples and centralized power in his own hands. His people, the folktales say, prospered mightily, and within a century other Hawaiian islands were acquiring even more impressive kings. Maui's ruler Kiha-a-Pi'ilani (who reigned around 1590), the legends say, was not just a great ruler, a fierce warrior, a fine surfer, and extremely good-looking; he was also an agricultural reformer who cleared forests and planted huge fields of sweet potatoes, as well as a peacemaker who judged his people fairly.

On Hawaii as in Eurasia, however, the course of productive war never did run smooth. The handsome King Kiha only got to be the ruler because he fell out with his older brother (who, the story runs, had thrown a bowl of fish and octopus in Kiha's face) and split the kingdom in civil war. Out of collapse, though, came further growth. Kiha won because 'Umi, king of the Big Island—and another famous planter of sweet potatoes—was eager to extend his influence onto Maui and sent troops to help the usurper.

In many ways, the Hawaiian wars of unification were strikingly like the productive wars that Eurasians had fought in the millennia leading up to A.D. 200—and strikingly *un*like the cycle of productive and counter-productive wars that Eurasians were trapped in between A.D. 200 and 1400. The obvious reason for this is that there were no steppes and horses on Hawaii. As a result, for every step backward, like Maui's civil war, Hawaiian productive war subsequently took two steps forward. By the 1610s, rulers were regularly trying to get multiple islands under their control. Waikiki Beach became the favored landing spot for invasions of Oahu; centuries before the first tourist stretched out on its perfect sands, a king of Maui, a high priest from Oahu, and several thousand soldiers all bled to death there.

In the eighteenth century, war pushed the eight islands into just three kingdoms, capable of fielding armies up to fifteen thousand strong and, in one case, a fleet of twelve hundred canoes. "Had contact with the West been delayed for another century," speculates Patrick Kirch, the leading archaeologist of Hawaii, "one of these polities would have won out and gained control over the entire archipelago." This was productive war with a vengeance.

Most farmers who left the lucky latitudes in search of new land, however, were not fortunate enough to be moving into places like the Pacific, full of uninhabited but fertile islands. More often, people were already living wherever migrants went. Sometimes local foragers ran away as farmers arrived, but if they did so, they would only find that more farmers would keep coming, clearing and plowing up more forest, until the natives ran out of places to run to. And when the cage closed, hunter-gatherers faced tough choices.

One option was to fight, burning outlying farms in bitter, generations-long guerrilla wars. The Navajo would wage just such an on-again, off-again war in the American Southwest, beginning in 1595 against the Spaniards, continuing against the Mexican government, and only ending in 1864, when the United States applied overwhelming force, devastating Navajo lands and expelling the survivors. It was just one among thousands of separate struggles. Most are now forgotten, but all ended the same way. Foragers who kept fighting were eventually annihilated, enslaved, or herded into reservations. The only alternative to destruction was assimilation, with foragers copying what the newcomers did and turning into farmers themselves. Assimilation became the second of the great forces that spread farming, caging, productive war, and Leviathans across the planet.

The most interesting example of assimilation may be Japan. Initially, migration was more important, with Koreans bringing rice and millet to Kyushu, Japan's southernmost island, around 2500 B.C. Kyushu was something of a hunter-gatherer paradise, with abundant wild foods that supported thousands of foragers; perhaps because of this, farming made little headway for nearly two thousand years. Only around 600 B.C., when new migrants from Korea arrived with metal weapons, did the farming frontier surge across to the main island of Honshu.

The Japanese islands are much bigger than the Hawaiian, and so caging took longer to work its magic. It was helped, though, by three more waves of Korean immigrants between A.D. 400 and 600. These newcomers are most famous for bringing writing and Buddhism to Japan, but their crossbows, cavalry, and iron swords were even more important. The agricultural frontier moved north across Honshu, but as it did so, assimilation pushed back. Japanese chiefs seized on the ready-made revolution in military affairs imported by Korean migrants to create their own homegrown Leviathan, the state of Yamato. By 800 it had conquered most of Kyushu and Honshu.

Over the next eight centuries, productive war united the whole archipelago. As in Hawaii, it was a bumpy ride, but each time Leviathan fell, it came back bigger and stronger than before. Yamato broke apart in the ninth and tenth centuries, and by 1100 the countryside had been overrun with private armies of the hired swords known as samurai. Fighting only turned productive again in the 1180s, when one warlord defeated the rest, got the samurai under control, and set himself up as shogun, or military governor.

In theory, the country was run by emperors who traced their ancestry back to gods, but shoguns—usually hard, self-made men who had risen through the army's ranks—actually called the shots. It was a messy arrangement, but it worked surprisingly well. After conquering almost all of what we now call Japan, the shoguns oversaw investments in agriculture. Productivity and population boomed, and in 1274 and 1281, Japan even beat off Mongol invasions.

The shoguns then learned, like so many rulers in the lucky latitudes, how easily productive war could turn counterproductive when nomads were involved. To mobilize the resources needed to stop the Mongols, the shoguns had to cut so many deals with samurai and local lords that these overmighty subjects lost all reason to fear Leviathan. Across the next three hundred years, Japan slithered into its own version of feudal anarchy. By the sixteenth century (the period that Akira Kurosawa's famous film *The Seven Samurai* is set in), villages, city neighborhoods, and Buddhist temples were all hiring their own samurai. Warlords filled the countryside with castles, and violence spiked up well past anything Cadfael was used to.

Not until the 1580s did the pendulum swing back. In the years that Kiha was subduing Maui and 'Umi was uniting Hawaii, a Japanese warlord named Oda Nobunaga stormed his rivals' castles and deposed the shogun. His successor, Hideyoshi, went further still, pushing through one of the most amazing disarmaments in history. Announcing that he wanted to "benefit the people not only in this life but in the life hereafter," he bullied his subjects into handing over their weapons so he could melt them down to make nails and bolts for a Buddha statue twice as tall as the Statue of Liberty. Government troops went on "sword hunts" to make sure that everyone shared in Hideyoshi's benefits.

Hideyoshi was not being entirely forthright, however. After disarming the people, he ramped up productive war by invading Korea, intending to swallow it and China into a single great East Asian Empire. The casualties were enormous, and when Hideyoshi died in 1598, his plan collapsed and his generals fought a civil war. Even so, his pacification of the homeland stuck. The government even demolished most of Japan's castles: in Bizen Province, for instance, the two hundred forts that had been built by 1500 had dwindled to one by 1615. For the next quarter millennium Japan was one of the least violent lands on earth. Even books describing weapons were banned.

By A.D. 1500, migration and assimilation had pushed farming, caging, productive war, and Leviathans far beyond their original homeland in the lucky latitudes, but in some places a third force intervened: independent invention. Several parts of the world outside the lucky latitudes had at least a few potentially domesticable plants and animals, and foragers in these regions eventually had their own agricultural revolutions and revolutions in military affairs. Despite a time lag thousands of years long, they began moving down the same path that people in the lucky latitudes had already trodden.

Africa is a striking case in point. Migration and assimilation certainly played big parts in bringing agriculture to the continent: Africa's first farmers were settlers from the Hilly Flanks who carried wheat, barley, and goats to the Nile Valley around 5500 B.C. (Figure 3.10). As Egyptian farmers spread into what we now call Sudan, Nubian foragers emulated them, turning to agriculture of their own accord. Eventually, when Egyptian armies pressed southward after 2000 B.C., the Nubians discovered productive war and formed their own kingdoms. In the seventh century B.C. a Nubian king—Taharqa of Napata—even conquered Egypt.

Productive war was just as messy on this frontier as anywhere else, regularly turning counterproductive and bringing on collapse, only to reverse itself and create a still stronger Leviathan. By 300 B.C., Napata was in decline, and a great new city was flourishing at Meroë. By A.D. 50, Meroë too was past its glory days, and the rulers of an even greater city at Aksum

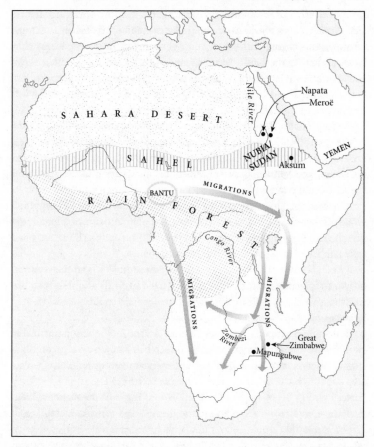

Figure 3.10. The not-so-dark continent: sites in Africa mentioned in this chapter

were raising stone pillars a hundred feet high and sending armies across the Red Sea into what is now Yemen.

Given time, migration and assimilation might have carried caging and productive war all the way down Africa's east coast, but homegrown caging overtook them. By 3000 B.C., people in the Sahel, the dusty grasslands that run across Africa between the southern edge of the Sahara Desert and the northern edge of the rain forest, had domesticated sorghum, yams, and the oil palm. What happened next is controversial: some archaeologists argue that eastern and southern Africans also began inventing agriculture independently, but most think that after 1000 B.C. Bantu-speaking farmers from western and central Africa migrated east and south, taking ranching, farming, and caging with them and fighting with iron weapons as they went. (Whether the Bantu learned ironworking from the Mediterranean world or invented it for themselves is yet another source of controversy.)

Whatever the details, though, by Cadfael's day productive war was bringing forth Leviathans everywhere from the mouth of the Congo River to the banks of the Zambezi, setting off local revolutions in military affairs. In the thirteenth century, for instance, archaeologists have detected new styles of fighting in the Congo Basin, involving larger forces, stronger command and control, big war canoes, and new iron stabbing spears for hand-to-hand combat.

Once again, the path toward larger, safer societies was bumpy and bloody. In southeast Africa, for example, population boomed, and a kingdom called Mapungubwe emerged in the twelfth century. By 1250, it had fallen, replaced by the new city of Great Zimbabwe. By 1400, Great Zimbabwe had subdued the Shona-speaking tribes around it and the city had grown to fifteen thousand residents, protected by walls and towers so impressive that the first Europeans to see their ruins could not believe that Africans had built them.

Fifteenth-century Hawaii, Japan, and Africa (and every point in between) were all different, of course, and each had its own unique combination of migration, assimilation, and independent invention. But when we step back from the details to look at the big picture, we see much the same pattern almost everywhere. Leviathan was taking over the planet. Whenever the evidence allows us to see the details, war was producing bigger governments that drove down rates of violent death and increased prosperity. Having started down the path of caging and productive war thousands of years later than the lucky latitudes, most of the rest of the world still lagged far behind the Leviathans in Eurasia's core in A.D. 1400, but thanks to the cycle of productive and counterproductive wars that had grown up along the edge of the steppes since A.D. 200, the gap was narrowing.

Natural Experiments

I have saved until last the most interesting case of all, America (Figure 3.11). Unlike Japan, the Pacific islands, and Africa, all of which were heavily impacted by emigration from Eurasia's lucky latitudes, America

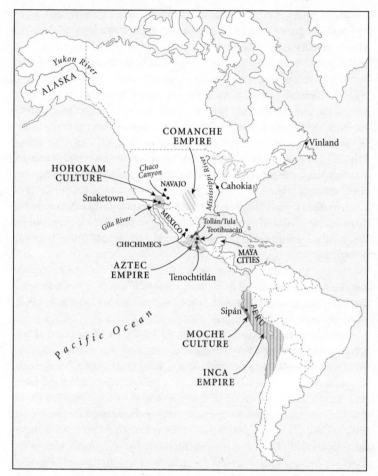

Figure 3.11. Sites in the Americas mentioned in this chapter

largely lost contact with the Old World after its initial colonization from Siberia some fifteen thousand years ago. A few daredevils did breach the barriers, such as the Vikings who settled Vinland around A.D. 1000 and the Polynesians who reached the West Coast soon after, but with just one exception, to which I will return in a moment, none of them had much impact. As a result, we can think of the New and Old Worlds as two independent natural experiments. Comparing their histories gives us a real test of the theory that productive war and Leviathan are universal human responses to caging, rather than the legacies of a distinctive Western (or even Eurasian) way of war.

When the Spanish conquistador Hernán Cortés showed up in Mexico in 1519, some six thousand years had passed since Mesoamericans had invented farming. If we count six thousand years from the establishment of farming in Eurasia's Hilly Flanks around 7500 B.C., we get to 1500 B.C., by which time Egypt's pharaohs were fielding thousands of chariots carrying bronze-clad archers firing composite bows. But the Aztecs defending Tenochtitlán against Cortés had no chariots or bronze. They fought on foot, wearing padded cotton suits and wooden helmets. Their bows were crude, and their most frightening weapons were oak sticks studded with flakes of a sharp volcanic glass called obsidian. Clearly, military affairs had unfolded on different schedules in the New World and the Old—which looks bad for this book's argument that productive war is a universal human response to caging.

Some of these differences are easy to explain, though. The Aztecs did not invent chariots because they could not: wild horses had gone extinct in the Americas around 12,000 B.C. (suspiciously soon after humans arrived), and with no horses to pull them, there could be no chariots. But what of bronze spearheads and armor? In the Old World, these appeared along-side the first cities and governments (around 3500 B.C. in Mesopotamia, 3000 B.C. in Egypt, 2500 B.C. in the Indus Valley, and 1900 B.C. in China); in the New World, they did not. The oldest known American experiments with metal date from around 1000 B.C., and by the time of the first Leviathans a millennium later, Moche metalworkers could produce objects like the beautiful gold ornaments buried with the so-called Lords of Sipán. But at no point did Native Americans think of alloying copper with other metals to make bronze weapons—or, if some enterprising smith did come up with the concept, it didn't catch on.

The American experience with bows and arrows is even odder. I mentioned in Chapter 2 that arrowheads go back more than sixty thousand years in Africa. But the people who crossed the land bridge from Siberia into America fifteen thousand years ago did not bring the bow with them, and no one in America reinvented it. The first arrowheads in America, found on the banks of the Yukon River in Alaska, date from around 2300 B.C. They were made in a style that archaeologists call the Arctic Small Tool Tradition, imported by a new wave of immigrants from Siberia. Archery then spread excruciatingly slowly across North America, taking thirty-five hundred years to reach Mexico. When Cortés arrived, Mesoamericans had only been using bows for about four centuries, and the Aztecs' simple self bows would have looked laughably old-fashioned to Egyptian pharaohs.

This sounds like an open-and-shut case that cultural differences determined everything, proving—depending, I suppose, on your politics—either that Eurasians were more rational (and therefore, perhaps, better) than Native Americans or that they were more violent (and therefore, perhaps, worse). But arguments like these have their problems too. Mesoamericans developed the problem-solving skills needed to produce remarkable calendars, raised-field farming, and irrigation. Calling these people irrational—or just less rational than Europeans—is not very convincing.

Neither is suggesting that Native American cultures were less violent than Europeans. For many years, archaeologists treated the ancient Maya as poster children for peace, arguing that because we had found few fortifications around their cities, they must have settled their disputes nonviolently. That theory collapsed almost the minute the Mayan script was deciphered. Its main topic was war. Mayan kings fought just as much as European ones.

Some historians point instead to what the Aztecs called Flower Wars, campaigns designed to minimize casualties on both sides. These, they argue, show that Native Americans looked at fighting as a kind of performance, in contrast to the European focus on decisive battle. But this is a misunderstanding: Flower Wars were more like limited wars than ritual wars. A Flower War was a cheap way to show enemies that resistance was futile. "If that failed," says Ross Hassig, the leading expert on Aztec warfare, "the flower war was escalated . . . shifting from demonstrations of prowess to wars of attrition." Aztecs, like Europeans, tried to win wars on the cheap, but when that did not work, they did whatever it took.

So why did New and Old World military methods follow such different paths? Frankly, we don't really know, because historians have spent remarkably little time asking such big comparative questions. But in the current state of the debate, the most compelling explanation may be a deceptively simple idea offered by the biologist turned geographer Jared Diamond in his book *Guns, Germs, and Steel.*

· The Americas, Diamond points out, basically run north–south across the globe, while Eurasia runs east–west (Figure 3.12). In Eurasia, people could move back and forth along the lucky latitudes, sharing ideas and

Figure 3.12. Geography as destiny: the north–south arrangement of the Americas versus the east–west arrangement of Eurasia

institutions, without having to leave this band of roughly similar ecological zones (what geographers call a biome). In much of the Americas, by contrast, people could not move very far to the east or the west within a biome; to fan out along the continent's long axis, they would have to go north or south, crossing daunting deserts and dense jungles.

This, Diamond suggests, would have had two consequences. First, because it was so much more difficult to move north–south across biomes than east–west along them, the communities of people able to share ideas and institutions would have been smaller in the New World than in the Old. If Eurasia had larger communities of metalworkers than the Americas, producing for markets that were larger too, we should perhaps not be surprised that Eurasians came up with useful ideas like bronze a lot faster than Americans. And second, Diamond suggests, when people did come up with useful ideas, they would be able to spread them farther and faster along the biomes in the Old World than across the biomes in the New.

This seems to fit the facts quite well. By the time Mesopotamians came up with bronze weapons in the fourth millennium B.C., they already had contacts stretching as far as India and the Mediterranean, linking more people than any comparable network in America would do before the Inca Empire in the fifteenth century A.D. And once Mesopotamians had bronze weapons, the idea spread quickly along the lucky latitudes. Within fifteen hundred years, people in what we now call China and Britain had bronze weapons too.

The jury is still out on why Native Americans didn't invent bronze weapons, but Diamond's thesis seems to be the best contender, and it explains the odd pattern of American archery even better. For reasons as yet unknown, prehistoric hunters had abandoned the bow as they moved northward across the biomes separating Africa from Siberia and then moved back southward through America. It took tens of thousands more years for the bow to spread all the way to the eastern end of Siberia. When bows did finally reach the Americas, being carried across the Bering Strait into Alaska around 2300 B.C., they took twice as long to pass through all the biomes separating Alaska from Mexico as Eurasian bronze weapons had needed to travel roughly the same distance within just a few biomes from Mesopotamia to England.

If Diamond is right that geography mattered more than culture in creating these differences, one further pattern should also be visible. We should find that while the pace of change was slower in America than Eurasia, its general direction—from farming to caging to productive war to Leviathan—was the same.

Broadly speaking, that is just what we do find. In the countries we now call Mexico and Peru, people domesticated what plants and animals were available by about 4500 B.C. At first, change came almost as quickly as in the Old World. In the Middle East it took roughly four thousand years to get from the first farmers to the first Leviathans (at Uruk and Susa, around 3500 B.C.); in the New World, it took roughly four and a half thousand to get to Teotihuacán and the Moche culture, around 100 B.C.

The Eastern and Western Hemispheres both went through similar two-steps-forward-for-one-step-back processes, producing strings of revolutions in military affairs. In Mesoamerica, Teotihuacán apparently introduced the first regular, disciplined formations, as well as hugely increasing the size of armies. By A.D. 150, little bands without helmets, shields, or armor gave way to forces perhaps ten thousand strong. Some men, at least, started wearing quilted cotton helmets, which, although they may not sound very safe, could apparently be quite effective against stone axes.

By A.D. 450, armies were probably twice as big, with elite troops wearing quilted cotton armor as well as helmets. Compared with the revolutions in military affairs in first-millennium-B.C. Eurasia, the American improvements were unimpressive, but Teotihuacán was nonetheless treading the same path as the Old World Leviathans. And, just like the Eurasian empires, Teotihuacán eventually fell, with its urban core sacked and burned around A.D. 650, probably by invaders from western Mexico. In further parallels with the Eastern Hemisphere, Mesoamerican military organization then collapsed. Post-Teotihuacán wall paintings show no armor at all, and a proliferation of hilltop forts suggests that law and order broke down.

Mesoamerican war turned productive again in the tenth century. A group called the Toltecs carved out a large kingdom, ruled from the city of Tollán (also known as Tula). Toltec fighters wore more cotton armor than Teotihuacános and introduced a new weapon that archaeologists call the curved club, made of oak studded with flakes of obsidian. The Toltec Empire probably never matched the scale of Teotihuacán's and certainly did not last as long. In the twelfth century, migrants from farther north overwhelmed it, burning Tollán around A.D. 1179. (Some of these invaders, the Chichimecs, might have brought the bow and arrow to Mexico at this time.) Mesoamerica then fell back into constant wars between small city-states until the fifteenth century, when another group of northern newcomers— the Aztecs—renewed productive war.

We know more about the Aztecs than any earlier American society. Their success depended as much on diplomacy and clever marriages as on fighting, but when they did fight, they did it better than Teotihuacános or Toltecs. Aztec armies marched in multiple divisions, each about eight thousand strong, capable—like the corps in Napoleon's armies—of advancing and fighting on separate lines and then concentrating quickly. Logistics improved even more, with defeated enemies now being required to provide supplies. A professional officer corps took shape, and even ordinary soldiers got basic training.

Battles began with slingshots and archery from the wings before shock troops closed for hand-to-hand combat, protected by thick cotton armor, large shields, and wooden helmets covered in feathers. The shock troops attacked in loose formations so they could swing "broadswords," four-foot-long oak sticks studded with rows of obsidian teeth, and advanced in two ranks, the first of elite aristocratic fighters and the second of veteran commoners. Commanders rotated the two groups in and out of combat to avoid exhaustion and tried to keep a big reserve, to be committed at the decisive moment to extend the line and outflank the enemy.

Aztec armies built the biggest empire Mesoamerica had seen. Its population boomed, to perhaps 4 million, with 200,000 in the capital city, Tenochtitlán. Agriculture reached new heights, trade networks stretched farther than ever before, and households prospered. We have no way of knowing how safe Aztecs were, but surviving scraps of poetry suggest that they certainly *felt* safe. "Proud of itself is the city of Mexico-Tenochtitlán," went one song. "Here no one fears to die in war. This is our glory!"

In the Old World, emigration, assimilation, and independent invention spread farming and caging beyond their original homelands in the lucky latitudes. If Diamond's theory is correct, we should expect the same thing to have happened in the New, only more slowly, because of the challenges of crossing biomes, and once again this seems to be what the evidence shows. To take just one example, not until A.D. 500 did corn, squash, and beans make their way from Mexico northward to the river valleys that cut across the scorched deserts of the American Southwest. The region was wetter in those days, but even so, rainfall was unreliable, and the only way to farm the parched land was by digging irrigation canals. Nothing cages people quite like lack of water, and by A.D. 700 hundreds were congregating in the best locations and fighting fiercely as population grew. Eighth- and ninth-century sites are full of skulls shattered by stone axes, arrowheads lodged in ribs, and villages burned to the ground.

After 900, though, the fighting apparently stopped. Archaeologists often call this the Chaco Phenomenon, after the impressive sites in Chaco Canyon, New Mexico, but Pax Chacoa might be a better label. People concentrated in even larger clusters (perhaps ten thousand in Chaco Canyon), built bigger houses with more storerooms, and traded farther afield.

The Pax Chacoa lasted until about 1150, and then it too ended. Driven perhaps by a worsening climate, people abandoned big communities such as Chaco Canyon and Snaketown on the Gila River in Arizona. They fought more, failed to maintain their irrigation ditches, and gave up long trading trips. And on the process went. Even more impressive towns grew up on the Gila in the thirteenth century, often decked out with ceremonial ball courts strikingly like examples in Mesoamerica, but the Hohokam culture (as these sites are called) fell apart too by 1450.

We could pile up more examples, such as the extraordinary Native American city at Cahokia on the Mississippi, but these few, I hope, are enough to make the point. Differences in geography shaped how the process worked in each specific place, but everywhere in the world that farming could get a toehold, the cage closed rapidly between A.D. 200 and 1400, creating productive war.

The one big exception to this pattern was, as we have seen, the Eurasian lucky latitudes. Here geography changed its meanings in the early first millennium A.D. as the agrarian empires became entangled with steppe nomads, trapping the now not-so-lucky latitudes in a cycle of productive and counterproductive wars.

Between A.D. 200 and 1400, Eurasia's formula of horses plus steppes plus agrarian empires was unique. Possibly, given time, the formula and the disastrous cycle it yielded would have been replicated elsewhere. In the eighteenth century, when European horses arrived on the steppe-like Great Plains in North America, the Comanche Indians carved out a nomad empire that—despite all the cultural differences between Native Americans and Mongols—historians regularly liken to a smaller version of Genghis Khan's. Eventually, perhaps, similar nomad empires might have arisen on the steppes of Argentina and South Africa.

But as it was, Eurasia paid a high price for being trapped in this cycle between A.D. 200 and 1400 while so much of the world was experiencing productive war. The enormous lead in development that Eurasians had built up over the previous ten thousand years was steadily whittled away. The gap between, say, Ming China and the Incas in the fifteenth century remained huge, but if the trends of 200–1400 had gone on long enough, that would have changed. Other things being equal, the twenty-first-century world might have been one in which the heirs of Great Zimbabwe had unified much of sub-Saharan Africa and were fighting fierce cavalry battles in the Nile Valley as they pushed their way toward the Mediterranean. Or one where iron-armed Mexican armies were bringing the last free farmers of North America under control and building fleets to battle the famous sailors of the Polynesian Empire. And one in which empires kept rising and falling along Eurasia's lucky latitudes without ever getting the upper hand over the steppe nomads.

Given another half-dozen centuries, the rest of the world might have caught up with Eurasia. But Eurasia did not give the rest of the world another half-dozen centuries.

The Happy Few

In 1415, a handful of Europeans put the world on notice that the clock was running out.

That October, a cold, miserable English army huddled between two damp forests near Agincourt in northern France. For two weeks it had been dragging its wagons through the mud, trying to escape a French host that outnumbered it four to one. But now it was trapped.

As was the custom, the English king stepped forward to cheer his men up before the slaughter. "This day is called the feast of Crispian," Shakespeare imagined him telling them. On this day, said Henry V, they would win one of the great victories of all time, so great, indeed, that

> He that shall live this day, and see old age,
> Will yearly on the vigil feast his neighbours,
> And say, "To-morrow is Saint Crispian";
> Then will he strip his sleeve and show his scars,
> And say, "These wounds I had on Crispin's day"
>   . . .
> This story shall the good man teach his son;
> And Crispin Crispian shall ne'er go by,
> From this day to the ending of the world,
> But we in it shall be rememberèd;
> We few, we happy few, we band of brothers.

And so it turned out. By lunchtime, the English had killed ten thousand French for the loss of just twenty-nine of their own. French corpses, the chroniclers said, were stacked so high that men could not climb across them, with many a knight ennobled just that morning drowning in gore beneath a pile of the dead.

Yet much as it pains someone who grew up in England to admit it, the story that the good man should really be teaching his son about 1415 involves an entirely different band of brothers, fighting under a fierce Mediterranean sun rather than a steady French drizzle. That summer, a flotilla had left Lisbon, crossed the narrow waters to Morocco, and stormed the city of Ceuta. This battle was even more one-sided than Agincourt, leaving several thousand Africans dead as against only eight Portuguese, but this was not what made it special. Ceuta's importance, only recognized long afterward, was that this was the first time since the Roman Empire that European productive war had gone intercontinental.

European warriors had crossed the seas before—Vikings to America, crusaders to the Holy Land—but they had always gone to get away from their masters and carve out their own little kingdoms, independent of any larger Leviathan. At Ceuta, by contrast, Portugal's King John was expanding Lisbon's rule into Africa. It was a small beginning, but over the next five hundred years Europeans would blast their way out of the cycle of productive and counterproductive wars to take three-quarters of the planet under their rule. Europeans were about to become the happy few.

4

THE FIVE HUNDRED YEARS' WAR:
EUROPE (ALMOST) CONQUERS
THE WORLD, 1415–1914

The Men Who Would Be Kings

One Saturday night in the 1880s—"a pitchy black night, as stifling as a June night can be," says the storyteller—two Englishmen, Daniel Dravot and Peachey Carnehan, stride into a newspaper office in northern India. "The less said about our professions the better," they announce; the only thing they care about tonight is how to get to Kafiristan (Figure 4.1).

"By my reckoning," says Dravot, "it's the top right-hand corner of Afghanistan, not more than three hundred miles from Peshawar. They have two-and-thirty heathen idols there, and we'll be the thirty-third and fourth . . . And that's all we know, except that no one has gone there, and they fight; and in any place where they fight, a man who knows how to drill men can always be a King."

Disguised as a deranged Muslim priest and his servant, with twenty Martini-Henry rifles hidden on the backs of two camels, Dravot and Carnehan drag themselves through sandstorms and blizzards until, in a big level valley crusted with snow, they spy two bands of men shooting it out with bows and arrows. "'This is the beginning of the business,'" says Dravot, "and with that he fires two rifles at the twenty men, and drops one of them at two hundred yards from the rock where he was sitting. The other men began to run, but Carnehan and Dravot sits on the [ammunition] boxes picking them off at all ranges, up and down the valley."

The survivors cower behind what cover they can find, but Dravot "walks over and kicks them, and then he lifts them up and shakes hands all round

Figure 4.1. Locations in Asia mentioned in this chapter

to make them friendly like. He calls them and gives them the boxes to carry, and waves his hand for all the world as though he was King already."

Dravot now sets about becoming a stationary bandit. First, "he and Carnehan takes the big boss of each village by the arm and walks them down into the valley, and shows them how to scratch a line with a spear right down the valley, and gives each a sod of turf from both sides of the line." Then, rounding up the villagers, "Dravot says—'Go and dig the land, and be fruitful and multiply,' which they did." Next, "Dravot leads the priest of each village up to the idol, and says he must sit there and judge the people, and if anything goes wrong he is to be shot." Finally, "he and Carnehan picks out twenty good men and shows them how to click off a rifle, and form fours, and advance in line, and they was very pleased to do so." In each village Carnehan and Dravot come to, "the Army explains that unless the people wants to be killed they had better not shoot their little matchlocks"; and soon enough, they have pacified Kafiristan, and Dravot is planning to present it to Queen Victoria.

Rudyard Kipling made up Dravot, Carnehan, Kafiristan, and its two-and-thirty heathen idols in 1888 for his short story "The Man Who Would Be King," to titillate readers hungry for ripping yarns of imperial derring-do. But what made the tale such a hit, and still worth reading today, was that the nineteenth century's truth was really no stranger than Kipling's fiction.

Take, for instance, James Brooke, a wild young man who joined the British East India Company's army at sixteen. After taking a bad wound fighting in Burma, he bought a ship, loaded it with cannons, and sailed it to Borneo in 1838. Once there, he helped the sultan of Brunei put down a rebellion. The grateful ruler made Brooke his governor in Sarawak Province, and by 1841 Brooke had parlayed this into his own kingdom. His descendants—the White Rajahs—ruled for three generations, finally handing Sarawak to the British government in 1946 in return for a (very) generous pension. To this day, the best-known pub in Sarawak—the Royalist—is named after Brooke's ship.

It was the hope of emulating Brooke, Kipling had his heroes say, that drew them to Kafiristan, "the [last] place now in the world that two strong men can Sar-a-whack." But they were not the first to try Sar-a-whacking in central Asia. In 1838, the very year that Brooke arrived in Brunei, an American adventurer named Josiah Harlan had already had a go. After losing in love, Harlan had signed up as a surgeon with the British East India Company and served in the same Burmese War as Brooke. When this ended, he drifted across India, eventually talking the maharaja of Lahore into giving him two provinces to govern. From there Harlan led his own army into Afghanistan to depose the prince of Ghor, a notorious slave trader. Overawed by Harlan's disciplined troops, the prince of Ghor offered him a deal: he would give Harlan his throne, so long as Harlan kept him on as his vizier.

Harlan grabbed the chance and raised the Stars and Stripes in the mountains of central Asia. But his monarchical tenure turned out to be as short as Dravot's in Kafiristan. Within weeks of his elevation to royalty, Britain occupied Afghanistan and threw the new-made prince out. Returning to the United States, Harlan almost persuaded Jefferson Davis (then secretary of war) to send him back to Afghanistan to buy camels for the army; once there, Harlan hoped, he could renew his tenure as prince of Ghor. When this fell through, he tried importing Afghan grapes into America and then raised a regiment for the Union in the Civil War, but an ugly court-martial cut this career short too. He died in San Francisco in 1871.

Men like Brooke, Harlan, Dravot, and Carnehan would have been unimaginable in any age before the nineteenth century, but by that time the globe had changed out of all recognition. Between the Portuguese capture of Ceuta in 1415 and the era of "The Man Who Would Be King," Europeans waged a Five Hundred Years' War on the rest of the world.

The Five Hundred Years' War was as ugly as any, full of trails of tears and wastelands. It was fiercely denounced by modern-day Calgacuses on every continent, but it had its Ciceros too, who constantly drove home one big point: that this was the most productive war in history. By 1914, Europeans and their colonists ruled 84 percent of the land and 100 percent of the sea. In their imperial heartlands, around the shores of the North Atlantic, rates of violent death had fallen lower than ever before and standards of living had risen higher. As always, the defeated fared less well than the victors, and in many places colonial conquest had devastating consequences. But once again, when we step back from the details to look at the larger picture, a broad pattern emerges. On the whole, the conquerors did suppress local wars, banditry, and private use of deadly force, and began making their subjects' lives safer and richer. Productive war carried on working its perverse magic, but this time on a global scale.

Top Guns

What carried Europeans from Ceuta to Kafiristan was a new revolution in military affairs, fueled by two great inventions. Neither invention, though, was made in Europe.

The first invention was the gun. I mentioned in the previous chapter that Chinese chemists had been experimenting with low-grade gunpowder since the ninth century, making fireworks and incendiaries. In the twelfth or thirteenth century, some now-anonymous tinkerer worked out how to add saltpeter to make real gunpowder. Instead of burning, this would explode when set alight, and if packed into a sufficiently strong chamber, it could blast a ball or arrow out of a tube fast enough to kill someone.

Our first sighting of a true gun may be in the unlikely setting of a Buddhist shrine near Chongqing, China's fastest-growing city. Sometime around 1150, worshippers decorated this sanctuary by carving figures into the cave walls. It is all very conventional stuff, showing lines of demons standing on banks of clouds, and in another conventional touch the sculptor gave several of the demons weapons. One has a bow, another an ax, another still a halberd, and four have swords. But one holds what looks for all the world like a crude cannon, spitting out a little cannonball in a blast of smoke and flame.

This carving is controversial. Some historians think it proves that twelfth-century Chinese armies used guns; others, that it shows that guns existed but were so rare that the sculptor had never seen one (if you hold a metal bombard the way the carved demon is doing, they point out, it will fry the skin off your palms); others still, that the demon is actually holding a musical instrument and that guns had not yet been invented. But however we come down on this issue, no one can dispute that guns were in use a century or so later, because archaeologists have found one—a simple, foot-long bronze tube buried near a battlefield in Manchuria no later than 1288 (Figure 4.2).

The 1288 gun would have been unpredictable, painfully slow to load, and wildly inaccurate, but bigger, better versions were soon in use. They were particularly popular in southern China, where much of the Yangzi Valley was in open rebellion against the country's Mongol rulers by the 1330s. Innovations came thick and fast, and within a decade or two the rebels had learned how to get the best out of the newfangled weapons. The first trick was to deploy them in large numbers (by 1350 the rebel state of Wu had turned out hundreds of cast-iron cannons, dozens of which survive); the second, to adopt combined-arms tactics. On the eve of his decisive battle against the Mongols, fought on Lake Boyang in 1363, the rebel leader Zhu Yuanzhang laid out the correct methods for his captains. "When

Figure 4.2. The start of something big: the oldest surviving genuine gun, abandoned on a Manchurian battlefield in 1288

you approach the enemy ships," he ordered, "first fire the firearms, then the bows and crossbows, and when you reach their ships, then attack them with hand-to-hand weapons." Zhu's men did what he said, and five years later he became the first emperor of the Ming dynasty.

People on the receiving end of new weapons regularly copy them, and guns were no exception. Koreans had guns in their fortresses by 1356. It took another century for firearms to make their way around the Himalayas to India, but they were definitely used at the siege of Mandalgarh in 1456. By 1500, bronze cannons were being cast in Burma and Siam, and after a delay (caused, perhaps, by Korean officials' efforts to keep firearms from them) Japanese too took up the gun in 1542.

The most surprising story, though, is the gun's rapid success in distant Europe. In 1326—less than forty years after the first definite example of a Chinese gun, and thirty years *before* the first definite Korean case—two officials in Florence, five thousand miles to the west, were already being ordered to obtain guns and ammunition (Figure 4.3). The next year, an illustrator in Oxford painted a picture of a small cannon in a manuscript. No invention had ever spread so quickly.

The supply side was crucial to this rapid diffusion. After their brutal thirteenth-century conquests, the Mongol khans created something of a Pax Mongolica on the steppes, which traders exploited to move goods from one end of Eurasia to the other. Marco Polo was merely the most famous of these merchants. By carrying around goods (above all, silk) and ideas (especially Christianity), they tied East and West together; by carrying microbes (the Black Death), they also brought disaster to all. But of all the blessings and curses they carried, none was quite as important as the gun.

That said, the demand side was also important. Europeans were more enthusiastic about guns than anyone else on earth, immediately seeing ways to use them and throwing themselves into making improvements. In 1331, just five years after the first reference to firearms at Florence, other Italians were using cannons in sieges. In 1372, guns actually breached city walls in France.

Something remarkable was happening. Innovation in gun use slowed in East Asia after about 1350, but in Europe it only accelerated. As demand grew, Europeans invented new ways to mine saltpeter, cutting its cost in half by the 1410s. Metalworkers responded by making bigger, cheaper wrought-iron guns that used more powder and could fire heavier cannonballs, and in the seven years after Agincourt, English gunners showed

Figure 4.3. Locations in Europe mentioned in this chapter (the borders of the Ottoman Empire are those of A.D. 1500)

heavy artillery's value by blasting the stone castles of Normandy into gravel.

Their experiences also underlined the drawbacks of big guns, though. While they were fine for sieges, huge bombards were so heavy to move and slow to fire that they were basically useless on battlefields. Even if an army could drag its cannons into position, after firing a single shot, the guns could be overrun by cavalry long before they could be reloaded. It was no accident that despite using a dozen big guns to batter Harfleur into submission in 1415, Henry V took none to Agincourt itself.

Within twenty years, the restless minds of artillerymen had hit on a brilliantly simple solution. Followers of the Czech religious rebel Jan Hus made dozens of small cannons and lashed them to wagons. They then pulled the wagons to the battlefield and chained them together, creating a miniature, mobile fortress (usually called by the Dutch word *laager*). The guns fired just as slowly as ever, but now pike- and swordsmen behind the wagons could hold off charging horsemen until the cannons were ready to shoot again.

In 1444 laager tactics almost caused a major military upset. For a century and a half, the Ottomans—one of the many groups of Turkic steppe warriors that had migrated into the lucky latitudes during the Middle Ages—had been expanding from their base in Anatolia. After overrunning most of the Balkans, their mounted archers now threatened Hungary. The pope declared a crusade, and a Christian coalition (including a Transylvanian contingent led by the brother of Vlad "the Impaler" Dracul) blocked the Turks' path at Varna in modern-day Bulgaria.

The Turks were the best soldiers in Europe and outnumbered their enemies two to one, so the battle should have been a walkover. But as wave after wave of Ottoman riders were shot down trying to break into the Christian laager, Turkish morale began to crack. For a moment the battle hung in the balance, and had the young Hungarian king not decided to charge into the heart of the Turkish line and get himself and five hundred knights killed, the Ottoman advance might actually have been stopped.

As it was, the Ottomans not only swallowed up Hungary but also drew the right lessons from this close-run thing. They began hiring Christian gunners and by 1448 were ready to turn laager tactics back against the Hungarians. Another five years after that, a Hungarian gunnery expert on the Ottoman payroll deployed dozens of medium-sized cannons to pound holes in the walls of Constantinople, ending the Byzantine Empire.

And still the improvements kept coming. Europeans learned to moisten gunpowder, leaving it to dry into granules ("corns") that exploded much more fiercely. At first no cannons were strong enough to contain the force of corned powder, but by the 1470s an arms race between France and Burgundy produced shorter guns with thicker barrels, using corned powder to fire iron rather than stone balls. Hungarians found a different use for the stronger powder, putting tiny amounts into handheld guns called arquebuses ("hook guns," so called after a hook used to reduce recoil).

The new weapons got a spectacular trial run in 1494. That year the French king, Charles VIII, obsessed with launching a crusade to take back the Holy Land, took it into his head that invading Italy was the logical first step. In most ways his campaign was a disaster, but it showed that the new guns had revolutionized war. With a few dozen up-to-date, lightweight cannons, Charles blew away everything in his path. For centuries, losers on the battlefield had always had the option of hiding in a castle and hoping to sit out the resulting siege, but Italians now learned (as Machiavelli, who lived through the war, put it) that "no wall exists, however thick, that artillery cannot destroy in a few days."

The first result was a spike in the number of battles, because any army that yielded the open countryside and retreated to its fortresses was now bound to lose. Between 1495 and 1525, western Europeans fought a dozen major engagements, a rate unprecedented since antiquity. But over the next decades that changed, as advances in offense called forth defensive responses. Europeans now abandoned the high stone walls that had held attackers at bay since the days of prehistoric Jericho. Instead, they raised low, sloping earth banks that deflected or absorbed cannonballs. The new walls were easier for infantry to climb over, but the solution to this problem was also to hand. "Our first care," Machiavelli observed around 1520, "is to make our walls crooked . . . [so] that if the Enemy attempts to approach, he may be opposed and repulsed just as well in the flank as in the front."

Over the next century, expensive new walls, shaped like starfish and studded with projecting ravelins, bastions, and hornworks, spread across Europe. With defeated armies again able to retreat into impregnable fastnesses, battles abruptly lost their appeal. Between 1534 and 1631, western Europeans hardly ever risked head-on clashes, and when they did do so, it was usually while one side was trying to relieve a siege. "We make war more like foxes, than like lyons," said an English soldier, "and you will have twenty sieges for one battell."

It all sounds like another Red Queen story, with Europeans running faster and faster just to stay in place, pouring out blood and gold on increasingly terrible but ultimately pointless wars. Yet as in the case of the invention of fortifications, metal arms and armor, and all the other ancient revolutions in military affairs that we saw in Chapter 2, nothing could be further from the truth. Western Europeans could not outpace each other, but they did pull ahead of everyone else on the planet.

For centuries, Europeans had been on the defensive against Mongols, Turks, and other invaders. The fall of Constantinople in 1453 sent shock waves through the continent, and in 1529 a Turkish army reached the gates of Vienna. A generation later, Europe's prospects looked darker still. "Can we doubt what the result must be," the leading European negotiator in Constantinople gloomily asked himself, on comparing Christendom's "empty treasury, luxurious habits, exhausted resources, [and] broken spirits" with the Turks' "unimpaired resources, experience and practice in arms, veteran soldiery, [and] uninterrupted sequence of victories"?

To most people's surprise, it turned out that the answer was yes. Even as the ambassador was writing, the military balance of power was shifting Europe's way. In 1600, the Turkish commander in Hungary gloomily reported that "most of the troops of these accursed ones [that is, Christians] are on foot and arquebusiers. Most of the troops of Islam are horsemen, and not only are their infantrymen few, but experts in the use of the arquebus are rare. For this reason, there is great trouble in battles and sieges."

Europeans had been steadily increasing the numbers of gunners in their armies for a century. The trend accelerated after the 1550s, when Spaniards introduced a new kind of handgun, the musket, which threw a two-ounce lead ball hard enough to pierce plate armor a hundred paces away. In the 1520s, infantry with edged weapons—pikes, swords, halberds—had typically outnumbered arquebusiers three to one, but a century later the ratio of shot to pike had been reversed. Cavalry, its medieval dominance over, had been relegated to scouting, skirmishing, and guarding the flanks. Horsemen rarely made up more than one-tenth of a seventeenth-century army.

And so we have yet another paradox. Around 1415, the Mongols and Ming China had the most powerful armies on earth, and Henry V and the other kings of Europe lagged far behind. By 1615—and perhaps even by 1515—that was turning around, and few armies in the world could have stood against European firepower. Europeans had got the top guns, and Asians, who had invented gunnery, had not.

Why did China not keep its early lead in firearms and go on to wage its own Five Hundred Years' War on the world? This is probably the single most important question in the whole of military history, but there is little agreement on the answer.

The most popular theory, versions of which we have encountered in earlier chapters, is that Europeans were the beneficiaries of a unique Western way of war. They had inherited it from ancient Greece, and it was responsible for their gunpowder revolution. "The critical point about firearms and explosives is not that they suddenly gave Western armies hegemony," the military historian Victor Davis Hanson suggests, "but that such weapons were produced in quality and great numbers in Western rather than in non-European countries—a fact that is ultimately explained by a longstanding Western cultural stance toward rationalism, free inquiry, and the dissemination of knowledge that has its roots in classical antiquity." Europe's takeoff, he concludes, was "logical given the Hellenic origins of European civilization."

At this stage in the book, you will not be surprised to hear that I am unconvinced. I tried to show in Chapter 2 that there was no such thing as an ancient Western way of war, because the ways Greeks and Romans fought were not uniquely Western. They were just the local (Mediterranean) versions of a pattern found all across the Eurasian lucky latitudes, which we might call the productive way of war. I went on in Chapter 3 to argue that everywhere from China to the Mediterranean this ancient productive way of war unraveled in the first millennium A.D. in the face of the rise of cavalry. If these claims are correct, then Hanson's suggestion that continuities in the Western way of war explain Europe's gunpowder takeoff must be incorrect, and when we look closely at what happened in sixteenth-century Europe, there is just too much that the Western way of war theory does not explain.

Other historians have gone into detail on this, so I will concentrate on just a couple of issues. If it is really the case that "it is this Western desire for a single, magnificent collision of infantry, for brutal killing with edged weapons on a battlefield between free men, that has baffled and terrified our adversaries from the non-Western world for more than 2,500 years" (Hanson's words), why was the new European style of fighting all about standing at a distance and firing guns rather than closing to use edged weapons? If the Western way of war has always been about "the absolute destruction of the enemy's forces in the field" and "the *desire* to deliver fatal blows and then steadfastly to endure, without retreat, any counter response," why did Europeans fight so few battles in the century between 1534 and 1631? And why, if "for the past 2,500 years . . . there has been a peculiar practice of Western warfare, a common foundation and continual way of fighting, that has made Europeans the most deadly soldiers in the history of fighting," had Europeans spent a whole millennium—from roughly A.D. 500 through 1500—in general retreat before raiders and invaders from Asia and North Africa?

Some historians propose a very down-to-earth answer to all these questions. Europe's firearms revolution, they argue, had nothing to do with cultural traditions: Europeans simply got good with guns because they fought a lot. Europe, the theory runs, was divided into lots of little states that were always at each other's throats. China, by contrast, was a unified empire for most of the time between 1368 and 1911. As a result, the

Chinese rarely fought and had little reason to invest in improving guns. For the feuding Europeans, however, investing in better guns was literally a matter of life and death. Therefore it was Europeans, not Chinese, who perfected the gun.

But this too leaves important questions unanswered. Despite its unity, China fought a lot between 1368 and 1911, often on a scale that dwarfed Europe's squabbles. In 1411 and again in 1449, emperors sent armies half a million strong against the Mongols. Fighting against pirates filled much of the sixteenth century, a terrible struggle with Japan devastated the Korean peninsula in the 1590s, and in 1600 a quarter of a million men were mobilized against a revolt in Sichuan. So why did none of these wars spur European-type innovations in firearms?

The real issue, the historian turned attorney Kenneth Chase explains in his magnificent book *Firearms: A Global History to 1700*, was not how many but what kinds of wars Europeans and Asians fought. The first guns were clumsy, slow things, their rates of fire measured in minutes per shot rather than shots per minute. They only really worked against clumsy, slow targets, such as city walls, which is why the first great advances were in siege artillery.

The hotbed of innovation was initially southern China, because the wars against the Mongol overlords of the mid-fourteenth-century Yangzi Valley would be won by storming fortresses and sinking big ships fighting in the constrained space of a river. For both these jobs, early guns were excellent. But when the fighting ended in 1368, the main theater of war shifted to the steppes in northern China. Here there were few forts to bombard, and slow-firing guns were useless against fast-moving cavalry. Chinese generals, being rational men, spent their money on extra horsemen and a great wall rather than incremental improvements in firearms.

Europe—at least when it came to gunnery—had more in common with southern than with northern China. It was full of forts, had plenty of broken landscapes that constrained armies' movements, and, because it was so far from the steppes (which made cavalry expensive), its armies always included a lot of slow-moving infantry. In this environment, tinkering with guns to squeeze out small improvements made a great deal of sense, and by 1600 so many improvements had accumulated that European armies were becoming the best on earth.

If Ming dynasty emperors had had a crystal ball and could have seen that by the seventeenth century firearms would be effective enough to defeat nomad cavalry, they would surely have taken the long-term view and made the investments to come up with corned powder, muskets, and wrought-iron cannons. But in the real world, no one can foresee the future (hard though some of us try). All we can do is respond to the immediate challenges that face us. Europeans invested in guns because it made sense at the time; Chinese did not invest in guns, because it did not make sense at the time; and because of all this good sense, Europe (almost) conquered the world.

Payback

Europeans had learned about guns in the fourteenth century because travelers, traders, and fighters had carried them westward across Eurasia, and in the sixteenth century Asians learned about improved European guns because travelers, traders, and fighters carried them back east again. It was payback, of a kind.

The Ottomans, who straddled the boundary between Europe and Asia, learned about European guns first. Turkish firepower usually lagged behind European but did stay decades ahead of gunnery in lands farther east and south. It was artillery mounted on wagons that slaughtered Persia's finest horsemen at Chaldiran in 1514 and Egypt's at Marj Dabiq two years later, giving the Ottomans mastery of the Middle East.

A generation later, Muscovy—another state straddling the boundary between Europe and Asia—also learned to apply Western guns. Since the thirteenth century, Russians had been buying survival with annual bribes to the Mongols, but in the sixteenth Tsar Ivan the Terrible took revenge. Russians had learned the basics of gunnery in bloody wars against Sweden and Poland, and Ivan swept down the Volga River, using artillery to smash Mongol stockades in his way. By his death in 1584 he had doubled the size of Moscow's empire, but this was just the beginning. In 1598, Russian fur trappers armed with newfangled muskets crossed the Ural Mountains; by 1639, they were gazing on the Pacific Ocean.

Other things being equal, caravans would presumably have carried advanced European guns east along the Silk Roads all the way to China, but they were overtaken by the second great invention of this age—the ocean-going ship.

As in the case of guns, the basic technology was pioneered in Asia but perfected in Europe. Magnetic compasses, for instance, were in Chinese skippers' hands by 1119. Picked up by Arab merchants on the Indian Ocean, they reached Italians in the Mediterranean by 1180. Over the next three centuries, East Asian shipwrights made further breakthroughs in rigging, steering, and hull construction. By 1403, China had the world's first dry docks, housing the biggest sailing ships ever built. Packed with watertight compartments, sealed with waterproof paint, and supported by freshwater tankers, these ships could have gone anywhere Chinese sailors wanted, and between 1405 and 1433 the famous admiral Zheng He led hundreds of them, manned by tens of thousands of sailors, to East Africa, Mecca, and Java.

Compared with this, Western ships looked very rough-and-ready, but—as with guns—Europeans took Asian ideas in radically different directions. Once again, the driving force was very basic: Europe's geography presented different challenges from Asia's, and in trying to rise to them, Europeans found enormous advantages in their relative backwardness.

Western Europe looked like the worst-placed part of Eurasia's lucky latitudes in the fifteenth century—just "a distant marginal peninsula," one economist has called it, far from the real centers of action in South and East Asia. European merchants were acutely conscious of the riches of China and India and for centuries had been seeking easy routes to the booming markets of the Orient. If anything, though, the situation seemed to be getting worse after 1400. The Mongol kingdoms were disintegrating, making the Silk Roads across the steppes more dangerous, while tolls imposed by the Ottomans had made the alternative route (overland from Syria to the Persian Gulf) more expensive. The best solution seemed to be to get to Asia by sailing around the bottom of Africa, bypassing the intervening kingdoms, but no one knew if that was even possible.

No part of Europe was better placed to find out than Portugal, and in the years after the capture of Ceuta, Portuguese ships nosed their way down Africa's west coast. It was hard going; oar-powered galleys ruled the roost in the Mediterranean but were ill suited to the distances and winds on the Atlantic. So serious did this seem that Prince Henry, one of the conquerors of Ceuta and third in line to the Portuguese throne, took personal charge of the push to produce better ships.

The project quickly paid off, in the form of caravels. These tiny ships, typically just fifty to a hundred feet long and displacing barely fifty tons, would have looked ridiculous to Zheng He, but they did the job. Their shallow bottoms could get into silty African river mouths, their square sails made them fast, and their lateen sails made them nimble. In 1420, Portuguese ships discovered Madeira and in 1427 the Azores; within a few years these islands were filled with flourishing plantations. In 1444 sailors reached the Senegal River, giving them access to gold from African mines. In 1473 they crossed the equator, and in 1482 they arrived at the mouth of the mighty Congo (Figure 4.4).

Everything was going famously, but once past the Congo, caravels (and newer, bigger versions called carracks) found themselves facing strong headwinds. Progress stalled, until Europe's sailors—afraid of nothing—found two solutions. First, in 1487, Bartolomeu Dias hit on the dramatic idea of *volta do mar*, "returning by sea." This meant plunging into the uncharted Atlantic in the hope of catching winds that would catapult him past the

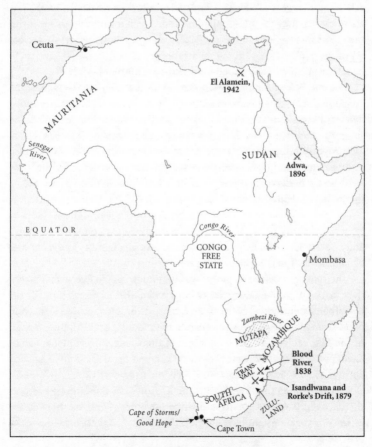

Figure 4.4. Locations in Africa mentioned in this chapter

bottom of Africa. Triumphant, he rounded what we now call the Cape of Good Hope. Dias, however, called it the Cape of Storms (the experience of trying to sleep through some of its howling gales makes me think Dias's name was the right one), but whatever we call the cape, the Portuguese sailors mutinied rather than go on in such foul weather. It was left to Vasco da Gama, in 1498, to take a second expedition around the bottom of Africa and into the Indian Ocean.

The second solution, Christopher Columbus's, was even more drastic. Like all educated Europeans, Columbus knew that the earth was round and that—in theory—by sailing west from Portugal, he would eventually get to the East. Most educated Europeans also knew that the world was about twenty-four thousand miles around, which meant that this route to the Indies was too long to be profitable. Columbus, however, refused to accept this, insisting that three thousand miles of sailing would get him to Japan. In 1492 he finally raised funds to prove his point.

Columbus went to his grave believing he had sailed to the land of the great khan, but it gradually became clear that his accidental discovery of a new world was more exciting. There was serious money to be made from shipping America's wealth—gold, silver, tobacco, even chocolate—back to Europe and shipping Africans to America to produce these fine things. European mariners transformed the Atlantic from a barrier into a highway.

It was a dangerous highway, though. Like the Mediterranean before the Roman conquest or the steppes before the Mongols, the Atlantic was largely beyond Leviathan's laws. Once a ship was out of sight of Cádiz or Lisbon, anything went. Anyone with a small ship, a couple of cannons, and no scruples could help himself (or occasionally herself) to the plunder of continents. The golden age of pirates had begun.

The sixteenth century's global war on piracy, fought everywhere from the Caribbean to the Taiwan Strait, was yet another asymmetric struggle. Leviathans could always win if they wanted to, but the take, hold, and build strategy that Pompey the Great had invented in the Mediterranean in the first century B.C. cost money. On the whole, governments calculated, putting up with pirates cost less than making war on them, so why bother? Clever bureaucrats could even turn piracy to their own ends, extracting bribes for turning a blind eye or even appointing the cutthroats as "privateers," legally entitled to rob other countries' ships. A few unwary voyagers might have to walk the plank, but that seemed a small price to pay.

The voyagers, however, thought this was a very high price, and so they did the obvious thing: they armed their ships. Caravels and carracks could carry a few cannons, but by 1530 Portuguese shipbuilders were producing a new type, the galleon, which was basically a floating firing platform (Figure 4.5). The galleon's long and narrow hull, four masts, and small fore- and aftercastles made it fast, but the real gain came from lining its sides with cannons, blasting away from gunports cut in the hull just above the waterline, hurling eight-pound iron balls five hundred yards.

For two thousand years, captains had fought by closing, ramming, and boarding, but now they learned to draw alongside and pour shot into the enemy through curtains of acrid smoke. There was still plenty of work for cutlass and dagger, but now men were more likely to be killed by "splinters"—an innocuous-sounding word for jagged, foot-long shards of oak that sprayed in every direction, tearing off arms and heads, whenever a cannonball ripped through a hull. One witness to the carnage spoke of

Figure 4.5. Floating firing platforms: French and Portuguese galleons engage off the coast of Brazil, probably in 1562.

decks "much dyed in blood, their masts and tackle being moiled with brains, hair, pieces of skulls."

Guns did not just hold pirates at bay, though. They also became a source of profit in their own right, because Asians would pay well for these vicious weapons. Several of da Gama's men jumped ship and set up as gunmakers to the sultan of Calicut, selling him four hundred cannons within a year. In 1521 the first Portuguese to reach China were also casting guns for local markets, and by 1524 Chinese craftsmen were making their own versions and corning powder.

The extreme case was Japan. When a storm blew three Portuguese ashore in 1542, they promptly sold their state-of-the-art muskets to a local lord and taught his metalworkers how to make more. By the 1560s Japanese guns were as sophisticated as anything in Europe and equally effective at making traditional fortifications obsolete. By contrast with Europe, though, defense did not run as quickly as offense in Japan, perhaps because advanced guns had appeared so suddenly rather than evolving over two centuries as in Europe. But whatever the cause, as we saw in Chapter 3, a single government controlled the whole archipelago by the 1580s.

European-style guns were such a hit that Asia's military men soon called all modern firearms by the generic label "Frankish" (*farangi* in Persia, *firingi* in India, *folangji* in China). They also adopted European tactics, learning that wagons bristling with modern muskets and cannons could actually defeat steppe horsemen.

Prince Zahir al-Din Muhammad Babur's experience was typical. Fighting with bows and spears, his Afghan followers failed to hold Samarkand and Kabul when Uzbek horsemen attacked between 1501 and 1511, and he had to flee to India. Once there, Babur hired Ottoman advisers, who urged him to buy guns and wagons, and in 1526 he regained everything in the shattering victory of Panipat. The Mughal Empire that he founded would become the biggest in India's history.

Chinese soldiers seem to have discovered the wagon laager independently. "Wagons," the commander of Beijing's defenses observed in the 1570s, "can serve as the walls of a camp; they can take the place of armor. When enemy cavalry swarms around, it has no way to pressure them; they are truly like walls with feet or horses without [need for] fodder. Still, everything depends on the firearms. If the firearms are lost, how can the wagons stand?"

Sometimes the firearms did get lost and the wagons did not stand; as late as 1739, Afghan horsemen overwhelmed the musketeers of Mughal

India, sacked Delhi, and carried off the Mughals' sapphire-studded Peacock Throne. But overall, between roughly 1550 and 1750 an astonishing thing happened. Armed with the new guns, the empires of the lucky latitudes finally mastered the steppes, breaking the cycle of productive and counterproductive wars.

The way the emperors did this was not by sending infantry to chase horsemen deep into the wilderness, which remained as expensive as ever, but by sending farmers to nibble away at the edges of the grasslands. Digging ditches, building palisades, and firing muskets, peasants channeled the nomads' movements and fenced the riders in, until eventually the nomads ran out of places to hide. Only then did emperors commit their new artillery, light enough to be dragged far onto the steppes.

> Cannon to right of them,
> Cannon to left of them,
> Cannon in front of them
> Volley'd and thunder'd . . .

wrote the poet Tennyson of the most famous battle between horse and gun; but scenes much like the Light Brigade's ride to disaster at Balaclava were acted out countless times on the steppes in the seventeenth and eighteenth centuries. Storm'd at with shot and shell, into the mouth of hell rode the nomads. Few came back.

Russians and Ottomans pinched off the western end of the steppes between 1500 and 1650; in central Asia, Mughals and Persians pushed the Uzbeks and Afghans back between 1600 and 1700; and in the east, China swallowed up the endless wastes of Xinjiang between 1650 and 1750. By 1727, when Russian and Chinese officials met at Kiakhta to sign a treaty fixing their borders in Mongolia, the gunpowder empires had effectively shut down the steppe highway.

With the nomads removed from the equation, productive war quickly resumed. From Turkey to China, extraordinary empires flourished behind the safety of the closed steppe. With their central Asian flanks secured, the Ottomans conquered North Africa and advanced to the Danube. Russia absorbed Siberia, the Safavid dynasty created the biggest empire Persia had seen in a thousand years, the Mughals took over almost all of India, and the Qing dynasty pushed China's borders out beyond even those of the modern People's Republic.

The details varied enormously, but despite including more than their fair share of drunks, drug addicts, and degenerates, the emperors were forced to follow the ancient script and turn into stationary bandits. They hired bureaucrats, paid their armies instead of leaving them to plunder, and—since shot and shell (not to mention harems and opium) cost money—found ways to promote farming and trade, the main sources of taxes. "Look with favor on the merchants," a typical Ottoman official urged his sultan. "Always care for them; let no one harass them; for through their trading the land becomes prosperous."

Most officials went on taking bribes and oppressing the poor, but a few began clarifying property rights, setting reasonable taxes, and encouraging investment. They promoted wonderful new crops—potatoes, sweet potatoes, peanuts, squash, corn—from the Americas, which raised yields dramatically. By investing in roads and bridges, arresting bandits, and passing business-friendly laws, governments made it practical for farmers to grow cash crops such as cotton, coffee, and silk. By 1600, the Yangzi Delta probably had the world's most productive farmers, and those in southern India and Bengal might not have been far behind.

The new rules worked well for the sultans and shahs, who were able to build their Taj Mahals and mosques, but how much better-off all this governing left ordinary Asians is unclear. There are hints that wages rose as Leviathans expanded and fell as governments broke down, but much more study of the obscure and confusing sources scattered in archives from Istanbul to Beijing will be needed before we can say for sure.

We are on safer ground in asserting that governments reduced violence. In Persia, the worst case, tribal feuds paralyzed the country until the sixteenth century. "For years," Shah Tahmasp lamented in 1524, "I was forced patiently to watch the bloodshed between the tribes and I tried to see what was the will of God in these events." But seventy years later, Shah Abbas took a stronger line. "As soon as he came to the throne," his biographer recorded, "he called for the principal highway robbers to be identified in each province and he then set about eliminating this class of people." Abbas's hands-on approach to security (he personally beheaded one troublemaker in 1593) worked; in the 1670s a French traveler marveled that "the Roads are so safe all over Asia, especially in *Persia*."

In China, we actually have some statistics. For the first half of its history, between 1368 and 1506, the Ming dynasty built up Leviathan, and just 108 episodes of banditry or rebellion are recorded from these years. Between 1507 and 1644, however, Ming bureaucrats steadily lost their grip, and the incident sheet balloons to 522 entries. Equally striking, bandits before 1506 tended to loot, rape, kill, and then run away before government forces showed up. After 1506 they tended to stand their ground against troops, and often won.

Eventually, in 1644, Ming rule collapsed altogether. But although millions—perhaps tens of millions—died in the subsequent Ming-Qing cataclysm (as historians call it), this horrific episode was different from earlier dynastic collapses. This time, the breakdown did not bring multiple waves of horsemen pouring out of the steppes to exploit the situation; China did not slide into recurring bloody crises. Instead, the new Qing dynasty restored the frontiers, crushed the rebels, and built an even stronger Leviathan.

To anyone living in 1650 or even 1700, it could easily have looked as if Asia had been the big winner since guns had been invented. Asians had given guns and oceangoing ships to Europe, but Europeans had repaid the gift with interest by improving the ships and then using them to carry equally improved guns back to Asia. Using European-style guns, Asians had then revived productive war, closing the steppes and building bigger, safer, and richer empires than ever before. In Europe, by contrast, not even the Ottoman Empire had managed to pull far enough ahead in the ever-accelerating arms race to conquer everyone else, and the continent remained a fragmented, squabbling mess of kings, princes, tsars, and even a few republics. Gazing in awe at the splendors of the East, no few Europeans concluded that they were falling further behind.

Drill, Baby, Drill

They were wrong. Far from falling behind, Europeans were in fact leaping ahead, and all by virtue of staying in place.

What I mean by this rather tortured formulation is that Europeans learned to line up soldiers and sailors and get them to stand their ground, which allowed them to get the most out of their firepower. By 1650, Europeans had discovered the fundamental principles behind pre-mechanical gunpowder warfare, and over the next 150 years they perfected them. Asian empires might have been reviving productive war, but Europeans were reinventing it, lock, stock, and smoking barrel.

As late as 1590, the biggest weakness of European armies and fleets was that their muskets and cannons were still so slow and inaccurate that, given luck and good timing, sudden onrushes of cavalry or pirates could overwhelm them before they could reload. The solution, legend has it, came to

Count William Louis of Nassau (co-commander of the Dutch army, fighting a grueling war for independence from Spain) in 1594, while he was reading an ancient Roman account of the best use of javelins.

William Louis dashed off a letter to his cousin Maurice (Figure 4.6). Competent musketeers, William Louis pointed out, can fire off a volley every thirty seconds or so. But what if, instead of all shooting at once, they formed up six ranks deep and fired one rank at a time, like Roman javelineers? The first rank could fire, turn on their heels, and march back through the other ranks. While they were countermarching, the second rank could fire; then, while it countermarched, the third fired; and so on. By the time the sixth rank had fired and countermarched, the first would be ready to fire again. Instead of one big volley every thirty seconds, the musketeers now fired one small volley every five seconds—close enough to a continuous hail of musket balls to stop cavalry or pirates in their tracks.

This, it turned out, was harder to do in practice—against enemies who shot back—than it sounded in theory, but in the 1620s Swedish soldiers

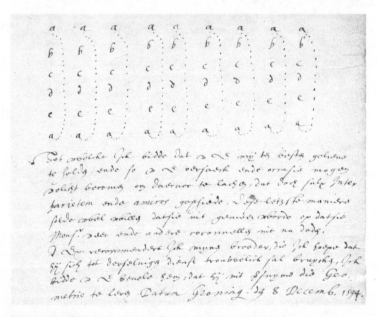

Figure 4.6. The secret of Europe's success: Count William Louis of Nassau's famous December 1594 letter to his cousin Maurice, explaining the principles of volleying

finally got volleying to work the way William Louis said it should. Sweden's king Gustavus Adolphus made the breakthrough by turning the Dutch ideas on their heads. Instead of having his men shoot, then countermarch, Gustavus had them march ten paces forward, then shoot, and then stay where they were to reload. Next, as a Scottish officer in Gustavus's army explained it, the other "rancks advance before them and give fire after the same manner, till the whole troop hath discharged and so to beginne againe as before . . . ever advancing to an enemie, never turning backe without death, or victorie."

Gustavus also saw that getting the best out of volleying infantry required reorganizing the rest of the army too. Field artillery should now be used in mass, with mobile batteries beefing up the infantry's hail of musket balls. Cavalry, however, should give up the gun. Sixteenth-century horsemen had typically ridden up to enemy infantry with a pistol in each hand, fired at close range, then galloped away, but continuous musketry made this suicidal. Gustavus returned riders to the age of cold steel, keeping his cavalry well away from infantry until a careless enemy left a flank open or a demoralized regiment turned and ran. Then the horsemen would charge home with slashing sabers.

To do all these tasks well, Gustavus realized, armies also needed to be a lot bigger. At Agincourt in 1415 the French probably fielded about 30,000 men, but as Gustavus's reforms spread across Europe, numbers exploded. In the 1640s, major powers were raising 150,000 men (about half the size of the Roman army in Agricola's day). France mustered 200,000 troops in the 1670s, 273,000 in 1691, and 395,000 in 1696. Between 1701 and 1713 a further 650,000 Frenchmen joined up, swelling the ranks until France had more soldiers than priests.

While Europe's generals worked out how to maximize firepower on land, its admirals solved the same problem at sea. There the goal was to get the most out of broadsides. Sixteenth-century fleets had tended to sail straight at the enemy, but because galleons carried nearly all their guns along their sides, there was very little shooting until the two fleets fell upon each other. Then the battle degenerated into a confused melee, in which gunners, blinded by smoke, were as likely to hit friendly ships as foes.

Between the 1630s and the 1650s, Dutch admirals came up with the line-ahead formation, a maritime version of volleying. Instead of charging straight at the enemy, ships now formed a nose-to-tail line and sailed parallel to their opponents, pouring out broadsides. The English, French, and Spanish, of course, quickly learned to do the same. Two fleets might sail alongside each other for hours, blasting away until night fell or one admiral broke off; or, if a gap opened in the enemy line, a fleet might sail through it, raking the vulnerable bow and stern of the ships on either side with broadside after broadside.

Admirals redesigned their fleets around this principle. Ships of the line (that is, those tough enough to be pounded in line-ahead formation) became a navy's backbone, while smaller ships screened the line, scouted, or—at least until about 1700—were used as fireships, deliberately set alight and pushed into the enemy line to cause chaos.

On land and sea, the key to these linear tactics was standardization. Already in 1599, Dutch quartermasters were giving every soldier the same kind of musket so they would take the same time to reload. Gustavus whittled the smorgasbord of sixteenth-century cannons down to just three types, throwing balls of three, twelve, or twenty-four pounds. And by adopting "seventy-fours," a French design with seventy-four cannons spread over two or three decks, admirals gained confidence that each vessel would respond to subtly shifting breezes in just the same way and keep its place in line.

Predictably, the hardest part of the war machine to standardize was the men. According to a Dutch manual of 1607, volleying involved forty-three separate steps, which musketeers had to memorize and perform perfectly under fire. Cannons had their own complicated routines, and keeping ships close-hauled in line-ahead formation was hardest of all. Thousands of able seamen had to scramble up rigging and reef, furl, tack, luff, reach, and beat at exactly the right moment—all while shrouded in smoke and peppered with shot. Men had to be made into interchangeable parts.

Four centuries on from this military revolution, delegates at the 2008 Republican National Convention came up with a catchy slogan to sum up their response to steeply rising gasoline prices. "Drill, baby, drill," they chanted, urging America to pump more oil from its own territories. No catchphrase could better describe the method that Gustavus Adolphus and his contemporaries came up with for standardizing men. Drill was the way to make them interchangeable. Relentless martinets (so called after Jean Martinet, a notoriously exacting French drillmaster) drilled soldiers in ramming powder, wadding, and musket balls down their muzzle-loaders till they could do it blindfolded, and sailors practiced tying knots till their fingers were raw. Men have never yet been turned completely into cogs in a machine, but seventeenth-century drillmasters came remarkably close.

The most difficult kinds of men to standardize were officers. The new system needed lots of them (Dutch armies shifted in the 1590s from companies of 250 soldiers with 11 officers to companies of 120 men with 12 officers, and the ten-to-one ratio remains standard to this day), but the obvious men for the job—the upper classes—tended to see themselves as aristocrats first and cogs in a machine a very distant second. "Our lives and possessions are the king's. Our soul is God's. Our honor is our own," one French officer wrote. Junior officers regularly dueled with their superiors over arcane points of etiquette, and being squeezed into uniforms that subsumed their individuality into standardized ranks struck most as a deep insult.

Well into the eighteenth century, officers dressed for battle as they would for a ball, in powdered wigs, buckled shoes, and satin breeches, trailing clouds of perfume. "Dear me," the heroine of one eighteenth-century comedy remarked, "to think how the sweet fellows sleep on the ground, and fight in silk stockings and lace ruffles." (At the Battle of Fontenoy in 1745, one French officer brought along seven spare pairs of silk stockings—just in case.) Not till 1747 did a group of young British naval officers, meeting secretly at a coffeehouse, hit on the idea "that a uniform dress is useful and necessary for the commissioned officers."

Sartorial anarchy aside, though, newly created military academies did start forging fairly professional officer classes after 1600. Samuel Pepys—diarist, man-about-town, and master administrator—overhauled English* naval training in 1677 and was clear about the goal: to produce officers of "sobriety, diligence, obedience to order and application to the study and practice of the art of navigation." With the possible exception of sobriety, he succeeded brilliantly, forcing every officer—no matter how well connected—to pass examinations in astronomy, gunnery, navigation, and signaling.

By 1700, the lines of fire that Europeans deployed on land and sea were unquestionably the most ferocious the world had ever seen. Their one weakness, Pepys observed, was "the want of money, [which] puts all things, and above all things the Navy, out of order." Keeping up with the arms race in standardized men and cannons was staggeringly expensive. Even in the

---

*By convention, historians speak of England and Scotland as separate countries before the Act of Union in 1707, and as Britain after that. (Ireland was added to the union in 1801.)

richest states, there was never enough money, and matching means and ends soon became the greatest challenge for governments.

The crudest solution was to cook the books. Governments blithely defaulted on debts, let inflation run riot, and, when all else failed, simply stopped paying their troops. That, however, usually went badly. Unpaid English sailors invented the concept of going on strike, literally striking their ships' sails so the fleet could not move until the government paid up. In 1667, with the fleet on strike and Pepys unable to work because of the "moan of the poor seamen that lie starving in the streets for lack of money," a Dutch fleet sailed up the Thames and burned or towed away England's best ships. Sailors' wives laid hands on members of Parliament in the streets of London, shrieking, "This is what comes of not paying our husbands!"

The alternative to lowering the costs of war was raising more revenues to pay for it, and governments pursued this tack even more vigorously. One technique, known as absolutism, involved sweeping away the clutter of privileges that nobles, cities, and clergymen had accumulated over the previous thousand years and allowing monarchs to tax everything in their realms. Naturally, this appealed strongly to kings, but those whose privileges were being swept away were less happy. All too often, the result was civil war.

When things went badly for kings, as they did in England in 1649 and France in 1793, they might end up losing their heads. But even when things went well, there was still never enough money. Not even France's Louis XIV, the greatest of the absolutists (who reputedly came up with the catchphrase *l'état, c'est moi*, "the state is me"), could actually raise enough money to batter all the kingdoms that combined to oppose him into submission. At his death in 1715, France was almost bankrupt.

A third approach was to mobilize money more efficiently. Here the Dutch led the way, creating a secondary market for government bonds. This allowed capitalists to buy pieces of the national debt, then sell them, along with the interest they paid, to other investors—much as banks today make mortgage loans and then sell them on. In combination with laws that soothed investors' fears about sovereign default, this gave Dutch governments the ability to raise more money, faster and cheaper than any rivals. The Dutch fought constantly in the seventeenth century, and their debt ballooned from 50 million guilders in 1632 to 250 million in 1752, but thanks to investor confidence the interest they paid steadily fell, dipping under 2.5 percent in 1747.

In 1694, England took this idea further, opening a national bank to manage the public debt and allocating specific taxes to pay interest on bonds. Sound public finance brought in extraordinary amounts of money; while a single major defeat could bring nations with poor credit to their knees, governments in Amsterdam and London seemed able to raise, drill, and commit new fleets and armies almost at will. To the English novelist Daniel Defoe, it felt as if "credit makes the soldier fight without pay, the armies without provisions."

Governments could hardly ask for more than this, yet most remained ambivalent about the new institutions. Then as now, financial instruments that looked wonderful to bankers could look alarming to everyone else, and then as now hardly anyone—including bankers—actually understood how the new tools really worked. In 1720 the South Sea Bubble in Britain and the Mississippi Bubble in France brought banks crashing down and left investors ruined. A Tea Party–style backlash set in, and although the eighteenth century had nothing quite like Wall Street versus Main Street, it did have Threadneedle Street (the Bank of England's address) versus the country estate. Aristocrats who had dominated politics for generations suspected (rightly) that business-friendly governments might leave them worse-off, and kings found it hard to give up the plunder-and-spend policies that had worked for them in the past.

The most constructive solution to the problems of funding fighting, however, came not from cooking the books, raising extra revenue, or mobilizing money more effectively but from putting the paradox of war to work. Kings trimmed back their increasingly lethal forces but wove webs of alliances to share the costs of campaigns. The result was something of a balance of power, raising the price of aggression (if a government upset the balance, others would band together to restore it) and lowering the price of survival (if one state was threatened with destruction, others would rescue it to keep the balance intact).

Paradoxically, because armed forces were now so deadly, the amount of killing they did declined. To avoid provoking hostile coalitions, rulers limited their wars, defining aims narrowly and using force carefully. Battles remained as gruesome as ever (in 1665, England's Duke of York was knocked off his feet by the detached head of the Earl of Burlington's second son), but wars—which European writers started calling *Kabinettskriege*, or "ministers' wars"—grew more orderly. "No longer is it nations which fight each other," a French politician observed in the 1780s, "but just armies and professionals; wars are like games of chance in which no one risks his all; what was once a wild rage is now just a folly."

In the classic case, seven European governments came together in a grand alliance in 1701 to stop the crowns of France and Spain from landing on a single royal head. Uniting Paris and Madrid would have created a superpower, shattering the balance; so, for a decade, volleys and broadsides blasted from Blenheim to Barbados to prevent this from happening. By 1710, the alliance clearly had the upper hand, but some of its members started worrying that crushing France and Spain would tip the balance of power too far in Britain's favor, so they switched sides to even things out. The fighting finally petered out in 1713–14.

Judged just by what was happening in western Europe, the coming of guns and the closing of the steppes had not been very productive at all. While it had freed Europe from the long cycle of productive and counterproductive wars by giving it the weapons to defeat the steppe horsemen, it had not revived productive war in the same way as had happened in Asia, where great new continental empires had formed since 1500. Western Europeans seemed bogged down in *un*productive war, in which kings and their cabinets besieged fortresses and exchanged frontier provinces but neither productively built up nor counterproductively broke down larger societies.

The War on the World

The three hundred years of war between 1415 and 1715 did little to change the map of western Europe, but they turned much of the rest of the globe upside down. Europe's conflicts spilled out across the oceans, and Europeans drifted into waging a war on the world. From Portugal to the Netherlands, rulers on Europe's Atlantic fringe grew very keen on overseas activity that they could tax, spending the gains on wars at home. The money that poured in paid for much of Europe's military revolution, and the military revolution in turn gave Europeans the weapons that made overseas expansion possible.

Cannons gave fifteenth-century sailors naval superiority everywhere they went and worked wonders for focusing the minds of reluctant trading partners. When haggling could not convince merchants in Mozambique and Mombasa to sell him supplies in 1498, Vasco da Gama found that gunfire could, and when Pedro Álvares Cabral reached India two years later (discovering Brazil along the way, when he sailed a little too far into the Atlantic while trying to get around Africa), his bombardment of Calicut—killing five hundred people—opened its markets promptly.

By 1506, Portugal had formulated a breathtakingly ambitious plan, elevating piracy to the level of grand strategy. Every ship trading in spices had to use a few key ports; so, Portuguese sailors reasoned, by shooting up and seizing Hormuz, Aden, Goa, and Malacca, they could turn the Indian Ocean into a private lake and tax every ship on it. Portugal would be rich beyond the dreams of avarice.

The plan almost, but not quite, came off. Part of the reason was military; because Portugal never managed to take Aden, Arab traders went on entering the Indian Ocean without paying duties. But the bigger problem was that there was more to overseas expansion than just winning battles. Four other forces—distance, disease, demography, and diplomacy—had as much to do with the outcome as did devastating firepower. How well Europeans fared in any part of the world was a function of the balance between these forces.

America, where the balance massively favored Europeans, saw the most extreme outcome. Distance and demography certainly worked against the interlopers, limiting the number of Europeans who could reach the New World to a tiny proportion of the number of Native Americans. But once Europeans arrived, the natives' stone blades, clubs, and cotton armor proved almost useless against steel swords, horses, and guns. Forty years after Columbus came ashore, a mere 168 Spaniards routed tens of thousands of Incas and captured King Atahuallpa at Cajamarca (Figure 4.7). Bullet-riddled skulls from sixteenth-century cemeteries testify vividly to firepower's triumph over distance and demography.

Like the Portuguese in the Indian Ocean, however, Spaniards in the Americas learned that firepower was not always enough. In 1520, Cortés's conquistadors only escaped an Aztec uprising by the skin of their teeth, and their sack of Tenochtitlán the next year had as much to do with diplomacy as with guns. Cortés certainly had diplomatic problems of his own, at one point having to fight a civil war against a rival conquistador, but these paled next to the divisions among Native Americans. In Mesoamerica, the Tlaxcalans and other victims of Aztec imperialism were all too happy to revolt, while in Peru, Pizarro faced an Inca Empire that was bitterly divided after a recent civil war. The bulk of the troops that took Tenochtitlán and Cusco were in fact natives.

The biggest factor in the Spaniards' success, however, was disease. For thousands of years, European and Asian farmers had been living alongside domesticated animals and evolving the unpleasant suite of microbes described in Chapter 3. Native Americans, who had very few domesticated

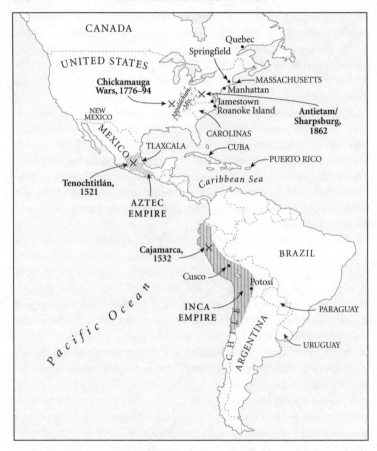

Figure 4.7. Sites in the Americas mentioned in this chapter

animals, had no resistance to these infections. They had a few horrible ailments of their own (including syphilis) to give back to the Spaniards, but the exchange of infections worked overwhelmingly in Europe's favor.

"Sores erupted on our faces, our breasts, our bellies," Aztec eyewitnesses said. "The sick were so utterly helpless that they could only lie on their beds . . . They could not get up to search for food, and everyone else was too sick to care for them, so they starved to death in their beds." Exact numbers are disputed, but a recent DNA study shows that the Native population shrank by at least half across the sixteenth and seventeenth centuries.

This demographic disaster left the invaders largely free to do what they wanted, which included looting the Aztecs and Incas, digging up the world's biggest deposit of silver at Potosí in the Andes, and importing African slaves to replace the lost Native labor. Savage struggles with Native Americans went on for centuries, but the biggest threat the Spaniards faced came not from indigenous resistance but from other Europeans who, by 1600, were trying to muscle in on their business.

These newcomers—mostly English, Dutch, and French—faced an uphill struggle. A few optimists thought there were more Aztec and Inca Empires waiting to be robbed and threw their lives away hunting for El Dorado, but most assumed that the Spaniards had already stolen everything worth stealing. (One report concluded that New Mexico contained nothing but "naked people, false bits of coral, and four pebbles.") The only ways to get rich, it seemed, were by hunting for new veins of precious metal ("the most disadvantageous lottery in the world," in Adam Smith's words) or plundering the ships carrying silver back to Spain.

That was certainly what the English thought. Walter Raleigh set up a pirate lair on Roanoke Island in 1585, but the colonists vanished without a trace. The gentlemen who settled at Jamestown in 1607 pinned their hopes on finding gold and jewels, but soon they too were disappointed and starving. Cut marks on the bones of a fourteen-year-old girl excavated in a garbage pit suggest that in the winter of 1609–10 they were reduced to eating corpses. But in 1612 the emaciated survivors made a great discovery: tobacco thrived in their swampy, malarial new home. Its leaves were not as sweet as the version Spaniards grew on Cuba, but it was cheap, and Englishmen were glad to buy it.

By then, French settlers in Quebec and Dutch in Manhattan were finding equally strong European markets for American fur, and the religious refugees who fled England for Massachusetts in the 1620s were happily selling timber for ships' masts to their former persecutors. By the 1650s, Puritans were also exporting food to the Caribbean, where plantation owners were turning over every scrap of land to sugar, a wonder drug that sold even better than tobacco. Commodities moved from west to east, and people—a "white plague," the historian Niall Ferguson calls them—flooded in the other direction.

Outside America, however, Europe's war on the world at first went less well, because the balance between distance, disease, demography, diplomacy, and firepower was less favorable. In West Africa, the source of slaves for American mines and plantations, Europeans again had overwhelming military dominance but consistently lost the war of microbes, thanks to yellow fever and malaria. Only where the disease environment was unusually favorable, as around Cape Town, did Europeans really have things their own way. After landing here in 1652, Dutch settlers pushed the local Khoekhoe farmers back fifty miles, and a smallpox epidemic in 1713 virtually ended native resistance.

But that was an exception. Usually, Europeans made little headway unless they got lucky diplomatic breaks. In southeast Africa, for example, Portuguese traders began moving up the Zambezi River in 1531, but the kingdom of Mutapa (one of the successors to Great Zimbabwe, which had declined in the 1440s) kept them at arm's length. Only around 1600, when a rebellion unnerved the Mutapan king, did that change. Fearing for his throne, the king invited in Portuguese soldiers and missionaries, and by the time he died in 1627, these advisers had such influence that they could handpick his successor.

As late as 1700, Europeans mostly had to content themselves with tiny toeholds along the coast, where merchants built forts and negotiated what deals they could with local communities. "You have three things we want," one African chief is supposed to have told a European trader: "powder, musket, and shot. And we have three things you want: men, women, and children." On this basis, between 1500 and 1800, Europeans bought something like twelve million people from warring African chiefs for shipment across the Atlantic.

Europe's position in Asia was initially even weaker. Disease gave Europeans no advantage: Eurasia's disease pools had largely merged since the Black Death of the fourteenth century, producing a balance that if anything worked against Europeans, who remained vulnerable to malaria in the tropics.

The vast distances separating Europe and Asia—eight thousand miles from Lisbon to Calicut, then another two thousand on to Malacca, and two thousand more to Guangzhou—were also hard to overcome. Dutch sailors found a shortcut in 1611 (trimming two thousand miles off the coastal route that the Portuguese had found to Southeast Asia by picking up the Westerlies near the Cape of Good Hope, taking them almost as far as Australia, and then cutting north), but even in 1620 a mere 20,000 or so Europeans faced nearly 200 million Asians around the Indian Ocean and another 100 million in China.

Asians could not stop European ships from coming, but until well into the seventeenth century they did not really want to. The sultan of Gujarat's view that "wars by sea are the affairs of merchants, and of no concern to the prestige of kings" was not far wrong. Portuguese carracks could pose existential threats to little city-states like Malacca, but to Turkey, Persia, India, China, and Japan they were more annoying than dangerous. Europeans were in the same category as pirates: both kinds of parasites might reduce imperial revenues by killing people in coastal towns, but so long as they stayed within limits, it was cheaper to ignore them than to fight them. There could even be advantages to courting them, particularly if an emperor needed to buy guns.

A two-speed economy took shape in the Indian Ocean. The great empires continued to dominate their own enormous internal markets, but Europeans inserted themselves around their edges and, so long as the empires ignored them, fought each other for shares of the rich international trade.

The fighting did not go well for Portugal. Ever since da Gama's day, the crown had kept traders on a short leash, and the kinds of commercial cartels that set up East India Companies in London (1600), Amsterdam (1602), and Paris (1674) barely existed in Lisbon. In principle, and often in practice, these private East India Companies carried all the costs of doing business in the Indian Ocean. The governor-general of the Dutch East India Company spelled it out in a letter to his directors in 1614: "Trade in Asia should be conducted and maintained under the protection and with the aid of your own weapons, and those weapons must be wielded with the profits gained by the trade. So trade cannot be maintained without war, nor war without trade."

The overburdened Portuguese government simply could not compete with this business model. By the 1650s, the Dutch had relieved it of its bases at Malacca and around Sri Lanka, and with the Portuguese effectively out of the picture, the Dutch turned on the English. "The trade of the world is too little for us two," an English seaman explained; "therefore one of us must down." Between 1652 and 1674, the two countries' fleets perfected the new line-ahead tactics in a string of grinding wars. Thanks in no small part to Pepys's labors at the Admiralty, England gradually came out on top, but by then France had emerged as a new rival.

Despite all the drama of these wars, though, the sultans, shahs, and emperors in Istanbul, Isfahan, Delhi, and Beijing paid little attention. One set of Europeans might replace another, but the larger balance of power was set in stone. As late as 1690, the Mughal Empire could slap down the English East India Company almost without effort when it felt that the interlopers were pushing a little too hard in Bengal. Half the men in an English invasion force died of disease that year, and the company had to swallow a humiliating peace.

The lesson seemed clear: Europeans had the edge on the battlefield, but unless they could combine that with an edge in the war of germs, it availed them little. Distance, disease, and demography made the Asian empires invulnerable. The most that Europeans could hope for was to fight over the crumbs that fell from their tables.

But then everything changed. Sooner or later, bad luck, bad blood, or bad judgment catches up with every empire, and in 1707 it was the Mughals' turn. After ruling India for almost half a century, the great Aurangzeb finally died. The occupant of the Peacock Throne had spent his last years falling out first with his own son and then with the rajas, nawabs, and minor sultans who did the actual work of running the subcontinent for him. At his passing, his former agents grabbed the opportunity to opt out of the Mughal organization. Law and order collapsed and violence spiked. It was every man for himself.

By 1720, local grandees were intriguing and fighting against each other, against their nominal overlords in distant Delhi, and against their own unhappy subjects. Players in this game of thrones ran up huge debts to finance their moves. "I am falling at [my creditors'] feet, till I have rubbed the skin from my forehead," one complained in the 1730s. Needless to say, the various East India Companies were only too happy to exploit this diplomatic opening by lending to the would-be nawabs—especially when they handed the money straight back to the companies to hire European troops.

But these were anxious days for the companies too. On the upside, companies that backed the right men could become kingmakers, perhaps even winning rights to administer and tax the lands around their coastal enclaves, but the downside was that all the fighting disrupted the trade that kept the companies going, threatening them with ruin. Tight-lipped men in tricorn hats slipped back and forth between European forts and rajas' palaces, betraying and being betrayed in turn in a murky world of shifting politics.

"The princes became independent," observed the British politician and philosopher Edmund Burke, "but their independence led to their ruin."

Few if any of the companies' men were actually seeking to ruin the princes, yet this was precisely what happened in the Carnatic region of southern India. Here things were even messier than usual, because the intriguing nawabs and sultans had the option of dealing not just with the British (based in Madras) but also with the French (in Pondicherry) and of playing the two East India Companies against each other. In 1744, when news arrived that Britain and France were again at war in Europe, both companies decided to put boots on the ground in the Carnatic, which promptly blew up in a multi-cornered conflict.

This Anglo-French confrontation added another wrinkle—Europe's ongoing revolution in military affairs—to the diplomatic opportunities presented by the Mughal meltdown. Had India fallen apart in the 1640s, Europeans might not have been strong enough to capitalize on it, but by the 1740s their professional armies were unstoppable. These forces were tiny, rarely more than three thousand men, and most troops were in fact local recruits rather than Europeans, but when it came to a fight, the well-armed, well-trained, highly disciplined company men consistently routed native armies ten times their size (even when the Indians brought along armored elephants). The Europeans were like a "wall which vomited fire and flame," a survivor of one battle said.

The Carnatic War raised the stakes for the companies. Whoever came out on top in the Anglo-French fighting would dispose of the entire Carnatic, not just its coastal trade, but it also became clear as the war dragged on that the costs for the companies would be enormous. Both companies had gone to India to make money, so commercial logic demanded a negotiated end to the war. In 1754 the French company began looking for an exit strategy. But the British did not.

For 150 years, Europe's great powers had fought over trade and colonies so they could make money to fund their wars at home. Britain had done better than anyone at this, becoming, one writer claimed in 1718, "the most considerable of any nation in the world [because of] the vastness and expansiveness of our trade." Yet if this were true, some Britons asked, did it not imply that conventional wisdom was wrong? Instead of trade in India being a means, contributing to the end of winning wars in Europe, perhaps wars in Europe should be the means, and winning more trade in India should be the end.

Really profound shifts in strategic thinking typically only come along every century or two, but one was now under way in London. Amid intense debate, a loose alliance of commercial interests dragged Britain in fits and starts toward a new business model, in which fighting in Europe was solely a way to distract France so that Britain could snap up its colonies and trade without interference.

The British government lent money and men to France's other enemies in Europe, while the British East India Company stayed the course in the Carnatic and bestowed the throne on its chosen nawab. The company then extorted massive kickbacks from him, seized his tax revenues, and swamped his economy with its agents. Money rolled in, and when a new, pro-French nawab in Bengal—the richest part of India—started making trouble in 1756, the company leaped at the chance to repeat its Carnatic strategy.

But the nawab struck first. He swept down on the company's base in Calcutta and on the pitchy, stifling night of June 20–21 crammed over a hundred prisoners into a cell made for eight. By dawn, half had suffocated or died from heatstroke. The company dispatched Robert Clive—an unlikable but undeniably daring hero of the Carnatic War—to avenge the Black Hole of Calcutta.

Clive did not just toss the nawab out of Calcutta; he also joined a Bengali uprising against him and, adding the company's men to the rebels, took on an army twenty times the size of his own. The resulting battle at Plassey was slightly farcical. The nawab's gunners accidentally blew up some of their own artillery, which stampeded the elephants dragging the guns. The rest of the nawab's army then ran away when the nawab's key ally— who also happened to be the company's pick as the next nawab—changed sides. The company now took over tax collection in Bengal, and Clive helped himself to a reward of £160,000 (as I write, the equivalent of about $400 million) from its treasury.

And Bengal was just the beginning. Over the next two years, Britain worked with its allies to keep France tied up in Germany while seizing for itself key Caribbean islands and the whole of Canada. A British army beat the French again in India, and the Royal Navy smashed the French fleet not once but twice. Rarely has a strategy been so successful. "Could it be believed," Burke asked the speaker of the House of Commons in 1783, "when I entered into existence [in 1729] or when you, a younger man, were born [1735], that on this day, in this House, we should be employed in discussing the conduct of those British subjects who had disposed of the power and person of the Grand Mogul?"*

---

*That is, the Mughal emperor.

The Invisible Fist

Between the Portuguese capture of Ceuta and Burke's speech in 1783, western Europeans had conquered millions of square miles of territory and tens of millions of people. They had reinvented productive war, rather than just reviving it; they took it global, creating entirely new kinds of bigger societies. And while their wars were raging across the oceans and in America, Asia, and Africa, in the western European homelands rates of violent death fell faster and further than ever before.

The fifteenth century was perhaps Europe's bloodiest since the fall of the Roman Empire a thousand years earlier, with bands of unemployed mercenaries ravaging France and Italy and civil war tearing England apart. "O piteous spectacle! O bloody times!" Shakespeare imagined the mad king Henry VI crying out in 1461, as fifty thousand men hacked at each other for hours in a snowstorm to decide his claim to the throne of England. And well he might cry out, given what archaeologists have found on the battlefield of Towton. One soldier, now known only as Towton 25, went down in a hail of blows that smashed his skull eight times. First came five stabs in the face, none of them fatal, but then a gigantic blow from behind ripped off the back of his skull and drove bone splinters through his brain. He fell forward, but another swipe flipped him over before a final sword stroke slashed his face in half, going in through an eye socket and bursting out through his throat (Figure 4.8).

But it could have been worse. His comrade Towton 32 took thirteen head wounds, one of them deliberately slicing off an ear. Nor were the contending kings immune. In 1485, in the last battle of the civil war, Richard III (identified in 2013 by his curved spine and DNA) was tied up, stabbed clean through the head with a sword, and hacked again with a halberd. Then, after he was dead, he was stabbed through his buttocks and tossed into a pit.

By the time Burke spoke in 1783, no one imagined that such violence could return to western Europe. Across the previous three centuries, government—desperate to raise cash for huge armies and navies, fierce new ships and guns, and professional officers and men—had reasserted itself. This was Elias's "civilizing process," the coming of an age of reason, order, and prosperity that would have astonished Kings Henry and Richard.

It was an uneven process. The seventeenth century saw another wave of failed states, prompting Hobbes to write *Leviathan*, but by 1783 pirates and highwaymen were becoming things of the past (Blackbeard was

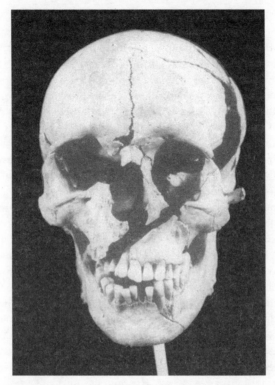

Figure 4.8. Bloody times: the skull of Towton 25, hacked apart by eight blows in 1461

shot—five times—in 1718 and Dick Turpin hanged in 1739), and homicide rates had collapsed. In the 1480s, roughly one western European in a hundred was being murdered; in the 1780s, that fate awaited just one in a thousand. Burke's England was probably the safest place the world had ever seen.

Western Europeans were, in a sense, rerunning the tape of ancient history. Like the Romans, Mauryans, and Han before them, they were creating bigger Leviathans. Just as in ancient times, the process was brutal and exploitative, but, again as in ancient times, in the long run it drove down rates of violent death and delivered prosperity. Intellectuals were acutely aware of this, devoting polemical pamphlets and learned treatises to what they called "the battle of the ancients and the moderns," arguing over whether—or when—they had surpassed the achievements of antiquity. (For what it is worth, the social development index that I describe in my earlier books *Why the West Rules—for Now* and *The Measure of Civilization* provides answers they might have liked: yes, and in 1720.) In another sense, though, Europeans were going well beyond the Romans: as with productive war, they did not so much revive Leviathan as reinvent it.

By building empires across the oceans instead of building a traditional territorial empire within their own continent, western Europeans created an entirely new kind of economy, which generated wealth on a staggering scale. Britain alone saw its exports boom from about £2 million in 1700 to nearly £40 million at the century's end.

What made the new economy different from anything seen before was the Atlantic Ocean. Europe's conquest of America had turned the northern part of the sea into a kind of Goldilocks Ocean, big enough to have very different ecologies and societies around its shores, but small enough that ships could cross it, trading at every point and generating steady profits (Figure 4.9).

Historians usually describe this as "triangular trade." A businessman could start in Liverpool with a boatload of textiles or guns and sail to Senegal, exchanging them, at a profit, for slaves. He could then carry the slaves to Jamaica and trade them (again at a profit) for sugar, which he could bring back to England to sell for more profits, before buying a new consignment of finished goods and setting off to Africa again. Alternatively, a Bostonian could take rum to Africa and swap it for slaves, bring the slaves to the Caribbean and exchange them for molasses, and then bring the molasses back to New England to make into more rum.

Europe's conquest of America had created something entirely unanticipated—an integrated intercontinental market, generating a geographical division of labor and making men rich on every shore. It gave each of the lands abutting the North Atlantic a comparative economic advantage and encouraged entrepreneurs to specialize—in capturing slaves in Africa, clearing plantations in the Caribbean and North America's southern states, and manufacturing in Europe and America's northern states.

To work well, the new economy needed new kinds of government that would make specialization easier. West Africa saw the rise of powerful kings; the Caribbean and the American South saw the coming of planter oligarchies; and in northwest Europe and the American Northeast, commercial elites challenged absolutist monarchs. Each shift generated conflict.

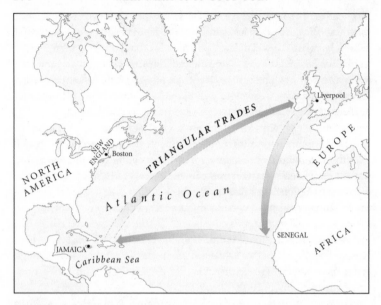

Figure 4.9. The Goldilocks Ocean: the triangular trades that generated unprecedented wealth, kick-started a market revolution in Europe, and transported twelve million Africans into slavery in the Americas

Africans raided their neighbors to abduct slaves, settlers in America seized the natives' lands, and Europeans boarded and sank each other's ships to seize trade routes.

Everywhere that the new Atlantic economy touched, all fixed, fast-frozen relations were swept away. In western Europe, cheap shipping brought a world of little luxuries within reach of everyday folk. By the eighteenth century, a man with a little cash in his pocket could do more than just buy another loaf of bread; he could get miraculous drugs—tea, coffee, tobacco, sugar—brought from distant continents, or homemade marvels such as clay pipes, umbrellas, and newspapers. And the same Atlantic economy that provided this bounty also produced people ready to give a man the cash he needed; because traders would buy every hat, gun, or blanket that they could get to ship to Africa or America, manufacturers were always willing to pay people to make more of them.

No longer did men automatically follow their fathers into farming if drifting into towns promised better wages. Some set their families to spinning and weaving to earn cash; others joined workshops and walked away from the fields. The details varied, but across the seventeenth and eighteenth centuries Europeans increasingly sold their labor to employers and worked longer hours. And the more they did so, the more sugar, tea, and newspapers they could buy—which meant more slaves dragged across the Atlantic, more acres cleared for plantations, and more factories and shops opened. Sales rose, economies of scale were achieved, and prices fell, opening this world of goods to even more western Europeans.

The real source of riches, the philosopher Adam Smith concluded in 1776 in his *Inquiry into the Nature and Causes of the Wealth of Nations*, was not plunder, conquest, or monopolies; it was the division of labor. This division of labor, he said, was itself the "consequence of a certain propensity in human nature . . . to truck, barter, and exchange one thing for another." In pursuing profit, people start to specialize on the jobs that they do particularly well or inexpensively and exchange the fruits of their labors for goods and services that other people produce particularly well or inexpensively. By creating markets for these goods and services, they simultaneously lower costs and raise quality, making everyone better-off. "It is not from the benevolence of the butcher, the brewer or the baker that we expect our dinner," Smith observed, "but from their regard to their own interest."

"By directing [his] industry in such a manner as its produce may be of the greatest value," Smith explained, a man "intends only his own gain; [but] he is in this, as in many other cases, led by an invisible hand to promote an end which was no part of his intention . . . By pursuing his own interest, he frequently promotes that of the society more effectually than when he really intends to promote it." The implication was obvious: the more that governments got out of people's way and left them free to truck, barter, and exchange, the better the invisible hand would work, and the better-off everyone would be.

Or would they? For five thousand years, one of the big perks of ruling had been the right to plunder successful subjects. Even the most assiduous stationary bandits sometimes gave in to the temptation, but the Smithian vision of the world now asked the mighty to make a bet. Stealing from your subjects, it advised rulers, gives you a bigger slice of the pie, but if you settle for a smaller slice, you will in the end eat more, because the pie will become much bigger. In those parts of western Europe where kings wielded the greatest power—particularly Spain—this did not sound very plausible. But in countries where kings were weaker—England, and especially the

Netherlands, which did not even have a king—governments were more willing to roll the dice by granting the nouveaux riches truckers, barterers, and exchangers more and more freedom to exploit the new Atlantic economy. (France, home of the original nouveaux riches, was somewhere in the middle.)

Fortunately for the delicate sensibilities of the wellborn, men who made money in trade could usually be relied upon to buy country estates and put on powdered wigs as soon as the opportunity presented itself. But capitalizing on the Atlantic economy did not just mean cutting deals with these people of no name; it also meant inviting them into the inner circle. Economic freedom led inexorably to demands for political freedom, and kings who tried to hold back the tide might lose their thrones (like England's James II, in 1688) or even their heads (like England's Charles I, in 1649, and France's Louis XVI, in 1793).

Yet not everything was wine and roses for the wealthy merchants either. The traditional way to rule a kingdom had involved farming out the right to collect taxes, judge disputes, and administer market monopolies to local worthies, who normally lined their own pockets but also kept government expenses down. Freeing people to truck, barter, and exchange meant sweeping away much of this archaic machinery and giving free rein to the invisible hand, but something had to replace the old way of guaranteeing law and order, and the only something available was central government. Allowing markets to work well was more complicated than it appeared. It was not just a matter of government stepping aside; rather, government had to step *in*, creating a whole new structure of more impartial functionaries, judges, and civil servants. Without this, the "open-access order" (as the noted social scientists Douglass North, John Wallis, and Barry Weingast call the new system in their book *Violence and Social Orders*) could not function.

We should not exaggerate the scale and speed of changes. Eighteenth-century governments remained tiny by twenty-first-century standards; the "better sort" expected, and generally received, deference; and almost everywhere, "democracy" was a dirty word. But all the same, ordinary people's interests began to matter more to rulers. The price of representation, however, was taxation, and more money meant that governments needed more managers—who, little by little, extended Leviathan's reach deeper into civil society. In England, which led the way in open access, the number of government pen pushers tripled between 1690 and 1782 and the tax take grew sixfold. "Let any gentleman but look into the Statute Books lying upon our Table," the Earl of Bath harrumphed in 1743. "It is monstrous, it is even frightful to look into the Indexes, where for several Columns together we see nothing but Taxes, Taxes, Taxes."

Despite the grumbling, by Smith's day it was clear that governments that laid bets on open access were doing better than those that did not. From Madrid to Constantinople, rulers carried on defending royal, aristocratic, and clerical prerogatives against merchants. They limited who could trade, they set up monopolies, and they went on seizing their subjects' goods. The payoffs: hunger, misery, and want as economies grew more slowly than people reproduced. In northwestern Europe, by contrast, rulers were far more willing to take a chance on the new ways of doing things. Holding their noses, they made deals with the moneymen. The payoff: economies that grew even faster than people could breed (Figure 4.10).

Even so, Smith saw, reordering relationships within nations was only the beginning. Rulers also needed to reorder the relations between nations. By forcing Asia, Africa, and America into a vastly expanded market, Smith acknowledged, European governments had added greatly to the world's wealth, but now the market had grown so big, he argued, that Europe "should voluntarily give up all authority over her colonies, and leave them to elect their own magistrates, to enact their own laws, and to make peace and war, as they might think proper." The Assyrian, Roman, or any other earlier empire would have been insane to abandon its provinces and rely

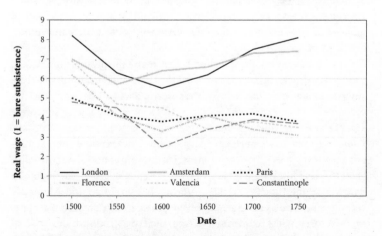

Figure 4.10. The wages of working for wages: the diverging average incomes of unskilled laborers in northwestern and southern Europe, 1500–1750

on trade to make it rich, but now, said Smith, freeing colonies to truck and barter as they saw fit would be a net gain for rulers.

"Such a measure," Smith admitted, "never was, and never will be, adopted by any nation in the world," but in 1776—the very year that *The Wealth of Nations* was published—Britain's American colonists relieved their motherland of the need to decide whether to follow Smith's advice by rebelling. Traditional-minded politicians assumed that losing the colonies would ruin Britain's Atlantic trade, but events soon showed that they were wrong and Smith was right. Anglo-American commerce regained its prewar level in 1789 and just kept growing.

Explaining this became, in many ways, *the* burning question of the late eighteenth century, and it has never really gone away since then. In a sense, it is the same question that I am trying to answer in this book. I have been arguing that in the ten thousand years since farming began, productive war has been the motor that made the world safer and richer, by creating Leviathans that in turn created bigger societies, pacified them internally, and allowed economies to grow. But the American Revolution seems to point in the opposite direction. By breaking a big chunk off the British Empire, the revolution was very much a counterproductive war (in the sense I have been using that expression), but instead of leading back to the kinds of calamities that we saw in Chapter 3, it made both Britain and the new United States richer than ever before. Perhaps what the American Revolution teaches us is that the whole argument of this book is wrong. Perhaps the real secret to a safer, richer world is just to set everyone free to pursue their own interests, without governments setting rules and enforcing them with violence.

This was certainly the conclusion that many intellectuals reached in the late eighteenth century. These were the years in which Rousseau challenged Hobbes, arguing that before governments had begun bothering them, people had lived in a peaceful and happy natural state. They were also the years in which Thomas Paine, in his bestselling pamphlet *Common Sense*, assured Americans that "government even in its best state is but a necessary evil." Some of America's revolutionaries—above all a group around Thomas Jefferson, known as Republicans—tried to put the new theory into practice. Others—above all a group around Alexander Hamilton, known as Federalists—pushed back against the idea that "government itself will become useless, and Society will subsist and flourish free from its shackles." The reality, the Federalist (and soon-to-be president) John Adams told Jefferson, was that men were slaves to their violent passions and that "Nothing but Force, and Power and Strength can restrain them."

Smith himself took a middle course. Just look, he said, at the Navigation Acts, which England passed in 1651. These laws, designed largely to exclude Dutch rivals from English colonial trade, were disastrous in purely economic terms. Shutting out the Dutch shrank England's markets and made everyone poorer. In strategic terms, however, the laws were vital, because growing Dutch power threatened England's very survival. "As defence," Smith pointed out, "is of much more importance than opulence, the act of navigation is, perhaps, the wisest of all the commercial regulations of England."

The Navigation Acts threw into sharp relief the fundamental problem of the Atlantic economy—a problem that it shared with every other part of the open-access order. Markets could not work well unless governments got out of them, but markets could not work at all unless governments got into them, using force to pacify the world and keep the Beast at bay. Violence and commerce were two sides of the same coin, because the invisible hand needed an invisible fist to smooth the way before it could work its magic.

The fifty years that followed the American Revolution gradually showed how to solve this conundrum—not by ridding the world of Leviathan, but by making a Leviathan that reached across the world. This Leviathan would be a novel kind of stationary bandit, one that stood above the fray and impartially umpired an international open-access order, preventing any lesser Leviathans from interfering with the invisible hand. What the new, business-friendly rulers of northwestern Europe were doing within their countries, a new, business-friendly super-Leviathan would do between countries. It would act as a globocop, an impartial policeman providing security for all and leaving economic self-interest to bring people together in larger and larger markets. In return for giving up plunder and monopolies, the globocop would become the most privileged player in a hugely expanded market, and if all went well, it would end up much richer than traditional Leviathans had ever been.

Once again, war was reaching a culminating point. Since reinventing productive war in the fifteenth century, Europeans had conquered more of the planet and created bigger markets than anyone had done before, but the strategies that had brought them so much success were now leading toward disaster. To thrive in the new world of global trade that productive war had made, governments had to embrace the open-access order. As

Smith foresaw, no nation in the world was ready to adopt such measures wholeheartedly, and even after its defeat in North America, Britain went on aggressively extending its control of India. However, Britain's governments did begin to see that they did not have to rule North America to get the benefits of a bigger society; they just had to rule the waves (it is no coincidence that "Rule, Britannia!"—the soundtrack to this chapter—was first sung in 1740). Britain edged, little by little, toward being a globocop, using its invisible fist to police the sea-lanes, clearing the way for the invisible hand of the market to do its job.

Productive war and Leviathans had not become obsolete. Rather, they were just evolving into new and more powerful forms. Unfortunately, it would take another generation of killing before the world learned this lesson.

War and Perpetual Peace

"In 1793, a force appeared that beggared all imagination. Suddenly war again became the business of the people."

This, thought Clausewitz (who lived through the events), was the real legacy of the late eighteenth century. Not for nothing did the United States' Founding Fathers open their draft constitution in 1787 with the words "We the People": it was the people in arms, not paid professionals or mercenaries, who rose against the British. Lacking their enemies' wealth and organization, the American revolutionaries had raised armies by enthusing them with patriotism instead of paying them and had run rings around the rigid, ponderous professionals. The open-access order was now opening war, as well as markets and politics, to the energies of the masses. A new revolution in military affairs was beginning.

This was not well understood at first, although it should have been. Many European observers insisted that there had in fact been nothing special about the American Revolution. Far from being a people united, they pointed out, Americans had actually been deeply divided over rebelling, and the rebels might well have lost without interventions by French and Spanish fleets and the Baron von Steuben, a German officer who trained the Continental Army to fight more like professionals.

Even when Europeans did recognize that the Americans had waged a novel kind of people's war, they rarely thought that it mattered much. The postrevolutionary United States, they observed, was a puny military power. As late as 1791, the outnumbered Miami Indians annihilated an American army near the headwaters of the Wabash River. They killed six hundred white soldiers and stuffed their mouths with soil to satisfy their land hunger. If this was what people's war brought, many Europeans concluded, they could do without it.

When Europeans *were* impressed by the American Revolution, it was more for its outpouring of announcements that the new republic had transcended war than for the way it had fought. Even George Washington, who knew more about battles than most men, felt able to tell a French correspondent that "it is time for the age of Knight-Errantry and mad-heroism to be at an end," because "the humanizing benefits of commerce, would supersede the waste of war and the rage of conquest; . . . as the Scripture expresses it, 'the nations learn war no more.'"

By the mid-1790s, Europe's literary salons were awash with proposals for world peace, often explicitly inspired by the American example. None, though, had quite the impact of Immanuel Kant's little pamphlet *Perpetual Peace*. Kant was probably Europe's most famous philosopher, renowned almost as much for his austere lifestyle (he liked to end his single meal of the day with laughter, he said, not because he enjoyed laughing, but because it was good for his digestion) as for his brilliant, closely argued monographs (even other philosophers initially found his eight-hundred-page *Critique of Pure Reason* impenetrable). *Perpetual Peace*, however, was neither austere nor dense. Kant even opened it with a little joke: his title, he said, came from the "satirical inscription on a Dutch innkeeper's sign upon which a burial ground was painted."

Despite the gallows humor, Kant's point was that perpetual peace was also possible in the here and now. The reason, he said, was that open-access republics were better at commerce than closed-access monarchies, and "if the consent of the citizens is required in order to decide that war should be declared," as it is in republics, then "nothing is more natural than that they would be very cautious in commencing such a poor game." And as republics renounced war, each "may and should for the sake of its own security demand that the others enter with it into a constitution similar to the civil constitution, for under such a constitution each can be secure in his right. This would be a league of nations." War would be no more.

Perpetual Peace remains hugely influential, regularly assigned (sometimes along with *Coming of Age in Samoa*) in college classes. But by the time it came out, in 1795, it was already clear that something was wrong with the argument. Far from ushering in perpetual peace, republicanism had plunged Europe into war.

In one of the eighteenth century's greater ironies, the catalyst was the military aid Louis XVI of France had lavished on the American revolutionaries in order to weaken Britain. He had borrowed heavily and by 1789 could no longer meet the interest payments. His efforts to raise cash set off a taxpayers' revolt, which quickly turned violent. The revolutionaries locked up the king and his wife, Marie Antoinette, and then sent both of them plus 16,592 of their fellow citizens to the guillotine.

Horrified, Europe's great powers rallied in a grand coalition to restore the status quo, and in 1793 the French revolutionaries, suddenly scared, unleashed a people's war, the force that beggared Clausewitz's imagination. "The full weight of the nation was thrown into the balance," said Clausewitz. "The resources and efforts now available for use surpassed all conventional limits; nothing now impeded the vigor with which war could be waged." A million Frenchmen joined up.

Kant may have been right that the citizens of republics would be very cautious in commencing such a poor game as war, but once they did commence it, they went about it with a violent rage that paid professionals largely lacked. America's Revolutionary War had seen relatively few massacres outside the campaigns in the Carolinas, but the French Revolutionary Wars were fought in frenzies of self-righteousness, directed particularly against enemies within. "We are bearing fire and death," a French officer wrote to his sister in 1794. "One volunteer killed three women with his own hands. It is atrocious, but the safety of the Republic demands it imperatively."

The revolutionary army slaughtered a quarter of a million countryfolk (considered counterrevolutionaries) that year. Finding guns and guillotines too slow, they took to tying civilians up and throwing them into rivers. "What a revolutionary torrent the Loire has become," the commander joked, before adding, apparently sincerely, that "it is out of a principle of humanity that I am purging the land of liberty of these monsters."

Against the trained troops of their Prussian, Austrian, and Russian enemies, however, the revolutionaries had a harder time, just as the American revolutionaries had initially had against the British and their Hessian mercenaries. The French people's army was huge, undisciplined, and—having beheaded or chased into exile most of its reactionary officers—usually poorly led. Only its excellent artillery, which had retained a backbone of nonaristocratic, prerevolutionary officers, saved it from disaster. By 1796, one of these officers—a short, quarrelsome provincial named Napoleone Buonaparte—had even worked out how to turn a people's army into a war-winning weapon.

"No more maneuvers, no more military art, just fire, steel, and patriotism," revolutionaries had proclaimed, but Napoleon's genius lay in turning this rhetoric into reality. Abandoning the clumsy supply trains that slowed down professional armies, Napoleon's men lived off the land, buying or stealing what they needed. No one had tried this since the seventeenth century, because forces had grown too big to be fed from farms along their line of march. Napoleon, however, broke his army down into corps and smaller divisions, each marching on a separate line. Each could fight a stand-alone battle if it had to, but the key to victory was that the columns could converge rapidly when the enemy was spotted, allowing Napoleon to concentrate overwhelming force.

Once on the battlefield, Napoleon followed the same principles. His men could rarely perform elaborate linear tactics as well as old-school professionals, so he did not ask them to. Instead, swarms of skirmishers sniped at the enemy's neat lines while the mass of French infantry ran forward in ragged columns, covered by barrages of shot and shell. When the columns got close to the opposition, they could quickly spread out into rough lines and fire off good enough volleys, substituting numbers for precision, or they could keep going, barreling into the enemy line with fixed bayonets. Even professionals regularly threw down their muskets and ran rather than receive the revolutionaries' charge.

Right around the time Kant was writing *Perpetual Peace*, France drifted—without too much deliberation—from waging people's wars in defense of the revolution to waging them to extend it. In 1796, Napoleon swept through northern Italy. In 1798 he invaded Egypt, and in December 1800, French armies stopped just fifty miles short of Vienna. In 1807, three years after Kant died, Napoleon occupied his hometown of Königsberg.

People's war in Europe had taken a very different path from the American version. After the British surrendered at Yorktown in 1781, the Americans had beaten their bayonets into plowshares. The Revolutionary generals had gone back to their farms, and Jefferson and like-minded Republicans had stubbornly resisted centralized power, taxes, a national debt, standing armies, and all the other tools of Leviathan.

To some Americans, this showed that they were cut from a different, more virtuous cloth than the corrupt Europeans. However, the fact that the United States lurched back toward Leviathan whenever it did perceive danger—as in the late 1790s, when fears of a French invasion flared up—suggests that the real difference was one of political geography. The United States faced few existential threats after 1781. In their absence, it could get away with being a military midget and even with engaging in arguments about whether it needed a Leviathan at all. European governments, on the other hand, faced predatory neighbors on every side. The slightest weakness could prove fatal, and republics had to fight just as hard as monarchies if they were to survive.

On both continents, the rise of patriotic passions was part of the larger rise of open-access orders, but European people's war diverged even further from the American brand when Napoleon discovered that it could be decoupled from republicanism. A quiet coup in 1799 effectively made him France's monarch, and in 1804 he very publicly crowned himself emperor. From now on, France's mass armies fought for the very old-fashioned cause of imperial expansion. George Washington had believed that commerce was making war redundant, but Napoleon never felt that way. In fact, after 1806 he tried to prove just the opposite, using war to overwhelm commerce by requiring defeated foes to join the "Continental System"—basically, a trade embargo intended to bankrupt Britain by shutting it out of Europe's markets.

It took almost ten more years of war, involving some of the biggest battles in European history (600,000 men fought at Leipzig in 1813), to show that Napoleon was wrong. The only way for war to defeat commerce was for French fleets to seize control of the seas and terminate Britain's trade, but because this trade was so profitable, Britain could always build more and better ships and train more and better sailors than France. Napoleon's naval efforts came to nothing, and because Britain's global commerce survived, Europeans quickly found that they needed British trade more than Britain needed them. One nation after another found ways to get around the Continental System and keep dealing in England's markets.

Napoleon's fights to enforce the system soon took him beyond the culminating point of people's war. Since 1799, he had shown that he could co-opt people's war to make himself an emperor, but Europe's more established monarchs now learned how to do the same to bring him down. When Napoleon occupied Spain in 1808 to keep it inside the Continental System, he was sucked into a quagmire of popular revolt (Figure 4.11), and Spanish insurgents, stiffened by British regulars, tied down hundreds of thousands of French troops for the next six years.

Worse followed when Napoleon, still trying to enforce the system, invaded Russia. (As mentioned in Chapter 3, it was this blunder that inspired Clausewitz to come up with his theory of culminating points: enraged

Figure 4.11. People's war: Spanish insurgents wage *guerrilla* ("little war") on French troops in Madrid, May 2, 1808.

when his native Prussia submitted to France, he joined the Russian army in 1812 as a volunteer and realized that his own anti-French anger was just part of a vast reaction that Napoleon had himself created by going too far.) The tide turned rapidly: just two years after Napoleon took Moscow, the Russians had taken Paris and Napoleon was in exile. But the tide then turned again, and in a hundred dramatic days in 1815, Napoleon stormed back into France, raised another army, and almost—but not quite—broke the British at Waterloo before being bundled back into a much more remote exile.

So it was that Britain's newfangled, open-access empire of trade survived the great challenge posed by Napoleon's marriage of old-school militarism and up-to-date people's war. By the time Bonaparte died, in 1821 (helped along, some said, by British poison), Britain bestrode much of the world like a colossus. Acting as a globocop was paying off: policing the waterways with British warships cost money, but it was worth it, because between 1781 and 1821 Britain's exports tripled and its workers became the most productive on the planet.

Britain was becoming a nation unlike any seen before—and also solving a problem that had never been seen before.

The Sun Never Sets

Bigger markets, Smith had argued, made for a finer division of labor, which lifted productivity, profits, and wages in a virtuous spiral. But what would happen when tasks had been subdivided as finely as possible and no further efficiency gains could be squeezed out?

Smith had not worried unduly about this, because the problem had never arisen. But by the time Napoleon died, his successors were worrying very much indeed. The high wages that British workers earned were already pricing some of their goods out of European markets. The only way for British firms to stay in business, it seemed, was to pay their workers less, and the average Londoner of the early nineteenth century was earning 15 percent less than his grandparents had. Having won the war, Britain seemed to be losing the peace.

Thomas Malthus, David Ricardo, and a string of other political economists speculated that there was an iron law of wages. The division of labor, imperial expansion, and becoming a globocop might all push wages up for a while, but in the end income would always be driven back down to the edge of starvation. The nineteenth century, some predicted, would be an age of misery. But this did not happen, because an odd concatenation of forces compelled the invisible hand and invisible fist to work together in new ways.

The story starts with clothes. Because everyone needs them, textiles are a major sector in all premodern economies, and because sheep do well in wet, grassy countries, Britons had for centuries worn wool. But as it made inroads into Asia, Britain's East India Company saw an opportunity and started shipping rolls of brightly colored, inexpensive cotton cloth back to the home isles. It was a huge hit.

Wool merchants, unhappy about this competition, struck back by doing the kind of thing that Smith hated most: distorting the market by lobbying Parliament to ban Indian cotton. Cotton cannot grow in Britain, so clothiers responded by importing raw cotton (which was still legal) from the Caribbean colonies and spinning and weaving it in Britain, but British workers could not do the job as cheaply (or, frankly, as well) as Indians. In the 1760s, thirty pieces of woolen clothing were being sold for every one of cotton.

The bottleneck in cotton production was spinning, the labor-intensive, repetitive job of twisting cotton fibers together to make strong, even thread, and it was opened (according to legend) in 1764, when a spinning wheel belonging to one James Hargreaves fell over. As he watched it continue turning for several seconds as it lay on its side, Hargreaves said, he had an epiphany: he could make a machine that flipped a spindle from vertical to horizontal and then back again, over and over, replacing the human fingers that laboriously twisted the fibers. In fact, a single machine could have dozens of spindles, doing the job faster than a human.

Hargreaves had hit on a solution to the downside of high wages: he would augment human labor with machine power, raising productivity. Hargreaves's spinning jenny was a hit (perhaps too much so; Hargreaves was unable to enforce his patent), and in 1779 a vastly superior device (Crompton's mule) also came onto the market, spinning cotton that was not only cheaper but also finer than anything made in India.

All this seems very far from the history of war, but before its relevance becomes clear, we must stray still farther from the battlefield, into the world of underground streams. In the eighteenth century, coal-mine owners were also facing the problem of high (by the standards of the day) wages. As wages rose, Britons had more babies; as population grew, people cut down forests to clear farmland; and as wood grew scarce, coal replaced it for heating and cooking. All this was good news for colliers, who dug their mines deeper to bring up ever more coal, but by 1700 mine after mine was flooding. Paying high-priced laborers to bail out the diggings was ruinously expensive, as was using high-priced land to grow oats to feed dozens of horses pulling bucket chains. The answer, first installed at a coal mine in 1712, was an engineering marvel—a machine that substituted cheap coal for expensive muscles. It burned coal to boil water, making steam that drove a piston that pumped water out of the mine shaft, allowing more coal to be dug up and burned.

Coal and clothes came together in 1785, when the first cotton mill owner hooked up his mules, jennies, and throstles to steam engines. Productivity exploded. The price of spun cotton fell from 38 shillings per pound in 1786 to under 7 shillings in 1807, but sales grew even faster. In 1760, Britain had imported 2.5 million pounds of raw cotton; by 1787 that jumped to 22 million pounds (in 1837 it reached 366 million pounds). Steam power then leaped from industry to industry as engineers figured out new applications. British wages, which had been sliding since the 1740s as Smithian improvements ran into diminishing returns, stabilized, and after 1830 surged upward. The Industrial Revolution had arrived.

Steam power smashed the last barriers to European commerce. For centuries, the vast distances separating Europe from East Asia had kept Western trade to a mere trickle, while the interiors of Africa and Asia had been beyond the merchants' reach altogether. Steam changed that. Engineers immediately saw that steam engines could be mounted on wheels and that these wheels could paddle ships across oceans and carry trains down tracks. Steam could do the work of the winds and waves in transport, much as it was doing the work of muscles in manufacturing. Steam could swallow space.

The British led the way. "The earth was made for Dombey and Son to trade in," announced Charles Dickens in his great novel—*Dombey and Son*—of pride, prejudice, and global commerce. "The sun and moon were made to give them light. Rivers and seas were formed to float their ships; rainbows gave them promise of fair weather; winds blew for or against their enterprises; stars and planets circled in their orbits, to preserve inviolate a system of which they were the centre . . . A.D. had no concern with anno Domini, but stood for anno Dombei—and Son."

Dickens wrote these words in 1846 (anno Domini, that is). In 1838 a British steamship had crossed the Atlantic in fifteen days, ignoring headwinds and currents to average an unheard-of ten miles per hour. The next year, an even more extraordinary ship sailed from England for China: the *Nemesis*, an all-iron steamship, armed with cannons and rockets. So odd did this boat seem that even its captain conceded that just "as the *floating* property of wood . . . rendered it the most natural material for the construction of ships, so did the *sinking* property of iron make it appear, at first sight, very ill adapted for a similar purpose."

The *Nemesis* was on its way to East Asia because of an extraordinarily sordid quarrel. Chinese governments, deeply suspicious of Western traders, had for generations penned them into tiny enclaves in Macao and Guangzhou and limited what they could buy and sell. The merchants, however, found that whatever the Chinese government might say, Chinese customers were eager for their goods, especially opium. Since the world's best opium grew in British-controlled India, business was good—until, in 1839, Beijing declared a war on drugs.

Chinese officials confiscated a fortune in opium from British drug dealers. After some dubious lobbying, the dealers persuaded the government in London to demand compensation, plus a base at Hong Kong, and the right for traders and merchants (including drug dealers) to enter other ports. The Chinese—understandably—refused, confident that distance would protect them, but the *Nemesis* and a small British fleet quickly showed that this assumption no longer held.

The technological gap between the two sides in this Opium War was just astonishing. Chinese junks, one British officer observed, looked "exactly as if the subjects of [medieval] prints had assumed life and substance and colour, and were moving and acting before me unconscious of the march of the world through centuries, and of all modern usage, invention, or improvement." Chinese forts crumbled under the intruders' guns, and in 1842 Beijing gave Britain what it demanded.

Steamships now flooded China's coastal cities with Western goods, and in 1853 an American flotilla, looking for coaling stations, steamed boldly into Tokyo Bay. It cowed the Japanese government without even firing a shot. Back in Washington, the president ignored his commodore's suggestion that he now annex Taiwan, but the lesson was clear: no country with a coastline was now safe from the West.

Nor, for that matter, were countries without coastlines. What steamships did at sea and up rivers, railroads did in the interior. Here, though, aggression was spearheaded less by Europeans than by their settlers overseas. Europe's governments had discovered early on that colonists separated from home by thousands of miles felt little need to follow orders. Since the sixteenth century, Lisbon, Madrid, London, and Paris had issued rafts of regulations on trade, tea, slaves, and stamps, but Brazil, Mexico, Massachusetts, and Quebec had ignored them. Even when kings' demands were quite mild—that colonists pay for their own defense, for instance—white settlers regularly refused and fought back against efforts to coerce them. After Britain lost the United States, it only held on to Canada, South Africa, Australia, and New Zealand by giving them most of what the American rebels had demanded. France sold off its last North American holdings in 1803; by 1825, Spain had lost all its American holdings except Cuba and Puerto Rico, and at that point Portugal's stake had been wiped out altogether.

European governments had hesitated to push inland, worrying about the costs of conquest, and sometimes even about the rights of local people. The white settlers, however, had fewer qualms. Americans were streaming across the Appalachians even before the ink was dry on the Declaration of Independence, and the Chickamauga Wars (1776–94) began a century of attacks on natives. In the 1820s white Australians followed the same path, conquering Tasmania and breaking into their continent's interior. In the 1830s, South African Boers struck out on their own to escape British regulation and at the Battle of Blood River shot dead three thousand Zulus for a loss of just three wounded Afrikaners. In the 1840s New Zealanders went to war with the Maori and the United States reached the Pacific, finally stretching from sea to shining sea.

A great native retreat was under way, but what turned it into a rout was the railroad. In the 1830s Americans laid down twice as much track as the whole of Europe combined, then doubled this in the 1840s and tripled it again in the 1850s. The iron horse moved millions of migrants westward and carried the supplies the army needed as it herded Native Americans into ever-more-remote reservations. By the 1880s, railroads were also bringing miners from Cape Town to dig up gold and diamonds in Transvaal and taking Russian settlers and soldiers to Samarkand. In 1896 a British army striking into Sudan to crush an Islamist uprising even built a railway as it went.

The last barrier to Western expansion—disease—collapsed between 1880 and 1920. In the space of a single lifetime, doctors isolated and conquered cholera, typhoid, malaria, sleeping sickness, and the Black Death. Only yellow fever (responsible for thirteen out of every fourteen deaths in the Spanish-American War of 1898) held out until the 1930s.

The consequences were felt all over the tropics, but most powerfully in Africa. As late as 1870, hardly any Europeans had gone more than a day or two's walk from the coast, but by 1890 steamships and railroads were moving thousands of them inland, and medicine was keeping them alive when they got there. For centuries, the only way to get ivory, gold, slaves, and anything else Europeans wanted had been by cutting deals with long chains of African chiefs, each of them taking a slice of the profits, but now the Europeans could take charge themselves.

As often happens, solving one problem just created another. Quinine and vaccines worked just as well on French and Belgians as on English and Americans, with the result that traders who braved deserts, jungles, and hostile natives kept finding that other Europeans had got there ahead of them. In a rerun of what had happened in America and India centuries earlier, the men on the ground lobbied their governments to take over great slices of Africa and keep other westerners out.

Annexation often needed only a few hundred Western soldiers. Africans and Asians had worked hard at catching up with European firepower since the 1750s (after a particularly hard-fought battle in India in 1803, the British commander confessed, "I never was in so severe a business in my life or anything like it, and pray to God, I never may be in such a situation again"), but Western firepower just kept getting better. In the 1850s, proper rifles—that is, guns with grooves inside the barrel to make bullets spin, increasing their range and accuracy—came into general use, with devastating results.

Steam-powered factories churned out rifles by the ten thousands, each one perfectly machined and far less likely to misfire than preindustrial muskets. Americans particularly shone at this mass production; British observers were astonished in 1854 when a workman at the Springfield Armory in Massachusetts randomly chose ten muskets made at the factory across the previous decade, disassembled them, threw the parts into a box, and reassembled them into ten perfectly working guns. The British immediately bought American machinery and founded the Enfield Armoury. "There is nothing that cannot be produced by machines," Samuel Colt told them.

When both sides had rifles and knew how to use them, as in the American Civil War, thousands of men could be mowed down in minutes. September 17, 1862, remains the single bloodiest day in the history of American armies, with nearly twenty-three thousand men killed or wounded at the Battle of Antietam (usually called Sharpsburg in the South). In Africa and Asia, though, Europeans rarely faced much return fire from rifles. General Henry Havelock's comment in 1857 after annihilating a huge Indian army that ambushed his tiny British column—"In ten minutes the affair was decided"—could be applied to dozens of mid-century slaughters, from Senegal to Siam. The Gatling gun (patented 1861), Carnehan and Dravot's beloved Martini-Henry rifle (introduced 1871), and the fully automatic Maxim gun (patented 1884) made the firepower gap between the West and the rest so wide (Figure 4.12) that only rank incompetence, of the kind British officers exhibited against the Zulus at Isandlwana in 1879 and Italians against Ethiopians at Adwa in 1896, could close it.

By the nineteenth century's end, Western armies went more or less wherever they wanted, and Western navies had even more freedom. European ships had had no serious rivals since the seventeenth century, but the nineteenth-century introduction of steel-plated steamships and explosive shells made resistance futile. The first clash of ironclads, the point-blank shoot-out between the *Monitor* and the *Merrimack** during the American Civil War, had amazed onlookers, but by the 1890s battleships were displacing fifteen thousand to seventeen thousand tons, steaming at sixteen knots, carrying four twelve-inch guns, and fighting duels at five miles' range. European governments spent fortunes on these ships, only for them to become

---

*The *Monitor* and the *Merrimack* were both originally Union ships, but after the *Merrimack* was sunk, the Confederates raised its wreck and refitted it as an ironclad, launched under the name CSS *Virginia*.

Figure 4.12. Mind the gap: by 1879, when this photograph was taken, the fire-power gap between Western and non-Western armies was enormous. Here, the Zulu prince Dabulamanzi kaMpande (center) and his men display their motley collection of shotguns, hunting rifles, and antique muskets. Dabulamanzi would soon be repulsed from Rorke's Drift, despite outnumbering the defenders ten to one. Only when Western officers were extremely incompetent could non-Western armies win.

instantly obsolete in 1906, when Britain launched HMS *Dreadnought*, complete with turbine engines, eleven-inch armor, and ten twelve-inch guns. Five years later British battleships switched from coal to oil, and by then, with a single exception that I will return to in Chapter 5, the maritime gap between the West and the rest was absolutely unbridgeable.

When I was a little boy, my grandmother had a battered globe that must have been made right around this time. Its paper surface was bubbled and peeling, but it fascinated me. British newspapers in the 1960s were full of stories of national humiliation and the retreat from empire, but here, in this little time capsule, everything was different. Two-fifths of the planet was colored pink, for the British Empire. "On her dominions the sun never sets," Scotland's oldest newspaper had rejoiced as early as 1821. "While sinking from the waters of Lake Superior, his eye opens upon the Mouth of the Ganges" (Figure 4.13).

Altogether, Europeans or their former colonists ruled five-sixths of the world, but not even Granny's globe captured the full magnitude of Europe's victory in the Five Hundred Years' War. Western dominion was so profound that historians regularly suggest that the word "empire" does not

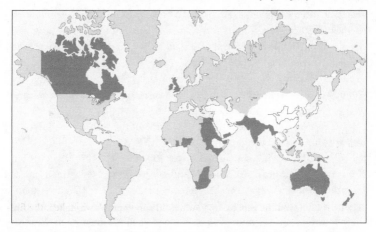

Figure 4.13. The scale of victory: by 1900, Europeans had conquered 84 percent of the earth's surface (shown in light gray; British Empire shown in dark gray).

really do it justice. Rather, they propose, we should think of a nineteenth-century "world-system," in which formal empires ruled from European capitals were just one—and not necessarily the most important—part of a wider web of connections binding the entire earth.

This was not exactly Adam Smith's vision of a world held together by self-interest, but it was closer to it than the empires of earlier ages. By 1850 the invisible hand and the invisible fist were cooperating in entirely new ways. The Royal Navy kept the seas free and punished people who offended against the open-access order (between 1807 and 1860, it effectively shut down the Atlantic slave trade, seizing sixteen hundred ships and returning the 150,000 slaves on them to West Africa), but the system was so big that there was never any possibility of Britain directly ruling it. The home islands were undoubtedly its center, but what coordination London did impose depended on providing incentives to the formally independent parts to act in ways that kept the system as a whole going.

The goal toward which Britain tried to nudge the world-system was simple enough. "The great object of the Government in every quarter of the world," the prime minister told Parliament in 1839, "was to extend the commerce of the country." But doing this nudging was anything but simple. British leaders had to coordinate four wildly different tools. The first was the United Kingdom itself, home to the biggest industrial economy on earth and a booming population that sent out more migrants than any other nation. The Royal Navy, stronger than the next-strongest two or even three fleets combined, kept open the sea-lanes for emigrants, imports, and exports—meaning not only cotton, steel, and machines but also a seductive soft power, which gave the world business suits, sandwiches, and soccer as well as Dickens, Darwin, and Kipling.

The second tool, located on the other side of the world, was India. As well as running an enormous trade deficit with Britain, as early as the 1820s the subcontinent paid for an army of over 200,000 men. This was, in effect, Britain's strategic reserve. When Napoleon needed to be thrown out of Egypt in 1799, or Chinese markets forced open in 1839, or the shah of Persia bullied in 1856, or Russia shut out of Afghanistan in 1879 (or, for that matter, when Rommel needed to be stopped at El Alamein in 1942), most of the men who did the job were Indians.

The flood of British emigrants—altogether, about twenty million of them—built the third tool, resource-rich white settler colonies on other continents. Their explosive economic growth mattered more and more as the nineteenth century wore on, and in the twentieth their young men were as important as India's in defending the world-system.

Finally, there was a fourth tool: a sprawling network of capital, experts, shipping, telegraphs, financial services, and investment. This vast, invisible empire extended far beyond the areas colored pink on the globe. Entire countries—Argentina, Chile, Persia—became so dependent on British markets and money that historians often call them an informal empire. They did not take direct orders from British politicians, but they rarely dared defy British financiers. By the 1890s, shipping and services brought three-quarters as much money into Britain as merchandise exports.

Keeping this elaborate world-system working was a tricky balancing act. It required Asian empires to remain weak, Europe to remain at peace (or at least not to be forced into a single, hostile empire by a new Napoleon waging people's wars), and the United States to remain strong but cooperative. And since Britain could rarely compel any of these actors to play their appointed parts, everything depended on a delicate mixture of gunboat diplomacy, market pressure, and enlightened self-interest.

There were constant crises. The worst was in India, where a great mutiny in 1857 might have expelled the British altogether had it been better led. In Europe, an ugly war had to be fought in Crimea between 1854 and

1856 to stop Russia from disrupting the balance of power, and on the American front war scares were constant. In 1844, arguments over the latitude of the U.S.-Canadian border grew so heated that "Fifty-four forty or fight!" became a presidential campaign slogan. In 1859, troops dug in and gunboats were sent to the same border after a British pig wandered into an American potato patch. And in 1861, with America's house divided against itself, war loomed again when Union sailors boarded a British ship.

But war never came. While damping down an earlier crisis in 1858, this time over British sailors boarding American ships, the American president, James Buchanan, had reminded Congress that "no two nations have ever existed on the face of the earth which could do each other so much good or so much harm." Congress agreed, and after making due allowance for local circumstances, most governments in Asia and Europe came to similar conclusions. For almost everyone, there was more to gain from buying into the British system than from trying to break it.

Pax Britannica

"I think there's an enormous amount to be proud of in what the British Empire did," Britain's prime minister, David Cameron, said in 2013. "But of course," he added, "there were bad events as well as good ones."

He was speaking at Amritsar, where, nearly a century earlier, British troops had gunned down thousands of unarmed Indian protesters, killing 379 of them. Immediately, Cameron's words were assailed from every side. To some, they smacked of hand-wringing liberal self-loathing; to others, they indicated his gross insensitivity and nostalgia for imperialism.

Prime ministers expect to be pilloried for everything they say, but there is probably no way to try to evaluate the legacy of Europe's Five Hundred Years' War without being accused of political bias. Accepting that, I will steel myself for the worst and come right to the point: the Five Hundred Years' War was the most productive—in the sense I have used that word in this book—war the world had so far seen, creating the biggest, safest, and most prosperous society (or world-system) yet. In 1415, the globe had been fragmented, with each continent dominated by a cluster of regional powers. By 1914, this ancient mosaic was gone, replaced by just three or four powers with truly global reach (France, Germany, the United States, and, of course, the United Kingdom), tightly linked in a system dominated by Britain. Europe had (almost) conquered the world.

The marriage of invisible hand and invisible fist made the modern world-system very different from any premodern empire, but the Five Hundred Years' War that created it had nevertheless followed a broadly familiar pattern. First came a conquest phase, driving up rates of violent death; next, in many cases, came an era of rebellion, with more great bloodlettings; and finally came an age of peace and prosperity as violence declined and economies were reconstructed on a larger scale.

The timing of the phases depended on where you lived. The wave of conquest broke on South and Central America in the sixteenth century, on North America in the seventeenth through nineteenth centuries, on India in the eighteenth and nineteenth centuries, on China in the mid-nineteenth century, and on Africa in the late nineteenth century, with the major rebellions generally coming hard on the heels of the end of the conquests.

The effects varied as much as the timing. In the Americas, invaders visited unspeakable horrors on the natives (and, it should be said, the natives repaid them in kind when they could), but, as we saw earlier in this chapter, the great killer was disease. If, as I think we should, we count the victims of pestilence and famine among the war dead, the figures are shocking. Between 1500 and 1650, the Native population of the New World fell by half. Those historians who call the conquest an "American holocaust" have a point.

In South Asia, the East India Company's conquests from the 1740s onward must have killed hundreds of thousands of natives, usually for minimal losses on the European side. Out of a population that started this period around 175 million and steadily grew, however, all the shooting and sabering can only have added a fraction of 1 percent to the death rate. One historian has claimed that the British massacred some 10 million people after the 1857 mutiny, or 1 Indian in 25, but although the reprisals were savage enough to shock many Britons, almost all experts put the true figure almost an order of magnitude lower. A death toll running into the hundreds of thousands remains appalling, but even at their worst the British killed less than 1 Indian in 250.

As in the European conquest of the Americas, the biggest killer was not direct violence but its consequences, which in India meant famine more often than disease. Between the Great Bengal Famine of 1769–70 and the All-India Famine of 1899–1900, a horrifying thirty to fifty million Indians starved. Roughly a billion people lived in India across these 130 years, and so one in twenty or one in thirty people died from war-related famines—*if*, that is, this horror should be laid entirely at the British door.

Bad weather, particularly El Niño events, was the immediate cause of most of these disasters, but some historians argue that a combination of the disruption caused by conquest and the callousness and/or stupidity of the conquerors turned unavoidable climate-driven crises into entirely avoidable human catastrophes. The blame game has been ugly ever since it began in the 1850s, but even the most anti-European critic would have to concede that the conquest of India was much less lethal than that of America.

In China, the pattern was different again. European (and, to a lesser degree, Japanese) invasions between the 1840s and the 1890s killed hundreds of thousands. About 750 million people lived in China across this half century, meaning that the wars directly killed roughly one person in a thousand, but here the biggest death toll began when the Qing dynasty fell apart and rebels rose up all over China. These civil wars took tens of millions of lives. China's population fell by 10 percent between 1840 and 1870, with violence and its train of starvation and disease causing most of this loss.

To complete this catalog of horrors, we should note the huge variations between the experiences of different parts of Africa. In some places, Europeans met almost no resistance and had minimal impact on the people they supposedly ruled. The vast French holdings in West Africa, for instance, were something of a virtual empire, in which virtually no officials administered virtually no subjects in the virtually empty wastes of the Sahara Desert. But in other places, the story was gruesome. The extreme case was the Congo Basin, seized by Belgium in 1884. Here a brutal system of punishing natives for not delivering rubber quotas might have cut the population in half by 1908, mostly through starvation and disease.

No one can deny that the Five Hundred Years' War made the world more dangerous for the people being conquered. Europeans, like ancient Romans, regularly created wastelands. But—again like the Romans—the legacy of war was peace. In most cases, once the gun smoke had cleared, shattered institutions had been rebuilt, and new antibodies had evolved, the conquered found themselves ruled by powerful new Leviathans that aggressively suppressed violence—much as Dravot and Carnehan did in Kafiristan.

To many westerners, this civilizing mission made imperialism a moral cause. "Take up the White man's burden," Kipling urged the United States in 1899,

> Send forth the best ye breed
> Go bind your sons to exile
> To serve your captives' need . . .
>
> Take up the White man's burden,
> In patience to abide,
> To veil the threat of terror
> And check the show of pride;
> By open speech and simple,
> An hundred times made plain.
> To seek another's profit,
> And work another's gain.

Within days of its publication, the poem was inspiring parodies ("Pile on the brown man's burden," went one, "To gratify your greed; Go, clear away the 'niggers,' Who progress would impede"), and it is hard to read Kipling's words today without squirming. Yet he was far from alone in seeing the world this way. Thousands of official memos, deposited in dusty or mildewed district offices from Mauritania to Malaya, record the earnestness with which functionaries at every level threw themselves into veiling the threat of terror and checking the show of pride. "These petty principalities are enjoying the full measure of British protection and are in a state of the most profound tranquility," wrote one Lieutenant Murray in an 1824 report, looking back on ten years of pacification in Nepal. "Murder is seldom committed and robbery unknown, and several Rajas are content and their subjects receiving all the blessings of a mild and happy rule. The cultivation has improved in a fourfold degree, and the mountains are clad in stepped verdure to the base."

But did Murray—or Kipling—know what he was talking about? Or were both men simply lying to justify an empire from which they profited at the subjects' expense? Answering this question is difficult, not least because of the sheer variety of places in the nineteenth-century world-system. In Australia, where Europeans almost annihilated the natives, or Ascension Island, uninhabited by any vertebrate before the British arrived, pacification was a very different business from, say, in Indochina, where a few thousand Frenchmen parachuted into the middle of thirty million natives.

And even within a single region, it could be hard to tell what was going on. As usual, India is the best-known (and most controversial) case. Here the East India Company, focused on maximizing profits, threw itself into pacification. The same Mughal breakdown that had given the company its opening in the 1740s had also filled the subcontinent with warring princes, and—although reliable statistics are once again sorely lacking—all the evidence suggests that rates of violent death had leaped up as law and order broke down. The squabbling nawabs and sultans had hired thousands of irregular cavalry to fight each other, and, thrown out of work, many of them turned into bandits, terrorizing the peasantry. Eighteenth-century India's roads were infested with highwaymen (some said to be *thugees*, members of a cult devoted to strangling travelers in honor of the goddess Kali), and the countryside was awash with guns.

Like any competent stationary bandit, the company cracked down on these roving bandits. But—like all too many stationary bandits—the company's activities were so violent (and profitable) that observers often wondered whether the cure was not worse than the disease. Heaps "of rupees, sacks of diamonds, Indians tortured to disclose their treasure," one London pamphleteer lamented; "cities, towns and villages ransacked and destroyed, jaghires and provinces purloined; Nabobs dethroned, and murdered, have found the delights and constituted the religions of the Directors and their servants."

Already in 1773, the British government tried to regulate the company into being a better stationary bandit. The company's officers "shall not accept, receive or take directly . . . from any of the *Indian* princes or Powers, or their Ministers or Agents (or any of the natives of *Asia*) any Present, Gift, Donation, Opportunity or Reward," Parliament ruled. The men on the ground, however, took little notice until in 1786 Parliament decided on its own crackdown. It impeached Warren Hastings, the company's governor, charging him with high crimes and misdemeanors—basically, with making a wasteland.

Edmund Burke led the charge, for all the world like Cicero come again to bring down the modern-day equivalent of the venal Roman governor Verres. "I impeach him in the name of the English nation," he thundered, "whose ancient honour he has sullied. I impeach him in the name of the people of India, whose rights he has trodden under foot, and whose country he has turned into a desert. Lastly, in the name of human nature itself, in the name of both sexes, in the name of every age, in the name of every rank, I impeach the common enemy of all."

And that was just Burke's opening statement. The trial went on, with one lurid revelation after another, for seven shameful years. In the end, despite an ocean of evidence, the House of Lords acquitted Hastings, but it was no victory for the company. Britain had had enough of this kind of pacification. Parliament passed another India Act, taking over the right to appoint governor-generals and setting the stage for the rise of the famously incorruptible Indian Civil Service.

The Parliament in London, like Leviathans in every age, remained more interested in lowering its administrative costs than in creating open-access order among its subjects. In one notorious case, begun in 1808, the judge who prosecuted a particularly vicious English settler for beating and starving an Indian servant to death seemed less worried that the defendant's actions were "injurious . . . to the peace and happiness of our native subjects" than that he had "defied my authority [and] conducted himself in a manner highly disrespectful to the Court."

But whatever their motives, judges sent out from Britain did gradually roll back the company's rough-and-ready martial law and reduce the violence of Indian life. The most visible consequence was a blanket ban on the Hindu ritual of sati, in which a widow would throw herself onto her husband's funeral pyre. Several Mughal emperors had legislated against sati ("in all lands under Mughal control, never again should officials allow a woman to be burned," Aurangzeb had ruled in 1663), with some success, but the British blanket ban of 1829 more or less eradicated it.

Documents written by educated Indians in the eighteenth and nineteenth centuries have little to say about rates of violent death, but a remarkable number of their authors seem to have concluded that the British Empire was, on balance, no bad thing. The extraordinary Calcutta-based scholar Rammohun Roy, for instance, embraced British liberalism, education, and law and joined the British crusade against sati. Roy did not hesitate to criticize the Europeans; he rebuked the British in 1823 for being slow to teach the "useful sciences" to Bengalis and had a smart put-down for a bishop of Calcutta who mistakenly congratulated him on converting from Hinduism to Christianity ("My lord," Roy said, "I did not abandon one superstition merely to take up another"). But when all was said and done, Roy thought that the ideal outcome for India would be to remain within the British Empire, in a position like Canada's. "India, in a like manner [as the Canadians]," he wrote in 1832, "will feel no disposition to cut off its connection with England, which may be preserved with so much mutual benefit to both countries."

Other Indians—such as the members of the Young Bengal movement, who shocked their elders in the 1830s by championing Tom Paine over Hindu scriptures—went much further in their admiration of all things Anglo. But their opinions, just like Roy's and Lieutenant Murray's, remain mere impressions. Until social historians do the kind of painstaking archival work that vindicated Elias's claims about Europeans becoming less violent, or until physical anthropologists catalog much more skeletal evidence of violent trauma, we have to continue to rely on qualitative evidence, just as we do in studying ancient times. But even so, the weight of the documentation does seem to be overwhelming. Despite their smugness, Kipling and Murray really were onto something. Once the conquests died down and the rebellions were suppressed, European empires generally drove down rates of violent death.

That said, the colonies and frontiers always remained rougher than Europe's imperial heartland. By 1900, homicide was taking the life of only one western European in sixteen hundred, but one American in every two hundred was still dying violently at that point. And even within the white settler colonies, there were stark differences between the urban cores and the wilder peripheries: murder was no more common in New England than in old England, but parts of the West and the South were ten times as dangerous. (According to one story, a southerner, quizzed about this by a Yankee, "replied that he reckoned there were just more folks in the South who needed killing.")

The likelihood of being killed in war fell almost as fast as the chance of being murdered. When we throw in all the battles, sieges, and feuds, about one western European in twenty was dying violently around 1415, but between 1815 and 1914, Europeans fought few major wars. The muddy, bloody Crimean War of 1853–56 killed 300,000, the Franco-Prussian War of 1870–71 another 400,000 or more, and the Russo-Turkish War of 1877–78 a further half million. This was a lot of slaughter, and yet, even after adding in every single war, less than one European in fifty (and probably closer to one in a hundred) can have died in conflict between 1815 and 1914.

Wars within and between white settler colonies (as opposed to wars they waged against nonwhites) were almost as rare. In the Americas, the horrific War of the Triple Alliance between 1864 and 1870 (in which Argentina, Brazil, and Uruguay blocked Paraguayan expansion) claimed about half a million lives, and the American Civil War (1861–65) took closer to three-quarters of a million. In Africa, the Second Boer War (1899–1902) killed at least sixty thousand. Overall, Europeans who settled overseas were more likely to die violently than those who stayed home, but not much more so.

The Five Hundred Years' War was far bigger than the wars that built the ancient empires. Mass armies with iron weapons had allowed the Romans, Han, Parthians, and Mauryans to project power on a subcontinental scale, but oceangoing ships, guns, and steam power extended Europeans' reach across the entire planet. Ancient wars produced societies tens of millions strong, with rates of violent death, I suggested, in the 2–5 percent range, but the Five Hundred Years' War produced societies hundreds of millions strong, with rates of violent death in the European core in the 1–3 percent range. Rates were slightly higher in the American and Australasian white settler colonies, and those in direct-rule colonies higher still.

Patchy data, lack of scholarly study, and the sheer variety of places involved—ranging from hells on earth such as the Congo through Margaret Mead's Samoa to sleepy outposts in Nepal—combine to make meaningful estimates of rates of violent death in the nineteenth-century empires almost impossible. This means that the number I offer in Figure 4.14—somewhere between 2.5 and 7.5 percent—is perhaps the most speculative in this whole book. It simply means that on average, nineteenth-century direct-rule colonies in Africa, Asia, and Oceania were more violent than the ancient empires but less violent than Eurasia in the age of migrations. One day, archival research and skeletal studies will allow us to make much better estimates, but we are not there yet.

What Calgacus said about Rome's wars of conquest was just as true of Europe's: both made wastelands. But on the other hand, what Cicero said about Rome's empire was also true of Europe's: both eventually drew their subjects into larger economic systems, which, in most cases, made them better-off. It is hard to argue with the economist Daron Acemoglu and the political scientist James Robinson when they say in their influential recent book, *Why Nations Fail*, that "the profitability of European colonial empires was often built on the destruction of independent polities and indigenous economies." And yet, as Figure 4.15 shows, this was what economists like to call creative destruction. As new economic systems replaced old ones, income and productivity rose all over the world after

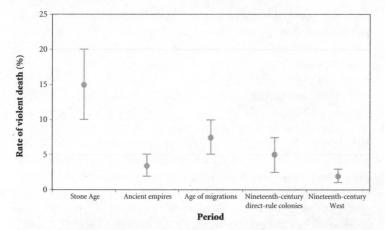

Figure 4.14. Getting better most of the time, version 1: estimates of rates of violent death, showing the range for each period (10–20 percent for Stone Age societies, 2–5 percent for ancient empires, 5–10 percent for Eurasia in the age of migrations, 1–3 percent for the nineteenth-century West, and 2.5–7.5 percent for Europe's direct-rule colonies) and its midpoint

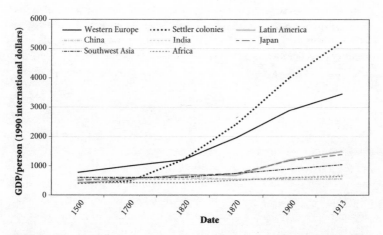

Figure 4.15. Getting better most of the time, version 2: productivity per person per year, 1500–1913, as calculated by the economist Angus Maddison and expressed in 1990 "international" dollars (an artificial unit commonly used to sidestep the problems of calculating conversion rates over long periods of time)

1870. There were certainly exceptions (the Congo again springs to mind), and the bulk of the gains did flow to the rulers of the new world-system. But as the nineteenth century drew to a close, the rising tide of the Five Hundred Years' War was lifting all the boats, making the world richer than ever as well as safer.

So it was that in August 1898, Nicholas II, tsar of all the Russias, drew what seemed to be the obvious conclusion and ordered his foreign minister to make an unprecedented announcement to the dignitaries who danced attendance on his court. "The preservation of a general peace and a possible reduction in the excessive armaments that now burden every nation," it said, "are ideals toward which all governments should strive." Nicholas therefore proposed an international conference—"a happy overture to the century ahead"—to discuss the end of war and mass disarmament.

General delight ensued. Baroness Bertha von Suttner, author of the international bestseller *Lay Down Your Arms* (one of Tolstoy's favorites) and soon to become the first woman to win the Nobel Peace Prize, called Nicholas "a new star in the cultural heavens," and in 1899—on the tsar's birthday, in fact—130 diplomats convened at a sylvan château near The Hague, in the doggedly neutral Netherlands, to work everything out.

After two months of dining, dancing, and decreeing, they emerged with a string of agreements, if not to end war, then at least to limit its barbarity. They agreed, enthusiastically, that another meeting was called for. This duly convened in 1907 at the same delightful spot, and such was its success that everyone made firm plans to gather there again—in 1914.

5

STORM OF STEEL:
THE WAR FOR EUROPE, 1914–1980s

Cosmos into Chaos

The *Daily Mail* has never been the mouthpiece of Britain's chattering classes ("produced by office-boys for office-boys," one prime minister acidly remarked around 1900), but a century ago it was the country's bestselling broadsheet, and Norman Angell—its Paris editor—was a man accustomed to being listened to. Even he, though, was astonished at the success of his book *The Great Illusion* when it appeared in 1910.

Angell was a character. After abandoning an expensive Swiss boarding school at seventeen, he had run off to California, where he tried his luck at pig-farming, ditch-digging, cattle-ranching, and mail-carrying. But then he drifted back to Europe, and now, approaching respectable middle age, he turned more Kantian than Kant himself. Updating *Perpetual Peace* for the twentieth century, he asked: "What is the real guarantee of good behaviour of one state to another?" His answer: "It is the elaborate interdependence which, not only in the economic sense, but in every sense, makes an unwarrantable aggression of one state upon another react upon the interests of the aggressor." War, he concluded, had put itself out of business. "The day for progress by force has passed," he pronounced; from now on, "it will be progress by ideas or not at all."

Angell joined the long list of prophets with terrible timing. In 1914, the same politicians who had praised his book and attended the Hague peace conferences set off World War I, and over the next four years they killed fifteen million people. The civil wars that dragged on for another four years killed another twenty million, and between 1939 and 1945 the greatest war of all killed fifty to a hundred million more. Angell was perhaps the worst prophet ever.

But then again . . . if Angell could have come back a century after he wrote, he might have claimed to be the *best* prophet of all time. In 2010 the planet was more peaceful and prosperous than ever before. The risk of violent death had fallen well below one in a hundred (in western Europe, below one in three thousand). People typically lived twice as long, ate well enough to grow four inches taller, and earned four times as much as their great-grandparents had in 1910.

The twentieth century was the best of times and it was the worst of times, what the great historian Eric Hobsbawm called an "age of extremes," combining the bloodiest war ever fought with the greatest peace ever known. Angell went on writing books for another forty years after *The Great Illusion* came out but never really did explain this paradox.

The easiest way out of the conundrum, which Angell sometimes took, was to insist that the big story was that the world really was going the way he (and Kant) had said, but that bad luck had intervened. Given the way the First World War began, in an absolute avalanche of bad luck, this seemed rather reasonable. If Austria's Archduke Franz Ferdinand had just decided not to go to Sarajevo on June 28, 1914 (Figure 5.1), he would not have been murdered, Austria would not have declared war on Serbia, and Russia, Germany, France, and Britain would have stayed at peace too. Or if the head of Austrian security that day had not published the archduke's route through Sarajevo in advance, let him ride in an open-topped car going at ten miles an hour, and refused to have any of the seventy thousand troops on maneuvers nearby serve as security details because their uniforms would be dirty, the terrorist plot would surely have failed. If the security chief had not then forgotten to tell the drivers of the first two cars in the archduke's convoy about a change in the route; if he had not stopped them and had the whole convoy back up, so that it was moving even slower as it passed the assassin Gavrilo Princip; if he had put the archduke's bodyguard on the side of the car facing the crowd, rather than the side facing the empty road; if another Serb had not attacked the policeman who grabbed Princip's hand as he pulled his revolver . . . if any of these things had gone differently, there would have been no July Crisis. The Guns of August would not have fired. And come December, a million young men would still have been alive. Accident has a lot to answer for.

When the war was over, the politicians who had led their people into it

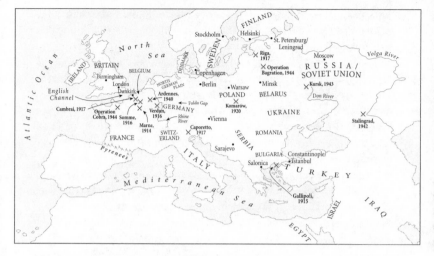

Figure 5.1. The great wars: the fight for Europe, 1910s-1980s

embraced this argument, rushing to reassure readers that the catastrophe had not been their fault. "The nations in 1914 slithered over the brink into the boiling cauldron of war without any trace of apprehension or dismay," Britain's wartime prime minister, David Lloyd George, claimed in his memoirs. Going one better, Winston Churchill (first lord of the Admiralty in 1914) suggested that the war had been a force of nature, beyond anyone's control. "One must think of the intercourse of nations in those days," he wrote in 1922,

> as prodigious organizations of forces active or latent which, like planetary bodies, could not approach each other in space without giving rise to profound magnetic reactions. If they got too near, the lightnings would begin to flash, and beyond a certain point they might be attracted altogether from the orbits in which they were restrained . . . and plunge Cosmos into Chaos.

And yet the letters, diaries, and cabinet minutes that politicians actually wrote during the doomed summer of 1914 reveal something entirely different. Europe's leaders were not slithering, sliding, or suffering from magnetic attraction. In reality, they coldly, calmly, and with all due calculation considered the risks and, one after another, concluded that war was their best option. Even after it was clear what the costs of war would be, more countries kept coming in—Turkey late in 1914, Italy and Bulgaria in 1915, Romania in 1916, and the United States in 1917. And in 1939, with no illusions left at all, the politicians condemned tens of millions more to death.

Should we conclude that all these politicians, with all their years of education and experience, were in fact fools, so blinded by irrational fears and hatreds that they could not see where their peoples' best interests lay? Judging from the number of books with titles like *The March of Folly*, many historians would answer yes. But this is superficial: the twentieth century's leaders were neither wiser nor more foolish than those of other ages, neither more nor less predisposed to think that force would solve their problems than the men we met in Chapters 1–4. The reason that the last century combined such violence with such peace and prosperity was that the legacy of the Five Hundred Years' War was more complicated than Angell—and many writers since his time—realized.

Unknown Unknowns

"When constabulary duty's to be done, to be done," the chorus sings in Gilbert and Sullivan's comic opera *The Pirates of Penzance*, "a policeman's lot is not an 'appy one." Audiences hooted with laughter when the show first went onstage in 1879, but the masters of the world-system were perhaps not amused.

For two generations, Britain had (usually) been willing and able to play globocop because, as late as 1860, it was the only truly industrialized economy on earth. British factories turned out better, cheaper goods than anyone else's, and so long as the seas were safe for free trade, these could always find buyers. Britons could then use their profits to purchase food wherever it was best and cheapest, and the farmers selling the food could use the profits from these sales to buy more British goods, allowing the British to buy more food . . . and so on. Britain had the money to play globocop, and needed to play globocop to keep making money.

Everyone involved prospered, but Britain prospered most of all. Its gross domestic product (GDP) almost tripled between 1820 and 1870, increasing from 5 percent to 9 percent of the world's total (today it is 3 percent). Ships and bases to keep the sea-lanes open cost money, but the British economy grew so fast that they seemed like a bargain, costing just sixpence out of every pound of wealth being produced—less than 3 percent of GDP.

By the 1870s, though, Britain was finding constabulary duty less happy, not because it was doing it badly, but because it was doing it too well. As

British profits accumulated, the same free trade that allowed Britain to prosper also allowed the country's capitalists to invest their surplus wealth wherever it promised to bring the highest returns—which, much of the time, meant financing industrial revolutions in other countries. Relying heavily on British loans (often using British money to buy British machines that could produce goods that would compete with British exports), a string of countries industrialized after 1870. That Britain's ancient rival France would go this way surprised no one, but civil wars in the United States (1861–65) and Japan (1864–68) and wars of unification in Germany (1864–71) also produced centralized governments that aggressively pursued industrialization (Figure 5.2). In 1880, Britain still accounted for 23 percent of the world's manufacturing and trade, but by 1913 this had fallen to 14 percent.

In purely economic terms, this was in fact good for Britain, because as the world industrialized, the pie got bigger. Fourteen percent of the world's manufacturing and trade in 1913 added up to a lot more than 23 percent in 1870. Further, Britain was moving up the value chain. It had shifted from agriculture toward more profitable industries after the 1780s, and in the 1870s it shifted again, abandoning investment in industry for greater profits from services (particularly banking, shipping, insurance, and foreign loans). Britain's GDP more than doubled between 1870 and 1913, and with all this extra wealth Britain (and other industrializing nations) could afford

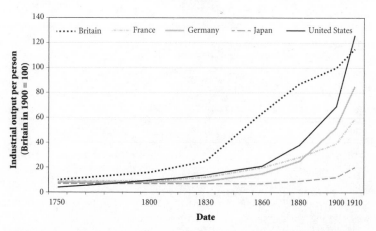

Figure 5.2. Dark satanic mills: industrial output per person in five major economies, 1750–1913 (Britain's output in 1900 is treated as 100 points)

to expand its open-access order aggressively. Germany led the way, introducing health insurance and old-age pensions for workers in the 1880s, and by 1913 most industrialized nations had followed. Free primary education, universal male suffrage, and eventually votes for women became the norm.

Strategically, though, the economic triumph was a disaster for Britain, because its strategy, much like the strategies of the ancient empires seventeen centuries earlier, had overshot its culminating point. The United States' economy outgrew Britain's in 1872, and in 1901 so did Germany's (Figure 5.3). Every newly wealthy government now built a modern fleet to project its power and prestige. Britain stayed in front, more than quadrupling the size and firepower of its navy between 1880 and 1914, but its share of global gunnery nonetheless declined (Figure 5.4). The globocop could take on any plausible combination of enemies but could no longer intimidate everyone at once.

If Britain was the world's policeman, we might think of the new industrial giants as being rather like urban gangs. The globocop, like any cop, had to decide whether to confront these rivals, cut deals with them, or do some combination of the two. Britain could wage trade wars on its rivals, wage shooting wars on them, or make concessions. The first two options threatened to ruin the free trade that made Britain rich; the third, to strengthen the rivals so much that Britain would no longer be able to play globocop.

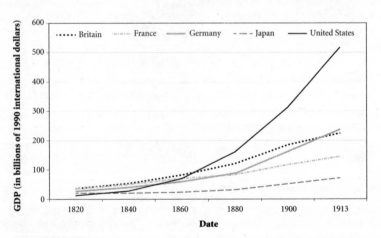

Figure 5.3. The rise of the rest: the size of five major industrial economies, 1820–1913

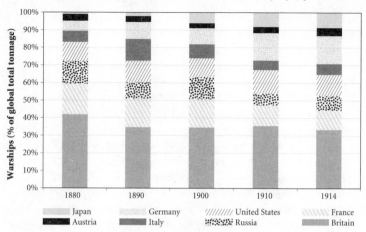

Figure 5.4. Unhappy lot: the decline of the globocop's naval power relative to Germany, Japan, and the United States, 1880–1914

Matters came to a head first with the United States. The 1823 Monroe Doctrine had in theory banned European meddling in American waters, but in the 1860s the prospect of the Royal Navy intervening in the Civil War remained Abraham Lincoln's worst nightmare. By the 1890s, though, it was clear to all that Britain was no longer strong enough to project power into the western Atlantic while also meeting its other obligations. Facing facts, London initiated a "great rapprochement" with Washington. The globocop effectively took on a deputy, giving it its own beat.

Britain retreated even further in eastern waters. Japan was the only non-Western country that had succeeded in responding to the European on-slaught by industrializing itself, and in the 1890s it was without doubt the greatest power in northeast Asia. Its fleet was not yet one of the world's top half-dozen, but given the distance separating Britain from the western Pacific, London concluded in 1902 that the only way to maintain some influence on the far side of the globe was a formal naval agreement, the first in Britain's history, with Japan.

Exactly a hundred years later, the U.S. defense secretary Donald Rumsfeld would tell journalists, "There are known unknowns, that is to say, we know there are some things we do not know; but there are also unknown unknowns—the ones we don't know we don't know." So long as the nineteenth century had a single, stable globocop, strategic problems were mostly known unknowns. When the Russians threatened Constantinople in 1853, or the Indians mutinied in 1857, or the Confederates fired on Fort Sumter in 1861, they did not know what the globocop would do to protect the world-system, but they did know it would do something. By the 1870s, however, unknown unknowns were multiplying. It became harder to predict whether the globocop would do anything at all. Uncertainty increased, and few could foresee the consequences of their actions. British strategists knew this, but given the grim alternatives, they kept taking on deputies. Their next deal, an entente cordiale agreed on in 1904, entrusted the Mediterranean to France so that Britain could concentrate on the biggest unknown unknown of all: Germany.

What made Germany so unknowable was its geography. In the same year that Britain cut its deal with France, Halford Mackinder—geographer, explorer, and the first director of the London School of Economics—gave an extraordinary public lecture. Twentieth-century history, he announced, would be driven by the balance between three vast regions. At the center of the story was what he called the heartland—"the pivot region of the world's politics, that vast area of Euro-Asia which is inaccessible to ships, but in antiquity lay open to the horse-riding nomads" (Figure 5.5).

Until the fifteenth century, Mackinder explained, raiders from the steppe heartland had dominated the rich civilizations of China, India, the Middle East, and Europe, which he called the inner rim. Beyond this inner rim, he also identified an outer rim, which counted for little—until, after 1500, European ships drew this huge region together. By the eighteenth century, outer-rim powers were projecting force into the inner rim, contesting the heartland's control of it, and in the nineteenth the outer rim's strength was so great that it penetrated into the heartland itself (British troops were marching into Tibet even as Mackinder delivered his lecture). Control of the outer rim's seas delivered domination of both the inner rim and the heartland—and therefore the world.

British politicians did not like sharing the outer rim with the United States, Japan, and France, but they gambled that they could strike deals with like-minded men who faced outer-rim problems much like Britain's own. Germany, though, was a different matter. It belonged to the inner rim, which gave it direct access to the heartland. Seen from London, a strong, united, industrialized Germany looked like the kind of place that might turn the heartland's resources against the outer rim. "If Germany were to ally herself with Russia," Mackinder worried, it "would permit of the

Figure 5.5. Mackinder's map: the heartland, inner rim, and outer rim

use of vast continental resources for fleet-building, and the empire of the world would then be in sight."

Seen from St. Petersburg, however, the other side of the same coin seemed more urgent—the danger that Germany might get the upper hand against France and Britain and then turn the outer rim's resources against the heartland. The real risk was not of Germany's allying with Russia; it was of Germany's conquering Russia. Napoleon had tried this, but reaching all the way from the outer rim to Moscow had been too much for him. Germany, however, might find the reach from the inner rim more manageable.

Politicians in Berlin saw a third dimension. To them, the big danger was not that Germany would exploit the outer rim or the heartland; it was that the outer rim and the heartland would combine to crush Germany between them, which had almost happened several times since the eighteenth century. That, German leaders concluded, had to be prevented at all costs, and this simple strategic fact largely explains twentieth-century Germany's tragic history.

The three visions of where Germany fit into the world pointed toward very different ways of arranging European politics, but initially the Germans had things their own way. They owed much of this success to Otto von Bismarck, arguably the least scrupulous but most clear-sighted diplomat of the nineteenth century. Bismarck saw that Germans needed to be violent in the 1860s. Short, sharp wars against Denmark, Austria, and France turned the muddle of weak German principalities into the strongest national state in the inner rim. But having won these wars, Bismarck saw that in the 1870s Germans needed to renounce violence. The best way to escape being squeezed between the heartland and the outer rim was to keep everyone else off balance, which meant making and breaking alliances in eastern and central Europe, placating Britain, and isolating France.

Bismarck kept all these balls in the air into the 1880s, but the proliferation of unknown unknowns as Britain's position deteriorated made such subtle juggling increasingly difficult. In 1890 a young new kaiser fired his aged chancellor and began wondering—as did heads of state everywhere—whether force might not, after all, be the best solution to the problems his nation faced in this uncertain world. He ordered his generals to plan preemptive wars, just in case, and German politicians played on the risk of war to distract voters' attention from the class conflicts at home caused by rapid industrialization. Bosses and workers might hate each other, but so long as both hated foreigners more, all might yet be well.

Germany's leaders found themselves taking chances that would have seemed insane in Bismarck's day, because the alternatives looked worse. Grabbing African colonies and building battleships were bound to provoke Britain, but not grabbing and building appeared to be the path to encirclement. At best, that might mean Germany's rivals could shut it out of overseas markets; at worst, it might mean war on two fronts. Germany had to do everything it could to break the circle, and yet everything it did just seemed to push its enemies closer together. With unknown unknowns multiplying and rumors of war weighing on all minds, continental powers bought more weapons, conscripted more of their young men, and kept them under arms longer—even though that threatened to turn the rumors into reality.

By 1912 the kaiser and his advisers felt that drastic measures were the only options left. Sometimes they talked about forging a United States of Europe, dominated of course by Germany; at other times, as a Viennese newspaper put it on Christmas Day 1913, they envisioned "a central European customs union that the western states would sooner or later join, like it or not. This would create an economic union that would be equal, or perhaps even superior, to America." In London or Washington, this sounded like fighting talk.

None of this made war inevitable in 1914. Franz Ferdinand could easily have survived June 28; calmer heads could easily have prevailed in the weeks that followed. Most people, in fact, thought calmer heads *had* prevailed: investors in the bond markets showed little anxiety until late July, and politicians and generals went ahead with their summer vacations. With just slightly better luck, the abiding memory of 1914 would have been its fine weather, not its killing fields.

But what would have happened then? Avoiding war in 1914 would not have revived the globocop, because the continuing spread of industrial revolutions around the world—caused by the globocop's success—would have made its position steadily less tenable. Unknown unknowns would have kept on multiplying. New crises would have followed the crisis of 1914, just as the Balkan crisis of 1914 had itself followed Moroccan crises in 1905 and 1911 and another Balkan crisis in 1912–13. Had every diplomat in twentieth-century Europe been a Bismarck born again, perhaps they could have carried on defusing emergencies indefinitely, but this was the real world, and its diplomats were, on average, no better and no worse than those of earlier ages. Every crisis was in effect a roll of the dice, and sooner or later—if not in the 1910s, then surely in the 1920s—some king or minister was going to conclude that war was, after all, the least bad solution to whatever problems were pressing on him.

And so, a month after Princip shot Franz Ferdinand, the Austro-Hungarian Empire declared war on Serbia, banking on the kaiser's assurance that he had "considered the question of Russian intervention and accepted the risk of a general war." After all, the German chancellor mused, the alternative was "self-castration." A week later most of Europe was on the march. There was no slithering over brinks, no planets spinning from their orbits; it was just a world in which the globocop had lost its grip.

The Storm Breaks

"The general aim of the war," said a document drafted for the German chancellor a month into the fighting, "is security for the German Reich in west and east for all imaginable time." To achieve that, "France must be so weakened as to make her revival as a great power impossible for all time [and] Russia must be thrust back as far as possible from Germany's eastern frontier and her domination over the non-Russian vassal peoples broken." Annexations would follow in Belgium and France, former Russian provinces would become German satellites, and British goods would be shut out of French markets. The goal was a counterproductive war, breaking the larger alliance that encircled Germany and dealing the globocop a terrible—perhaps fatal—blow.

Whether Germany went to war with this plan in mind or only formulated it in reaction to the terrible casualties of the first few weeks of fighting remains unclear, but either way the Germans were taking gigantic, terrifying risks. Bismarck's worst-case scenario came to pass in 1914, exposing Germany to the full weight of the heartland and the outer rim, and the German General Staff concluded that their one hope was to exploit their central position and industrial organization to knock France out of the war before Russia could mobilize.

Pulling off an administrative masterstroke, German bureaucrats commandeered eight thousand trains and rushed 1.6 million men and half a million horses to the western frontier. From there they swept through neutral Belgium, marching and fighting without rest. By September 7, the vanguard was across the Marne River, just twenty miles from Paris. On the map, it looked as if the war were almost won, with the French army being enveloped and forced away from its capital, but Helmuth von Moltke, the German chief of staff, was about to discover how modern warfare really worked. His twentieth-century Leviathan had called up a million-man army, which was now spread across a hundred miles, but he only had nineteenth-century ways of communicating with it. Radios were rare and unreliable, telephones were worse, and there were virtually no spotter planes.

Moltke had no idea what was actually happening in September 1914. Reports took days to reach him. One would say the French were collapsing; the next, that they were counterattacking. With no other way to find out what was going on, Moltke put a staff officer into a car and sent him to the front. "If the pessimistic [Lieutenant Colonel] Hentsch had crashed into a tree . . . somewhere on his journey of 8 September," another German officer later lamented, "or if he had been shot by a French straggler, we would have had a ceasefire two weeks later and thereafter would have received a peace in which we could have asked for everything." But Hentsch did reach the front and, horrified by the risks the men on the ground were taking, prevailed on them to order a retreat.

Despite a century of hindsight, we are no better placed today than Moltke was in 1914 to know whether Hentsch snatched defeat from the jaws of victory or saved the Germans from catastrophe. But to men who thought triumph was within their grasp, the decision to retreat was devastating. It came "like a bolt of thunder," said the commander of the 133rd

Reserve Infantry Regiment. "I saw many men cry, the tears rolled down their cheeks; others simply expressed amazement." Moltke had a nervous breakdown.

Germany's great gamble had not paid off, and it had no Plan B. However, the alliance opposing it was little better-off. Its own Plan A had been, just as the Germans expected, to crush Germany between simultaneous attacks from France and Russia, but by October the Russians had suffered a string of defeats, and the French were lucky still to be in the war. The Anglo-Franco-Russian alliance did have a Plan B, in which Britain's huge fleet would bottle up Germany's battleships in their harbors, impose a naval blockade, and snap up the enemy's overseas colonies. With the exception of East Africa, where an extraordinary German colonel was still waging guerrilla war when hostilities in Europe had ended, all this went smoothly, but unfortunately Plan B could only produce victory very slowly, by starving Germany's people and industry.

Churchill, in charge at the Admiralty, pushed for a more decisive use of naval supremacy. The admirals had rejected an invasion of northern Germany as too risky, but Churchill insisted that amphibious operations could instead split open the Central Powers' soft underbelly. A landing at Salonica (ignoring the detail that Greece was neutral) got nowhere; another in Iraq led to a humiliating surrender; and a third, at Gallipoli, was such a disaster that it almost ended Churchill's career. By 1915, even the most determined navalists recognized that the war would be won or lost on land.

But how to do that? There is a saying that generals always refight the last war, but initially Europe's military men were even further behind the times. The Boer and Russo-Japanese Wars had shown that armies could not survive in the open against modern firepower, and as long ago as the 1860s the last stages of the American Civil War had revealed that troops who dug trenches were almost immovable. Yet in 1914, the armies massed their men, unfurled their flags, and charged, much as they had in Napoleon's day. *Offensive à outrance* was their motto: "Attack to excess."

Just three weeks into the war, a young French lieutenant named Charles de Gaulle was shot leading one such charge in Belgium. "The enemy's fire was precise and concentrated," he later wrote. "Second by second the hail of bullets and the thunder of shells grew stronger. Those who survived lay flat on the ground, amid the screaming wounded and the humble corpses. With affected calm, the officers let themselves be killed standing upright . . . but all to no purpose. In an instant it had become clear that not all the courage in the world could withstand this fire." Ernst Jünger, who served Germany with much the same reckless bravery that de Gaulle displayed for France, coined the perfect label for this as the title of his war memoirs (to my mind, the finest ever written): *Storm of Steel*.

After the war, it became a commonplace that the de Gaulles and Jüngers had been "lions led by donkeys"—heroes sent to their deaths by champagne-swilling buffoons who knew little and cared less about the horrors at the front. In reality, though, leaders learned from their mistakes just as quickly as those of earlier ages and rapidly modified their methods. In France, it was obvious by October 1914 that with millions of men crammed into a three-hundred-mile front, continuous lines of trenches from Switzerland to the North Sea were perfectly possible, and once both sides had dug trenches, the overriding question became how to break through them.

At first, the answer seemed obvious. "Breaking through the enemy's lines," the British commander concluded in January 1915, "is largely a question of expenditure of high-explosive ammunition. If sufficient ammunition is forthcoming, a way can be blasted through the line. If the attempt fails . . . either more guns must be brought up, or the allowance of ammunition per gun must be increased."

This put the emphasis on the home front. He who channeled his economy most efficiently into churning out guns and shells, it appeared, would win the day. In every country, production soared as governments took over everything from munitions and transport to food and wages. Women had to be lured out of the home and into fields and factories to replace the men drafted into the armies; food had to be rationed and distributed; production had to be rationalized to give the armies just enough of everything they needed. All this meant more bureaucrats, more taxes, and more regulation. Leviathans exploded.

But despite it all, neither side could make a decisive breakthrough. Once again, the Red Queen pattern seemed to be at work. The armies' offensive powers improved dramatically. Millions of shells were manufactured, tens of millions of horses were coaxed and beaten to drag them to the front (Germany alone lost a million horses during the war, more to exhaustion and starvation than to enemy fire), and artillerymen became more sophisticated, mixing short, intense barrages with long, sustained ones and firing creeping barrages that moved forward just ahead of advancing infantry. But for every improvement attackers made, defenders found a response. They dug multiple lines of trenches, four or five miles deep. They manned the forward positions lightly, rotating troops in and out of the line to keep them fresh. Most men stayed back out of artillery range, letting the enemy capture the front lines and counterattacking when the assault outran its artillery cover.

The real issue, generals realized as early as 1915, was that Moltke's problem went all the way down. Once battle was joined, commanders could not control their armies. If their men did overrun enemy defenses, hours might pass before headquarters heard about it, and the opportunity to commit fresh reserves and exploit the opening would be lost. "Generals were like men without eyes, without ears and without voices," the historian John Keegan observed.

In this age of science, both sides turned to technology for ways to beat the Red Queen. Germany led the way, using tear gas in Poland in January 1915. It was not a success; the day was so cold that the gas froze. But when they tried chlorine gas on the Western Front three months later, the results were dramatic. A light breeze carried the poisonous green clouds into trenches full of unsuspecting French and African troops. Chlorine is a nasty way to kill: it burns the lungs, stimulating them to overproduce fluids; gassed men drown. Although the gas killed only about two hundred men (a mere handful by the bloody standards of World War I), thousands more ran away "like a flock of sheep," a German officer observed. The rout left a gap nearly five miles wide, but unfortunately for the Germans their own troops were nearly as surprised as the enemy's and failed to push through the opening. By the second day of the attack, all surprise was lost, and because chlorine is soluble, the Canadians who plugged the gap in the line could neutralize it by just tying wet rags over their faces.

Gas pervades popular memories of World War I ("If you could hear," wrote Wilfred Owen, "at every jolt, the blood / Come gargling from the froth-corrupted lungs, / Obscene as cancer, bitter as the cud / Of vile, incurable sores on innocent tongues"), but to armies that expected it, it was more a nuisance than a game changer. Less than one in eighty of the war dead died from gassing, and only one war pension in a hundred was gas related.

Britain tried a different technological fix: tanks. H. G. Wells had written a short story titled "The Land Ironclads" back in 1903, and engineers were already discussing armored, tracked vehicles by December 1914. The internal combustion engine was still in its infancy, and the technical challenges of moving several tons of steel over trenches and shell holes were enormous, but by September 1916 almost fifty tanks were ready to fight. Thirteen of them broke down before the battle began, but the Germans fled at the mere sight of the others, which advanced two miles before they, too, broke down. In late 1917, Britain massed 324 tanks on a five-mile front at Cambrai and pushed forward four miles—a massive advance for World War I—before they got stuck. British church bells were rung in celebration, but the German line held.

Other innovations were less spectacular, but arguably more important. When the war started, artillerymen often had little patience with technicians who wanted to bring too much science to their craft. "My boy, this is war, this is practical stuff!" one subaltern remembered being told. "Forget all that nonsense they taught you at 'The Shop'! If it's cold, cock her up a bit!"* By 1917, though, fire control had improved by an order of magnitude—much of it owed to the war's other great technical advance, aviation. There had been no aircraft at all until 1903, and none was used in war until 1911, but by 1918 two thousand planes were buzzing above the western front, correcting artillery fire, attacking enemy infantry, and even shooting each other down.

Yet still the great breakthrough did not come. Despairing, in 1916 generals resorted to making the body count an end in itself. When the Germans attacked at Verdun in February, instead of trying to break through, they aimed to bleed the French white. Seven hundred thousand men died in a few square miles of mud over the next nine months. Nor did the British really expect to break through when they attacked along the Somme River that July; their aim was just to distract the Germans from Verdun. By lunchtime on the first day, 20,000 Britons had been killed, and over the next four months another 300,000 followed them.

Germany generally had the better of this war of attrition, killing more men than it lost and doing it more cost effectively. By one gruesome calculation, Britain, France, Russia, and (eventually) the United States spent $36,485.48 for every enemy soldier they killed, while Germany and its allies spent just $11,344.77 per corpse. Where German efficiency broke down, however, was in the realm of strategy. After starting the war with no Plan B, Germany soon had too many Plan Bs. Some generals argued that Germany should concentrate on knocking out Russia. On the eastern front, they pointed out, the challenge was not how to break through—there was so much room for maneuver that armies regularly did this—but how to sustain advances in a land largely lacking railways and roads. Solving that problem, they suggested, would be much easier than finding a way through

---

*That is, raise the trajectory of the barrel slightly.

the trenches in France. Other generals, though, argued that Russia was a sideshow; the only way to win the war was by breaking the British and the French, whereupon the Russians would fold too.

First one faction, then the other gained the upper hand, dissipating German efforts, and to make things worse, other influential voices hoped to win the war outside Europe. "Our consuls in Turkey and India," the kaiser wrote in 1914, "must rouse the whole Muslim world into wild rebellion against this hateful, mendacious, unprincipled [British] nation of shopkeepers." The jihad went nowhere, but in 1915 the navy started pressing another global strategy. Since Britain depended even more than Germany on imports, the admirals observed, why not use submarines to close its trade routes?

After much back-and-forth, in February 1917 Germany committed to sinking merchant ships on sight, regardless of what flag they flew. German leaders knew that this would probably bring the United States into the war, but as they saw it, Americans were virtually combatants already. Before the war, Britain had dominated the world-system by exporting capital and industrial goods, but now Britain was importing a quarter-billion dollars' worth of American war matériel every month. Adding insult to injury, much of the money to do this was borrowed on the New York markets. German economists calculated that if they cut this Atlantic lifeline, Britain could only fight for another seven or eight months. Provoking the Americans might lead to defeat, but, they pointed out, doing nothing would definitely lead to defeat. To hedge their bets, however, the Germans came up with the staggeringly bad idea of offering to bankroll a Mexican invasion of the United States. This was the final straw, and in April 1917 the Americans declared war on Germany.

This was the moment of decision. The United States was throwing its weight behind Britain and France at the very moment that attrition and a focus on the east were beginning to work for Germany. By early 1917, Russia had lost three million dead (one-third of them civilians), and its army was disintegrating. A mutiny in March (known, thanks to the old-fashioned Russian calendar, as the February Revolution) overthrew the tsar, and the October Revolution (in November) brought Bolshevik agitators to power. Russians now turned to fighting each other, and Germany bullied the new Soviet Union into surrendering its non-Russian territories.

This produced borders uncannily like those that followed the Soviets' final collapse in 1991, except that in 1918, Poland, Ukraine, Belarus, and the Baltic States received assorted German royals as rulers. "German prestige," explained Erich von Ludendorff (Germany's quartermaster general and, by this point, virtual dictator), "demands that we should hold a strong protecting hand, not only over German citizens, but over all Germans." This included Germans in the Austro-Hungarian Empire, which was now more or less a satellite of Berlin. Had Ludendorff won the war, a Greater Germany would have stretched from the English Channel to the Don Basin, which would surely have meant the end of the British globocop.

Russia's collapse freed up half a million Germans to fight in the west before the American flood could arrive. But even more important, the fighting in Russia also showed how to solve the fundamental problem of command and control.

I have mentioned several times the military historian Victor Davis Hanson's theory of a Western way of war, stretching from ancient Greece to modern Europe and America, which wins battles with "a single, magnificent collision of infantry." What the Germans discovered in 1917, though, was a "modern system" of war-fighting (as the strategist Stephen Biddle calls it) in which infantry does just the opposite, not colliding magnificently, but "reducing exposure to hostile fire"; seeking not concentration and shock but "cover, concealment, [and] dispersion."

This modern way of war once again revolutionized military affairs. It tapped into the energies of people's war by pushing initiative down the ranks, into the hands of noncommissioned officers and even individual storm troops (as Germans called the new kind of soldier). Given proper training, these men could be relied on to exercise their own initiative without officers around to drive them forward. Small groups would sneak across no-man's-land, rushing through the killing fields by exploiting shell holes, tree stumps, and whatever other cover survived (Figure 5.6).

Storm troops carried light but powerful weapons—the first submachine guns and flamethrowers—but the modern way of war was not about technology. It was about surprise. Instead of intense shelling, giving the game away, attacks now opened with short blasts of gas, enough to sow confusion among defenders scrambling to fit their masks ("Gas! Gas! Quick, boys!—An ecstasy of fumbling, / Fitting the clumsy helmets just in time"), but not enough to give them time to prepare for what was coming. The storm troops then infiltrated into the trenches, bypassing well-organized defenders and crawling forward to find command posts and artillery. These they hit hard, decapitating the enemy organization and throwing everything into confusion. For most of the defenders, the first sign of trouble was shooting coming from *behind* them.

Figure 5.6. To the green fields beyond: German storm troops infiltrating through the ruined French village of Pont-Arcy, May 27, 1918

By then, a second wave of Germans was already assaulting the strong-points left behind by the first, but when all went well, this was not even necessary. Surrounded, getting no orders, and with no idea where the real battle was happening, armies regularly ran away or gave up. A British officer who had been on the receiving end of the new German tactics called the effect "strategic paralysis." "To attack the nerves of an army, and through its nerves the will of its commander," he learned, "is more profitable than to batter to pieces the bodies of its men."

The first time the Germans tried storm-troop warfare, at Riga in September 1917, the entire Russian line collapsed. At Caporetto in Italy six weeks later, the panic (immortalized in Ernest Hemingway's novel *A Fare-well to Arms*) was even more overwhelming. At one point, one German lieutenant—Erwin Rommel—captured fifteen hundred Italians with the help of just five of his own men. In all, a quarter of a million Italians surrendered, and the Germans and Austrians surged forward sixty miles.

These, though, were just rehearsals. By the end of 1917, the only thing that mattered was caving in the Western Front before too many Americans arrived. Ludendorff saw no option but to bet the house on breaking the British line, pushing the globocop's troops back into the Channel ports,

and driving the French to the negotiating table. In March 1918, he rolled
the dice one last time.

Just two days into the attack, the British Fifth Army folded. Thousands
of men threw away their rifles and ran, leaving thousands more behind
them, permanently (Figure 5.7). The kaiser gave every schoolchild in Germany a victory vacation, but unlike at Riga or Caporetto, this time the
defenders kept their heads and rushed reserves into the gap. As the German advance slowed to a crawl, Ludendorff attacked a new section of the
line, and in early May the British position was once more critical. "With
our backs to the wall," the order came down, "and believing in the justice
of our cause, each one of us must fight on to the end . . . There must be no
retirement."

There was in fact quite a lot of retirement, but the British again blunted
the attacks. Ludendorff made another push, pressing the French so hard
that Americans, fresh from the Atlantic crossing, had to be thrown in. The
French fell back, recommending that the U.S. Marines follow them, only
to receive the immortal reply: "Retreat? Hell, we just got here." The position held. Ludendorff had lost.

It was now the Germans who buckled under the weight of attrition.
Each side lost around half a million men in the spring of 1918, and a hor-

Figure 5.7. Some corner of a foreign field that is forever England: British dead
at Songueval, March 1918

rendous new enemy, Spanish influenza, was raging through both armies (the H1N1 virus probably evolved in crowded army camps in 1917–18 and killed fifty million to a hundred million people by the end of 1919). But while the Allies could replace their casualties—700,000 Americans were already in France, with twice as many more on the way—Germany could not. The Anglo-Franco-American alliance planned huge new offensives for 1919, talking of parachute drops far behind German lines and armored breakouts using thousands of tanks (although whether the planes and tanks of 1919 were up to this remains an open question), but in the end Britain's old Plan B—of starving the enemy into submission—beat these grandiose schemes to the finish line. In the fall of 1918, famine gripped Germany. Soldiers and sailors mutinied. Bolsheviks seized cities. Civil war began.

At the front, German soldiers began giving up in huge numbers. Americans netted 13,251 in a single day, and between April and October 1918 the German army shrank by a million men. Ludendorff had a breakdown at the end of September; the kaiser fired him and then fled into exile. Finally, on November 11, the shooting stopped on the Western Front. "At eleven o'clock this morning," Prime Minister David Lloyd George told Parliament, "came to an end the cruellest and most terrible war that has ever scourged mankind. I hope we may say that thus, this fateful morning, came to an end all wars."

Peace Without Victory

Why was Lloyd George so badly wrong? Some blame the Treaty of Versailles for being too harsh, leaving Germany seeking revenge. Others blame it for being too soft, leaving Germany intact instead of reversing its 1871 unification. Others still blame the U.S. Congress for refusing to ratify the treaty or Britain and France for scheming to exploit it. The truth, though, is much simpler. Real peace required a strong globocop.

Germany had not gotten the counterproductive war it wanted, which would have broken up the European alliance against it and crippled the British globocop, but neither had Britain gotten a productive war restoring its pre-1870 prominence. Britain came out of the war virtually untouched by shot, shell, or bomb, with an economy second only to the United States', with the largest fleet in the world, and, after gobbling up various German colonies, with an empire that ruled roughly a quarter of the planet. But the price of victory had been ruinous. More than a third of a millennium had passed since Pepys had grumbled that "want of money puts all things, and above all things the Navy, out of order," but it was even truer in 1919 than it had been in 1661. Britain's debts were twice as large as its gross national product. They were smaller than the burden the nation had borne after the wars against Napoleon, to be sure, but in 1815 Britain had been the world's only industrializing economy, and in 1919 it was not. Nineteenth-century Britain, its GDP growing by leaps and bounds, had steadily paid down its debt, but trying to repeat that feat in the twentieth century by slashing spending and raising taxes only brought on recession.

By 1921, British unemployment was over 11 percent, and inflation passed 21 percent. Strikes wasted eighty-six million workdays, and the economy—which had shrunk by nearly a quarter since the war ended (Figure 5.8)—was smaller than it had been in 1906. Deep spending cuts drove the chief of the Imperial General Staff to despair that "in no single theatre are we strong enough—not in Ireland, nor England, nor on the Rhine, nor in Constantinople, nor Batoum, nor Egypt, nor Palestine, nor Mesopotamia, nor Persia, nor India." Unable to fund its fleet, Britain accepted naval parity with the United States in 1922, achieved by voluntarily scrapping more ships than the Royal Navy had ever lost in a battle. "We cannot alone act as the policeman of the world," the leader of the Conservative Party conceded.

The United States, on the other hand, supported its mega-fleet while spending just 1 percent of GDP on defense, because American output surged steadily upward in the 1920s while other economies struggled through

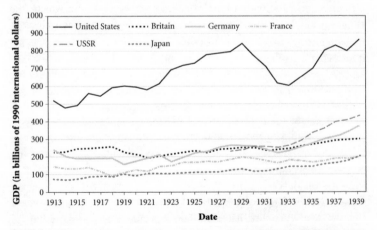

Figure 5.8. The shape of unknown unknowns: the wild rides of the world's biggest economies, 1913–39 (Soviet figures are unreliable before 1928)

boom-and-bust cycles. By 1929 American foreign investment had almost matched Britain's peak level of 1913, and its global trade was worth 50 percent more. "The change since 1914 in the international position of the United States," the *New York Times'* financial editor noted in 1926, was "perhaps the most dramatic transformation of economic history."

The United States seemed ready to drive Britain out of its job as globocop, but this was the last thing on most Americans' minds. Some adhered to Thomas Jefferson's hope for "peace, commerce, and honest friendship with all nations, entangling alliances with none"; others worried more about avoiding entangling expenses; but others still, including President Woodrow Wilson, dreamed of something completely different.

The goal of fighting, Wilson told the Senate in January 1917, must be "peace without victory," because "victory would mean peace forced upon the loser, a victor's terms imposed upon the vanquished." As Wilson saw it, "only a peace between equals can last," meaning that "the guarantees exchanged must neither recognize nor imply a difference between big nations and small, between those that are powerful and those that are weak." In place of one mighty empire acting as globocop, Wilson proposed a league of nations, "a single and overwhelming powerful group of nations who shall be the trustee of peace in the world."

On the face of it, this did not look so new. Kant, of course, had talked about something similar, and just a few years before Wilson's speech the former president Theodore Roosevelt had suggested replacing the old-fashioned globocop with a kind of community globocop, in which "the efficient civilized nations—those that are efficient in war as well as in peace—shall join in a world league for the peace of righteousness . . . to act with the combined military strength of all of them against any recalcitrant nation." Some even imagined an international air force that would bomb aggressors to the negotiating table.

But when the League of Nations took shape in 1919, it looked nothing like this. It had no coercive powers. Its achievements in bringing refugees home, stabilizing currencies, and gathering statistics were extraordinary, but it could not fill the vacuum left by the British globocop. Many critics suspected that not competing with Britain was in fact the whole point of the exercise; after all, they observed, when Lloyd George declared, "I am for a league of nations," he had added, "In fact . . . the British Empire *is* a league of nations." The league's constitution was based largely on British proposals, and one of its first acts was to approve British and French "mandates"—in effect, colonies—in much of the Arab world.

The U.S. Congress wanted nothing to do with it, seeing it as just one more entangling alliance; Jawaharlal Nehru, India's future prime minister, wrote from a British jail that "the League of Nations . . . looks forward to a permanent dominance by these Powers over their empires"; and Lenin denounced it as a "stinking corpse" and "an alliance of world bandits." The only real alternative to a globocop, the Soviets announced in 1919, was communism itself, which would "destroy the rule of capital, make war impossible, abolish state frontiers, [and] change the entire world into one cooperative community."

The problem with the communist solution, however, was that the Bolsheviks had been killing from the moment they seized power, and seemed to relish it. "Comrade!" Lenin wrote to one commissar in August 1918. "Hang (and I mean hang so that the *people can see*) *not less than 100* known kulaks [prosperous peasants], rich men, bloodsuckers . . . Do this so that for hundreds of miles around the people can see, tremble, know and cry: they are killing and will go on killing the bloodsucking kulaks . . .

"Yours, Lenin.

"P.S. Find tougher people."

In March 1919, when Lenin called the League of Nations a stinking corpse, more than five million men were fighting a particularly horrible civil war in the new Soviet Union. This ultimately killed even more Russians (perhaps eight million, counting deaths from famine and disease) than the Germans had done. Britain and France had decided as early as May 1918 that they had to intervene, and serious fighting began on November 11, the very day that quiet fell on the Western Front. In 1919 a quarter of a million foreign troops (mostly British, Czech, Japanese, French, and American, but including Polish, Indian, Australian, Canadian, Estonian, Romanian, Serbian, Italian, Greek, and even Chinese contingents) served on Russian soil.

If the league really had been a capitalist conspiracy, Lenin and his henchmen would not have lasted long enough to condemn it. But as it was, with no globocop overseeing operations, the interventions in the Russian Civil War broke down in disorder. By mid-1920, all forces but the Japanese had withdrawn, and Soviet armies were bearing down on Warsaw. After gobbling up Poland, the Soviets planned to carry communism to Germany, which had just finished putting down its own Bolshevik revolution. For a few weeks in the summer of 1920 it looked as if Lenin's boast that the red flag would sweep away state frontiers might actually come true, but as the Red Army outran its supplies, the Poles rallied and hurled it back. At the end of August, Polish horsemen even won Europe's last big cavalry battle, at Komarów. Twenty-five thousand men charged and countercharged, sabers drawn, much as mounted warriors had been doing for the previous two thousand years, but this time they did it with machine guns clattering and high explosive shells bursting all around them.

Over the next few years, the Soviets quietly dropped their talk of world revolution. Sporadic fighting continued over the carcasses of the empires cast down by World War I, but for a while at least, the world seemed to be getting along just fine without a globocop. International trade recovered, and by 1924 incomes in most places were back where they had been in 1914. The world was finally putting the horrors of the war behind it. Between 1921 and 1927, the Dow Jones index of American stocks quadrupled; between 1927 and 1929 it almost doubled again, peaking at 381.17 points on September 3, 1929.

Ten years later to the day, Britain and France once again declared war on Germany.

Death of a Globocop

The nineteenth-century world-system finally died over the last weekend of October 1929.

Despite eighty-five years of arguments, we still don't know exactly how it started. "The 1929 crisis is a substantial curiosity," says the financial historian Harold James, "in that it was a major event, with truly world-historical consequences (the Great Depression, even perhaps the Second World War), but no obvious causes." For whatever reason, Wall Street traders lost their heads on Wednesday, October 23. Four billion dollars of wealth (the equivalent of $53 billion today) evaporated. By Thursday lunchtime, another $9 billion of American riches had evaporated. Then the markets rallied, buoyed by an alliance of bankers buying up the shares no one wanted, but on Monday the roof really fell in. By Tuesday afternoon the Dow had lost almost a quarter of its value, and by the summer of 1932 a dollar of stock bought at the market's peak on September 3, 1929, was worth just eleven cents.

The decade between September 3, 1929, and September 3, 1939, saw global finance melt down, sweeping away what was left of the integration that had made the nineteenth-century world-system work. Into the 1870s and even beyond, Britain had regularly acted as the lender of last resort, accepting that being a globo–credit union was part of the globocop's job.

But now there was no globocop; it was every government for itself. One after another, they walled off their economies, raising barriers against competition and financial contagion. The United States alone introduced twenty-one thousand tariffs to keep out imports, and by the end of 1932 international trade had shrunk to one-third of what it had been in 1929.

It was this that killed Britain's last pretensions to playing globocop. Like everyone else, governments in London retreated behind tariffs. Defense spending fell even further, and in 1932 the chiefs of staff admitted that the navy could no longer defend the empire east of Suez. War, they conceded, would "expose to depredation, for an inestimable period, British possessions and dependencies, including those of India, Australia and New Zealand."

Not surprisingly, the possessions and dependencies being so exposed reacted badly. The white settler dominions made it clear that London should not take their support for granted if another war came, and India, for so long a central pillar in the world-system, began going its own way. Britain opened negotiations with Gandhi's noncooperation movement in 1930, and in 1935 it made major concessions to Indian political parties.

The 1930s collapse shook the British ruling class to its core. "It is the virtue of the Englishman," a Cambridge don had written in 1913, "that he never doubts," but over the next twenty years this certainty faded fast. Even to its rulers, the whole globocop exercise was starting to seem just a little bit pointless. The most eloquent doubter was surely George Orwell, an Old Etonian whose five-year stint in the empire's police force in Burma turned him into one of Britannia's fiercest critics. However, he was hardly alone. "All over India," he observed, "there are Englishmen who secretly loathe the system of which they are a part." Once, he wrote, he had shared a compartment on an overnight train ride with an (English) officer of the Indian Education Service. "It was too hot to sleep," he said, "and we spent the night in talking."

> Half an hour's cautious questioning decided each of us that the other was "safe"; and then for hours, while the train jolted slowly through the pitch-black night, sitting up in our bunks with bottles of beer handy, we damned the British Empire—damned it from the inside, intelligently and intimately. It did us both good. But . . . when the train crawled into Mandalay, we parted as guiltily as any adulterous couple.

The empire still had its boosters, of course. "There are Englishmen who reproach themselves with having governed [India] badly," one of these admirers wrote. "Why? Because the Indians show no enthusiasm for their rule. I claim that the English have governed India very well, but their error is to expect enthusiasm from the people they administer."

This fan was Adolf Hitler. The solution to the world's uncertainties, he insisted, was force, not self-doubt, and as the democracies of the 1930s struggled with sluggish growth, faction-ridden ruling coalitions, unemployment, and social unrest, it began to look as if he might be right. Violent strongmen (some on the left, but most on the right) seized power in Europe, East Asia, and Latin America. All made the same bet: that without a globocop, force was the solution to their problems.

In many ways, the Soviet Union was the model for them all. Its leaders seemed to have discovered the secret of success in the uncertain postwar world: that more violence worked better than less violence. Stalin shot tens of thousands of his subjects, locked a million in gulags, shipped millions more around his empire, and confiscated so much grain that ten million starved, and as he did so, the closed, inward-turned, centrally planned Soviet economy grew by 80 percent between 1929 and 1939. This dwarfed the performance of the open-access, globally linked, capitalist economies. Britain expanded by a respectable 20 percent across the same decade, but France managed only 3 percent, and the United States just 2 percent.

Cheered by the success of internally directed violence, and undeterred by the fact that he had just had all the best officers in the Red Army shot, Stalin turned violence outward in 1939. He sent troops into Finland, the Baltic States, Poland, and Manchuria, and on the last of these fronts the Soviets clashed with an equally aggressive Japan, which, after prospering as a commercial power since the 1870s, had been hard-hit by the new barriers to trade in the 1930s. "Our nation seems to be at a dead-lock," Lieutenant Colonel Ishiwara Kanji observed, "and there appears to be no solution for the important problems of population and food"—unless, that is, Japan adopted Ishiwara's solution: "the development of Manchuria and Mongolia [whose] natural resources will be sufficient to save [Japan] from the imminent crisis" (Figure 5.9).

Ishiwara and a gaggle of junior officers went rogue, invading Manchuria (then part of China) in 1931 without any orders to do so. Ishiwara half expected to be court-martialed, but when it became clear that the invasion was going well and that there was no invisible fist to punish them, politicians in Tokyo—themselves drowning in unknown unknowns—also embraced force. When the League of Nations insisted that they withdraw, they instead withdrew from the league.

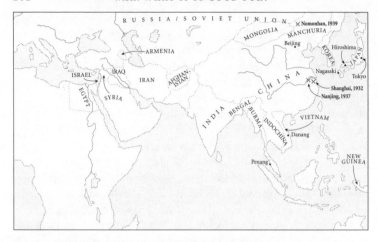

Figure 5.9. End of empire: the wars for Asia, 1931–83

British and American politicians fulminated but did nothing. A Japanese attack on Shanghai in 1932 did shock Britain into dropping the budgeting assumption (in place since 1919) that it would not have to fight a major war within the next decade, but still Britain hesitated to rearm, largely out of fear of stoking inflation.

Five years later, Japan struck again, overrunning northern China. Once more, violence paid. With newly conquered markets to sell in and burgeoning armies to provision, Japan saw its GDP grow more than 70 percent in the 1930s. "We really got busy," one munitions worker remembered. "By the end of 1937, everybody in the country was working. For the first time, I was able to take care of my father. War's not bad at all, I thought" (Figure 5.10).

Japan outdid the Soviets at externally directed violence. After storming Nanjing in southern China in December 1937, Japanese soldiers raped and murdered perhaps a quarter of a million people. "We took turns raping them," one soldier confessed. "It would be all right if we only raped them. I shouldn't say all right. But we always stabbed and killed them." When a Tokyo journalist recoiled at seeing men hanging by their tongues from hooks, an officer explained things to him. "You and I have diametrically different views of the Chinese. You may be dealing with them as human beings, but I regard them as swine. We can do anything to such creatures."

Back in 1904, when Halford Mackinder predicted that the struggle

Figure 5.10. "War's not bad at all": burned children in Shanghai's bombed-out railway station, 1937

between the inner rim, the outer rim, and the heartland would dominate the twentieth century, he was already worrying that Japan might follow a path like the one Ishiwara recommended. "Were the Chinese," he speculated, "organized by the Japanese, to overthrow the Russian Empire and conquer its territory, they might constitute the yellow peril to the world's freedom just because they would add an oceanic frontage to the resources of the great continent, an advantage as yet denied to the Russian tenant of the pivot region."

When Mackinder was delivering his famous lecture in 1904, Japan was pressing from the outer into the inner rim, fighting Russia for access to Manchuria, but thirty-five years later Manchuria was completely under its control. There was no immediate danger of Japan's invading the heartland, and a tough, undeclared war with Stalin in the summer of 1939 saw Soviet tanks inflict a sharp defeat on the Japanese at Nomonhan. But the conquest of coastal China—to Mackinder, the prerequisite for conquering the heartland—was moving ahead. Japan seemed to be working from Mackinder's script: by taking over Manchuria and China, Ishiwara announced, "the Japanese people can become rulers of Asia and be prepared to wage the final and decisive war against the various white races."

All this was alarming—very alarming—but what worried defenders of the status quo most was, once again, Germany. The Versailles settlement had created a buffer zone of small states in eastern Europe, but Germany's strategic problem (and opportunities) had not gone away. It was still sandwiched between the Russian heartland and the Franco-British outer rim, and violence seemed as plausible a policy in the 1930s as it had been in the 1910s.

Back in 1917, the kaiser had compared Europe with the ancient Mediterranean. Because Rome's victory over Carthage in the First Punic War of 264–241 B.C. had failed to resolve the two powers' real issues, he observed, a more terrible—but also more decisive—Second Punic War had to be fought twenty years later. Germany too, he predicted, would have to fight a Second Punic War. All it needed was a Hannibal—and in 1933 it got one.

The Tempest

"Germany's problem," Hitler told his advisers in 1937, "could be solved only by the use of force." This, he argued as early as 1925 in his book *Mein Kampf,* meant that Germany had to refight the First World War, and this time get it right.

Germany's 1914 strategy, Hitler thought, had been basically correct, and in the war to come, the army would once again strike west while marking time in the east. After overthrowing the outer-rim powers of France and Britain, Germany would turn on the Soviet Union. At that point, though, Hitler went beyond the thinking of the 1910s. In 1917, Ludendorff had insisted that anywhere that Germans lived, from the Rhine to the Volga, was part of a "Greater Germany," but Hitler imagined what the historian Niall Ferguson calls a "Greatest Possible Germany," where *only* Germans lived. This would give the German race *Lebensraum,* or "living space," where sturdy Teutonic farmers would go forth and multiply free from the taint of lesser races.

Success, Hitler said, depended on learning two great lessons from World War I and then going beyond them. The first came originally from British officers, who, in 1918, had seen that combining German storm-troop tactics with their own style of massed tank attacks and (insofar as the technology of the day allowed it) close air support could make trench warfare obsolete. The idea, the maverick military theorist Captain Basil Liddell

Hart explained, was to make the fight more fluid, with success coming *"above all* in the 'follow-through'—the way that a break-through . . . is exploited by a deep strategic penetration; carried out by armoured forces racing on ahead of the main army, and operating *independently."*

Lack of funds and a certain amount of stick-in-the-mudness meant that the interwar British, French, and American armies did little to develop this bold vision, but Soviet generals did pick it up. Organizing tanks into large armored corps for independent operations, they planned to wage what they called "deep battle," pushing far behind the enemy front in just the way suggested by Liddell Hart; but Stalin had most of these officers shot in 1937, and their replacements, understandably, tried to avoid radical ideas that might attract the great man's attention.

Only in Germany, where the strict limits imposed by the Treaty of Versailles had left military men with no option but to innovate, did the doctrine of combined-arms breakouts—what journalists later labeled "blitzkrieg," or lightning war—really take hold. By the time Hitler started flooding the army with money in the mid-1930s, its leaders had embraced blitzkrieg, and its engineers were building tanks, aircraft, and radios that (unlike the weapons of 1918) could withstand the stresses of mobile war. Germany's temporary monopoly on the new tactics gave Hitler a real chance to grab victory before anyone else realized what was going on.

Blitzkrieg meant embracing risk and chaos, turning the storm of steel into a true tempest. Bombers and parachutists would sow disorder deep in the enemy's rear, attacking civilians as often as soldiers and choking the roads with refugees. Up at the front, squads of infantry covered by intense artillery fire and swooping dive-bombers would probe for gaps in the enemy line, slipping between strongpoints or turning open flanks. Tanks and trucks would surge through the openings, and now the real fight would begin. Armored columns would fan out miles behind enemy positions, racing to overrun command centers before reserves could concentrate, cut off, and crush the penetrations. Eventually, the breakthrough would outrun its supplies, but by then a second echelon of armor would have burst through. If necessary, a third would follow, always keeping the defenders off balance, until, sooner rather than later, confusion overwhelmed everything and the enemy's will collapsed.

Blitzkrieg worked exactly as advertised. Poland's armies disintegrated before Britain and France could even mobilize, and France itself, which had fought so long and hard in World War I, collapsed completely in May 1940 when a thousand German tanks burst through a carelessly guarded stretch of the front. Three weeks later, Winston Churchill gave the greatest speech of his career, insisting, "We shall go on to the end." But when his war secretary secretly gathered senior officers in a hotel room to ask whether their troops "could be counted on to continue to fight in all circumstances," the answer shocked him. "No one dared," one of the officers recalled, "to estimate any exact proportion."

Britain, of course, did fight on, but twelve months later Germany looked even closer to winning the war. With more than four thousand tanks driving east, the Soviet army seemed to be crumbling as abruptly as the French had. The "Russians lost this war in the first eight days," the German chief of staff announced. Stalin promptly had a mini-breakdown and fled to his country estate, where—on the eighth day—the rest of the Politburo came looking for him. "We found him in an armchair in the small dining room," one of them wrote. "He looked up and said, 'What have you come for?' He had the strangest look on his face and the question itself was pretty strange." Stalin, his henchmen realized, thought they had come to execute him before surrendering to the Germans.

But the Soviets too fought on, because—and this was the second lesson Hitler took from World War I—wars are not lost on battlefields alone. Despite (or because of?) his experiences in the trenches as the army collapsed in 1918, Hitler shared the popular view that Germany had never been defeated in the field. It had failed, he was certain, because traitors had stabbed it in the back—from which he drew the conclusion that this time around, Germany had to strike the would-be traitors before the war even began. He started with communists, rounded up by the thousands in 1933. Next came rivals on the extreme right, murdered en masse in 1934, and then, on a larger scale still, all groups judged insufficiently German.

"The main thing," Hitler said in private in 1938, "is that the Jews are driven out." The Roman Empire had expelled the Jews from their homeland two thousand years earlier, and Europeans had periodically persecuted them ever since, but the Nazis, once again, took things further. The Jews' homelessness, Hitler argued, made them the absolute opposite of Germans, who had a sacred bond to the soil. Jewish rootlessness and commercial greed would corrupt the coming thousand-year Reich and must therefore be eradicated. Almost the minute they invaded Poland in 1939, German troops started shooting Jews. When that proved too slow and expensive, they converted trucks to act as mobile gas chambers. Hitler probably took the decision to round up and murder every Jew in Europe in July 1941, soon after he attacked the Soviet Union. Hitler's inner circle, agreeing with their master that Europe's other *Untermenschen*—"subhumans"—would also have to go, floated plans to cut off the food supply to Russian cities, starving tens of millions of people to death over the coming winter.

This was people's war taken to the extreme, and it made World War II unique. There had been orchestrated massacres in World War I (in Serbia, Belgium, Africa, and above all Armenia), but such calculated barbarism, on such a scale, was—as Churchill put it—"a monstrous tyranny, never surpassed in the dark, lamentable catalogue of human crime." Not all of Hitler's genocidal plans came off, but the Nazis still murdered at least twenty million civilians.

That is why, in the introduction to this book, I raised what I called the what-about-Hitler problem. If it is true, as I have been claiming, that war has been productive, creating bigger societies that pacify themselves internally and generate economic growth, then what about Hitler? His Greatest Possible Germany would have been the biggest society the continent had seen since the Roman Empire, yet it would also have impoverished most of its subjects and made their lives much more dangerous—the exact opposite of productive war.

I suggested in the introduction that the solution to the what-about-Hitler problem is fairly obvious once we take a long-term perspective on history. Since caging began ten thousand years ago, conquerors have been making wastelands, but they or their successors then faced a harsh choice between turning into stationary bandits and being replaced by new conquerors, who would face exactly the same choice. Churchill predicted that if Hitler beat Britain, "the whole world, including the United States, including all that we have known and cared for, will sink into the abyss of a new Dark Age, made more sinister, and perhaps more protracted, by the lights of perverted science." All the evidence, though, suggests that Hitler's regime would in fact have had to make the same choice between stationary banditry and extinction as every other regime in history.

Hitler always recognized that winning the war in Europe would not be the end of his struggle. "For a foreseeable period of about one to three generations," he predicted, eastern Europe would provide scope for the German race to grow, but after that it would need to expand again, probably overseas. At that point, somewhere between the 1970s and the 2030s, Hitler's successors would fight a Third World War, in which Germany would crush whatever remained of the British Empire and take dominion over the globe.

Perhaps because they were so convinced that traitors rather than the arrival of American troops had cost them victory in 1918, few Nazi leaders ever understood that the real problem for their long-term plans was the United States, not Britain. Nothing else can explain why, just days after Japan attacked Pearl Harbor, Hitler declared war on the Americans rather than hoping that the war in the Pacific would distract them from Europe. "What does the USA amount to anyway?" asked Hermann Göring, the head of the German air force. Churchill, however, saw exactly what it amounted to. "Now at this very moment I knew the United States was in the war, up to the neck and in to the death," he said of hearing the news about Pearl Harbor. "So we had won after all!"

Hitler had been making vague plans to attack the United States since 1938, and periodically ordered German factories to start building long-range bombers that could reach New York and great surface fleets to contest the Atlantic, only to cancel the commissions as more pressing problems arose. Whether he would have gotten more serious had he beaten Britain and the Soviets in 1940–41, we can only speculate; but such speculation is useful, I think, because as soon as we ask this question, we see why the Nazis, like all rulers since productive war began, would quickly have been forced to choose between becoming stationary bandits and being defeated.

Had Hitler built bombers and fleets in earnest and tried to wage a transatlantic war, he would soon have run into the same difficulties that Japan encountered in the Pacific. The first was that once the Americans worked out how to survive blitzkrieg, the struggle would turn into a long, logistical slogging match; and the second, that even with all the resources of an enslaved Europe to draw on, Hitler could not win this.

In some ways, Hitler's position was rather like Napoleon's, 135 years earlier. Both men tried to conquer Europe by wedding the modern energies of people's war to an old idea of empire, using violence to unify the European inner rim and then close it off from the commercial, open-access orders of the outer rim. This, I suggested in Chapter 4, was already a losing strategy when Napoleon tried it around 1805, because the vast wealth being generated by the Atlantic economy meant that real power now came from getting the invisible hand and the invisible fist to work together. Because Britain was doing this and Napoleon was not, the emperor never stood much chance of prevailing over the nation of shopkeepers. By the time Hitler reran a more extreme, bloodthirsty version of the strategy around 1940, the odds against it were even steeper. It is perhaps no coincidence that Hitler, exactly like Napoleon, was turned back at the English Channel, in the snows before Moscow, and in the sands of Egypt. Both men suffered the same fate because both men were trying to do the same thing.

If Hitler had broken Britain, he would just have found himself facing the United States' even bigger and more dynamic open-access order. Like the hunter-gatherers confronting farmers in prehistory, or the stateless societies struggling against ancient empires, the autocrats of the nineteenth and twentieth centuries were on the wrong side of history.

Rather than creating the thousand-year Reich that Hitler so often spoke of, a Nazi victory in Europe would have set up a situation very like the real-world Cold War that took shape after 1945. A totalitarian European empire and an open-access American order would have glared at each other from behind fences of nuclear missiles, struggling for influence over Latin America and the carcasses of the old British and French Empires. They would have sponsored coups, waged proxy wars, and wooed each other's allies (Nixon might have flown to Tokyo in 1972 to split Japan from Germany, rather than flying to Beijing to split China from the Soviet Union). They might even have had their own Petrov moments.

There would have been differences too, of course. Had Hitler won, the European empire would have been ruled from Berlin, not Moscow, and would have run all the way to the Atlantic, rather than stopping at the Iron Curtain. Hitler and his successors might have been more willing than Stalin and his to risk nuclear war. And without western Europe in its orbit, the United States would surely have found it harder to prevail. But in the end, the Nazis would still have faced the same core problem as the communists, of how to compete with a dynamic, open-access outer-rim order, and been confronted with exactly the same choices. They could have recognized the strengths of the open-access economy and begun imitating it, as mainland China did after Mao's death in 1976, or they could have ignored it and collapsed, as the Soviet Union did in 1989.

I will have much more to say about the Cold War in the last parts of this chapter; here I will content myself with observing that these are the reasons why I conclude that the what-about-Hitler problem is not really a problem at all (for the theory that I am advancing in this book, that is, not for the people who lived through his reign of terror). Hitler's regime was an extreme case in the annals of atrocity. A Nazi victory would have been a disaster, condemning decades of Europeans to the grip of the Gestapo and the death camps, driving the rate of violent death back up to levels not seen for centuries. But even so, the Nazis would have remained subject to the same iron laws as every other government in history. As the decades lengthened into generations, the need to compete commercially and militarily with the open-access order would have forced Hitler's successors to make a choice between defeat and turning into stationary bandits. In the 2010s, I hazard to suggest, Europe might still have been a dark continent where secret police kicked in doors in the middle of the night, but the downward march of violent death rates would have resumed. Hitler could have slowed the civilizing process, but he could not have stopped it altogether.

As it was, of course, Hitler did not win. Had he handled the Stalingrad campaign better in 1942, he could still have prevailed, and even in the summer of 1943, when he launched the biggest tank battle in history at Kursk, he still stood a chance. But by then his enemies had learned not only to survive blitzkrieg but also to mount their own versions. Committing their enormous economies to total war, they overwhelmed Germany and Japan (Figure 5.11). Thousand-bomber raids pounded the Axis homelands day and night, paralyzing their economies and killing about a million civilians (including a hundred thousand in Tokyo in a single night). When the German army invaded the Soviet Union in 1941, it needed 600,000 horses to haul its guns and supplies, greatly slowing its advance,

Figure 5.11. Overwhelmed: a German artilleryman despairs as the biggest tank battle in history, at Kursk in July 1943, ends Hitler's hopes of defeating the Soviet Union.

but by 1944 the Allied armies were fully motorized. Now it was the turn of veteran German forces to disintegrate as American tanks broke out after the D-Day landings (Operation Cobra) and Soviet armor smashed its way through to the German frontier, annihilating Hitler's Army Group Center (Operation Bagration). With their cities in flames, Hitler shot himself and Japan's emperor broadcast his first-ever speech to his people. "The war situation," he conceded, "has not developed necessarily to Japan's advantage." With that, the tempest was over.

Learning to Love the Bomb

The Second World War was the most destructive ever fought. When we include those who starved, succumbed to disease, and were murdered in German, Soviet, and Japanese camps, it claimed fifty million to a hundred million lives, as compared with fifteen million dead in World War I and another twenty million in the civil wars that followed it. World War II turned much of Europe and East Asia into wastelands and cost something like $1 trillion (as I write, in 2013, the equivalent of perhaps $15 trillion, the entire annual output of the United States or the European Union). And yet, in a paradox as striking as any in the history of conflict, World War II also managed to be among the most productive ever fought.

That was because the war began the process of clearing away the chaos left by the demise of the British globocop. This, needless to say, was not the end Churchill had had in mind when he asked for the British people's blood, toil, tears, and sweat. In August 1941, before the United States had even entered the war, he had rushed back from a secret meeting with President Franklin Delano Roosevelt to boast to the cabinet that he had "a plain and bold intimation that after the war, the US will join with us in policing the world until the establishment of a better order." But this was not to be. There was a popular saying during the war that Britain provided the time, Russia provided the men, and America provided the money to defeat Hitler, but by November 1943, when Churchill, Stalin, and Roosevelt held their first group meeting, time was already on the Allies' side. Only men and money now mattered, and Churchill found himself sidelined.

Far from sharing global condominium with the United States, Britain woke up from celebrating victory over Germany and Japan to the worst economic hangover in its history. Its debts were much worse than in 1918, its economy completely distorted by war production, and its very food supply dependent on American loans. "It was extraordinarily unreal, even absurd, and shabby," a left-wing journalist wrote in his diary in December 1945 after spending two days watching Parliament debate the terms of a new American bailout. "Speakers took up their position, but the only reality was the fear which none of them dared to express—the fear of the consequences if cigarettes and films and spam were not available from America."

Absurd and shabby it might have been, but unreal it was not. Britain had gone broke fighting Germany. To pay its debts, it had to put exports ahead of consumption, and food rationing actually got stricter after 1945. When eggs became freely available in 1950, there was euphoria. "What this means to us only an English housewife can understand," one diary records; "at last actually we could beat up two eggs and put them in a cake . . . THE FIRST TIME FOR TEN YEARS."

Trapped between insolvency and demands to expand the open-access order into an expensive welfare state, Britain soon found running its old empire an unaffordable luxury. Back in 1916, a German general commanding Turkish troops defending Iraq against a mostly Indian army fighting for the British Empire had written home that "the hallmark of the twentieth century must be the revolution of the colored races against the colonial imperialism of Europe," but it took another world war to fulfill his prophecy.

British rule never recovered from its failure to stand up to Japan. The scene at Penang in Malaya in December 1941 was fairly typical: as Japanese spearheads infiltrated past the British fortifications, the European defenders left without firing a shot, abandoning their local allies to the invaders' tender mercies. Out of the dozens of Asian civil servants who had actually run the town on Britain's behalf, only one was even told about the evacuation, and he was then turned out of the boat to make room for the British commandant's car. It was, thought a young British woman caught up in the rout, "a thing which I am sure will never be forgotten or forgiven."

Although two and a half million Indians volunteered to fight for the empire while only a few thousand joined the Japanese army (often so they could get out of prisoner-of-war camps), the London government nevertheless had no illusions about being able to keep control in the subcontinent after the war ended. It pulled out in indecent haste in 1947, and by 1971 Britain ruled virtually nothing east of Suez (or east of Dover, for that matter).

"Great Britain has lost an empire and has not yet found a role," the former American secretary of state Dean Acheson famously remarked in 1962, but that was not entirely true. The ex-globocop in fact transitioned remarkably smoothly to being the main supporter of the new power that had taken its job, probably because Britain really had very few options. Less than a year after Hitler's suicide, Churchill could already see that "an Iron Curtain has descended across the [European] continent." The war had not been productive enough to install a new globocop, but it did set up two new hemispherical cops.

During the Five Hundred Years' War, Europe had (almost) conquered the world, and now the Soviet Union and the United States had between them conquered Europe. They had divided the continent down the middle, solving the great strategic problem posed by a mighty Germany forever fearful of being crushed between the outer rim and the heartland by tearing the country in two. Seen in isolation, the First World War had been very much a counterproductive war, crippling the British globocop, but from the vantage point of 1945 it now looked more like the opening round in a longer productive war, which was moving toward replacing the nineteenth-century globocop with a much stronger twentieth-century version. Many thoughtful observers concluded that there would have to be one more great productive war, with the two hemispherical cops fighting it out until just one globocop remained standing.

But one thing stood in the way of this outcome: the bomb.

Splitting the atom had changed everything. The biggest artillery bombardments in the world wars had typically lobbed fifteen to twenty thousand tons of high explosives at enemy trenches over the course of several days, but the individual bombs dropped on Hiroshima and Nagasaki concentrated these barrages into single blasts and also poisoned the survivors with lethal neutrons and gamma rays. With just two bombs, the United States killed more than 150,000 people. A war between two nations with large nuclear arsenals (in 1986, the peak year, the United States and the Soviet Union had seventy thousand warheads between them) was beyond anything that could be imagined. It would be truly counterproductive war, laying lands waste for thousands of years to come. Even Stalin found the thought unbearable.

The question, then, was what to do about it. One possibility was that the world would be scared straight: after looking into the abyss, it might finally beat its swords into plowshares. Albert Einstein wrote to *The New York Times* less than a month after Hiroshima and Nagasaki explaining that this was the only option. An earnest committee at the University of Chicago issued guidelines for a world government. Hope even flared that the United Nations, the League of Nations' successor, would make war redundant.

But all these answers begged the same question: What happens when the nuclear giants fall out? The idea that the United Nations' Atomic Energy Commission would control all atom bombs collapsed when the Americans and the Soviets could not agree on inspection protocols, and by 1947 confidence in the power of talk was disappearing. Soviets called the United Nations "not so much a world organization as an organization for the Americans"; American officials, watching the delegates' antics, dismissed it as "the monkey house."

Another possibility was that the world might be scared violent. Pushing the lesser-evil logic to its horrifying limits, some Americans pointed out that since they had not only atom bombs but also bombers that could reach enemy cities, while the Soviets had neither, it made sense to fight a one-sided nuclear war now rather than a much worse, two-sided one later. Churchill even contemplated a plan (called, quite rightly, Operation Unthinkable) to follow up nuclear attacks by having the recently surrendered German army reinvade Russia.

The flaw with this thinking was that during the four years that the United States had the world's only atomic bombs, it did not have enough of them to defeat the Soviets. The Joint Chiefs of Staff calculated in 1948 that if they dropped all 133 of their bombs on Soviet cities, they would kill three million people—a horrifying number, but not enough to shatter a nation that had survived twenty-five million deaths during World War II. Not until 1952, when American physicists set off a thermonuclear ("hydrogen") bomb with a blast equal to seven hundred Hiroshimas, was the United States in a position to kill tens of millions of communists, but by then—thanks as much to their spies as their scientists—the communists had a bomb of their own (Figure 5.12).

Never one to give up easily, the newly elected president, Dwight Eisenhower, told his National Security Council in 1953 that there was "no sense merely shuddering at the enemy's capacity." Rather, "we presently really have to face the question of whether or not we would really have to throw everything at once against the enemy." One study he commissioned confirmed that "virtually all of Russia would be nothing but a smoking, radiating ruin at the end of two hours." Another, however, pointed out that if Soviet bombers made one-way suicide flights—reasonable behavior for crews whose homes were now radiating ruins—they could drop a hundred atom bombs on American cities and kill about eleven million people.

Figure 5.12. Changing the equation: Joe-1, the first Soviet atomic test, August 29, 1949

There would be furious dogfights far above the North Pole, and many, perhaps most, of the Soviet bombers would be shot down. But these were still not odds Eisenhower wanted to gamble with, and when the Soviets unveiled genuine long-range bombers in 1954 and their own hydrogen bomb in 1955, the calculus became even less attractive. A fairly standard hydrogen bomb, with a blast equivalent to a million tons of TNT, would kill everyone and level every building within three miles. Up to six miles out, clothes would burst into flames, and people would be tossed through the air at lethal speeds. Eleven miles away, anyone caught in the open could get second-degree burns and radiation poisoning. By the late 1950s, the Soviets had hundreds of these bombs and the Americans had thousands.

Neither scared straight nor scared violent, Americans plumped in 1947 for a middle course, which came to be called containment. As they (rightly) saw it, the United States was an outer-rim power. It had taken the open-access order much further than nineteenth-century Britain by renouncing direct rule (other than its rule over the nearly 3.8 million square miles it had conquered within North America) altogether. In fact, most Americans thought of their country as an anti-empire, fighting imperialism in the name of freedom. But even so, as the historian Niall Ferguson has acutely observed in his books *Colossus* and *Empire*, the United States' strategic situation after 1945 was strikingly like Britain's a century earlier.

Like Britain, the United States ruled the seas (and now the skies too), maintained military bases around the world, and exercised overwhelming economic power. Because it was the leader of a constellation of allies, rather than the ruler of provinces or client kingdoms, it relied more on coups and cooperation with local militaries than on sending gunboats to keep its followers in line, even though this meant that the followers often had at least some freedom to pursue policies that Washington did not like. But the price of opposing the United States on serious matters—as Britain and France discovered when they invaded Egypt without permission in 1956—was higher than its allies were typically willing to pay. Everything was always up for negotiation, but on the whole, the allies did more or less what Washington wanted—which is why so many people, friends as well as foes, called the postwar world an American Empire.

Within this alliance/empire, peace fell hard and fast. In part, this was because the United States rarely allowed its allies the freedom to fight each other (which, given that most of the world's democracies were in the American Empire, largely explains the phenomenon known as democratic peace). But peace also triumphed within national boundaries. The war had done wonders for popular respect for government and revulsion against political violence. The immediate postwar decades were a golden age of law and order: just one Scandinavian in five thousand and one Briton in four thousand died violently between 1950 and 1974, and while the American homicide rate—one in seven hundred—remained higher than Europe's, it had still fallen 50 percent since the 1930s. The 1950s might have been dull, but they were very, very safe.

They were also very, very prosperous. At a great gathering in the woods of New Hampshire in July 1944, Americans had laid the foundations of a new international economic order to replace the one that died between September 3, 1929, and September 3, 1939, and the United States began pouring cash into Europe's devastated economies. Most went to wartime allies, but, with the free-trade principle taken beyond anything nineteenth-century Britain had tried, vast amounts also went to West Germany, Japan, and Italy. By 1951 the United States had given away $26 billion, equivalent to roughly 10 percent of its annual GDP.

"It was," observes the strategist Robert Kagan, "the perfect capitalist solution to a problem that was strategic as well as economic." Like Adam Smith's butcher, brewer, and baker, the American Empire acted not out of benevolence but from regard for its own interest. The flood of capital into Europe stimulated effective demand for American food and goods, and after a short, sharp depression as economies shifted from war- to peacetime production, the American Empire enjoyed the biggest, most broadly shared economic boom in history (Figure 5.13). In Britain, where being allowed to buy eggs had caused such joy in 1950, by 1960 more than a quarter of all families owned a car, and by 1965 it was more than a third. Car ownership remained more than twice as common in the United States, but few Europeans were complaining.

Each world war had seen Leviathans extending their tentacles deep into civil society so they could mobilize their resources to win, taking responsibility for organizing everything from munitions production to hospitals and child-rearing. After 1918, most voters viewed all this as infringements on their freedoms, electing governments that rushed to shed the burdens of enforcing high tax rates and running their citizens' lives. By 1945, though, many western Europeans (and some, though not quite as many, Americans) had come to see big government very differently—not as a

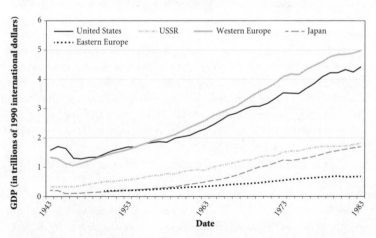

Figure 5.13. Let the good times roll: the biggest economic boom in history begins, 1943–83 (eastern European data are generally unreliable before 1950).

form of oppression, but as a tool of freedom. Big government had won the war against Hitler, and now, perhaps, it could win wars against poverty and injustice. To the horror of many conservatives, voters started electing governments committed to national health services, social security, state-funded university education, state-owned industries, steeply progressive taxation, and legal protections for previously marginalized groups.

As empires went, most members of the American version concluded, this was not so bad.

Getting to Petrov

The American Empire had no need to push into the Eurasian heartland, but it did need to protect and expand free markets all around the inner rim, and especially in western Europe. Its policy of containment meant leaving the Soviets to get on with whatever they liked in their own heartland but contesting all communist advances into the inner rim. If the United States could not be a globocop, it could at least be a globobouncer.

From the heartland, predictably, containment looked like encirclement. Almost everywhere the Politburo looked, from Scandinavia to Japan, American allies locked them in, their wealth and freedom tempting inner-rim nations into America's orbit, threatening the future of communism. Moscow's ideologues did their best to compete in the war of ideas, and the various five-year plans generated economic growth that would have been impressive in any earlier age. But from the minute they conquered eastern Europe, the Soviets had to rely heavily on force, much as the tsars had before them.

Repression made sense for a heartland power. Far from the great flows of oceanic trade and unable to generate as much prosperity as an outer-rim empire, the Soviets had a much harder time than the Americans or even the British before them in buying loyalty with higher living standards. At its peak in 1953 (the last year of Stalin's life), the gulag system housed 2.5 million prisoners. Stalin had even briefly reopened the Nazi concentration camp at Buchenwald, killing a further ten thousand or so people there. In two known cases, families had one child executed by Hitler and the other by Stalin.

Soviet statistics are notoriously unreliable, but, depressing as the thought is, communist police states do seem to have driven violent crime down to extremely low levels. However, they clearly also made the Soviet Empire's subjects miserable, and the huge spending required to support all the machinery of repression distorted the economy. Soviet living standards did rise, roughly doubling between 1946 and 1960, but American income roughly tripled in the same period.

In addition to all these drawbacks, the resources lavished on the million Soviet troops needed to occupy eastern Europe created a distinctly threatening impression on the American side of the Iron Curtain, and with each superpower suspecting the other's intentions (often with good cause), the inevitable outcome was constant conflicts of interest around the inner rim. In the twilight struggle that ensued, fought as much by spies and policemen as by insurgents and armies, the United States and the Soviet Union both discovered—to paraphrase Marx—that while they made their own strategies, they could not always do so in ways of their own choosing. Both superpowers had to work closely with allies, and the tail often seemed to be wagging the dog. Soviets complained that their East German clients dragged them into crises they did not want, and the first secretary-general of NATO—the North Atlantic Treaty Organization, formed on a Norwegian initiative in 1949—joked that the alliance was a cynical western European conspiracy "to keep the Russians out, the Americans in, and the Germans down."

At the other end of Eurasia, the alliance politics were messier still. For years, Mao Zedong had been bombarding Moscow with requests for help in the Chinese civil war, and Kim Il Sung had been demanding permission to invade South Korea. Stalin, worried about provoking Washington, had stalled both men, but when Mao surprised everyone by hoisting the red flag over Beijing in 1949, Stalin found the temptation of expelling the United States from the Pacific inner rim altogether just too tempting. He approved the Korean War in 1950.

It took three years, three million dead, and American threats of atomic attacks on China to end the fighting. The United States had hung on in the inner rim, but at a terrible cost, and in 1954 Eisenhower rolled out a new, zero-tolerance version of containment called the New Look (a bizarre choice of name, borrowed from Christian Dior's 1947 line of full-skirted fashions). Official explanations were studiedly vague, but it seemed to add up to massive nuclear retaliation against any attack, anywhere. Ground forces would be cut to a bare minimum, serving only as trip wires for nuclear weapons. NATO's commander in Europe was blunt. We "are basing all our planning on using atomic and thermonuclear weapons in our defence," he wrote. "With us it is no longer: 'They may possibly be used.' It is very definitely: 'They will be used.'"

So long as the Soviets accepted that war would be suicidal for them but merely *almost* suicidal for the Americans, the New Look more or less returned the initiative to Washington, at least against Moscow and Beijing (which got the bomb in 1964). But thanks to the strange tail-wagging-the-dog logic of the nuclear standoff, weaker communist countries felt able to take more risks, knowing that the United States would rather lose its arguments with them than be seen as the vicious bully that had gone nuclear against a minnow. In 1954, Eisenhower had to acknowledge that he would not use nuclear weapons against Ho Chi Minh in Indochina.

The speed with which the nuclear revolution in military affairs unfolded made stable strategies almost impossible. In 1945 the United States and the Soviet Union had both scooped up as many of Hitler's rocket scientists as they could and set them to work designing intercontinental ballistic missiles (ICBMs). In 1957 the Soviets narrowly won the race ("Our Germans are better than their Germans," the film *The Right Stuff* has Khrushchev boast), using one of their first working rockets to fire a 184-pound steel ball, the Sputnik, into orbit. Inside was a radio transmitter, which did nothing but beep, but that was enough to fill Americans with despair. "Listen now," NBC warned, "for the sound that will forever separate the old from the new."

But like nearly everything in this brave new world, the Soviet lead was short-lived. Two years later the United States also had working ICBMs, and in 1960 both sides mastered the art of launching them from submarines. This ruled out the possibility of a first strike killing enough of the enemy's missiles to prevent him from shooting back and shifted the calculus again.

In the early 1960s, the United States still had a nine-to-one nuclear superiority over the Soviets (Figure 5.14), and the Department of Defense projected that an American first strike would be able to kill 100 million people, probably bringing down the Soviet Union. However, the report went on, a Soviet counterstrike against the bigger cities of the United States and its allies would kill 75 million Americans and 115 million Europeans, bringing down most of the rest of the Northern Hemisphere.

The age of mutual assured destruction, with its almost too perfect acronym, MAD, had arrived. Massive retaliation now meant that the United States, as well as the Soviet Union, would be committing suicide, which naturally made the New Look rather less attractive. Unknown unknowns were returning. In 1961, wondering whether the newly installed president, John F. Kennedy, would really risk New York to save his stake in Berlin, the Soviets pushed harder than usual in the endless confrontation over that

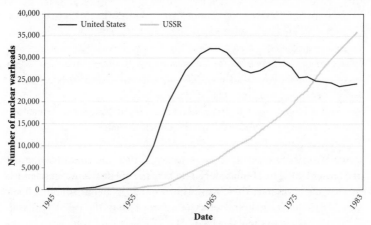

Figure 5.14. Overkill: Soviet and American nuclear arsenals, 1945–83

divided city. Fear clutched the world as politicians postured and threatened. Finally, the communists compromised and built a wall down the middle of the city, but the next year things got even worse. "Why not throw a hedgehog at Uncle Sam's pants?" Khrushchev asked, and sent Soviet missiles to Cuba. For thirteen heart-stopping days, the worst-case scenario seemed to have arrived. It was like the 1910s all over again, but this time with doomsday devices.

The world woke up with a start to what it had wrought. In the liberal democracies of the American alliance, millions marched in campaigns for nuclear disarmament, sang protest songs, and lined up to see *Dr. Strangelove. Coming of Age*–ism's assumption that war was good for absolutely nothing, under any circumstances, swept the field.

But none of this solved the planet's problem. As in every earlier age, so long as anyone thought that force might be the least bad answer to their problems (or so long as anyone thought that someone else might be thinking that), no one dared forgo weapons, and as with every vicious new weapon since the first stone ax, once the bomb had been invented, it could not be "disinvented" (Eisenhower's word). If all the warheads in the world were scrapped, they could be replaced in a matter of months—which might mean that banning the bomb would be the most dangerous action imaginable, because a treacherous enemy might secretly rebuild its arsenal and launch a devastating first strike before its rule-abiding rival could make enough bombs to deter it.

Despite the runaway success of "War" and dozens of lesser protest songs in the late 1960s, most people apparently agreed with this logic. No nuclear-armed electorate ever voted in a party preaching disarmament. When the British Labour Party did promise to ban the bomb, it went down to an epic defeat (one of its own Members of Parliament called its manifesto "the longest suicide note in history").

The cold-eyed men who handled the realities of nuclear war looked for more practical solutions. Some of these, such as installing a direct phone line (via relays in London, Copenhagen, Stockholm, and Helsinki) between Washington and Moscow, were easy. Others, such as reducing the immense stockpiles of warheads, were not. The United States stopped expanding its arsenal in 1966, but the Soviets did not follow suit for twenty years. (As one American secretary of defense observed, "When we build, they build; when we stop, they build.")

The most difficult step of all was finding strategies to contest the inner rim without bringing on the end of days. The American answer was a new policy of flexible response. Instead of threatening to kill hundreds of millions over any disagreement, the United States would react in proportion to the threat. But how would it decide what was proportionate? This definitional issue quickly raised its head in the wake of the European empires' retreat from Southeast Asia. Americans agreed that keeping a foothold in the inner rim in this distant corner of the world was not important enough for nuclear war, but was it worth the bones of American soldiers? In his first year in office, Kennedy had grumbled, "The troops will march in; the crowds will cheer . . . Then we will be told we have to send in more troops. It's like taking a drink." All the same, he sent eight thousand advisers to South Vietnam. Two years later, there were twice as many. Four years after that, U.S. marines splashed ashore at Danang, and by 1968 half a million Americans were fighting in Vietnam (Figure 5.15).

Putting boots on the ground just brought on a flood of further decisions. Was interning civilians, a tried-and-true method for cutting off supplies to insurgents, proportionate? Yes, the White House decided. What about bombing North Vietnam? Sometimes. Or invading North Vietnam? No, because that might provoke Soviet escalation. Bombing and raiding communist positions in supposedly neutral Cambodia struck President Nixon as proportionate, but many Americans disagreed. Riots broke out; the National Guard shot four dead in Ohio. Consequently, when it came to the bigger step of interrupting communist supplies by building a fortified line across Laos—a militarily obvious move, which, South Vietnamese

Figure 5.15. Search and destroy: the U.S. 1st Air Cavalry Division scours the coastal lowlands of Binh Dinh Province, South Vietnam, in the endless hunt for insurgents (January or February 1968).

generals argued, would "cut off the North's front from its rear"—no president would say yes.

The war dragged on, ultimately killing three or more million people. But despite this unsatisfactory beginning, NATO applied flexible response to Europe too. Here, war would mean the mother of all blitzkriegs. Under cover of the biggest air and artillery bombardment in history, seven thousand Soviet tanks would smash into the thin defensive screen along the inner German frontier, while crack troops arriving by parachute or helicopter sowed chaos a hundred miles to the rear. As the opening battles raged, those NATO planes that survived the initial air raids would strike all the way to Poland to shatter the second, third, and fourth echelons of Soviet armor before they reached the battlefield, while infantry hunkered down to blunt the first wave of Soviet tanks before it could break through the Fulda Gap or across the North German Plain.

NATO generals pinned their hopes on the apparent lessons of Egypt and Syria's attack on Israel in 1973, when, for a few days, poorly led and trained Arab infantry armed with wire-guided antitank missiles had fought superbly led and trained Israeli tank crews to a standstill. It took less than two weeks for the Israelis to adapt, counterattack, and annihilate the Arab armies, but NATO gambled that their troops could hold out longer—long enough, the hope was, for American forces to rush across the Atlantic, pick up pre-positioned heavy equipment, and drive the Soviets back.

This was much the way General John Hackett (a former commander of British forces in West Germany) imagined a war playing out in his widely read 1978 novel, *The Third World War*. In his story, flexible response worked perfectly. After seventeen days of conventional battle the Soviet offensive stalled, and with American troops arriving to stiffen the line and even push back, the Soviets escalated. They launched a single SS-17 missile with a nuclear warhead, destroying Birmingham, England. Three hundred thousand died. NATO responded proportionately, with a nuclear strike on Minsk. The unstable Soviet regime then collapsed.

I happened to be living in Birmingham in 1978 (about two miles from Winson Green, Hackett's ground zero), and I did not like his prophecy one bit. But the reality, as the general knew perfectly well, would probably have been much worse. NATO anticipated being the first to go nuclear, using "tactical" devices (often equivalent to half a Hiroshima) to stop break-throughs and also to signal that the attack must end. If Moscow ignored the message, bigger bombs, shells, and warheads (typically worth half a dozen Hiroshimas) would be used, and if there was still no response by the time Soviet tanks were sixty miles into West Germany, the gloves would come off.

Unfortunately, the Soviets showed not the slightest intention of thinking about H-bombs as subtle signals. Their plan called for tanks to reach the Rhine in two weeks and the English Channel and Pyrenees after another four. To accomplish this, the first echelon would use twenty-eight to seventy-five nuclear weapons to rip holes in the NATO line, and the second would fire another thirty-four to a hundred during its armored break-out. Expecting NATO to reply in kind, Soviet troops were equipped to fight on battlefields drenched in chemicals and radiation, concentrating quickly for attacks and then dispersing. West Germany would suffer several hundred Hiroshimas, killing most of the people who lived there. By that point, the ICBMs would be roaring over the North Pole. As Moscow saw it, a few days of total war would devastate both homelands, but once the warheads were used up, conventional fighting would continue until one side could go on no longer.

The official Soviet line was optimistic (probably, given what we now know about their atrocious infrastructure and organization, overoptimistic) about winning, but no one was actually looking forward to a war like this. Consequently, amid fierce debates, both superpowers started drifting toward an understanding (dressed up with the name "détente") that would allow them to muddle through despite the inadequacy of flexible response as a strategy of deterrence. Talks about limiting nuclear weapons began in 1969, and in the 1970s the Soviets made concessions on human rights. Americans sold them grain and lent them dollars to make up for the mushrooming failures of collective farms and communist economies, and astronauts and cosmonauts joined hands in orbit.

It all looked good, but none of it altered the realities. Two semi-global empires with enough firepower to destroy civilization remained locked in a competition over the inner rim; the inner rim continued to be run largely by unstable, unreliable proxies with their own agendas; and neither side could afford to lose.

The strategic tug-of-war surged first one way, then the other. In 1972, President Richard Nixon scored a gigantic coup when Moscow's former client Mao decided that he did not hate the United States as much as he hated the Soviet Union. The strategic net tightened around Russia—but just a year later, the newest Arab-Israeli war wiped out many of the United States' gains. Arab oil producers quadrupled their prices, tipping the American alliance into economic crisis while flooding the oil-exporting Soviet Union with cash. The economic slowdown, anxieties over how to handle nuclear parity with the Soviets, and recriminations over the Vietnam War formed a toxic brew, shattering America's quarter-century-old strategic consensus over containment. Conservatives began arguing that only cutting back welfare spending and the bureaucracies that administered it could revive economic growth, without which containment would not work, and the Watergate scandal convinced many liberals that they did not hate the Soviets as much as they hated Nixon. With political gridlock paralyzing defense policies, the United States stood by as North Vietnam finally overran the South.

By the late 1970s, the United States was in retreat everywhere. Communists were winning civil wars (and even an election) in Africa and Latin America, as well as hearts and minds in Europe. One Christmas—1976, I think—one of my uncles, an unemployed steelworker, actually gave me a copy of Mao's little red book. In 1979 noncommunist radicals in Iran got in on the game too, hurling the Great Satan out of yet another part of the inner rim. The final straw came as the year ended, with the Soviets invading Afghanistan—still the strategic bridge linking heartland and inner rim in South Asia, just as it had been when Russia and Britain had contested it a century earlier.

Détente collapsed. The United States rearmed furiously, deploying deadly new cruise missiles in Europe and talking up technologies that would slice through Soviet defenses like a knife through butter. Paranoia turned to panic in Moscow in 1982, when Israelis used American-made computerized weapon systems to destroy seventeen of Syria's nineteen Soviet-made surface-to-air missile sites and to shoot down ninety-two of its Soviet planes for the loss of three (or six, depending who was counting) of their own. And while any sensible scientist could have told the Soviets that decades would pass before "Star Wars" (an American system for shooting ICBMs down with lasers) or Assault Breaker (a long-range rocket that scattered masses of computer-guided bomblets to destroy entire armored divisions before they got to the front line) would actually work, in the febrile atmosphere of early 1980s Moscow, assuming the worst was a way of life.

It all came to a head in November 1983, just six weeks after Stanislav Petrov had had to decide whether to believe his own computer algorithm when it said that the Americans were launching their missiles. Convinced that NATO was planning a first strike, the neurotic, diabetic Soviet premier, Yuri Andropov—confined to bed by his failing kidneys—pressured the KGB to find evidence of it. Ever dutiful, his spies reported back that a lot of American and British civil servants seemed to be working late in their offices. The only possible conclusion: the United States must be planning to use an upcoming military exercise in western Europe as cover for an attack. Soviet aircraft in East Germany were armed with live nuclear weapons. Leave was canceled. Even military weather forecasts were suspended, lest they give something away.

Fortunately, the one sure thing in the Cold War was that no one could keep a secret. "When I told the British," a senior KGB officer later reminisced to interviewers, "they simply could not believe that the Soviet leadership was so stupid and narrow-minded as to believe in something so impossible." Opinions vary as to whether Andropov really was this stupid and narrow-minded, but American fear of Soviet fear reached the point that Reagan felt the need to dispatch General (later National Security Adviser) Brent Scowcroft to Moscow to persuade Andropov to step back from the brink.

Once again, millions marched to ban the bomb. Bruce Springsteen released his remake of "War." Anyone not worrying about the end of the world was not paying attention.

And yet here we are, thirty years on, safer and richer than ever. Against all the odds and in defiance of the trends of the last ten thousand years, the war to end war—and humanity itself—did not come. For every twenty nuclear warheads threatening our survival when Petrov picked up the phone in 1983, there is now (in mid-2013) just one. The chance of a megawar killing a billion people in the next few years seems close to zero.

How did we make it through these dangerous days? And how long will our luck hold out? These, it seems to me, are among the most important questions anyone can ask. The answers, though, lie in a place we rarely look.

6

RED IN TOOTH AND CLAW: WHY THE CHIMPS OF GOMBE WENT TO WAR

Killer Apes and Hippie Chimps

January 7, 1974

In the early afternoon, a war party from Kasekela slipped unseen across the border into Kahaman territory. There were eight raiders, moving silently, purposefully, on a mission to kill. By the time Godi of Kahama saw them, it was too late.

Godi leaped from the tree where he had been eating fruit and ran, but the attackers fell on him. One pinned Godi facedown in the mud; the others, screaming with rage, punched and tore at him with their fangs for a full ten minutes. Finally, after hurling rocks at his body, the war party headed deeper into the forest.

Godi was not dead, yet, but blood was pouring from dozens of gashes and punctures in his face, chest, arms, and legs. After lying still for several minutes, mewling in pain, he crawled into the trees. He was never seen again.

This was the first time that scientists had seen chimpanzees from one community deliberately seek out, attack, and leave for dead a chimpanzee from another. In 1960, Jane Goodall had set up the world's first project to study chimpanzees in the wild at Gombe in Tanzania (Figure 6.1), and for a decade she had delighted readers of *National Geographic* and viewers of her television specials with stories of the gentle, wise David Greybeard, the canny Flo, the mischievous Mike, and all their chimpanzee friends. But now the chimps were revealed as murderers.

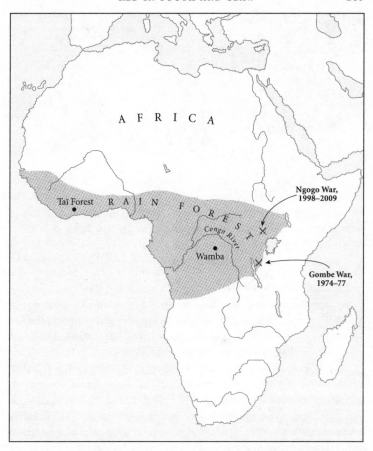

Figure 6.1. The cradle of war: sites in Africa mentioned in this chapter

Worse followed. Over the next three years, the Kasekelans beat to death all six males and one female in the Kahama community. Two more Kahaman females went missing, presumed dead; three more, beaten and raped, joined the Kasekelans; and finally, the Kasekelans took over Kahama's territory. Godi's death had been the first blow in a war of extermination (Figure 6.2).

News of the Gombe War rocked the world of primatology. The implications, it seemed, were enormous. We humans share more than 98 percent

Figure 6.2. Killer apes? Four chimpanzees (at left) bully, threaten, and charge a fifth chimpanzee (at right) in the primate park at Arnhem Zoo in the Netherlands (late 1970s).

of our DNA with chimpanzees. When two closely related species behave in the same way, there is always a good chance that they have inherited this trait from a shared ancestral species. Since we only have to go back 7.5 million years (not long to an evolutionary biologist) to find the last common ancestor of chimpanzees and humans, the obvious conclusion seemed to be that humans are hardwired for violence.

The 1970s were the golden days of *Coming of Age*–ism, and, not surprisingly, this finding did not sit well with everyone. Some scholars blamed the messenger. Goodall, they insisted, had caused the war. In her efforts to get the chimpanzees comfortable around humans, she had fed them bananas, and competition over this rich food, the critics suggested, had corrupted the chimps' naturally peaceful society and turned it violent.

The ensuing debate was just as bitter as the quarrels I described in Chapter 1 over the anthropologist Napoleon Chagnon's account of the fierce Yanomami, but Goodall did not have to wait as long as Chagnon to be proved right. In the 1970s and '80s, dozens of other scientists plunged into the African rain forest to live among apes (my account of the Gombe War and much else in the opening section of this chapter draws on the book *Demonic Males* that one of these scientists, Goodall's former graduate student Richard Wrangham, co-authored with Dale Peterson). Developing more sophisticated, less intrusive methods of observation, they soon showed that chimpanzees wage war whether humans feed them or not.

Even as you read these words, gangs of male chimpanzees are patrolling the boundaries of their territories everywhere from the Ivory Coast to Uganda, systematically hunting for foreign chimps to attack. They move silently and deliberately, not even taking time to eat. The most recent study, in Uganda, used GPS devices to track dozens of raids and twenty-one kills made by the Ngogo chimpanzee community between 1998 and 2008, ending in the annexation of a neighboring territory (Figure 6.3).

The chimps' only weapons are fists, teeth, and the occasional rock or branch, but even an elderly chimp can hit harder than a heavyweight boxer, and their razor-sharp fangs can be four inches long. When they find enemies, they fight to kill, biting through fingers and toes, breaking bones, and ripping off faces. On one occasion, primatologists looked on in horror as attackers tore open their victim's throat and yanked out his windpipe.

So *Lord of the Flies* would seem to have gotten it right: the Beast is part of us, close, close, close. But, as usually happens in new scientific fields, it quickly turned out that things were more complicated. When I brought up the *Lord of the Flies* theory in Chapter 1, I immediately had to add that a trip across the South Seas to another island, Samoa, put things in an entirely different perspective. There, Margaret Mead found evidence that convinced

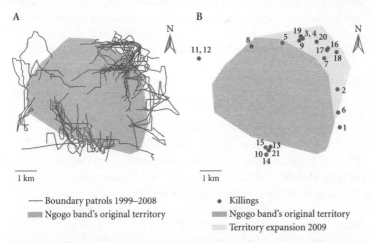

Figure 6.3. The Ngogo War, 1998–2009. Ngogo chimpanzees launched dozens of raids into neighboring territories (black lines on the map at left), killing twenty-one chimpanzees before annexing the area that had seen the heaviest fighting (shaded area on the map at right).

her that she had stumbled onto a Pacific paradise, where violence rarely reared its ugly head. In a similar way, if we leap six hundred miles across the mighty Congo River from Gombe to a different patch of African rain forest, called Wamba, it feels as if we have followed Alice through the looking glass into Wonderland.

On December 21, 1986, the primatologist Gen'ichi Idani was sitting at the edge of a clearing. He was waiting to see a party of apes pass through, but to his astonishment, not one but two parties simultaneously showed up. If Idani had been at Gombe, things might have turned very nasty in the next few minutes. There would have been threatening hoots between the parties, followed by mock charges and branch-waving. Under the wrong circumstances, there might have been fighting and death.

At Wamba, though, none of that happened. The two parties sat down a few yards apart and stared at each other. After half an hour, a female from what the primatologists were calling the P-group got up and ambled across the open ground toward a female from the E-group. A moment passed, and then the two females lay down facing each other. Each spread her legs; they pressed their genitals together. They started moving their hips from side to side, faster and faster, rubbing their clitorises together and grunting. Within minutes both apes were panting and shrieking, hugging each other tightly, and going into spasms. For a tense moment both fell silent, staring into each other's eyes, and then they collapsed, exhausted.

By this point, the distance between the two parties had dissolved. Almost all the apes were sharing food, grooming, or having sex—male with female, female with female, male with male, young with old, with hands, mouths, and genitals mingling indiscriminately. They were making love, not war (Figure 6.4).

Over the next two months, Idani and his colleagues watched the P- and E-groups repeat this scene some thirty times. Not once did they see anything like the violence of the Gombe chimpanzees—but that was because the apes of Wamba were not chimpanzees. Not the same kind of chimpanzees, anyway. Technically, the Wamba apes were pygmy chimpanzees (*Pan paniscus*), while the Gombe apes were regular chimpanzees (*Pan troglodytes*).

To the untrained eye the two species are almost indistinguishable, the pygmy variety being just slightly smaller, with arms and legs a little longer and thinner, mouths and teeth a little smaller, faces a little blacker, and hair parted in the middle (primatologists only identified *Pan paniscus* as a

Figure 6.4. Hippie chimps: two female bonobos in the Congo Basin engaging in what scientists call genito-genital rubbing

separate species in 1928). The differences between them, though, help us answer the fundamental question of what war is good for, and what will happen to humanity in the twenty-first century.

Pygmy chimpanzees (to avoid confusion, scientists usually call them bonobos; journalists often call them hippie chimps) and regular chimpanzees (usually just called chimpanzees, without any qualifying adjective) have almost identical DNA, having diverged from their shared ancestor just 1.3 million years ago (Figure 6.5). Even more surprisingly, the two kinds of apes are genetically equidistant from humans. If chimpanzee wars suggest that humans might be natural-born killers, bonobo orgies suggest we could equally well be natural-born lovers. Rather than pulling out their swords and stabbing at the Graupian Mountain, Agricola and Calgacus might have torn off their togas and rubbed their genitals together.

Explaining why there was stabbing rather than rubbing in A.D. 83 will also show us why, after ten thousand years of regularly choosing war over words, we did *not* go ahead and blow the world to pieces in the later twentieth century. It will also hint at how we might maintain this record in the twenty-first. But it is a long story—3.8 billion years long, in fact.

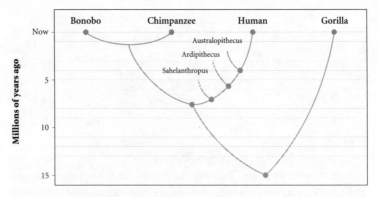

Figure 6.5. The family tree: the divergence of the great apes from our last shared ancestor fifteen million years ago

The Game of Death

In the beginning, there were blobs.

At least, that is what biologists often call them: short chains of carbon-based molecules held together by crude membranes. These blobs began forming about 3.8 billion years ago, through chemical reactions between simple proteins and nucleic acids. The blobs grew by absorbing chemicals, and when they got too big for their membranes, they split into multiple blobs. Each time a blob split, its component chemicals knew how to re-combine into new blobs because the ground plan for blobbishness was encoded in ribonucleic acid (RNA), which told proteins what to do. Un-dramatic as it sounds, this was the beginning of life.

Darwin famously defined evolution as "descent with modification." RNA (or, in complicated life-forms such as ourselves, DNA, deoxyribonu-cleic acid) copies genetic code almost—but not quite—perfectly, introduc-ing random genetic mutations. Most of these made little difference to the blobs; a few were catastrophic, causing the blobs to break apart (killing them, we might say); and others made the blobs replicate better. Over time—a *lot* of time—more efficient blobs outreproduced less efficient blobs.

Evolution may be the one thing in the world that is even more para-doxical than war. Natural selection is a competition, but the biggest re-wards go to cooperation, resulting—to cut this 3.8-billion-year-long story short—in the evolution of ever-more-complex carbon-based life-forms that cooperate and compete in extraordinary ways.

Three hundred million years of random genetic mutations produced blobs able to cooperate well enough to form cells (more sophisticated bundles of carbon-based molecules clustered around strings of DNA). Cells outcompeted blobs for access to energy in the earth's primeval oceans, and by 1.5 billion years ago had become much more complicated. For the previous 2 billion years, all life had reproduced by cloning, and mistakes in genetic copying were the only source of modification. The new cells, however, could cooperate by sharing the information in their DNA—that is, by sexual reproduction. Sex massively increased the variation in the gene pool, sending evolution into overdrive. By 600 million years ago, some cells were sharing genetic information so thoroughly that they could band together by the millions to make multicellular organisms (our own bodies contain about 100 billion cells each).

The cells in these animals cooperated by taking on different functions. Some turned into gills and stomachs to process energy in new ways; others into blood, to carry this energy around the body; and others still into shells, cartilage, and bones. By 400 million years ago, some fish found their gills turning into lungs and their fins into feet; they invaded the land.

The cells in fins or feet did not compete with those in stomachs or bones; instead, they cooperated to make a creature that could compete more successfully against other clusters of cells to get the energy that all such animals needed. The result was an evolutionary arms race. It took hundreds of millions of years, but some cells specialized to be sensitive to light, sound, touch, taste, or smell, and the resulting eyes, ears, skin, tongues, and noses gave animals information on where to go and what to do. Nerves carried this information to a single point, normally at the front end of the animal, where they knotted together into tiny brains.

Animals that became aware of their own bodies—where their skin was, where they themselves ended and the rest of the world began—tended to compete better than those unaware of such boundaries, and those aware of their own awareness competed better still. The brain became conscious of the animal it was lodged within as an individual; it formulated hopes, fears, and dreams. The animal became an "I," and mind came into the world.

That the blind, undirected process of descent with modification has over the last three billion years turned carbon blobs into poets, politicians, and Stanislav Petrov does seem like something of a miracle, and we need hardly be surprised that until Darwin's day almost every human who ever lived saw the hand of god(s) behind the wonder of life. But this astounding story also had a darker side.

Around 400 million years ago, the mouths of some fish sprouted cartilaginous teeth, sharp enough—and set in jaws strong enough—to tear the flesh of other animals. These proto-sharks had found a shortcut in the competition for energy. They could steal the energy locked up in other animals' bodies by eating them, and if they bumped into other proto-sharks competing for the same piece of food or the same sexual partner, they could fight. Teeth raised competition to a new level, and other animals responded by growing scales for defense, speed for fleeing, and teeth of their own (or stings, poison sacs, and—on land—claws and fangs) for striking back. Violence had evolved.

This did not turn the world into a free-for-all. When one animal runs into another that can fight back, it thinks twice before attacking. Animals that are heavily armed with fangs and claws will growl, bare their teeth, or puff up feathers or fur rather than simply assaulting one another. If bravado fails and the rival does not crawl, run, swim, or fly away, things may reach the point of locking horns or butting heads until one contestant recognizes that it is losing and yields. But tussling like this is a risky business, regularly causing serious injuries, and every species has evolved ways to avoid actual fighting through elaborate signals of submission, such as groveling, presenting bellies or rears, and even urinating with fear.

Explaining this behavior will provide the key to making sense of much of the behavior we saw among our own species in Chapters 1–5, but to get to the answers, we must turn from biology to mathematics. Imagine, mathematicians say, two animals simultaneously coming across a tasty morsel or available mate. Will they fight? All kinds of factors will play into the decision, and no two animals will act in exactly the same way. Take my own two dogs. One, Fuzzy, thinks everyone is his friend, and he turns every encounter into a frenzy of tail-wagging, sniffing, and licking. The other, Milo, assumes that every other dog (except Fuzzy) is out to get him. There will be snarling, lunging, and straining at the leash; given the chance, he will bite first and sniff later.

And yet, mathematicians observe, behind the almost infinite variety of animal personalities and actual encounters, there are patterns. Fighting has consequences for the participants' genetic success. The effects can be direct, as when the winner passes on genes by procreating or the loser drops out of the gene pool by getting injured or dying, but more often they are indirect. A winner might eat, storing energy for procreating later, or win prestige, becoming more attractive to mates and more intimidating to rivals. A loser might go hungry or lose face.

Few animals (including humans) calculate quite so coldly when a confrontation gets going; instead, we are taken over by hormones that have evolved precisely to help us make quick decisions. Chemicals flood our brains. We panic and run away, wag tails and approach, or see red—"the mad blood stirring," said Shakespeare—and lash out in anger. The choices each animal makes, though, affect its chances of transmitting genes to the next generation, and thanks to the relentless logic of natural selection, behaviors that favor transmission gradually replace those that don't.

We might think of these confrontations, the mathematicians suggest, as games, and assign points on a league table of genetic success for the different moves an animal might make. Game theory (which is what scientists call this exercise) simplifies reality wildly, but it helps us see how each species—including humans—evolves its own balance between fight, fright, and flight.

I will borrow an example from the evolutionary biologist Richard Dawkins. Let us say, he proposes in his bestselling book *The Selfish Gene*, that an animal that wins a confrontation picks up 50 points in the race for genetic success while one that loses gets 0. Getting hurt costs a player 100 points, and a long confrontation that wastes time (which could be more profitably spent eating or mating somewhere else) costs the animal 10 points.

If the two animals facing off are doves (not real doves; this is mathematics, so "dove" is a symbol, standing for an animal that never fights), they will not come to blows. They both want the mate, food, or status under dispute, though, so a standoff ensues, with much puffing up and hard staring. This goes on until one bird loses patience and flies off. The winner then gets 50 points, but loses 10 for time wasted, for a net gain of +40. The dove that backs down scores −10 (0 gained and 10 points lost for its time). The average outcome of such face-offs, repeated millions of times over thousands of years, is +15 points (the winner's 40 points added to the loser's −10, divided by 2).

But what if one of the doves is actually a hawk? (Again, this is a mathematical hawk, which just means an animal that always fights.) The hawk neither stares nor puffs up; it attacks, and the dove flees. If every confrontation this hawk gets into is against a dove, the hawk always scores 50 points (with no points lost, because no time has been wasted)—much more than the +15 a dove averages with its strategy. The result: hawkish genes spread through the dovish population.

But now the paradox of evolution kicks in. As the number of hawks increases, it becomes more likely that a hawk will find itself facing another hawk rather than a dove, and both will attack. One hawk will win (+50 points; for simplicity's sake, I will assume it is unhurt), and the other will be wounded, losing 100 points. The overall yield (50–100, shared between the two animals) is –25 points.

In this situation, the remaining doves do rather well. Because they always flee, they always score 0 points, which is a lot better than the –25 that the hawks are making. Dove genes start spreading back through the population. The scoring system Dawkins deployed in this game means that the gene pool will drift toward a sweet spot—what biologists call an evolutionarily stable strategy—at which five out of every twelve animals act like doves and the other seven like hawks.

Random mutations, luck, and all kinds of other forces constantly push the actual numbers away from this balance, only for the game of death to pull them back again. Each species, including our own, will have outliers—its Fuzzys and Milos—but most members are somewhere in the middle, nudged by the game of death toward the evolutionarily stable strategy, with its own distinctive form of violence.

The abstract game of death lays bare the principles behind the use of force in every kind of animal. It suggests that our own violence, like that of other creatures, must be an evolutionary adaptation, descended with modification from the habits of ancestors millions of years ago. But at the same time, game theory also shows us the peculiarities of human violence. We regularly kill rather than just chase off enemies. Since winners who fight to the death face more risks than winners who accept submission, killers should on average get lower payoffs from the game of death than non-killers. He who fights and runs away lives to fight another day, and so does he who recognizes signals of submission and lets the loser go.

So why, we have to ask, when Godi jumped out of his tree at Gombe in 1974 and ran for dear life, did the Kasekelans chase him, pin him down, and beat him to death? Why did they go on to kill the rest of the Kahaman males? Why have chimpanzees embraced lethal violence as part of their evolutionarily stable strategy? And why have we?

A Little Help from My Friends

Part of the answer is obvious. The attack that killed Godi differed in one crucial way from the abstract experiments of game theory: it was eight against one. The Kahaman chimp never stood a chance, and his attackers knuckle-walked away with barely a scratch on them. One of the Kasekelans was so old that his teeth were worn down to stumps, but at those odds he happily joined in the bloodbath.

Eight-to-one attacks are a special kind of violence, only possible for animals that can cooperate to form gangs. It has taken an awful lot of evolution to produce this blend of cooperation and competition. Three and a half billion years ago, some blobs evolved to cooperate so well that they could become cells, which could compete for energy more effectively than crude blobs. Around 1.5 billion years ago, some cells worked together so well that they could reproduce sexually, generating more mutations and offspring than asexual cells. By 600 million years ago, some of these complex cells were cooperating so much that they formed multicelled animals, with yet more advantages in the competition to pass on their genes. But only in the last 100 million years have some of these animals raised cooperation still higher, forming multi-animal societies.

Biologists call these organisms social animals. All birds and mammals are at least slightly social, in that mothers and their young form strong bonds, but a few dozen species go well beyond this. They form permanent communities with anywhere from dozens to billions of members, each one of whom has his or her own functions in a larger division of labor. Only social animals can form gangs and engage in an activity like killing Godi.

Humans, the cleverest animals on earth, are highly social. So too are dolphins, killer whales, and nonhuman apes, which also stand out for brainpower. But before we jump to the conclusion that braininess causes sociability, we should bear in mind that ants—arguably the most sociable animals of all—are also among the stupidest. Although ant cooperation reaches such heights that biologists call their colonies superorganisms, with millions of insects acting together as if they made up one giant animal, ant experts also call these superorganisms "civilization by instinct," because individual ants have such sketchy mental lives that the knot of nerve endings in an ant's head barely counts as a brain at all ("ganglion" is the preferred term).

Some ten thousand species of ants are known, and far more wait to be classified. Some of these species are very peaceful, while others fight constantly. Just as some cells in an animal's body turn into blood while others become teeth, some female ants in each colony turn into reproductive queens while others become sterile workers, and in warlike species some also grow up to be soldiers. Without ever really thinking about what they are doing, they wage savage wars driven by smell.

Since there are so many kinds of ants, there are many different patterns, but one of the commonest is that soldier ants "smell" the workers in their colony by tapping them with their antennae (which function rather like our noses). If foragers go out in the morning but do not come back, the absence of their smells triggers a response that sends the soldiers rushing out to confront whatever is detaining the foragers. After about one-fifth of the soldiers have marched out, the remaining four-fifths react to the new chemical balance in the air by staying put as a reserve in case some other ant colony should exploit their absence to seize the unoccupied nest.

If the expeditionary force finds that enemy ants are killing the missing foragers, it does not just rush to attack the foe. Instead, the soldier ants do more tapping and smelling, and if this tells them that they outnumber the enemy, they charge, clamping their jaws around the hostile ants' abdomens and breaking them in two (Figure 6.6). If the odds seem balanced, they will have a standoff, waving their feelers, and if they sense that they are outnumbered, they run home. When the imbalance in numbers is extreme, the stronger force might storm the weaker's nest, massacring its queen and soldiers and carrying off its babies to raise as slaves.

Biologists draw three broad conclusions from this. First, since some species of unintelligent ants and some species of highly intelligent apes wage lethal gang warfare while other species do not, powerful brains are neither necessary nor sufficient for this kind of behavior. Second, we can conclude that sociability *is* necessary for lethal gang warfare, because only sociable animals can form gangs, cooperating to attack enemies at such unfair odds that they can safely fight to the death. The third conclusion, however, is that sociability by itself is not a sufficient cause for lethal violence, because some species of sociable apes and ants do not form murderous mobs.

For animals to make killing part of their evolutionarily stable strategy, some other factor must be driving up the payoff from lethal aggression, and the natural histories of ants and apes suggest that this secret ingredient is territory. When animals have valuable territories to compete over, the payoff from killing enemies rises. Each time the chimpanzees of Kasekela raided into Kahama during the Gombe War, the Kahama chimps retali-

Figure 6.6. Six-legged soldiers: *Plectroctena* ants battling to the death in Tanzania

ated by raiding back into Kasekela. If the Kasekelans had scared Godi but let him get away on January 7, 1974, they could have been confident he would have joined the next raid against them. But if they killed him, they could be certain he would not. And if they killed all the Kahaman males, they could take over their land and surviving females.

Here we confront one of the biggest paradoxes of war. Territoriality drove up the payoff from killing for those ants and apes sociable enough to be able to do it safely, but when, at the end of the Ice Age, population growth and farming began caging human societies in the lucky latitudes, this extreme version of territoriality pushed our ancestors into productive war, which raised the payoffs from *not* killing defeated enemies. Instead, societies that recognized signals of submission and absorbed losers became safer and richer and outcompeted their rivals until—eventually—one of them turned into a globocop.

I will return to this odd outcome toward the end of the chapter. For now, though, I want to focus on the facts that—for all their differences—chimpanzees, bonobos, and humans are all sociable and territorial and all descend from a shared ancestor (usually called proto-Pan, from the Greek words for ancestral ape). Clearly, this ancestral species had the potential to develop wildly different evolutionarily stable strategies. Something happened 7 or 8 million years ago to set chimpanzees and humans on the road toward violence; then, around 1.3 million years ago, something else happened to push bonobos away from using violence against their own kind (although they do hunt monkeys for meat, and in one disturbing case, several adult bonobos were seen to cannibalize a dead bonobo baby, with the baby's mother leading the way). Finally, in the last 10,000 years, yet another development made us humans react to caging by becoming less violent. But what?

Planet of the Apes

I want to look first at the chimpanzee/bonobo split, which, study of the two apes' DNA tells us, began around 1.3 million years ago. This makes it much more recent than the human/proto-Pan split (dating back some 7.5 million years). Unfortunately, though, we know less about it, because fossils do not survive well in the tropical rain forest where it happened. This forces us to work with indirect lines of evidence.

DNA analysis suggests that as recently (on an evolutionary scale) as 2 million years ago, the now-extinct proto-Pans roamed over a central African rain forest the size of the continental United States. But nothing lasts forever, and as the climate fluctuated over the following half-million years, a great inland lake in East Africa burst its banks. The water flowed north and west toward the Atlantic, turning into what is now the mighty, mile-wide Congo River (Figure 6.7). Impassable to apes, this split proto-Pan's kingdom in two. By 1.3 million years ago, apes north of the Congo were evolving into chimpanzees and those south of the river into bonobos.

The forests on either side of the river were not wildly different, and apes in both places ate mostly fruit, seeds, and (when they could catch them) monkeys. South of the Congo, however, the apes that eventually evolved into bonobos expanded their diet by eating young leaves and shoots. Their bodies adapted to this diet, growing teeth with long shearing edges to tear up their greens. Bonobos do not find leaves and shoots as tasty as fruits, seeds, and monkey meat, but leaves and shoots are more plentiful, and they keep bonobos full between real meals. Leaves and shoots, says the biological anthropologist Richard Wrangham, are bonobo "snack food."

Just why bonobos fill up on these snacks and chimpanzees do not remains controversial, but in their book *Demonic Males*, Wrangham and his co-author Dale Peterson suggest that it is because gorillas—who also eat

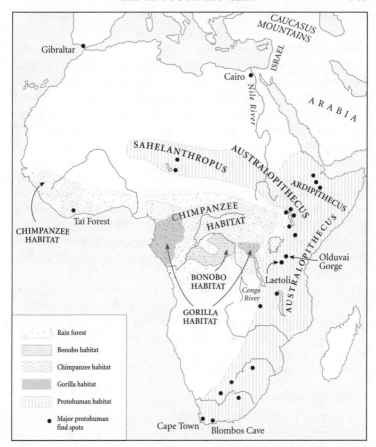

Figure 6.7. Planet of the apes: the ranges of modern chimpanzees, bonobos, and gorillas, and major sites with protohuman fossils between one million and six million years old

shoots and leaves—went extinct south of the Congo but hung on north of it. This left the southern branch of proto-Pan without competitors for shoots and leaves, and so any random genetic mutation that made it easier for an ape to eat this extra food flourished. The mutations spread through the gene pool, and proto-Pan began evolving into bonobos. North of the river, however, proto-Pan still lived alongside gorillas, and since no hundred-pound proto-Pan that challenged the proverbial four-hundred-pound gorilla for a leaf would last long enough to pass on its genes, chimpanzees did not evolve to eat these foods.

Other primatologists suggest different explanations, such as small differences between the two sides of the Congo in climate or the concentration of good foods, which might have made growing new kinds of teeth and adapting to new foods worthwhile for bonobos but not for chimpanzees. Eventually, as techniques improve and data pile up, scientists will surely answer this question. For our purposes, though, what really matters is not the cause of the divergence in diets but its consequences, because—unlikely as it may sound—snacks sent bonobos down the path toward peace and love while chimps took off along the hard road of violence.

Because they can fill up on leaves and shoots when they cannot find fruits and their other favorite foods, bonobos can travel in large, stable groups (typically about sixteen animals). Chimpanzees, however, regularly have to split up into very small groups of two to eight animals, because they cannot find enough fruit to feed larger parties. Godi's disastrous decision to strike off on his own in 1974 was entirely typical for a chimpanzee but would have been very eccentric for a bonobo. The result, of course, is that bonobos almost never find themselves outnumbered eight to one.

But that is not all. Chimpanzee groups also tend to split up in very specific ways when they go foraging. Males can travel faster than females (especially females burdened with babies), and so males often head off in single-sex groups. Female chimps, however, often resort to foraging individually, because they move too slowly to cover enough ground in a day to find enough food to support a bigger group. All this is in striking contrast to the snack-rich bonobos. As well as being large and stable, their foraging parties normally have roughly equal numbers of males and females.

At this point, the absence of snacks in chimpanzee-land turns ugly. Groups of half a dozen males are regularly running into isolated females. The males do not always rape the females, but it happens with alarming regularity. At these odds, females have no real chance of fighting off attackers; what fighting does take place instead tends to be among the males, over who gets access to the female.

Over the last million-plus years, male chimpanzees have evolved two very specific features because of their inability to subsist on snacks: hawkishness and huge testicles. Because rape is always an option, males who will fight are more likely to pass on their genes than males who will not, and because females often end up having sex with multiple males in a single day, males who have large testes (to pump out the biggest possible load of sperm, increasing the odds of being the lucky fellow who fertilizes the egg) have a reproductive advantage over those who do not.

So important is this quirk of ape evolution that biologists have created an entire subfield called sperm competition theory. On average, chimpanzee testicles weigh a whopping quarter pound, while gorillas, despite having bodies four times as big, have testicles weighing just an ounce. This is because each alpha-male gorilla monopolizes a harem of females and faces little competition from other gorillas' sperm.

Bonobos have huge testicles too, because male bonobos, like male chimpanzees, are locked in competition to impregnate females who have multiple sexual partners. Unlike what goes on among chimps, however, bonobo sperm competitions are almost entirely nonviolent. Males rarely outnumber females, and if a male courts his intended too aggressively, other females are likely to gang up on him, chasing him away with hoots and threats. (Female chimpanzees do sometimes cooperate against rapists, but nowhere near so effectively.)

Male bonobos win the sperm competition not by fighting each other but by making themselves agreeable to females. One of the best methods, it seems, is to be a good son; bonobo mothers use their friendships among the females to make sure that their own sons find girlfriends. In the land of the bonobos, mama's boys finish first.

Across a million or so years, the payoffs of dovishness soared among bonobos. The meek inherited the rain forest, and bonobos of both sexes evolved to be smaller, more delicate, and just plain *nicer* than chimpanzees. "In all my experience," Robert Yerkes (the founding father of primatology) said of Prince Chim, the first bonobo in captivity, "I have never met an animal the equal of Prince Chim in approach to physical perfection, alertness, adaptability, and agreeableness of disposition." Whether Prince Chim felt the same way about Yerkes, who locked him up in Cambridge, Massachusetts, and trained him to eat with a fork at a miniature table, we will never know.

The Naked Ape

The evolutionary paths that led to Chim and Yerkes branched about 7.5 million years ago. Around then, apes living at the edges of the great central African rain forest began evolving away from proto-Pan and toward us—the only animals with the capacity to cage their own Beast.

Once again, food seems to have been at the center of things. Because fruit trees thin out in these dry borderlands, giving way first to mixed woodland and then to open savannas, apes had to find new things to eat if they were to live there. Since adversity is the mother of evolutionary invention, all kinds of genetic mutations flourished as the apes adapted. Anthropologists have given these creatures wonderful, exotic names— *Sahelanthropus* north of the rain forest, *Ardipithecus* east of it, and different kinds of *Australopithecus* all around it—but I will call them collectively protohumans.

To the nonexpert eye, protohuman bones look much like any other ape's, but great changes were under way. Over a few million years, molar teeth grew bigger and flatter, thickly coated with enamel. This made them ideal for crunching up hard, dry foods, and chemical analysis shows that the foods in question were tubers and the roots of grasses. These are good sources of carbohydrates and are available even in dry spells, when the aboveground parts of plants shrivel up—*if* apes can dig them up and chew them. Any mutation that made paws nimbler would therefore make protohumans fatter, stronger, and probably better at fighting too, and altogether more likely to spread their genes through the population.

The anatomy of ankles and finds of actual footprints, left by protohumans taking strolls through soft ash and mud that then hardened into stone, show that the shift was under way by four million years ago. Protohumans had begun walking on their hind legs, freeing up their front legs to turn into arms. These creatures were certainly still very different from us, however. They were only four feet tall, probably covered in hair, and still spent a lot of time in trees. They rarely—if ever—made stone tools and certainly could not talk, and it is a fair bet that the males still had testicles on the chimpanzee/bonobo scale.

But however apelike they were, they more than made up for it by mutating toward bigger and bigger brains. Four million years ago, the average *Australopithecus* sported twenty-two cubic inches of gray matter (less than modern chimpanzees, which typically have twenty-five cubic inches). By three million years ago, this had increased to twenty-eight cubic inches, and another million years after that, to thirty-eight. (Today we average eighty-six cubic inches.)

It might seem self-evident that big brains are better than small ones, but the logic of evolution is more complicated. Brains are expensive to run. Our own typically make up 2 percent of our body weight but use up 20 percent of the energy we consume. Mutations producing bigger brains only spread if the brain tissue that is added pays for itself by bringing in the extra food it needs. In the middle of the rain forest, this was rarely the case, because apes did not need to be Einsteins to find leaves and fruit. In the dry woodlands and savanna, however, brainpower and food supply rose together in a virtuous spiral. Smart woodland apes dug up roots and tubers, which paid for bigger brains; the even smarter apes this produced figured out better ways to hunt, and meat paid for even more of the expensive gray cells.

Armed with all this brainpower, protohumans went straight to work on inventing weapons. Modern chimpanzees and bonobos have been known to use sticks and stones to catch food and hit each other, but by 2.4 million years ago protohumans had already realized that they could bash pebbles together to make sharp cutting edges. Telltale marks show that they used these choppers (as archaeologists call them) to slice meat off animal bones, although so far we have found no signs that they used them to slice each other.

Biologists conventionally treat the combination of brains over thirty-eight cubic inches and the ability to make tools as the threshold at which apes became *Homo* ("mankind" in Latin), the genus to which we, *Homo sapiens* ("wise man"), belong, and over the next half-million years *Homo* began looking and acting much more like us. Around 1.8 million years ago, in the space of a few thousand generations—the blinking of an evolutionary eye—average adult height shot up above five feet. Bones became lighter, with jaws that protruded less and noses that protruded more. Sexual dimorphism—the size difference between males and females—declined toward the range we find among modern people, and protohumans shifted permanently from tree to ground living.

The label that biologists use for these new creatures is *Homo ergaster*, "working man," chosen to reflect their skill at making tools and weapons. Some of these can be quite beautiful, made from carefully selected stones and finished with delicate touches from wood and bone "hammers"—all of which required careful coordination, forward planning, and, of course, bigger brains still (fifty-three cubic inches by 1.7 million years ago).

Homo ergaster paid for its huge head with a peculiar trade-off: its guts got smaller. Earlier protohumans had rib cages that flared out at the bottom, like those of modern apes, to accommodate enormous intestines, but *Homo ergaster*'s ribs were more like ours (Figure 6.8). This left less room for yards of digestive tubing, which poses a difficult question for anthropologists. Apes have huge bowels so they can digest the fibrous raw plants

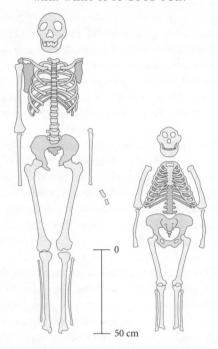

Figure 6.8. *La bella figura*: on the left, the best-preserved *Homo ergaster* skeleton so far found (known as the Turkana Boy), belonging to a boy roughly ten years old who died 1.5 million years ago; on the right, the famous Lucy, an adult female *Australopithecus afarensis* who lived 3.2 million years ago

they live on. Smaller guts would mean that *Homo ergaster* was extracting less energy from its food—but its bigger brain called for *more* energy. So what was going on?

The answer, we can be fairly certain, is that *Homo ergaster* was the first protohuman that could make fire at will and used this new skill to cook. Cooking makes food easier to digest, which made enormous intestines, along with the huge flat teeth and powerful jaws earlier protohumans had needed to chew up raw tubers, roots, and grass, redundant. All now disappeared.

This, Richard Wrangham suggests in his marvelous book *Catching Fire*, was as much of a turning point in the evolution of human violence as snacks were for bonobos. Anytime a chimpanzee catches a monkey or finds a particularly tasty breadfruit, Wrangham has observed in his many years in the rain forest, males materialize from all around, and fighting frequently breaks out. Even sweet-natured bonobos find it difficult to enjoy a morsel of monkey brain without being besieged by jostling beggars. It is hard, Wrangham observes, to imagine how either kind of ape could have cooked food without it all being stolen—in which case this adaptation would not have paid off and would not have spread through the population. This forces us to conclude, Wrangham suggests, that when cooking caught on, it did so as part of a package deal with another great change—the shift from living in large, sexually promiscuous troops (like chimpanzees or bonobos) to male-female pair-bonding.

When chimpanzees and bonobos look for food, it is every ape for itself, with males and females active as both hunters and gatherers. Among modern human hunter-gatherers, though, men typically do nearly all the hunting and women nearly all the gathering, and they then share the food with each other and their offspring. The details vary according to where in the world people live, but in pretty much every hunter-gatherer society, woman's work includes cooking and man's work includes threatening or even attacking anyone trying to steal the couple's food. This raises the costs of theft, changing the evolutionarily stable strategy. Families replace troops as the foundation of society, with elaborate rules of sharing and etiquette evolving to take care of the elderly, orphans, and others without their own home and hearth.

These changes must have revolutionized protohuman intimacy. As our ancestors shifted from apelike sex lives to pair-bonding, proto-men's best strategy for passing on their genes shifted too, from fighting their way to the front of the line and flooding proto-women with semen toward skill at courting and providing. If *Homo ergaster* males still had quarter-pound testicles, they would have been as much of an expensive luxury as enormous intestines. Proto-men still faced sperm competition from seducers and rapists, and could not get away with gonads as tiny as alpha-male gorillas', but by modern times our testes had shrunk to just 1.5 ounces.

Along with huge scrotums, proto-men also lost a rather revolting feature of bonobo and chimpanzee penises: a little spur on the side that works to scoop any old deposits of semen out of a partner's vagina before inserting a new one. The fact that bonobos and chimpanzees both have these spurs strongly suggests that our last shared ancestor had them too and that protohumans lost their spurs because they no longer needed them. In their place, proto-men grew supersized phalluses. The average human erection is about six inches long, but chimpanzees and bonobos manage just three inches, and gorillas a meager inch and a quarter. Proto-women returned the compliment by growing breasts that look like mountains compared with the molehills on other apes.

These anatomical peculiarities led Desmond Morris, a onetime keeper of primates at London Zoo, to conclude in his famous book *The Naked Ape* that humans are "the sexiest primate alive" (this was fifty years ago, before primatologists had discovered what bonobos get up to). Remarkably, zoologists cannot seem to agree on why human breasts and penises ballooned ("The inability of twentieth-century science to formulate an adequate Theory of Penis Length," Jared Diamond dryly muses, is "a glaring failure"), but the obvious guess is that shifting from fighting for mates to courting them put a high priority on sending signals of sexual fitness, both to the opposite sex and to same-sex rivals. What better way to do that than by flaunting ostentatiously enormous organs?

By 1.3 million years ago, the point at which bonobos and chimpanzees began diverging, protohumans had already evolved very, very far from other apes. Just how that affected strategies of trauma, though, remains controversial, because we currently have nowhere near enough fossil skeletons to get a sense of how many protohumans were bludgeoned, stabbed, and otherwise done to death. To date, only one body dating back more than a million years bears traces of lethal trauma, and even that is not a certain case of deliberate killing. Only in the last half-million years, when skeletons become much more common, do we find unambiguously fatal wounds.

But given the similarities between the ways chimpanzees and modern humans fight, we can make some fairly secure speculations. In both populations, violence is overwhelmingly the preserve of young males, who are likely to be bigger, stronger, and angrier than females or old males. There is a saying that when you have a hammer, every problem looks like a nail, and to young male chimps and humans, wrapped in muscles and soaked in testosterone, many problems look like ones that force will solve. Primatologists tell us that males commit well over 90 percent of assaults among chimpanzees, and policemen tell us that the human statistics are very similar. Young males (human or chimpanzee) will fight over almost anything, with sex and prestige as the major flash points and material goods a rather distant third, and they are most likely to turn homicidal when they get together in gangs that outnumber their enemies.

Evolutionists cannot at this point prove that humans and chimpanzees inherited the practice of lethal male gang violence from proto-Pan, but it is certainly the most economical conclusion. If that is right, we should probably also conclude that starting about 1.8 million years ago, pair-bonding made fighting less useful than courting as a mating strategy among *Homo ergaster* but did not reduce its value as a way to deal with rival communities of protohumans. Bonobos, by contrast, began evolving in an entirely different direction 1.3 million years ago, as female solidarity reduced the payoffs to male violence across the board. (Pair-bonding might actually have reduced the scope for bonobo-like group solidarity among proto-women.)

As archaeologists excavate more skeletons, the details will become clearer, but the one thing we can already be certain about is that the proto-humans' new evolutionarily stable strategy was hugely successful. *Homo* went forth and multiplied as no ape had done before. Over the course of a thousand centuries, our ancestors spread across much of Africa, and a thousand centuries more of gradual extensions of their grazing ranges took them as far as what we now call England and Indonesia (the earliest skeleton with signs of violence in fact comes from Java). They moved into environments utterly different from the East African savanna, and, predictably, mutations flourished. Almost every year now brings an announcement that archaeologists or geneticists have discovered yet another new species of protohuman in Asia or Europe.

By half a million years ago, one of these protohuman variants—known, after its original find spot in Germany, as Heidelberg Man—had evolved brains almost as big as ours, and over the next few hundred thousand years Neanderthals (also named after an original find spot in Germany) actually grew brains bigger than ours, albeit flatter, with some areas therefore less developed. One or both species might have communicated in ways we would call speech, and they definitely found new ways to kill, using resin and sinews taken from other animals to attach stone spearheads to wooden shafts.

Archaeologists have found enough Neanderthal skeletons to know that they were very, very violent. At least two skulls bear healed traces of non-fatal stabbings. Stone spearheads are common on Neanderthal sites, and head and neck traumas even more so. The closest parallel to Neanderthal bone breakage patterns comes in fact from modern rodeo riders—but since there were no bucking broncos a hundred thousand years ago, we probably have to assume that Neanderthals got hurt fighting. Possibly all these fights were against their prey, but since their prey sometimes included other Neanderthals—the evidence of occasional cannibalism is overwhelming— it is hard not to suspect that the big-brained Neanderthals were the most violent of all the great apes. Clever, well armed, and extraordinarily strong (two leading archaeologists describe them as "combining [the physique] of a powerful wrestler with the endurance of a marathon runner"), by 100,000 B.C. they had extended their range from central Asia to the Atlantic.

But then along came us.

2.7 Pounds of Magic

Inside your head is a little piece of magic. Nothing else in nature can compare with the 2.7 pounds of water, fat, blood, and protein pulsing away inside your skull, guzzling energy and fairly crackling with electricity. Four hundred million years in the making, this brain sets us apart from every other animal on earth and has changed everything about the place of force in our lives.

Archaeologists and geneticists agree that this miracle of nature took on its fully modern form in Africa somewhere between 200,000 and 50,000 years ago. This was a time when new twigs were sprouting off the protohuman branch of the tree of life with particular vigor, perhaps because an extremely unstable climate kept changing the payoffs in the games of life and death.

It was a wild ride: temperatures 200,000 years ago were distinctly cooler than today's (on average, perhaps 3°F lower), but then, amid many wild zigs and zags, they tumbled into a genuine ice age. By 150,000 years ago, the world was 14°F colder than today. Mile-thick glaciers blanketed much of northern Asia, Europe, and America, tying up so much water that the sea level fell three hundred feet below what we are used to. No one could live on the glaciers, and the vast arid steppes around their edges, where winds howled and dust storms raged, were little better. Even near the equator, summers were short, water was scarce, and low levels of atmospheric carbon dioxide stunted plant growth.

Humans that looked just like us, with high, domed skulls, flat faces, and small teeth, first walked the earth in these years. Excavated fossil remains and DNA studies both agree on this, suggesting that the first modern humans evolved in East Africa between 200,000 and 150,000 years ago. The odd thing about the earliest finds, though, is that while these great apes chipped stone tools, hunted and gathered, and fought and mated, little we find on their sites is very different from what we find on sites belonging to Neanderthals or other protohumans. Just why this is remains hotly debated, but it was not until after the world had warmed up for a few millennia and then crashed into another ice age that humans started acting like us as well as looking like us.

Beginning between 100,000 and 70,000 years ago, odd things start turning up on archaeological sites. People were now decorating themselves, something previous protohumans did not do. They collected eggshells and spent hours chipping and grinding little disks out of them. Using just a pointed bone, they would drill a hole through the middle of each disk and string hundreds together in necklaces. They swapped these ornaments with each other, sometimes trading them across hundreds of miles.

Protohumans were acting a lot less proto and a lot more human. They gathered ocher, a kind of iron ore, and used it to draw bold red lines on cave walls and probably on each other's bodies. At Blombos Cave in South Africa someone even scratched simple geometric patterns onto a little stick of ocher seventy-five thousand years ago—making it not just the oldest known work of art but also a work of art used for making other works of art.

People coaxed their fingers into producing tiny tools, lighter and subtler than anything seen before, and then used some of the tools as weapons. The oldest known carved bones include fishhooks, and among the oldest known stone bladelets (as archaeologists call the tiny tools) are arrowheads and javelin points. Bird and fish bones from caves along Africa's southern shores show that people used these devices to kill prey that had previously been beyond their reach (remains of their shoulder and elbow joints suggest that Neanderthals, for all their fierceness, could not throw very well, let alone shoot arrows).

Like Neanderthals, early *Homo sapiens* also occasionally ate their own kind, using stone blades to carve the flesh off meaty long bones and stone hammers to crack bones to extract marrow and the tastiest treat of all, the miraculous human brain. A steady trickle of bashed-in skulls uncovered by archaeologists strongly suggests that humans were killing each other, but we have to wait until thirty thousand years ago to find decisive evidence. This comes not from mutilated skeletons but from the famous paintings that *Homo sapiens* began leaving on cave walls in northern Spain and southern France. These are things of exquisite beauty. "None of us could paint like that," Picasso is supposed to have said when he first saw them. "After Altamira, all is decadence." However, some of them have a dark side too, showing unmistakable scenes of humans shooting each other with arrows.

Archaeologists excavating sites between 100,000 and 50,000 years old occasionally find objects that look distinctly modern, such as jewelry or art, but sites younger than 50,000 years almost always include such artifacts. People were doing new things, finding new ways to do old things, and inventing multiple ways to do everything. From Cape Town to Cairo, pre-50,000-B.C. sites all look rather alike, with much the same kinds of finds used in much the same kinds of ways. Post-50,000-B.C. sites, however, vary wildly. By 30,000 B.C., the Nile Valley alone hosted half a dozen distinct regional styles of stone tools.

Humans had invented culture, using their great, fast brains to weave webs of symbols that not only communicated complex ideas—Neanderthals and perhaps even *Homo ergaster* could do that—but also preserved them through time. Modern humans, unlike any other animal on earth, could change how they thought and lived in ways that accumulated, with one idea leading to another and mounting up across the generations.

Culture is a product of the biological evolution of our big, fast brains, but culture itself also evolves. Biological evolution is driven by genetic mutations, with the mutations that work best replacing those that do not across thousands or even millions of years. Cultural evolution, however, moves much faster, because unlike the biological version, it is directed. People face problems, their little gray cells go to work, and ideas come out. Most ideas, like most genetic mutations, end up making little difference to the world, and some are downright harmful, but over time ideas that work well outcompete those that do not.

Imagine, for instance, that you were a young hunter in the Nile Valley thirty thousand years ago. In my made-up game of death earlier in this chapter, I used "doves" as symbols for animals that never fight and "hawks" for those that always fight; here, I will use "sheep" to represent people who follow the herd and "goats" for those who don't. Our young hunter is a goat, certain that he knows best, and he thinks up a new design for arrowheads. Let us say that his version has longer tangs, so that it will stay lodged in the flank of a wounded antelope better than the old style. To his astonishment, though, his sheepish associates pooh-pooh his idea, telling him that the ancestors didn't need long tangs, so neither do we.

Like fight and flight in the dove-and-hawk game, innovation and conservatism both have costs and benefits. Innovators pay a price: it takes time to learn to make new arrowheads and to use them properly (costing, let us say, 10 points), and—perhaps more seriously—going against the way things have always been done might lose them respect (−20 points). Other men might not want to cooperate on hunts with someone so quirky, in which case the goatish inventor might actually end up with less meat, despite having better technology (another −10 points). In the end, he might just let the whole thing drop.

Unless, that is, the gains outweigh the losses. If his arrowheads really do produce more kills, he not only gains weight by eating more (say, +20 points) but also can gain prestige by sharing antelope steaks generously (+25 points). Such a successful man might get more sex (a further +10 points), which will put the balance firmly in the black (at +15 points). Over several generations he might spread his ingenious, goatish genes through the little hunter-gatherer group; but cultural change will overtake biological change long before that happens, because the other men in the band will simply copy his arrowheads. The inventor's tally of points and luck with the ladies will then decline, but perhaps not quite back to zero, because now everyone is eating better—unless, of course, the hunters' new technology is so effective that it kills off all the antelopes, setting off new chains of consequences . . .

Like the dove-and-hawk game, this is fun to play. We can make the story branch off in all kinds of directions, because even small changes in the payoffs produce big changes in the results. But the point, as with the earlier game, is that in real life the sheep-and-goat game is played over and over, with different results each time. If the costs of going against tradition are high in the inventor's band, the arrowhead will not catch on, but if it really is a better arrowhead, people in other bands will also think of it, and before long it will catch on somewhere else. Goatish bands might then outhunt sheepish ones, forcing the latter either to switch arrowheads after all, or change their diet, or fight the innovators—or in an uncaged landscape they could just move away.

Culture wars of this kind are uniquely human. Although some other animals can be said to have cultures (particularly chimpanzees, among whom each community does things slightly differently from its neighbors), none seem to be capable of cumulative cultural change. The evolutionary consequences of culture have been a bit like those of the rise of sexual reproduction 1.5 billion years ago: where sex sped up genetic mutation, culture sped up innovation. Both mechanisms vastly increased the diversity of outcomes, allowing cells or humans to cooperate and compete on a bigger scale.

Armed with brains powerful enough for cultural evolution, modern humans conquered the world. A few *Homo sapiens* had drifted out of

Africa just before 100,000 years ago, when culture was still a fragile flower, and perhaps because of this these early emigrants only got as far as what we now call Israel and Arabia. There they lived alongside Neanderthals, although not necessarily happily: the oldest known fatality from a spear thrust, around 100,000 years ago, was one of these pioneers. But a second wave, which broke out of Africa about 70,000 years ago, took the full package of modern human behavior with it and spread across the planet fifty times as fast as the protohumans who had left Africa nearly 1.6 million years earlier.

Culture gave the new migrants huge advantages over protohumans. When modern humans arrived in Siberia thirty thousand years ago, for instance, it was even colder than it is now. But unlike other animals, they did not have to wait millennia while their genes evolved toward hairiness to keep them warm. Instead, they invented bone needles and gut threads and sewed fitted clothes. There might have been conservatives who preferred traditional, ill-fitting skins to this new look, but the first winter either changed their minds or killed them.

This process explains not only why there is so much cultural variety around the world (slight variations in local conditions, combined with the random generation of good enough ideas, produced countless different evolutionarily stable strategies) but also why there is so much similarity (competing cultures tend to converge on a few winning strategies). And as well as being humanity's best tool for adapting to new environments, culture was the greatest force for transforming those environments. It transformed them so much, in fact, that all the protohumans in the world went extinct.

It is unsettling to think about what this involved. On the one hand, there is no hard evidence that our ancestors actively drove protohumans extinct, and DNA analysis hints that there might have been cooperation between species. The Neanderthal genome, sequenced in 2010, shows that *Homo sapiens* and Neanderthals mixed their body fluids sufficiently often that 1–4 percent of the DNA of everyone of Asian or European descent comes from Neanderthal ancestors, while 6 percent of the DNA in Australian Aboriginals and New Guineans comes from Denisovans, a kind of protohuman that was only discovered in March 2010. On the other hand, we have no way to tell how many of these couplings were rapes—or whether, when we find smashed Neanderthal skulls, the hand that wielded the murder weapon belonged to another Neanderthal or to a *Homo sapiens*. But whether or not modern humans hunted down their rivals, it is all too easy to imagine how our inventiveness would have made life impossible for slower-witted kin who needed the same food.

Whatever the chain of cause and effect, it is a depressing coincidence that as our kind of humans spread, every other kind fled. By twenty-five thousand years ago, Neanderthals had retreated to a few inaccessible caves at Gibraltar and in the Caucasus Mountains, and by twenty thousand years ago they were gone altogether. Other kinds of protohumans hung on, on isolated islands, until 18,000 B.C., and people claim to see Yetis even today, but all the hard evidence says that we are alone and have been since the coldest point of the last ice age, two hundred centuries ago.

This was just the beginning of the ways culture would transform the planet. I spent a page or two in Chapter 2 talking about how, when the most recent ice age ended around 9600 B.C., plants multiplied madly and animals—including humans—ate them and multiplied madly too. For all animals except humans, these good times lasted only a few generations, until their own numbers outran their increased food supply and hunger returned. The humans in the lucky latitudes, though, were able to respond by evolving culturally, domesticating plants and animals to increase their food supply.

When I talked about the beginnings of agriculture in Chapter 2, I called it one of the two or three great turning points in human history, in part because the new and crowded farming landscapes made it harder for losers in the game of death to run away. This turned territoriality into caging, but whereas territory gave ants and apes reasons to fight to the death, caging had more complicated effects on us. In fact, it created the new evolutionarily stable strategy that I have been calling productive war. This rewarded people who kept killing until their rivals lost their will to resist, but beyond that point it rewarded people who accepted their defeated enemies' signals of submission rather than slaughtering them. Cultural evolution turned killers into conquerors, ruling over larger, safer, and richer societies.

Chimpanzees do incorporate some defeated enemies into their own communities, as the Kasekela chimps did with the last surviving Kahaman females at the end of the Gombe War in 1977. But chimpanzees lack the flexible brainpower for cumulative cultural evolution. There are no simian cities or ant empires, because communities that grow too large break apart, rather like the carbon blobs in the early earth's oceans. This, in fact, was how the Kasekela and Kahama chimpanzee bands originally emerged. When Jane Goodall set up her research station at Gombe in 1960, there was only one community of chimps, but this grew and then split in two in the early 1970s.

Humans, by contrast, can organize themselves to live in larger and more complex groups without having to evolve biologically into a whole new kind of animal. In the increasingly competitive caged world of the post–Ice Age lucky latitudes, bigger communities could generally outcompete smaller ones, but holding big groups together required leaders to foster internal cooperation so that the group could compete better against outsiders.

So it was that Leviathans became part of the human evolutionarily stable strategy. Once again, we can see a pale shadow of human behavior among chimpanzees, who fight less often when they live in communities with a well-established alpha male than in bands where the hierarchy is unsettled. And like human leaders who turn into stationary bandits as they pursue their self-interest, really entrenched alpha males can be surprisingly impartial and even altruistic toward the weak. The extreme case may be Freddy, a supremely secure alpha-male chimp in the Taï Forest in West Africa. The wildly popular Disney nature documentary *Chimpanzee* shows Freddy feeding and caring for an orphaned baby chimp named Oscar, even though this cost Freddy time that he would ordinarily have spent patrolling the borders with other adult males. According to the film, though, all ended well, with Freddy's troop seeing off a raid by the neighboring community, whose chief—the villainous Scar—had failed to prevent rifts from growing among his followers.*

Like so many great leaders—most famously, perhaps, Abraham Lincoln—Freddy set an example of cooperation that perhaps helped his team of rivals work together well. Yet Freddy will not be founding a dynasty that steadily drives down rates of lethal violence in the Taï Forest. To do that, he and his troop would need to evolve biologically into animals that, like humans, can evolve culturally. Alpha-male chimps cannot reorganize their societies to build on their predecessors' accomplishments any more than they can foster revolutions in military affairs. Only we can do these things.

---

*I say "according to the film" because, Richard Wrangham tells me, while Freddy, Scar, and their different behavior patterns are all real enough, the two chimps actually live on opposite sides of Africa—Freddy in the Ivory Coast, and Scar in Uganda. The filmmakers took a little artistic license and stitched two separate tales together. The moral of the story, though, seems to survive this flexible approach to reality.

And these things, as we saw in Chapters 1–5, are precisely what we have done in the last ten thousand years. We have made bigger societies that constantly revolutionize their military affairs. Fortifications, metal arms and armor, discipline, chariots, massed iron-armed infantry, cavalry, guns, battleships, tanks, aircraft, nuclear weapons—the list goes on and on, with each advance allowing us to wage ever-fiercer wars; but to compete in these conflicts, our bigger societies have also had to find ways to get their members to cooperate better, which has pushed them toward stationary bandits, internal peace, and prosperity. In this peculiar, paradoxical way, war has made the world safer and richer.

The Pacifist's Dilemma

In *The Better Angels of Our Nature*, perhaps the best book on the modern decline of violence since Norbert Elias's *Civilizing Process*, the psychologist Steven Pinker illustrates his arguments about the increasing peacefulness of Europe and North America since A.D. 1500 with a game that he calls "the Pacifist's Dilemma." The basic format is much like the hawk-and-dove and sheep-and-goat games that I played earlier in this chapter. Pinker assumes that anytime there is a dispute to be resolved, the payoff of cooperating is +5 points for each player. The payoff of attacking an unsuspecting player and just taking what you want is +10 points, while the cost of suffering such an attack is a disproportionate –100 points. (If you have ever been mugged, that will make sense.) As we might expect, the fear of losing 100 points is enough to make everyone trigger-happy, even though the payoff when both players attack is –50 points all around (both players get hurt, and neither gets what he or perhaps she wants). Everyone would like the +5 payoff from cooperating but settles for the –50 of fighting to avoid getting the –100 of being mugged.

And yet, over the past few centuries, fighting has been declining, and the world has been drifting toward +5. As Pinker points out, the logic of the game of death means the only possible explanation is that the payoffs have changed over time. Either the rewards of peace or the costs of fighting (or both) have risen so much that the number of situations in which force pays off has shrunk, and we have responded by using force less and less often.

The changes those of us now in middle age have seen during our own lifetimes are frankly quite remarkable. A few years ago, while I was directing an archaeological excavation in Sicily, the topic of fighting came up one evening over dinner. One of the students on the dig—a big, strapping lad in his early twenties—commented that he couldn't imagine what it would feel like to hit someone. I thought he was joking, until it became clear that almost no one at the table had ever raised a hand in anger. For a moment, I felt as if I had stepped into an episode of *The Twilight Zone*. I had hardly been a wild child, but there was no way I could have gotten through high school back in the 1970s without throwing the occasional punch. Admittedly, students from Stanford University may be near one extreme of the nonviolent spectrum (psychologists call such people WEIRD— "Western, educated, industrialized, rich, and democratic"), but even so they belong to a broader trend. We are living in a kinder, gentler age.

Pinker suggests that five factors have changed the payoffs from violence, making force less attractive. First, he says, comes our old friend Leviathan. Governments have become stationary bandits, penalizing aggressors. In his Pacifist's Dilemma game, even quite a small penalty of −15 points would push the payoff from winning a fight down from +10 to −5 points, which would be less than the +5 average from being peaceful. This would soon have Leviathan's subjects burying the hatchet.

But government, Pinker argues, was just the first step. Commerce has also increased the payoffs from peace. If gains from trade were to add 100 points to each player's payoff whenever they both chose cooperation over fighting,* Pinker observes, the resulting score of +105 points would dwarf the +10 that anyone would score by winning a war (let alone the −50 he would suffer from a war that dragged on without victory).

And then, Pinker says, there is feminization. In every documented human society, males are responsible for nearly all the violent crime and war-making. Throughout history, men—and male values—have dominated, but in the last few centuries, beginning in Europe and North America and then spreading around the world, women have been increasingly empowered. We have not gone as far as bonobos, among whom females keep aggressive males in their place, but, Pinker suggests, feminism has reduced the payoff from violence by making machismo look ridiculous rather than glorious. If, he speculates, 80 percent of the payoff from successful violence is psychological, then the growing importance of feminine values would drive the gains from victories down from +10 to +2 points. This is

---

*A hundred points strikes me as overoptimistic, given what we know about the scale of commerce in most periods of history, but since the numbers in these games are all made up, it hardly seems worth quibbling.

well under the +5 points that everyone gets for being peaceful, and would quickly turn pacifism into the new evolutionarily stable strategy.

Nor is that all. Since the eighteenth-century Enlightenment, Pinker goes on to suggest, empathy has become increasingly important. "I feel your pain" is not just New Age nonsense; seeing other people as fellow humans has raised not only the psychological payoffs from helping them but also the costs of hurting them. If choosing peaceful cooperation gives each player just an extra 5 points' worth of pleasure, it would raise both sides' payoff from working together to +10 points, and then any reduction at all for guilt from causing pain would drive the payoff of aggression down below +10 points. Peace, love, and understanding would win the day.

Finally, Pinker suggests, science and reason have also changed payoffs. Since the seventeenth-century scientific revolution, we have learned to view the world objectively. We understand how the universe began, that the earth goes around the sun, and how life evolved. We have found the Higgs boson and even invented game theory. Knowing that cooperation is more rational than using force must raise the psychological payoff from the former while reducing the payoff from the latter.

It is hard to disagree with any of Pinker's points, but I think we can actually go further. In the introduction to this book, I suggested that long-term global history is one of our most powerful tools for making sense of the world, and I now want to suggest that by limiting his focus to western Europe and North America in the last five hundred years, Pinker actually saw only part of the picture. If we instead look at the entire planet across the last hundred thousand years, we find that the story is simultaneously more complicated and much simpler than Pinker suggests.

What makes the story more complicated is that the Euro-American decline in violence in the last half millennium was not a onetime event. In Chapters 1 and 2, we saw that rates of violent death also fell in the age of ancient empires, tumbling by the end of the first millennium B.C. to perhaps just one-quarter of what they had been ten thousand years earlier. Between A.D. 200 and 1400, rates of violence then rose again in Eurasia's lucky latitudes, where the bulk of the world's population lived (Chapter 3), before a second great pacification—the one Pinker focuses on—began (Chapters 4 and 5). Well before 1900, the risk of violent death had fallen even lower than in the days of the ancient empires, and since then it has just carried on sliding (Figure 6.9).

What makes the story simpler than Pinker's, however, is that when we compare the ancient and the modern periods of declining violence and

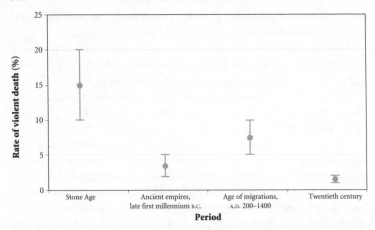

Figure 6.9. The big picture: rates of violent death, 10,000 B.C.–A.D. 2000

contrast them with the intervening medieval period of rising violence, we find that we only need one factor, not five, to explain why violence declined. That factor, you will probably not be surprised to hear at this point in the book, is productive war.

Pinker recognizes that "a state that uses a monopoly on force to protect its citizens from one another may be the most consistent violence-reducer," but the reality seems simpler to me. For ten thousand years, productive war has always been the prime mover in reducing violence, creating bigger societies ruled by Leviathans, which, to survive in competition with other Leviathans, have to turn into stationary bandits that punish unauthorized violence. Pinker's other four factors—commerce, feminization, empathy, and reason—are always consequences of the peace brought by productive war, not independent causes in their own right.

This is most obvious in the case of commerce. In ancient times and again after A.D. 1500, the invisible hand increased the benefits of commercial cooperation—but only because the invisible fist had already raised the costs of using force. Whether we look at the ancient Roman, Han, and Mauryan Empires or the early-modern European ones, the fist always preceded the hand. When the fist failed in Eurasia after about A.D. 200 and steppe nomads overwhelmed the ancient empires, the hand failed with it. Only when European ships and guns conquered the oceans did global trade take off, reaching dizzying heights in the age of the nineteenth-century globocop. When the globocop faltered in the early twentieth century, trade contracted and violence surged, and as we will see in Chapter 7, the installation of a new globocop since 1989 has driven a new age of commercial expansion.

The long-term pattern is clear. Leviathan raises the costs of force, making peace pay off better than violence, and the more peaceful that conditions become, the easier it is for commerce to flourish, increasing the payoffs to be won by cooperating.

Empathy and rationalism were also consequences of productive war in ancient as well as modern times. Enlightened eighteenth-century gentlemen penning pamphlets arguing that universal sympathy was bringing about perpetual peace regularly appealed to Roman writings to justify their ideas, for the very good reason that Roman gentlemen had often held very similar views. But in neither case was empathy or rationalism a prime mover in the decline of violence. As we saw in Chapters 1 and 2, the nonviolent messages of Confucianism, Buddhism, Stoicism, and Christianity won mass followings only after the wars of conquest that created the Han, Mauryan, and Roman Empires had passed their peaks; similarly, Europe's eighteenth- and nineteenth-century age of empathy and rationalism came after the worst parts of the Five Hundred Years' War had already passed. These intellectual movements justified and explained worlds that Leviathan was already making safer, rather than themselves creating peace, and as we saw in Chapter 3, when the Leviathans collapsed in the first millennium A.D. and violence returned, no philosophical system was able to stop it.

Feminization is even more clearly a consequence rather than a cause of the decline of violence. The empowerment of women played little part in the ancient decline and is hard to spot in the modern version until the nineteenth or even the twentieth century, by which time Leviathan had already driven rates of violent death lower than ever before. Perhaps it is only when societies are so pacified that violent death falls below 2 percent that women become sufficiently empowered to challenge male aggression. This was never consistently achieved anywhere before about A.D. 1750–1800, but the moment this level was reached, in Europe and some of its settler colonies, we begin to see signs of feminization.

Sticking with the payoffs Pinker assigned in the Pacifist's Dilemma (+5 for each player when he cooperates, +10 for winning a fight, −100 for losing a fight, and −50 all around when both sides fight), I now want to look at how the game might play out. The 15-point penalty that Leviathan imposes on aggressors makes cooperation much the best game in town. The result is that productive war drives violence down, and as this happens,

Pinker's other four factors also come into play, acting as multipliers. First, peace encourages commerce (this was clearly happening in several of the ancient empires by 200 B.C., and in modern Europe by A.D. 1700), and even a much smaller bonus than the huge 100-point bump that Pinker suggested would make a big difference. It only takes 10 points to give peaceful merchant societies a payoff of +15, far ahead of the next-best option of –5 (for winning a fight and then being punished by Leviathan). Pinker does not suggest a score for rationality but does have empathy yield 5 points for the peacemakers. If we share these 5 points between rationality and empathy, the payoff for being peaceful goes up to +20, and when rates of violence fall really low, as they were doing in Europe by 1800, feminization kicks in and makes force even less attractive.

The whole process depends on Leviathan's being strong enough not only to punish its own subjects but also to defend them, because, of course, the game of death that Leviathan is playing with its subjects is nestled into other games that Leviathan is playing with its neighbors. A Leviathan that wins productive wars, picking up +10 points each time, will eventually dominate its neighborhood, swallowing up its former rivals. It will turn into something like the Roman Empire, within which trade, empathy, and so on flourish on a much larger scale. Eventually, it may even become a globocop.

Reality, of course, is messier than simplifying games such as the Pacifist's Dilemma. In the late nineteenth century, as we saw in Chapter 5, the globocop ran into unanticipated feedback loops as its success in running an international system made everyone richer, which stimulated new industrial revolutions, which then created rivals that undercut the globocop's ability to punish rule breakers. By 1914, several players had concluded that the payoffs from using force had risen back above the payoffs from peaceful cooperation—with catastrophic results. And then things got worse: in the 1930s, the Pacifist's Dilemma abruptly morphed into a game of hawk-and-dove. Most European governments, traumatized by the bloodletting of World War I, consistently pursued peace at any price, which left the field free for Hitler to turn hawkish. He almost won the game in 1940, again in 1941, and a third time in 1942, before the British, Soviets, and Americans finally figured out how to play. Once that happened, of course, the game's unforgiving logic could only lead one way, and by 1945 the Allies had beaten Hitler at his own violent game. Most of Europe and East Asia were in ruins, about a hundred million people were dead, and the United States had the bomb.

Payoffs now changed out of all recognition, because nuclear weapons began driving the penalty for using force up toward infinity. According to the cold rules of the game, even without a single globocop to impose penalties, force could only have positive payoffs if it was applied so timidly—in insurrections, coups, and limited wars—that it did not provoke a violent countermove. If either superpower did anything that challenged the other's survival, both would lose the game. Logic therefore demanded that force become obsolete, and, following the logic, the Soviets and Americans managed for decade after decade not to go to war. But the problem, as Ronald Reagan memorably put it, was that having two nuclear-armed hemispherical cops instead of one globocop was "like having two westerners standing in a saloon aiming their guns at each other's heads—permanently." Everything would be fine, so long as neither gunslinger ever had a bad day.

Getting Past Petrov

Game theory got its big break in the incongruously beautiful setting of Santa Monica, California. Realizing in the early 1950s that the game of death had taken an alarming turn, the American government outsourced to the RAND Corporation the job of figuring out—objectively and scientifically—how to avoid blowing up the world. RAND's solution was to lure away from Ivy League universities one brilliant mathematician after another and set them to calculating the payoffs from every conceivable move in the game.

These chalkboard warriors were a quirky crowd of geniuses. The best known today is John Nash, the hero, if that is the right word, of the bestselling book and film *A Beautiful Mind*. Nash had proved that payoffs could be set up so that bitter rivals would work their way toward a mutually satisfactory balance (what mathematicians call a Nash equilibrium) without resorting to force. This suggested that nuclear deterrence really should work, so long as the people playing the game remained steely-eyed and rational. Nash's own judgment, however, did not inspire confidence. He began hearing voices, had his security clearance revoked after he was arrested for indecent exposure in a men's room, and then turned into a schizophrenic recluse.

Fortunately, the men who made the decisions about nuclear war and peace were less brilliant but more grounded than Nash. But in the absence of a globocop, and with unknown unknowns thicker on the ground than ever before, even someone as stolid as Dwight Eisenhower soon found himself losing sleep, drinking milk for his ulcers, and suffering heart troubles that put him in the hospital. The tiniest miscalculation or accident could mean the end. In theory—in games played on a blackboard over and over again—deterrence made perfect sense, but in reality the fate of the world hung on the snap judgments of men like Petrov. Deterrence lacked stability, and without that, there can of course be no evolutionarily stable strategy.

Throughout history, the only stable solution to the game of death has always been for someone to win it, meaning that the only way to get past moments like Petrov's was for one hemispherical cop to defeat the other. The Cold War's arms race, proxy wars, spies, and coups were all attempts to find a game changer, a gradual or sudden shift in the balance of power that would bring the other side to its knees (or prevent the other side from bringing us to our knees). In the early 1980s, many Soviet strategists began worrying that precision weapons would undo them (the expression "revolution in military affairs" was in fact coined by Soviet analysts to describe this new technology). They were right, although not in the way they expected.

The American computerization of war changed the military balance in Europe enough for Moscow to start exploring ways to fight without going nuclear, but hindsight has revealed that what mattered most about Star Wars, Assault Breaker, and the other newfangled weapons was that countering them would be really, really complicated and costly. The Soviet economy could churn out tanks, Kalashnikovs, nuclear warheads, and ICBMs but could not rise to—or pay for—the computers and smart munitions that promised to dominate 1990s battlefields.

This leap in the costs of war came at the worst possible time for Moscow. Much of the Soviets' success in the 1970s had been paid for by oil exports, driven to sky-high prices by war and revolution in the Middle East, but between 1980 and 1986 the cost of a barrel of oil fell by almost 80 percent, wiping out much of Moscow's disposable income. Adding to the Kremlin's woes, while the productivity of American workers surged by 27 percent between 1975 and 1985 and that of western Europeans by 23 percent, Soviet citizens' output grew just 9 percent, and their eastern European subjects only performed 1 percent better. Communist farms were so inefficient that productivity barely rose at all. Consequently, grain imports (especially from the United States and Canada) more than doubled, paid for largely by huge loans from banks in the American alliance. One debt crisis followed another.

"Force," Clausewitz famously insisted, is "the *means* of war; to impose our will on the enemy is its object." Therefore, Clausewitz concluded, we should not hesitate to kill if that seems like the best way to break the enemy's will to resist, but when killing is not the best way, we should not waste our time doing it. The brilliance of the grand strategy of containment that the United States unveiled in the late 1940s was that it recognized this. Most of the time, American policy makers rejected the dovish claim that two hemispherical cops could coexist indefinitely, and most of the time they also rejected the hawkish counterclaim that victory would come if the United States just waged its proxy wars more aggressively. Instead, they followed a middle course that played to American strengths.

The United States had inherited Britain's mantle as the great outer-rim power and with it Britain's role as a liberal Leviathan, promoting free markets, elections, and speech. The way to leverage liberal strength, American strategists realized, was to wage liberal war, using freedom as a weapon to undermine the Soviets' will to resist. The United States could only wage this kind of war if it had an invisible fist to back up the invisible hand, and so, divisive and distasteful as this was, Washington had to keep building hydrogen bombs, fighting proxy wars, and cozying up to dictators. But through it all, American leaders had to remember that bombs, battles, and brutality would not by themselves deliver victory—that could only be delivered by the Soviet Empire's own subjects as they waited in line at the store, cursed at cars that would not start, and bought Bruce Springsteen LPs on the black market. Little by little, the invisible hand would choke the will out of communism.

The plan was hardly a secret. As early as 1951, the American sociologist David Riesman had both mocked and celebrated it in a short story called "The Nylon War." In it, the Pentagon top brass sells liberal war to the White House by explaining that "if allowed to sample the riches of America, the Russian people would not long tolerate masters who gave them tanks and spies instead of vacuum cleaners." The president agrees, the air force rains stockings and cigarettes from the Russian skies, and communism collapses.

The reality was, of course, not so simple, but little by little, Stalin and his successors came to understand the importance of stockings. A year after Riesman's story came out, the Soviet premier told China's foreign minister ("jokingly," the transcript says) that "the main armament of the Americans . . . is nylons, cigarettes, and other goods for sale . . . No, the Americans don't know how to wage war." Before the decade was out, however, the Soviets had learned that the only way to win the Nylon War was for their own ideologues to push back, denying the truth of American claims and highlighting capitalism's unfairness. Thanks to the fact that nuclear weapons meant that a shooting war would effectively be suicide, the Soviets never seriously considered the path chosen by hundreds of rulers in earlier times, who had responded to economic decline by attacking their more prosperous neighbors and taking their rich provinces or trade routes. Instead, Soviet leaders let the liberal war of attrition grind on until it broke their empire apart.

The Politburo let this happen not because the apparatchiks had all been listening to "War" but because they knew force could not solve their problem. Invading West Germany or South Korea would not make the Soviet Empire as rich and productive as the American; it would just bring on Armageddon. For thirty years, the Soviets managed to paper over most of the cracks, convincing many of their subjects (and even some outsiders) that the empire was flourishing, but by the 1980s this was no longer possible.

By then, egg rationing and the other indignities of 1940s austerity were just distant memories for most western Europeans, but in eastern Europe it was all too easy to feel that they were on their way back. "It was a struggle to get basic things like washing powder," a Polish nurse remembered. "I had to wash my hair with egg yolks because there was no shampoo . . . If we didn't have information about life elsewhere, that would have been different. But we were conscious of the way [other] people lived." And if anyone still had doubts that the Soviet bloc was losing the economic war, the meltdown of the Chernobyl nuclear reactor swept them away in 1986, flooding Ukraine with radiation and exposing the incompetence and dishonesty of the Soviet regime in a way that could not be covered up.

"We can't go on like this," Mikhail Gorbachev had confessed to his wife in 1985, just hours before he was appointed Soviet premier. Desperate times call for desperate measures, and Gorbachev, recognizing that the Soviet Empire's will to resist was ebbing away, staked everything on one big bet. He would restart economic growth by promoting restructuring (perestroika) and transparency (glasnost) while—at all costs—avoiding recourse to violence, which could only end badly.

Many Americans assumed that this must be another clever move in the game of death (so clever, in fact, that they could not quite figure out what the Soviets might be trying to do). "I was suspicious of Gorbachev's motives," National Security Adviser Brent Scowcroft later confessed. "My fear," he explained, "was that Gorbachev could talk us into disarming without the Soviet Union having to do anything fundamental to its own military structure and that, in a decade or so, we could face a more serious military threat than ever before."

There were times when it looked as if Scowcroft might be right. In October 1986, Reagan and Gorbachev sat across a table in Reykjavík and actually started talking about banning all nuclear weapons. This threw American defense experts into a panic. The Soviets might be terrified of NATO's new, high-tech arsenal, but Americans—who knew that few of these wonder weapons were yet in service—were equally terrified that without nuclear deterrence their conventional forces in Europe would be hard-pressed to hold off the much larger Soviet armies. Gorbachev, however, was not trying to trick anyone, and it slowly became clear that he really was serious about playing the game without using force. No one knew what to make of it.

"Did we see what was coming when we took office [in January 1989]?" George Bush the Elder later asked, admitting, "No, we did not." And if Bush *had* somehow seen how 1989 would turn out, and had claimed in his inauguration address that before his term ended he would oversee the collapse of the Soviet Empire and Russia's retreat to the borders Germany had imposed on it in 1918, everyone would have thought that this arch-realist, former CIA director had gone completely mad. For more than forty years, the United States had been scheming, plotting, and killing, all to break the Soviets' will, but when the endgame finally arrived, it took everyone by surprise.

A few months after Bush's inauguration, an official committee in Hungary concluded that the country's 1956 rebellion against the Soviets had been a "popular uprising against an oligarchic system of power which had humiliated the nation." In Stalin's day, such a report would have been equivalent to a collective suicide note. Even under Khrushchev or Brezhnev, the consequences could have been serious. But not only did Gorbachev not have anyone shot; he tacitly signaled agreement.

Encouraged, in June 1989 the Hungarians gave a retrospective public funeral to a former premier whom the Soviets *had* shot. Two hundred thousand mourners turned out, but still Moscow made no move. Without consulting anyone, the Hungarian prime minister announced that budgetary problems prevented him from renewing the barbed wire along the border with Austria, and since the old wire violated health and safety rules, it would have to be rolled up. A hole, hundreds of miles wide, was about to appear in the Iron Curtain. In a panic, East German communists asked the Kremlin to intervene, only to be told, "We can't do anything."

Any amount of concession, Gorbachev reasoned, was better than risking the collapse of the whole Soviet system by using force. Not everyone agreed, and in December, Romania's thuggish dictator, Nicolae Ceauşescu, had his troops shoot demonstrators. The country rose against him, the Soviets did nothing, and on Christmas Day he and his wife were themselves shot.

East German communists, scrambling and bungling almost as badly, lurched in the other direction and threw open the gates of the Berlin Wall. East Germans rushed west; West Germans strolled east; all kinds of people danced on top of the wall or took hammers to it; and nothing happened. "How could you shoot at Germans who walk across the border to meet other Germans on the other side?" Gorbachev asked the next day. "The policy had to change."

The events in Romania suggested that Gorbachev was right, but by the summer of 1989 the Soviets probably had no winning moves left. Changing one policy just led to irresistible pressure on the next policy. Less than three months after the Berlin Wall came down, East Germany's prime minister told Gorbachev that the two Germanys wanted to merge into one. This could only happen, Gorbachev replied, if the unified Germany were demilitarized and neutral. A proposal was put to the Americans, but Bush refused to withdraw the quarter of a million American personnel in West Germany. Gorbachev pulled his 300,000 troops out of East Germany anyway, and the new, reunited Germany joined NATO.

With the benefit of hindsight, it is perhaps not surprising that once the Germans, Poles, Hungarians, Czechs, Slovaks, Romanians, and Bulgarians had walked away from the Soviet Empire, the Estonians, Lithuanians, Latvians, Belarusians, Ukrainians, Armenians, Georgians, Azeris, Chechens, Kazakhs, Uzbeks, Turkmen, Kyrgyz, Tajiks, and Mongolians would follow. What does still seem remarkable, though, is that the Russians themselves decided that they wanted nothing more to do with their own empire and announced their withdrawal from the Soviet system. On Christmas Day 1991, Gorbachev signed a decree formally dissolving the Soviet Union.

By playing the game without violence, Gorbachev got a bad payoff, but the only obvious alternative—using force to hold the eastern Europeans down and to resist any American effort to roll back the empire—would have paid off much, much worse. Russia had been defeated, getting shoved unceremoniously out of the inner rim and even out of much of the heartland, but at least this had happened with barely a shot being fired. Five hundred million lives had been on the line during Petrov's moment of

Figure 6.10. A lot to smile about: Mikhail Gorbachev and Ronald Reagan bring down the curtain on the Cold War, and a billion people live to fight another day.

truth in 1983, but when the end of the Cold War finally came, fewer than three hundred people actually died.

The United States had won the greatest and most unexpected triumph in the history of productive war (Figure 6.10). The world had a new globocop.

⟹⬦⟸

THE LAST BEST HOPE OF EARTH:
AMERICAN EMPIRE, 1989–?

Can't Get There from Here

Monday, November 26, 2012, was a modern miracle. For an entire day (in fact, from 10:30 on Sunday night until 10:20 on Tuesday morning), not a single person was shot, stabbed, or otherwise done to death anywhere in New York City. There had been no such day since comprehensive data collection began in 1994, at which point the Big Apple averaged fourteen killings each day. In fact, we have to go back more than fifty years, to a time when records were spotty and the city had half a million fewer people, to find another day without violent death. All in all, in 2012 just one New Yorker in twenty thousand died violently—probably an all-time low.

New York is not, of course, the only place in America. In Chicago, murders rose by one-sixth in 2012, while San Bernardino, California—where half the homeowners owe more than their houses are worth and the city government has gone bankrupt—saw killings jump 50 percent ("Lock your doors and load your guns," the city attorney advised). And as 2012 drew to a close, a psychopath in Newtown, Connecticut, gunned down twenty schoolchildren, six staff members, his own mother, and then himself. Yet New York was more typical than Newtown: despite the nightmarish exceptions, the nation's murder rate fell in 2012.

In fact, New York is fairly typical not just of the United States but also of much of the world. Homicide is in general retreat. Roughly 1 human in every 13,000 was murdered in 2004; by 2010, the figure had fallen to just over 1 in every 14,500. Deaths in war went the same way. Interstate wars—

typically the biggest and bloodiest conflicts—almost disappeared. Civil wars in the wake of state failures continue (in 2012, civil war killed about 1 Syrian in every 400), but the statistics suggest that these conflicts are becoming rarer too.

Averaged across the planet, violence killed about 1 person in every 4,375 in 2012, implying that just 0.7 percent of the people alive today will die violently, as against 1–2 percent of the people who lived in the twentieth century, 2–5 percent in the ancient empires, 5–10 percent in Eurasia in the age of steppe migrations, and a terrifying 10–20 percent in the Stone Age (Figure 7.1). The world is finally getting to Denmark, and Denmark itself—where just 1 person per 111,000 was murdered in 2009, representing a lifetime risk of violent death of just 0.027 percent—gets more Danish every day. Most wonderful of all, for every twenty nuclear warheads in the world in 1986—when Bruce Springsteen rerecorded "War"—there is now only one. Fifty years ago, Strategic Air Command (charged with delivering nuclear weapons) was at the cutting edge of the U.S. Air Force; nowadays, most air force officers consider going into the nuclear branch career suicide.

Nor is that the end of the good news. As has happened so often across the last few thousand years, falling rates of violence have gone hand in hand with rising prosperity. When the United States took over as undisputed globocop in 1989, the average human being generated just over $5,000

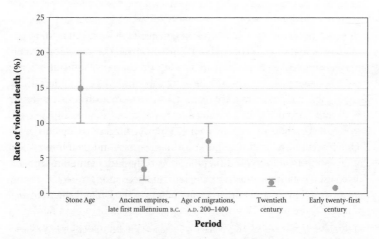

Figure 7.1. Almost there: rates of violent death, 10,000 B.C.–A.D. 2013

of wealth.* By 2011, the most recent year with complete data, that had doubled. Asia had benefited most, with coastal China, parts of Southeast Asia, and a few regions in India going through their own industrial revolutions. These fueled the greatest migration of peasants into cities in history, lifting more than two billion people out of absolute poverty (defined by the World Bank as surviving on less than $1 per day). Latin America, Africa, and eastern Europe initially went backward, thanks to debt crises, the AIDS epidemic, and postcommunist collapse, respectively, but all have gained ground since 2000 (Figure 7.2).

Figures 7.1 and 7.2 are remarkable graphs, showing that the world is getting not just safer and richer but also—as inequalities between the continents decline—fairer. Even more remarkable, however, is the explanation for all this good news, argued throughout this book: that productive war has made the planet a better place. This is a paradoxical, counterintuitive, and frankly disturbing notion (and, as I mentioned in the introduction, not one that crossed my mind before I started studying the long-term history of war). But the evidence of archaeology, anthropology, history, and evolutionary biology seems conclusive.

Violence evolved 400 million years ago as a way to win arguments (initially, between proto-sharks that wanted to eat other fish and other fish that did not want to be eaten). It has been a hugely successful adaptation, and almost all animals now use it. Some have even evolved to use violence collectively, and when territory is involved, this violence can be lethal. War has come into the world.

Human history is one of the shorter twigs on the evolutionary tree, but it is by far the most unusual. We alone can evolve culturally as well as genetically, responding to changes in the payoffs from the game of death by altering our behavior rather than waiting thousands of generations for natural selection to change us. Because of this, since the end of the last ice age we have found ways to use violence that—paradoxically—have lowered the payoffs from using further violence.

When the world warmed up after 10,000 B.C., animals and plants of all kinds reacted by reproducing. For most species, hard times returned when hungry mouths outran food supplies, but in the lucky latitudes humans solved this problem by evolving culturally and becoming farmers. Farming had its costs, but it also supported many more people, and the resulting

*Measured in 1990 international dollars, a standard unit of comparison. At current market exchange rates, global GDP/capita in 2011 was more like $12,000.

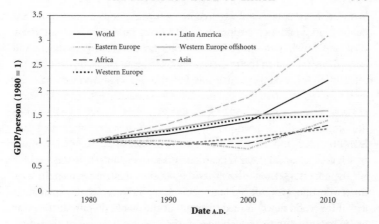

Figure 7.2. The rich get richer, and the poor get richer faster: the speed at which wealth grew in different parts of the world between 1980 and 2010. Globally, the average person was 2.2 times richer in 2010 than in 1980, but the average Asian was three times richer. Africans and Latin Americans got poorer in the 1980s and eastern Europeans in the 1990s, but all have gained on northwestern Europeans and their settler colonies (Australia, Canada, New Zealand, and the United States) since 2000.

crowding created caging. For chimpanzees and probably for ice-age humans too, territoriality meant that the highest payoffs in the game of death came from killing competing groups, but caging meant that incorporating defeated enemies into larger societies paid off better still. "Incorporation" is a bland word for a process that included so much plunder, rape, enslavement, and displacement, but because competition rewarded conquerors who turned themselves into stationary bandits, the long-term result of all this violence was pacification and rising prosperity.

By 3500 B.C., stationary bandits were evolving into genuine Leviathans, able to raise taxes and punish recalcitrant subjects. The process began in what we now call the Middle East because that was also where farming had begun, and it was therefore the place where caging and competition had gone furthest; but over the next few thousand years most of the lucky latitudes moved the same way.

Each region in the Old World's lucky latitudes went through a similar sequence of revolutions in military affairs (although, for reasons we saw in Chapter 3, and above all the absence of horses, the sequence in the New

World differed somewhat). First came fortifications, as an answer to endemic raiding; attackers responded by learning how to besiege walls they could not climb. Next, in Eurasia, came bronze, for offensive weapons and defensive armor. Then there was discipline, to persuade wild young men to attack despite the danger and to stand their ground against murderous enemies. By 1900 B.C., herders on Eurasia's steppes learned to harness horses to chariots, bringing speed and fluidity to battlefields. By 1200 B.C., warriors around the Mediterranean found ways to fight back, but in the first millennium B.C. the initiative shifted toward masses of iron-armed infantry, which conquered huge empires all across Eurasia's lucky latitudes.

Each revolution was a race between offense and defense, but, as I have insisted throughout this book, war was never a case of what evolutionists call the Red Queen Effect. The race did not leave everyone in the same place, because it transformed the societies that ran it. Every revolution required Leviathans to get stronger, and stronger Leviathans drove down rates of violent death still further.

Nor do the facts fit comfortably with the theory of a unique Western way of war, invented by the Greeks in ancient times and raising European fighters above everyone else in the world. In reality, people all across the lucky latitudes invented a single productive way of war, and what it produced was stronger Leviathans, safety, and wealth. In the first millennium B.C., people got to Chang'an, Pataliputra, and Teotihuacán as well as Rome.

Another theme in this book, though, is that everything in war is paradoxical. By the end of the first millennium B.C., Eurasia's productive wars were reaching what Clausewitz called a culminating point, at which behavior that previously produced success started delivering disaster. The ancient empires' expansion increasingly entangled them with the steppes. Here, highly mobile horsemen could cover vast distances and strike into the empires almost at will, but the great infantry armies that had created the empires struggled to survive at all on the arid grasslands. From China to Europe, cavalry came to dominate the battlefield, and for more than a thousand years—from roughly A.D. 200 through 1400—the lucky latitudes and steppes were locked in a terrible cycle of productive and counterproductive wars. For every productive war that produced bigger, safer, and richer societies, a counterproductive war broke them down again. Leviathans lost their teeth, rates of violent death rose, and prosperity fell.

One day, not too far away, physical anthropologists will have studied enough skeletons to put precise numbers on these rates, but for the time being, we have to rely on the impressionistic evidence that I reviewed in Chapters 1–3. For prehistory, we can combine analogies from twentieth-century Stone Age societies with the small but growing body of skeletal evidence, but for the ancient empires and the age of steppe migrations we have to rely largely on the societies' own literary accounts. I argued in Chapters 1 and 2 that these writings make it almost certain that the ancient empires reduced rates of violent death and in Chapter 3 that rates rose again after about A.D. 200, but at the moment there is frankly no way to know precisely *how much* they rose and fell.

My own estimates—that the risk of violent death was in the 2–5 percent range in the ancient empires, rising to 5–10 percent in the times of feudal anarchy—will doubtless be proved wrong as evidence accumulates, but that, it seems to me, is how scholarship is supposed to work. One researcher makes conjectures; another comes along and refutes them, putting better conjectures in their place. But if nothing else, I hope this first stab at putting actual numbers on the table will provoke others to disprove them by collecting better data and devising better methods that reveal where I went wrong.

The story only moves onto a firmer numerical footing in the middle of the second millennium A.D., when Leviathans—especially in Europe—once again revived as guns closed the steppe highway and long-distance shipping opened up the oceans. Both inventions were made in East Asia but perfected in western Europe, where they broke the cycle of productive and counterproductive wars.

The reason for this, I suggested in Chapter 4, once again had more to do with geography than with a Western way of war. On the one hand, Europe's political geography—with lots of small kingdoms, constantly at war—rewarded societies that built better guns; on the other hand, Europe's physical geography—the fact that it was twice as close as East Asia to the Americas—made it easier for Europeans than for Asians to discover, plunder, and colonize the New World. Europeans began their Five Hundred Years' War on the world not because they were more dynamic (or more wicked) than anyone else but because geography made it easier for them than for anyone else.

The Five Hundred Years' War forced Europeans to reinvent productive war, because the sheer size of the societies their conquests produced changed the rules of the game. In an age of intercontinental empires, they discovered, the wealth of nations could be increased most not by plundering or even taxing downtrodden subjects but by using state power to make as many people as possible as free as possible to trade in bigger and bigger markets.

Beginning in northwestern Europe, relentless competition forced Leviathans to embrace open-access order, which brought the market's invisible hand and government's invisible fist into harmony. Britain, after stumbling into an industrial revolution in the 1780s, emerged as the first globocop, its ships, money, and diplomats policing a worldwide order. But although rates of violent death fell to new lows and prosperity climbed toward new highs, even the globocop had a culminating point. The Pax Britannica produced so many rivals that the globocop could no longer do its job. After 1914, the worst wars in history overthrew it—only for the United States to emerge as victor seventy-five years later, at the head of an even bigger open-access order, producing even lower rates of violent death and even more wealth.

This is a big story, only visible if we look at all of human history across the entire planet and pursue all four of the approaches (personal, military-historical, technical, and evolutionary) that I identified in the introduction. This alone, I suggest, will show what war has been good for—and what the costs have been.

The answer to the question in this book's title is both paradoxical and horrible. War has been good for making humanity safer and richer, but it has done so through mass murder. But because war *has* been good for something, we must recognize that all this misery and death was not in vain. Given a choice of how to get from the poor, violent Stone Age to the peace and prosperity of Figures 7.1 and 7.2, few of us, I am sure, would want war to be the way, but evolution—which is what human history is—is not driven by what we want. In the end, the only thing that matters is the grim logic of the game of death.

Looking at how that logic has played out since the end of the Ice Age, it seems obvious where it should take us next. We have moved from bands of foragers via Leviathans to a globocop; the next step, surely, should be to a world government that drives the payoffs from violence down to zero. Everyone should get to Denmark, and despite all the horrors in its pages this book should have a happy ending after all—almost as happy, in fact, as the ending of Norman Angell's *Great Illusion*, which I mentioned at the start of Chapter 5. In 1910, when that book appeared, there had been no major great-power wars for ninety-five years. Across that period, global incomes had doubled, and in Europe, at least, the murder rate had halved.

The implication, Angell and his admirers concluded, was that a world without war was just around the corner.

It was not, but *The Great Illusion* remains worth reading anyway, because the reasons Angell was wrong apply to our own age too. As we saw in Chapter 5, the nineteenth century's march toward Denmark was unsustainable. The better the globocop did its job, the more rivals it created, and the more rivals it created, the more difficult its job became. Figure 7.2 suggests that history is repeating itself. The American colossus bestrides the world in the 2010s even more completely than the British version bestrode it in the 1860s, but the United States seems to be rerunning the United Kingdom's experience. The better that Washington keeps global order, the richer and stronger its potential rivals become. Unknown unknowns are proliferating and gamblers are already taking chances. The closer we get to Denmark, the further away it seems.

The first time I ever visited New England, a lifetime resident told me an ancient joke about the orneriness of the region's residents. A tourist (in most versions, from New York) gets hopelessly lost in darkest Massachusetts (or perhaps Maine). After driving in circles for an hour, he stops to ask directions. A wizened local reflects on, but then rejects, one possible route after another. Finally, with a weary shake of his head, he tells the tourist, "You can't get there from here."

Unhelpful advice, to be sure, but the similarities between Figure 7.2 and the graphs that opened Chapter 5 suggest it might be a better description of the world we live in than Angell's upbeat interpretation. Perhaps we face not a Red Queen Effect but a Tortoise and Hare Effect. By running very fast, humanity *has* gotten somewhere: rates of violent death have fallen, and prosperity has risen. But although we keep getting closer to Denmark, we will never quite get there from here. The Hare races forward, but the Tortoise always crawls just a little farther ahead, creating new rivals, new unknown unknowns, and perhaps even new storms of steel. So much for the happy ending.

In this final chapter, I want to suggest that neither Angell's happy ending nor the New Englander's unhappy one is actually much of a guide to the shape of things to come. Angell's idea—that economic interconnection makes war unthinkable—was wrong a hundred years ago, and it is still wrong today, but so too is the New Englander's claim that we can't get there from here.

We seem to be making the worst of all possible worlds for ourselves.

On the one hand, it will be even less stable than the 1870s–1910s, when the previous globocop was in decline; on the other, its weapons will be even deadlier than those of the 1940s–80s, when the United States and the Soviet Union threatened humanity with mutual assured destruction. Despite the steady decline in rates of violent death over the last forty years, and despite the unlikeliness of a new world war in the mid-2010s, the next forty years promise to be the most dangerous in history.

But if we step back from the details and look at the coming decades in the same way that we looked at the long-term history of violence in Chapters 1–6, rather different parts of the picture come into focus. In spite of everything, this broader perspective suggests, we really might get there from here—even if "there" is not where we expected.

Venus and Mars

For many years, the U.S. government regularly published a pamphlet called the Defense Planning Guidance, summarizing its official position on grand strategy. Most Guidances were rather bland documents, but in February 1992, just two months after the Soviet Union dissolved, the committee charged with drafting a new Guidance did something outrageous. It told the truth.

What it drafted was a how-to guide for globocops. While the United States could not "assum[e] responsibility for righting every wrong," it conceded, "we will retain the preeminent responsibility for addressing selectively those wrongs which threaten not only our interests, but those of our allies or friends, or which could seriously unsettle international relations." This meant accomplishing one big thing:

> Our first objective is to prevent the reemergence of a new rival, either on the territory of the former Soviet Union or elsewhere, that poses a threat on the order of that posed formerly by the Soviet Union. This . . . requires that we endeavor to prevent any hostile power from dominating a region whose resources would, under consolidated control, be sufficient to generate global power. These regions include Western Europe, East Asia, the territory of the former Soviet Union, and Southwest Asia.

Promptly leaked to the press, the draft set off a political firestorm. What it was talking about was "literally a Pax Americana," complained the future vice president Joe Biden, which "won't work." Chastened, the Department of Defense toned down the final version, but whatever we call it, a Pax Americana is precisely what the United States has been pursuing for the last twenty-odd years (several of them with Joe Biden in the White House).

The lesson that politicians should have learned from the Pax Britannica was that an American version *would* work, at least for a few decades. Overall, the American experience since 1989 has been strikingly like Britain's in the late nineteenth century, and even the apparent exceptions are of the kind that only goes to prove the rule.

The most extraordinary of these apparent exceptions is surely western Europe, the first of the four potential problem spots that the 1992 planners worried about. The parallels between this region's experiences with the British and the American globocops are obvious enough. In the later nineteenth century, western European economies prospered in markets guaranteed by the British globocop, and a wealthy, powerful Germany became Britain's deadliest rival in the 1890s. In the later twentieth century, western Europe's economies once again flourished in markets guaranteed by the American globocop, and plenty of politicians—in Europe even more than in the United States—became alarmed that the reunited Germany would continue rerunning the historical script. ("People say, 'It is a terrible thing that Germany is not working,'" one French official half joked, "but I say, 'Really? When Germany is working, six months later it is usually marching down the Champs Elysées.'")

But that did not happen. Instead, western Europe moved in a direction that at first sight seems to challenge not only the analogy between American and British global power but also virtually every argument in this book. Far from turning into a rival to the globocop, western Europe has almost entirely renounced force as a policy tool. A truly astonishing thing is happening. For the first time in history, huge numbers of people—500 million so far—are coming together to form a bigger, safer, richer society without being forced to do so (Figure 7.3).

It has been an epochal transformation, albeit a quiet one. I spent my first twenty-seven years living through it (assuming, for the sake of argument, that we count Britain as part of western Europe) without realizing that it was happening. Nothing, in fact, used to make me turn the TV off quite as quickly as yet another announcement from the bureaucrats in Brussels about what I was allowed to eat or drink and what size container it would come in.

But I—as well as the millions of others who shared my lack of interest in all things European—was very wrong. Dullness was the whole point of

Figure 7.3. A world (almost) without war: locations in Europe mentioned in this chapter. Countries marked dark gray belong to the European Union and the eurozone; those marked light gray, to the European Union only (as of 2014).

the European Community (as it was called until it rebranded itself as the European Union in 1993). Old-fashioned Leviathans had used violence to create political unity and then used politics (and, when necessary, more violence) to create economic unity, but western Europe now turned history's most successful formula around. In committee meeting after committee meeting, its unsung heroes spun a web of rules and regulations that bound its members together in an economic unit and then began using economics to create a political unit. "The final goal," the former head of the German Bundesbank explained in 1994, "is a political one . . . to reach any type of political unification in Europe, a federation of states, an association of states or even a stronger form of union." In this agenda, "the economic union is [merely] an important vehicle to reach this target."

This was simultaneously the dullest and most daring trick that statesmen had ever attempted, and for fifteen years after the signing of the crucial treaty at Maastricht in 1992 it seemed to be working. Europe remained a mosaic of independent states, but from Ireland to Estonia most Europeans shared a single currency and central bank, accepted rulings from a European court and parliament, and crossed borders without passports. Until 2010, at least, the tedious path of consensus-building really did seem to be getting Europe there from here.

At that point, however, the countries that had adopted the euro as their currency plunged into a debt crisis (or, more accurately, a balance-of-payments crisis between the highly productive North and the less productive South) and discovered the limits of a rules-based union. An old-style Leviathan could have used force to solve the problems, as Britain did when it sent gunboats to extract debt payments from Greece in 1850, but in the new Europe no German tanks would be rolling through the streets of Athens to restore fiscal discipline.

Relying on the invisible hand of the market rather than the invisible fist of military power to enforce its rules, the European Union seemed to be teetering on the brink of an abyss. In late 2011 the Swiss bank UBS worried publicly about a descent into violence. "Almost no modern fiat currency monetary unions," their analysts observed, "have broken up without some form of authoritarian or military government, or civil war." Sobering stuff, and yet as I write, in mid-2013, the much-criticized policy of masterly inactivity—doing just enough to keep indebted countries afloat, but no more—does seem to be averting disaster. Despite skyrocketing unemployment, violent street protests, and political crisis, Greece has hung on within the eurozone, and despite mounting pressure on Ireland, Portugal, Spain, Italy, and even France, none has collapsed. Far from breaking Europe apart, the crisis may yet become an opportunity to push political centralization further. Without shooting anyone, Europe's administrators might succeed where Napoleon and Hitler failed.

The Nobel Committee recognized this in 2012 by awarding its Peace Prize to the entire European Union. And well they might—the EU's citizens murder each other less often than any other people on earth; its governments have abolished the death penalty; and it has abandoned war within its borders and almost given it up beyond them too. Europeans outside the EU still sometimes see positive payoffs from force, as Russia showed in its Five-Day War against Georgia in 2008, but within the EU few seem to agree. The EU's Common Security and Defence Policy does recognize the right to use force, but only Britain and France have done so, and always to restore peace in collapsing former colonies. Even when there were clear humanitarian arguments for military action, as in Kosovo in 1999, western European governments moved with a caution that often infuriated their American partners. The surreal face-off between Sweden and Belarus in 2012—when a Swedish plane parachuted eight hundred teddy bears onto Minsk, each clutching a little sign saying "Free Speech Now," and Belarus counterattacked by firing the generals in charge of its border patrol and air force—might be more typical of the new European way of war.

In 2003, opinion pollsters found that only 12 percent of French and Germans thought that war was ever justified, as against 55 percent of Americans, and in 2006 respondents in Britain, France, and Spain even told pollsters that the warlike Americans were the greatest threat to world peace. "On major strategic and international questions today," the strategist Robert Kagan concluded, "Americans are from Mars and Europeans are from Venus."

The growing contrast between European and American attitudes to violence has occasioned much comment, but there is no mystery about it. Europeans are from Venus *because* Americans are from Mars. Without the American globocop protecting the peace, Europe's dovish strategy would be impossible. But on the other hand, without European dovishness, the United States could not afford to go on as globocop. If the European Union had acted more hawkishly over the past fifteen years, the costs of countering it would already be undermining the American position, just as the costs of countering Germany undermined the British globocop a hundred years ago. Mars and Venus need each other.

Between 1945 and 1989, the best way for western Europe to play the game of death was by being warlike enough to help deter the Soviet Union but not so warlike as to alarm the Americans (disagreement over exactly where that sweet spot was partly explains France's departure from NATO's unified command structure in 1966). Since 1989, though, facing no serious security risks at all and being able to rely on the United States to punish any and all hawks, western Europe has become even more dovish (disagreement over which hawks needed punishment partly explains the spike in European anti-Americanism in 2003). The result: unlike British governments a century ago, American administrations have never had to worry that their money and protection were nourishing European rivals that would challenge their ability to act as a globocop.

Europe's move toward Venus has not, of course, abolished the tensions between the outer rim, the inner rim, and the heartland that Mackinder identified a century ago. Since the seventeenth century, British grand strategy has revolved around engaging with the wider world while preventing any single power from dominating continental Europe. "We have no eternal allies and we have no perpetual friends," said Lord Palmerston, the foreign secretary, in 1848; only "our interests are eternal and perpetual." Following this logic, he would have understood why Britain stayed out of the eurozone, will hold a referendum on European Union membership by 2017, and is sometimes markedly less Venusian than its neighbors.

Eastern Europeans also have doubts about Venus. Caught along the line separating the heartland from the inner rim, and lacking natural barriers to protect them from their mighty German and Russian neighbors, they too find that centuries-old strategic concerns have not gone away. Like Britain, several eastern European governments seek to balance their fears of a German-dominated European Union by leaning even more toward the American globocop. The paradox of power being what it is, however, the United States does not want its best friends leaning *too* far away from the European Union, because that would threaten the calm that America needs if it is to do its job.

Western Europe has not transcended the game of death. Rather, it has played the game skillfully, reaping the rewards offered to doves by the presence of a globocop that punishes hawks. Nor has the United States become a rogue nation; it too has played the game skillfully, reaping the rewards of European dovishness to maintain its position as globocop. The European Union richly deserved its 2012 Peace Prize, but when the Nobel Committee gave the 2009 prize to Barack Obama, it might have done better to award it to all American presidents since 1945. Collectively, they have made Europe's experiment possible.

America's Boer War

If western Europe is the region where the United States has done best at avoiding creating a rival, southwest Asia has some claims to be the one where it has done worst. The United States has fought three wars here (four if we count the 2012 air strikes on Libya) since the Berlin Wall came down, and will be lucky to get through the 2010s without fighting a fourth (or fifth). In this region, the similarities between the problems of the new and the old globocops are especially strong.

That is true even though southwest Asia's strategic significance has changed out of all recognition across the last hundred years. In Mackinder's time, the Ottoman and Persian Empires mattered most to the globocop because they lay astride its communications through the Suez Canal to India (Figure 7.4). From the Caucasus to the Hindu Kush, British and Russian explorers and spies jostled for decades in what Kipling called "the Great Game." Russian armies swallowed up what are now the -stans of central Asia; British redcoats swallowed, but could not keep down, Afghanistan.

What changed the Great Game into the version we now play was of course oil. For decades after the world's first well was sunk at Titusville, Pennsylvania, in 1859, the United States remained the center of production, but drilling started in southwest Asia in 1871, and Russian pioneers soon struck black gold at Baku in Azerbaijan. Western oilmen followed, with a British speculator buying up rights to two-thirds of the oil in Persia in 1901 and Standard of California opening the first Saudi oil field in 1933. Production boomed in the 1960s to meet American, European, and Japanese demand, and by the mid-1970s oil was sucking more than $400 million of outside money to the shores of the Persian Gulf every day.

Western newspapers went wild with stories of Arab millionaires buying up historic landmarks, but on the face of it there was little danger that America's success in creating a free market for the oil it needed would also create a southwest Asian rival. With their tiny middle classes, restricted educational systems, and endemic corruption, not even the richest oil-

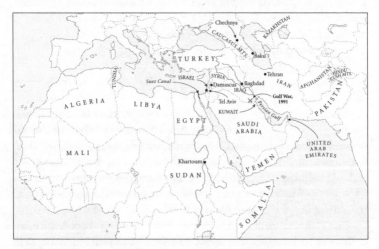

Figure 7.4. The new great game, from Algeria to Afghanistan

producing countries of the 1960s were in any position to have their own industrial revolutions or create diversified, modern economies.

Because of this, oil money did not empower broad citizenries, as American aid had in Europe after World War II. Instead, it flowed largely into the hands of narrow elites, whose repression, dishonesty, and incompetence provoked growing anger. The United States, anxious to keep the sources of its oil out of Soviet clutches, found itself propping up dictators, juntas, and absolutist kings; critics regularly charged that it was now running the same kind of informal empire that Europeans had used to dominate the Middle East in the nineteenth and early twentieth centuries.

Oil oligarchs tried to channel popular discontent into nationalism and hatred of Israel, but mullahs and ayatollahs did much better at hijacking the rage to serve Islamic fundamentalism (and, of course, hatred of Israel too). Few Islamists saw the United States as their primary enemy, and even during the Iranian hostage crisis some Americans still hoped to befriend the religious radicals (improbable as it now seems, *Time* magazine named Ayatollah Khomeini as its 1979 Man of the Year). But the revolutionaries quickly discovered that there was no way to fight American puppets without fighting America too, and before 1979 was over, Iran had branded the United States the Great Satan.

Unintended consequences abounded as the globocop tried to manage this angry new Islam. Far from the Persian Gulf's oil fields, American aid proved crucial to sustaining Afghan resistance against the Soviet occupation of the 1980s, but instead of earning goodwill, this just created a well-armed, battle-hardened legion of Arab jihadists. These men, ready to wage holy war against any foe, exploited the chaos left by the struggle against communism to turn Afghanistan into an Islamist safe haven.

Worse was to come. Back in the heart of oil country, the United States rushed troops to the Gulf in 1990 to protect Saudi wells after Saddam Hussein invaded Kuwait. Given that Saddam had spent the 1980s waging war on revolutionary Iran, brutally repressing Islamists inside Iraq, and trying to develop nuclear weapons, Washington's move ought to have won Arab hearts and minds; but the presence of unbelievers on Arabia's sacred soil instead made many Muslims suspect American motives even more.

The 1991 Gulf War and the tight sanctions that followed stopped Iraq from becoming the kind of southwest Asian rival that the drafters of the Defense Planning Guidance had feared. But over the next decade, American strategists (and almost everyone else) were blindsided by the way radical Islam mutated. All the forces shaking up the Muslim world—oil money, opposition to Arab rulers, jihad in Afghanistan, outrage at Americans in Saudi Arabia, unending hostility toward Israel—came together in one man, Osama bin Laden. "Under your supervision," he wrote in an open letter to Americans in 2002,

> the governments of [Muslim] countries which act as your agents, attack us on a daily basis . . . You steal our wealth and oil at paltry prices because of your international influence and military threats. This theft is indeed the biggest theft ever witnessed by mankind in the history of the world . . . Your forces occupy our countries; you spread your military bases throughout them; you corrupt our lands, and you besiege our sanctities, to protect the security of the Jews.

By this point, bin Laden's organization, al-Qaeda, had declared war on the United States on behalf of all Muslims and killed three thousand Americans.

Since the late 1990s, al-Qaeda has presented the globocop with a new kind of rival. In most ways, it is much weaker than the nation-states that the drafters of the 1992 Guidance worried about. If al-Qaeda or an affiliate gets hold of a nuclear weapon, it could potentially kill a thousand times as many people as it murdered on September 11, but a nuclear-armed Iraq could have done—and, should it arise, a nuclear-armed Iran may yet do—much worse. Southwest Asian governments with tax revenues and plenty of space to hide their weapons can amass hundreds of warheads rather than one or two. They can build missiles able to deliver death as far away as Europe, should they so desire. Given a few more years and the right friends, nowhere on earth would be safe. Al-Qaeda, however, cannot do this, unless it finds a state sponsor, and it will never pose the kind of threat to the American globocop that Germany and the United States posed to the British globocop a century ago.

Al-Qaeda does, though, very much resemble a different kind of threat that the British world-system also faced in the late nineteenth century. Then as now, terrorism and religious fundamentalism were popular responses to the globocop. Anarchists and Islamists both enjoyed an earlier golden age between the 1880s and 1910s, their bullets and bombs carrying off tsars and presidents. Muhammad Ahmad, known to the British as the Mad Mahdi, created an old-time al-Qaeda in Sudan. In 1883 his followers massacred to the last man a ten-thousand-strong Egyptian army and its British leader, and the following year they took Khartoum and killed another British general. Britain did not overthrow Islamist rule in Sudan until 1899 and kept troops there until 1956.

Bin Laden had a lot in common with the Mad Mahdi but was much more dangerous, because he had a real plan. Knowing that al-Qaeda could never directly threaten the United States' survival, he instead crafted a two-part, indirect approach. His first step was to use violence to overthrow any government, from Algeria to Indonesia, that he judged insufficiently Islamist (what al-Qaeda calls "the near enemy"), thus creating a caliphate of all the faithful; the second, to entangle the United States ("the distant enemy") in wars it could not afford and did not understand, until it tired of propping up non-Islamist regimes. "Then," al-Qaeda's number two man explained, "history would make a new turn, God willing, in the opposite direction against the empire of the United States and the world's Jewish government."

As I write, in mid-2013, it looks as if history is failing to take this turn. Far from overthrowing the near enemy, al-Qaeda has inspired fear and loathing all across the Middle East by murdering more Arabs than Americans. Its affiliates may be able to profit from disorder in Libya and Syria, but Afghanistan, Sudan, and Somalia, which all had Islamist regimes before bin Laden's war began, have since shed them, and the countries where Islamists have put serious pressure on governments—Algeria, Mali, Yemen, Pakistan—all lie well outside the strategically crucial, oil-rich Gulf region. Only Pakistan, with its nuclear arsenal, poses a real threat to global order ("A stable Afghanistan is not essential; a stable Pakistan is essential," President Obama's former special adviser on the region liked to say).

The United States' grand strategy against al-Qaeda's war on its near enemy was to defang the Islamists' appeal by promoting democratic reforms—to "send forth the news," President Bush (the Younger) said, "from Damascus to Tehran, that freedom can be the future of every nation. The establishment of a free Iraq at the heart of the Middle East," he insisted, "will be a watershed event in the global democratic revolution."

Arguably, the fall of tyrants in Tunisia, Libya, Egypt, and Yemen since 2011 has vindicated this strategy—although, as Bush himself recognized, "modernization is not the same as Westernization; representative governments in the Middle East will reflect their own cultures." Freed from authoritarian rulers, Arab voters consistently elected Islamists, but as I write, the consequences are still unclear. In Egypt the army abandoned a dictator to his fate in 2011 but overthrew an elected Islamist president two years later. In Libya, Islamist extremists took root during the civil war that ended Qaddafi's rule and, using weapons looted from his regime, spread jihad into Mali. Syria, much like Somalia and Lebanon before it, has disintegrated into a land of warlords, some of them just as violent as al-Qaeda. Overall, the emerging post–Arab Spring world looks somewhat democratic but highly unstable. It is largely Islamist, largely poor, badly governed, mistrustful of America, and even more mistrustful of Israel. It is hard to know who, out of Bush and bin Laden, would have liked it less.

The second part of al-Qaeda's plot, to suck the United States into so many ruinous wars that it would turn its back on the vast Islamic inner rim, started well. Bin Laden judged rightly that by hitting the United States so hard in 2001, he would leave Americans no option but to invade Afghanistan to root him out. This saddled the United States with its longest-ever war, and while the American decision to make an invasion of Iraq part of its response to terrorism was hardly a direct response to the events of September 11, the march on Baghdad was precisely the kind of overreaction that bin Laden had hoped for.

Where bin Laden went disastrously wrong, though, was in thinking that an overcommitted United States would either bankrupt itself or back away from southwest Asia. Instead, it stayed the course, killed bin Laden, and largely managed to "disrupt, dismantle, and defeat al Qaeda" (Barack Obama's definition of the goal). The cost of doing this, though, was to be dragged into yet another set of problems strikingly like those the British globocop wrestled with a century earlier.

The war the United States got when it invaded Iraq in 2003 was, in a remarkable number of ways, a kind of rerun of the Boer War that Britain fought against the South African Republic and Orange Free State between 1899 and 1902. The Boer and Iraq Wars were both preemptive, launched to head off future aggression. In both 1899 and 2003, critics often blamed war on an unholy alliance of self-interested politicians and businessmen greedy for natural resources—gold and diamonds in South Africa, oil in Iraq. The politicians leading the two globocops into war, however, often saw themselves as humanitarians, not materialists, fighting to protect the downtrodden (Shiites and Kurds in Iraq, black Africans in the Boer War), but regardless of which interpretation held the most truth, Britain and the United States both found that their decisions to use force divided opinion at home and turned old allies against them.

Where the Boer and Iraq Wars differed most was in their opening stages. In 2003 the United States overwhelmed Iraq's army, while in 1899 Britain blundered into defeat after defeat, sending soldiers in closed ranks across open terrain into withering artillery and rifle fire. Within eighteen months, though, the British had enough boots on the ground to bludgeon the Boer armies to pieces—only to find, as the Americans would do 103 years later, that their foes melted away and became insurgents.

The British army in 1900 and the American in 2003 were built to fight conventional wars, and at first both found counterinsurgency heavy going. For the British, it meant chasing tiny detachments, which the Boers called commandos, across vast stretches of veld. "We lived in momentary expectation of the order, 'Saddle-up!'" one officer recalled. "Many a time we did saddle-up, but however quick we might be we were never quick enough." In a similar mood more than a century later, a U.S. marine told his newly arrived commanding officer: "Sir, we patrol until we hit an IED, then we call in a medevac* and go back; and then we do it again the next day."

Both armies learned quickly. New commanders (Herbert Kitchener for the British, David Petraeus for the Americans) worked out counterinsurgency strategies and got the upper hand. But both globocops paid a price for this success, because the obvious way to fight irregular enemies was to turn to what Vice President Dick Cheney called "the dark side," and this was highly unpopular at home and among allies.

The United States spied on its own citizens, detained prisoners indefinitely, and denied them the protection of the Geneva Conventions. It tortured some of its captives and shipped others to countries that recognized no restraints at all, and even after these methods were renounced, targeted killings by remotely piloted aircraft continued to excite opposition. But compared with Britain's treatment of South Africans, Americans never got very dark at all. Kitchener burned thousands of farms, shot the insurgents' cattle, and herded their families into concentration camps. Roughly a quarter of the detainees—overwhelmingly women and children—died of disease and starvation.

Overall, despite missteps, the United States handled its version of the Boer War much better than the British handled the original, squandering far less blood and gold and inflicting less pain. Of roughly 1.5 million American troops who served in Iraq, fewer than 5,000 died; Britain sent similar numbers to South Africa but lost 22,000 (mostly from disease). Roughly one Iraqi civilian in every three hundred died violently during the American occupation, the vast majority at the hands of other Iraqis

---

*IED: improvised explosive device (that is, a homemade bomb). Medevac: medical evacuation helicopter.

and foreign militants in sectarian fighting, but Britain was ten times as murderous, killing one South African in thirty during the Boer War. America's war was also more cost-effective. The final bill, after the interest on borrowing is paid off, may be about $2.4 trillion, or roughly one-sixth of the U.S. GDP in 2011, but Britain's £211 billion tab for the Boer War represented one-third of its 1902 GDP.

In the end, Britain and the United States both won their Boer Wars, but to do this, both had to define down what victory meant. Britain drove South Africa's prewar leader Paul Kruger into exile, only to hand over much of what he had wanted to postwar South African governments run by former insurgents. Similarly, the United States toppled Saddam, only to see Iraqis elect governments with strong ties to the insurgents and Iran.

The lesson seems to be that it is easy for a globocop to get into a Boer-type war in a resource-rich part of the inner rim but difficult, divisive, and expensive to get out again. A determined globocop will probably always be able to win a Boer War, but a globocop that makes a habit of fighting Boer Wars will probably not hang on to its job for long.

Britain learned these lessons and avoided further Boer Wars. Time will tell whether the United States can follow the same path. On the positive side, al-Qaeda and its affiliates are in general retreat, and American dependence on Persian Gulf oil is declining (thanks to greater efficiency and booming domestic production, American energy imports in 2014 should be smaller than at any time since 1987). But on the negative side, the Afghan War looks likely to end even less satisfactorily than the Iraq War, the Arab Spring has spawned economic collapse and—particularly in the diplomatic debacle over Syria in September 2013—damaged American credibility, and Iran is close to acquiring nuclear weapons—which, Henry Kissinger warned during the darkest days of the Iraq War, "would be one of the worst strategic nightmares that America could imagine." Since then, tight sanctions, assassinations of scientists, and fiendishly clever cyberattacks have driven Iran to the negotiating table, but they cannot undo the nuclear advances it has already made.

If Iran ever puts a live warhead on a missile, it risks war with Israel and perhaps with the United States too. But it does not need to go that far, because it can probably bully and blackmail its neighbors simply by being known to be capable of going nuclear at short notice. Possibly the United States and southwest Asia would learn to live with this, just as the United States and northeast Asia have (so far) lived with a nuclear North Korea. Equally possibly, though, an almost-nuclear Iran would send wealthy neighbors—Turkey, Saudi Arabia, the United Arab Emirates—rushing to the almost-nuclear threshold too. At that point, Israel and/or the United States might well feel that another preemptive war—the mother of all Boer Wars—would be less bad than the risk of a Middle Eastern nuclear war.

Currently, southwest Asia consumes almost one-sixth of the American military budget. Given the continuing threats from terrorism, Islamism, and the Iranian nuclear program, plus (at least in the short term) the continuing importance of the region's oil, this seems unlikely to fall anytime soon, even assuming that the United States avoids another Boer War. Such costs will perhaps be bearable if southwest Asia remains America's major military focus; but of all the uncertainties in the coming decade, this seems the least certain of all.

The Inevitable Analogy

"When it comes to predicting the nature and location of our next military engagements," Secretary of Defense Robert Gates told West Point cadets in 2011, "our record has been perfect. We have never once gotten it right."

But that has not stopped military men from trying. Plans, after all, have to be made and weapon systems procured, and in the 1990s, with the Soviet Union gone and the number of interstate conflicts falling, one expert after another concluded that there would be no more big wars. The struggles in Iraq and Afghanistan after 2001 seemed to confirm this prognosis. From here on out, it would be counterinsurgency all the way.

So it was that when I had an opportunity in early 2012 to visit the U.S. Army National Training Center at Fort Irwin, California,* I found myself in the middle of a mock Middle Eastern village, complete with mosques and Arabic-speaking actors. I joined a party on an unfinished, windblown rooftop to watch troops trying their hand at taking "Afghan" elders to a meeting—only for make-believe jihadists to ambush them in the alleys. A bomb went off in a trash can with a deafening blast. Snipers opened up from windows and hillsides. A Humvee broke down, blocking a crucial intersection. It was unbelievably loud, dusty, and confusing (Figure 7.5), but the convoy finally fought its way out.

Fort Irwin, a chunk of the Mojave Desert as big as the state of Rhode Island, is the last place American troops go before deploying overseas. For

---

*I would like to offer my thanks once again to General (retired) Karl Eikenberry and the soldiers at Fort Irwin for arranging this visit.

Figure 7.5. Real war games: all hell breaks loose in 2011 in a mock Middle Eastern village at the U.S. Army National Training Center, Fort Irwin, California.

more than thirty years, it has been a barometer of American thinking about coming engagements. Had I shown up in 1980, when the center opened, I would have seen long-range shoot-outs between hundreds of tanks, skies full of fighters, and entire infantry battalions storming drab replicas of central European towns. But that all changed in 2005, when concerns about counterinsurgency took over. All the fake apartment blocks were torn down, except for one ersatz town, saved for old times' sake. In their place, the imitation minarets and madrassas that I saw rose from the sand.

If I get a chance to make another visit anytime soon, the scenery in the Mojave Desert will have changed yet again. Counterinsurgency was the face of battle while the globocop was strong enough to deter all rivals from trying anything else, but how much longer, the army is now asking, will that hold true? Hoping for the best but planning for the worst, the center is bringing back the tanks. Middle Eastern mock-ups are making way for a range of scenarios, from blitzkrieg breakthroughs to gunfights with gangsters. The new settings could represent almost any place from Syria to South Korea, but major wars are definitely back on the army's agenda.

Despite the globocop's travails in southwest Asia, it is increasingly looking as if the region where it is failing most seriously at preventing the rise of strategic rivals is actually East Asia. Along the continent's outer rim— the chain of islands from Japan to Jakarta (Figure 7.6)—the struggle has generally gone well. In some ways, in fact, developments in outer-rim East Asia have been very like those in western Europe. Japan, like West Germany,

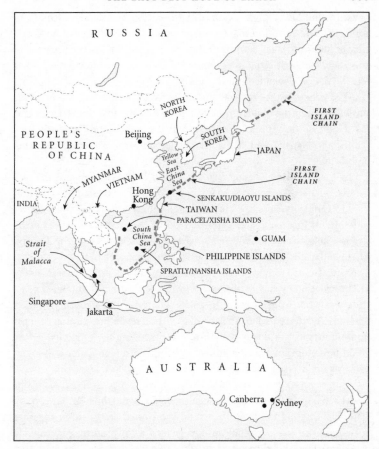

Figure 7.6. Island chains: how the world looks from Beijing

was demilitarized and occupied in 1945 and then partially remilitarized and admitted to world markets under American supervision. South Korea, Taiwan, Hong Kong, and Singapore all followed suit, turning into economic giants, but even in the 1980s, when Japan was booming even faster than West Germany and its holdings of U.S. Treasury bonds had reached enormous heights, American anxiety about having created a Japanese rival remained muted.

East Asia's inner rim, however, has been a different story. The People's Republic of China controls not only thousands of miles of inner-rim coastline but also a great swath of the Eurasian heartland, putting it in much the same position that Germany would have been in had it won either of the world wars. For two millennia, this setting made China one of the world's biggest economies, but since the Industrial Revolution it has left the nation dependent on importing natural resources and exporting finished products through the outer rim. Every year, $5 trillion in goods passes through the South China Sea, investing not just the Strait of Malacca but also tiny specks of rock such as the Spratly and Paracel Islands (called the Nansha and Xisha Islands in Chinese) with huge strategic significance.

By the time Mao Zedong seized power in 1949, it looked as if the successive outer-rim globocops had encircled China with island chains that could strangle its economy. Mao's initial response was to seek drastic remedies. In his first five years, he tried to loosen the globocop's grip by sending millions of men to fight in Korea and threatening to invade Taiwan, but in both cases American nuclear blackmail persuaded him to back down. Next, he decided to ignore geopolitics and to jump-start a Chinese industrial revolution by sheer willpower. However, when he commanded peasants to switch from farming to backyard ironworking, twenty million starved. Undeterred, Mao proclaimed a cultural revolution, urging younger communists to tear down everything old (including the economy) before building a utopia fueled by nothing more solid than Mao Zedong Thought. Once again, disaster ensued.

Things got so bad by 1972 that Mao felt compelled to signal his openness to change in the grandest possible way. For some time, Richard Nixon had been angling to bring China and the United States closer together to oppose the Soviet Union; now, to general astonishment, Mao invited America's former red-baiter in chief to Beijing. "This was the week that changed the world," Nixon grandiloquently announced, but in fact it was only after Mao was safely dead that saner counsels really prevailed in China. By that point, in the late 1970s, China's economy needed to grow by 8 percent every year for decades to avoid famines even worse than the ones it had already endured. Recognizing this, Deng Xiaoping opened China to the world economy. Since China could not break the island chains by force (it had virtually no navy, and the vast People's Liberation Army, old-fashioned at the best of times, had come close to collapse during the Cultural Revolution), this meant making nice with the globocop.

Deng's policies unleashed environmental devastation and rampant corruption, but they also delivered the goods. During the 1990s, a staggering 150 million farmers fled the impoverished interior for factories near the coast, effectively creating a new Chicago every year. Moving to a city typically raised a worker's income by 50 percent, and because the new urbanites still needed to eat, those who stayed on the farm and sold food to the cities also saw wages rise by 6 percent per year. By 2006, China's economy was nine times bigger than it had been when Mao died thirty years earlier.

But this was just the beginning. Fourteen thousand new cars were hitting China's roads every day in 2006, and nearly fifty-three thousand miles of new roads were being built for them to drive on. By 2030, officials estimated, these cars and roads would bring another 400 million peasants into the cities, and to accommodate them, China would erect more than half of all the homes being built on the planet. Between 1976 and 2006, China's share of the world's economic output more than tripled, from 4.5 to 15.4 percent. Across the same years the American share declined, and although the United States was still ahead, producing 19.5 percent of the world's GDP, there was no denying that the globocop now had a rival.

The United States let China become such a rival for the same reason that the United Kingdom let Germany and the United States itself become rivals in the late nineteenth century: it made the globocop richer too. In fact, China's rise was an extraordinarily good financial deal for America. Because Chinese imports were so inexpensive, most American workers saw their living standards improve, even though their wages were stagnant; and because China lent much of its profits back to the United States by buying a trillion dollars' worth of Treasury bonds, Americans never ran out of money to keep buying Chinese imports. As a final touch, cheap Chinese goods exerted deflationary pressures that prevented cheap Chinese credit from setting off rampant inflation. Everybody won.

So mutually rewarding was the relationship between the globocop and its Asian friend that the historian Niall Ferguson and the economist Moritz Schularick christened it "Chimerica"—a marriage of China and America. What made the name so apt, though, was that Chimerica was also a chimera, a dream from which the world would eventually wake up. In economics as in strategy, every action has a culminating point, beyond which, Clausewitz observed, "the scale turns and the reaction follows."

The scale was already turning by 2004, when *BusinessWeek* magazine announced that "the China Price" had become "the three scariest words in U.S. industry," and the turn was complete by 2008, when economic logic reasserted itself and Western asset bubbles burst. In April 2009, with the bottom of the abyss still not in sight, the leaders of the world's twenty biggest economies met in London to craft a response. Their best hope, one of their British hosts suggested, was that a joke doing the rounds of the meeting would turn out to be true: "After [the Tiananmen Square crisis in] 1989 capitalism saved China. After 2009 China saved capitalism."

Be careful what you wish for, the saying goes. China's part in helping to save capitalism made "the China Price" into the scariest three words for American diplomats as well as industrialists. China has become a massive body in the financial firmament, and its economic gravity is pulling the western Pacific into a Sinocentric orbit. Before 2009 was over, South Korea, Japan, and even Taiwan had all made very public overtures to Beijing. Vital links in the island chain around China were close to snapping.

The big question was what this would mean for the globocop. Not much, said Beijing, which, since 2004, had been describing China's growing influence as a "Peaceful Rise." China, it insisted, was joining—not challenging— the American world-system and would accept its rules. And just in case "Peaceful Rise" still sounded alarming, Beijing softened its image still further in 2008 by changing the label to "Peaceful Development." This, spokesmen explained, was part of an ancient Chinese strategic culture, rooted in Confucianism. Rather than using force to resolve disputes, China had always relied on virtue, showing by its humane example that cooperation would make everyone better-off.

Americans have often made similar claims about their own policies. As long ago as 1821, John Quincy Adams argued that the United States made its mark on the world through the "benignant sympathy of her example." But despite these fine words, the United States has regularly resorted to force, and throughout history, in fact, geopolitical shifts on the scale of China's takeoff have always been accompanied by massive violence. Europe's rise between the fifteenth and the nineteenth centuries had involved a Five Hundred Years' War, and the shift in the economic center of gravity from Europe to North America between 1914 and 1945 set off a storm of steel. Perhaps this time will be different, but if drawing the western Pacific into a Sinocentric orbit also means drawing the region out of the American orbit, the consequences for the globocop could be fatal—very like, perhaps, those Britain would have suffered if Germany had defeated France in 1914 and shut it out of a western European customs union.

China's leaders are neither uniquely virtuous (as the Confucian argument implies) nor uniquely vicious (as their shriller critics sometimes suggest). They are just like leaders throughout the world and throughout history—but that is precisely what makes the situation alarming. China, like everyone else, has to play the game of death. Since the 1980s it has mostly played the game well, which means (as it always means) being dovish when that works and hawkish when it does not. Far from substituting Confucius for Mackinder, China is (in the words of the journalist Robert Kaplan) an "über-realist power."

Recognizing its military weakness, diplomatic isolation, and strategic vulnerability, for a generation after Mao's death China avoided confrontations while pouring money into military modernization. Between 1989 and 2011, spending grew almost sevenfold, while the American defense budget—despite vast outlays on the Global War on Terror—grew by just one-quarter.*

"The inevitable analogy," says the strategist Edward Luttwak, is between China today and Germany in the 1890s. But while both countries spent massively to turn industrial might into military might, China's spending has been smarter than Germany's. Kaiser Wilhelm challenged the United Kingdom directly by building a battleship fleet, but China is challenging the United States asymmetrically.

Chinese investment has gone mostly into submarines, mines, and short-range ballistic missiles. These cannot contest American dominance of the oceans, but they can make the waters right around China too dangerous for the United States to operate in. According to one senior Chinese adviser, Beijing "is looking for more strategic space in the western part of the Pacific, so that American strategic weapons will not be able to pass through the Yellow Sea and the East China Sea." Success may be close: war games played by the RAND Corporation in 2009 suggested that already by 2013 China would be able to win an air war over Taiwan. Its thousands of missiles would quickly suppress land-based Taiwanese fighters, and with American planes forced to operate from carriers deployed out of missile range ("over the horizon," in military-speak) or from distant Guam, a mainland invasion of Taiwan would stand a good chance of success.

None of this would matter if China could rely on economic gravity to resolve all disputes in its favor, but strategy being what it is, that is not happening. By 2010, China's growing power had so alarmed its neighbors that some were banding together to stand up to the giant. Predictably, as

---

*If we measure instead from its low point in 1998 to its peak in 2010, American defense spending almost doubled, but even that is less than one-third of the Chinese proportional increase.

dovish behavior stopped yielding results, China turned more hawkish. A series of standoffs with Japan, the Philippines, Vietnam, and even India followed. Around one uninhabited atoll after another, aircraft buzzed each other, frigates were blasted with fire hoses, and fishermen were arrested. "China Ready for Worst-Case Diaoyu* Scenario," the *Global Times* (more or less an organ of the Chinese Communist Party) warned.

In mid-2011, as governments all around the Pacific Rim weighed their options, I had the good fortune to be invited to Canberra for a meeting of the Australian Strategic Policy Institute.[†] Seen from Canberra, the dilemmas were particularly acute. When the rest of the West had fallen into recession in 2009, Australia had not, largely because China's continued hunger for its coal and iron fueled a mining and commodities boom. By 2011, the country was unique among rich nations in being in its twentieth straight year of economic growth. To many Australians, this suggested—as the institute's director, Major General Peter Abigail, put it—"that Australia will at some stage need to make a choice between its primary economic partner [China] and its primary security partner [the United States]."

During the darkest days of the global financial crisis, Australia had already hinted at what its choice would be. "The Government's judgement," a Defence White Paper had announced in 2009, "is that strategic stability in the region is best underpinned by the continued presence of the United States." But the problem, as Australian journalists mercilessly pointed out, was that the official thinking was a mess: after insisting on the primacy of Australia's security partner, the bulk of the white paper was about how to stay in its economic partner's good graces.

The meeting I went to had been called to try to straighten out this muddle before the government published its next Defence White Paper. The discussion was open and engaged, ranging from the nature of strategy to urbanization and energy, but through it all there was a palpable discomfort in the room. Every option seemed to bring more costs than benefits. A split with its economic partner would ruin Australia. A split with its security partner would leave Australia unable to stand up to China. And if, miracle of miracles, Australia managed to keep all these balls in the air, a continuing mining boom would ruin it anyway by distorting its economy.

Personally, I left Canberra even less certain about what would happen next than I had been when I arrived, but behind the scenes more impor-

---

*The Diaoyu Islands (Senkakus in Japanese) are claimed by both China and Japan.
[†]I would like to thank the institute once again for this invitation.

tant conversations were going on. At first, these conversations also seemed to be more decisive: forsaking ambiguity, the Australian government announced that "Australia and the United States are seeking to align their respective force postures in ways that serve shared security interests." In November 2011, Barack Obama flew to Canberra. "Let there be no doubt," he told the Parliament. "In the Asia-Pacific of the twenty-first century, the United States of America is all in . . . We will allocate the resources necessary to maintain our strong military presence in the region . . . We will keep our commitments." Over the months that followed, discussions much like those in Canberra went on all along the island chains. One government after another followed Australia's lead and stiffened its spine. A flurry of collective security agreements followed, and some nations made major policy shifts. Myanmar turned its back on China and embraced Washington (and democracy); Japan talked of rearming and even of fighting China over the Senkaku Islands.

But no sooner had these new certainties taken shape than they began dissolving. In May 2013, Australia's new Defence White Paper abandoned the recent tough talk and cut back military spending sharply. "Whereas the Chinese saw the [previous] plan as a red rag," Rory Medcalf of Sydney's Lowy Institute for International Policy observed, "it is tempting to caricature Australia's new strategy as raising a white flag." This, apparently, was just the conclusion that the People's Liberation Army did reach. "U.S. power," its newly appointed deputy chief of staff told a Communist Party newspaper, "is on the decline, and leading the Asia-Pacific is beyond its grasp."

Perhaps I was right to be confused in Canberra. Nothing is clear in the western Pacific because the fog of unknown unknowns is denser here than anywhere else on earth. And yet it is here that the most important decisions have to be made. "If we get China wrong," one Washington insider admitted, "in thirty years that's the only thing anyone will remember."

Breaking the Chains

The worst way the United States could get China wrong is the same as the worst way that Britain could have gotten Germany wrong a century ago: by getting into a war with it.

To experts in Washington, the most easily imaginable military scenario is that China might grab the Senkakus, Spratlys, Paracels, or some similarly isolated piece of real estate, perhaps in the hope that a weak American response would lead its allies to desert it, breaking the island chains. However, hardly anyone thinks this scenario will actually happen. In 2011, *Foreign Policy* magazine asked a group of experts to rate the likelihood of a Sino-American war in the next decade, on a scale from 1 (impossible) to 10 (certain). No one gave a score above 5, and the average was just 2.4. Nonexperts agree; that same year, the Pew Research Center found that only 20 percent of Americans saw China as the greatest international threat—although that did represent a doubling since 2009, and China scored higher than any other country (in second place, with 18 percent, was North Korea).

The reason this island-grabbing scenario seems so unlikely is that despite China's military buildup, American dominance remains overwhelming. Aggression would call down on China a counteroffensive that American planners call "AirSea Battle." The United States has well-developed plans for cyberwar and would open with a massive electronic strike, paralyzing China's power grids and finances, blinding its satellites and surveillance, and jamming its command-and-control systems. Cruise and ballistic missiles, guaranteed to land within five or ten yards of their targets even after flying thousands of miles, would crater China's military runways and annihilate its surface-to-air defenses. Virtually undetectable stealth planes— B-2 bombers, F-22 fighters, and eventually F-35s too—would streak deep into the interior, flattening missile launchpads. China would lose the initiative within hours, and while American admirals might still hesitate to sail close to the Chinese coast, their naval aircraft and missiles would sink any Chinese ship foolish enough to put to sea and would pulverize any breach in the island chain.

Experts in Beijing seem to agree that island-grabbing would be unwise. In fact, they suggest, the real security risk is not a speculative Chinese attack but a preemptive American one. In the 1950s, American presidents sent tanks to the Yalu River and twice threatened nuclear war. Even the level-headed premier Hu Jintao sometimes felt besieged; observing in 2002 that the United States had "strengthened its military deployments in the Asia-Pacific region, strengthened the US-Japan military alliance, strengthened strategic cooperation with India, improved relations with Vietnam, inveigled Pakistan, strengthened a pro-American government in Afghanistan, increased arms sales to Taiwan, and so on," he suggested that "they have extended outposts and placed pressure points on us from the east, south, and west." To some Chinese generals, the harsh logic of the game of death seems to be encouraging the United States to exploit its military lead while it still can, launching an unprovoked attack on its rising rival to win itself another generation as globocop.

That, though, is surely the least likely future of all. Globocops, like real cops, pay huge reputational costs for brutalizing the innocent. Democratic globocops pay higher costs still, and when the intended victim is also the globocop's banker—as China is for the United States—beating him up becomes a truly terrible idea. The Pax Americana, like the Pax Britannica before it, is as much a diplomatic and financial balance as a military one, and winning a preemptive war would hurt the Americans almost as much as the Chinese.

If anyone gained from such a war, it would probably be Russia, the fourth region that the drafters of the Defense Planning Guidance worried about back in 1992. For a decade, their fears of Russian revanchism seemed misplaced, because the country fell off an economic cliff. Output declined by 40 percent in the 1990s and real wages by 45 percent. The government defaulted on its debts in 1998, and living standards tumbled so far that in 2000 the average Russian died younger than his or her grandparents. Russia hung on to the world's biggest nuclear arsenal, but it was not even clear whether its missiles still worked, and its soldiers put up a wretched showing against Islamists in Chechnya.

But since the 1990s much has changed. Fueled by oil and gas exports, GDP per person doubled between 2000 and 2012. The Kremlin has announced a $600 billion modernization of its submarines and missiles, and it is carving a smaller, nimbler expeditionary force out of the ruins of the old Red Army. Russia remains much less threatening than the Soviet Union and may become less threatening still if, as the World Bank expects, its oil revenues fall after 2015. But even so, if American aggression pushed China into Russia's arms, that would be among the worst of all possible outcomes for the globocop. A Russo-Chinese axis controlling the Eurasian heartland and a great stretch of its inner rim would be Mackinder's worst nightmare.

For some years, Russia and China have been cooperating loosely to block American plans in Syria, Iran, Pakistan, and North Korea, but the two countries' differences—over Russian arms sales to Vietnam and India, Chinese access to Russian oil and gas, and competition in mineral-rich Kazakhstan and Mongolia—have so far obstructed anything deeper. Far from buying itself more time to act as globocop, if the United States was to beat China on the battlefield, it would overshoot the culminating point of its strategy, leaving Beijing with nowhere to turn but Moscow and bringing on just the strategic disaster it was trying to avert.

The obvious conclusion to draw is that despite all the saber-rattling and policy-pivoting since 2009, the costs of using force are prohibitively high for everyone involved, and the payoffs equally low. It is hard to imagine anyone starting a great-power war in East Asia in the 2010s—just as it was hard to imagine anyone doing so in Europe back in the 1870s, when the British globocop began showing the first signs of losing its grip. It took another forty years of relative decline, in which Britain's economy grew more slowly than those of its rivals, before anyone was willing to push matters all the way to the brink. And that, I would suggest, is the historical analogy that we need to worry about. If the forty years between the 2010s and the 2050s do unfold like the forty between the 1870s and the 1910s, they will be the most dangerous in history.

There is, of course, no guarantee that history will repeat itself. Much could change in the next four decades. Chinese growth might stall, as Japan's did in the 1990s. Or the American economy might get new legs, invigorated perhaps by its ongoing revolution in extracting gas and oil from shale and tar sands. This promises (or threatens—environmentalists decry the dirtiness of the new fracking technology) to release vast supplies of energy from what once seemed unprofitable sources. Some economists also suggest that a "third industrial revolution" in nanotechnology and three-dimensional printing will boost American productivity even more dramatically. The United States might then confound its critics, as it has often done before. Plenty of people wrote America off back in the 1930s, only to see it come back and defeat the Nazis in the 1940s. Others wrote it off again in the 1970s, only for it to defeat the Soviets in the 1980s. Who is to say that the United States will not continue the forty-year cycle, recovering from its 2010s woes to get the better of China in the 2020s?

Current trends, however, make such sunny prognostications look rather unlikely. Chinese growth will probably slow over the next few decades, but most economists think it will nonetheless remain faster than American economic expansion. The Organisation for Economic Co-operation and Development (OECD), for instance, foresees Chinese growth coming down from 9.5 percent in 2013 to 4.0 percent in 2030, but in no year, it predicts, will the American economy expand by more than 2.4 percent. The Congressional Budget Office is gloomier still, setting a ceiling for American annual growth of 2.25 percent in the 2020s, and some financial analysts foresee long-term American growth averaging just 1.0–1.4 percent per year.

Most predictions expect China's economy to outgrow America's sometime between 2017 and 2027 (probably in 2019, and almost certainly by

2022, says *The Economist*). According to the accountants at Pricewater-houseCoopers, China's GDP will be 50 percent bigger than the United States' in the 2050s, while the OECD's economists think the gap will be more like 70 percent. And by that point, both sets of experts agree, India's economy will also be catching up with—or overtaking—America's (Table 7.1).

One of the reasons that American military dominance is so overwhelming in the mid-2010s is that the United States not only has a bigger economy than China (roughly $15 trillion versus $12 trillion in 2012, calculated at purchasing power parity) but also spends more of it (4.8 percent versus 2.1 percent) on preparing for war. But that too is changing. Chinese military investment, after more than doubling between 1991 and 2001 and then tripling again in the next decade, will probably slow in the 2010s; but American spending will actually shrink. After failing to find a plan to deal with its $16.7 trillion debt mountain—$148,000 per taxpayer—the American government imposed across-the-board cuts on itself in March 2013. Military spending, which stood at $690 billion in 2012, was capped at $475 billion; by 2023, it will be lower in real terms than it was in 2010.

It will take China decades to catch up with the American military budget (in 2012, the gap was $228 billion at purchasing power parity), and even then it will probably not have wiped out the lead in morale, command and control, and all-around effectiveness that American forces have built up across a century of preeminence. But that, perhaps, is not the most important point. Britain ceased to be an effective globocop long before any

	2011	2030	2050
United States	13.6	21.2	38.8
China	10.8	33.3	66.2
India	4.1	13.3	43.4
	2012	2030	2060
United States	15.2	23.4	38.0
China	11.3	30.6	53.9
India	4.5	13.7	34.7

Table 7.1. The post-American world? Top, PricewaterhouseCoopers's estimates of GDP in the United States, China, and India, 2011–50 (in trillions of 2011 U.S. dollars at purchasing power parity [PPP]); bottom, the Organisation for Economic Co-operation and Development's estimates, 2012–60 (in trillions of 2005 U.S. dollars at PPP)

individual foreign power could have beaten its navy in a straight fight, and much the same fate awaits the United States as soon as it can no longer afford armed forces powerful enough to intimidate everyone at once. The 2010s, warns Michael O'Hanlon of the Brookings Institution, will probably force "dramatic changes in America's basic strategic approach to the world . . . [and] while hardly emasculating the country or its armed forces, [the cuts] would be too risky for the world in which we live."

"The most significant threat to our national security," the outgoing chairman of the U.S. Joint Chiefs of Staff warned in 2010, "is our debt." But this in fact understates the problem in two big ways: first, debt is just a symptom of the deeper issue of American relative economic decline (Figure 7.7); and second, the United States' economic problems threaten the entire world's security, not just its own.

If the downward trend of the last sixty years continues for another forty, the United States will lose the economic dominance it needs to be a globocop. Like Britain around 1900, it may have to farm out parts of its beat to allies, multiplying unknown unknowns. To the rising powers of the 2010s and probably the 2020s too, any move that risks war with the United States smacks of madness. But the payoffs may look very different to the rising powers of the 2030s and 2040s. Absent an American economic revival, the

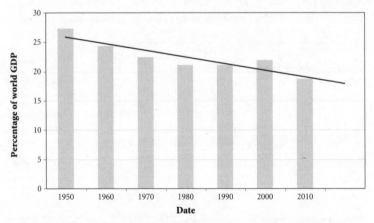

Figure 7.7. Slippery slope: the economic decline of the United States relative to the rest of the world—gradual in the 1950s–70s, partially reversed in the 1980s–90s, and precipitous since 2000

2050s may have much in common with the 1910s, with no one quite sure whether the globocop can still outgun everyone else.

The Years of Living Dangerously

"We are headed into uncharted waters," warns the National Intelligence Council in *Global Trends 2030*, the 2012 edition of the strategic foresight report that it presents every four years to the newly elected or reelected American president.* The real issue in the 2010s, they suggest, is not just that the United States has failed to prevent the emergence of a new rival; it is that the great-power politicking that worried the drafters of the Defense Planning Guidance twenty years ago is in fact just the tip of a much bigger iceberg of uncertainty.

Deep below the surface, says the council, are seven "tectonic shifts," playing out slowly across the coming decades: the growth of the global middle class, wider access to lethal and disruptive technologies, the shift of economic power toward the East and the South, unprecedented and widespread aging, urbanization, food and water pressures, and the return of American energy independence. Not all of these will work against the globocop's interests, but at the very least all seem likely to complicate its job. Nearer the surface, the council sees six "game-changers . . . questions regarding the global economy, governance, conflict, regional instability, technology, and the role of the United States." Any of these could blow up at any point, rearranging the geopolitical landscape in a matter of weeks. And right on the waterline, says the council, operating on even shorter timescales, comes a bevy of "black swans"—everything from pandemics, through solar storms that cripple the world's electricity supply, to the collapse of the euro.

The unstable years between 1870 and 1914 had uncertainties of their own, but, the council points out, we have now added an entirely new challenge: climate change. Of the hundred billion tons of carbon dioxide that humans have pumped into the air since 1750, a full quarter was belched out between 2000 and 2010. On May 10, 2013, the carbon dioxide in the

*I would like to thank Mat Burrows, former counselor to the director of the National Intelligence Council, and Banning Garrett, director of the Strategic Foresight Initiative at the Atlantic Council, for inviting me to make presentations to their organizations in July 2011 and to join several of their Silicon Valley meetings since then.

atmosphere briefly peaked above four hundred parts per million, its highest level in 800,000 years. Average temperatures rose 1.5°F between 1910 and 2010, and the ten hottest years on record have all been since 1998.

So far, the effects have been fairly small, but the worst impacts have come in what the council calls an "arc of instability" (Figure 7.8). The news from this crescent of poor, arid, politically unstable, but often energy-rich lands is mostly bad. Water flow in the mighty Euphrates River, which irrigates much of Syria and Iraq, has declined by one-third in recent decades, and the water table in its drainage basin dropped by a foot each year between 2006 and 2009. In 2013, Egypt even hinted at war if Ethiopia went ahead with a giant dam on the Nile. Extreme weather will roil the arc with more droughts, more crop failures, and millions more migrants. It is a recipe for more Boer Wars.

The greatest uncertainty, though, is that climate change is an unknown in the fullest sense: scientists simply do not know what will happen next. In 2013, NASA reported that "the five-year mean global temperature has been flat for a decade" (Figure 7.9). This might be good news, meaning that temperatures are less sensitive to carbon levels than climatologists had

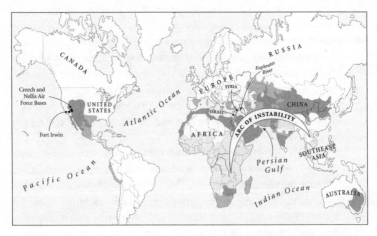

Figure 7.8. Feeling the heat: the darker the shading on a region, the more vulnerable it is to drought. Rich countries, such as the United States, China, and Australia, can pump water from wet regions to dry ones, but poor countries—above all, those inner-rim nations in the arc of instability—cannot. Trouble may be looming if temperatures resume their upward trend in the next few decades.

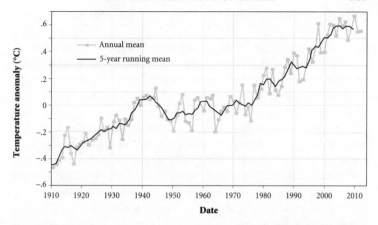

Figure 7.9. Strategic science: NASA estimates of global warming, 1910–2010. The gray line shows the average annual temperature and the black line the five-year running average, which—to many scientists' surprise—has flattened off since 2002.

thought—in which case, global warming might stay at the low end of the estimates, adding just 1°F between 1985 and 2035. Or it might be bad news, meaning that the carbon-climate relationship is more volatile than had been thought—in which case, temperatures will suddenly spike up from their 2002–12 plateau. Few scientific debates have so much strategic significance, but, in what might be a sign of more uncertainty to come, budget cuts forced the CIA to close its Center on Climate Change and National Security at the end of 2012, just days before the *Global Trends 2030* report was published.

But in spite of all this doom and gloom, the National Intelligence Council remains relatively optimistic about the outlook as far forward as 2030, the end point of its study. The globocop will probably face mounting financial pressures but will still be able to do its job; consequently, while "major powers might be drawn into conflict, we do not see any . . . tensions or bilateral conflict igniting a full-scale conflagration." Further, the potential death toll from great-power conflicts is currently declining. There are no longer enough nuclear warheads in the world to kill us all: an all-out nuclear exchange in the mid-2010s might kill several hundred million people—more than World War II, but much less than the billion-plus whose lives hung in the balance when Petrov had his moment of truth. And as the

2010s go on, the scale of possible slaughter will probably fall further. All the great powers (except China) plan more nuclear reductions, and in 2013 the United States ruled out any possibility of short-term rearmament by putting its new Los Alamos plutonium production facility on hold because of money problems.

As well as getting scarcer, warheads have gotten smaller. The bomb is a seventy-year-old technology, invented in an age when explosives tossed out of the back of a plane were lucky to land within half a mile of what they were aimed at. Multimegaton blasts solved the targeting problem by leveling entire cities, but today, when precision-guided munitions can strike within a few feet of their intended victims, these huge, expensive hydrogen bombs look like a solution to a problem that no longer exists. Accurate, low-yield nuclear warheads—or even smart conventional bombs—have largely replaced them.

Even more remarkably, the computers that make smart bombs possible are also giving us antimissile defenses that actually work. There is still a long way to go, and no shield could currently hold off a serious attack by hundreds of missiles equipped with decoys and countermeasures; but in sixteen tests since 1999, the U.S. Ground-Based Midcourse Defense system hit half of the ICBMs sent against it. In November 2012, Israel's Iron Dome system did better still, shooting down 90 percent of the slower, short-range rockets fired from the Gaza Strip (Figure 7.10).

In the next decade or two, the computerization of war will go much further, and—initially, at least—almost everything about it will make war less bloody. When the Soviet Union tried to suppress Afghan insurgents in the 1980s, it shelled and carpet bombed their villages, killing tens of thousands of people. Since 2002, by contrast, the United States has handed over more and more of its own counterinsurgency in that country to remotely piloted aircraft. Like precision-guided missiles, drones—as they are commonly called*—are cheaper than alternative tools (about $26 million for a top-of-the-line MQ-9 Reaper as against an anticipated $235 million for an F-35 fighter) and kill fewer people. Estimates of civilian deaths from drone strikes in Afghanistan and Pakistan have become a political football, and

---

*Here, as so often, terminology is contentious. "Remotely piloted aircraft (RPAs)" is the preferred air force term, emphasizing that these are still aircraft and do still have pilots. The army and the navy speak of unmanned aerial vehicles (UAVs), while civilians tend to say "drones." Being a civilian, I will say "drones" too, although in military circles "drone" conventionally means a robotic vehicle used for gunnery practice.

Figure 7.10. Iron Dome: an Israeli antimissile missile on its way to shoot down an incoming rocket over Tel Aviv, November 17, 2012

vary from the low hundreds to the low thousands, but even the highest figures are much lower than the carnage any other method of going after the same targets (say, by using Special Forces or conventional air raids) would have produced.

By 2011, air force drones had logged a million active-service flight hours, flying two thousand sorties in that year alone. The typical mission involves drones loitering fifteen thousand feet above a suspect, unseen and un-heard, for up to three weeks. Sophisticated cameras (which account for a quarter of the cost of an MQ-1 Predator) record the target's every move, beaming pictures back through a chain of satellites and relay stations to Creech Air Force Base in Nevada. Here, two-person crews sit in cramped but cool and comfortable trailers (I had the opportunity to visit one in 2013*) for hour after hour, watching the glowing monitors to establish the suspects' "patterns of life."

Much of the time, the mission goes nowhere. The suspect turns out to be just an ordinary Afghan, falsely fingered by an angry or hypervigilant

*Once again, I thank General (retired) Karl Eikenberry for arranging this visit, and the personnel at Nellis and Creech Air Force Bases for making it so informative.

neighbor. But if the cameras do record suspicious behavior, ground forces are called in to make an arrest, usually in the dead of night to reduce the risk of a shoot-out. If alert insurgents—woken by the roar of helicopters and Humvees—creep or run away ("leakers" and "squirters," air force pilots call them), a drone "sparkles" them with infrared lasers, invisible to the naked eye but allowing troops with night-vision gear to make arrests at their own convenience. The mere possibility of attracting drones' attention has hamstrung jihadists: the best plan, an advice sheet for Malian insurgents warned in 2012, was to "maintain complete silence of all wireless contacts" and to "avoid gathering in open areas"—hardly a recipe for effective operations.

Drones have become the eyes and ears of counterinsurgency in Afghanistan, and in about 1 percent of missions they also become its teeth. Tight rules of engagement bind air force crews, but when a suspect does something clearly hostile—such as setting up a mortar in the back of a truck—the pilot can squeeze a trigger on a joystick back in Nevada, killing the insurgent with a precision-guided Hellfire missile. (In Pakistan and Yemen, where the United States is technically not at war, the CIA has separate, secret drone programs. With different rules of engagement and fewer options to use ground forces, these probably use missiles and bombs more often than the air force, but here too, civilian casualties fell sharply between 2010 and 2013.)

Drones are the thin end of a robotic wedge, which is breaking apart conventional fighting done by humans. The wedge has not widened as quickly as some people expected (in 2003, a report from the U.S. Joint Forces Command speculated that "between 2015 and 2025 . . . the joint force could be largely robotic at the tactical level"), but neither has it gone as slowly as some naysayers thought. "It is doubtful that computers will ever be smart enough to do all of the fighting," the historian Max Boot argued in 2006, leading him to predict that "machines will [only] be called upon to perform work that is dull, dirty, or dangerous."

The actual outcome will probably be somewhere between these extremes, with the trend of the last forty years toward machines taking over the fastest and most technically sophisticated kinds of combat accelerating in the coming forty. At present, drones can only operate if manned aircraft first establish air superiority, because the slow-moving robots would be sitting ducks if a near-peer rival contested the skies with fighters, surface-to-air missiles, or signal jammers. Flying a drone over Afghanistan from a trailer in Nevada is an odd, out-of-body experience (I was given a few minutes on a simulator at Creech Air Force Base), because the delay between your hand moving the joystick and the aircraft responding can be as much as a second and a half as the signal races around the world through relay stations and satellite links. Better communications, or putting the pilots in trailers in theater, can shorten the delay, but the finite speed of light means it will never go away. In the *Top Gun* world of supersonic dogfights, milliseconds matter, and remotely piloted aircraft will never be able to compete with manned fighters.

The solution, an air force study suggested in 2009, might be to shift from keeping humans in the loop, remotely flying the aircraft, to having them merely "on the loop." By this, the air force means deploying mixed formations, with a manned plane acting as wing leader for three unmanned aircraft. Each robot would have its own task (air-to-air combat, suppressing ground fire, bombing, and so on), with the wing leader "monitoring the execution of certain decisions." The wing leader could override the robots, but "advances in AI [artificial intelligence] will enable systems to make combat decisions and act within legal and policy constraints without necessarily requiring human input."

Unmanned jet fighters are already being tested, and in July 2013 one even landed on the rolling deck of an aircraft carrier (Figure 7.11), one of the most difficult tasks a (human) navy flier ever has to perform. By the late 2040s, the air force suggests, "technology will be able to reduce the time to complete the OODA [observe, orient, decide, and act] loop to micro- or nano-seconds." But if—when—we reach that point, the obvious question will come up: Why keep humans on the loop at all?

The answer is equally obvious: because we do not trust our machines. If the Soviets had trusted Petrov's algorithms in 1983, perhaps none of us would be here now, and when the crew of the USS *Vincennes* did trust their machines in 1988, they shot down an Iranian passenger jet, killing 290 civilians. No one wants more of that. "We already don't understand Microsoft Windows," a researcher at Princeton University's Program on Science and Global Security jokes, and so "we're certainly not going to understand something as complex as a humanlike intelligence. Why," he goes on to ask, "should we create something like that and then arm it?"

Once again, the answer is obvious: because we will have no choice. The United Nations has demanded a moratorium on what it calls "lethal autonomous robotics," and an international Campaign to Stop Killer Robots is gaining traction, but when hypersonic fighter planes clash in the 2050s,

Figure 7.11. Look, no hands! A Northrop Grumman X-47B robot stealth fighter roars past the USS *George H. W. Bush* in 2013, just before becoming the first unmanned plane ever to land itself on the deck of an aircraft carrier.

robots with OODA loops of nanoseconds will kill humans with OODA loops of milliseconds, and there will be no more debate. As in every other revolution in military affairs, people will make new weapons because if they do not, their enemies might do so first.

Battle, the former U.S. Army lieutenant colonel Thomas Adams suggests, is already moving beyond "human space" as weapons become "too fast, too small, too numerous, and . . . create an environment too complex for humans to direct." Robotics is "rapidly taking us to a place where we may not want to go, but probably are unable to avoid." (I heard a joke at Nellis Air Force Base: the air force of the future will consist of just a man, a dog, and a computer. The man's job will be to feed the dog, and the dog's job will be to stop the man from touching the computer.)

Current trends suggest that robots will begin taking over our fighting in the 2040s—just around the time, the trends also suggest, that the globocop will be losing control of the international order. In the 1910s, the combination of a weakening globocop and revolutionary new fighting machines (dreadnoughts, machine guns, aircraft, quick-firing artillery, internal combustion engines) ended a century of smaller, less bloody wars and set off a storm of steel. The 2040s promise a similar combination.

Opinions vary over whether this will bring similar or even worse results than the 1910s saw. In the most detailed (or, according to taste, most speculative) discussion, the strategic forecaster George Friedman has argued that hugely sophisticated space-based intelligence systems will dominate war by 2050. He expects American power to be anchored on a string of these great space stations, surrounded and protected by dozens of smaller satellites, in much the same way that destroyers and frigates protect contemporary aircraft carriers. These orbiting flotillas will police the earth below, partly by firing missiles but mainly by collecting and analyzing data, coordinating swarms of hypersonic robot planes, and guiding ground battles in which, suggests Friedman, "the key weapon will be the armored infantryman—a single soldier, encased in a powered suit . . . Think of him as a one-man tank, only more lethal."

The focus of mid-twenty-first-century fighting—what Clausewitz called the *Schwerpunkt*—will be cyber and kinetic battles to blind the space flotillas, followed by attacks on the power plants that generate the vast amounts of energy that the robots will need. "Electricity," Friedman speculates, "will be to war in the twenty-first century as petroleum was to war in the twentieth." He foresees "a world war in the truest sense of the word—but given the technological advances in precision and speed, it won't be total war." What Friedman means by this is that civilians will be bystanders, looking on anxiously as robotically augmented warriors battle it out. Once one side starts losing the robotic war, its position will quickly become hopeless, leaving surrender or slaughter as the only options. The war will then end, leaving not the billion dead of Petrov's day, or even the hundred million of Hitler's, but, Friedman estimates, more like fifty thousand— only slightly more than die each year in automobile accidents in the United States.

I would like to believe this relatively sunny scenario—who wouldn't?— but the lessons of the last ten millennia of fighting make it difficult. The first time I raised the idea of revolutions in military affairs, back in Chapter 2, I observed that there is no new thing under the sun. Nearly four thousand years ago, soldiers in southwest Asia had already augmented the merely human warrior by combining him with horses. These augmented warriors—charioteers—literally rode rings around unaugmented warriors plodding along on foot, with results that were, in one way, very like what Friedman predicts. When one side lost a chariot fight around 1400 B.C., its foot soldiers and civilians found themselves in a hopeless position. Surrender and slaughter were their only options.

New kinds of augmentation were invented in first-millennium-B.C. India, where humans riding on elephants dominated battlefields, and on the steppes in the first millennium A.D., where bigger horses were added to humans to produce cavalry. In each case, once battle was joined, foot soldiers and civilians often just had to wait as the pachyderms or horsemen fought it out, hoping for the best. Once again, whoever lost the animal-augmented fight was in a hopeless position.

But there the similarities with Friedman's scenario end. Chariots, elephants, and cavalry did not mount surgical strikes, skillfully destroying the other side's chariots, elephants, and cavalry and then stopping. Battles did not lead to cool calculations and the negotiated surrender of defenseless infantry and civilians. Instead, wars were no-holds-barred frenzies of violence. When the dust settled after the high-tech horse and elephant fighting, the losers regularly got slaughtered whether they surrendered or not. The age of chariots saw one atrocity after another; the age of elephants was so appalling that the Mauryan king Ashoka foreswore violence in 260 B.C.; and the age of cavalry, all the way from Attila the Hun to Genghis Khan, was worse than either.

All the signs—particularly on the nuclear front—suggest that major wars in the mid-twenty-first century will look more like these earlier conflicts than Friedman's optimistic account. We are already, according to the political scientist Paul Bracken, moving into a Second Nuclear Age. The First Nuclear Age—the Soviet-American confrontation of the 1940s–80s—was scary but simple, because mutual assured destruction produced stability (of a kind). The Second Age, by contrast, is for the moment not quite so scary, because the number of warheads is so much smaller, but it is very far from simple. It has more players than the Cold War, using smaller forces and following few if any agreed-on rules. Mutual assured destruction no longer applies, because India, Pakistan, and Israel (if or when Iran goes nuclear) know that a first strike against their regional rival could conceivably take out its second-strike capability. So far, antimissile defenses and the globocop's guarantees have kept order. But if the globocop does lose credibility in the 2030s and after, nuclear proliferation, arms races, and even preemptive attacks may start to make sense.

If major war comes in the 2040s or '50s, there is a very good chance that it will begin not with a quarantined, high-tech battle between the great powers' computers, space stations, and robots but with nuclear wars in South, southwest, or East Asia that expand to draw in everyone else. A Third

World War will probably be as messy and furious as the first two, and much, much bloodier. We should expect massive cyber, space, robotic, chemical, and nuclear onslaughts, hurled against the enemy's digital and antimissile shields like futuristic broadswords smashing at a suit of armor, and when the armor cracks, as it eventually will, storms of fire, radiation, and disease will pour through onto the defenseless bodies on the other side. Quite possibly, as in so many battles in the past, neither side will really know whether it is winning or losing until disaster suddenly overtakes it or the enemy—or both at once.

This is a terrifying scenario. But if the 2010s–50s do rerun the script of the 1870s–1910s, with the globocop weakening, unknown unknowns multiplying, and weapons growing ever more destructive, it will become increasingly plausible.

The New England saying, then, may be true: perhaps we really can't get there from here.

Unless, that is, "there" isn't where we think it is.

Come Together

The secret of strategy is knowing where you want to go, because only then can you work out how to get there. For more than two hundred years, campaigners for peace have been imagining "there"—a world without war—in much the way that Kant did, as something that can be brought into being by a conscious decision to renounce violence. Margaret Mead insisted that war is something we have invented, and therefore something we can uninvent. The authors of "War" suggested that standing up and shouting that war is good for absolutely nothing would end it. Political scientists tend to be less idealistic, but many of them also argue that conscious choice (this time, to build better, more democratic, and more inclusive institutions) will get us there from here.

The long-term history I have traced in this book, however, points in a very different direction. We kill because the grim logic of the game of death rewards it. On the whole, the choices we make do not change the game's payoffs; rather, the game's payoffs change the choices we make. That is why we cannot just decide to end war.

But long-term history also suggests a second, and more upbeat, conclusion. We are not trapped in a Red Queen Effect, doomed to rerun the self-defeating tragedy of globocops that create their own enemies until we destroy civilization altogether. Far from keeping us in the same place, all the running we have done in the last ten thousand years has transformed our societies, changing the payoffs in the game; and in the next few decades the payoffs look likely to change so much that the game of death will turn into something entirely new. We are beginning to play the endgame of death.

To explain what I mean by this rather cryptic statement, I want to step back from the horrors of war for a moment to take up some of the arguments in my two most recent books, *Why the West Rules—for Now* and *The Measure of Civilization*. As I mentioned at the end of Chapter 2, in these publications I presented what I called an index of social development, which measures how successful different societies have been at getting what they wanted from the world across the fifteen thousand years since the last ice age. The index assigned social development scores on a scale from 0 points to 1,000, the latter being the highest score possible under the conditions prevailing in the year A.D. 2000, where the index ended.

Armed with this index, I asked—partly tongue in cheek and partly not—what would happen if we projected the scores forward. As with any prediction, the results depend on what assumptions we make, so I took a deliberately conservative starting point, asking how the future will shape up if development continues increasing in the twenty-first century just at the pace it did in the twentieth. The result, even with such a restrictive assumption, was startling: by 2100, the development score will have leaped to 5,000 points. Getting from a caveman painting bison at Lascaux to you reading this book required development to rise by 900 points; getting to 2100 will see it increase by another *4,000* points.

"Mind-boggling" is the only word for such a prediction—literally, because one of the major implications of such soaring development is that the human mind itself will be transformed during the century to come. Computerization is not just changing war: it is changing everything, including the animals that we are. Biological evolution gave us brains so powerful that we could invent cultural evolution, but cultural evolution has now reached the point that the machines we are building are beginning to feed back into our biological evolution—with results that will change the game of death into an *end*game of death, with the potential to make violence irrelevant.

It is hard to imagine anything that could be more important for the future of war, but in conversations over the last year or two I have noticed a deep disconnect between how technologists and security analysts see the world. Among technologists, there seems to be no such thing as over-optimism; everything is possible, and it will all turn out better than we expect. In the world of international security, however, the bad is always about to get worse, and things are always scarier than we had realized. Security analysts tend to dismiss technologists as dreamers, so lost in uto-pian fantasies that they cannot see that strategic realities will always over-ride technobabble, and technologists often deride the security crowd as dinosaurs, so stuck in the old paradigm that they cannot see that comput-erization will sweep their worries away.

There are exceptions, of course. The National Intelligence Council's re-ports try to bring both points of view together, as does the recent book *The New Digital Age*, co-authored by the technologist Eric Schmidt and the se-curity expert Jared Cohen. Trying to build on their examples—schizophrenic as the experience can be—I devote the rest of this section to the technolo-gists' projections, turning to the reality check of security concerns in the section that follows. The combination produces a vision of the near future that is both uplifting and alarming.

The technologists' starting point is an obvious fact: computers power-ful enough to fly fighter jets in real time will be powerful enough to do a lot more too. Just how much more, no one can say for sure, but hundreds of futurists have made their best guesses anyway. Not surprisingly, no two agree on very much, and if there is anything we can be certain of, it is that these visions are at least as full of errors as the century-old science fiction of Jules Verne and H. G. Wells. But by the same token, when taken in bulk rather than tested one speculation at a time, today's futurists also resemble those of late-Victorian times in recognizing a set of broad trends trans-forming the world—and when it came to broad trends, Verne and Wells were arguably right more often than they were wrong.

The biggest area of agreement among contemporary futurists (and the mainstay of the *Matrix* movies) is that we are merging with our machines. This is an easy prediction to make, given that we have been doing it since the first cardiac pacemaker was fitted in 1958 (or, in a milder sense, since the first false teeth and wooden legs). The twenty-first-century version, how-ever, is much grander. Not only are we merging with our machines; through our machines, we are also merging with each other.

The idea behind this argument is very simple. Inside your brain, that 2.7 pounds of magic that I said so much about in Chapter 6, 10,000 trillion electrical signals flash back and forth every second between some twenty-two billion neurons. These signals make you who you are, with your unique way of thinking and the roughly ten trillion stored pieces of information that constitute your memory. No machine yet comes close to matching this miracle of nature—although the machines are gaining fast.

For half a century, the power, speed, and cost-effectiveness of computers have been doubling every year or so. In 1965, a dollar's worth of computing on a new, superefficient IBM 1130 bought one one-thousandth of a calculation per second. By 2010, the same dollar/second bought more than ten billion calculations, and by the time this book appears in 2014, the relentless doubling will have boosted that above a hundred billion. Cheap laptops can do more calculations, and faster, than the giant mainframes of fifty years ago. We can even make computers just a few molecules across, so small that they can be inserted into our veins to reprogram cells to fight cancer. Just a century ago, it would all have seemed like sorcery.

We only need to extend the trend line out as far as 2029, observes Ray Kurzweil (the best known of the technological futurists, and now director of engineering at Google too), to get scanners powerful enough to map brains neuron by neuron and computers powerful enough to run the programs in real time. At that point, Kurzweil claims, there will effectively be two of you: one the old, unimproved, biological version, decaying over time, and the other a new, unchanging, machine-based alternative. Better still, says Kurzweil, the machine-based minds will be able to share information as easily as we now swap files between computers, and by 2045, if the trends hold, there will be supercomputers powerful enough to host scans of all eight billion minds in the world. Carbon- and silicon-based intelligence will come together in a single global consciousness, with thinking power dwarfing anything the world has ever seen. Kurzweil calls this moment the Singularity—"a future period during which the pace of technological change will be so rapid, its impact so deep . . . that technology appears to be expanding at infinite speed."

These are extraordinary claims. Naturally, there are plenty of naysayers, including some leading scientists as well as rival futurists. They are often blunt; the Singularity is just "the Rapture for Nerds," says the science-fiction author Ken MacLeod, while the influential technology critic Evgeny Morozov thinks that all this "digito-futuristic nonsense" is nothing more than a "Cyber-Whig theory of history." (I am not entirely sure what that means, but it is clearly not a compliment.) One neuroscientist, speaking at a conference in 2012, was even more direct. "It's crap," he said.

Other critics, however, prefer to follow the lead of the famous physicist Niels Bohr, who once told a colleague, "We are all agreed that your theory is crazy. The question that divides us is whether it is crazy enough to have a chance of being correct." Perhaps, some think, Kurzweil is not being crazy enough. A 2012 survey of crystal-ball gazers found that the median date at which they anticipated a technological Singularity was 2040, five years ahead of Kurzweil's projection; while Henry Markram, the neuroscientist who directs the Human Brain Project, even expects to get there (with the aid of a billion-euro grant from the European Union) by 2020.

But when we turn from soothsaying to what is actually happening in laboratories, we discover—perhaps unsurprisingly—that while no one can predict the detailed results, the broad trend does keep moving toward the computerization of everything. I touched on some of this science in my book *Why the West Rules—for Now*, so here I can be brief, but I do want to note a couple of remarkable advances in what neuroscientists call brain-to-brain interfacing (in plain English, telepathy over the Internet) made since that book appeared in 2010.

The first requirement for merging minds through machines is machines that can read the electrical signals inside our skulls, and in 2011 neuroscientists at the University of California, Berkeley, took a big step in this direction. After measuring the blood flow through volunteers' visual cortices as they watched film clips, they used computer algorithms to convert the data back into images. The results were crude, grainy, and rather confusing, but Jack Gallant, the neuroscientist leading the project, is surely right to say, "We are opening a window into the movies in our minds."

Just a few months later, another Berkeley team recorded the electrical activity in subjects' brains as they listened to human speech, and then had computers translate these signals back into words. Both experiments were clumsy; the first required volunteers to lie still for hours, strapped into functional magnetic resonance imaging scanners, while the second could only be done on patients undergoing brain surgery, who had had big slices of their skulls removed and electrodes placed directly inside. "There's a long way to go before you get to proper mind-reading," Jan Schnupp, a professor of neuroscience at Oxford University, concluded in his assessment of the research, but, he added, "it's a question of when rather than if . . . It is conceivable that in the next ten years this could happen."

The second requirement for Internet-enabled telepathy is a way to transmit electrical signals from one brain to another, and in 2012 Miguel Nicolelis, a neuroscientist at Duke University, showed how this might be done, by getting rats in his native Brazil to control the bodies of rats in North Carolina. The South American rodents had been taught that when a light flashed, they would get snacks if they pressed a lever. Electrodes attached to their heads picked up this brain activity and sent it over the Internet to electrodes on the skulls of North American rodents—who, without the benefit of training or flashing lights, pressed the same lever and got a snack 70 percent of the time.

Seventy percent is far from perfect, rats' brains are much simpler than ours, and pressing a lever is not a very challenging task. But despite the myriad technical problems, one thing seems certain. Brain-to-brain interfacing is not going to stop at rats moving one another's paws over the Internet. It may well develop in ways entirely different from Kurzweil's vision—which Nicolelis calls "a bunch of hot air"—but it will continue to develop nonetheless. (Nicolelis, in fact, expects us to get to much the same place as does Kurzweil, but from the opposite direction: instead of uploading brain scans onto computers, he says, we will implant tiny computers into our brains.)

Since the experts cannot agree on the details, there is little to gain from arbitrarily picking one prophecy and running with it. However, there is even less to gain from pretending that nothing is happening at all. We might do best to heed the sage words of Richard Smalley, a Nobel Prize–winning chemist who is often called the father of nanotechnology. Smalley's Law (as I like to call it) tells us that "when a scientist says something is possible, they're probably underestimating how long it will take. But if they say it's impossible, they're probably wrong." However exactly it works, and whether we like the idea or not, brain-to-brain interfacing—as Lieutenant Colonel Thomas Adams, quoted a few pages ago, said of robotics on the battlefield—is taking us to a place where we may not want to go but probably are unable to avoid.

That place is nothing less than a new stage in our evolution. Beginning more than a hundred thousand years ago, the struggle for survival in a harsh, ice-age world created conditions in which freakish mutants with big brains—us—could outcompete and replace all earlier kinds of protohumans. This happened even though the protohumans that got replaced had themselves created the mutants, by having sex, which produced random genetic variations, some of which flourished under the relentless pressure of natural selection. It seems unlikely that protohumans wanted to create monsters that would drive them into extinction, but, evolution being what it is, they had no choice in the matter.

As ye sow, so shall ye reap; and now, a thousand centuries on, we are doing something rather similar to what the protohumans did, but doing it faster, through cultural rather than biological evolution. In our struggle for survival in a crowded, warming world, we are creating new kinds of freakish mutants with big brains, using machines to merge our unimproved, individual, merely biological minds into some sort of superorganism. What we are making is, in a way, the ultimate open-access order, breaking down every barrier between individuals. Age, sex, race, class, language, education, you name it—all will be dissolved in the superorganism.

Maybe the process will only go as far as sharing thoughts, memories, and personalities (Nicolelis's guess). Or maybe it will reach the point that individuality and physical bodies no longer mean much (Kurzweil's guess). Or maybe it will go even further, and what we condescendingly call "artificial intelligence" will completely supplant ineffective, old-fashioned animal intelligence. We cannot know, but if long-term history is any guide, we have to suspect that one way or another the mutants—the new version of us—will replace the old us as completely as the old us replaced Neanderthals.

Once again, it seems that there is no new thing under the sun. Brain-to-brain interfacing is just the latest chapter in an ancient story. Two billion years ago, bacteria began merging to produce simple cells. Another 300 million years after that, simple cells began merging into more complex ones, and after another 900 million years complex cells began merging into multicelled animals. At each stage, simpler organisms gave up some functions—some of their freedom, in a sense—in order to become more specialized parts of a bigger, more complex being. Bacteria lost bacteria-ness but gained cellness; cells lost cellness but gained animality and ultimately consciousness; and now, perhaps, we are about to lose our individual animality as we become part of something as far removed from *Homo sapiens* as we are from our ancestral cells.

The consequences for the game of death are, to put it mildly, enormous. Two thousand years ago, the Roman historian Livy told a story about a time when his city had been bitterly divided. The poor, he said, had risen up against the rich, calling them parasites. As tensions mounted, Menenius Agrippa, a prominent senator, entered the rebels' camp to make peace. "Once upon a time," Agrippa told them, "the parts of the human body did not all agree as they do now, but each had its own ideas." The stomach, the other organs felt, did nothing all day but grow fat from their efforts, "and so," Agrippa said, "they made a plot that the hand would not carry food to the mouth, nor would the mouth accept anything it was given, nor would the teeth chew. But while the angry organs tried to subdue the stomach, the whole body wasted away." The rebels got the point.

The further that brain-to-brain interfacing goes, the more Agrippa's parable will become reality. It might even push the payoffs from violence right down to zero. Should that come to pass, then the Beast, along with our basic animalness, will go extinct, and it will make no more sense for merged intelligences to solve disagreements violently (whatever "disagreements" and "violently" might then mean) than it does for me to cut off my nose to spite my face.

Or perhaps that is not what will happen. If the analogy between cells merging to create bodies and minds merging to create a superorganism is a good one, conflict might just evolve into new forms. Our own bodies, after all, are scenes of unceasing struggle. Pregnant women compete with their unborn babies for blood and the sugar it carries. If the mother succeeds too well, the fetus suffers damage or death; if the fetus succeeds too well, the mother may succumb to preeclampsia or gestational diabetes, potentially killing both parent and child. A superorganism may face similar conflicts, perhaps over which part of it gets access to the most energy.

About one person in forty currently also has fights going on inside his or her cells, where so-called B chromosomes feed off the body's chemicals but refuse to participate in swapping genes, and about one person in five hundred has cancer, with some cells refusing to stop replicating, regardless of the cost to the rest of the body. To protect ourselves from these scourges and against viruses that invade us from outside, our bodies have evolved multiple lines of microscopic defense. A superorganism may have to do something similar, perhaps even producing the equivalents of antibodies that can kill intruders or parts of its own body that go rogue. After all, as most of us have learned to our cost, machines are just as vulnerable to viruses as animals are.

There is plenty to speculate about. What we can be sure of, though, is that brain-to-brain interfacing and merging through our machines are accelerating. The old rules, by which we have been playing the game of death for a hundred thousand years, are reaching their own culminating point, and we are entering an entirely new endgame of death. If we play it badly, there is almost no limit to the horrors we can inflict on ourselves. But if we play it well, before the end of the twenty-first century the age-old dream of a world without war might become reality.

The Endgame of Death

"Everything in war is very simple," said Clausewitz, "but the simplest thing is difficult." So it will be in the endgame of death. Playing it well will be simple—but also terrifyingly difficult.

What makes the endgame simple is that once we know where "there" is and what war is good for, it is fairly obvious how—in theory—we get there from here. I have suggested that "there" is the computerization of every-thing, and that what war is good for is creating Leviathans and ultimately globocops that keep the peace by raising the costs of violence to prohibi-tive levels. From these premises, the conclusion seems to follow that the world needs a globocop, ready to use force to keep the peace until the computerization of everything makes globocops unnecessary. The only alternative to a globocop is a rerun of the script of the 1870s–1910s, but this time with nuclear weapons. And since the United States is the only plau-sible candidate for the job of globocop, it remains, as Abraham Lincoln said a century and a half ago, "the last best hope of earth." If the United States fails, the whole world fails.

As I write, in 2013, a great debate is under way in American policy circles, between those who believe the superpower should "lean forward" and those who urge it to "pull back." Leaning forward, say its supporters, means sticking to "a grand strategy of actively managing global security and promoting the liberal economic order that has served the United States exceptionally well for the past six decades," while pullers-back argue that "it is time to abandon the United States' hegemonic strategy and replace it with one of restraint . . . giving up on global reform and sticking to pro-tecting narrow national security interests . . . [which] would help preserve the country's prosperity and security over the long run."

Long-term history suggests that both camps are right—or at least half-right. The United States must lean forward and *then* pull back. As we saw in Chapter 4, when fifteenth-century Europeans launched their Five Hun-dred Years' War on the rest of the world, it was old-fashioned imperialists who led the charge, plundering and taxing the people they conquered. The success of the Five Hundred Years' War, however, produced societies so big that old-style imperialism passed its culminating point. By the eighteenth century, open-access orders that managed to get the invisible hand and the invisible fist working together were generating much more wealth and power than traditional kinds of empires. The result was the rise of the world's first globocop—only for its success at implementing and managing a worldwide open-access order to generate such rich, powerful rivals that the British system soon passed its own culminating point.

The result of this, as we saw in Chapter 5, was a storm of steel and the rise of a much more powerful American globocop. Now, the new globocop's success is moving the world toward what I have called the ultimate open-access order, in which the invisible hand may have no need for the invisible fist. That will mark the culminating point not just for the American globocop, but for *all* globocops. Right now, the United States is the indispensable nation, and it must lean forward, but as it approaches the culminating point of globocoppery, the United States will need to pull back. The Pax Americana will yield to a Pax Technologica (a phrase I borrow from the futurists Ayesha and Parag Khanna), and we will no longer need a globocop.

Everything, then, is very simple—until we start asking the kinds of questions that immediately occur to security analysts. At that point, we see just how difficult the simplest things can be. We cannot just wish away humanity's defense dilemmas by applying science. In fact, it would seem that merging with machines is itself the most destabilizing of all the tectonic shifts, game changers, and black swans considered in this chapter, because the process will be so uneven.

As I type these words, I am sitting just fifteen miles (as the crow flies) from San Jose, the heart of California's Silicon Valley. The newest neighbor to move onto my road up in the Santa Cruz Mountains is an engineer working on Google Glass; when I commute to my own workplace, I fairly often pass self-driving cars (which tend to stick to the posted speed limits). But if I lived in Congo or Niger, which tied for last place in the most recent (2013) United Nations Human Development Report, I doubt that I would have such neighbors or see such vehicles. San Jose is one of the world's richest and safest cities; Kinshasa, one of its poorest and most dangerous. And not surprisingly, places that are already safe and rich (especially San Jose) are moving toward the computerization of everything faster than those that are not.

Open-access orders thrive on inclusion, because the bigger their markets and the greater their freedoms, the better the system works. Because of this, technologists tend to be confident that over the medium to long term, the computerization of everything will break down barriers, making the world fairer. However, throughout history, early adopters—whether of farming, Leviathan, or fossil fuels—have always had the advantage over those who follow later. Open-access orders do not incorporate everyone on equal terms, nor is everyone equally enthusiastic about being incorporated. In the eighteenth century, the Europeans who colonized America brought Africans into the Atlantic open-access order primarily as slaves; in the nineteenth, industrialized Europeans and Americans frequently used guns to force other Africans and Asians into larger markets.

It is hard to imagine such crude kinds of bullying resurfacing in the twenty-first century (rich northerners scanning poor southerners' brains at gunpoint?), but in the short run computerization is likely to widen the gap between the First World and the rest. In the next decade or two it may cause more, not less, conflict as it dislocates economies and adds to the sense of injustice that already inspires Islamist violence. More terrorism, Boer Wars, and state failures may be looming.

Nor will the disruptive effects of brain-to-brain interfacing be limited to the poor South. The rather modest amount of computerization that the world's wealthiest countries have seen since the 1980s has already increased their inequality. Over the medium to long term, merging through machines should make this kind of distinction meaningless, but if—as seems quite possible—a narrow elite of wealth and talent leads the way in brain-to-brain interfacing, in the shorter term the new technocrats might come to tower over everyone else in ways that today's 1 percent can only dream of.

There is a story, admittedly of doubtful veracity, that the novelist F. Scott Fitzgerald once announced at a party that "the rich are different from you and me"—only for Ernest Hemingway to come back with the immortal put-down "Yes, they have more money." Now, however, Fitzgerald is about to get his revenge. Over the next few decades, a new kind of rich really will become different from the rest of us.

Just how different is every bit as disputed as anything else in the prediction business, but for my money you cannot beat the imaginative account by the nanotechnologist turned novelist (and adviser to the National Intelligence Council) Ramez Naam. In *Nexus*, the only work of fiction I have ever encountered that comes with an appendix on bioengineering, Naam tells us that the 2036 edition of *The Oxford English Dictionary* will include some unfamiliar words. One is "transhuman," defined as "a human being whose capabilities have been enhanced such that they now exceed normal human maxima in one or more important dimensions." Another is "posthuman," meaning "a being which has been so radically transformed by technology that it has gone beyond transhuman status and can no longer be considered human at all." Transhumans, according to Naam's *OED*, are "an incremental step in human evolution," while posthumans are "the next major leap in human evolution."

Naam's novel is set in 2040, and at that point, he suggests, rich countries will have not just plenty of transhumans but also the first few posthumans. He imagines growing conflicts. Idealistic, highly educated elite youths maneuver to give everyone the chance to tune in to posthumanity, turn on, and drop out; a conservative American globocop tries to control the technology and protect old ways of being human; and rising rivals—particularly China—try to exploit posthumans for strategic advantage. In the sequel, *Crux*, terrorists get in on the act too, using merged minds for political murder. The world edges toward war, and much blood is shed, by and from humans of all kinds.

Nexus and *Crux* are only stories, but they nicely capture the messiness of merging with and through machines and the complexity of the choices ahead. If, for instance, the globocop leans too far forward—say, by trying to control developments too tightly, or by holding on to its job past the culminating point—it will face mounting opposition, overstretch, and financial collapse, quite possibly bringing on precisely the military challenges that it will be trying to avoid. That is a surefire strategy for losing the endgame of death, and one of the reasons I spent so much time in earlier chapters looking at the theory of a Western way of war is that it seems to encourage just this kind of overconfidence about leaning forward. Thanks to the military legacy inherited from ancient Greece, Victor Davis Hanson assures us, "deadly Western armies have little to fear from any force other than themselves." But this, I argued, is not what long-term history shows. In fact, as the twenty-first century goes on, it will be non-Western armies that challenge the globocop most. Maintaining order will depend on sound judgment and skillful shepherding of resources, not the legacy of ancient Greece.

On the other hand, if leaning forward too far or too long will lose the endgame, pulling back too far or too soon will do so even faster. If the globocop goes absent without leave, the most relevant analogy for the coming years might be not the slowly mounting crises of the 1870s–1910s, but the abrupt catastrophe of the 1930s—that low, dishonest decade when the British globocop lay dying, Americans were unwilling to take its place, and reckless rivals gambled everything on violent solutions to their problems. In the long run, pulling back will be essential, but in the short run it will be catastrophic.

Everything will hang on the relative timing of the shift from the Pax Americana to a Pax Technologica and the mounting difficulties that the globocop will face—if current economic trends continue—in doing its job. I suggested earlier that in the 2010s and probably the 2020s too, the United States will remain largely unchallenged, but as the 2030s, 2040s, and 2050s go on, it will find it harder and harder to overawe rivals. I also noted that the majority opinion among the futurists is that merging with machines will reach the Singularity stage in the 2040s. If all of these guesses are right, we perhaps do not have too much to worry about. The world will become increasingly troubled, polarized, and tense as we head through the 2020s, but the globocop will remain strong enough to handle the stresses. As we enter the 2030s, the globocop will be feeling the strain, but it will by then be pulling back anyway as the Pax Technologica begins to make violence irrelevant to problem-solving; and in the 2040s and '50s, just at the point that the globocop ceases to be able to cope, the world will no longer need its services. All will be well.

But will the computerization of everything really proceed at this convenient pace? The 2040s are only thirty years away, and although the thirty years that have just passed saw dramatic technological changes, it is far from obvious that another three decades will merge us with our machines. But that misapprehension, the futurists insist, comes from failing to see that technological change is exponential, constantly doubling up, not linear. Imagine, they sometimes say, that you rent a summer cottage. When you arrive, there is a very pretty lily on the pond. A week later, there are two; another week after that, there are four. You then, reluctantly, have to go back to work, and two months pass before you can resume your vacation. When you get back to the cottage, more than a thousand lilies confront you. The four lilies you left have doubled and redoubled eight times; you can no longer see the pond under them.

Let us say, for the sake of argument, that one full lily's worth of technological transformation had happened by 1983, the year of Petrov's moment of truth, and that each lily reproduces once every half-dozen years. In 2013, as I write, the lilies have doubled five times, and we have 32 of them—a lot more than in 1983, but still far from filling the pond. By 2025, however, there will be 128, and by 2043—the eve of Kurzweil's date for the

Singularity—over 1,000. The original pond—that is, we unimproved, merely biological humans—will have disappeared under a carpet of trans- and posthuman techno-lilies.

The thirty-some lilies we have in the mid-2010s represent gadgets like Google Glass, the Internet, and rats moving each other's paws. These are nice additions to the ways humans have lived for the last fifty thousand years, but nothing more. The two hundred or so lilies of the late 2020s might add up to artificial intelligence that can sometimes pass for human, a touch of telepathy, and some people living their lives largely in virtual reality, but there will still be far more pond than lily. The knee of the curve, as statisticians call the point where the increases really take off, will come in the mid-2030s, by which time every year will see more change than happened in the whole period between the 1980s and the 2010s; and in the 2040s, when change becomes so rapid that it appears to be instantaneous, the globocop can retire.

The arithmetic only adds up, though, if the exponential improvements in computing power continue at the same speed as they have in the last fifty years—but that would break Smalley's Law, the premise that everything is possible but will take longer than we think. If Smalley's Law does apply to the computerization of everything, we might still be very far from finishing the endgame of death when the globocop loses its grip in the 2040s. Even a modest increase in the time techno-lilies need to reproduce, from the half-dozen years that I proposed to a decade, would push the knee of the technological curve back to the 2060s and delay any kind of Singularity into the 2080s.

If the globocop stumbles in the 2040s, a period of several decades will then ensue with neither a Pax Americana nor a Pax Technologica. Rather than merging into a single superorganism, a Smallean world might dissolve in the 2050s into multiple and incompatible brain-to-brain networks, each dominated by a different great power. We might see a high-tech version of the nineteenth-century scramble for Africa as the networks compete for neural market share, shutting their rivals out of different parts of the world. Climate change might by then be convulsing the arc of instability, the coming of killer robots might be shifting the balance of power, and the infrastructure and energy needs of merging with machines might be providing a whole new kind of target to attack. A nation that feels it has a temporary edge in the technological transformation might be tempted to gamble on using it to impose its will violently on everyone else, or, perhaps more likely, a government that is falling behind might go for broke, betting everything on attacking before the enemy's lead becomes unassailable.

Armageddon will be beckoning.

War! What Is It Going to Be Good For?

But that, I am confident, is not how the story will end.

The reason for my optimism is our track record, revealed so clearly by long-term history. We have not managed to wish war out of existence, but that is because it cannot be done. We have, however, been extremely good at responding to changing incentives in the game of death. For most of our time on earth, we have been aggressive, violent animals, because aggression and violence have paid off. But in the ten thousand years since we invented productive war, we have evolved culturally to become less violent—because that pays off even better. And since nuclear weapons came into the world in 1945, the incentives in the game have changed faster than ever before, and our reactions have accelerated along with them. As a result, the average person is now roughly twenty times less likely to die violently than the average person was in the Stone Age.

Imagine, for a moment, that I had written this book fifty years ago, publishing it not in 2014 but in 1964—less than three years after the Berlin crisis, two after the Cuban missile crisis, a few months before Mao tested his first atomic bomb, and a year before U.S. marines landed in South Vietnam. Imagine too that I had predicted in it that humanity was now so well attuned to changes in the game of death's payoffs that within twenty-five years the Soviet Union would renounce force, tear down the Berlin Wall, and then dissolve itself, all without firing a single shot, let alone a nuclear missile. Even if I had held myself back from speculating that Red China would embrace capitalism and turn into the world's second-biggest economy, I doubt that the reviewers would have been kind. But I would have been right. And now, back in the present, the same reasoning leads me to believe that we will play the endgame of death just as skillfully as we played the regular game.

What we need to do is simple but, as Clausewitz said, difficult, because humanity will only win the endgame of death if the Singularity arrives before the globocop fails. If we are really going to get there from here, the globocop must remain strong for as long as possible—which means that the United States must, for the next forty-plus years, maintain its military spending and readiness at levels that make it a credible Leviathan. It must be ready to threaten and even use force to preserve the global order, while neither spending so much that it breaks the political consensus in favor of leaning forward nor exploiting its advantages so aggressively that it alienates its allies. To meet all these challenges, Americans will need to get their financial house in order, sustain economic growth, and invest in basic science, all while continuing to find leaders of the same quality as those that carried the country through the Cold War. Simple, but difficult.

The faster the computerization of everything proceeds, the greater the likelihood that the Pax Americana turns into a Pax Technologica before the globocop's weakness leads to a new storm of steel. But even in the worst-case, Smalley's Law–type scenario, the United States must remain as ready to pay any price, bear any burden, and meet any hardship as it was when John F. Kennedy first recommended such a course in 1961. In September 2013, as this book goes into production, two-thirds of Americans are telling pollsters that they oppose any use of force in Syria; but if the United States (like Britain between the World Wars) wearies of its role as globocop, there is no Plan B.

On the whole, American efforts to preserve global order will directly benefit the country's many overseas allies, but sometimes, inevitably, they will not—which means that the allies, too, will have a major role to play in the endgame. Sometimes they will need to speak truth to power, telling the globocop things it does not want to hear; at other times they will need to back up the globocop with diplomacy, money, or even force of arms. Above all, they will need the wisdom to know when to subordinate their own local concerns to a global strategy, recognizing that the whole is greater than the sum of its parts.

The most difficult decisions of all, though, might be those that fall to the globocop's rivals. The more these rivals' wealth grows, the more their moves will affect how the endgame turns out. A hundred-plus years ago, the British globocop's two greatest rising rivals were Germany and the United States. Germany's Kaiser Wilhelm felt that the only options open to him were risky moves that undermined the global order, while the United States found ways to act in its own interests while still (mostly) shoring up the globocop. "Speak softly and carry a big stick," President Theodore Roosevelt advised; and as today's rising rivals acquire big sticks of their own, their leaders will have to choose between Roosevelt and Wilhelm as models. The United States can do much to influence these choices by making room for rivals' peaceful development while simultaneously deterring rash aggression; but in the end, the more that America's rivals lean toward Roosevelt, the more likely the world is to win the endgame of death.

Si vis pacem, said a famous Roman proverb, *para bellum*: If you want peace, prepare for war. Despite everything that has changed in the two thousand years since Calgacus and Agricola fought rather than talked at the Graupian Mountain, this has remained true. The song "War" got it wrong. War has *not* been good for absolutely nothing, because—uncomfortable as it is to face this fact—war is the only method humans have found for moving from tiny Stone Age bands with rates of violent death in the 10–20 percent range to today's vast, globalized society with a rate below 1 percent. War has made the planet peaceful and prosperous; so peaceful and prosperous, in fact, that war has almost, *but not quite*, put itself out of business. Hence the final paradox in this paradoxical tale: If we really want a world where war is good for absolutely nothing, we must recognize that war still has a part to play.

NOTES

All URLs were checked on September 22, 2013.

INTRODUCTION

4 "I am reporting to you": D. Hoffman 2009, p. 11.

5 You may not be: The phrase is regularly attributed to Trotsky but might in fact be just a mistranslation of a paraphrase of a letter he wrote to Albert Goldman in June 1940 (http://en.wikiquote.org/wiki/Leon_Trotsky#Misattributed).

6 "War!/Huh, good God": Norman Whitfield and Barrett Strong, "War" (1969). Whitfield and Strong originally wrote the song for the Temptations, who recorded it on their 1970 album *Psychedelic Shack* but never released it as a single. Edwin Starr rerecorded it later in 1970 and turned it into a number one hit.

7 peace *for* our time: Neville Chamberlain, speech from 10 Downing Street, September 30, 1938, reported in the *Times*, October 1, 1938, www.thetimes.co.uk/tto/archive/.

8 "Lord knows, there's got to be a better way": Whitfield and Strong, "War."

10 "a noncontradictory linear logic": Luttwak 2001, p. 2.

11 "war is always": Liddell Hart 1967, p. 368. Liddell Hart was here playing on Saint Paul's comments on evil (Romans 3:8). I shudder to think what he would have made of Google's corporate motto, "Don't be evil" (Google Code of Conduct, April 8, 2009, http://investor.google.com/corporate/code-of-conduct.html; Paul Buchheit and Amit Patel originally suggested this motto).

11 captured a terrorist: Professor Chris Bobonich, Stanford University, Fall 1999.

14 "the losses in life": Richardson 1960, pp. ix–x. These sentences were actually written by Richardson's editors, drawn out of his own more circuitous prose.

16 "In such condition": Thomas Hobbes, *Leviathan* (1651), chap. 17.

16 "On earth there is nothing like him": Job 41:33–34 (King James Version).

16 "The attaining": Hobbes, *Leviathan*, chap. 17.

17 "an equal stranger": Jean-Jacques Rousseau, *A Discourse upon the Origin and the Foundations of Inequality Among Mankind* (1755), pt. 1.

17 "Government . . . is not the solution": Ronald Reagan, first inaugural address, Washington, D.C., January 20, 1981, www.presidency.ucsb.edu/ws/index.php?pid=43130#axzz1iWuZS4P3.

17 "the ten most terrifying words": Ronald Reagan, "Remarks to Representatives of the Future Farmers of America," July 28, 1988, www.reagan.utexas.edu/archives/speeches/1988/072888c.htm. Reagan is often misquoted as saying, "The nine most

terrifying words in the English language are 'I'm from the government, and I'm here to help.'"

18 "One legislator": Ronald Reagan, "Address to the Republican State Central Committee Convention," September 7, 1973, http://en.wikiquote.org/wiki/Ronald _Reagan.

18 "war made the state": Tilly 1975, p. 42.

18 "Hobbes was closer to the truth": Gat 2006, p. 663.

18 "if Rousseau's primitive golden age": Keeley 1996, p. 178.

18 "Hobbes was right": Pinker 2002, p. 56.

19 "is a tale of six trends": Pinker 2011, p. xxiv.

20 "Generals gathered": Tony Iommi, "War Pigs," released on Black Sabbath's album *Paranoid* (Vertigo, 1970; Warner Brothers, 1971).

20 "Well . . . I did like it": Kathy St. John, personal communication, October 2008.

21 "O for a Muse of fire": William Shakespeare, *Henry V* (1599), 1.1.1.

23 "In the long run": Keynes 1923, p. 80.

23 "I work for a Government": Keynes to Duncan Grant, December 15, 1917, quoted in Moggridge 1992, p. 279.

23 "The table should be read": N. Ferguson 2004, p. 11.

25 "All the isms have become wasms": Cited in Andrew Roberts 2011, p. 10.

I. THE WASTELAND?

27 "Men of the North!": My version of Calgacus's speech is a loose and truncated translation of Tacitus's more formal Latin prose in *Agricola* 30 (published around A.D. 98). Tacitus describes his own version as merely being "the substance of what [Calgacus] is reported to have said" (*Agricola* 29), so I have felt free to take some liberties. There is no way to tell which, out of my English version and Tacitus's Latin one, is closer to Calgacus's Celtic original.

    Roman sources regularly use the word "Caledonia" for what we now call Scotland, but we do not know if the people who lived there thought of themselves as Caledonians. I have therefore had Calgacus call them "Men of the North" (with shades of George R. R. Martin). Tacitus also applied the word "Britanni" indiscriminately to people from what are now England, Wales, and Scotland; again, we do not know if the ancient peoples thought of themselves as Britons. Mattingly 2006; Mattingly 2011, pp. 81–93, 219–36.

31 No plan survives: Attributed to Helmuth von Moltke (also known as Moltke the Elder). His actual wording was more convoluted. Hughes 1995, pp. 43–45.

32 "the Britons scattered": Tacitus, *Agricola* 38.

33 "Let Asia think on this": Cicero, *Letters to My Brother Quintus* 1.1.34 (60/59 B.C.).

34 "Germans have no taste for peace": Tacitus, *Germania* 14 (A.D. 98).

35 "a narrative of recent events": Philip of Pergamum, *FGrH* 95 T1 (30s B.C.). Translation modified from Chaniotis 2005, p. 16. Other than this fragment, Philip's *History* has not survived.

37 "to exterminate": Polybius 10.15.

38 "went on killing": Jerusalem Talmud (composed ca. A.D. 200–400), Ta'anit 4:5.

39 "no one should count himself rich": Crassus, quoted in Plutarch, *Life of Crassus* 2 (published ca. A.D. 120).

39 "The readier men were": Tacitus, *Annals* 1.2 (left unfinished at Tacitus's death in A.D. 117).

39 "The ox roams": Horace, *Odes* 4.5.17–19 (published ca. 15 B.C.).

39 Rome "has provided us": Epictetus, *Discourses* 3.13.9 (published around A.D. 108).

39 "if a man were called": Edward Gibbon, *History of the Decline and Fall of the Roman Empire* (London, 1776), vol. 1, chap. 3.

40 "During an exchange": Tacitus, *Annals* 14.17.
40 "we [had] lived in peace and harmony": Bosnian Croat informant, cited in Goldhagen 2009, p. 212.
40 "commonwealth by *acquisition*": Hobbes, *Leviathan*, chap. 17.
41 "Formerly we suffered": Tacitus, *Annals* 3.25.
41 needed three years: Cicero, *Against Verres* 1.40 (published 70 B.C.).
43 "Who does not now recognize": Pliny the Elder, *Natural History* 14.2 (published A.D. 79).
43 "over-paid by the immense reward": Gibbon, *Decline and Fall*, vol. 1, chap. 3.
44 rulers are *stationary* bandits: Olson 2000, pp. 6–14.
45 "I came, I saw, I conquered": Julius Caesar, probably written in a letter to a friend in Rome, 47 B.C. (quoted in Plutarch, *Life of Caesar* 50. Suetonius, *The Deified Julius* 37, has a slightly different account).
45 "freed the inhabitants of Lagash": Uru'inimgina of Lagash, ca. 2360 B.C., trans. in J. Cooper 1986, no. 9.
46 "I, even I": *Corpus Inscriptionum Latinarum* 11.11284 (ca. A.D. 250–260), trans. in MacMullen 1974, p. 43.
47 "People": Rodney King, May 1, 1992, www.youtube.com/watch?v=2Pbyi0JwNug&playnext=1&list=PLB874144170217AF6&index=15.
47 "To jaw-jaw": Winston Churchill, speech at the White House, June 26, 1954, published in *The New York Times*, June 27, 1954, p. 1.
47 "With my pious hand": Philip of Pergamum, *FGrH* 95 T1 (30s B.C.). Translation modified from Chaniotis 2005, p. 16.
47 "clear, hold, and build": Taken from the discussion in Ricks 2009, pp. 50–51.
48 "Wild animals": Plutarch, *Life of Pompey* 28 (ca. A.D. 120).
49 "people living": Tacitus, *Agricola* 21.
49 "intangible factors": Nye 2011, p. 21.
49 "Grab 'em by the balls": Unnamed American officer in Vietnam (1965), cited in Karnow 1986, p. 435.
50 "Render therefore unto Caesar": Matthew 22:21 (King James Version).
50 "for . . . there is no power": Paul, Romans 13:1 (King James Version).
50 "What most men call 'peace' ": Plato, *The Laws* 626a (ca. 355 B.C.).
52 "Fancy thinking": Golding 1954, chap. 8.
53 "As the dawn begins": Mead 1928, pp. 14, 16, 19.
54 "Samoa . . . is a place": Ibid., p. 198.
54 "Warfare . . . is just an invention": Mead 1940.
55 "The excitement" . . . "looked up and gasped": Chagnon 1997, pp. 11–13.
55 "*Yanomamö* is the term": Borofsky 2005, p. 4.
55 "a good many incidents": Chagnon 1997, p. 9.
57 "A stunned silence": Ibid., p. 20.
58 "speaking their language": Mead 1928, p. 10.
58 "we just fibbed": Fa'apua'a Fa'amu, interview with Galea'i Poumele, November 13, 1987, trans. in Freeman 1989, p. 1020, with the original Samoan text at p. 1021n5.
59 "a happy, enthusiastic, sociable person": Diamond 2008, p. 75.
60 "disastrous war": Williams 1984 (1832), p. 128.
60 "All the districts": Ibid., p. 131.
63 "a mythical place": Fukuyama 2011, p. 14.

2. CAGING THE BEAST

64 "The Greeks had a word for it": Best known from the title of Zoë Akins's 1930 play, renamed *The Greeks Had a Word for Them* in the 1932 film version (which is also sometimes known as *The Three Broadway Girls*).

64 "The Persians were as brave": Herodotus, *The Histories* 9.62–63 (published ca. 430 B.C.).

65 "the Persians . . . had many men": Ibid., 7.210 (he actually makes this judgment in his account of the Battle of Thermopylae in 480 B.C.).

65 "For the past 2,500 years": V. D. Hanson 2001, p. 5.

66 "It is this Western desire": V. D. Hanson 1989, p. 9.

66 "a line of division": Keegan 1993, pp. 332–33.

69 "When one has questioned": From *Models on Sealing and Investigation* (late third century B.C.), trans. in Lewis 1990, p. 247.

71 "on conquering Kalinga" . . . "victory on all his frontiers": Ashoka, Major Rock Edict XIII, trans. in Thapar 1973, p. 256.

71 "good behavior": Ashoka, Major Rock Edict XI, trans. in Thapar 1973, pp. 254–55.

71 "officers of *dhamma*": Ashoka, Major Rock Edict V, trans. in Thapar 1973, p. 252.

71 "legislation has been less effective": Ashoka, Pillar Edict VII, trans. in Thapar 1973, p. 266.

71 "since [*dhamma* had been instituted], evil": Ashoka, Kandahar Bilingual Rock Inscription, Aramaic text, trans. in Thapar 1973, p. 260.

73 "the Chinese Pompeii": http://discovermagazine.com/2011/jan-feb/89.

73 Pliny grumbled: Pliny the Elder, *Natural History* 6.20.

74 "In no year": Ibid., 12.41.

78 "≠Gau grabbed his people": R. Lee 1979, p. 390.

79 "their earth scorched": Caesar, *Gallic War* 1.1, 11, 18.

80 "circumscription": Carneiro 1970.

80 "caging": M. Mann 1986, pp. 39–40.

81 "is what occurs": Krepinevich 1994, pp. 30–31.

81 "Is there any thing": Ecclesiastes 1:9–10 (King James Version).

83 "Just as the sky": Hopi story, trans. in Lomatuway'ma et al. 1993, pp. 275–97.

84 "so fast": Lewis Carroll, *Through the Looking-Glass, and What Alice Found There* (1871), chap. 2.

86 "Alas! . . . that day of mine": Trans. in Jacobsen 1976, pp. 77–78.

89 "next to death": Muhammad Ali, interview in Manila, October 1, 1975, quoted in www.nytimes.com/books/98/10/25/specials/ali-price.html.

90 "5,400 men" . . . "the cities": Sargon of Akkad (2330 B.C.), trans. in Kuhrt 1995, pp. 55, 53.

94 "the sun disappeared" . . . "the chariot fighters": *Mahabharata* 4 (47) 31.6–7, 18–20, cited in Drews 1992, p. 125.

96 "some swearing": William Shakespeare, *Henry V* (ca. 1599), 4.1.

106 "At the end of ten years": Sima Qian, *Shiji*, trans. in Bloodworth and Bloodworth 1981, p. 74.

107 "A king relies": *Arthashastra* 2.2.13 and 10.5.54, trans. in Rangarajan 1992, pp. 657, 659.

108 "the law of the fishes": *Mahabharata*, Shanti Parvan 67.16 (compiled between 400 B.C. and A.D. 450; discussed in Thapar 1984, pp. 117–18).

108 "A hundred and fifty thousand people": Ashoka, Major Rock Edict XIII (ca. 255 B.C.), trans. in Thapar 1973, p. 255.

3. THE BARBARIANS STRIKE BACK

112 "there are lots of cavalry": Vindolanda tablets 2.164 (written around A.D. 100), http://vindolanda.csad.ox.ac.uk/TVII-164.

114 "The empire": Augustus's will (A.D. 14), quoted in Tacitus, *Annals* 1.11.

114 "Even victory": Clausewitz, "The Culminating Point of the Attack," trans. in Howard and Paret 1976, p. 566.

114 "Beyond that point": Clausewitz, *On War* (1832), bk. 7, chap. 5, trans. in Howard and Paret 1976, p. 528.
114 "In the entire realm": Luttwak 2001, p. 16.
116 "If we remember": Clausewitz, *On War*, bk. 7, chap. 5, trans. in Howard and Paret 1976, p. 528.
117 "Life was thrown into chaos": Herodotus 1.106.
117 "neutralize": See L. Wright 2006, pp. 297–330.
120 "what you could call the 'falling domino' principle": President Dwight D. Eisenhower, news conference, April 7, 1954, www.mtholyoke.edu/acad/intrel/pentagon/ps11.htm.
122 "Recently . . . the Western Qiang": *Book of the Former Han* 94b, p. 3804 (published A.D. 111), trans. in Lewis 2009, p. 148.
122 "Even women bear halberds": *Book of the Later Han* 70, p. 2258 (published early fifth century A.D.), trans. in Lewis 2009, p. 263.
124 "You know": Summers 1982, p. 1.
124 "The Romans stayed calm": Cassius Dio, *Roman History* 72.7 (published ca. A.D. 230). The original version of this part of Dio's history has been lost, and it is now known only from a somewhat garbled summary prepared by the Byzantine scholar Ioannis Xiphilinos in the 1070s A.D.
125 "All the companies": Ammianus Marcellinus, *Histories* 25.1.12–13 (published ca. A.D. 380).
126 "When a Scythian kills": Herodotus 4.64.
127 "They have squat bodies": Ammianus Marcellinus, *Histories* 31.2.
128 "These strongest and bravest": *Book of the Later Han* 70, p. 2258, trans. in Lewis 2009, p. 263.
132 "a chaos unamenable": Toynbee 1957, p. 265.
135 "against all men": Treaty of Dover, March 10, 1101, trans. in Chaplais 1964, no. 1.
137 "This caused great wars": Regino of Prüm, *Chronicon*, bk. 2, entry for 888 (written around A.D. 906), trans. in Kirshner and Morrison 1986, p. 56.
138 "feudal anarchy": Adam Smith, *An Inquiry into the Nature and Causes of the Wealth of Nations* (1776), bk. 5, chap. 2, art. 3.
138 "great lords": Ibid., bk. 3, chap. 4.
139 "This rich wine": *Chronique de Bertrand du Guesclin* (late fourteenth century), line 7254. Quoted in Charrière 1839, p. 264.
139 "The city walls had collapsed": Yang Xuanzhi, *Memories of Luoyang* (A.D. 547), trans. in Jenner 1981, p. 142.
140 "Understand this truth": Prince of Gurgan, *The Book of Qabus* (ca. A.D. 1080), trans. in Morgan 1988, p. 12.
140 "The ruler depends": Emperor Taizong, *Zizhi Tongjian* 192, p. 6026, cited in Wechsler 1979, p. 131.
141 "Chang'an lies in silence": Wei Zhuang, *Lament of the Lady of Qin* (ca. A.D. 890), trans. in Kuhn 2009, p. 17.
143 "Keep peace with walls": Ammianus Marcellinus 31.6.4.
143 "From the walls": Priscus, *History*, frag. 6 (written ca. A.D. 475).
143 "captured more than a hundred cities": Anonymous, *Life of Hypatius* 104, trans. in Heather 2006, pp. 309–10.
144 "They even take the fat": Giovanni da Pian del Carpine, *Ystoria Mongalorum* (ca. A.D. 1250), trans. in Dawson 1955, pp. 37–38.
147 "to the sounds of trumpets": Giovanni Miniati da Prato, *Narrazione e disegna della terra di Prato*, cited in Origo 1957, p. 61.
147 "At this . . . the people rejoiced": Unnamed chronicler, cited in Huizinga 1955, p. 23.
150 "Had contact with the West": Kirch 2010, p. 117.

152 "benefit the people": Toyotomi Hideyoshi, Sword Collection Edict 2 (1588), trans. in Tsunoda et al. 1964, p. 320.

157 "If that failed": Hassig 1992, p. 146.

161 "Proud of itself": *Cantares mexicanos* (sixteenth century), cited in M. Smith 2003, p. 183.

163 "This day is called": Shakespeare, *Henry V*, 4.3, 40–60.

4. THE FIVE HUNDRED YEARS' WAR

165 "a pitchy black night": Rudyard Kipling, "The Man Who Would Be King," first published in the series Indian Railway Library 5 (Allahabad: A. H. Wheeler, 1888). I cite it from *The Bombay Edition of the Works of Rudyard Kipling* (London: Macmillan, 1913), with quotations from vol. 3, pp. 171, 174, 178–79, 186.

169 "When you approach the enemy ships": Zhu Yuanzhang, in *Veritable Records of the Ming*, Hongwu 12/6b (compiled ca. 1400), trans. in Chase 2003, p. 34.

173 "no wall exists": Niccolò Machiavelli, *Discourses on the First Decade of Titus Livy* 2.17 (written ca. 1517, published 1531).

173 "Our first care": Machiavelli, *The Art of War* 7.1 (written 1519–20, published 1521).

173 "We make war": Roger Boyle, Earl of Orrery, *A Treatise on the Art of War* (1677), p. 15, cited in Parker 1996, p. 16.

173 "Can we doubt": Ogier Ghiselin de Busbecq, letter 3 (1560), cited in Ross and McLaughlin 1953, p. 255.

174 "most of the troops": Lala Mehmed Pasha, memorandum to Grand Vizier Yemishchi Hasan Pasha (ca. 1600), quoted in Imber 2002, p. 284.

174 "The critical point": V. D. Hanson 1989, pp. 19, 20.

175 "it is this Western desire" . . . "the absolute destruction" . . . "the *desire* to deliver fatal blows": V. D. Hanson 1989, p. 9.

175 "for the past 2,500 years": V. D. Hanson 2001, p. 5.

178 "a distant marginal peninsula": Frank 1998, p. 2.

182 "much dyed in blood": Battle participant (1653), cited in Capp 1989, pp. 80–81.

182 "Wagons . . . can serve": Qi Jiguang, *Practical Arrangement of Military Training*, zaji 6/11b (1571), cited in Chase 2003, p. 165.

183 "Cannon to right of them": Alfred, Lord Tennyson, "The Charge of the Light Brigade" (1854).

184 "Look with favor on the merchants": Sinan Pasha (ca. 1450–1500), cited in Inalcik 1969, p. 102.

184 "For years": Tahmasp I, *Memoirs* (1524), cited in Dale 2010, p. 88.

184 "As soon as he came to the throne": Iskandar Beg Munshi, *History of Shah 'Abbas the Great* (ca. 1620), trans. in Savory 1978, p. 523.

184 "the Roads are so safe": Jean Chardin, *Travels in Persia, 1673–1677*, cited in Dale 2010, p. 113.

187 "rancks advance": Colonel Robert Monro, cited in M. Roberts 1965, p. 258.

188 "Drill, baby, drill": http://blogs.wsj.com/washwire/2008/09/03/steele-gives-gop-dele gates-new-cheer-drill-baby-drill/tab/article/.

189 "Our lives and possessions": Blaise de Montluc, *Commentaires* (1592), cited in David Bell 2007, p. 36.

189 "Dear me": Richard Brinsley Sheridan, *Saint Patrick's Day* (1775), 1.2.

189 "that a uniform dress": Philip Saumarez (1747), cited in Herman 2004, p. 261.

189 "sobriety, diligence, obedience": Samuel Pepys (1677), cited in Coote 2000, p. 271.

189 "the want of money": *The Diary of Samuel Pepys*, September 30, 1661, www.pepysdi ary.com/archive/1661/09/30/.

190 "moan of the poor seamen": Ibid., October 7, 1665, www.pepysdiary.com/archive /1665/10/07/.

190 "This is what comes": Ibid., June 14, 1667, www.pepysdiary.com/archive/1667/06/14/.
190 *l'état, c'est moi* : This bon mot may well be apocryphal, but if Louis did not say it, he should have done.
191 "credit makes the soldier fight": Daniel Defoe, *The Complete English Tradesman* (1725), vol. 1, chap. 25.
191 "No longer is it nations": Jean-Paul Rabaut Saint-Etienne, cited in David Bell 2007, p. 48.
194 "Sores erupted on our faces": As told by Aztec informants to Bernardino de Sahagún (1530s), cited in Léon-Portilla 2006, p. 85.
195 "naked people": Letter to Juan de Oñate (1605), cited in Kamen 2003, p. 253.
195 "the most disadvantageous lottery": Smith, *Wealth of Nations*, bk. 4, chap. 7, pt. 1.
195 "white plague": N. Ferguson 2003, pp. 59–113.
196 "You have three things we want": Unnamed African chief, cited in T.D. Lloyd 1984, p. 37.
197 "wars by sea": Sultan of Gujarat (1509), cited in Pearson 1987, p. 56.
197 "Trade in Asia": Jan Pieterszoon Coen, letter to Directors 17, December 27, 1614, cited in Parker 1996, p. 132.
197 "The trade of the world": Captain George Cocke, quoted in Pepys, *Diary*, February 2, 1664, www.pepysdiary.com/archive/1664/02/02/.
198 "I am falling": Peshwa Balaji Baji Rao (1730s), cited in L. James 1997, p. 10.
198 "The princes became independent": Edmund Burke, opening speech in the impeachment of Warren Hastings, London, February 15, 1788, cited in Bond 1859, p. 42.
199 "wall which vomited fire and flame": Bengali survivor of the Battle of Buxar (1764), cited in L. James 1997, p. 41.
199 "the most considerable of any nation": Anonymous author of *Magnae Britanniae Notitia; or, The Present State of Great Britain* (London, 1718), p. 33, cited in Colley 2009, p. 59.
200 $400 million: Calculated at www.measuringworth.com/ppoweruk/ using average earnings; if the amount is measured in terms of the retail price index, Clive merely walked off with $25 million.
200 "Could it be believed": Burke, debate on the India Bill, London, December 1783, cited in Parker 1996, p. 117.
201 "O piteous spectacle!": Shakespeare, *Henry VI, Part 3* (1591), 2.6.73.
205 "consequence of a certain propensity": Smith, *Wealth of Nations*, bk. 1, chap. 1.
205 "By directing [his] industry": Ibid., bk. 4, chap. 2.
206 "open-access order": North et al. 2009.
206 "Let any gentleman but look": William Pulteney, First Earl of Bath (1743), cited in Brewer 1989, p. 91.
207 "should voluntarily give up all authority": Smith, *Wealth of Nations*, bk. 4, chap. 7, pt. 3.
207 "Such a measure": Ibid.
207 "government even in its best state": Thomas Paine, *Common Sense* (1776), first section. Available at www.gutenberg.org.
207 "government itself will become useless": Alexander Hamilton, "Views on the French Revolution" (1794), cited in Wood 2009, p. 302.
209 "Nothing but Force": Ambassador John Adams to Thomas Jefferson, October 9, 1787, cited in Wood 2009, p. 214.
209 "As defence": Smith, *Wealth of Nations*, bk. 4, chap. 2.
210 "Rule, Britannia!": Lyrics by James Thomson and music by Thomas Arne, first performed in *The Masque of Alfred* (1740).
210 "In 1793, a force appeared": Clausewitz, *On War*, bk. 8, chap. 3, trans. in Howard and Paret 1976, p. 591.

210 "We the People": U. S. Constitution, Preamble (1787), www.archives.gov/exhibits /charters/constitution_transcript.html.

211 "it is time for the age of Knight-Errantry": George Washington to François-Jean de Beauvoir de Chastellux, April 25, 1788, cited in David Bell 2007, p. 74.

211 "satirical inscription": Immanuel Kant, *Perpetual Peace* (1795), www.constitution .org/kant/perpeace.htm.

212 "The full weight of the nation": Clausewitz, *On War*, bk. 8, chap. 3, trans. in Howard and Paret 1976, p. 592.

212 "We are bearing fire and death": Captain Dupuy to his sister, January 25, 1794, cited in David Bell 2007, p. 180.

212 "What a revolutionary torrent": Jean-Baptiste Carrier, December 20, 1793, cited in David Bell 2007, p. 182.

213 "No more maneuvers": Lazare Carnot (1794), cited in Howard 2009, p. 80.

218 "The earth was made for Dombey and Son": Charles Dickens, *Dealings with the Firm of Dombey and Son: Wholesale, Retail, and for Exportation* (1846), chap. 1.

218 "as the *floating* property": Bernard and Hall 1844, p. 6.

219 "exactly as if the subjects": Armine Mountain (1842), cited in Fay 1997, p. 222.

220 "I never was in so severe a business": General Gerard Lake, November 1803, cited in Barua 1994, p. 599.

221 "There is nothing": Samuel Colt, report to Parliament (1854), cited in McPherson 1988, p. 16.

221 "In ten minutes the affair was decided": Henry Havelock, July 12, 1857, cited in E. Stokes 1986, p. 59.

222 "On her dominions": *Caledonian Mercury,* October 15, 1821, p. 4.

223 "world-system": Darwin 2009.

223 "The great object": Henry John Temple, Viscount Palmerston, speech to Parliament, August 6, 1839, cited ibid., p. 36.

225 "Fifty-four forty or fight!": Slogan in James Polk's 1844 presidential campaign, cited in Foreman 2010, p. 25.

225 "no two nations have ever existed": President James Buchanan, December 1858, cited in Foreman 2010, p. 39.

225 "I think there's an enormous amount": Prime Minister David Cameron, interview at Amritsar, India, February 19, 2013, cited in www.dailymail.co.uk/news/article -2281422/David-Cameron-talks-pride-British-Empire-stops-short-giving-apology -Amritsar-massacre.html.

226 "American holocaust": Particularly Stannard 1993.

228 "Take up the White man's burden": Rudyard Kipling, "The White Man's Burden: The United States and the Philippine Islands," *McClure's,* February 12, 1899.

228 "Pile on the brown man's burden": Henry Labouchère, "The Brown Man's Burden," *Literary Digest,* February 1899, www.swans.com/library/art8/xxx074.html.

228 "These petty principalities": Lieutenant Murray, local commission report on Nepal (1824), cited in L. James 1997, p. 73.

229 "of rupees, sacks of diamonds": Anonymous pamphlet (1773), cited in L. James 1997, p. 49.

229 "shall not accept, receive or take directly": Regulating Act (1773), cited in L. James 1997, p. 52.

229 "I impeach him": Edmund Burke, opening speech in the impeachment of Warren Hastings, London, February 15, 1788, cited in N. Ferguson 2003, p. 55.

230 "injurious": Calcutta Supreme Court, circular order, July 10, 1810, cited in Kolsky 2010, p. 28.

230 "defied my authority": Judge J. Ahmuty, Calcutta, December 3, 1808, cited in Kolsky 2010, p. 27.

230 "in all lands": Aurangzeb, December 1663, cited in Ikram 1964, p. 236.

230 "useful sciences": Rammohun Roy (1823), cited in S. Bayly 1999, p. 459.

230 "My lord": Rammohun Roy, cited in Fernández-Armesto 2010, p. 740.

230 "India, in a like manner": Rammohun Roy (1832), cited in C. Bayly 2004, p. 293.

231 "replied that he reckoned": Hackney 1969, p. 908.

232 "the profitability of European colonial empires": Acemoglu and Robinson 2012, p. 271.

234 "The preservation of a general peace": Tsar Nicholas II, August 24, 1898, cited in Sheehan 2008, p. 22.

234 "a new star in the cultural heavens": Bertha Felicitas Sophie Freifrau von Suttner (Baroness von Suttner and Countess Kinsky von Wchinitz und Tettau), statement at the First Hague Conference, May 1899, cited in Sheehan 2008, p. 30.

5. STORM OF STEEL

235 "produced by office-boys": Lord Salisbury (prime minister 1895–1902), quoted in Fyfe 1930, p. 63.

235 "What is the real guarantee": Angell 1913 (originally published 1910), pp. 295, 361.

237 "The nations in 1914": Lloyd George 1933, p. 52.

237 "One must think of the intercourse of nations": Churchill 1931, pp. 27–28.

238 The March of Folly: Tuchman 1984.

238 "When constabulary duty's to be done": William Gilbert and Arthur Sullivan, The Pirates of Penzance. The opera premiered on December 31, 1879, in New York (perhaps a sign of the times) and came to London in 1880.

241 "There are known unknowns": Secretary of Defense Donald Rumsfeld, February 12, 2002, press briefing, Washington, D.C., www.defense.gov/transcripts/transcript.aspx?transcriptid=2636.

242 "the pivot region of the world's politics": Mackinder 1904, p. 434.

242 "If Germany were to ally herself": Ibid., p. 436.

244 "a central European customs union": Walther Rathenau, "Deutsche Gefahren und neue Zielen," Neue Freie Presse (Vienna), December 25, 1913, trans. in Fischer 1974, p. 14.

245 "considered the question": Kaiser Wilhelm II to Alexander Count Hoyos, July 4, 1914, trans. in Herwig 2009, p. 9.

245 "self-castration": Chancellor Theobald von Bethmann Hollweg, cited in Stevenson 2004, p. 34.

245 "The general aim of the war": Kurt Riezler, secret document prepared for von Bethmann Hollweg, September 9, 1914, trans. at www.wwnorton.com/college/history/ralph/workbook/ralprs34.htm.

246 "If the pessimistic [Lieutenant Colonel] Hentsch": Captain Edward Jenö von Egan-Krieger, who was present at Hentsch's visit to Second Army headquarters on September 8–9, 1914, but only published his account after his death in 1965. Trans. in Herwig 2009, p. 266.

246 "like a bolt of thunder": Lieutenant Colonel Schmidt, 133rd Reserve Infantry Regiment, September 9, 1914, trans. in Herwig 2009, p. 302.

247 "The enemy's fire": Charles de Gaulle, cited in de la Gorce 1963, p. 102.

248 "Breaking through the enemy's lines": General John French, minutes, January 1915, cited in Strachan 2003, p. 163.

249 "Generals were like men without eyes": Keegan 1998, p. 321.

249 "like a flock of sheep": Lieutenant Teller, April 22, 1915, cited in Corrigan 2003, p. 165.

249 "If you could hear": Wilfred Owen, "Dulce et Decorum Est" (1917), lines 21–24.

250 "My boy, this is war": Second Lieutenant Murray Rymer Jones, cited in Hart 2008, p. 20.

251 "Our consuls in Turkey and India": Kaiser Wilhelm II, July 30, 1914, cited in Strachan 2001, p. 696.

251 "German prestige": von Ludendorff 1920.

252 "a single, magnificent collision of infantry": V. D. Hanson 1989, p. 9.

252 "modern system": Biddle 2004, pp. 28, 35.

252 "Gas! Gas!": Owen, "Dulce et Decorum Est," lines 9–10.

253 "strategic paralysis": Major J. F. C. Fuller, memorandum, "Strategic Paralysis as the Object of the Decisive Attack," May 1918, cited in Watts and Murray 1996, p. 382.

253 "To attack the nerves of an army": Fuller, lecture given in London (1932), cited in Watts and Murray 1996, p. 382n35.

254 "With our backs to the wall": Field Marshal Sir Douglas Haig, "Backs to the Wall" Order, April 11, 1918, cited in Edmonds 1951, p. 305.

254 "Retreat?": Usually attributed to Captain Lloyd Williams, June 3, 1918, although some sources name Major Frederic Wise. Cited in Keegan 1998, p. 407.

255 "At eleven o'clock": Prime Minister David Lloyd George, speech to Parliament, November 11, 1918, cited in Hansard, November 11, 1918, col. 2463.

255 "want of money": Pepys, Diary, September 30, 1661, www.pepysdiary.com/archive /1661/09/30/.

256 "in no single theatre": Field Marshal Sir Henry Wilson (1921), cited in N. Ferguson 2006, p. 320.

256 "We cannot alone act": Andrew Bonar Law (1922), cited in N. Ferguson 2006, p. 320.

257 "The change since 1914": Noyes 1926, pp. 436–37.

257 "peace, commerce, and honest friendship": Thomas Jefferson, first inaugural address, Washington, D.C., March 4, 1801, http://en.wikisource.org/wiki/Thomas_Jefferson %27s_First_Inaugural_Address.

257 "peace without victory": President Woodrow Wilson, speech to the U.S. Senate, January 22, 1917, https://www.mtholyoke.edu/acad/intrel/ww15.htm.

257 "a single and overwhelming powerful group of nations": Woodrow Wilson, speech in London, September 1918, cited in Mazower 2012, p. 128.

257 "the efficient civilized nations": President Theodore Roosevelt, January 4, 1915, cited in www.theodoreroosevelt.org/TR%20Web%20Book/TR_CD_to_HTML342.html.

257 "I am for a league of nations": Lloyd George, September 1918, cited in Mazower 2012, p. 128.

258 "the League of Nations": Nehru 1942, p. 638.

258 "stinking corpse": Vladimir Lenin, Moscow, March 1919, cited in Mazower 2012, p. 177.

258 "destroy the rule of capital": Nikolai Bukharin, Moscow, March 1919, cited in Degras 1965, p. 35.

258 "Comrade!": Lenin to the Bolsheviks of Penza, August 1918, cited in N. Ferguson 1998, p. 394.

259 "The 1929 crisis": H. James 2009, pp. 47–48.

260 "expose to depredation": British Chiefs of Staff, October 1932, cited in N. Ferguson 2006, p. 321.

260 "It is the virtue of the Englishman": Goldsworthy Lowes Dickinson (1913), cited in J. Morris 1978, p. 306.

260 "All over India": Orwell 1937, chap. 9.

260 "There are Englishmen who reproach themselves": Adolf Hitler, Mein Kampf (Munich: Eher, 1924).

261 "Our nation": Lieutenant Colonel Ishiwara Kanji (1932), cited in Yasuba 1996, p. 553n30.

262 "We really got busy": Anonymous Japanese worker, quoted in Taya Cook and Cook 1992, p. 49.

262 "We took turns raping them": Azuma Shiro, interviewed for the film In the Name of the Emperor (1995), cited in I. Chang 1997, p. 49.

262 "You and I": Lieutenant Colonel Tanaka Ryukichi, Nanjing, December 1937, cited in N. Ferguson 2006, p. 477.

263 "Were the Chinese": Mackinder 1904, p. 437.

264 "the Japanese people": Ishiwara (1932), cited in Totman 2000, p. 424.

264 Second Punic War: Kaiser Wilhelm II, mentioned in a letter from Admiral Henning von Holtzendorff to Chancellor Georg Michaelis, September 14, 1917, trans. in Lutz 1969, pp. 47–48.

264 "Germany's problem": Hitler, meeting at the Reich Chancellery, Berlin, November 5, 1937, cited in Evans 2005, p. 359.

264 "Greatest Possible Germany": N. Ferguson 2006, p. 315.

265 *above all* in the 'follow-through' ": Liddell Hart 1965, vol. 1, p. 164.

265 "deep battle": Citino 2004, p. 79.

266 "We shall go on to the end": Churchill, speech to Parliament, June 4, 1940, quoted in Churchill 1949, p. 104.

266 "could be counted on" . . . "No one dared": Secretary of War Anthony Eden and Brigadier Charles Hudson, secret meeting in York, June 5, 1940, cited in Andrew Roberts 2011, p. 88.

266 "Russians lost this war": General Franz Halder to Louise von Benda, July 3, 1941, cited in Weinberg 2005, p. 267.

266 "We found him in an armchair": Anastas Mikoyan, memoirs, June 30, 1941, cited in Bullock 1993, p. 722.

266 "The main thing": Adolf Hitler to Joseph Goebbels, July 25, 1938, cited in Evans 2005, p. 577.

267 "a monstrous tyranny": Churchill, speech to the House of Commons, May 13, 1940, cited in Churchill 1949, p. 24.

267 "the whole world": Churchill, speech to the House of Commons, June 18, 1940, cited in Churchill 1949, p. 198.

267 "For a foreseeable period": Hitler, meeting at the Reich Chancellery, Berlin, November 5, 1937, cited in Evans 2005, p. 359.

268 "What does the USA amount to anyway?": Hermann Göring, cited in Weinberg 2005, p. 238.

268 "Now at this very moment": Churchill 1950, p. 539.

271 "The war situation": Emperor Hirohito, radio broadcast, August 15, 1945, cited in Frank 1999, p. 320.

271 "a plain and bold intimation": Churchill, cabinet minutes, August 1941, cited in Mazower 2012, p. 195.

271 "It was extraordinarily unreal": Malcolm Muggeridge, *Diary,* December 16, 1945, cited in Kynaston 2007, p. 133.

272 "What this means to us": Vere Hodgson, diary, March 19, 1950, cited in Kynaston 2007, p. 510.

272 "the hallmark of the twentieth century": General Colmar von der Goltz, letter (1916), cited in Strachan 2003, p. 123.

272 "a thing": J. A. Quitzow, "Penang Experiences" (January 27, 1942), cited in Bayly and Harper 2004, p. 120.

272 "Great Britain has lost an empire": Dean Acheson, speech at West Point Military Academy, December 5, 1962.

273 "an Iron Curtain has descended": Winston Churchill, speech at Westminster College, Fulton, Missouri, March 5, 1946, www.nato.int/docu/speech/1946/s460305a_e.htm.

274 "the monkey house": Undersecretary of State Dean Acheson (1946), cited in Mazower 2012, p. 222.

274 Operation Unthinkable: N. Ferguson 2006, p. 592.

274 "no sense merely shuddering": President Dwight D. Eisenhower, National Security Council meeting, September 24, 1953, cited in E. Thomas 2012, p. 102.

274 "virtually all of Russia": Captain William Brigham Moore, Offutt Air Force Base, Nebraska, March 15, 1954, quoted in Rosenberg and Moore 1981, p. 25.

276 *Colossus*: N. Ferguson 2004a. *Empire*: N. Ferguson 2003.

277 "It was . . . the perfect capitalist solution": Kagan 2012, p. 40.

279 "to keep the Russians out": General Hastings Lionel Ismay, 1st Baron Ismay (1949), cited in D. Reynolds 1994, p. 13.

279 "are basing all our planning": Montgomery 1954, p. 508.

280 "Our Germans": Kaufman and Wolfe 1980, p. 33. The phrase appears in the film version of *The Right Stuff* (Warner Bros., 1983) but not in Tom Wolfe's novel.

280 "Listen now": NBC broadcast, October 5, 1957, cited in E. Thomas 2012, p. 253.

281 "Why not throw a hedgehog": Nikita Khrushchev, April 1962, cited in Fursenko and Naftali 1997, p. 171.

281 "disinvented": Eisenhower, March 1953, cited in Rosenberg 1983, p. 27.

282 "the longest suicide note in history": Labour MP Gerald Kaufman, June 1983, cited in Marr 2007, p. 450.

282 "When we build": Secretary of Defense Harold Brown, statement to a joint meeting of the House and Senate Budget Committees, January 31, 1979, cited in Odom 1988, p. 115.

282 "The troops will march in": President John F. Kennedy, interview with Arthur Schlesinger, October 1961, cited in E. Thomas 2012, pp. 408–9.

283 "cut off the North's front from its rear": General Cao Van Vien, April 1972, cited in Summers 1982, p. 119.

286 "When I told the British": Colonel Oleg Gordievsky (KGB resident designate in London and double agent, 1982–85), quoted in Sebestyen 2009, p. 88.

6. RED IN TOOTH AND CLAW

294 "descent with modification": Charles Darwin, *On the Origin of Species by Means of Natural Selection* (London: John Murray, 1859), chap. 4.

297 "the mad blood stirring": Shakespeare, *Romeo and Juliet* (1599), 3.1.4.

299 "civilization by instinct": Hölldobler and Wilson 2010.

302 "snack food": Wrangham and Peterson 1996, p. 223.

305 "In all my experience": Yerkes 1925, chap. 13. Yerkes did not know that Chim was a bonobo. Bonobos had only been recognized as a separate species in 1928, and Yerkes thought he was just dealing with an unusually nice chimp.

310 "the sexiest primate alive": D. Morris 1967, p. 63. Nearly fifty years of research has left *The Naked Ape* badly out of date, but it is still well worth reading.

310 "The inability": Diamond 1992, p. 75.

312 "combining [the physique] of a powerful wrestler": Stringer and Andrews 2012, p. 157.

313 "None of us could paint like that": This sentiment is regularly attributed to Picasso, but Bahn (2005) suggests that it is apocryphal. Picasso was apparently not very interested in the cave paintings.

319 "the Pacifist's Dilemma": Pinker 2011, p. 678.

320 "Western, educated": Henrich et al. 2010.

322 "a state that uses a monopoly": Pinker 2011, p. 680.

325 "like having two westerners": Ronald Reagan, March 23, 1983, cited in Gaddis 2005a, p. 225.

326 "Force . . . the *means* of war": Clausewitz 1976, p. 75.

327 "if allowed to sample the riches": Riesman 1964 (first published 1951), p. 64.

327 "the main armament of the Americans": Stalin to Zhou Enlai, August 1952, quoted from a transcript provided to me by David Holloway.

328 "It was a struggle": Alina Pienkowska, undated interview, cited in Sebestyen 2009, pp. 217–18.

328 "We can't go on like this": Gorbachev 1995, p. 165.

328 "I was suspicious of Gorbachev's motives": Bush and Scowcroft 1998, pp. 13–14.

329 "Did we see what was coming": Ibid., p. xiii.

329 "popular uprising against an oligarchic system": Hungarian report, June 1989, cited in G. Stokes 1993, p. 100.

329 "We can't do anything": Interview on the CNN television series *Cold War* (1998), episode 23, cited in Gaddis 2005a, p. 241.

330 "How could you shoot": Gorbachev, interview on the CNN television series *Cold War* (1998), episode 23, cited in Gaddis 2005a, p. 250.

7. THE LAST BEST HOPE OF EARTH

332 "Lock your doors and load your guns": City attorney of San Bernardino, California, quoted in Friend 2013, p. 29.

339 "You can't get there from here": I owe this insight to Dick Granger, December 1983.

340 "assum[e] responsibility": Zalmay Khalilzad and Scooter Libby, February 18 draft of the 1992 *Defense Planning Guidance*, www.gwu.edu/~nsarchiv/nukevault/ebb245 /index.htm.

340 "literally a Pax Americana": Senator Joseph Biden, quoted in *Washington Post*, March 11, 1992, p. A1, www.yale.edu/strattech/92dpg.html.

341 "People say, 'It is a terrible thing'": Unnamed French official, quoted in *Financial Times*, October 17, 2002, and cited in Kagan 2003, p. 63.

342 "The final goal": Helmut Schlesinger (1994), cited in Deo et al. 2011, p. 16.

343 "Almost no modern fiat currency": Deo et al. 2011, p. 1.

344 "Free Speech Now": Quoted from Belarusian News Photos, August 2012, www.bnp .by/shvedy-dejstvitelno-sbrosili-na-belarus-plyushevyx-medvedej-na-parashyutax.

344 "On major strategic and international questions": Kagan 2003, p. 3.

345 "We have no eternal allies": Lord Palmerston, speech to the House of Commons, reported in *Hansard*, March 1, 1848, col. 122.

346 "the Great Game": Rudyard Kipling, *Kim* (London: Macmillan, 1901), chap. 12.

348 "Under your supervision": Osama bin Laden, "Letter to America," mid-November 2002, cited in www.guardian.co.uk/world/2002/nov/24/theobserver.

349 "Then . . . history would make a new turn": Ayman al-Zawahiri, *Knights Under the Prophet's Banner* (2001), cited in L. Wright 2006, p. 46.

349 "A stable Afghanistan": Special Adviser Richard Holbrooke, cited in Sanger 2012, p. 132.

349 "send forth the news": President George W. Bush, speech at the U.S. Chamber of Commerce, November 6, 2003, http://georgewbush-whitehouse.archives.gov/news /releases/2003/11/20031106-2.html.

349 "modernization is not": Ibid.

350 "disrupt, dismantle, and defeat al Qaeda": President Barack Obama, speech at the White House, March 27, 2009, www.whitehouse.gov/the_press_office/Remarks-by -the-President-on-a-New-Strategy-for-Afghanistan-and-Pakistan/.

351 "We lived in momentary expectation": Major F. M. Crum (First Battalion, King's Royal Rifles), *Memoirs of an Unconventional Soldier* (1903), cited in Citino 2002, p. 60.

351 "Sir, we patrol until we hit an IED": Unnamed U.S. marine to Brigadier General Larry Nicholson, February 2009, quoted in Chandrasekaran 2012, p. 4.

351 "the dark side": Vice President Dick Cheney, interview on *Meet the Press*, NBC, September 16, 2001, available at www.youtube.com/watch?v=X56PBAEkzYg.

352 "would be one of the worst": Henry Kissinger to Michael Gerson, September 2005, cited in Woodward 2006, p. 409.

353 "When it comes to predicting": Secretary of Defense Robert Gates, speech at West Point, February 25, 2011, www.defense.gov/speeches/speech.aspx?speechid=1539.

356 "This was the week that changed the world": President Richard Nixon, toast at a dinner in Shanghai, February 27, 1972, cited in D. Reynolds 2000, p. 329.

357 "Chimerica": Ferguson and Schularick 2007.

357 "the scale turns and the reaction follows": Clausewitz, *On War*, bk. 7, chap. 5, trans. in Howard and Paret 1976, p. 528.

357 "the China Price": *BusinessWeek*, December 6, 2004, p. 104.

358 "After . . . 1989 capitalism saved China": Foreign Secretary David Miliband, interview with *Guardian*, cited in "May the Good China Preserve Us," *Economist*, May 21, 2009, www.economist.com/node/13701737.

358 "Peaceful Rise": Zheng 2005.

358 "Peaceful Development": Dai 2010.

358 "benignant sympathy of her example": John Quincy Adams, speech to the House of Representatives, July 4, 1821, http://fff.org/explore-freedom/article/john-quincy-adams-foreign-policy-1821/.

359 "über-realist power": R. Kaplan 2012, p. 196.

359 "The inevitable analogy": Luttwak 2012, p. 56.

359 "is looking for more strategic space": Shi Yinhong, professor of international relations at Renmin University, May 28, 2013, cited in www.nytimes.com/2013/05/29/world/asia/china-to-seek-more-equal-footing-with-us-in-talks.html?ref=world&_r=1&.

360 "China Ready for Worst-Case Diaoyu Scenario": *Global Times*, January 11, 2013, www.globaltimes.cn/content/755170.shtml.

360 "that Australia will at some stage": Abigail 2012, p. 74.

360 "The Government's judgement": Commonwealth of Australia 2009, p. 43.

361 "Australia and the United States": Hawke and Smith 2012, p. 53.

361 "Let there be no doubt": Barack Obama, speech to the Australian Parliament, Canberra, November 17, 2011, www.whitehouse.gov/the-press-office/2011/11/17/remarks-president-obama-australian-parliament.

361 "Whereas the Chinese saw": Rory Medcalf, director of the international security program of the Lowy Institute, Sydney, May 7, 2013, http://thediplomat.com/2013/05/07/breaking-down-australias-defense-white-paper-2013/.

361 "U.S. power . . . is on the decline": Lieutenant General Qi Jianguo, "An Unprecedented Great Changing Situation," *Study Times*, January 21, 2013, trans. by James Bellacqua and Daniel Hartnett at www.cna.org/sites/default/files/research/DQR-2013-U-004445-Final.pdf.

361 "If we get China wrong": Unidentified American diplomat, quoted in Sanger 2012, p. xix.

362 *Foreign Policy* magazine asked a group: www.foreignpolicy.com/articles/2011/02/22/the_future_of_war.

362 the Pew Research Center found: http://people-press.org/files/legacy-pdf/692.pdf.

362 "AirSea Battle": Krepinevich 2010; van Tol et al. 2010.

362 "strengthened its military deployments": Hu Jintao, comments in 2001 in private discussions, trans. in Gilley and Nathan 2003, pp. 235–36.

364 "third industrial revolution": Rifkin 2011.

366 "dramatic changes": O'Hanlon 2013, pp. 30, v.

366 "The most significant threat": Admiral Michael Mullen, interview with CNN, August 25, 2010, www.cnn.com/2010/US/08/27/debt.security.mullen/index.html.

367 "We are headed into uncharted waters": National Intelligence Council 2012, pp. v, 3.

367 "game-changers" and "arc of instability": National Intelligence Council 2008, p. 61.

368 "the five-year mean global temperature": Hansen et al. 2013, p. 1.

369 "major powers might be drawn into conflict": National Intelligence Council 2012, p. xii.

371 "patterns of life": Unclassified briefing by Colonel James Hecker, 432nd Air Wing, Creech Air Force Base, Nevada, March 5, 2013.

372 "maintain complete silence": Quoted in Byman 2013, p. 40.

372 "between 2015 and 2025": Joint Forces Command 2003, p. 5.

372 "It is doubtful": Boot 2006, p. 442.

373 "on the loop": U.S. Air Force 2009, p. 41.

373 "We already don't understand Microsoft Windows": Mark Gubrud, research associate at Princeton University's Program on Science and Global Security, interview with *Mother Jones*, May 3, 2013, www.motherjones.com/politics/2013/05/campaign-stop-killer-robots-military-drones.

373 "lethal autonomous robotics": United Nations 2013.

374 "human space": Adams 2011, p. 5.

375 "the key weapon": G. Friedman 2009, pp. 202, 211.

380 "a future period": Kurzweil 2005, pp. 5, 24.

380 "the Rapture for Nerds": MacLeod 1998, p. 115.

380 "digito-futuristic nonsense": Evgeny Morozov, www.newrepublic.com/article/books-and-arts/magazine/105703/the-naked-and-the-ted-khanna#.

381 "It's crap": Unnamed neuroscientist, Swiss Academy of Sciences meeting, Bern, January 20, 2012, www.nature.com/news/computer-modelling-brain-in-a-box-1.10066.

381 "We are all agreed": Niels Bohr to Wolfgang Pauli, Columbia University, 1958, cited in *Economist*, August 24, 2013, p. 71.

381 "We are opening a window": Jack Gallant, professor of neuroscience at the University of California, Berkeley, September 2011, quoted at www.sciencedaily.com/releases/2011/09/110922121407.htm.

381 "There's a long way to go": Jan Schnupp, professor of neuroscience at Oxford University, February 1, 2012, quoted at www.dailymail.co.uk/sciencetech/article-2095214/As-scientists-discover-translate-brainwaves-words–Could-machine-read-innermost-thoughts.html.

382 "a bunch of hot air": Miguel Nicolelis, professor of neuroscience at Duke University, February 18, 2013, quoted at www.technologyreview.com/view/511421/the-brain-is-not-computable/.

382 "when a scientist says": Richard Smalley, October 2000, quoted in washingtonmonthly.com/features/2000/0010.thompson.html.

383 "Once upon a time": Livy, *History of Rome* 2.32 (translation mine).

385 "Everything in war is very simple": Clausewitz, *On War*, bk. 1, chap. 7, trans. in Howard and Paret 1976, p. 119.

385 "the last best hope of earth": President Abraham Lincoln, second annual message to Congress, December 1, 1862, www.presidency.ucsb.edu/ws/?pid=29503.

385 "lean forward": Brooks et al. 2013, p. 142.

385 "pull back": Posen 2013, pp. 117–18.

385 "a grand strategy": Brooks et al. 2013, p. 42.

385 "it is time to abandon": Posen 2013, pp. 117–18.

386 Pax Technologica: Khanna and Khanna 2012.

387 "the rich are different from you and me": F. Scott Fitzgerald and Ernest Hemingway (possibly 1936), as discussed at www.nytimes.com/1988/11/13/books/l-the-rich-are-different-907188.html.

387 "transhuman": Naam 2013a, p. 23.

388 "deadly Western armies": V. D. Hanson 2001, p. 24.

392 two-thirds of Americans are telling pollsters: www.cnn.com/2013/09/09/politics/syria=poll=main/index.html.

392 "Speak softly and carry a big stick": Theodore Roosevelt (then governor of New York) to Henry L. Sprague, January 26, 1900, www.loc.gov/exhibits/treasures/images/at0052as.jpg.

393 *Si vis pacem*: Unattributed Roman proverb. The closest version preserved in Roman literature is "Qui desiderat pacem, praeparet bellum," in Vegetius, *On Military Matters* (ca. A.D. 400).

FURTHER READING

There are more books and essays on the history of war than anyone could read in a dozen lifetimes, and so in this section I simply list the works that have had the most influence on my own thinking. One of the joys of being an academic is that I get paid to read books about things I am interested in, and so even though I have pruned the list several times, it still runs to hundreds of titles.

Within this mass of scholarship, though, I want to single out just a dozen works without which I probably never would have written this book: Azar Gat's *War in Human Civilization* (2006), the unchallenged starting point for all serious studies of the long-term history of war; Jared Diamond's *Guns, Germs, and Steel* (1997) and Robert Wright's *Nonzero* (2000), wonderful examples of how to combine evolution and history; Richard Wrangham and Dale Peterson's *Demonic Males* (1996), still the best book on primate and human violence; Lawrence Keeley's *War Before Civilization* (1996), which opened a new chapter in the study of prehistoric war; Steven Pinker's *Better Angels of Our Nature* (2011), a magnificent account of modern violence; Edward Luttwak's *Strategy* (2001) and Rupert Smith's *Utility of Force* (2005), which bring Clausewitz's theorizing together with the modern history of war; Kenneth Chase's *Firearms* (2003), a neglected classic of comparative military history; Paul Kennedy's *Rise and Fall of the Great Powers* (1987) and Niall Ferguson's *Empire* (2003), which offer grand visions of war in the last few hundred years; and, last but certainly not least, John Keegan's *Face of Battle* (1976), to my mind the finest history of the battlefield experience yet written.

Because the literature is so large, almost every topic I touch on is controversial, making it virtually impossible to say anything of substance without going against the judgment of at least some specialists. Where debates are particularly contentious, or where I go against the majority opinion among experts, I indicate this, but sadly space does not allow for exhaustive bibliographies on every point.

My list combines studies aimed at general readers, academic overviews, and pieces of detailed research on specific points. Whenever possible I cite recent works in English that provide large bibliographies of their own. Except when referring to short essays in newspapers, I cite works by the author's last name and date of publications; full details can be found in the bibliography that follows.

All URLs were checked on September 22, 2013.

·INTRODUCTION

Events of September 26, 1983: I draw on the account in D. Hoffman 2009, pp. 6–11. We still do not know exactly where Soviet missiles were pointed in 1983, in part because many Russian missiles are still pointing at the same targets. I would like to thank David Holloway for discussing this episode with me.

Likely casualties from nuclear war in the 1980s: Daugherty et al. 1986; B. Levi et al. 1987/88. U.S. war game: Bracken 2012, pp. 82–88.

Thompson and Smith 1980 convey the mood of Europe's antinuclear movements, and Sabin 1986 is excellent on the British context that I experienced as a student. Nuclear stockpiles in 1986: Norris and Kristensen 2006, p. 66.

Lesser-evil arguments: Pinker 2011, pp. 507-8, 557.

Civilizing Process: Elias 1982 (1939). Homicide statistics: Eisner 2003, elaborated in Spierenburg 2008. Roth 2009 extends the analysis to the United States.

War Before Civilization: Keeley 1996, developed further in LeBlanc and Register 2003 and Gat 2006, pp. 3–145. Brian Ferguson 2013 challenges these estimates of prehistoric mortality.

Statistics of Deadly Quarrels: Richardson 1960. Several scholars have offered complicated (but not, to my mind, very convincing) refutations of Richardson's conclusion that humans have become less warlike since 1820; Wilkinson 1980 discusses their arguments.

Databases of death: Since there are now so many (and there are doubtless more out there that I am unaware of), I divide these into four broad categories: war, genocide, terrorism, and homicide. This is somewhat arbitrary, though, because the categories merge into each other and different researchers define them differently (Rudy Rummel, for instance, classifies Nazi massacres of civilians in eastern Europe as genocide, while most databases treat them as war deaths). Because of definitional differences and the inherent ambiguities and gaps in the evidence, no two databases come up with exactly the same numbers.

Deaths from war: Brecke 1999, 2002; Cederman 2003; Clodfelter 1993; Eck and Hultman 2007; Eckhardt 1992; Ganzel and Schwinghammer 2000; Gleditsch et al. 2002; Hewitt et al. 2008; Human Security Centre 2005, 2006; Human Security Report Project 2007, 2008, 2009, 2011, www.hsrgroup.org/; Lacina 2009; Lacina et al. 2006; Levy 1983; Peace Research Institute of Oslo, www.prio.no/CSCW/Datasets/Armed-Conflict/Battle-Deaths; Sarkees 2000; Singer and Small 1972; Sorokin 1957; Steckel and Wallis 2009; Stockholm International Peace Research Institute 2012; Uppsala Conflict Data Project, www.prio.no /CSCW/Datasets/Armed-Conflict/UCDP-PRIO, with discussion in Themnér and Wallensteen 2012; M. White 2011, http://users.erols.com/mwhite28/; Q. Wright 1942.

Deaths from genocide: Harff 2003, 2005; One-Sided Violence Dataset, www.pcr.uu.se /research/ucdp/datasets/; Rummel 1994, 1997, 2002, 2004.

Deaths from terrorism: National Consortium for the Study of Terrorism and Responses to Terrorism, www.start.umd.edu/gtd/.

Deaths from homicide: Eisner 2003; Krug et al. 2002; Spierenburg 2008; Roth 2009.

Overall levels of violence: Global Peace Index, www.visionofhumanity.org/. Extreme cases: Gerlach 2010.

Analyses of databases and categories of analysis: Chirot and McCauley 2006; Dulic 2004;

Lacina and Gleditsch 2005; Levy and Thompson 2011; Long and Brecke 2003; Ober-
meyer et al. 2008; Adam Roberts 2010; Roberts and Turcotte 1998; Spagat et al. 2009.
Disagreements over death toll in Afghanistan since 2001: http://atwar.blogs.nytimes.com
    /2012/08/21/calculating-the-human-cost-of-the-war-in-afghanistan/.
War in Human Civilization: Gat 2006. *Sex at Dawn*: Ryan and Jethá 2010 (to be read with
    the equally impassioned response *Sex at Dusk* [Saxon 2012]). *The End of War*: Horgan
    2012. *War, Peace, and Human Nature*: Fry 2013. *Winning the War on War*: Goldstein
    2011. *Better Angels*: Pinker 2011. *World Until Yesterday*: Diamond 2012.
Leviathan and its critics: Parkin 2007. French alternatives: David Bell 2007, pp. 52–83.
War and the state: Tilly 1975, 1985.
Fifty thousand books on the American Civil War: Keeley 1996, p. 4.
Hitler and the Nazi Leviathan: Evans 2005; Mazower 2008.
Menu of types of imperialism: N. Ferguson 2004, pp. 7–13.

I. THE WASTELAND?

Battle at the Graupian Mountain: This calls for a long note. To begin with, we do not know
    for sure where the battle at the Graupian Mountain was fought. Like most historians since
    St. Joseph (1978), though, I suspect it was on the slopes of Bennachie in Aberdeenshire.

Nor can we be certain exactly what happened in it. Each detail in my account is based
    on real events and passages in ancient texts, but we do not know whether all, some, or
    none of them actually happened on that day—or, for that matter, on any day (Lendon 1999
    discusses the rhetorical complexities of Roman battle accounts). Overall I rely on the one
    major source for the battle, Tacitus's *Agricola* 29–38 (published around A.D. 98), and aug-
    ment it with details of Caledonian tactics and weapons from other Roman sources (par-
    ticularly Tacitus, *Agricola* 11 and *Germania* 4; Strabo, *Geography* 4.5.2, 7.1.2; Diodorus of
    Sicily 5.30.5; and Julius Caesar, *The Gallic War* 5.14). I also draw on the enormous modern
    literature on Roman tactics (Goldsworthy 1996, 2003, and 2006 are excellent accounts),
    modern models of how ancient battles could plausibly have worked (Sabin 2000, 2007),
    and the battle analyses by W. S. Hanson 1987, pp. 129–39, and Campbell 2010.

Since few modern authors have been in a cavalry charge, and ancient accounts are
    very generic, I draw on Winston Churchill's (1930, chap. 15) eyewitness description of
    the last major cavalry charge by a British regiment, at Omdurman in 1898, in my de-
    scription of the auxiliaries' attack.

I have Calgacus slip on a mail shirt before joining battle because, while Roman
    writers repeatedly say that Britons fought unarmored, chain mail has been found in
    several pre-Roman graves (Mattingly 2006, p. 48). By A.D. 83, Caledonian chiefs would
    probably have worn mail to fight.

Tacitus's attitude toward Roman imperialism was, to put it mildly, complicated
    (Sailor 2011, Woolf 2011). He married Agricola's daughter, consistently praised Agricola
    for spreading Roman civilization, and criticized the emperor Domitian for abandoning
    Agricola's conquests in Britain; at the same time he used the idealized simplicity of the
    peoples outside the empire to highlight Rome's decadence, described the incorpora-
    tion of the Britons into the empire as slavery, and wrote a stirring speech for Calgacus.
On the Roman Empire generally, volumes 8–11 of the second edition of the *Cambridge An-
    cient History* (published 1989-2000) provide enormous detail, while Woolf 2012 gives a fine
    overview. Gat 2006, pp. 3–322, is excellent on the evolution of ancient war and government.
Tel Aviv skulls: Cohen et al. 2012. Peruvian skeletons: Arkush and Tung 2013. *The Routledge*

Handbook of the Bioarchaeology of Human Conflict (Knüsel and Smith 2013) appeared while this book was in production but has some excellent essays.

Everyday barbarian violence: Caesar, *Gallic Wars* 6.16–24; Tacitus, *Germania* 13–15; Strabo, *Geography* 4.4. Shields and spears for Germans like togas for Romans: Tacitus, *Germania* 13. Wicker cages: Caesar, *Gallic Wars* 6.16.

Mattingly 2006 and 2011 argue that Roman writers misrepresented the people they conquered, and Hingley 2000 and 2005 discuss how Victorian attitudes toward empire colored Roman archaeology.

Rome, violence, and the eastern Mediterranean: Chaniotis 2005; Eckstein 2006, pp. 79–117. Bandits: Shaw 1984. Pirates: de Souza 1999.

Western societies before the Roman conquest: Wells 1999. The Bog Man (a.k.a. Pete Marsh): Brothwell 1986. Human sacrifice, heads, and so on: K. Sanders 2009. Alken Enge: www.sciencedaily.com/releases/2012/08/120814100302.htm.

Danebury: Cunliffe 1983. Fin Cop: www.dailymail.co.uk/sciencetech/article-1378190 /Iron-Age-mass-grave-reveals-slaughter-women-children.html.

Death, enslavement, and Rome's wars: Harris 1979 remains the classic account. Epirus, 167 B.C.: Livy 45.33–34. Sack of cities: Polybius 10.15 (describing events in 209 B.C.). Caesar in Gaul: Goldsworthy 2006, pp. 184–356. Deaths in the Gallic War: Plutarch, *Life of Julius Caesar* 15; Pliny the Elder, *Natural History* 7.92. Casualties in the Jewish War of A.D. 66–73: Josephus, *Jewish War* 6.420. Casualties in the revolt of A.D. 132–135 (also known as the Bar Kochba Revolt): Cassius Dio 69.14. Few ancient statistics are reliable, and casualty totals could be wildly inflated. However, they were certainly high enough to make Calgacus's point.

Violence in first-century-B.C. Rome has been analyzed in detail: See Lintott 1968; Nippel 1995; Riggsby 1999; and Harries 2007.

Elias on the Roman Empire: Elias 1992, pp. 222–29.

Roman aristocrats remaking themselves: Gleason 1995; Harris 2004. Pax Romana: Woolf 1993. Parchami 2009 compares the Paces Romana, Britannica, and Americana, as I do in later chapters of this book, but concentrates more on theories of empire than on their consequences. Decline in piracy: Braund 1993.

Verres: Cicero, *Against Verres* (published 70 B.C.).

Roman economic growth: Bowman and Wilson 2009; Scheidel and Friesen 2009; Scheidel 2010, 2012. On maritime trade, Harris and Iara 2011. I would like to thank Richard Saller, Walter Scheidel, Rob Stephan, John Sutherland, and Peter Temin for discussions on this topic. I discuss the different kinds of evidence and elaborate my own views in I. Morris 2013, pp. 66–80.

What Roman emperors actually did: Millar 1977. Suetonius, *The Twelve Caesars* (published ca. A.D. 120), has graphic descriptions of the sins of Caligula, Nero, Tiberius, and Domitian.

Roving and stationary bandits: McGuire and Olson 1996; Olson 2000. Differences between gangsters and government: Tilly 1985. Diamond 2012, pp. 79–118, has a fine account of how governments change law and suppress violence.

Uru'inimgina's laws: J. Cooper 1986, pp. 70–78.

Rodney King: *Report of the Independent Commission on the Los Angeles Police Department* (1991), www.parc.info/client_files/Special%20Reports/1%20-%20Chistopher%20Commi sion.pdf. Beating videotape: www.youtube.com/watch?v=0w-SP7iuM6k&feature=related.

Pompey: Seager 2002.

Casualties in Iraq, 2006–9: The precise numbers are debated, but most sources agree on the pattern. I use data from the Iraq Coalition Casualty Count (http://icasualties.org/)

and Iraq Body Count (www.iraqbodycount.org/database/). Petraeus and counterinsurgency: F. Kaplan 2013.

Hard, soft, and smart power: Nye 2011.

Decline of violence in Greek cities: van Wees 1998. Hitting slaves: Old Oligarch 1.10. Athens and fifth-century cities: I. Morris 2009. *Koina*: Mackil 2013 is the best account, although her analysis differs from mine. Ptolemy VIII and Attalus III: I follow the accounts in Gruen 1984, pp. 592–608 and 692–709. The most important texts are translated in Austin 1981, nos. 214 and 230.

Lord of the Flies: Golding 1954. Golding and the Pacific: Carey 2010, p. 110.

Coming of Age in Samoa: Mead 1928.

Levitating the Pentagon: Norman Mailer's fictionalized *Armies of the Night* (1968) is an extraordinary read.

Yanomami: Chagnon 1997. Since 1970, Chagnon and Timothy Asch have also released twenty-two superb films about the Yanomami: www.anth.ucsb.edu/projects/axfight/up dates/yanomamofilmography.html. Homicide and reproduction: Chagnon 1988. Among the Waorani people of Ecuador, where rates of violence are even higher than among the Yanomami, murderous men also outbreed the peaceful: Beckerman et al. 2009.

Criticisms of Chagnon: Tierney 2000, 2001. Accusations about massacres: www.bbc.co.uk /news/world-latin-america-19413107; www.bbc.co.uk/news/world-latin-america-19460663. Borofsky 2005 tries to be evenhanded, while Dreger 2011 forcefully refutes Tierney's accusations. José Padilha's 2010 film *Secrets of the Tribe* even alleges that some of Chagnon's critics had illegal sexual relations with Yanomami children. Chagnon 2013 is a very readable account of what he calls "two dangerous tribes—the Yanomamö and the anthropologists."

Criticisms of Margaret Mead: Freeman 1983, 1989, 1999. There are many defenses too (for example, Shankman 2009).

Anthropological fieldwork as artistic performance: Faubion et al. 2009, with references to other examples.

Twentieth-century death rates: See sources listed for the introduction to this book.

Violence in Stone Age societies: Keeley 1996, LeBlanc and Register 2003, and Gat 2006 are excellent overviews. Several papers in Fry 2013 (especially B. Ferguson 2013) insist that Keeley, LeBlanc and Register, and Gat got it wrong, but I am unconvinced. Nivette 2011 usefully lists the main anthropological studies, emphasizing variations as well as the generally high level of violence. Several separate cross-cultural surveys of war in small-scale societies (Otterbein 1989; Ross 1983, 1985) found that 85–90 percent of these societies went to war in most years. Arkush and Allen 2006 is a good review of archaeological finds.

New Guinean driver: Diamond 2008. Lawsuit: Baltar 2009; www.stinkyjournalism.org /latest-journalism-news-updates-149.php#. Case dismissed: Jared Diamond's personal communication, February 3, 2012.

The Hidden Life of Dogs: E. M. Thomas 1993. *The Harmless People*: E. M. Thomas 1959. Death rates: Knauft 1985, p. 379, table E, suggests that 1.3 percent of the San and 1.3 percent in Detroit died violently (San figures for 1920–55; American for 1980). McCall and Shields 2008 discuss the San case. *The Gods Must Be Crazy*: In Afrikaans, Ster Kinekor, 1980; general release in English, 20th Century Fox, 1984.

Violence in small-scale societies caused by contact with the West: B. Ferguson 1992, 1995, and 2013, with references to earlier papers.

Samoan hillforts: Best 1993 (a few radiocarbon dates are much earlier, including one of 1500±80 BP from Luatuanu'u; but, as Best points out, p. 433, the early dates lack clear associations with the forts). Legends of Samoan-Tongan wars: Ella 1899. Samoan and Tongan archaeology: Kirch 1984. Clubs and war canoes: Krämer 1995, p. 391.

Former military men in archaeology: Wheeler 1958 is a classic. Koukounaries: Schilardi 1984.

Ice Man: On the original discovery, Spindler 1993; the arrowhead, Pertner et al. 2007; the fatal blow, Nerlich et al. 2009, Gostner et al. 2011; red blood cells, Janko et al. 2012; ritual burial theory, Vanzetti et al. 2010.

Crow Creek: Zimmerman and Bradley 1993; Willey 1990; Willey et al. 1993. Sacred Ridge: Potter and Chuipka 2010; www.sciencenews.org/view/feature/id/64465/title/Massacre _at_Sacred_Ridge.

The Origins of Political Order: Fukuyama 2011.

2. CAGING THE BEAST

Battle of Plataea: Lazenby 1993 gives a good account. Briant 2002, pp. 535–42, discusses the Persian perspective.

Western way of war: V. D. Hanson 1989, 2001; Keegan 1993.

Scarre and Fagan 2007 give a concise overview of early civilizations.

New World states: Smith and Schreiber 2005, 2006, with references. Human sacrifice and militarism at Teotihuacán: Sugiyama 2005. Roman gladiators: Futrell 2006. Roman gladiator skeletons: Kanz and Grossschmidt 2006. Wari burial: news.nationalgeo graphic.com/news/2013/06/130627-peru-archaeology-wari-south-america-human -sacrifice-royal-ancient-world. In the best treatment of Mesoamerican warfare, Ross Hassig (1992, p. 60) asks, "Was there a Pax Teotihuacana?" and answers, "Probably not."

Parthia: Curtis and Stewart 2007.

Han China generally: Lewis 2007. Han warfare: Lewis 1990. Unification of China: Hsu 1965; Lewis 1999. Yin Shang: Loewe 2006, pp. 166–67. Comparison of Roman and Han law: Turner 2009. Peacefulness of Han China: Loewe 1974; Loewe and Wilson 2005; Lewis 2000, 2007.

Discovery of the *Arthashastra*: Shamasastry 1967, p. vi. Murder, *Arthashastra* 4.7; rules for investigating assault, 3.19; doctors, 2.36.10; cruelty to animals, 3.10.30–34; types of violence, 4.10–11; spitting and vomiting, 3.19.2–4 (= Rangarajan 1992, pp. 427–30, 435, 329, 292, 438–39, 437). Problems of interpretation: Thapar 1973, pp. 218–25; Mukherjee 2000, pp. 159–64.

Greek sources on India: the surviving fragments are translated at www.sdstate.edu/proj ectsouthasia/upload/Megasthene-Indika.pdf.

Law-abiding Indians: Megasthenes frag. 27 (reported in Strabo 15.1.53–56); no devastation or massacres, frag. 1 and 33 (Diodorus of Sicily 2.36; Strabo 15.1.40); feet back to front, frag. 29 (Strabo 15.1.57); dogs, frag. 12 (Strabo 15.1.37).

Ashoka's urban officers: Major Rock Edict V. Rural officers: Pillar Edict IV. Tours of inspection: Major Rock Edict VIII. Ashoka's reign: Thapar 1973. Ashoka and Buddhism: Seneviratna 1994.

Nature of the Mauryan Empire: Compare Mookerjee 1966, Mukherjee 2000, and Thapar 2002, pp. 174–208. On the archaeology, Allchin 1995, pp. 187–273; Chakrabarti 1999, pp. 262–318.

Han standards of living: Hsu 1980; Wang 1982.

Sanyangzhuang: Kidder et al. 2012. Roman silk dresses: Pliny, *Natural History* 6.20.

Mauryan economic growth: Megasthenes frag. 1 (Diodorus of Sicily 2.36); Thapar 2002, pp. 188–89; Allchin 1995, pp. 200–221, 231–37; J. Marshall 1951, pp. 26, 87–110.

Mauryan economy: Saletore 1973. Standards of living: Allchin 1995. Bhita: J. Marshall 1911–12. Taxila: J. Marshall 1951. The Mauryan phase at Taxila is stratum II.

Marvels of India: Megasthenes frags. 1, 16, and 59 (quoted in Diodorus of Sicily 2.36; Pliny, *Natural History* 8.14.1; Aelian, *History of Animals* 16.2). Roman trade with India: Tomber 2008; Pliny, *Natural History* 6.26, 12.41. Muziris papyrus: Rathbone 2001. GDP of Roman Empire: Scheidel and Friesen 2009 estimate 20 billion sesterces. Cost of Roman army: Duncan-Jones 1994. Excavations at Muziris: Cherian et al. 2007; www .hindu.com/2011/06/12/stories/2011061254420500.htm.

Origins of agriculture: Diamond 1997 is the clearest account and G. Barker 2006 the fullest. ≠Gau's band: R. Lee 1979, pp. 390–91. Aedui and Helvetii: Goldsworthy 2006, pp. 184–204, has a good account.

Circumscription: Carneiro 1970. Caging: M. Mann 1986, pp. 46–49. Keith Otterbein 2004 argues the opposite view—that violence declines with the shift from hunting to farming—but the evidence seems to point the other way.

Roman crucifixion: Appian, *Civil Wars* 1.120 (published ca. A.D. 150), on the mass crucifixion of Spartacus's followers in 71 B.C. Maslen and Mitchell 2006 explain the grisly mechanics. Zias and Sekeles 1985 describe an actual first-century-A.D. crucifixion victim, found with an iron nail still lodged in one foot.

Casualties in 1991 Gulf War: Keaney and Cohen 1998. Revolution in military affairs since the 1970s: Martinage and Vickers 2004. Krepinevich 1994, Knox and Murray 2001, and Boot 2006 all put this in the context of the last seven centuries.

Stone Age battles: Q. Wright 1942, pp. 62–88, and Turney-High 1949 are the classic statements of the ritualized war theory. As so often, Keeley 1996, LeBlanc and Register 2003, and Gat 2006 put things straight. Raiding in the American Southwest: LeBlanc 1999.

Red Queen Effect: Van Valen 1973; Ridley 1993.

Early fortifications: Jericho: Bar-Yosef 1986; McClellan 2006. Mersin: Garstang 1956. Uruk: Liverani 2006.

Relations between Uruk, Tell Brak, and Habuba Kabira: Rothman 2001. Tell Brak fighting: http://news.nationalgeographic.com/news/2007/09/070907-syria-graves.html. Early Egypt: Wengrow 2006.

Thrilla in Manila: www.youtube.com/watch?v=D_y7FiCryb8. War and society in Sumer: Kuhrt 1995, pp. 29–44. Sargon of Akkad: Liverani 2003.

Indus civilization and collapse: Rita Wright 2009.

Domestication of horses and invention of chariots: Anthony 2009; Outram et al. 2009. Chariot warfare: Chakravarti 1941, pp. 22–32; Drews 1988, 1992; Shaughnessy 1988. The *Nova* documentary "Building Pharaoh's Chariot" (http://video.pbs.org/video /2331305481/), first shown in 2013, is excellent. Weight: Piggott 1983, p. 89.

Earliest bows and arrows: Brown et al. 2012; Lombard 2011.

Solomon's chariots: 1 Kings 10:29. Slave price: Exodus 21:32. Hittite text: *Instructions of Kikkuli* (Nyland 2009). Numbers of chariots: Drews 1992, pp. 106n6 and 133–34.

Scale of Fertile Crescent wars and state power after 1600 B.C.: Hamblin 2006; Spaliger 2005; van de Mieroop 2007, pp. 119–78, 2011; pp. 151–239.

Peace and prosperity in the chariot age: See, for example, Akkermans and Schwartz 2003, pp. 327–59; Kemp 2012; Cline 2010; von Falkenhausen 2006.

Sword types: D. H. Gordon 1953. Second-millennium-B.C. European warfare: Harding 2000, pp. 275–85; Kristiansen 2002; Kristiansen and Larsson 2005, pp. 212–47. There is some debate over where the new sword styles came into use; I follow Drews 1992, pp. 192–208, and Harding 2000.

Collapse of Bronze Age societies: Drews 1992; Cline 2013. Decline in trade: S. Murray

2013. I try to quantify the decline in population and living standards after 1200 B.C. in Greece (admittedly an extreme case) in I. Morris 2007.

Adoption of iron: Snodgrass 2006, pp. 126–43.

Revival of states in Assyria and Israel: Kuhrt 1995, pp. 385–546; van de Mieroop 2007, pp. 195–231.

Origins of cavalry: Anthony 2009; Anthony and Brown 2011.

Amazons: Herodotus 4.110–17; Mayor, forthcoming. Scythian warrior women: Guliaev 2003.

Tiglath-Pileser III: Tadmor and Yamada 2011 collect the main evidence. Empires of western Eurasia: Morris and Scheidel 2009; Cline and Graham 2011.

Despite the prominence of war in ancient texts, there is a surprising amount of controversy over how armies actually fought. On Assyria, see Archer 2010; G. Fagan 2010; Nadali 2010; Scurlock 1997. On Persia, see Briant 1999; Tuplin 2010. On Greece, see V. D. Hanson 1989; van Wees 2004; Kagan and Viggiano 2013. On Macedon, see Hamilton 1999; A. Lloyd 1996. On republican Rome, see Keppie 1984; Goldsworthy 2003.

Punic Wars: Goldsworthy 2000; Miles 2011.

Size of states: There are many ways to count, so for the sake of consistency I have used a single set of figures, based on Taagepera 1978, 1979.

Ancient Chinese war: Lewis 1990, 1999; di Cosmo 2011; Sawyer 2011. Battle of Changping: Sima Qian, *Shiji* 73, pp. 2333–35, trans. in B. Watson 1993, pp. 122–24. First Emperor: Portal 2007. Qin and Han law: Hulsewé 1955, 1985.

Ancient Indian war: Chakravarti 1941; Dikshitar 1987; Thapliyal 2010. Mailed infantry: *Arthashastra* 9.2.29, trans. in Rangarajan 1992, p. 644. Elephants: Kistler 2007.

Rise of Ganges states: Allchin 1995, pp. 99–151; Chakrabarti 1999; Eltsov 2008; Erdosy 1988; Raychaudhuri 1996, pp. 85–158; Thapar 1984.

Social development index: I. Morris 2010, 2013.

3. THE BARBARIANS STRIKE BACK

Vindolanda letters: Bowman and Thomas 1994 and http://vindolanda.csad.ox.ac.uk/. Weather, nos. 234, 343; beer, no. 190; socks, no. 346; food, nos. 301, 302. Bowman 1994 discusses the letters. Afghanistan e-mails and blogs: Burden 2006; Tupper 2010.

Domitian's jealousy: Tacitus, *Agricola* 39–40. Rome's strategic situation: Luttwak 1976, pp. 51–126.

Roman defeat of A.D. 9: Wells 2003, with nice illustrations in the 2009 special edition of the magazine *Ancient Warfare*. Kalkriese park: www.kalkriese-varusschlacht.de/.

Clausewitz: Howard 2002 is an excellent introduction.

Distance costs in the Roman Empire: http://orbis.stanford.edu/.

Chinese frontiers: C. Chang 2007; Hsieh 2011. Xuanquan: www.dartmouth.edu/~ear lychina/research-resources/conferences/changsha-bamboo-documents.html. Very few of the texts have yet been translated; I draw on Hsieh 2011, pp. 221–38.

Steppe nomads: Beckwith 2009 and Golden 2011 give good short reviews of the history, and J. D. Rogers 2012 discusses the forms of nomadic states. Dani and Masson 1992 (vols. 2–4), Harmatta 1994, Litvinsky 1996, and Sinor 1990 go into more detail. Di Cosmo 2002b and Hildinger 2001 focus on the military aspects, and E. Murphy 2003 and Jordana et al. 2009 present skeletal evidence for high levels of violence.

Assyrian cavalry: Dalley 1985. Fall of Assyria: Liverani 2001; Melville 2011. Murder of Scythian leaders in 590s B.C.: Herodotus 1.106.

Contemporary asymmetric wars: I have found Burke 2011, Coll 2004, Clarke 2007, and Joint Chiefs of Staff 2012 helpful. Neutralizing bin Laden: Coll 2004, pp. 369–584; L. Wright 2006, pp. 297–330.

Darius's lack of cavalry in 513 B.C.: Herodotus 4.136.

Han cavalry: C. Chang 2007, pp. 177–81. Wudi's wars: Loewe 1986, pp. 152–79.

Strategies for dealing with steppe nomads: Barfield 1989; di Cosmo 2002a.

CIA cash handouts: Woodward 2003, pp. 139–50. Tora Bora bribes: Burke 2011, p. 69.

Western way of war: See sources listed under Chapter 2.

Persian shift toward cavalry: Tuplin 2010. Han cavalry: Chang 2007, pp. 177–81. Shakas, Yuezhi, and Kushans: Liu 2001; Mukherjee 1981, 1988. Kushan sculptures of horse archers: Lebedynsky 2006, p. 62.

Qiang wars: Lewis 2007, pp. 147–51, 253–64.

Germanic societies: Todd 1992; Wells 1999. Sarmatian women: Herodotus 4.117.

Gothic migrations: Heather 1996, pp. 11–50. Marcus Aurelius and the Marcomannic wars: Birley 1987.

Sasanid cavalry: Farrokh 2005, 2009.

Evolution of the Roman army, A.D. 200–400: Elton 2007; Rance 2007. Troop strengths in the late Roman Empire are hotly debated; see Treadgold 1995, pp. 55–57.

Second-century-A.D. plagues: McNeill 1976, pp. 93–119; Stathakopoulos 2007. Climate change: McCormick et al. 2012.

Fall of Han China: Beck 1986. China after the Han: Dien 1990, 2007; Lewis 2009a.

Rome's third-century crisis: Duncan-Jones 2004; Scheidel 2002; Witschel 2004.

Sasanid Persia: Daryaee 2009; Dignas and Winter 2007. Satavahana: R. K. Sharma 1999.

So far as I know, no recent book treats the crises of all Eurasia's empires between A.D. 200 and 600 comparatively, but Christian 1998, pp. 209–303, gives a useful survey from the perspective of the steppe nomads.

Size of states, A.D. 1–1400: For the sake of consistency, I use the sizes listed in Taagepera 1979. His data set skips over some periods and is light on South Asian cases; I have measured these from published maps.

Toynbee: McNeill 1989. Scientific approaches seeking regularities in steppe history: Turchin 2003, 2006, 2009, 2010; Turchin and Nefedov 2009.

Counterrevolution in military affairs: Bloch 1961 and Ganshof 1961 are now extremely dated but remain valuable (see below on their critics). Herlihy 1970 is a fine collection of primary sources, and Halsall 2003 is good on the military situation in western Europe.

Battle of Hastings: Howarth 1981 remains the classic account. Medieval military indiscipline: Morillo 2006.

European medieval war: Contamine 1984; Verbruggen 1997, 2004. Bachrach 2006, 2011 argues that cavalry were never important in western Europe, but this is a minority view.

Justinian: Maas 2005; O'Donnell 2008. Seventh-century crisis: Haldon 1997; Howard-Johnston 2010. Muslim conquests and the caliphate: H. Kennedy 2004, 2007. Charlemagne: Barbero 2004; McKitterick 2008.

Multiple ties of dependence in western Europe: Bloch 1961, pp. 211–18. De Coucy: Tuchman 1978, pp. 246–83.

Criticisms of describing Europe as feudal: E. Brown 1974; S. Reynolds 1994.

Debates over feudalism outside western Europe: China, Graff 2002a, pp. 37, 256; Lewis 2009a, pp. 54–85. India, R. S. Sharma 1985, 2001; Chattopadhyaya 2010. Abbasid caliphate: M. Gordon 2001; H. Kennedy 2001. Byzantium: Haldon 1993; Treadgold 1997. On western Eurasia as a whole, Wickham 2005.

Violence in late Roman and medieval Europe: Tuchman 1978 is a wonderful read; see also Halsall 1998; Canning et al. 2004, pp. 9–89; W. Brown 2010; McGlynn 2010; Shaw 2011.

Sixth- and seventh-century China: Twitchett 1979; Graff 2002a, pp. 92–204; Lewis 2009b. Cavalry and relations with the steppes: Skaff 2012. Battle of the Iron Mountain: Graff 2002a, pp. 183–89; 2002b.

Chang'an in 883: Kuhn 2009, pp. 16–17. Fall of the Tang: Somers 1979.

Earliest gunpowder weapons: Needham 1986; Chase 2003, pp. 30–33; Lorge 2008, pp. 32–44.

Hun siege warfare: Heather 2006, pp. 300–312. Nicopolis: Poulter 1995. Mongol siege warfare: T. May 2007, pp. 77–79. Siege of Baghdad: T. May 2007, pp. 130–34. Sieges of Xiangyang and Fancheng: Lorge 2005, pp. 83–87.

Battles of Tarain: Sarkar 1960, pp. 32–37. Medieval Indian cavalry: Bhakari 1980, pp. 55–61.

Increasing organization of nomad empires: Di Cosmo 1999; Chaliand 2004.

Battle of the Indus: T. May 2007, p. 123. Second Battle of Homs: Amitai-Preiss 1995, pp. 179–201.

Nomadic death toll: Several of the sections in M. White 2011, pp. 59–153, discuss the numbers killed by steppe nomads and the empires that fought back against them. White is right to criticize the recent trend among historians to downplay the scale of slaughter, but some of his own estimates (such as thirty-six million for the Tang breakdown of 755–763 and forty million for Genghis Khan) seem very high.

Tamerlane: Manz 1989.

Western European homicide: Eisner 2003, with discussion in Spierenburg 2008, pp. 1–42.

Cadfael: Twenty-one books by Ellis Peters, beginning with *A Morbid Taste for Bones* (London: Macmillan, 1977) and ending with *Brother Cadfael's Penance* (London: Headline, 1994).

Spread of farming outside the lucky latitudes: G. Barker 2006 is excellent on the details.

Spread of caging across the Pacific: Kirch 1984, using the revised chronology in Kirch 2010, pp. 126–27. Productive war on Hawaii: Kirch 2010; Kolb and Dixon 2002. Sahlins 2004 has a fine account of the great wars of eighteenth-century Hawaii, stressing their similarities to the Peloponnesian War in fifth-century-B.C. Greece.

Navajo wars: McNitt 1990; Trafzer 1990.

War and state formation in Japan: Berry 1989; Farris 1996; Ferejohn and Rosenbluth 2010; Friday 2003; Ikegumi 1997; Turnbull 2002, 2012; and, last but not least, James Clavell's epic novel *Shogun* (1975) and the accompanying TV miniseries (NBC, 1980), set in the early seventeenth century. Hideyoshi's invasion of Korea: Swope 2009. Tearing down castles and banning books: Parker 1996, pp. 144–45.

African state formation: Ehret 2002. Great Zimbabwe: Pikirayi and Vogel 2001.

Natural experiments in history: Diamond and Robinson 2010.

Aztec weapons: Hassig 1988; Pohl 2001. Extinction of New World horses: Haynes 2009. Andean copper-working ca. 1000 B.C.: Kolata 1993, pp. 61–62. Lords of Sipán: Alva and Donnan 1993.

European culture more rational than Native American: V. D. Hanson 2001, pp. 170–232. Native American cultures more peaceful than European: P. Watson 2012.

Mesoamerican calendars: Aveni 2001; Hassig 2001. Raised fields and irrigation: Sanders et al. 1979, pp. 252–81.

Maya decipherment: Coe 2012. Maya war: Webster 1999.

Aztec Flower Wars: Compare Keegan 1993, pp. 110–11, with Hassig 1992, pp. 145–46.

Continental axes: Diamond 1997, pp. 360–70. Biomes: Ricklefs 2001. Turchin et al. 2006 and Laitin et al. 2012 have tried testing Diamond's theory against data for the spread of other institutions and even languages, with results that suggest that continental axes may be important in many other ways.

Arrival of the bow in Alaska: B. Fagan 2012, p. 63. Arrival in Mexico: Hassig 1992, p. 119.

Teotihuacán: See references for Chapter 2, and Cowgill 2013 on the city's fall. Toltecs: Diehl 1983; Smith and Montiel 2001. Aztecs: M. Smith 2003. Violence in Aztec society: Carrasco 1999. Mesoamerican warfare and state formation: Brown and Stanton 2003; Eeckhout and Le Fort 2005; Hassig 1988, 1992; Sherman et al. 2010; Webster 1999.

American Southwest: Cordell and McBrinn 2012. Southwestern war: LeBlanc 1999; Rice and LeBlanc 2001. Cahokia: Pauketat 2004.

Comanche Empire: Hämäläinen 2008 (with pp. 243 and 352 on the Mongol analogy).

Agincourt: See J. Barker 2007 and the superb account in Keegan 1976, pp. 79–116 (with pp. 106–7 on the implausibility of the stacks of corpses); and, of course, Shakespeare's *Henry V*. Kenneth Branagh's 1989 film version is one of the all-time great war movies. The precise casualties are debated: See Reid 2007, pp. 275–76.

Ceuta: Boxer 1969, pp. 15–19.

4. THE FIVE HUNDRED YEARS' WAR

Not many books treat the period 1415–1914 as a unit in its own right, but several excellent studies cover most of the period or discuss it as part of a longer story. I have benefited particularly from Chase 2003, Cipolla 1965, Headrick 2010, P. Kennedy 1987, Lorge 2008, McNeill 1982, Parker 1996, C. Rogers 1995, and Simms 2013. On the British Empire, volumes 1–3 of *The Oxford History of the British Empire* are the standard reference works.

Kafiristan: Rudyard Kipling, "The Man Who Would Be King," first published in the series Indian Railway Library 5 (Allahabad: A. H. Wheeler, 1888), reissued many times since, and made by John Huston into a memorable film starring Michael Caine and Sean Connery (Allied Artists, 1975).

James Brooke: Runciman 1960. Josiah Harlan: Macintyre 2004.

Early Chinese guns: Chase 2003, pp. 30–55; Lorge 2008, pp. 69–75. Dazu Cave: Lu et al. 1988. Manchurian gun: Needham et al. 1986, pp. 111–26, 147–92.

Early Indian guns: Khan 2004. Persian guns: Woods 1999, pp. 114–20. Oxford illustration: Hall 1997, pp. 43–44.

There are many fine studies of Europe's gunpowder takeoff. Hall 1997, P. Hoffman 2011, and Lorge 2008 differ from my interpretation in important ways.

Western way of war: Lynn 2003 offers an extended rebuttal of Hanson's arguments.

Firearms: A Global History to 1700: Chase 2003.

Ivan the Terrible: De Madariaga 2006. Chinese shipbuilding: Needham 1971. Zheng's voyages: Dreyer 2006. European shipbuilding: Gardiner and Unger 2000. Voyages of exploration: Fernández-Armesto 2006. Henry the Navigator: Russell 2000. Pirate wars: Earle 2003. European guns in Asia: Chase 2003; Lorge 2008. Victories over steppe nomads: Perdue 2005.

Ottoman, Safavid, and Mughal Empires: Dale 2010; Hathaway 2004; Streusand 2010.

Safavid prosperity: Floor 2000. Mughal prosperity: Richards 1994. Ottoman prosperity: Inalcik and Quataert 1994.

Productivity of Yangzi Delta around 1600: Allen et al. 2011. Southern India and Bengal: Parthasarathi 2011, pp. 68–78. New World crops: C. Mann 2011.

Evidence for Asian wages: Pamuk 2007, with references. Debates over India: Parthasarathi 2011, pp. 37–46; Broadberry and Gupta 2006; R. Allen 2007.

Abbas I: Blow 2009. Beheading in 1593: Dale 2010, p. 93.

Violence in Ming literature: Robinson 2001. Statistics of Ming violence: Tong 1991.

Ming-Qing cataclysm: Struve 1993. Death toll: M. White 2012, pp. 223–30, although his estimate of twenty-five million seems very high.

European musketry, drill, volleying, and training: See particularly Parker 1996 and C. Rogers 1995.

In recent years, some historians have downplayed the novelty of European military reforms (for example, P. Wilson 2009, pp. 186–87) or the scale of Europe's military lead over other cultures (for example, Black 1999), but I do not find their arguments very compelling.

New naval tactics: De Glete 1999.

Seven spare pairs of silk stockings: David Bell 2007, p. 39.

English navy, Pepys, and finance: J. D. Davies 2008.

Kabinettskrieg: Duffy 1987. Flying head: Hainsworth and Churches 1998, p. 125.

Financial solutions: Bonney 1999, with comparisons outside western Europe in Yun-Castalilla et al. 2012.

The financial crashes of 1720: N. Ferguson 2008, pp. 119–75, has a fine account.

Portuguese Empire: Boxer 1969. Spanish Empire: Kamen 2003.

Bullet holes in Inca skeletons: Murphy et al. 2010. Columbian exchange: Crosby 1972, 2003; C. Mann 2011. American population collapse: C. Mann 2005. The estimate of 50 percent comes from mitochondrial DNA: O'Fallon and Fehren-Schmitz 2011.

Jamestown cannibalism: Horn et al. 2013.

India before 1750: Asher and Talbot 2006.

British wars in India: Judd 2010; S. Gordon 1993. R. Cooper 2003 argues that Maratha armies were just as effective as British, but this would make the outcomes hard to explain.

Battle of Towton: Boylston and Knüsel 2010. Richard III: www.dailymail.co.uk/news/article-2273535/500-years-grisly-secrets-Richard-IIIs-lost-grave-revealed-King-discovered-car-park-stripped-tied-suffered-humiliation-wounds-death.html.

Pacification in Europe, 1500–1750: Elias 1982 (1939); Spierenburg 2008; Pinker 2011. Market economies and social change in western Europe: Braudel 1981–84 remains the best account. Europeans working harder: De Vries 2008.

Atlantic economy: Findlay and O'Rourke 2007. Numbers of Africans shipped across Atlantic: Inikori and Engermann 1992. War, politics, and trade: Tracy 1991. Growth of trade: Findlay and O'Rourke 2007, pp. 227–364. Statistics: pp. 260, 314.

Adam Smith: Phillipson 2010.

Transformation of late-seventeenth-century England: Pincus 2010. Open-access order: North et al. 2009. Acemoglu and Robinson 2012 develop similar ideas. Freedom and government in eighteenth-century England: Brewer 1989.

European wages: R. Allen 2001, 2003.

Early American Republic: Wood 2009.

British Empire in the eighteenth century: C. Bayly 1989; P.J. Marshall 1998–2000.

People's war: David Bell 2007. American people: Wood 1991. American Revolutionary War: Among many excellent accounts, my favorites are Middlekauff 2007 and Ferling 2009.

Eighteenth-century philosophers on perpetual peace: David Bell 2007, pp. 52–83.

French Revolutionary Wars: Blanning 1996. Massacres: Broers 2008. Napoleonic wars: Rothenberg 2006. Naval wars: Mostert 2008.

Although now very dated, Eric Hobsbawm's trilogy (1962, 1975, 1987) on the nineteenth-century world remains one of the great reads in historical literature.

Industrial Revolution: R. Allen 2009; Wrigley 2010.

Opium War: Fay 2003.

Technological change and imperialism: Headrick 2010.

White settler colonies: Duncan Bell 2007; Belich 2009.

Gap between European and other armies: Callwell 1909 is the classic eyewitness account. David 2006 describes British experiences; Porch 2000 warns against exaggeration.

American Civil War: The literature is overwhelming. McPherson 1988 puts the war in context; Keegan 2009 offers a fresh perspective on the events.

Isandlwana: David 2004, pp. 124–58. Adwa: Jonas 2011.

Naval gap between the West and the rest: Herwig 2001.

Nineteenth-century Britain and the world-system: N. Ferguson 2003; Darwin 2009.

On death tolls, see in general M. White 2011, with references. Population figures taken from Maddison 2003. New World death rates from disease: See above. American holocaust: Stannard 1993. Misra 2008 says ten million were killed in the Indian Mutiny, but most historians put the figure well under one million (see David 2006). Famines and Indian death rates: Fieldhouse 1996. Davis 2001 blames the famines strongly on Britain. Congo: Hochschild 1998.

Reception of Kipling's "White Man's Burden": Gilmour 2002.

Indian anarchy and the East India Company's crackdown: Washbrook 1999. Violent crime in India: Fisch 1983, Yang 1985, and Singha 1998 document courts' aggressive crackdowns on interpersonal violence. More recent studies, such as Kolsky 2010 and T. Sherman 2010 (the latter taking the story into the twentieth century), however, tend to focus on British violence against Indians rather than broader efforts to suppress violence. Wiener 2008 looks at Australia, Kenya, and the Caribbean as well as India.

Rammohun Roy: Sen 2012.

Historians' evaluations of the British Empire vary wildly. Gott 2011 is the most negative that I have seen.

Decline in European violence: Spierenburg 2008. American violence: Roth 2009. Casualties in wars: M. White 2011.

Nineteenth-century economic growth: Frieden 2006, pp. 13–123.

Figure 4.17: Data from Maddison 2003.

Hague conferences: Sheehan 2008, pp. 22–26.

5. STORM OF STEEL

The Great Illusion: Angell 1910 (the book was frequently reissued in expanded versions; like most historians, I use the fourth edition, of 1913). On Angell himself: Ceadel 2009.

Twentieth century as age of extremes: Hobsbawm 1994.

Sarajevo: Dedijer 1966 remains the standard academic analysis, and D. Smith 2009 gives an up-to-date general treatment.

Casualties in 1914: Stevenson 2004, pp. 75–76.

Decisions to go to war in 1914: There are excellent analyses in Hamilton and Herwig 2003, McMeekin 2011, Stevenson 2004, pp. 3–36, and Strachan 2001, pp. 1–102. On ways war might not have broken out, Beatty 2012.

March of Folly: Tuchman 1984.

British GDP: Maddison 2010. Growth of new industrial and naval powers: Broadberry

1998; P. Kennedy 1987, pp. 194–249; Trebilock 1981. American and German wars of the 1860s compared: Förster and Nagler 1999. Centrality of finance to the late-nineteenth-century British world-system: Cain and Hopkins 2000.

Figure 5.1: Data from Bairoch 1982. Figure 5.2: Data from Maddison 2003. Figure 5.3: Data from P. Kennedy 1987, table 20.

British intervention and the American Civil War: H. Fuller 2008; Foreman 2010. Great rapprochement: Perkins 1968. British and American navies: O'Brien 1998. Britain's naval alliances: Sumida 1989.

Geography and strategy: Mackinder 1904, with Kearns 2009.

Germany before 1871: Sheehan 1989; C. Clark 2006. Bismarck: Lerman 2004. A.J.P. Taylor's *Bismarck* (1967) nowadays seems very old-fashioned but remains a great read. Germany after 1890: P. Kennedy 1980; C. Clark 2009. German strategic intentions: Fritz Fischer 1967, 1974 set off a bitter debate by suggesting that Germany aimed at world domination in 1914. Strachan 2001, pp. 52–54, has a concise review of the debate, and Mulligan 2010 gives a general picture of the whole period 1870–1914.

Bond markets in summer 1914: N. Ferguson 1998, pp. 186–97.

Crises of 1905–13: Jarausch 1983.

General course of World War I: The literature is enormous. My favorites are Strachan 2003 for a brief account, Stevenson 2004 for a mid-length study, and Strachan 2001 for a comprehensive treatment of the first year of the war.

On the Schlieffen Plan, see Zuber 2011, to be read with the spirited debate in the journal *War in History*, beginning with Zuber's 1999 paper. On the eastern front, Stone 1975 and Showalter 1991 remain classics.

Germany's "September Program": Fischer 1967; N. Ferguson 1998, pp. 168–73.

Germany's defeat on the Marne in 1914: Herwig 2009.

The war at sea: Strachan 2001, pp. 374–494; Massie 2003. Africa: Strachan 2001, pp. 495–643; Paice 2010.

Methods of fighting in 1914: Howard 1985. *Storm of Steel*: Jünger 2003, trans. from the 1961 German edition. Jünger first published *In Stahlgewittern* in 1920 but heavily revised the text in later editions. Lions led by donkeys: A. Clark 1962 is a classic account. Military learning in World War I: Doughty 2008; Lupfer 1981; W. Murray 2011, pp. 74–118; Travers 2003.

War economies: Broadberry and Harrison 2005; Chickering and Förster 2000.

Horses: The Royal National Theatre's adaptation of Michael Morpurgo's 1982 novel, *War Horse*, first staged in 2007, gives an extraordinarily powerful impression of this side of the war. The 2011 film version directed by Steven Spielberg is less memorable.

Command and control: Sheffield 2001; Sheffield and Todman 2008. Technological fixes: Travers 1992; Echevarria 2007. Gas casualties: Corrigan 2003, pp. 173–74. Tanks: Childs 1999. War in the air: M. Cooper 1986.

Attrition: Harris and Marble 2008. Cost per kill: N. Ferguson 1998, p. 336.

Jihad: Aksakal 2011. Submarine war: Halpern 1994. Atlantic lifeline: Burk 1985.

Russia's collapse: Figes 1997.

Modern system: Biddle 2004. Storm troops: Gudmundsson 1995 (Griffith 1996 argues that British troops mastered infiltration tactics earlier than the Germans). *A Farewell to Arms*: Hemingway 1929. Germany's 1918 offensive: Zabecki 2006; Hart 2008. Allied counteroffensive: Boff 2012.

British plans for 1919: J.F.C. Fuller 1936, pp. 322–36. Surrendering: N. Ferguson 2004, debated in Dollery and Parsons 2007 and A. Watson 2008. H1N1 flu and German collapse: Barry 2004; Price-Smith 2009, pp. 57–81.

Interwar world: P. Kennedy 1987, pp. 275–343; N. Ferguson 1998, pp. 395–432; Frieden 2006, pp. 127–72. British financial situation after 1918: Boyce 1987; N. Ferguson 2001, pp. 45–47, 125–27.

Wilson and the League of Nations: R. Kennedy 2009; Mazower 2012, pp. 116–53.

Russian Civil War: Figes 1997, pp. 555–720; Lincoln 1999. (My own sense of these events was indelibly imprinted by David Lean's 1965 film of Boris Pasternak's novel *Doctor Zhivago*, starring Omar Sharif and Julie Christie.) Russo-Polish War: N. Davies 2003.

Crash of 1929 and subsequent banking crisis: H. James 2009, pp. 36–97.

Decline of confidence in the British Empire: J. Morris 1978, pp. 299–318, is a classic account.

Soviet violence: Conquest 2007; Naimark 2010; Snyder 2010. Soviet economy: Davies et al. 1994. Ishiwara: Peattie 1975. Japanese invasion of China: Mitter 2013. Rape of Nanjing: I. Chang 1997. Russo-Japanese war of 1939: S. Goldman 2012.

General course of World War II: The literature is so big, says Max Hastings 2007, p. 559, that "a catalogue of relevant titles becomes merely an author's peacock display." With that caveat, my favorite readable recent mid-length surveys are Beevor 2012, Evans 2009, Hastings 2011, and Andrew Roberts 2011, and on the details Weinberg 2005. N. Davies 2006 is good on the messiness of the outcome.

Development of Hitler's thought: Kershaw 2000.

Development of blitzkrieg: Muller 1996, W. Murray 1996, and Gat 2000, suggesting that British stick-in-the-mudness was less of an issue than tank theorists such as Liddell Hart and Fuller liked to claim. On the practice of blitzkrieg, Guderian 1992 (1937) is the classic, although Guderian never used the word *blitzkrieg* in his book. It seems to have been coined by a journalist at *Time* magazine in 1939. (The famous passage in which Guderian says that he took his ideas from Liddell Hart does not appear in the original German text, apparently being inserted later at Liddell Hart's suggestion—Guderian 1992, p. 16.)

Fall of France: E. May 2001. Bloch 1999 (1946), an eyewitness account by a brave man caught up in the disaster, is subjective but powerful.

Why Germany nearly won: Mercatante 2012.

Hitler's use of violence against internal enemies: The literature is vast, but Evans 2005 is a good starting point. Massacres in World War I: Hull 2005; Kramer 2007. Greatest Possible Germany: N. Ferguson 2006, p. 315. Starving Russian cities: Weinberg 2005, p. 267.

How the Allies won: Overy 1995. Learning in World War II: W. Murray 2011, pp. 119–261. Allied economies: Harrison 1998; on the United States, Herman 2012 is very readable.

If Hitler had won: On this, novelists have the most interesting things to say (especially R. Harris 1992 and Sansom 2012).

Visions of an Anglo-American world order: Ryan 1987. American thinking about Europe: Harper 1996. Soviet thinking about Europe: Applebaum 2012.

Collapse of Britain's Asian Empire: Bayly and Harper 2004.

Cold War generally: There are excellent short accounts in D. Reynolds 2000 and Gaddis 1997 and 2005a. Leffler and Westad 2010 provide rich detail, and CNN's twenty-four-part TV documentary *The Cold War* (1998) has excellent footage and interviews. Cold War outside Europe: Westad 2005; Brands 2010.

The bomb: Rhodes 1987, 1996, and 2007 are required reading.

World government: Baratta 2004. United Nations: Mazower 2012.

U.S. nuclear strategy: Rosenberg 1983; Jervis 1990; Freedman 2003. Soviet nuclear strategy: Garthoff 1958; Holloway 1994; Fursenko and Naftali 2006. European nuclear strategy: Heuser 1997. Effects of a one-megaton bomb: Freedman 2003, p. xiii. Containment: Gaddis 2005b.

Democratic peace: Doyle 1983 elaborates Kant's *Perpetual Peace* into a philosophical account of why twentieth-century democracies rarely went to war, but the theory remains controversial among political scientists (Kinsella et al. 2005). Western murder levels: Eisner 2003, table 1; Roth 2009, figure I.1. More generally, Spierenburg 2008, pp. 165–205; and Roth 2009, pp. 435–68.

American affluence and Europe: De Grazia 2006. Car ownership: Figures from Sandbrook 2005, p. 121; and Patterson 1996, p. 71.

Figure 5.13: Data from Maddison 2003. "Western Europe" shows Maddison's twenty-nine-nation scores, and "Eastern Europe" his seven-nation scores. Maddison combined East and West German data; I have treated Germany as part of western Europe, which means that Figure 5.9 understates eastern European performance (though not enough to change the shape of the graph dramatically). Eastern European data are unreliable before 1950.

Soviet repression: Applebaum 2003, 2012. Buchenwald: M. White 2012, p. 390. Families with one child executed by Hitler and a second by Stalin: Snyder 2010, p. 149. Soviet murder levels: Pridemore 2007, p. 121. Soviet economic growth: Spufford 2010 is a quirky, fascinating account.

Lowe 2012 does a fine job comparing postwar eastern and western Europe.

Casualty estimates for 1962: N. Friedman 2000, pp. 284–85.

Figure 5.14: Data from Norris and Kristensen 2006; Kristensen and Norris 2012, 2013.

Berlin crisis: Kempe 2011. Cuban missile crisis: Fursenko and Naftali 1998. Peace movements: Wittner 2009. *Dr. Strangelove*: Columbia Pictures, 1964.

Vietnam: Among the studies written before the Vietnamese archives opened up, Karnow 1997 stands out; among those written since the opening, Nguyen 2012 is excellent. Strategy: Summers 1982; Krepinevich 1986.

Likely forms of war in Europe in the 1960s–80s: Dinter and Griffith 1983. N. Friedman 2000, pp. 271–442, is good on the larger strategic picture, and Hoffenaar et al. 2012 on the various armies' planning. *The Third World War*: Hackett et al. 1978. I take the numbers of Soviet nuclear weapons to be used from their 1983 war plan (N. Friedman 2000, pp. 424–25).

Much of the American debate over détente took place in the pages of journals such as *Commentary* and *Foreign Affairs*. Broader 1970s situation: N. Ferguson et al. 2010.

Afghanistan: Feifer 2009. China's reorientation: Lüthi 2008; Macmillan 2008. American 1980s military buildup: Zakheim 1997. November 1983 war scare: Rhodes 2007, pp. 154–67.

6. RED IN TOOTH AND CLAW

On evolution and human behavior generally, E. O. Wilson 1975 remains the classic theoretical work. Diamond 1997 and Robert Wright 2000 are (to my mind) the most interesting historical applications.

Ape and human war: Wrangham and Peterson 1996 is fundamental. Ape and human politics: De Waal 1982.

Gombe War: Goodall 1986, pp. 503–16; Wrangham and Peterson 1996, pp. 5–18.

Similarities of human and chimpanzee genome: Chimpanzee Sequencing and Analysis Consortium 2005 (the 98 percent similarity figure obscures several technical difficulties). Divergence of humans and chimpanzees from a shared ancestor seven to eight million years ago: Landergraber et al. 2012.

Criticisms of Goodall: See particularly Power 1991, with discussion in Wrangham 2010

(Goodall's team was in fact the first to highlight the distortions introduced by feeding chimpanzees [Wrangham 1974]). Chagnon debates: See Chapter 1 above.

Chimpanzee wars observed since the 1970s: Wrangham 2010; M. Wilson 2013. Ngogo War: Mitani et al. 2010. A few primatologists and anthropologists continue to question the reality of chimpanzee wars (for example, Sussman and Marshack 2010; B. Ferguson 2011).

Extreme chimpanzee violence: De Waal 1986; Goodall 1991. De Waal 1982 does a wonderful job of putting the violence in perspective.

Wamba encounters: Idani 1991; Wrangham and Peterson 1996, pp. 209–16. Bonobos (pygmy chimpanzees/*Pan paniscus*): De Waal 1997; Furuichi and Thompson 2008. Bonobo genito-genital rubbing: Fruth and Hohmann 2000.

Origins of life and single-celled organisms: There are many recent accounts (Dawkins 2004 is a fascinating, quirky example), but Margulis and Sagan 1987 remains hard to beat. Dawkins 1989, Dennett 1995, and Coyne 2009 are my favorite treatments of the workings of biological evolution, and Christian 2004 and Robert Wright 2000 link the biological story to human history. Evolution of consciousness: Dennett 1991; Hofstadter 2007.

Game theory: Poundstone 1992 engagingly describes the field's history, calling the classic technical exposition, von Neumann and Morgenstern's daunting *Theory of Games and Economic Behavior* (1944), "one of the most influential and least-read books of the twentieth century" (p. 41). Schelling 1960 may be the best point of entry for readers interested in military applications.

Evolutionarily stable strategies: Maynard Smith 1982 is the best account, and Dawkins 1989, pp. 68–87, has an extremely clear summary. Violent outliers among humans: Raine 2013.

Psychological bases of human violence: Anderson and Bushman 2002.

Importance of numbers in chimpanzee attacks: Wilson et al. 2012.

Social animals: De Waal and Tyack 2003. Game theory has a lot to say on the evolution of sociability (Axelrod 1984 is a classic), and Shultz et al. 2011 discuss the evolution of primate sociality. Cooperation and competition: Bowles and Gintis 2010.

Ants: Hölldobler and Wilson 1990; D. Gordon 2000. Superorganisms: Hölldobler and Wilson 2008. Army ants: Gotwald 1995. Ant communication: D. Gordon 2010.

Territoriality: Wrangham and Peterson 1996.

Bonobo cannibalism: Fowler and Hohmann 2010.

Fossil evidence for evolution of modern apes: Klein 2009, pp. 112–26. The only chimpanzee fossils yet found come from the drier climate of Kenya, at the extreme eastern end of their range (McBrearty and Jablonski 2005).

Formation of Congo River: J. Thompson 2003, with Caswell et al. 2008, p. 11, on dating. Divergence of chimpanzee and bonobo DNA: Caswell et al. 2008. Congo River as an obstacle to gene flows: Eriksson et al. 2004.

Reasons for divergence of chimpanzee and bonobo diets: Wrangham and Peterson 1996, pp. 220–30; Potts 2004; Furuichi 2009; Hohmann et al. 2010. Sapolsky 2006 provides more evidence on how quickly changes in the environment can affect primate violence, this time among baboons.

Chimpanzee rape: There is a long-running debate between evolutionists and feminists over whether rape is an adaptation that allows otherwise uncompetitive males to spread their genes or a tool of male oppression; the answer, not surprisingly, seems to be that it is both at once (Muller and Wrangham 2009).

Chimpanzee sperm competition: Diamond 1992, pp. 72–75. Boesch 2009 emphasizes the methods female chimpanzees have developed to exploit male sexuality and aggression for their own reproductive ends. Gorillas: Fossey 1983; Harcourt and Stewart 2007. Sperm competition theory: Birkhead 2002.

Minimal sexual violence among bonobos: Hohmann and Fruth 2003. Importance of female bonobo coalitions: Furuichi 2011. Importance of mothers in regulating bonobo sexual competition: Surbeck et al. 2011.

Prince Chim: Yerkes 1925. Yerkes's famous Primate Laboratory was based at Yale University, but Chim died before Yerkes moved there from Harvard in 1925.

Human evolution generally: Klein 2009 is strong on the details; Stringer and Andrews 2012 is beautifully illustrated. Our knowledge of *Sahelanthropus*, *Ardipithecus*, and *Australopithecus* (not to mention several newly identified genera) is improving rapidly: See White et al. 2009; Dirks et al. 2012; Haile-Selassie et al. 2012; Berger et al. 2013. *Australopithecus* brain: http://meeting.physanth.org/program/2013/session16/bienvenu -2013-the-endocast-of-sahelanthropus-tchadensis-the-earliest-known-hominid-7-ma -chad.html.

Teeth, tubers, and roots: Lee-Thorp et al. 2012. Bipedalism: Klein 2009, pp. 271–78.

Expensive brain tissue: Aiello and Wheeler 1995; Fish and Lockwood 2003. Brain growth in the last three million years: McHenry and Coffing 2000. Tool use among apes: Roffman et al. 2012; Sanz et al. 2013.

Early *Homo*: Aiello and Antón 2012. *Homo ergaster/erectus*: Antón 2003. Climate and evolution of *H. ergaster*: Magill et al. 2012. Brains: Rightmire 2004.

Early use of fire: Berna et al. 2012.

Cooking and pair-bonding: Wrangham 2009. Bonobo monkey hunts: Surbeck and Hohmann 2008.

On all matters (human) breast- and penis-related: Yalom 1998; Hickman 2012. Penis, testicle, and breast size: Diamond 1992, pp. 72–76.

Skeletal evidence of protohuman violence: Wu et al. 2011, with table S2 (available at www .pnas.org/content/suppl/2011/11/14/1117113108.DCSupplemental/pnas.201117113SI .pdf#nameddest=ST2), containing fifty-three examples; Walker 2001.

Patterns of violence among Stone Age humans: Keeley 1996; Gat 2006. Similarities to chimpanzee violence: Wrangham and Glowacki 2012. Similarities between human and chimpanzee gangs of young adult males: Wrangham and Wilson 2004. Chimpanzees are usually hostile toward members of other communities, but de Waal 1989 describes ape strategies for resolving conflicts without violence. Chimpanzee mortality rates: Hill et al. 2001; M. Wilson 2013. Males and violence: Ghiglieri 1999.

Spread of protohumans out of Africa: Klein 2009, pp. 279–372, gives an exhaustive overview. Discovery of new species: Meyer et al. 2012. Heidelberg Man communication: Martinez et al. 2012. Stone spearheads: Wilkins et al. 2012.

Neanderthals: Mithen 2005. Stab wounds: Shanidar 3 and St. Césaire 1, mentioned in Walker 2001, p. 585. Stone weapons: Lazuén 2012. Bone breakage patterns: Berger and Trinkaus 1995. Cannibalism: Klein 2009, pp. 574–76.

The modern brain: J. Allen 2009; Pinker 1997.

The Ice Age and its end: N. Roberts 1998; Mithen 2003.

Evolution of fully modern humans: Klein 2009, pp. 615–751. Shea 2011 discusses variability and modernity in *Homo sapiens* behavior before fifty thousand years ago.

I explain my views on cultural evolution (this is the expression generally used in American English; in British English, social evolution is more common) and its relationship to biological evolution more fully in my book *The Measure of Civilization* (I. Morris 2013, pp. 6–24, 252–63). Whiten 2011 and Whiten et al. 2011, which I had not read when

I wrote *The Measure of Civilization*, are valuable analyses of how human culture evolves and its relationship to culture among other apes.

Chimpanzee culture: Wrangham 2006; Boesch 2012. Bonobo culture: Hohmann and Fruth 2003.

Fatal spear thrust 100,000 years ago (Skhul skeleton 9): Walker 2001, p. 585.

Evolution of diversity of human cultures: Foley and Mirazón Lahr 2011.

Neanderthal genome: Green et al. 2010. Denisovan DNA: Rasmussen et al. 2011. Neanderthal extinction: Finlayson 2010.

Chimpanzee stable dominance hierarchy: De Waal 1982.

Freddy, Oscar, and Scar: *Chimpanzee* (Disneynature 2012, directed by Alastair Fothergill and Mark Linfield).

Pacifist's Dilemma: Pinker 2011.

Game theory and 1950s–60s nuclear strategy: Poundstone 1992; Freedman 2003, pp. 165–78. John Nash: Nasar 1998.

NATO and Soviet war aims in the 1980s: Odom 1988; Heuser 1998.

"The Nylon War": Riesman 1951.

The final stages of the Cold War remain controversial, but in addition to the sources cited for Chapter 5, I have found Gaidar 2007, Grachev 2008, and Sebestyen 2009 helpful for seeing the crisis from the Russian side.

7. THE LAST BEST HOPE OF EARTH

Homicides in New York: www.cnn.com/2012/11/28/justice/new-york-murder-free-day /index.html. Chicago: www.huffingtonpost.com/2013/01/28/chicago-homicide-rate -201_n_2569472.html. San Bernardino: Friend 2013. Newtown: www.nytimes.com /2012/12/16/nyregion/gunman-kills-20-children-at-school-in-connecticut-28-dead-in -all.html. U.S. rates: www.fbi.gov/about-us/cjis/ucr/crime-in-the-u.s/2012/preliminary -semiannual-uniform-crime-report-january-june-2012.

Global statistics for 2004: Geneva Declaration on Armed Violence and Development, www.genevadeclaration.org/fileadmin/docs/Global-Burden-of-Armed-Violence-full -report.pdf. Global statistics for 2010: United Nations Office on Drugs and Crime, www.unodc.org/unodc/en/data-and-analysis/homicide.html. Global rate of violent death for 2012: World Health Organization, www.who.int/violence_injury_prevention/vio lence/en/. Syrian civil war: www.cnn.com/2013/01/02/world/meast/syria-civil-war/index .html. Frequency of interstate wars: Uppsala Conflict Data Program and Peace Research Institute of Oslo, www.pcr.uu.se/research/ucdp/datasets/ucdp_prio_armed_conflict _dataset/. Downward trend in civil wars: Hegre 2013, drawing on Peace Research Institute of Oslo data.

Number of nuclear warheads: See Kristensen and Norris 2012a, 2012b. The best-known index of the risk of annihilation, the *Bulletin of the Atomic Scientists*' "Doomsday Clock" (www.thebulletin.org/content/doomsday-clock/timeline), is rather misleading: it is currently set at five minutes to midnight, closer to the apocalypse than it was during the Cuban missile crisis.

Nuclear weapons as career suicide: Panel discussion at Nellis Air Force Base, Nevada, March 5, 2013.

GDP per person: Maddison 2010. Figure 7.2 is based on these data, brought up to date with World Bank data (http://data.worldbank.org/indicator/NY.GDP.PCAP.CD) converted to Maddison's metric of 1990 Geary-Khamis international dollars.

Problems of the American globocop: Ikenberry 2011. Similarities (and differences) between the British and the American globocops: N. Ferguson 2003, 2004a.

First draft of 1992 Defense Planning Guidance: www/gwu.edu/~nsarchiv/nukevault /ebb245/index.htm. *New York Times* leak and reactions, March 8, 1992: www.nytimes .com/1992/03/08/world/us-strategy-plan-calls-for-insuring-no-rivals-develop.html.

American foreign relations since 1989: Herring 2011, pp. 899–964. United States and Europe: R. Kagan 2002.

EU and U.S. GDPs: Maddison 2010.

European integration: Gillingham 2003. Fiscal integration: H. James 2012. UBS report: Deo et al. 2011. On German policy, *The Economist*'s special report on Germany (June 15, 2013) is excellent, as is the *Financial Times*' special report on the future of the European Union (May 15, 2013). The OECD's Economic Outlook Web page (www.oecd.org /eco/economicoutlook.htm) is valuable for following events.

European demilitarization: Sheehan 2008. Common Security and Defence Policy: Deighton 2011; http://eeas.europa.eu/cfsp/index_en.html; and comments by Catherine Ashton at a lunch at Stanford University on May 7, 2013.

Belarus incident: www.nytimes.com/2012/08/02/world/europe/in-belarus-a-teddy-bear -airdrop-vexes-lukashenko.html?_r=1&ref=europe.

Opinion poll in 2003: Sheehan 2008, p. xvi. Opinion poll in 2006: www.guardian.co.uk /world/2006/jun/15/usa.iran.

European strategic realities: R. Kaplan 2012. U.S. pressure on Britain to remain in Europe: www.independent.co.uk/news/world/politics/barack-obama-piles-pressure-on-david -cameron-over-eu-exit-8458116.html.

The Great Game: Hopkirk 1990 is a wonderful account.

Oil and southwest Asia: Yergin 1991.

Spending on oil in mid-1970s: Based on Yergin 1991, pp. 792–93.

United States and Iran: Milani 2011. Ayatollah Khomeini as Man of the Year: *Time*, January 7, 1980 (www.time.com/time/specials/packages/article/0,28804,2019712_2019694 _2019594,00.html). *Time* received more than fourteen thousand letters of complaint.

Bin Laden and al-Qaeda: L. Wright 2006 is excellent.

Boer War: Pakenham 1979 remains the best treatment. Iraq War: The literature is vast, but Ricks 2006 and 2009 are good introductions.

American torture: Greenberg 2005. Drone killings: Cavallaro et al. 2012; http://openchan nel.nbcnews.com/_news/2013/02/04/16843014-justice-department-memo-reveals-legal -case-for-drone-strikes-on-americans?lite.

U.S. casualties in Iraq: www.defense.gov/news/casualty/pdf. Iraqi civilian casualties: www .iraqbodycount.org/analysis/numbers/ten-years/. Costs of Boer War: Pakenham 1979, compared with British GDP from Maddison 2010.

Declining U.S. oil imports: U.S. Energy Information Administration, www.eia.gov/fore casts/steo/report/us_oil.cfm. Imports peaked at 12.5 million barrels per day in 2005; the 1987 level was 6 million barrels.

Slowing down Iran's nuclear program: Sanger 2012, pp. 141–240, www.foreignpolicy.com /articles/2013/11/19/stuxnets_secret_twin_iran_nukes_cyber_attack. Iranian nuclear options: Bracken 2012, pp. 155–60.

End of big wars: Hammes 2006. Gray 2005 summarizes and criticizes the predictions.

Middle Eastern villages at Fort Irwin: www.good.is/posts/picture-show-iraq-in-the-mojave/.

American anxieties about Japanese economic growth: Vogel 1980.

Five-trillion-dollar trade through South China Sea: Luttwak 2012, p. 206.

Maoist economic disasters: Diktötter 2010; MacFarquhar and Schoenhals 2006.

Chinese economic growth and fragility: Fenby 2012; Beardson 2013; Shambaugh 2013. The detail about deforestation comes from Economy 2004, p. 64, and the estimates of growth by 2030 from Economy 2007.

China as a military rival to the United States: Out of a huge recent literature, I have found R. Kaplan 2012 and Luttwak 2012 particularly useful.

Peaceful Rise: Zheng 2005. Peaceful Development: Dai 2010.

Chinese strategic culture: Yan 2011; Ye 2010. Confucian politics: Jiang 2013.

Military spending, 1989–2011: Data from the SIPRI Military Expenditure Database, http://milexdata.sipri.org. Chinese armed forces: Department of Defense 2012, 2013.

China-Germany analogy: Luttwak 2012, pp. 56–67.

RAND war games: Shlapak et al. 2009.

The proceedings of the ASPI conference (*Global Forces 2011*) are available at www.aspi.org .au/publications/publications_all.aspx. Australian 2009 Defence White Paper: www .defence.gov.au/whitepaper/. Reactions: Lyon and Davies 2009.

U.S.-Asia pivot: Clinton 2011.

Estimates of risk of Sino-American war: www.foreignpolicy.com/articles/2011/02/22/the _future_of_war. Pew poll: http://people-press.org/reports/pdf/692.pdf. Feldman 2013 is a good analysis of U.S.-China relations.

AirSea Battle: Krepinevich 2010; van Tol et al. 2010, with debates at http://thediplomat .com/the-naval-diplomat/2013/08/19/airsea-battle-vs-offshore-control-can-the-us -blockade-china. U.S. cyberwar plans: www.guardian.co.uk/world/interactive/2013/jun /07/obama-cyber-directive-full-text.

China's strategic options: Tellis and Tanner 2012; Bracken 2012, pp. 195–211.

Russia since 1989: M. Goldman 2008. Military modernization: www.reuters.com/article /2012/07/30/us-russia-putin-navy-idUSBRE86T1D320120730; www.foreignpolicy.com /articles/2012/09/05/building_a_better_bear. Declining revenues: www.worldbank.org /en/country/russia/overview.

Shale revolution: M. Levi 2013. Third industrial revolution: Rifkin 2011.

Estimates of economic growth, 2010–60: OECD, www.oecd.org/eco/outlook/lookingto2060 .htm; Congressional Budget Office, www.cbo.gov/publications/43907. Lower esti-mates: www.economist.com/blogs/buttonwood/2012/11/economic-outlook; Pricewater-houseCoopers, www.pwc.com/en_GX/gx/world-2050/assets/pwc-world-in-2050-report -january-2013.pdf; *Economist*, www.economist.com/blogs/graphicdetail/2013/06/daily -chart-0.

Chinese and American military budgets: http://milexdata.sipri.org.

Global trends to 2030: National Intelligence Council 2012. Arc of instability: National Intelligence Council 2008.

Carbon dioxide levels: http://co2now.org. Possible consequences: L. Smith 2010; www .sciencemag.org/site/special/climate2013/.

Euphrates: "Less Fertile Crescent," *Economist*, March 9, 2013, p. 42, www.economist.com /news/middle-east-and-africa/21573158-waters-babylon-are-running-dry-less-fertile -crescent. Egypt and Ethiopia: www.reuters.com/article/2013/06/10/us-ethiopia-egypt -nile-war-idUSBRE95911020130610.

Mean temperatures, 2002–12: Hansen et al. 2013; "A Sensitive Matter," *Economist*, March 30, 2013, pp. 77–79, www.economist.com/news/science-and-technology/21574461-cli mate-may-be-heating-up-less-response-greenhouse-gas-emissions.

CIA climate change office closes: http://eenews.net/public/Greenwire/2012/11/19/1.

Number of nuclear warheads: Kristensen and Norris 2012, 2013. U.S. plutonium facility put on hold: www.lasg.org/press/2013/NWMM_22Feb2013.html. Ground-Based Mid-course Defense: www.mda.mil/system/gmd.html. Iron Dome: http://nation.time.com /2012/11/19/iron-dome-a-missile-shield-that-works/#ixzz2Ci0JS7Us.

I learned a great deal about the drone program from my visit to Creech Air Force Base, Nevada, on March 5, 2013. The PBS *Nova* television show "The Rise of the Drones" (www.pbs.org/wgbh/nova/military/rise-of-the-drones.html) gives a good account of its history, and a pair of papers (Byman 2013, Cronin 2013) in *Foreign Affairs* 92.4 (July/ August 2013) present the main issues in the public debate.

MQ-9 unit cost: www.dod.mil/pubs/foi/logistics_material_readiness/acq_bud_fin/SARs /DEC%202011%20SAR/MQ-9%20UAS%20REAPER%20-%20SAR%20-%2031%20DEC %202011.pdf. F-35 unit cost: www.defense-aerospace.com/article-view/feature/141238 /**f_35-lot-5-unit-costs-exceed-$223m.html.

Civilian casualties of drones: www.propublica.org/article/everything-we-know-so-far -about-drone-strikes, with links to competing estimates. Casualties in Pakistan: http:// natsec.newamerica.net/drones/pakistan/analysis; www.thebureauinvestigates.com/2013 /07/22/get-the-data-the-pakistan-governments-secret-document/.

Singer 2009 is an excellent introduction to robotic warfare. Official reports: Joint Forces Command 2003, U.S. Air Force 2009. Call for a moratorium: United Nations 2013; www.hrw.org/news/2013/05/28/us-take-lead-against-lethal-robotic-weapons. Campaign to Stop Killer Robots: www.stopkillerrobots.org. Most recent (November 2012) statement of U.S. policy on lethal drones: www.dtic.mil/whs/directives/corres/pdf /300009p.pdf.

War in 2050: G. Friedman 2009.

Second Nuclear Age: Bracken 2012.

Social development index: I. Morris 2010, 2013.

Combination of technology and security perspectives: National Intelligence Council 2008, 2012; Schmidt and Cohen 2013.

Brains and the Singularity: Kurzweil 2005, 2013. Survey of predictions: http://fora.tv/2012 /10/14/Stuart_Armstrong_How_Were_Predicting_AI. Human Brain Project: www .humanbrainproject.eu; www.wired.com/wiredscience/2013/05/neurologist-markam -human-brain/all/.

Criticisms of Singularity theories: See particularly Morozov 2013. Kurzweil 2013, pp. 266–82, addresses some of the objections.

Berkeley movie experiment: www.sciencedaily.com/releases/2011/09/110922121407.htm, with footage at www.youtube.com/watch?v=nsjDnYxJ0bo. Berkeley speech experiment: www.plosbiology.org/article/info:doi/10.1371/journal.pbio.1001251. Rat telepathy: www.nature.com/srep/2013/130228/srep01319/full/srep01319.html, with discussion at http://singularityhub.com/2013/03/11/brains-of-two-rats-linked-half-way-across-the -world/.

Human superorganism: Robert Wright 2000.

Competitions within our bodies: Ridley 1996, pp. 11–34, has a clear account.

Policy debate: Brooks et al. 2013; Posen 2013.

Pax Technologica: Khanna and Khanna 2012.

Computerization and wealth inequality: http://krugman.blogs.nytimes.com/2012/12/08 /rise-of-the-robots/?_r=0; Cowen 2013.

Nexus and *Crux*: Naam 2013a, 2013 b.

BIBLIOGRAPHY

Abigail, Peter. "Australia's Next Defence White Paper: An ASPI Update." In *Global Forces 2011*, pp. 71–81. Canberra: Australian Strategic Policy Institute, 2012. Available at www.aspi.org.au/publications/publications_all.aspx.

Acemoglu, Daron, and James Robinson. *Why Nations Fail: The Origins of Power, Prosperity, and Poverty*. New York: Crown, 2012.

Adams, Thomas. "Future Warfare and the Decline of Human Decisionmaking." *Parameters* 41.4 (2011), pp. 5–19. www.carlisle.army.mil/USAWC/Parameters/Articles/2011 winter/Adams.pdf.

Aiello, Leslie, and Susan Antón, eds. "Human Biology and the Origins of *Homo*," supplement, *Current Anthropology* 53.S6 (2012), pp. S267–S478.

Aiello, Leslie, and Peter Wheeler. "The Expensive-Tissue Hypothesis: The Brain and the Digestive System in Human and Primate Evolution." *Current Anthropology* 36 (1995), pp. 199–221.

Akkermans, Peter, and Glenn Schwartz. *The Archaeology of Syria*. Cambridge, U.K.: Cambridge University Press, 2003.

Aksakal, Mustafa. " 'Holy War Made in Germany'? Ottoman Origins of the 1914 Jihad." *War in History* 18 (2011), pp. 184–99.

Aldhouse-Green, Miranda. *Dying for the Gods: Human Sacrifice in Iron Age and Roman Europe*. Stroud, U.K.: Tempus, 2001.

Allchin, F. Raymond. *The Archaeology of Early Historic South Asia*. Cambridge, U.K.: Cambridge University Press, 1995.

Allen, John. *Lives of the Brain: Human Evolution and the Organ of Mind*. Cambridge, Mass.: Belknap Press, 2009.

Allen, Robert. "The Great Divergence in European Wages and Prices from the Middle Ages to the First World War." *Explorations in Economic History* 38 (2001), pp. 411–47.

———. "Poverty and Progress in Early Modern Europe." *Economic History Review* 56 (2003), pp. 403–43.

———. "India in the Great Divergence." In Timothy Hatton et al., eds., *The New Comparative Economic History*, pp. 9–32. Cambridge, Mass.: Harvard University Press, 2007.

———. *The British Industrial Revolution in Global Perspective*. Cambridge, U.K.: Cambridge University Press, 2009.

Allen, Robert, et al. "Wages, Prices, and Living Standards in China, 1738–1925: In

Comparison with Europe, Japan, and India." *Economic History Review* 64.S1 (2011), pp. 8–38.

Alva, Walter, and Christopher Donnan. *The Lords of Sipán*. Los Angeles: Fowler Museum, 1993.

Amitai-Preiss, Reuven. *Mongols and Mamluks: The Mamluk-Ilkhanid War, 1260–1281*. Cambridge, U.K.: Cambridge University Press, 1995.

Anderson, Craig, and Brad Bushman. "Human Aggression." *Annual Review of Psychology* 53 (2002), pp. 27–51.

Angell, Norman. *The Great Illusion: A Study of the Relation of Military Power to National Advantage*. 4th ed. London: G. P. Putnam's Sons, 1913.

Anthony, David. *The Horse, the Wheel, and Language: How Bronze Age Riders from the Eurasian Steppes Shaped the Modern World*. Princeton, N.J.: Princeton University Press, 2009.

Anthony, David, and Dorcas Brown. "The Secondary Products Revolution, Horse-Riding, and Mounted Warfare." *Journal of World Prehistory* 24 (2011), pp. 131–60.

Antón, Susan. "Natural History of *Homo erectus*." *Yearbook of Physical Anthropology* 46 (2003), pp. 126–70.

Applebaum, Anne. *Gulag: A History of the Soviet Camps*. New York: Penguin, 2003.

——. *Iron Curtain: The Crushing of Eastern Europe, 1944–1956*. New York: Doubleday, 2012.

Archer, Robin. "Chariotry to Cavalry: Developments in the Early First Millennium." In Fagan and Trundle 2010, pp. 57–80.

Arkush, Elizabeth, and Mark Allen, eds. *The Archaeology of Warfare: Prehistories of Raiding and Conquest*. Gainesville: University Press of Florida, 2006.

Arkush, Elizabeth, and Tiffany Tung. "Patterns of War in the Andes from the Archaic to the Late Horizon: Insights from Settlement Patterns and Cranial Trauma." *Journal of Archaeological Research* 21 (2013), pp. 307–69.

Asher, Catherine, and Cynthia Talbot. *India Before Europe*. Cambridge, U.K.: Cambridge University Press, 2006.

Austin, Michel. *The Hellenistic World from Alexander to the Roman Conquest*. Cambridge, U.K.: Cambridge University Press, 1981.

Aveni, Anthony. *Skywatchers*. 2nd ed. Austin: University of Texas Press, 2001.

Axelrod, Robert. *The Evolution of Cooperation*. New York: Basic Books, 1984.

Bachrach, Bernard. "Verbruggen's 'Cavalry' and the Lyon-Thesis." *Journal of Medieval Military History* 4 (2006), pp. 137–63.

——. *Early Carolingian Warfare: Prelude to Empire*. Philadelphia: University of Pennsylvania Press, 2011.

Bahn, Paul. "A Lot of Bull: Pablo Picasso and Ice Age Art." *Munibe* 57 (2005), pp. 217–23. www.aranzadi-zientziak.org/fileadmin/docs/Munibe/200503217223AA.pdf.

Bairoch, Paul. "International Industrialization Levels from 1750 to 1980." *Journal of European Economic History* 11 (1982), pp. 269–333.

Baltar, Michael. " 'Vengeance' Bites Back at Jared Diamond." *Science* 324 (2009), pp. 872–74.

Baratta, Joseph. *The Politics of World Federation*. Westport, Conn.: Praeger, 2004.

Barbero, Alessandro. *Charlemagne: Father of a Continent*. Berkeley: University of California Press, 2004.

Barfield, Thomas. *The Perilous Frontier: Nomadic Empires and China, 221 BC–AD 1757*. Oxford: Blackwell, 1989.

Barker, Graeme. *The Agricultural Revolution in Prehistory*. Oxford: Oxford University Press, 2006.

Barker, Juliet. *Agincourt: Henry V and the Battle That Made England*. Boston: Back Bay Books, 2007.

Barry, John. *The Great Influenza*. New York: Penguin, 2004.

Barua, Pradeep. "Military Developments in India, 1750–1850." *Journal of Military History* 58 (1994), pp. 599–616.

Bar-Yosef, Ofer. "The Walls of Jericho: An Alternative Interpretation." *Current Anthropology* 27 (1986), pp. 157–62.

Bayly, Christopher. *Imperial Meridian: The British Empire and the World, 1780–1830.* London: Longman, 1989.

———. *The Birth of the Modern World, 1780–1914.* Oxford: Blackwell, 2004.

Bayly, Christopher, and Tim Harper. *Forgotten Armies: Britain's Asian Empire and the War with Japan.* London: Allen Lane, 2004.

Bayly, Susan. "The Evolution of Colonial Cultures: Nineteenth-Century Asia." In Porter 1999, pp. 447–69.

Beardson, Timothy. *Stumbling Giant: The Threats to China's Future.* New Haven, Conn.: Yale University Press, 2013.

Beatty, Jack. *The Lost History of 1914: Reconsidering the Year the Great War Began.* London: Walker, 2012.

Beck, B. J. Mansfeld. "The Fall of the Han." In Twitchett and Loewe 1986, pp. 317–76.

Beckerman, Stephen, et al. "Life Histories, Blood Revenge, and Reproductive Success Among the Waorani of Ecuador." *Proceedings of the National Academy of Sciences* 106 (2009), pp. 8134–39.

Beckwith, Peter. *Empires of the Silk Road: A History of Central Eurasia from the Bronze Age to the Present.* Princeton, N.J.: Princeton University Press, 2009.

Beevor, Antony. *The Second World War.* Boston: Little, Brown, 2012.

Belich, James. *Replenishing the Earth: The Settler Revolution and the Rise of the Anglo-World, 1783–1939.* Oxford: Oxford University Press, 2009.

Bell, David. *The First Total War: Napoleon's Europe and the Birth of Warfare as We Know It.* Boston: Houghton Mifflin, 2007.

Bell, Duncan. *The Idea of Greater Britain: Empire and the Future of World Order, 1860–1900.* Princeton, N.J.: Princeton University Press, 2007.

Berger, Lee, et al. "*Australopithecus sediba.*" *Science* 340 (2013), pp. 163–200.

Berger, Thomas, and Erik Trinkaus. "Patterns of Trauma Among the Neandertals." *Journal of Archaeological Science* 22 (1995), pp. 841–52.

Berna, Francesco, et al. "Microstratigraphic Evidence of In Situ Fire in the Acheulean Strata of Wonderwerk Cave, Northern Cape Province, South Africa." *Proceedings of the National Academy of Sciences* 109 (2012), pp. 1215–20.

Bernard, W. D., and W. H. Hall. *Narrative of the Voyages and Services of the Nemesis, 1840 to 1843.* Vol. 1. London: H. Colburn, 1844.

Berry, Mary. *Hideyoshi.* Cambridge, Mass.: Harvard University Press, 1989.

Best, Simon. "At the Halls of the Mountain Kings: Fijian and Samoan Fortifications: Comparison and Analysis." *Journal of the Polynesian Society* 102 (1993), pp. 385–447.

Bhakari, S. K. *Indian Warfare: An Appraisal of Strategy and Tactics of War in the Early Medieval Period.* New Delhi: Munshiran Manoharlal, 1980.

Biddle, Stephen. *Military Power: Explaining Victory and Defeat in Modern Battle.* Princeton, N.J.: Princeton University Press, 2004.

Birkhead, Tim. *Promiscuity: An Evolutionary History of Sperm Competition.* Cambridge, Mass.: Harvard University Press, 2002.

Birley, Anthony. *Marcus Aurelius: A Biography.* 2nd ed. New Haven, Conn.: Yale University Press, 1987.

Black, Jeremy. *Warfare in the Eighteenth Century.* Washington, D.C.: Smithsonian, 1999.

Blanning, Timothy. *The French Revolutionary Wars, 1787–1802.* London: Hodder & Stoughton, 1996.

Bloch, Marc. *Feudal Society.* 2 vols. Trans. L. A. Manyon. First published in French, 1939–40. London: Routledge, Kegan Paul, 1961.

———. *Strange Defeat: A Statement of Evidence Written in 1940.* First published in French, 1946. New York: Norton, 1999.

Blow, David. *Shah Abbas: The Ruthless King Who Became an Iranian Legend.* London: I. B. Tauris, 2009.

Boesch, Christophe. *The Real Chimpanzee: Sex Strategies in the Forest.* Cambridge, U.K.: Cambridge University Press, 2009.

———. *Wild Cultures: A Comparison Between Chimpanzee and Human Cultures.* Cambridge, U.K.: Cambridge University Press, 2012.

Boesche, Roger. *The First Great Political Realist: Kautilya and His Arthashastra.* Lanham, Md.: Lexington Books, 2003.

Boff, Jonathan. *Winning and Losing on the Western Front: The British Third Army and the Defeat of Germany in 1918.* Cambridge, U.K.: Cambridge University Press, 2012.

Bond, E. A., ed. *Speeches of the Managers and Counsel in the Trial of Warren Hastings.* Vol. 1. London: Longman, Brown, Green, Longmans & Roberts, 1859.

Bonney, Richard, ed. *The Rise of the Fiscal State in Europe, c. 1200–1815.* Oxford: Oxford University Press, 1999.

Boot, Max. *War Made New: Technology, Warfare, and the Course of History, 1500 to Today.* New York: Gotham Books, 2006.

Borofsky, Robert. *Yanomami: The Fierce Controversy and What We Can Learn from It.* Berkeley: University of California Press, 2005.

Bowles, Samuel, and Herbert Gintis. *A Cooperative Species: Human Reciprocity and Its Evolution.* Cambridge, U.K.: Cambridge University Press, 2011.

Bowman, Alan. *Life and Letters on the Roman Frontier.* London: British Museum Press, 1994.

Bowman, Alan, and J. D. Thomas. *The Vindolanda Writing Tablets (Tabulae Vindolandenses* II*).* London: British Museum Press, 1994.

Bowman, Alan, and Andrew Wilson, eds. *Quantifying the Roman Economy.* Oxford: Oxford University Press, 2009.

Boxer, C. R. *The Portuguese Seaborne Empire, 1415–1825.* 2nd ed. London: Hutchinson, 1969.

Boyce, Robert. *British Capitalism at the Crossroads, 1919–1932.* Cambridge, U.K.: Cambridge University Press, 1987.

Boylston, Anthea, and Christopher Knüsel, eds. *Blood Red Roses: The Archaeology of a Mass Grave from the Battle of Towton, AD 1461.* 2nd ed. Oxford: Oxbow, 2010.

Bracken, Paul. *The Second Nuclear Age: Strategy, Danger, and the New Power Politics.* New York: Times Books, 2012.

Brands, Hal. *Latin America's Cold War.* Cambridge, Mass.: Harvard University Press, 2010.

Braudel, Fernand. *Civilization and Capitalism, 15th–18th Century.* 3 vols. Trans. Siân Reynolds. New York: Harper and Row, 1981–84.

Braund, David. "Piracy Under the Principate and the Ideology of Imperial Eradication." In Rich and Shipley 1993, pp. 195–212.

Brecke, Peter. "Violent Conflicts 1400 A.D. to the Present in Different Regions of the World." 1999. www.inta.gatech.edu/peter/PSS99_paper.html.

———. "Taxonomy of Violent Conflicts." 2002. www.inta.gatech.edu/peter/taxonomy.html.

Briant, Pierre. "The Achaemenid Empire." In Raaflaub and Rosenstein 1999, pp. 105–28.

———. *From Cyrus to Alexander: A History of the Persian Empire.* Winona Lake, Ind.: Eisenbrauns, 2002.

Broadberry, Stephen. "How Did the United States and Germany Overtake Britain? A Sectoral Analysis of Comparative Productivity Levels, 1870–1990." *Journal of Economic History* 58 (1998), pp. 375–407.

Broadberry, Stephen, and Bishnupriya Gupta. "The Early Modern Great Divergence: Wages, Prices, and Economic Development in Europe and Asia, 1500–1800." *Economic History Review,* n.s. 59 (2006), pp. 2–31.

Broadberry, Stephen, and Mark Harrison, eds. *The Economics of World War I.* Cambridge, U.K.: Cambridge University Press, 2005.

Broers, Michael. "The Concept of 'Total War' in the Revolutionary-Napoleonic Period." *War in History* 15 (2008), pp. 247–68.

Brooks, Stephen, et al. "Lean Forward: In Defense of American Engagement." *Foreign Affairs* 92.1 (January/February 2013), pp. 130–42.

Brothwell, Don. *The Bog Man and the Archaeology of People.* London: British Museum, 1986.

Brown, Elizabeth. "The Tyranny of a Construct: Feudalism and Historians of Medieval Europe." *American Historical Review* 79 (1974), pp. 1063–68.

Brown, Kathryn, and Travis Stanton, eds. *Ancient Mesoamerican Warfare.* Walnut Creek, Calif.: AltaMira, 2003.

Brown, Kyle, et al. "An Early and Enduring Advanced Technology Originating 71,000 Years Ago in South Africa." *Nature*, November 7, 2012. doi:10.1038/nature11660.

Brown, Warren. *Violence in Medieval Europe.* London: Longmans, 2010.

Bullock, Alan. *Hitler and Stalin: Parallel Lives.* New York: Vintage, 1993.

Burden, Matthew. *The Blog of War: Front-Line Dispatches from Soldiers in Iraq and Afghanistan.* New York: Simon & Schuster, 2006.

Burk, Kathleen. *Britain, America, and the Sinews of War, 1914–1918.* New York: Harper-Collins, 1985.

Burke, Jason. *The 9/11 Wars.* New York: Allen Lane, 2011.

Bush, George H. W., and Brent Scowcroft. *A World Transformed.* New York: Knopf, 1998.

Byman, Daniel. "Why Drones Work: The Case for Washington's Weapon of Choice." *Foreign Affairs* 92.4 (July/August 2013), pp. 32–43.

Cain, P. J., and Anthony Hopkins. *British Imperialism, 1688–2000.* 2nd ed. London: Longman, 2000.

Callwell, C. E. *Small Wars: Their Principles and Practice.* 3rd ed. London: War Office, 1909.

Campbell, Duncan. *Mons Graupius AD 83.* Oxford: Osprey, 2010.

Canning, Joseph, et al., eds. *Power, Violence, and Mass Death in Pre-modern and Modern Times.* Aldershot, U.K.: Ashgate, 2004.

Capp, Bernard. *Cromwell's Navy: The Fleet and the English Revolution, 1648–1660.* New York: Oxford University Press, 1989.

Carey, John. *William Golding: The Man Who Wrote "Lord of the Flies."* New York: Free Press, 2010.

Carneiro, Robert. "A Theory of the Origin of the State." *Science* 169 (1970), pp. 733–38.

Carrasco, David. *City of Sacrifice: The Aztec Empire and the Role of Violence in Civilization.* Boston: Beacon Press, 1999.

Caswell, Jennifer, et al. "Analysis of Chimpanzee History Based on Genome Sequence Alignments." *PLoS Genetics* 4 (2008). doi:10.1371/journal.pgen.1000057.

Cavallaro, James, et al. *Living Under Drones: Death, Injury, and Trauma to Civilians from US Drone Practices in Pakistan.* Stanford, Calif., and New York: Stanford Law School and NYU School of Law, 2012. Available at http://livingunderdrones.org/.

Ceadel, Martin. *Living the Great Illusion: Sir Norman Angell, 1872–1967.* Oxford: Oxford University Press, 2009.

Cederman, L.-E. "Modeling the Size of Wars: From Billiard Balls to Sandpiles." *American Political Science Review* 97 (2003), pp. 135–50.

Chagnon, Napoleon. "Life Histories, Blood Revenge, and Warfare in a Tribal Society." *Science* 239 (1988), pp. 985–92.

———. *Yanomamö.* 5th ed. New York: Harcourt Brace College Publishers, 1997.

———. *Noble Savages: My Life Among Two Dangerous Tribes—the Yanomamö and the Anthropologists.* New York: Simon & Schuster, 2013.

Chakrabarti, Dilip. *India: An Archaeological History.* New Delhi: Oxford University Press, 1999.

Chakravarti, P. K. *The Art of War in Ancient India*. First published 1941. Reprint, Delhi: Low Price Publishers, 2010.

Chaliand, Gerard. *Nomadic Empires from Mongolia to the Danube*. Trans. A. M. Berrett. New Brunswick, N.J.: Transaction, 2004.

Chandrasekaran, Rajiv. *Little America: The War Within the War for Afghanistan*. New York: Knopf, 2012.

Chang, Chun-shu. *The Rise of the Chinese Empire: Nation, State, and Imperialism in Early China, ca. 1600 B.C.–A.D. 8*. Ann Arbor: University of Michigan Press, 2007.

Chang, Iris. *The Rape of Nanking: The Forgotten Holocaust of World War II*. New York: Penguin, 1997.

Chaniotis, Angelos. *War in the Hellenistic World*. Oxford: Blackwell, 2005.

Chaplais, Pierre. *Diplomatic Documents Preserved in the Public Record Office*. Vol. 1, *1101–1307*. London: Public Record Office, 1964.

Charrière, E., trans. *Chronique de Bertrand du Guesclin* Vol. 1. Paris: Typographie du Firmin Didot Frères, 1839. http://archive.org/stream/chroniquedebert00saingoog#page /n8/mode/2up.

Chase, Kenneth. *Firearms: A Global History to 1700*. Cambridge, U.K.: Cambridge University Press, 2003.

Chattopadhyaya, B. *The Making of Early Medieval India*. 2nd ed. Oxford: Oxford University Press, 2010.

Cherian, P. J., et al. "The Muziris Heritage Project: Excavations at Pattanam—2007." *Journal of Indian Ocean Archaeology* 4 (2007), pp. 1–10.

Chickering, Roger, and Stig Förster, eds. *Great War, Total War: Combat and Mobilization on the Western Front, 1914–1918*. Cambridge, U.K.: Cambridge University Press, 2000.

Childs, David. *A Peripheral Weapon? The Production and Employment of British Tanks in the First World War*. Westport, Conn.: Praeger, 1999.

Chimpanzee Sequencing and Analysis Consortium. "Initial Sequence of the Chimpanzee Genome and Comparison with the Human Genome." *Nature* 437 (2005), pp. 69–87.

Chirot, Daniel, and Clark McCauley. *Why Not Kill Them All? The Logic and Prevention of Mass Political Murder*. Princeton, N.J.: Princeton University Press, 2006.

Christian, David. *A History of Russia, Central Asia, and Mongolia*. Vol. 1, *Inner Eurasia from Prehistory to the Mongol Empire*. Oxford: Blackwell, 1998.

——. *Maps of Time: An Introduction to Big History*. Berkeley: University of California Press, 2004.

Churchill, Winston. *My Early Life, 1874–1904*. New York: Charles Scribner's Sons, 1930.

——. *The World Crisis, 1911–1918*. Abr. ed. First published in 5 vols., 1923–31. New York: Charles Scribner's Sons, 1931.

——. *The Second World War*. Vol. 2, *Their Finest Hour*. Boston: Houghton Mifflin, 1949.

——. *The Second World War*. Vol. 3, *The Grand Alliance*. Boston: Houghton Mifflin, 1950.

Cipolla, Carlo. *Guns, Sails, and Empires: Technological Innovation and the Early Phases of European Expansion, 1400–1700*. New York: Random House, 1965.

Citino, Robert. *Blitzkrieg to Desert Storm: The Evolution of Operational Warfare*. Lawrence: University Press of Kansas, 2004.

——. *The Quest for Decisive Victory: From Stalemate to Blitzkrieg in Europe, 1899–1940*. Lawrence: University Press of Kansas, 2009.

Clark, Alan. *The Donkeys*. New York: Morrow, 1962.

Clark, Christopher. *Iron Kingdom: The Rise and Downfall of Prussia, 1600–1947*. Cambridge, Mass.: Belknap Press, 2006.

——. *Kaiser Wilhelm II: A Life in Power*. New York: Penguin, 2009.

Clarke, Richard. *Against All Enemies: Inside America's War on Terror*. New York: Free Press, 2007.

Clavell, James. *Shogun*. New York: Delacorte Press, 1975.

Cliff, Roger, et al. *New Opportunities and Challenges for Taiwan's Security*. Santa Monica, Calif.: RAND Corporation, 2011. www.rand.org/content/dam/rand/pubs/conf_pro ceedings/2011/RAND_CF279.pdf.

Cline, Eric, ed. *The Oxford Handbook of the Bronze Age Aegean*. Oxford: Oxford University Press, 2010.

———. *1177 B.C. The Year Civilization Collapsed*. Princeton, N.J. Princeton University Press, 2013.

Cline, Eric, and Mark Graham. *Ancient Empires*. New York: Cambridge University Press, 2011.

Clinton, Hillary. "America's Pacific Century." *Foreign Policy* 191 (November/December 2011). www.foreignpolicy.com/articles/2011/10/11/americas_pacific_century.

Clodfelter, Micheal. *Warfare and Armed Conflicts: A Statistical Reference*. 3 vols. London: McFarland, 1992.

Coe, Michael. *Breaking the Maya Code*. 3rd ed. London: Thames & Hudson, 2012.

Cohen, H., et al. "Trauma to the Skull: A Historical Perspective from the Southern Levant (4300BCE–1917CE)." *International Journal of Osteoarchaeology* 20 (2012). doi:10.1002 /oa.2258.

Coll, Steve. *Ghost Wars: The Secret History of the CIA, Afghanistan, and bin Laden, from the Soviet Invasion to September 10, 2001*. New York: Penguin, 2004.

Colley, Linda. *Britons: The Forging of a Nation, 1707–1837*. 3rd ed. New Haven, Conn.: Yale University Press, 2009.

Commonwealth of Australia. *Defending Australia in the Asia Pacific Century: Force 2030*. Canberra: Department of Defence, 2009.

Conquest, Robert. *The Great Terror: A Reassessment*. New York: Oxford University Press, 2007.

Contamine, Philippe. *War in the Middle Ages*. Trans. Michael Jones. Oxford: Blackwell, 1984.

Cooper, Jerrold. *Sumerian and Akkadian Royal Inscriptions: Pre-Sargonic Inscriptions*. Winona Lake, Ind: Eisenbrauns, 1986.

Cooper, Malcolm. *The Birth of Independent Air Power*. London: Unwin, 1986.

Cooper, Randolf. *The Anglo-Maratha Campaigns and the Contest for India*. Cambridge, U.K.: Cambridge University Press, 2003.

Coote, Stephen. *Samuel Pepys: A Life*. London: Hodder & Stoughton, 2000.

Cordell, Linda, and Maxine McBrinn. *Archaeology of the Southwest*. 3rd ed. Walnut Creek, Calif.: Left Coast Press, 2012.

Corrigan, Gerald. *Mud, Blood, and Poppycock: Britain and the First World War*. London: Cassell, 2003.

Cowen, Tyler. *Average Is Over: Powering America Beyond the Age of the Great Stagnation*. New York: Dutton, 2013.

Cowgill, George. "Possible Migrations and Shifting Identities in the Central Mexican Epiclassic." *Ancient Mesoamerica* 24 (2013), pp. 1–19.

Coyne, Jerry. *Why Evolution Is True*. New York: Viking, 2009.

Cronin, Audrey Kurth. "Why Drones Fail: When Tactics Drive Strategy." *Foreign Affairs* 92.4 (July/August 2013), pp. 44–54.

Crosby, Alfred. *The Columbian Exchange: Biological and Cultural Consequences of 1492*. Westport, Conn.: Westview Press, 1972.

———. *Ecological Imperialism: The Biological Expansion of Europe, 900–1900*. 2nd ed. Cambridge, U.K.: Cambridge University Press, 2003.

Cunliffe, Barry. *Danebury: Anatomy of an Iron Age Hillfort*. London: Batsford, 1983.

Curtis, Vesta Sarkhosh, and Sarah Stewart, eds. *The Age of the Parthians*. London: I. B. Tauris, 2007.

Dai Bingguo. "Adhere to the Path of Peaceful Development." *Waijiaobu Wangzhan*, December 6, 2010. Trans. Xinhua News Agency. http://china.usc.edu/ShowArticle.aspx ?articleID=2325.

Dale, Stephen. *The Muslim Empires of the Ottomans, Safavids, and Mughals*. Cambridge, U.K.: Cambridge University Press, 2010.

Dalley, Stephanie. "Foreign Chariotry and Cavalry in the Armies of Tiglath-Pileser III and Sargon II." *Iraq* 47 (1985), pp. 31–48.

Dani, A. H., and V. M. Masson, eds. *History of Civilizations of Central Asia*. 6 vols. Paris: UNESCO, 1992.

Darwin, John. *The Empire Project: The Rise and Fall of the British World-System, 1830–1970*. Cambridge, U.K.: Cambridge University Press, 2009.

Daryaee, Touraj. *Sasanian Persia: The Rise and Fall of an Empire*. London: Tauris, 2009.

Daugherty, William, et al. "The Consequences of 'Limited' Nuclear Attacks on the United States." *International Security* 10.4 (1986), pp. 3–45.

David, Saul. *The Indian Mutiny*. London: Penguin, 2003.

——. *Zulu: The Heroism and Tragedy of the Zulu War of 1879*. New York: Viking, 2004.

——. *Victoria's Wars: The Rise of Empire*. London: Penguin, 2006.

Davies, J. D. *Pepys's Navy: Ships, Men, and Organisation, 1649–1689*. Annapolis, Md.: Naval Institute Press, 2008.

Davies, Norman. *White Eagle, Red Star: The Polish-Soviet War, 1919–1920, and the "Miracle on the Vistula."* London: Random House, 2003.

——. *No Simple Victory: World War II in Europe, 1939–1945*. New York: Penguin, 2006.

Davies, R. W., et al., eds. *The Economic Transformation of the Soviet Union, 1913–1945*. Cambridge, U.K.: Cambridge University Press, 1994.

Davis, Mike. *Late Victorian Holocausts*. London: Verso, 2001.

Dawkins, Richard. *The Selfish Gene*. 2nd ed. Oxford: Oxford University Press, 1989.

——. *The Ancestor's Tale: A Pilgrimage to the Dawn of Evolution*. Boston: Houghton Mifflin, 2004.

Dawson, Christopher, ed. *The Mongol Mission: Narratives and Letters of the Franciscan Missionaries in Mongolia and China in the Thirteenth and Fourteenth Centuries*. New York: Sheed and Ward, 1955.

Dedijer, Vladimir. *The Road to Sarajevo*. New York: Simon & Schuster, 1966.

de Glete, Jan. *Warfare at Sea, 1500–1650: Maritime Conflicts and the Transformation of Europe*. London: Routledge, 1999.

Degras, Jane, ed. *The Communist International, 1919–1943: Documents* Vol. 2. London: Oxford University Press, 1965.

de Grazia, Victoria. *Irresistible Empire: America's Advance Through Twentieth-Century Europe*. Cambridge, Mass.: Harvard University Press, 2006.

Deighton, Anne. "The European Union, Multilateralism, and the Use of Force." In Strachan and Schepers 2011, pp. 315–32.

de la Gorce, Paul-Marie. *The French Army: A Military-Political History*. Trans. Kenneth Douglas. London: Weidenfeld and Nicolson, 1963.

de Madariaga, Isabel. *Ivan the Terrible*. New Haven, Conn.: Yale University Press, 2006.

Dennett, Daniel. *Consciousness Explained*. Boston: Little, Brown, 1991.

——. *Darwin's Dangerous Idea*. New York: Simon & Schuster, 1995.

Deo, Stephane, et al. "Euro Break-Up—the Consequences." *UBS Investment Research, Global Economic Perspectives*, September 6, 2011, pp. 1–18. Available at www.ubs.com /economics.

Department of Defense. *Quadrennial Defense Review Report February 2010*. Washington, D.C.: Department of Defense, 2010. www.defense.gov/qdr/.

——. *Annual Report to Congress: Military and Security Developments Involving the People's Republic of China 2012*. Washington, D.C.: Department of Defense, 2012. www .defense.gov/pubs/pdfs/2012_CMPR_Final.pdf.

——. *Military and Security Developments Involving the People's Republic of China 2013*. Washington, D.C.: Office of the Secretary of Defense, 2013. www.defense.gov/pubs/2013 _china_report_final.pdf.

de Souza, Philip. *Piracy in the Graeco-Roman World*. Cambridge, U.K.: Cambridge University Press, 1999.

De Vries, Jan. *The Industrious Revolution: Consumer Behaviour and the Household Economy, 1650 to the Present*. Cambridge, U.K.: Cambridge University Press, 2008.

de Waal, Frans. *Chimpanzee Politics: Power and Sex Among Apes*. Baltimore: Johns Hopkins University Press, 1982.

———. "The Brutal Elimination of a Rival Among Captive Male Chimpanzees." *Ethology and Sociobiology* 7 (1986), pp. 237–51.

———. *Peacemaking Among Primates*. Cambridge, Mass.: Harvard University Press, 1989.

———. *Bonobo: The Forgotten Ape*. Berkeley: University of California Press, 1997.

de Waal, Frans, and Peter Tyack, eds. *Animal Social Complexity: Intelligence, Culture, and Individualized Societies*. Cambridge, Mass.: Harvard University Press, 2003.

Diamond, Jared. *The Third Chimpanzee: The Evolution and Future of the Human Animal*. New York: HarperCollins, 1992.

———. *Guns, Germs, and Steel: The Fates of Human Societies*. 2nd ed. New York: Norton, 2005.

———. "Vengeance Is Ours." *New Yorker*, April 21, 2008, pp. 74–81.

———. *The World Until Yesterday: What Can We Learn from Traditional Societies?* New York: Viking, 2012.

Di Cosmo, Nicola. "State Formation and Periodization in Inner Asian History." *Journal of World History* 10 (1999), pp. 1–40.

———. *Ancient China and Its Enemies*. Cambridge, U.K.: Cambridge University Press, 2002a.

———, ed. *Warfare in Inner Asian History (500–1800)*. Leiden: Brill, 2002b.

———. *Military Culture in Imperial China*. Cambridge, Mass.: Harvard University Press, 2011.

Diehl, Richard. *Tula: The Toltec Capital of Ancient Mexico*. London: Thames & Hudson, 1983.

Dien, Albert, ed. *State and Society in Early Medieval China*. Stanford, Calif.: Stanford University Press, 1990.

———. *Six Dynasties Civilization*. New Haven, Conn.: Yale University Press, 2007.

Dignas, Beate, and Engelbert Winter. *Rome and Persia in Late Antiquity: Neighbours and Rivals*. Cambridge, U.K.: Cambridge University Press, 2007.

Dikshitar, V. R. *War in Ancient India*. Delhi: Motilal Banarsidass, 1987.

Diktötter, Frank. *Mao's Great Famine*. London: Bloomsbury, 2010.

Dinter, Elmar, and Paddy Griffith. *Not Over by Christmas: NATO's Central Front in World War III*. New York: Hippocrene, 1983.

Dirks, Paul, et al. "Geological Setting and Age of *Australopithecus sediba* from Southern Africa." *Science* 328 (2010), p. 205.

Dollery, Brian, and Craig Parsons. "Prisoner Taking and Prisoner Killing: A Comment on Ferguson's Political Economy Approach." *War in History* 14 (2007), pp. 499–512.

Doughty, Robert. *Pyrrhic Victory: French Strategy and Operations in the Great War*. Cambridge, Mass.: Harvard University Press, 2008.

Doyle, Michael. "Kant, Liberal Legacies, and Foreign Affairs." *Philosophy and Public Affairs* 12 (1983), pp. 205–35, 323–53.

Dreger, Alice. "*Darkness*'s Descent on the American Anthropological Association." *Human Nature* 22 (2011), pp. 225–46.

Drews, Robert. *The Coming of the Greeks: Indo-European Conquests in the Aegean and the Near East*. Princeton, N.J.: Princeton University Press, 1988.

———. *The End of the Bronze Age: Changes in Warfare and the Catastrophe ca. 1200 B.C.* Princeton, N.J.: Princeton University Press, 1992.

Dreyer, Edward. *Zheng He: China and the Oceans in the Early Ming Dynasty, 1405–1433*. New York: Pearson Longman, 2006.

Duffy, Christopher. *Military Experience in the Age of Reason*. London: Routledge, 1987.

Dulic, T. "Tito's Slaughterhouse: A Critical Analysis of Rummel's Work on Democide." *Journal of Peace Research* 41 (2004), pp. 85–102.

Duncan-Jones, Richard. "Economic Change and the Transition to Late Antiquity." In Simon Swain and Mark Edwards, eds., *Approaching Late Antiquity: The Transition from Early to Late Empire*, pp. 20–52. Oxford: Oxford University Press, 2004.

Earle, Peter. *The Pirate Wars*. New York: St. Martin's, 2006.

Echevarria, Antulio. *Imagining Future War: The West's Technological Revolution and Visions of Wars to Come, 1880–1914*. Westport, Conn.: Praeger, 2007.

Eck, K., and L. Hultman. "Violence Against Civilians in War." *Journal of Peace Research* 44 (2007), pp. 233–46.

Eckhardt, William. *Civilizations, Empires, and Wars: A Quantitative History of War*. Jefferson, N.C.: McFarland, 1992.

Eckstein, Arthur. *Mediterranean Anarchy, Interstate War, and the Rise of Rome*. Berkeley: University of California Press, 2006.

Economy, Elizabeth. *The River Runs Black: The Environmental Challenge to China's Future*. Ithaca, N.Y.: Cornell University Press, 2004.

———. "The Great Leap Backward?" *Foreign Affairs* 86.5 (2007), www.foreignaffairs.com /articles/62827/elizabeth-c-economy/the-great-leap-backward.

Edmonds, James. *A Short History of World War I*. Oxford: Oxford University Press, 1951.

Eeckhout, Peter, and Geneviève Le Fort, eds. *Wars and Conflicts in Prehispanic Meso-america and the Andes*. Oxford: John and Erica Hedges, 2005.

Ehret, Christopher. *The Civilizations of Africa: A History to 1800*. Charlottesville: University Press of Virginia, 2002.

Eisner, Manuel. "Long-Term Historical Trends in Violent Crime." *Crime & Justice* 30 (2003), pp. 83–142.

Elias, Norbert. *The Civilizing Process*. Trans. Edmund Jephcott. First published in German, 1939. Oxford: Blackwell, 1982.

Ella, S. "The War of Tonga and Samoa and the Origin of the Name Malietoa." *Journal of the Polynesian Society* 8 (1899), pp. 231–34.

Elton, Hugh. "Military Forces." In Sabin et al. 2007, pp. 270–309.

Eltsov, Piotr Andreevich. *From Harappa to Hastinapura: A Study of the Earliest South Asian City and Civilization*. Leiden: Brill, 2008.

Erdosy, George. *Urbanisation in Early Historic India*. Oxford: British Archaeological Reports, 1988.

Eriksson, J., et al. "Rivers Influence the Population Genetic Structure of Bonobos (*Pan paniscus*)." *Molecular Ecology* 13 (2004), pp. 3425–35.

Evans, Richard. *The Third Reich in Power*. New York: Penguin, 2005.

———. *The Third Reich at War*. New York: Penguin, 2009.

Fagan, Brian. *The First North Americans: An Archaeological Journey*. London: Thames & Hudson, 2012.

Fagan, Garrett. "'I Fell upon Him Like a Furious Arrow': Toward a Reconstruction of the Assyrian Tactical System." In Fagan and Trundle 2010, pp. 81–100.

Fagan, Garrett, and Matthew Trundle, eds. *New Perspectives on Ancient Warfare*. Leiden: Brill, 2010.

Farris, William Wayne. *Heavenly Warriors: The Evolution of Japan's Military, 500–1300*. Cambridge, Mass.: Harvard University Press, 1996.

Farrokh, Kaveh. *Sassanian Elite Cavalry, AD 224–642*. Oxford: Osprey, 2005.

———. *Shadows in the Desert: Ancient Persia at War*. Oxford: Osprey, 2009.

———. *Iran at War: 1500–1988*. Oxford: Osprey, 2011.

Faubion, James, et al., eds. *Fieldwork Is Not What It Used to Be: Learning Anthropology's Method in a Time of Transition*. Ithaca, N.Y.: Cornell University Press, 2009.

Fay, Peter Ward. *The Opium War, 1840–1842*. 2nd ed. Chapel Hill: University of North Carolina Press, 1997.

Feifer, Gregory. *The Great Gamble: The Soviet War in Afghanistan*. New York: Harper-Collins, 2009.

Feldman, Noah. *Cool War: The Future of Global Competition*. New York: Random House, 2013.

Fenby, Jonathan. *Tiger Head, Snake Tails: China Today, How It Got There, and Where It Is Heading*. New York: Simon & Schuster, 2012.

Ferejohn, John, and Frances Rosenbluth, eds. *War and State Building in Medieval Japan*. Stanford, Calif.: Stanford University Press, 2010.

Ferguson, Brian. "Savage Encounter: Western Contact and the Yanomami War Complex." In Brian Ferguson and Neil Whitehead, eds., *War in the Tribal Zone: Expanding States and Indigenous Warfare*, pp. 199–227. Santa Fe, N.M.: School of American Research, 1992.

———. *Yanomami Warfare*. Santa Fe, N.M.: School of American Research, 1995.

———. "Born to Live: Challenging Killer Myths." In Robert Sussman and C. R. Cloninger, eds., *Origins of Altruism and Cooperation*, pp. 249–70. Amsterdam: Springer, 2011.

———. "Pinker's List: Exaggerating Prehistoric War Mortality." In Fry 2013, pp. 112–31.

Ferguson, Niall. *The Pity of War: Explaining World War I*. London: Allen Lane, 1998.

———. *The Cash Nexus: Money and Power in the Modern World, 1700–2000*. New York: Basic Books, 2001.

———. *Empire: The Rise and Demise of the British World Order and the Lessons for Global Power*. New York: Basic Books, 2003.

———. *Colossus: The Price of America's Empire*. New York: Penguin, 2004a.

———. "Prisoner Taking and Prisoner Killing in the Age of Total War: Towards a Political Economy of Military Defeat." *War in History* 11 (2004b), pp. 148–92.

———. *The War of the World: Twentieth-Century Conflict and the Descent of the West*. New York: Penguin, 2006.

———. *The Ascent of Money: A Financial History of the World*. New York: Penguin, 2008.

Ferguson, Niall, and Moritz Schularick. "'Chimerica' and the Global Asset Market Boom." *International Finance* 10.3 (2007), pp. 215–39.

Ferguson, Niall, et al., eds. *The Shock of the Global: The 1970s in Perspective*. Cambridge, Mass: Harvard University Press, 2010.

Ferling, John. *Almost a Miracle: The American Victory in the War of Independence*. New York: Oxford University Press, 2007.

Fernández-Armesto, Felipe. *Pathfinders: A Global History of Exploration*. New York: Norton, 2006.

———. *The World: A History*. 2nd ed. Upper Saddle River, N.J.: Prentice Hall, 2010.

Fieldhouse, Donald. "For Richer, for Poorer." In P. J. Marshall, ed., *The Cambridge Illustrated History of the British Empire*, pp. 108–46. Cambridge, U.K.: Cambridge University Press, 1996.

Figes, Orlando. *A People's Tragedy: The Russian Revolution, 1891–1924*. London: Pimlico, 1997.

———. *The Crimean War: A History*. New York: Metropolitan Books, 2010.

Findlay, Ronald, and Kevin O'Rourke. *Power and Plenty: Trade, War, and the World Economy in the Second Millennium*. Princeton, N.J.: Princeton University Press, 2007.

Finlayson, Clive. *The Humans Who Went Extinct: Why Neanderthals Died Out and We Survived*. Oxford: Oxford University Press, 2010.

Fisch, Jörg. *Cheap Lives and Dear Limbs: The British Transformation of the Bengali Criminal Law, 1769–1817*. Wiesbaden: Franz Steiner, 1983.

Fischer, Fritz. *Germany's Aims in the First World War*. First published in German, 1961. New York: Norton, 1967.

———. *World Power or Decline? The Controversy over Germany's Aims in the First World War*. Trans. Lancelot Farrar et al. New York: Norton, 1974.

444   BIBLIOGRAPHY

Fish, Jennifer, and C. A. Lockwood. "Dietary Constraints on Encephalization in Primates." *American Journal of Physical Anthropology* 120 (2003), pp. 171–81.

Floor, Willem. *The Economy of Safavid Persia*. Wiesbaden: Reichert, 2000.

Foley, Robert, and M. Mirazón Lahr. "The Evolution of the Diversity of Cultures." *Philosophical Transactions of the Royal Society B* 366 (2011), pp. 1080–89.

Foreman, Amanda. *A World on Fire: Britain's Crucial Role in the American Civil War.* New York: Random House, 2010.

Förster, Stig, and Jorg Nagler, eds. *On the Road to Total War: The American Civil War and the German Wars of Unification, 1861–1871.* Cambridge, U.K.: Cambridge University Press, 1999.

Fossey, Dian. *Gorillas in the Mist.* Boston: Houghton Mifflin, 1983.

Fowler, Andrew, and Gottfried Hohmann. "Cannibalism in Wild Bonobos (*Pan paniscus*) at Lui Kotale." *American Journal of Primatology* 72 (2010), pp. 509–14.

Frank, Andre Gunder. *ReOrient: Global Economy in the Asian Age.* Berkeley: University of California Press, 1998.

Freedman, Lawrence. *The Evolution of Nuclear Strategy.* 3rd ed. London: Palgrave, 2003.

Freeman, Derek. *Margaret Mead and Samoa: The Making and Unmaking of an Anthropological Myth.* Cambridge, Mass.: Harvard University Press, 1983.

———. "Fa'apua'a Fa'amu and Margaret Mead." *American Anthropologist* 91 (1989), pp. 1017–22.

———. *The Fateful Hoaxing of Margaret Mead: A Historical Analysis of Her Samoan Research.* Boulder, Colo.: Westview Press, 1999.

Friday, Karl. *Samurai, Warfare, and the State in Early Medieval Japan.* London: Routledge, 2003.

Friedman, George. *The Next 100 Years: A Forecast for the 21st Century.* New York: Doubleday, 2009.

Friedman, Norman. *The Fifty Year War: Conflict and Strategy in the Cold War.* Annapolis, Md.: Naval Institute Press, 2000.

Friend, Tad. "Home Economics." *New Yorker*, February 4, 2013, pp. 26–33.

Fruth, Barbara, and Gottfried Hohmann. "Social Grease for Females? Same-Sex Genital Contacts in Wild Bonobos." In Volker Sommer and Paul Vasey, eds., *Homosexual Behaviour in Animals*, pp. 294–314. Cambridge, U.K.: Cambridge University Press, 2006.

Fry, Douglas, ed. *War, Peace, and Human Nature: The Convergence of Evolutionary and Cultural Views.* Oxford: Oxford University Press, 2013.

Fukuyama, Francis. *The Origins of Political Order: From Prehuman Times to the French Revolution.* New York: Farrar, Straus and Giroux, 2011.

Fuller, Howard. *Clad in Iron: The American Civil War and British Naval Power.* Westport, Conn.: Praeger, 2008.

Fuller, J. F. C. *Memoirs of an Unconventional Soldier.* London: Nicholson & Watson, 1936.

Fursenko, Aleksandr, and Timothy Naftali. *One Hell of a Gamble: Khrushchev, Castro, and Kennedy, 1958–1964: The Secret History of the Cuban Missile Crisis.* New York: Norton, 1998.

———. *Khrushchev's Cold War: The Inside Story of an American Adversary.* New York: Norton, 2006.

Furuichi, Takeshi. "Factors Underlying Party Size Differences Between Chimpanzees and Bonobos." *Primates* 50 (2009), pp. 197–209.

———. "Female Contributions to the Peaceful Nature of Bonobo Society." *Evolutionary Anthropology* 20 (2011), pp. 131–42.

Furuichi, Takeshi, and Jo Thompson, eds. *The Bonobos: Behavior, Ecology, and Conservation.* Amsterdam: Springer, 2008.

Futrell, Alison. *The Roman Games.* Oxford: Blackwell, 2006.

Fyfe, H. Hamilton. *Northcliffe, an Intimate Biography.* London: Allen and Unwin, 1930.

Gaddis, John Lewis. *We Now Know: Rethinking Cold War History*. Oxford: Oxford University Press, 1997.

———. *The Cold War: A New History*. New York: Penguin, 2005a.

———. *Strategies of Containment: A Critical Appraisal of American National Security Policy During the Cold War*. New York: Oxford University Press, 2005b.

Gaidar, Yegor. *Collapse of an Empire: Lessons for Modern Russia*. Trans. Antonina Bouis. Washington, D.C.: Brookings Institution Press, 2007.

Ganshof, François Louis. *Feudalism*. Trans. Philip Grierson. First published in French, 1947. London: Longmans, Green, 1952.

Ganzel, Klaus Jürgen, and Torsten Schwinghammer. *Warfare Since the Second World War*. Trans. P. G. Bach. London: Transaction Books, 2000.

Gardiner, Robert, and Richard Unger, eds. *Cogs, Caravels, and Galleons: The Sailing Ship, 1000–1650*. London: Chartwell Books, 2000.

Garstang, John. *Prehistoric Mersin: Yümük Tepe in Southern Turkey*. Oxford: Oxford University Press, 1953.

Garthoff, Raymond. *Soviet Strategy in the Nuclear Age*. New York: Praeger, 1958.

Gat, Azar. *British Armour Theory and the Rise of the Panzer Arm: Revising the Revisionists*. London: Macmillan, 2000.

———. *War in Human Civilization*. Oxford: Oxford University Press, 2006.

Gerlach, Christian. *Extremely Violent Societies: Mass Violence in the Twentieth-Century World*. Cambridge, U.K.: Cambridge University Press, 2010.

Ghiglieri, Michael. *The Dark Side of Man: Tracing the Origins of Male Violence*. New York: Basic Books, 1999.

Gilboy, George, and Eric Heginbotham. *Chinese and Indian Strategic Behavior: Growing Power and Alarm*. Cambridge, U.K.: Cambridge University Press, 2012.

Gilley, Bruce, and Andrew Nathan. *China's New Rulers: The Secret Files*. 2nd ed. New York: New York Review Books, 2003.

Gillingham, John. *European Integration, 1950–2003: Superstate or New Market Economy?* Cambridge, U.K.: Cambridge University Press, 2003.

Gilmour, David. *The Long Recessional: The Imperial Life of Rudyard Kipling*. New York: Farrar, Straus and Giroux, 2002.

Gleason, Maud. *Making Men: Sophists and Self-Presentation in Ancient Rome*. Princeton, N.J.: Princeton University Press, 1995.

Gleditsch, Nils Petter, et al. "Armed Conflict, 1946–2001: A New Dataset." *Journal of Peace Research* 39 (2002), pp. 615–37.

Golden, Peter. *Central Asia in World History*. Oxford: Oxford University Press, 2011.

Goldhagen, Jonah. *Worse Than War: Genocide, Eliminationism, and the Ongoing Assault on Humanity*. New York: PublicAffairs, 2009.

Golding, William. *Lord of the Flies*. London: Faber and Faber, 1954.

Goldman, Marshall. *Petrostate: Putin, Power, and the New Russia*. New York: Oxford University Press, 2008.

Goldman, Stuart. *Nomonhan, 1939: The Red Army's Victory That Shaped World War II*. Annapolis, Md.: Naval Institute Press, 2012.

Goldstein, Joshua. *Winning the War on War: The Surprising Decline in Armed Conflict Worldwide*. New York: Norton, 2011.

Goldsworthy, Adrian. *The Roman Army at War, 200 BC–AD 100*. Oxford: Oxford University Press, 1996.

———. *The Fall of Carthage: The Punic Wars, 265–146 BC*. London: Cassell, 2000.

———. *The Complete Roman Army*. London: Thames & Hudson, 2003.

———. *Caesar: Life of a Colossus*. New Haven, Conn.: Yale University Press, 2007.

Goodall, Jane. *The Chimpanzees of Gombe: Patterns of Behavior*. Cambridge, Mass.: Harvard University Press, 1986.

———. "Unusual Violence in the Overthrow of an Alpha Male Chimpanzee at Gombe." In

Toshisada Nishida et al., eds., *Topics in Primatology*. Vol. 1, *Human Origins*, pp. 131–42. Tokyo: University of Tokyo Press, 1991.

Gorbachev, Mikhail. *Memoirs*. New York: Doubleday, 1995.

Gordon, D. H. "Swords, Rapiers, and Horse-Riders." *Antiquity* 27 (1953), pp. 67–78.

Gordon, Deborah. *Ants at Work: How an Insect Society Is Organized*. New York: Norton, 2000.

——. *Ant Encounters: Interaction Networks and Colony Behavior*. Princeton, N.J.: Princeton University Press, 2010.

Gordon, Matthew. *The Breaking of a Thousand Swords: A History of the Turkish Military of Samarra (AH 200–275/819–889 CE)*. Albany: State University of New York Press, 2001.

Gordon, Stewart. *The Marathas, 1600–1818*. Cambridge, U.K.: Cambridge University Press, 1993.

Gostner, Paul, et al. "New Radiological Insights into the Life and Death of the Tyrolean Ice Man." *Journal of Archaeological Science* 38 (2011), pp. 3425–31.

Gott, Richard. *Britain's Empire: Resistance, Repression and Revolt*. London: Verso, 2011.

Gotwald, William. *Army Ants: The Biology of Social Predation*. Ithaca, N.Y.: Cornell University Press, 1995.

Grachev, Andrei. *Gorbachev's Gamble: Soviet Foreign Policy and the End of the Cold War*. Cambridge, U.K.: Polity, 2008.

Graff, David. *Medieval Chinese Warfare, 300–900*. London: Routledge, 2002a.

——. "Strategy and Contingency in the Tang Defeat of the Eastern Turks, 629–630." In Di Cosmo 2002, pp. 33–71.

Gray, Colin. *Modern Strategy*. New York: Oxford University Press, 1999.

——. *Another Bloody Century: Future Warfare*. London: Weidenfeld and Nicolson, 2005.

Green, Richard, et al. "A Draft Sequence of the Neandertal Genome." *Science* 328 (2010), pp. 710–22.

Greenberg, Karen, ed. *The Torture Debate in America*. Cambridge, U.K.: Cambridge University Press, 2005.

Greene, Joshua, and Jonathan Haidt. "How (and Where) Does Moral Judgment Work?" *Trends in Cognitive Sciences* 6 (2002), pp. 517–23.

Griffith, Paddy. *Battle Tactics of the Western Front: The British Army's Art of Attack*. New Haven, Conn.: Yale University Press, 1996.

Grossman, Dave. *On Killing: The Psychological Cost of Learning to Kill in War and Society*. Rev. ed. Boston: Back Bay Books, 2009.

Gruen, Erich. *The Hellenistic World and the Coming of Rome*. 2 vols. Berkeley: University of California Press, 1984.

Guderian, Heinz. *Achtung—Panzer!* Trans. Christopher Duffy. First published in German, 1937. London: Cassell, 1992.

Gudmundsson, Bruce. *Stormtroop Tactics: Innovation in the German Army, 1914–1918*. Westport, Conn.: Praeger, 1995.

Guliaev, V. I. "Amazons in the Scythia: New Finds at the Middle Don, Southern Russia." *World Archaeology* 35 (2003), pp. 112–25.

Gurwood, John, ed. *The Dispatches of Field Marshal the Duke of Wellington During his Various Campaigns in India, Denmark, Portugal, Spain, the Low Countries, and France, from 1799 to 1818*. Vol. 2. London: John Murray, 1834.

Hackett, John, et al. *The Third World War, August 1985: A Future History*. London: Sidgwick & Jackson, 1978.

Hackney, Sheldon. "Southern Violence." *American Historical Review* 74 (1969), pp. 906–25.

Haile-Selassie, Yohannes, et al. "A New Hominin Foot from Ethiopia Shows Multiple Pliocene Bipedal Adaptations." *Nature* 483 (2012), pp. 565–69.

Hainsworth, Roger, and Christine Churches. *The Anglo-Dutch Naval Wars, 1652–1674*. Stroud, U.K.: Sutton, 1998.

Haldon, John. *Byzantium in the Seventh Century.* Cambridge, U.K.: Cambridge University Press, 1997.

Hall, Bert. *Weapons and Warfare in Renaissance Europe: Gunpowder, Technology, and Tactics.* Baltimore: Johns Hopkins University Press, 1997.

Halpern, Paul. *A Naval History of World War I.* London: Routledge, 1994.

Halsall, Guy, ed. *Violence and Society in the Early Medieval West.* Woodbridge, U.K.: Boydell Press, 1998.

———. *Warfare and Society in the Barbarian West, 450–900.* London: Routledge, 2003.

Hämäläinen, Pekka. *The Comanche Empire.* New Haven, Conn.: Yale University Press, 2008.

Hamblin, William. *Warfare in the Ancient Near East to 1600 BC.* London: Routledge, 2006.

Hamilton, Charles. "The Hellenistic World." In Raaflaub and Rosenstein 1999, pp. 163–91.

Hamilton, Richard, and Holger Herwig, eds. *The Origins of World War I.* Cambridge, U.K.: Cambridge University Press, 2003.

Hammes, Thomas. *The Sling and the Stone: On War in the 21st Century.* Minneapolis: Zenith Press, 2006.

Handel, Michael. *Masters of War: Classical Strategic Thought.* 3rd ed. London: Routledge, 2000.

Hansen, James, et al. "Global Temperature Update Through 2012," January 15, 2013. www.nasa.gov/pdf/719139main_2012_GISTEMP_summary.pdf.

Hanson, Victor Davis. *The Western Way of War: Infantry Battle in Ancient Greece.* New York: Oxford University Press, 1989.

———. *Carnage and Culture: Landmark Battles in the Rise of Western Power.* New York: Anchor, 2001.

Hanson, William S. *Agricola and the Conquest of the North.* London: Batsford, 1987.

Harcourt, Alexander, and Kelly Stewart. *Gorilla Society: Conflict, Compromise, and Co-operation Between the Sexes.* Chicago: University of Chicago Press, 2007.

Harding, Anthony. *European Societies in the Bronze Age.* Cambridge, U.K.: Cambridge University Press, 2000.

Harff, B. "No Lessons Learned from the Holocaust? Assessing the Risks of Genocide and Political Mass Murder Since 1955." *American Political Science Review* 97 (2003), pp. 57–73.

———. "Assessing Risks of Genocide and Politicide." In M. Marshall and Ted Gurr, eds., *Peace and Conflict 2005.* College Park, Md.: Center for International Development and Conflict Management, 2005.

Harmatta, Janos, ed. *History of Civilizations of Central Asia.* Vol. 2, *The Development of Sedentary and Nomadic Civilizations, 700 BC to 250 AD.* Paris: UNESCO, 1994.

Harper, John Lamberton. *American Visions of Europe: Franklin Delano Roosevelt, George F. Kennan, and Dean Acheson.* Cambridge, U.K.: Cambridge University Press, 1996.

Harries, Jill. *Law and Crime in the Roman World.* Cambridge, U.K.: Cambridge University Press, 2007.

Harris, Paul, and Sanders Marble. "The 'Step-by-Step' Approach: British Military Thought and Operational Method on the Western Front, 1915–1917." *War in History* 15 (2008), pp. 17–42.

Harris, Robert. *Fatherland.* New York: Book Club Associates, 1992.

Harris, William. *War and Imperialism in Republican Rome, 327–70 BC.* Oxford: Clarendon Press, 1979.

———. *Restraining Rage: The Ideology of Anger Control in Classical Antiquity.* Cambridge, Mass.: Harvard University Press, 2004.

Harris, William, and Kristine Iara, eds. *Maritime Technology in the Ancient Economy.* Portsmouth, R.I.: Journal of Roman Archaeology, 2011.

Harrison, Mark. *The Economics of World War II: Six Great Powers in International Comparison.* Cambridge, U.K.: Cambridge University Press, 1998.

Hart, Peter. *1918: A Very British Victory*. London: Weidenfeld and Nicolson, 2008.

Hassig, Ross. *Aztec Warfare: Imperial Expansion and Political Control*. Norman: University of Oklahoma Press, 1988.

——. *War and Society in Ancient Mesoamerica*. Berkeley: University of California Press, 1992.

——. *Time, History, and Belief in Aztec and Colonial Mexico*. Austin: University of Texas Press, 2001.

Hastings, Max. *The Korean War*. New York: Simon & Schuster, 1987.

——. *Inferno: The World at War, 1939–1945*. New York: Knopf, 2011.

Hathaway, Jane. *The Arab Lands Under Ottoman Rule, 1516–1800*. London: Longmans, 2008.

Hawke, Allan, and Ric Smith. *Australian Defence Force Posture Review 2012*. Canberra: Australian Government, 2012.

Haynes, Gary, ed. *American Megafaunal Extinctions at the End of the Pleistocene*. Amsterdam: Springer, 2009.

Headrick, Daniel. *Power over Peoples: Technology, Environments, and Western Imperialism, 1400 to the Present*. Princeton, N.J.: Princeton University Press, 2010.

Heather, Peter. *The Goths*. Oxford: Blackwell, 1996.

——. *The Fall of the Roman Empire: A New History of Rome and the Barbarians*. New York: Oxford University Press, 2006.

Hegre, Håvard, et al. "Predicting Armed Conflict, 2010–2050." *International Studies Quarterly* 55 (2013). http://folk.uio.no/hahegre/Papers/PredictionISQ_Final.pdf.

Hemingway, Ernest. *A Farewell to Arms*. New York: Scribner's, 1929.

Henrich, Joseph, et al. "The Weirdest People in the World?" *Behavioral and Brain Sciences* 33 (2010), pp. 61–135.

Herlihy, David, ed. *The History of Feudalism*. Atlantic Highlands, N.J.: Humanities Press, 1970.

Herman, Arthur. *To Rule the Waves: How the British Navy Shaped the Modern World*. New York: Harper, 2004.

——. *Freedom's Forge: How American Business Produced Victory in World War II*. New York: Random House, 2012.

Herring, George. *From Colony to Superpower: American Foreign Relations Since 1776*. Oxford: Oxford University Press, 2011.

Herwig, Holger. "The Battlefleet Revolution, 1885–1914." In MacGregor Knox and Williamson Murray, eds., *The Dynamics of Military Revolution, 1300–2050*, pp. 114–30. Cambridge, U.K.: Cambridge University Press, 2001.

——. *The Marne, 1914: The Opening of World War I and the Battle That Changed the World*. New York: Random House, 2009.

Heuser, Beatrice. *NATO, Britain, France, and the FRG: Nuclear Strategies and Forces for Europe, 1949–2000*. Basingstoke, U.K.: Macmillan, 1997.

——. "Victory in a Nuclear War? A Comparison of NATO and WTO War Aims and Strategies." *Contemporary European History* 7 (1998), pp. 311–27.

Hewitt, J., et al., eds. *Peace and Conflict 2008*. Boulder, Colo.: Paradigm, 2008.

Hickman, Tom. *God's Doodle: The Life and Times of the Penis*. London: Square Peg, 2012.

Hildinger, Erik. *Warriors of the Steppe: A Military History of Central Asia, 500 B.C. to A.D. 1700*. New York: Da Capo, 2001.

Hill, Kim, et al. "Mortality Rates Among Wild Chimpanzees." *Journal of Human Evolution* 40 (2001), pp. 437–50.

Hingley, Richard. *Roman Officers and English Gentlemen: The Imperial Origins of Roman Archaeology*. London: Routledge, 2000.

——. *Globalizing Roman Culture: Unity, Diversity, and Empire*. London: Routledge, 2005.

Hobsbawm, Eric. *The Age of Revolution, 1789–1848*. New York: New American Library, 1962.

——. *The Age of Capital, 1848–1875*. New York: New American Library, 1975.

——. *The Age of Empire, 1875–1914*. New York: Vintage, 1987.

——. *The Age of Extremes: A History of the World, 1914–1991*. New York: Random House, 1994.

Hochschild, Adam. *King Leopold's Ghost*. New York: Mariner, 1998.

Hoffenaar, Jan, et al., eds. *Blueprints for Battle: Planning for War in Central Europe, 1948–1968*. Lexington: University Press of Kentucky, 2012.

Hoffman, David. *The Dead Hand: The Untold Story of the Cold War Arms Race and Its Dangerous Legacy*. New York: Random House, 2009.

Hoffman, Philip. "Prices, the Military Revolution, and Western Europe's Comparative Advantage in Violence." *Economic History Review* 64, Supplement 1 (2011), pp. 39–59.

Hofstadter, Richard. *I Am a Strange Loop*. New York: Basic Books, 2007.

Hohmann, Gottfried, and Barbara Fruth. "Use and Function of Genital Contacts Among Female Bonobos." *Animal Behaviour* 60 (2000), pp. 107–20.

——. "Culture in Bonobos? Between-Species and Within-Species Variation in Behavior." *Current Anthropology* 44 (2003), pp. 563–71.

——. "Intra- and Inter-sexual Aggression by Bonobos in the Context of Mating." *Behaviour* 140 (2011), pp. 1389–413.

Hohmann, Gottfried, et al. "Plant Foods Consumed by *Pan*: Exploring the Variation of Nutritional Ecology Across Africa." *American Journal of Physical Anthropology* 141 (2010), pp. 476–85.

Hölldobler, Bert, and Edward O. Wilson. *The Ants*. Cambridge, Mass.: Harvard University Press, 1990.

——. *Superorganism: The Beauty, Elegance, and Strangeness of Insect Societies*. New York: Norton, 2008.

——. *The Leafcutter Ants: Civilization by Instinct*. New York: Norton, 2010.

Holloway, David. *Stalin and the Bomb: The Soviet Union and Atomic Energy, 1939–1956*. New Haven, Conn.: Yale University Press, 1994.

Holman, Brett. "World Police for World Peace: British Internationalism and the Threat of a Knock-Out Blow from the Air, 1919–1945." *War in History* 17 (2010), pp. 313–32.

Hopkirk, Peter. *The Great Game: The Struggle for Empire in Central Asia*. London: John Murray, 1990.

Horgan, John. *The End of War*. San Francisco: McSweeney's, 2012.

Horn, James, et al. *Jane: Starvation, Cannibalism, and Endurance at Jamestown*. Jamestown, Va.: Jamestown Rediscovery Project, 2013.

Howard, Michael. "Men Against Fire: The Doctrine of the Offensive in 1914." In Peter Paret, ed., *The Makers of Modern Strategy*, pp. 510–26. Princeton, N.J.: Princeton University Press, 1985.

——. *War in European History*. Rev. ed. Oxford: Oxford University Press, 2009.

Howard, Michael, and Peter Paret, eds. *Carl von Clausewitz, On War*. Princeton, N.J.: Princeton University Press, 1976.

Howard-Johnston, James. *Witnesses to a World Crisis: Historians and Histories of the Middle East in the Seventh Century*. New York: Oxford University Press, 2010.

Howarth, David. *1066: The Year of the Conquest*. Harmondsworth, U.K.: Penguin, 1981.

Hsieh, Mei-yu. "Viewing the Han Empire from the Edge." PhD diss., Stanford University, 2011.

Hsu, Cho-yun. *Ancient China in Transition: An Analysis of Social Mobility, 722–222 B.C.* Stanford, Calif.: Stanford University Press, 1965.

——. *Han Agriculture: The Formation of Early Chinese Agrarian Economy (206 BC–AD 220)*. Seattle: University of Washington Press, 1980.

Huang, Ray. *1587, a Year of No Significance: The Ming Dynasty in Decline*. New Haven, Conn.: Yale University Press, 1981.

Hughes, Daniel, ed. *Moltke on the Art of War: Selected Writings*. New York: Ballantine, 1995.

Huizinga, Jan. *The Waning of the Middle Ages*. Harmondsworth, U.K.: Penguin, 1955.

Hull, Isabel. *Absolute Destruction: Military Culture and the Practices of War in Imperial Germany.* Ithaca, N.Y.: Cornell University Press, 2005.

Hulsewé, A. F. P. *Remnants of Han Law.* Vol. 1. Leiden: E. J. Brill, 1955.

———. *Remnants of Ch'in Law.* Leiden: E. J. Brill, 1985.

Human Security Centre. *Human Security Report 2005.* New York: Oxford University Press, 2005.

———. *Human Security Brief 2006.* Vancouver, B.C.: Human Security Centre, 2006.

Human Security Report Project. *Human Security Brief 2007.* Vancouver, B.C.: Human Security Report Project, 2007.

———. *Miniatlas of Human Security.* Washington, D.C.: World Bank, 2008.

———. *Human Security Report Project 2009.* New York: Oxford University Press, 2009.

———. *Human Security Report 2009/10.* New York: Oxford University Press, 2011.

Idani, Gen'ichi. "Cases of Inter-unit Group Encounters in Pygmy Chimpanzees at Wamba, Zaire." In Akiyoshi Ehara et al., *Primatology Today,* pp. 235–38. Amsterdam: Elsevier, 1991.

Ikegumi, Eiko. *The Taming of the Samurai.* Cambridge, Mass.: Harvard University Press, 1997.

Ikenberry, John. *Liberal Leviathan: The Origins, Crisis, and Transformation of the American World Order.* Princeton, N.J.: Princeton University Press, 2011.

Ikram, S. M. *Muslim Civilization in India.* Ed. Ainslee Embree. New York: Columbia University Press, 1964.

Imber, Colin. *The Ottoman Empire, 1300–1650: The Structure of Power.* London: Palgrave, 2002.

Inalcik, Halil. "Capital Formation in the Ottoman Empire." *Journal of Economic History* 29 (1969), pp. 97–140.

Inalcik, Halil, and Donald Quataert, eds. *An Economic and Social History of the Ottoman Empire, 1300–1914.* Cambridge, U.K.: Cambridge University Press, 1994.

Inikori, Joseph, and Stanley Engermann, eds. *The Atlantic Slave Trade: Effects on Economies, Societies, and Peoples in Africa, the Americas, and Europe.* Durham, N.C.: Duke University Press, 1992.

Jacobsen, Thorkild. *The Treasures of Darkness: A History of Mesopotamian Religion.* New Haven, Conn.: Yale University Press, 1976.

James, Harold. *The Creation and Destruction of Value: The Globalization Cycle.* Cambridge, Mass.: Harvard University Press, 2009.

———. *Making the European Monetary Union.* Cambridge, Mass.: Harvard University Press, 2012.

James, Lawrence. *Raj: The Making and Unmaking of British India.* New York: St. Martin's Griffin, 1997.

Janko, Marek, et al. "Preservation of 5300 Year Old Red Blood Cells in the Iceman." *Journal of the Royal Society Interface* (2012). doi:10.1098/rsif.2012.0174. http://rsif.royalsociety publishing.org/content/early/2012/04/26/rsif.2012.0174.full.

Jarausch, Konrad. *The Enigmatic Chancellor: Bethmann Hollweg and the Hubris of Imperial Germany.* New Haven, Conn.: Yale University Press, 1983.

Jelavich, Barbara. *History of the Balkans.* Vol. 2. Cambridge, U.K.: Cambridge University Press, 1983.

Jenner, W. J. F. *Memories of Loyang: Yang Hsüan-chih and the Lost Capital (493–534).* Oxford: Clarendon Press, 1981.

Jervis, Robert. *The Meaning of the Nuclear Revolution: Statecraft and the Prospect of Armageddon.* Ithaca, N.Y.: Cornell University Press, 1989.

Jiang Qing. *A Confucian Constitutional Order: How China's Ancient Past Can Shape Its Political Future.* Trans. Edmund Ryden. Princeton, N.J.: Princeton University Press, 2013.

Joint Chiefs of Staff. *Decade of War.* Vol. 1, *Enduring Lessons from the Past Decade of Operations.* Suffolk, Va.: Joint and Coalition Operational Analysis, 2012. http://blogs .defensenews.com/saxotech-access/pdfs/decade-of-war-lessons-learned.pdf.

Joint Forces Command. "Unmanned Effects (UFX): Taking the Human Out of the Loop." Rapid Assessments Process (RAP) Report 03-10, 2003. www.hsdl.org/?view& did=705224.

Jonas, Raymond. *The Battle of Adwa: African Victory in the Age of Empire*. Cambridge, Mass.: Harvard University Press, 2011.

Jordana, Xavier, et al. "The Warriors of the Steppes: Osteological Evidence of Warfare and Violence from Pazyryk Tumuli in the Mongolian Altai." *Journal of Archaeological Science* 36 (2009), pp. 1319–27.

Jorgenson, J. *Western Indians*. San Francisco: Freeman, 1980.

Judd, Denis. *The Lion and the Tiger: The Rise and Fall of the British Raj, 1600–1947*. New York: Oxford University Press, 2010.

Jünger, Ernst. *Storm of Steel*. Trans. Michael Hofmann. First published in 1920; this translation from the final (1961) edition. London: Allen Lane, 2003.

Kagan, Donald, and Gregory Viggiano, eds. *Men of Bronze: Hoplite Warfare in Ancient Greece*. Princeton, N.J.: Princeton University Press, 2013.

Kagan, Robert. *Of Paradise and Power: America and Europe in the New World Order*. New York: Knopf, 2003.

——. *The World America Made*. New York: Knopf, 2012.

Kamen, Stanley. *Empire: How Spain Became a World Power, 1492–1763*. New York: Harper, 2003.

Kano, Takayoshi. *The Last Ape: Pygmy Chimpanzee Behavior and Ecology*. Stanford, Calif.: Stanford University Press, 1992.

Kanz, Fabian, and Karl Grossschmidt. "Head Injuries of Roman Gladiators." *Forensic Science International* 160 (2006), pp. 207–16.

Kaplan, Fred. *The Insurgents: David Petraeus and the Plot to Change the American Way of War*. New York: Simon & Schuster, 2013.

Kaplan, Robert. *The Revenge of Geography: What the Map Tells Us About Coming Conflicts and the Struggle Against Fate*. New York: Random House, 2012.

Karnow, Stanley. *Vietnam: A History*. New York: Penguin, 1986.

Kaufman, Philip, and Tom Wolfe. *The Right Stuff: A Screenplay from Tom Wolfe's Book*. University Park, Pa.: Script City, 1980.

Keaney, Thomas, and Eliot Cohen. *Gulf War Air Power Survey: Summary Report*. Philadelphia: Diane, 1998.

Kearns, Gerard. *Geopolitics and Empire: The Legacy of Halford Mackinder*. New York: Oxford University Press, 2009.

Keegan, John. *The Face of Battle: A Study of Agincourt, Waterloo & the Somme*. New York: Viking Press, 1976.

——. *A History of Warfare*. New York: Vintage, 1993.

——. *The First World War*. New York: Vintage, 1998.

——. *The American Civil War*. New York: Vintage, 2009.

Keeley, Lawrence. *War Before Civilization: The Myth of the Peaceful Savage*. New York: Oxford University Press, 1996.

Keller, Andreas, et al. "New Insights into the Tyrolean Iceman's Origin and Phenotype as Inferred by Whole-Genome Sequencing." *Nature Communications* 3 (2012). doi:10.1038 /ncomms1701.

Kemp, Barry. *The City of Akhenaten and Nefertiti: Amarna and Its People*. London: Thames & Hudson, 2012.

Kempe, Frederick. *Berlin 1961: Kennedy, Khrushchev, and the Most Dangerous Place on Earth*. New York: Putnam's, 2011.

Kennedy, Hugh. *The Armies of the Caliphs: Military and Society in the Early Islamic State*. London: Routledge, 2001.

——. *The Great Arab Conquests*. Philadelphia: Da Capo, 2007.

Kennedy, Paul. *The Rise and Fall of British Naval Mastery*. London: Allen Lane, 1976.

——. *The Rise of Anglo-German Antagonism, 1860–1914*. Boston: Allen Unwin, 1980.

——. *The Rise and Fall of the Great Powers*. New York: Vintage, 1987.

Kennedy, Ross. *The Will to Believe: Woodrow Wilson, World War I, and America's Strategy for Peace and Security*. Kent, Ohio: Kent State University Press, 2009.

Keppie, Lawrence. *The Making of the Roman Army: From Republic to Empire*. London: Routledge, 1984.

Kershaw, Ian. *Hitler, 1889–1936: Hubris*. New York: Norton, 2000.

Keynes, John Maynard. *A Tract on Monetary Reform*. London, 1923.

Khan, Iqtidar Alam. *Gunpowder and Firearms: Warfare in Medieval India*. New Delhi: Oxford University Press, 2004.

Khanna, Ayesha, and Parag Khanna. *Hybrid Reality: Thriving in the Emerging Human-Technology Civilization*. TED Books, 2012.

Kidder, Tristram, et al. "Sanyangzhuang: Early Farming and a Han Settlement Preserved Beneath Yellow River Flood Deposits." *Antiquity* 86 (2012), pp. 30–47.

Kinsella, David, et al. "No Rest for the Democratic Peace." *American Political Science Review* 99 (2005), pp. 453–72.

Kirch, Patrick. *The Evolution of Polynesian Chiefdoms*. Cambridge, U.K.: Cambridge University Press, 1984.

——. *How Chiefs Became Kings: Divine Kingship and the Rise of Archaic States in Ancient Hawai'i*. Berkeley: University of California Press, 2010.

Kirshner, Julius, and Karl Morrison, eds. *University of Chicago Readings in Western Civilization*. Vol. 4, *Medieval Europe*. Chicago: University of Chicago Press, 1986.

Kistler, John. *War Elephants*. Lincoln, Neb.: Bison Books, 2007.

Klein, Richard. *The Human Career: Human Biological and Cultural Origins*. 3rd ed. Chicago: University of Chicago Press, 2009.

Knauft, Bruce. *Good Company and Violence: Sorcery and Social Action in a Lowland New Guinea Society*. Berkeley: University of California Press, 1985.

Knox, MacGregor, and Williamson Murray, eds. *The Dynamics of Military Revolution, 1300–2050*. Cambridge, U.K.: Cambridge University Press, 2001.

Knüse, Christopher, and Martin Smith, eds. *The Routledge Handbook of the Bioarchaeology of Human Conflict*. London: Routledge, 2013.

Kolata, Alan. *The Tiwanaku*. Oxford: Blackwell, 1993.

Kolb, Michael, and B. Dixon. "Landscapes of War: Rules and Conventions of Conflict in Ancient Hawai'i (and Elsewhere)." *American Antiquity* 67 (2002), pp. 514–34.

Kolsky, Elizabeth. *Colonial Justice in British India: White Violence and the Rule of Law*. Cambridge, U.K.: Cambridge University Press, 2010.

Kramer, Alan. *Dynamic of Destruction: Culture and Mass Killing in the First World War*. Oxford: Oxford University Press, 2007.

Krämer, Augustin. *The Samoa Islands*. Vol. 2, *Material Culture*. First published in German, 1902. Honolulu: University of Hawai'i Press, 1995.

Krentz, Peter. "Casualties in Hoplite Battles." *Classical Antiquity* 4 (1985), pp. 13–20.

Krepinevich, Andrew. *The Army and Vietnam*. Baltimore: Johns Hopkins University Press, 1986.

——. "Cavalry to Computer: The Pattern of Military Revolutions." *National Interest* 37 (1994), pp. 30–42.

——. *Why AirSea Battle?* Washington, D.C.: Center for Strategic and Budget Assessment, 2010. www.csbaonline.org/publications/2010/02/why-airsea-battle/.

Kristensen, Hans, and Robert Norris. "Chinese Nuclear Forces, 2011." *Bulletin of the Atomic Scientists* 67.6 (2011), pp. 61–87.

——. "Russian Nuclear Forces, 2012." *Bulletin of the Atomic Scientists* 68 (2012), pp. 87–97.

——. "US Nuclear Forces, 2013." *Bulletin of the Atomic Scientists* 69.2 (2013), pp. 77–86.

Kristiansen, Kristian. "The Tale of the Sword: Swords and Swordfighters in Bronze Age Europe." *Oxford Journal of Archaeology* 21 (2002), pp. 319–32.

Kristiansen, Kristian, and Thomas Larsson. *The Rise of Bronze Age Society: Travels, Transmissions, and Transformations*. Cambridge, U.K.: Cambridge University Press, 2005.

Krug, Etienne, et al. *World Report on Violence and Health*. Geneva: World Health Organization, 2002.

Kuhn, Dieter. *The Age of Confucian Rule: The Song Transformation of China*. Cambridge, Mass.: Harvard University Press, 2009.

Kuhrt, Amélie. *The Ancient Near East*. 2 vols. London: Routledge, 1995.

Kurzweil, Ray. *The Singularity Is Near: When Humans Transcend Biology*. New York: Viking, 2005.

———. *How to Create a Mind: The Secret of Human Thought Revealed*. New York: Viking, 2013.

Kynaston, David. *Austerity Britain, 1945–51*. London: Bloomsbury, 2007.

Lacina, Bethany. *Battle Deaths Dataset, 1946–2009: Codebook for Version 3.0*. Oslo: Center for the Study of Civil War and International Peace Research Institute, 2009.

Lacina, Bethany, and Nils Petter Gleditsch. "Monitoring Trends in Global Combat: A New Dataset in Battle Deaths." *European Journal of Population* 21 (2005), pp. 145–66.

Lacina, Bethany, et al. "The Declining Risk of Death in Battle." *International Studies Quarterly* 50 (2006), pp. 673–80.

Laitin, David, et al. "Geographic Axes and the Persistence of Cultural Diversity." *Proceedings of the National Academy of Sciences* 110 (2012). doi:10.1073/pnas.1205338109.

Landergraber, Kevin, et al. "Generation Times in Wild Chimpanzees and Gorillas Suggest Earlier Divergence Times in Great Ape and Human Evolution." *Proceedings of the National Academy of Sciences* 109 (2012), pp. 15716–21.

Lazenby, J. F. *The Defence of Greece, 480–479 BC*. Warminster, U.K.: Aris & Phillips, 1993.

Lazuén, Talía. "European Neanderthal Stone Hunting Weapons Reveal Complex Behavior Long Before the Appearance of Modern Humans." *Journal of Archaeological Science* 39 (2012), pp. 2304–11.

Lebedynsky, Iaroslav. *Les Saces: Les "scythes" d'Asie, VIII siècle av. J.-C.–IV siècle apr. J.-C.* Paris: Errance, 2006.

LeBlanc, Steven. *Prehistoric Warfare in the American Southwest*. Salt Lake City: University of Utah Press, 1999.

LeBlanc, Steven, and Katherine Register. *Constant Battles: Why We Fight*. New York: St. Martin's Press, 2003.

Lee, Richard. *The !Kung San: Men, Women, and Work in a Foraging Society*. Cambridge, U.K.: Cambridge University Press, 1979.

Lee, Wayne, ed. *Warfare and Culture in World History*. New York: New York University Press, 2011.

Lee-Thorp, Julia, et al. "Isotopic Evidence for an Early Shift to C_4 Resources by Pliocene Hominins in Chad." *Proceedings of the National Academy of Sciences* 109 (2012). doi:10.1073/pnas.1204209109.

Leffler, Melvyn, and Odd Arne Westad, eds. *The Cambridge History of the Cold War*. 3 vols. Cambridge, U.K.: Cambridge University Press, 2010.

Lendon, John. "The Rhetoric of Combat: Greek Military Theory and Roman Culture in Julius Caesar's Battle Descriptions." *Classical Antiquity* 18 (1999), pp. 273–329.

Léon-Portilla, Miguel. *The Broken Spears: The Aztec Account of the Conquest of Mexico*. Rev. ed. Boston: Beacon Press, 2006.

Lerman, Katharine. *Bismarck*. London: Longmans, 2004.

Levi, Barbara, et al. "Civilian Casualties from 'Limited' Nuclear Attacks on the USSR." *International Security* 12.3 (1987/88), pp. 168–89.

Levi, Michael. *The Power Surge: Energy, Opportunity, and the Battle for America's Future*. New York: Oxford University Press, 2013.

Levy, Jack. *War in the Modern Great Power System, 1495–1975*. Lexington: University Press of Kentucky, 1983.

Levy, Jack, and William Thompson. *The Arc of War: Origins, Escalation, and Transformation*. Chicago: University of Chicago Press, 2011.

Lewis, Mark Edward. *Sanctioned Violence in Early China*. Albany: State University of New York Press, 1990.

———. "Warring States: Political History." In Michael Loewe and Edward Shaughnessy, eds., *The Cambridge History of Ancient China*, pp. 587–650. Cambridge, U.K.: Cambridge University Press, 1999.

———. "The Han Abolition of Universal Military Service." In Hans van de Ven, ed., *Warfare in Chinese History*. Leiden: E. J. Brill, 2000.

———. *The Early Chinese Empires: Qin and Han*. Cambridge, Mass.: Harvard University Press, 2007.

———. *China Between Empires: The Northern and Southern Dynasties*. Cambridge, Mass.: Harvard University Press, 2009a.

———. *China's Cosmopolitan Empire: The Tang Dynasty*. Cambridge, Mass.: Harvard University Press, 2009b.

Li, Bozhong. *Agricultural Development in Jiangnan, 1620–1850*. New York: St. Martin's Press, 1997.

Liddell Hart, Basil. *The Memoirs of Captain Liddell Hart*. 2 vols. London: Cassell, 1965.

———. *Strategy*. 2nd ed. London: Faber and Faber, 1967.

Lincoln, W. Bruce. *Red Victory: A History of the Russian Civil War, 1918–1921*. New York: Da Capo, 1999.

Lintott, Andrew. *Violence in Republican Rome*. London: Croom Helm, 1968.

Litvinsky, B. A. *History of Civilizations of Central Asia*. Vol. 3, *The Crossroads of Civilizations, AD 250 to 750*. Paris: UNESCO, 1996.

Liu, Xinru. *Ancient India and Ancient China: Trade and Religious Exchanges, AD 1–600*. Delhi: Oxford University Press, 1988.

———. "Migration and Settlement of the Yuezhi-Kushan." *Journal of World History* 12 (2001), pp. 261–92.

Liverani, Mario. "The Fall of the Assyrian Empire." In Susan Alcock et al., eds., *Empires*, pp. 374–91. Cambridge, U.K.: Cambridge University Press, 2001.

———. *Akkad, the First World Empire*. Padua: Sargon, 2003.

———. *Uruk: The First City*. London: Equinox, 2006.

Livi-Bacci, Massimo. *The Population of Europe: A History*. Trans. Cynthia De Nardi Ipsen and Carl Ipsen. Oxford: Blackwell, 2000.

Lloyd, Alan. "Philip II and Alexander the Great: The Moulding of Macedon's Army." In Alan Lloyd, ed., *Battle in Antiquity*, pp. 161–98. London: Duckworth, 1996.

Lloyd, T. O. *The British Empire, 1558–1983*. Oxford: Oxford University Press, 1984.

Lloyd George, David. *War Memoirs of David Lloyd George, 1914–1918*. Vol. 1. Boston: Houghton Mifflin, 1933.

Loewe, Michael. *Crisis and Conflict in Han China, 104 BC to AD 9*. London: George Allen and Unwin, 1974.

———. "The Former Han Dynasty." In Twitchett and Loewe 1986, pp. 103–221.

———. *The Government of the Qin and Han Empires, 221 BCE–220 CE*. Indianapolis: Hackett, 2006.

Loewe, Michael, and Eva Wilson. *Everyday Life in Early Imperial China*. Indianapolis: Hackett, 2005.

Lomatuway'ma, M., et al., eds. *Hopi Ruin Legends*. Lincoln: University of Nebraska Press, 1993.

Lombard, Marlize. "Quartz-Tipped Arrows Older Than 60 ka: Further Use-Trace Evidence from Sibudu, Kwazulu-Natal, South Africa." *Journal of Archaeological Science* 58 (2011), pp. 1918–30.

Long, William, and Peter Brecke. *War and Reconciliation: Reason and Emotion in Conflict Resolution*. Cambridge, Mass.: MIT Press, 2003.

Lorge, Peter. *War, Politics, and Society in Early Modern China, 900–1795*. London: Routledge, 2005.

——. *The Asian Military Revolution: From Gunpowder to the Bomb*. Cambridge, U.K.: Cambridge University Press, 2008.

Lovejoy, Paul. *Transformations in Slavery: A History of Slavery in Africa*. 2nd ed. Cambridge, U.K.: Cambridge University Press, 2000.

Lowe, Keith. *Savage Continent: Europe in the Aftermath of World War II*. New York: St. Martin's Press, 2012.

Lu, Gwei-djen, et al. "The Oldest Representation of a Bombard." *Technology and Culture* 29 (1988), pp. 594–605.

Lupfer, Timothy. *The Dynamics of Doctrine: The Changes in German Tactical Doctrine During the First World War*. Leavenworth, Kans.: U.S. Army Command, 1981.

Lüthi, Lorenz. *The Sino-Soviet Split: Cold War in the Communist World*. Princeton, N.J.: Princeton University Press, 2008.

Luttwak, Edward. *The Grand Strategy of the Roman Empire*. Baltimore: Johns Hopkins University Press, 1976.

——. *Strategy: The Logic of War and Peace*. Rev. ed. Cambridge, Mass.: Belknap Press, 2001.

——. *The Grand Strategy of the Byzantine Empire*. Cambridge, Mass.: Belknap Press, 2009.

——. *The Rise of China vs. the Logic of Strategy*. Cambridge, Mass.: Belknap Press, 2012.

Lutz, Ralph Haswell, ed. *The Causes of the German Collapse in 1918*. London: Archon Books, 1969.

Lynn, John. *Battle: A History of Combat and Culture*. Boulder, Colo.: Westview Press, 2003.

Lyon, Rod, and Andrew Davies. *Assessing the Defence White Paper 2009*. Canberra: Australian Strategic Policy Institute Policy Analysis Paper 41, 2009. Available at www.aspi.org.au/publications/publications_all.aspx.

Maas, Michael, ed. *The Cambridge Companion to the Age of Justinian*. Cambridge, U.K.: Cambridge University Press, 2005.

MacFarquhar, Roderick, and Michael Schoenhals. *Mao's Last Revolution*. Cambridge, Mass.: Harvard University Press, 2006.

Macintyre, Ben. *The Man Who Would Be King: The First American in Afghanistan*. New York: Farrar, Straus and Giroux, 2004.

Mackil, Emily. *Creating a Common Polity: Religion, Economics, and Politics in the Making of the Greek Koinon*. Berkeley: University of California Press, 2013.

Mackinder, Halford. "The Geographical Pivot of History." *Geographical Journal* 23 (1904), pp. 421–37.

MacLeod, Ken. *The Cassini Division*. New York: Orbit, 1998.

Macmillan, Margaret. *Nixon and Mao: The Week That Changed the World*. New York: Random House, 2008.

MacMullen, Ramsay. *Roman Social Relations, 50 B.C. to A.D. 284*. New Haven, Conn.: Yale University Press, 1974.

Maddison, Angus. *Statistics on World Population GDP and Per Capita GDP, 1–2008 AD* (2010). www.ggdc.net/maddison/Maddison.htm.

Magill, Clayton, et al. "Ecosystem Variability and Early Human Habitats in Eastern Africa." *Proceedings of the National Academy of Sciences* 110 (2012). doi:10.1073/pnas.1206276110.

Mahan, Alfred Thayer. *The Influence of Sea Power upon History, 1660–1783*. Boston: Little, Brown, 1890.

Mailer, Norman. *Armies of the Night: History as a Novel/The Novel as History*. New York: New American Library, 1968.

Mann, Charles. *1491: New Revelations of the Americas Before Columbus*. New York: Knopf, 2005.

——. *1493: Uncovering the New World Columbus Created*. New York: Knopf, 2011.

Mann, Michael. *The Sources of Social Power.* Vol. 1, *A History of Power from the Beginning to A.D. 1760.* Cambridge, U.K.: Cambridge University Press, 1986.

——. *The Sources of Social Power.* Vol. 3, *Global Empires and Revolution, 1890–1945.* Cambridge, U.K.: Cambridge University Press, 2012.

Marcus, George, and Michael Fischer. *Anthropology as Cultural Critique: An Experimental Moment in the Human Sciences.* Chicago: University of Chicago Press, 1988.

Margulis, Lynn, and Dorion Sagan. *Microcosmos: Four Billion Years of Microbial Evolution.* London: Allen & Unwin, 1987.

Marlantes, Karl. *What It Is Like to Go to War.* New York: Atlantic Monthly Press, 2011.

Marr, Andrew. *A History of Modern Britain.* London: Macmillan, 2007.

Marshall, John. "Excavations at Bhita." *Annual Report of the Archaeological Survey of India* (1911–12), pp. 29–94.

——. *Taxila: An Illustrated Account of Archaeological Excavations.* 3 vols. Cambridge, U.K.: Cambridge University Press, 1951. Reprint, Varanasi: Bhartiya, 1975.

Marshall, P. J., ed. *The Writings and Speeches of Edmund Burke.* Vol. 6, *India: The Launching of the Hastings Impeachment, 1786–88.* Oxford: Oxford University Press, 1991.

——. "Britain and the World in the Eighteenth Century: I–III." *Transactions of the Royal Historical Society,* 6th ser., 8 (1998), pp. 1–18; 9 (1999), pp. 1–16; 10 (2000), pp. 1–16.

Martinage, Robert, and Michael Vickers. *The Revolution in War.* Washington, D.C.: Center for Strategic and Budget Assessment, 2004. www.csbaonline.org/publications/2004/12/the-revolution-in-war/.

Martinez, Ignacio, et al. "On the Origin of Language: The Atapuerca Evidence." Paper delivered at the Eighty-First Annual Meeting of the American Association of Physical Anthropologists, Portland, Ore., April 12, 2012. www.physanth.org/annual-meeting/2012/aapa-meeting-program-2012.

Marx, Karl. *Pre-capitalist Economic Formations.* Trans. Jack Cohen. London: Lawrence & Wishart, 1964. Written in German, 1857–58, but not published.

Maslen, M. W., and Piers Mitchell. "Medical Theories on the Cause of Death in Crucifixion." *Journal of the Royal Society of Medicine* 99 (2006), pp. 185–88.

Massie, Robert. *Castles of Steel: Winning the Great War at Sea.* New York: Ballantine, 2003.

Mattingly, David. *An Imperial Possession: Britain in the Roman Empire.* London: Penguin, 2006.

——. *Imperialism, Power, and Identity: Experiencing the Roman Empire.* Princeton, N.J.: Princeton University Press, 2011.

May, Ernest. *Strange Victory: Hitler's Conquest of France.* New York: Hill & Wang, 2001.

May, Timothy. *The Mongol Art of War: Chinggis Khan and the Mongol Military System.* London: Pen & Sword, 2007.

Maynard Smith, John. *Evolution and the Theory of Games.* Cambridge, U.K.: Cambridge University Press, 1982.

Mayor, Adrienne. *Amazons in Love and War.* Princeton, N.J.: Princeton University Press, 2014.

Mazower, Mark. *Hitler's Empire: How the Nazis Ruled Europe.* New York: Penguin, 2008.

——. *Governing the World: The Rise and Fall of an Idea, 1815 to the Present.* New York: Penguin, 2012.

McAlpin, Michelle. "Famine, Epidemics, and Population Growth: The Case of India." *Journal of Interdisciplinary History* 14 (1983), pp. 351–66.

McBrearty, Sally, and Nina Jablonski. "First Fossil Chimpanzee." *Nature* 437 (2005), pp. 105–8.

McCall, Grant, and Nancy Shields. "Examining the Evidence from Small-Scale Societies and Early Prehistory and Implications for Modern Theories of Aggression and Violence." *Aggression and Violent Behavior* 13 (2008), pp. 1–9.

McClellan, Thomas. "Early Fortifications: The Missing Walls of Jericho." *Baghdader Mitteilungen* 18 (2006), pp. 593–610.

McCormick, Michael, et al. "Climate Change During and After the Roman Empire: Reconstructing the Past from Scientific and Historical Evidence." *Journal of Interdisciplinary History* 43 (2012), pp. 169–220.

McGlynn, Sean. *By Sword and Fire: Cruelty and Atrocity in Medieval Warfare.* London: Cassell, 2010.

McGrew, William, et al., ed. *Great Ape Societies.* Cambridge, U.K.: Cambridge University Press, 1996.

McGuire, Martin, and Mancur Olson. "The Economics of Autocracy and Majority Rule: The Invisible Hand and the Use of Force." *Journal of Economic Literature* 34 (1996), pp. 72–96.

McHenry, Henry, and Catherine Coffing. "*Australopithecus* to *Homo*: Transformations in Body and Mind." *Annual Review of Anthropology* 29 (2000), pp. 129–46.

McKitterick, Rosamond. *Charlemagne: The Formation of European Identity.* Cambridge, U.K.: Cambridge University Press, 2008.

McLaughlin, Raoul. *Rome and the Distant East: Trade Routes to the Ancient Lands of Arabia, India, and China.* London: Continuum, 2010.

McMeekin, Sean. *The Russian Origins of the First World War.* Cambridge, Mass.: Belknap Press, 2011.

McNeill, William. *Plagues and Peoples.* New York: Anchor, 1976.

———. *The Pursuit of Power: Technology, Armed Force, and Society Since AD 1000.* Chicago: University of Chicago Press, 1982.

———. *Arnold J. Toynbee: A Life.* New York: Oxford University Press, 1989.

McNitt, Frank, *Navajo Wars: Military Campaigns, Slave Raids, and Reprisals.* Albuquerque: University of New Mexico Press, 1990.

McPherson, James. *Battle Cry of Freedom: The Civil War Era.* New York: Oxford University Press, 1988.

Mead, Margaret. *Coming of Age in Samoa: A Psychological Study of Primitive Youth for Western Civilization.* New York: William Morrow, 1928.

———. "Warfare Is Only an Invention—Not a Biological Necessity." *Asia* 3 (1940), pp. 402–5.

Melville, Sarah. "The Last Campaign: The Assyrian Way of War and the Collapse of the Empire." In Lee 2011, pp. 12–33.

Mercatante, Steven. *Why Germany Nearly Won: A New History of the Second World War in Europe.* Westport, Conn.: Praeger, 2012.

Meyer, Matthias, et al. "A High-Coverage Genome Sequence from an Archaic Denisovan Individual." *Science* 338 (2012), pp. 222–26.

Middlekauff, Robert. *The Glorious Cause: The American Revolution, 1763–1789.* New York: Oxford University Press, 2007.

Milani, Abbas. *The Myth of the Great Satan: A New Look at America's Relations with Iran.* Stanford, Calif.: Hoover Institution Press, 2011.

Miles, Richard. *Carthage Must Be Destroyed.* New York: Penguin, 2011.

Millar, Fergus. *The Emperor in the Roman World.* London: Duckworth, 1977.

Miller, David. *The Cold War: A Military History.* London: Pimlico, 1998.

Misra, Amaresh. *War of Civilisations: India, A.D. 1857.* 2 vols. New Delhi: Rupa, 2008.

Mitani, John, et al. "Lethal Intergroup Aggression Leads to Territorial Expansion in Wild Chimpanzees." *Current Biology* 20.12 (2010), pp. R507–8.

Mithen, Steven. *After the Ice: Global Human History, 20,000–5000 BC.* Cambridge, Mass.: Harvard University Press, 2003.

———. *The Singing Neanderthals.* London: Weidenfeld and Nicolson, 2005.

Mitter, Rana. *China's War with Japan, 1937–1945: The Struggle for Survival.* London: Allen Lane, 2013.

Moggridge, Donald. *Maynard Keynes: An Economists' Biography*. London: Routledge, 1992.

Mohan, C. Raja. *Samudra Manthan: Sino-Indian Rivalry in the Indo-Pacific*. New York: Carnegie Foundation, 2012.

Montefiore, Simon Sebag. *Stalin: The Court of the Red Tsar*. New York: Knopf, 2004.

Montgomery, Bernard. "A Look Through a Window at World War III." *Journal of the Royal United Services Institute* 99 (1954), pp. 505–9.

Mookerjee, R. K. *Chandragupta Maurya and His Times*. Delhi: Motilal Banarsidass, 1966.

Moore, Gordon. "Cramming More Components onto Integrated Circuits." *Electronics* 38.8 (August 19, 1965), pp. 114–17. ftp://download.intel.com/research/silicon/moorespaper.pdf.

Morgan, David. *Medieval Persia, 1040–1797*. London: Longman, 1988.

Morillo, Stephen. "Expecting Cowardice: Medieval Battle Tactics Reconsidered." *Journal of Medieval Military History* 4 (2006), pp. 65–73.

Morozov, Evgeny. *To Save Everything, Click Here: The Folly of Technological Solutionism*. New York: PublicAffairs, 2013.

Morris, Desmond. *The Naked Ape: A Zoologist's Study of the Human Animal*. London: Corgi, 1967.

Morris, Ian. "The Greater Athenian State." In Ian Morris and Walter Scheidel, eds., *The Dynamics of Ancient Empires*, pp. 99–177. New York: Oxford University Press, 2009.

——. *Why the West Rules—for Now: The Patterns of History, and What They Reveal About the Future*. New York: Farrar, Straus and Giroux, 2010.

——. *The Measure of Civilization: How Social Development Decides the Fate of Nations*. Princeton, N.J.: Princeton University Press, 2013.

——. *Foragers, Farmers, and Fossil Fuels: How Values Evolve*. Princeton, N.J.: Princeton University Press, in press.

Morris, James [Jan]. *Farewell the Trumpets: An Imperial Retreat*. London: Faber and Faber, 1978.

Mostert, Noël. *The Line upon a Wind: The Great War at Sea, 1793–1815*. New York: Norton, 2008.

Muchembled, Robert. *A History of Violence: From the End of the Middle Ages to the Present*. Cambridge, Mass.: Polity, 2012.

Mueller, John. *The Remnants of War*. Ithaca, N.Y.: Cornell University Press, 2004.

Mukherjee, B. N. *Mathura and Its Society—the Saka-Pahlava Phase*. Calcutta: J. B. Enterprises, 1981.

——. *The Rise and Fall of the Kushana Empire*. Calcutta: J. B. Enterprises, 1988.

——. *The Character of the Maurya Empire*. Calcutta: J. B. Enterprises, 2000.

Muller, Martin, and Richard Wrangham, eds. *Sexual Coercion in Primates and Humans*. Cambridge, Mass.: Harvard University Press, 2009.

Muller, Richard. "Close Air Support: The German, British, and American Experiences, 1918–1941." In Murray and Millett 1996, pp. 144–90.

Mulligan, William. *The Origins of the First World War*. Cambridge, U.K.: Cambridge University Press, 2010.

Murphy, Eileen. *Iron Age Archaeology and Trauma from Aymyrlyg, South Siberia*. British Archaeological Reports International Series 1152. Oxford: Archaeopress, 2003.

Murphy, Melissa, et al. "Violence and Weapon-Related Trauma at Puruchuco-Huaquerones, Peru." *American Journal of Physical Anthropology* 142 (2010), pp. 636–49.

Murray, Sarah. "Trade, Imports, and Society in Early Greece, 1300–900 BC." PhD diss., Stanford University, 2013.

Murray, Williamson. "Armored Warfare: The British, French, and German Experiences." In Murray and Millett 1996, pp. 6–49.

——. *Military Adaptation in War with Fear of Change*. Cambridge, U.K.: Cambridge University Press, 2011.

Murray, Williamson, and Allan Millett, eds. *Military Innovation in the Interwar Period.* Cambridge, U.K.: Cambridge University Press, 1996.

Naam, Ramez. *Nexus: Mankind Gets an Upgrade.* New York: Angry Robot, 2013a.

———. *Crux: Upgrade in Progress.* New York: Angry Robot, 2013b.

Nadali, Davide. "Assyrian Open Field Battles: An Attempt at Reconstruction and Analysis." In J. Vidial, ed., *Studies on War in the Ancient Near East,* pp. 153–63. Münster: Ugarit, 2010.

Naimark, Norman. *Stalin's Genocides.* Princeton, N.J.: Princeton University Press, 2010.

Nasar, Sylvia. *A Beautiful Mind: The Life of Mathematical Genius and Nobel Laureate John Nash.* New York: Simon & Schuster, 1998.

National Intelligence Council. *Global Trends 2025: A Transformed World.* Washington, D.C.: Government Printing Office, 2008. Available at www.dni.gov/nic/globaltrends.

———. *Global Trends 2030: Alternative Worlds.* Washington, D.C.: Office of the Director of National Intelligence, 2012. Available at www.dni.gov/nic/globaltrends.

Needham, Joseph. *Science and Civilisation in China.* Vol. 4, *Physics and Physical Technology.* Pt. 3, *Civil Engineering and Nautics.* Cambridge, U.K.: Cambridge University Press, 1971.

Needham, Joseph, et al. *Science and Civilisation in China.* Vol. 5, *Chemistry and Chemical Technology.* Pt. 5, *Military Technology, the Gunpowder Epic.* Cambridge, U.K.: Cambridge University Press, 1986.

Nehru, Jawaharlal. *Glimpses of World History: Being Further Letters to His Daughter, Written in Prison, and Containing a Rambling Account of History for Young People.* New York: John Day, 1942.

Nerlich, Andreas, et al. "New Evidence for Ötzi's Final Trauma." *Intensive Care Medicine* 35 (January 2009), pp. 1138–39.

Nguyen, Lien-Hang. *Hanoi's War: An International History of the War for Peace in Vietnam.* Chapel Hill: University of North Carolina Press, 2012.

Nippel, Wilfried. *Public Order in Ancient Rome.* Cambridge, U.K.: Cambridge University Press, 1995.

Nivette, Amy. "Violence in Non-state Societies: A Review." *British Journal of Criminology* 51 (2011), pp. 578–98.

Norris, Robert, and Hans Kristensen. "Global Nuclear Stockpiles, 1945–2006." *Bulletin of the Atomic Scientists,* July/August 2006, pp. 64–66.

North, Douglass, et al. *Violence and Social Orders: A Conceptual Framework for Interpreting Recorded Human History.* Cambridge, U.K.: Cambridge University Press, 2009.

Noyes, Alexander. *The War Period of American Finance.* New York: Putnam's, 1926.

Nye, Joseph. *The Future of Power.* New York: PublicAffairs, 2011.

Nyland, Ann. *The Kikkuli Method of Horsetraining.* Rev. ed. Sydney: Maryannu Press, 2009.

Obermeyer, Ziyad, et al. "Fifty Years of Violent War Deaths from Vietnam to Bosnia: Analysis of Data from the World Health Survey Programme." *British Medical Journal* 336 (2008), pp. 1482–86.

O'Brien, Phillips Payson. *British and American Naval Power: Politics and Policy, 1900–1936.* Westport, Conn.: Praeger, 1998.

Odom, William. "Soviet Military Doctrine." *Foreign Affairs* 67.2 (Winter 1988), pp. 114–34.

O'Donnell, James. *The Ruin of the Roman Empire.* New York: HarperCollins, 2008.

O'Fallon, Brendan, and Lars Fehren-Schmitz. "Native Americans Experienced a Strong Population Bottleneck Coincident with European Contact." *Proceedings of the National Academy of Sciences* 108 (2011), pp. 20444–48.

O'Hanlon, Michael. *A Moderate Plan for Additional Defense Budget Cuts.* Washington, D.C.: Brookings Institution, Policy Paper 30, February 2013. www.brookings.edu/~/media/Research/Files/Papers/2013/1/defense%20budget%20cuts%20ohanlon/defense%20budget%20cuts%20ohanlon.pdf.

Olson, Mancur. *Power and Prosperity*. New York: Basic Books, 2000.

Origo, Iris. *The Merchant of Prato: Daily Life in a Medieval Italian City*. Harmondsworth, U.K.: Penguin, 1957.

Orwell, George. *The Road to Wigan Pier*. London: Gollancz, 1937.

Otterbein, Keith. *The Evolution of War: A Cross-Cultural Study*. 3rd ed. New Haven, Conn.: Human Relations Area Files Press, 1989.

———. *How War Began*. College Station: Texas A&M University Press, 2004.

Outram, Alan, et al. "The Earliest Horse Harnessing and Milking." *Science* 323 (2009), pp. 1332–35.

Overy, Richard. *Why the Allies Won*. New York: Norton, 1995.

Paice, Edward. *World War I: The African Front*. New York: Pegasus, 2010.

Pakenham, Thomas. *The Boer War*. London: HarperPerennial, 1979.

Pamuk, Sevket. "The Black Death and the Origins of the 'Great Divergence' Across Europe, 1300–1600." *European Review of Economic History* 11 (2007), pp. 289–317.

Parchami, Ali. *Hegemonic Peace and Empire: The Pax Romana, Britannica, and Americana*. London: Routledge, 2009.

Parker, Geoffrey. *The Military Revolution: Military Innovation and the Rise of the West, 1500–1800*. 2nd ed. Cambridge, U.K.: Cambridge University Press, 1996.

Parkin, Jon. *Taming the Leviathan: The Reception of the Political and Religious Ideas of Thomas Hobbes in England, 1640–1700*. Cambridge, U.K.: Cambridge University Press, 2007.

Parthasarathi, Prasannan. *Why Europe Grew Rich and Asia Did Not: Global Economic Divergence, 1600–1850*. Cambridge, U.K.: Cambridge University Press, 2011.

Patterson, James. *Grand Expectations: The United States, 1945–1974*. New York: Oxford University Press, 1996.

Pauketat, Timothy. *Ancient Cahokia and the Mississippians*. Cambridge, U.K.: Cambridge University Press, 2004.

Payne, James. *A History of Force: Exploring the Worldwide Movement Against Habits of Coercion, Bloodshed, and Mayhem*. Sandpoint, Idaho: Lytton, 2004.

Pearson, M. N. *The Portuguese in India*. Cambridge, U.K.: Cambridge University Press, 1987.

Peattie, Mark. *Ishiwara Kanji and Japan's Confrontation with the West*. Princeton, N.J.: Princeton University Press, 1975.

Perdue, Peter. *China Marches West: The Qing Conquest of Central Eurasia*. Cambridge, Mass.: Harvard University Press, 2005.

Perkins, Bradford. *The Great Rapprochement: England and the United States, 1895–1914*. London: Athenaeum, 1968.

Pertner, A., et al. "Radiologic Proof of the Iceman's Cause of Death (ca. 5,300 BP)." *Journal of Archaeological Science* 34 (2007), pp. 1784–86.

Phillipson, Nicholas. *Adam Smith: An Enlightened Life*. New Haven, Conn.: Yale University Press, 2010.

Piggott, Stuart. *The Earliest Wheeled Transport*. Ithaca, N.Y.: Cornell University Press, 1983.

Pikirayi, Innocent, and Joseph Vogel. *The Zimbabwe Culture: Origins and Decline of Southern Zambezian States*. Walnut Creek, Calif.: AltaMira Press, 2001.

Pincus, Steve. *1688: The First Modern Revolution*. New Haven, Conn.: Yale University Press, 2010.

Pinker, Steven. *How the Mind Works*. New York: Norton, 1997.

———. *The Blank Slate: The Modern Denial of Human Nature*. New York: Viking, 2002.

———. *The Better Angels of Our Nature: Why Violence Has Declined*. New York: Viking, 2011.

Pohl, John. *Aztec Warrior, AD 1325–1521*. Oxford: Osprey, 2001.

Porch, Douglas. *Wars of Empire*. Washington, D.C.: Smithsonian, 2000.

Porter, Andrew, ed. *The Oxford History of the British Empire*. Vol. 3, *The Nineteenth Century*. Oxford: Oxford University Press, 1999.

Posen, Barry. "Pull Back: The Case for a Less Activist Foreign Policy." *Foreign Affairs* 92.1 (January/February 2013), pp. 116–28.

Potter, James, and Jason Chuipka. "Perimortem Mutilation of Human Remains in an Early Village in the American Southwest." *Journal of Anthropological Archaeology* 29 (2010), pp. 507–23.

Potts, R. "Paleoenvironmental Basis of Cognitive Evolution in Great Apes." *American Journal of Primatology* 62 (2004), pp. 209–28.

Poulter, Andrew. *Nicopolis ad Istrum: A Roman, Late Roman, and Early Byzantine City: Excavations, 1985–1992*. London: Society for the Promotion of Roman Studies, 1995.

Poundstone, William. *Prisoner's Dilemma: John von Neumann, Game Theory, and the Puzzle of the Bomb*. New York: Random House, 1992.

Power, Margaret. *The Egalitarians—Human and Chimpanzee: An Anthropological View of Social Organization*. Cambridge, U.K.: Cambridge University Press, 1991.

Price-Smith, Andrew. *Contagion and Chaos: Disease, Ecology, and National Security in the Era of Globalization*. Cambridge, Mass.: MIT Press, 2009.

Pridemore, William. *Ruling Russia: Law, Crime, and Justice in a Changing Society*. Lanham, Md.: Rowman and Littlefield, 2007.

Qing, Jiang. *A Confucian Constitutional Order: How China's Ancient Past Can Shape Its Political Future*. Princeton, N.J.: Princeton University Press, 2012.

Raaflaub, Kurt, and Nathan Rosenstein, eds. *War and Society in the Ancient and Medieval Worlds*. Cambridge, Mass.: Harvard University Press, 1999.

Raaflaub, Kurt, et al. *Origins of Democracy in Ancient Greece*. Berkeley: University of California Press, 2007.

Raine, Adrian. *The Anatomy of Violence: The Biological Roots of Crime*. New York: Pantheon, 2013.

Rance, Philip. "Battle." In Sabin et al. 2007, pp. 342–78.

Rangarajan, L. N., ed. and trans. *Kautilya, The Arthashastra*. New Delhi: Penguin Books India, 1992.

Rasmussen, Morten, et al. "An Aboriginal Australian Genome Reveals Separate Human Dispersals into Asia." *Science* 334 (2011), pp. 94–98.

Rathbone, Dominic. "The 'Muziris' Papyrus (SB XVIII 13167): Financing Roman Trade with India." In *Alexandrian Studies II in Honour of Mostafa el Abbadi*, pp. 39–50. Bulletin de la Société d'Archéologie d'Alexandrie 46. Alexandria, 2001.

Raychaudhuri, Hemchandra. *Political History of Ancient India*. 8th ed. Delhi: Oxford University Press, 1996.

Reid, Peter. *Medieval Warfare: Triumph and Domination in the Wars of the Middle Ages*. New York: Carroll & Graf, 2007.

Reynolds, David. *Origins of the Cold War: International Perspectives*. New Haven, Conn.: Yale University Press, 1994.

———. *One World Divisible: A Global History Since 1945*. New York: Norton, 2000.

Reynolds, Susan. *Fiefs and Vassals: The Medieval Evidence Reinterpreted*. Oxford: Oxford University Press, 1994.

Rhodes, Richard. *The Making of the Atomic Bomb*. New York: Simon & Schuster, 1987.

———. *Dark Sun: The Making of the Hydrogen Bomb*. New York: Simon & Schuster, 1996.

———. *Arsenals of Folly: The Making of the Nuclear Arms Race*. New York: Knopf, 2007.

———. *Twilight of the Bombs: Recent Challenges, New Dangers, and the Prospects for a World Without Nuclear Weapons*. New York: Vintage, 2010.

Rich, John, and Graham Shipley, eds. *War and Society in the Roman World*. London: Routledge, 1993.

Richards, John. *The Mughal Empire*. Cambridge, U.K.: Cambridge University Press, 1994.

Richardson, Lewis Fry. *Statistics of Deadly Quarrels*. Pacific Grove, Calif.: Boxwood Press, 1960.

Ricklefs, Robert. *The Economy of Nature*. 5th ed. New York: Freeman, 2001.

Ricks, Thomas. *Fiasco: The American Military Adventure in Iraq*. New York: Penguin, 2006.

———. *The Gamble: General Petraeus and the American Military Adventure in Iraq, 2006–2008*. New York: Penguin, 2009.

Ridley, Matthew. *The Red Queen: Sex and the Evolution of Human Nature*. New York: Penguin, 1993.

———. *The Origins of Virtue: Human Instincts and the Evolution of Cooperation*. New York: Penguin, 1996.

Riesman, David. *Abundance for What?* Garden City, N.Y.: Doubleday, 1964.

Rifkin, Jeremy. *The Third Industrial Revolution: How Lateral Power Is Transforming Energy, the Economy, and the World*. New York: Palgrave Macmillan, 2011.

Riggsby, Andrew. *Crime and Community in Ciceronian Rome*. Austin: University of Texas Press, 1999.

Rightmire, G. Philip. "Brain Size and Encephalization in Early- to Mid-Pleistocene *Homo*." *American Journal of Physical Anthropology* 124 (2004), pp. 109–23.

Roberts, Adam. "Lives and Statistics: Are 90% of War Victims Civilians?" *Survival* 52 (2010), pp. 115–36.

Roberts, Andrew. *The Storm of War: A New History of the Second World War*. New York: Harper, 2011.

Roberts, D., and D. Turcotte. "Fractality and Self-Organized Criticality of Wars." *Fractals* 6 (1998), pp. 351–57.

Roberts, Michael. *Gustavus Adolphus: A History of Sweden, 1611–1632*. Vol. 2. London: Longman, Green, 1965.

Roberts, Neil. *The Holocene: An Environmental History*. 2nd ed. Oxford: Wiley-Blackwell, 1998.

Robinson, David. *Bandits, Eunuchs, and the Son of Heaven: Rebellion and the Economy of Violence in Mid-Ming China*. Honolulu: University of Hawai'i Press, 2001.

Roffman, Itai, et al. "Stone Tool Production and Utilization by Bonobo-Chimpanzees (*Pan paniscus*)." *Proceedings of the National Academy of Sciences* 109 (2012), pp. 14500–3.

Rogers, Clifford, ed. *The Military Revolution Debate*. Boulder, Colo.: Westview Press, 1995.

Rogers, J. Daniel. "Inner Asian States and Empires: Theories and Synthesis." *Journal of Archaeological Research* 20 (2012), pp. 205–56.

Roscoe, Paul. "*Dead Birds*: The 'Theater' of War Among the Dani." *American Anthropologist* 113 (2011), pp. 56–70.

Rosen, Stephen. *War and Human Nature*. Princeton, N.J.: Princeton University Press, 2005.

Rosenberg, David. "The Origins of Overkill: Nuclear Weapons and American Strategy, 1946–1960." *International Security* 7.4 (1983), pp. 3–71.

Rosenberg, David, and William Brigham Moore. "'Smoking Radiating Ruin at the End of Two Hours': Documents on American Plans for Nuclear War with the Soviet Union, 1954–55." *International Security* 6.3 (1981), pp. 3–38.

Ross, M. "Political Decision-Making and Conflict: Additional Cross-Cultural Codes and Scales." *Ethnology* 22 (1983), pp. 169–82.

———. "Internal and External Conflict and Violence: Cross-Cultural Evidence and a New Analysis." *Journal of Conflict Resolution* 29 (1985), pp. 547–79.

Roth, Randolph. *American Homicide*. Cambridge, Mass.: Belknap Press, 2009.

Rothenberg, Gunther. *The Napoleonic Wars*. Washington, D.C.: Smithsonian, 2006.

Rothman, Mitchell, ed. *Uruk Mesopotamia and Its Neighbors*. Santa Fe, N.M.: School of American Research Press, 2001.

Royal Society. *Brain Waves* Module 3: *Neuroscience, Conflict, and Security*. London: Royal Society, 2012.

Rummel, Rudy. *Death by Government*. Piscataway, N.J.: Transaction, 1994.

——. *Statistics of Democide*. Piscataway, N.J.: Transaction, 1997.

——. "20th-Century Democide." 2002. www.hawaii.edu/powerkills/20TH.HTM.

——. "One-Thirteenth of a Data Point Does Not a Generalization Make: A Reply to Dulic." *Journal of Peace Research* 41 (2004), pp. 103–4.

Runciman, Steven. *The White Rajahs: A History of Sarawak from 1841 to 1946*. Cambridge, U.K.: Cambridge University Press, 1960.

Russell, Peter. *Prince Henry "the Navigator": A Life*. New Haven, Conn.: Yale University Press, 2000.

Ryan, Christopher, and Cacilda Jethá. *Sex at Dawn: How We Mate, Why We Stray, and What It Means for Modern Relationships*. New York: Harper Collins, 2010.

Ryan, Henry Butterfield. *The Vision of Anglo-America*. Cambridge, U.K.: Cambridge University Press, 1987.

Sabin, Philip. *The Third World War Scare in Britain: A Critical Analysis*. London: Macmillan, 1986.

——. "The Face of Roman Battle." *Journal of Roman Studies* 90 (2000), pp. 1–17.

——. *Lost Battles: Reconstructing the Great Clashes of the Ancient World*. London: Continuum, 2007.

Sabin, Philip, et al., eds. *The Cambridge History of Greek and Roman Warfare*. Vol. 2, *Rome from the Late Republic to the Late Empire*. Cambridge, U.K.: Cambridge University Press, 2007.

Sahlins, Marshall. *Apologies to Thucydides: Understanding History as Culture and Vice Versa*. Chicago: University of Chicago Press, 2004.

Sailor, Dylan. *Writing and Empire in Tacitus*. Cambridge, U.K.: Cambridge University Press, 2011.

Sakharov, Andrei. "The Danger of Thermonuclear War." *Foreign Affairs* 61.5 (Summer 1983), pp. 1001–16.

Saletore, R. N. *Early Indian Economic History*. London: Curzon Press, 1973.

Sandbrook, Dominic. *Never Had It So Good, 1956–63: A History of Britain from Suez to the Beatles*. London: Abacus, 2005.

Sanders, Karin. *Bodies in the Bog and the Archaeological Imagination*. Chicago: University of Chicago Press, 2009.

Sanders, William, et al. *The Basin of Mexico: Ecological Processes in the Evolution of a Civilization*. New York: Academic Press, 1979.

Sanger, David. *Confront and Conceal: Obama's Secret Wars and the Surprising Use of American Power*. New York: Crown, 2012.

Sansom, C. J. *Dominion*. London: Mantle, 2012.

Sanz, Crickette, et al. *Tool Use in Animals: Cognition and Ecology*. Cambridge, U.K.: Cambridge University Press, 2013.

Sapolsky, Robert. "A Natural History of Peace." *Foreign Affairs* 85.1 (2006), pp. 104–20.

Sarkar, Jadunath. *A Military History of India*. Calcutta: M. C. Sarkar & Sons, 1960.

Sarkees, Meredith. "The Correlates of War Data on War: An Update to 1997." *Conflict Management and Peace Science* 18 (2000), pp. 123–44.

Savory, Roger, trans. *History of Shah 'Abbas the Great*. Vol. 2. Boulder, Colo.: Westview Press, 1978.

Sawyer, Ralph. *Ancient Chinese Warfare*. New York: Basic Books, 2011.

Scarre, Christopher, and Brian Fagan. *Ancient Civilizations*. 3rd ed. Upper Saddle River, N.J.: Prentice Hall, 2007.

Scheidel, Walter. "A Model of Demographic and Economic Change in Egypt After the Antonine Plague." *Journal of Roman Archaeology* 15 (2002), pp. 97–114.

——. "The Monetary Systems of the Han and Roman Empires." In Walter Scheidel, ed., *Rome and China: Comparative Perspectives on Ancient World Empires*, pp. 137–207. New York: Oxford University Press, 2009.

——. "Real Wages in Early Economies: Evidence for Living Standards from 1800 BCE to 1300 CE." *Journal of the Economic and Social History of the Orient* 53 (2010), pp. 425–62.

——, ed. *The Cambridge Companion to the Roman Economy*. Cambridge, U.K.: Cambridge University Press, 2012.

Scheidel, Walter, and Steven Friesen. "The Size of the Economy and the Distribution of Income in the Roman Empire." *Journal of Roman Studies* 99 (2009), pp. 61–91.

Schelling, Thomas. *The Strategy of Conflict*. Cambridge, Mass.: Harvard University Press, 1960.

Schilardi, Demetrius. "The LHIIIC Period at the Koukounaries Acropolis, Paros." In J. A. MacGillivray and Robin Barber, eds., *The Prehistoric Cyclades*, pp. 184–206. Edinburgh: Edinburgh University Press, 1984.

Schmidt, Eric, and Jared Cohen. *The New Digital Age: Reshaping the Future of People, Nations, and Business*. New York: Knopf, 2013.

Scurlock, Joanne. "Neo-Assyrian Battle Tactics." In G. D. Young et al., eds., *Crossing Boundaries and Linking Horizons: Studies in Honor of Michael C. Astour on His 80th Birthday*, pp. 491–517. Bethesda, Md.: CDC Press, 1997.

Seager, Robin. *Pompey the Great: A Political Biography*. 2nd ed. Oxford: Wiley-Blackwell, 2002.

Sebestyen, Oleg. *Revolution 1989: The Fall of the Soviet Empire*. New York: Random House, 2009.

Sen, Amiya. *Rammohun Roy: A Critical Biography*. New York: Penguin, 2012.

Seneviratna, Anuradha, ed. *King Asoka and Buddhism*. Kandy, Sri Lanka: Buddhist Publication Society, 1994.

Shamasastry, Rudrapatnam, trans. *Arthashastra of Kautilya: Translation*. 8th ed. Mysore: University of Mysore Oriental Library Publications, 1967.

Shambaugh, David. *China Goes Global: The Partial Power*. New York: Oxford University Press, 2013.

Shankman, Paul. *The Trashing of Margaret Mead: Anatomy of an Anthropological Controversy*. Madison: University of Wisconsin Press, 2009.

Sharma, R. K. *Age of the Satavahanas*. 2 vols. Delhi: Aryan Books International, 1999.

Sharma, R. S. "How Feudal Was Indian Feudalism?" *Journal of Peasant Studies* 12 (1985), pp. 19–43.

——. *Early Medieval Indian Society: A Study in Feudalisation*. Leiden: Brill, 2001.

Shaughnessy, Edward. "Historical Perspectives on the Introduction of the Chariot into China." *Harvard Journal of Asiatic Studies* 48 (1988), pp. 189–237.

Shaw, Brent. "Bandits in the Roman Empire." *Past & Present* 105 (1984), pp. 3–52.

——. *Sacred Violence: African Christians and Sectarian Hatred in the Age of Augustine*. Cambridge, U.K.: Cambridge University Press, 2011.

Shea, John. "*Homo* Is as *Homo* Was." *Current Anthropology* 52 (2011), pp. 1–35.

Sheehan, James. *Where Have All the Soldiers Gone? The Transformation of Modern Europe*. Boston: Houghton Mifflin, 2008.

Sheffield, Gary. *Forgotten Victory: The First World War: Myths and Realities*. London: Headline, 2001.

Sheffield, Gary, and Dan Todman, eds. *Command and Control on the Western Front*. London: History Press, 2008.

Sherman, Jason, et al. "Expansionary Dynamics of the Nascent Monte Albán State." *Journal of Anthropological Archaeology* 29 (2010), pp. 278–301.

Sherman, Taylor. *State Violence and Punishment in India*. London: Routledge, 2010.

Shlapak, David, et al. *A Question of Balance: Political Context and Military Aspects of the China-Taiwan Dispute*. Santa Monica, Calif.: RAND Corporation, 2009. Available at www.rand.org/topics/taiwan.html.

Showalter, Dennis. *Tannenberg: Clash of Empires*. Hamden, Conn.: Archon Books, 1991.

Shultz, Susanne, et al. "Stepwise Evolution of Stable Sociability in Primates." *Nature* 479 (2011), pp. 219–22.

Simms, Brendan. *Europe: The Struggle for Supremacy, from 1453 to the Present.* New York: Basic Books, 2013.

Singer, Joel David, and Melvin Small. *The Wages of War, 1816–1965: A Statistical Handbook.* New York: Wiley & Sons, 1972.

Singer, P. W. *Wired for War: The Robotics Revolution and Conflict in the 21st Century.* New York: Penguin, 2009.

Singha, Radhika. *A Despotism of Law: Crime and Justice in Early Colonial India.* Delhi: Oxford University Press, 1998.

Sinor, Denis. *The Cambridge History of Early Inner Asia.* Cambridge, U.K.: Cambridge University Press, 1990.

Skaff, Jonathan Karam. *Sui-Tang China and Its Turko-Mongol Neighbors: Culture, Power, and Connections, 580–800.* New York: Oxford University Press, 2012.

Smith, David J. *One Morning in Sarajevo: 28 June 1914.* London: Phoenix, 2009.

Smith, Laurence. *The World in 2050: Four Forces Shaping Civilization's Northern Future.* New York: Dutton, 2010.

Smith, Michael. *The Aztecs.* 2nd ed. Oxford: Blackwell, 2003.

Smith, Michael, and Lisa Montiel. "The Archaeological Study of Empires and Imperialism in Prehispanic Central Mexico." *Journal of Anthropological Archaeology* 20 (2001), pp. 245–84.

Smith, Michael, and Katharina Schreiber. "New World States and Empires: Economic and Social Organization." *Journal of Anthropological Research* 13 (2005), pp. 189–229.

———. "New World States and Empires: Politics, Religion, and Urbanism." *Journal of Anthropological Research* 14 (2006), pp. 1–52.

Smith, Rupert. *The Utility of Force: The Art of War in the Modern World.* New York: Vintage, 2005.

Snodgrass, Anthony. *Archaeology and the Emergence of Greece.* Edinburgh: Edinburgh University Press, 2006.

Snyder, Timothy. *Bloodlands: Europe Between Hitler and Stalin.* New York: Basic Books, 2010.

Sokolovsky, V. D. *Soviet Military Strategy.* 3rd ed. Ed. Harriet Fast Scott. London: Macdonald and Jane's, 1975.

Somers, Robert. "The End of the T'ang." In Twitchett and Fairbank 1979, pp. 682–788.

Sorokin, Pitirim. *Social and Cultural Change: A Study of Change in Major Systems of Art, Truth, Ethics, Law, and Social Relationships.* Boston: Extending Horizons, 1957.

Spagat, Mike, et al. "Estimating War Deaths: An Arena of Contestation." *Journal of Conflict Resolution* 53 (2009), pp. 934–50.

Spaliger, Anthony. *War in Ancient Egypt: The New Kingdom.* Oxford: Blackwell, 2005.

Spencer, Herbert. "Progress: Its Law and Cause." *Westminster Review* 67 (1857), pp. 445–85.

Spierenburg, Pieter. *A History of Murder: Personal Violence in Europe from the Middle Ages to the Present.* Cambridge, U.K.: Polity, 2008.

Spindler, Konrad. *The Man in the Ice.* New York: Three Rivers Press, 1993.

Spoor, F., et al. "Implications of New Early *Homo* Fossils from Ileret, East of Lake Turkana, Kenya." *Nature* 448 (2007), pp. 688–91.

Springborg, Patricia, ed. *The Cambridge Companion to Hobbes's "Leviathan."* Cambridge, U.K.: Cambridge University Press, 2007.

Spufford, Francis. *Red Plenty: Industry! Progress! Abundance! Inside the Fifties' Soviet Dream.* London: Faber and Faber, 2010.

Stannard, David. *American Holocaust: The Conquest of the New World.* New York: Oxford University Press, 1993.

Stathakopoulos, Dionysios. *Famine and Pestilence in the Late Roman and Early Byzantine Empire.* Burlington, Vt.: Ashgate, 2004.

Steckel, Rick, and John Wallis. "Stones, Bones, and States: A New Approach to the Neolithic Revolution." 2009. www.nber.org/~confer/2007/daes07/steckel.pdf.

Stefflre, Volney. "Long-Term Forecasting and the Problem of Large-Scale Wars." *Futures* 6 (1974), pp. 302–8.

Stevenson, David. *Cataclysm: The First World War as Political Tragedy.* New York: Basic Books, 2004.

St. Joseph, J. K. "The Camp at Durno, Aberdeenshire, and the Site of Mons Graupius." *Britannia* 9 (1978), pp. 271–87.

Stockholm International Peace Research Institute. *SIPRI Yearbook 2012: Armaments, Disarmament, and International Security.* New York: Oxford University Press, 2012.

Stokes, Eric. *The Peasant Armed: The Indian Rebellion of 1857.* Ed. Christopher Bayly. Oxford: Clarendon Press, 1986.

Stokes, Gale. *The Walls Came Tumbling Down: The Collapse of Communism in Eastern Europe.* New York: Oxford University Press, 1993.

Stone, Norman. *The Eastern Front, 1914–17.* New York: Charles Scribner's Sons, 1975.

Strachan, Hew. *The First World War.* Vol. 1, *To Arms.* Oxford: Oxford University Press, 2001.

———. *The First World War.* London: Simon & Schuster, 2003.

———. "Strategy in the Twenty-First Century." In Strachan and Schepers 2011, pp. 503–23.

Strachan, Hew, and Sybille Schepers, eds. *The Changing Character of War.* Oxford: Oxford University Press, 2011.

Streusand, Douglas. *The First Gunpowder Empires: The Ottomans, Safavids, and Mughals.* Boulder, Colo.: Westview Press, 2010.

Stringer, Chris, and Peter Andrews. *The Complete World of Human Evolution.* 2nd ed. London: Thames & Hudson, 2012.

Struve, Lynn, ed. *Voices from the Ming-Qing Cataclysm.* New Haven, Conn.: Yale University Press, 1993.

Sugiyama, Saburo. *Human Sacrifice, Militarism, and Rulership: Materialization of State Ideology at the Feathered Serpent Pyramid, Teotihuacán.* Cambridge, U.K.: Cambridge University Press, 2005.

Sumida, Jon Tetsuro. *In Defense of Naval Supremacy: Finance, Technology, and British Naval Policy, 1899–1914.* London: Routledge, 1989.

———. *Inventing Grand Strategy and Teaching Command.* Baltimore: Johns Hopkins University Press, 1997.

Summers, Harry. *On Strategy: A Critical Analysis of the Vietnam War.* Novato, Calif.: Presidio Press, 1982.

Surbeck, Martin, and Gottfried Hohmann. "Primate Hunting by Bonobos at KuiKotale, Salonga National Park." *Current Biology* 18 (2008), pp. R906–7.

Surbeck, Martin, et al. "Mothers Matter! Maternal Support, Dominance Status, and Mating Success in Male Bonobos (*Pan paniscus*)." *Proceedings of the Royal Society* Series B 278 (2011), pp. 590–98.

Sussman, Robert, and Joshua Marshack. "Are Humans Inherently Killers?" *Global Nonkilling Working Papers* 1 (2010), pp. 7–26.

Swope, Kenneth. *A Dragon's Head and a Serpent's Tail: Ming China and the First Great East Asian War, 1592–1598.* Norman: University of Oklahoma Press, 2009.

Taagepera, Rein. "Size and Duration of Empires: Growth-Decline Curve, 3000 to 600 BC." *Social Science Research* 7 (1978), pp. 180–96.

———. "Size and Duration of Empires: Growth-Decline Curve, 600 BC to 600 AD." *Social Science Research* 8 (1979), pp. 115–38.

Tadmor, Hayim, and S. Yamada. *The Royal Inscriptions of Tiglath-Pileser III (744–727 BC) and Shalmaneser III (726–722 BC), Kings of Assyria.* Winona Lake, Ind.: Eisenbrauns, 2011.

Taya Cook, Haruko, and Theodore Cook. *Japan at War: An Oral History.* New York: Free Press, 1992.

Taylor, A. J. P. *Bismarck: The Man and the Statesman*. New York: Vintage, 1967.

Taylor, Sherman. *State Violence and Punishment in India*. Cambridge, U.K.: Cambridge University Press, 2010.

Tellis, Ashley, and Travis Tanner. *Strategic Asia, 2012–13: China's Military Challenge*. Seattle: National Bureau of Asian Research, 2012.

Thapar, Romila. *Asoka and the Decline of the Mauryas*. 2nd ed. Delhi: Oxford University Press, 1973.

———. *From Lineage to State: Social Formations in the Mid-First Millennium B.C. in the Ganga Valley*. Delhi: Oxford University Press, 1984.

———. *Early India from the Origins to AD 1300*. Berkeley: University of California Press, 2002.

Thapliyal, Uma Prasad. *Warfare in Ancient India: Organizational and Operational Dimensions*. New Delhi: Manohar, 2010.

Thayer, Bradley. *Darwin and International Relations: On the Evolutionary Origins of War and Ethnic Conflict*. Lexington: University Press of Kentucky, 2004.

Themnér, Lotta, and Peter Wallensteen. "Armed Conflicts, 1946–2011." *Journal of Peace Research* 49 (2012), pp. 565–75.

Thomas, Elizabeth Marshall. *The Harmless People*. New York: Knopf, 1959.

———. *The Hidden Life of Dogs*. New York: Houghton Mifflin, 1993.

Thomas, Evan. *Ike's Bluff: President Eisenhower's Secret Battle to Save the World*. New York: Little, Brown, 2012.

Thompson, E. P., and Dan Smith, eds. *Protest and Survive*. Harmondsworth, U.K.: Penguin, 1980.

Thompson, Jo. "A Model of the Biogeographical Journey from *Proto-Pan* to *Pan paniscus*." *Primates* 44 (2003), pp. 191–97.

Tierney, Patrick. "The Fierce Anthropologist." *New Yorker*, October 9, 2000, pp. 50–61.

———. *Darkness at El Dorado: How Scientists and Journalists Devastated the Amazon*. New York: Norton, 2001.

Tilly, Charles. "Reflections on the History of European State-Making." In Charles Tilly, ed., *The Formation of National States in Western Europe*, pp. 3–83. Princeton, N.J.: Princeton University Press, 1975.

———. "War Making and State Making as Organized Crime." In Peter Evans et al., *Bringing the State Back In*, pp. 169–91. Cambridge, U.K.: Cambridge University Press, 1985.

Todd, Malcolm. *The Early Germans*. Oxford: Blackwell, 1992.

Tong, James. *Disorder Under Heaven: Collective Violence in the Ming Dynasty*. Stanford, Calif.: Stanford University Press, 1991.

Tooze, Adam. *The Wages of Destruction: The Making and Breaking of the Nazi Economy*. New York: Penguin, 2006.

Toynbee, Arnold. *A Study of History*. Vol. 2. Abr. ed. New York: Oxford University Press, 1957.

Tracy, James. *The Political Economy of Merchant Empires*. Cambridge, U.K.: Cambridge University Press, 1991.

Trafzer, Clifford. *The Kit Carson Campaign: The Last Great Navajo War*. Norman: University of Oklahoma Press, 1990.

Travers, Timothy. *How the War Was Won: Command and Technology in the British Army on the Western Front, 1917–18*. London: Routledge, 1992.

———. *The Killing Ground*. London: Pen & Sword, 2003.

Treadgold, Warren. *Byzantium and Its Army, 284–1081*. Stanford, Calif.: Stanford University Press, 1995.

———. *A History of the Byzantine State and Society*. Stanford, Calif.: Stanford University Press, 1997.

Trebilcock, Clive. *The Industrialization of the Continental Powers, 1780–1914*. London: Longman, 1981.

Tsunoda, Ryusaku, et al., trans. *Sources of Japanese Tradition*. 2 vols. New York: Columbia University Press, 1964.

Tuchman, Barbara. *A Distant Mirror: The Calamitous Fourteenth Century*. London: Macmillan, 1978.

———. *The March of Folly: From Troy to Vietnam*. New York: Knopf, 1984.

Tuplin, Christopher. "All the King's Horse: In Search of Achaemenid Persian Cavalry." In Fagan and Trundle 2010, pp. 101–82.

Tupper, Benjamin. *Greetings from Afghanistan, Send More Ammo: Dispatches from Taliban Country*. New York: NAL, 2010.

Turchin, Peter. *Historical Dynamics: Why States Rise and Fall*. Princeton, N.J.: Princeton University Press, 2003.

———. *War & Peace & War: The Life Cycles of Imperial Nations*. New York: Pi Press, 2006.

———. "A Theory for Formation of Large Empires." *Journal of Global History* 4 (2009), pp. 191–217.

———. "Warfare and the Evolution of Social Complexity: A Multilevel Selection Approach." *Structure and Dynamics* 4 (2010), pp. 1–37.

Turchin, Peter, and Sergey Nefedov. *Secular Cycles*. Princeton, N.J.: Princeton University Press, 2009.

Turchin, Peter, et al. "East–West Orientation of Historical Empires and Modern Nations." *Journal of World Systems Research* 12 (2006), pp. 218–29.

Turnbull, Colin. *War in Japan, 1467–1615*. Oxford: Osprey, 2002.

———. *Tokugawa Ieyasu*. Oxford: Osprey, 2012.

Turney-High, Harry. *Primitive War: Its Practice and Concepts*. Columbia: University of South Carolina Press, 1949.

Twitchett, Denis, and John K. Fairbank, eds. *The Cambridge History of China*. Vol. 3, *Sui and T'ang China, 589–906*. Pt. 1. Cambridge, U.K.: Cambridge University Press, 1979.

Twitchett, Denis, and Michael Loewe, eds. *The Cambridge History of China*, Vol. 1. *The Ch'in and Han Empires, 221 B.C.–A.D. 220*. Cambridge, U.K.: Cambridge University Press, 1986.

United Nations. "Report of the Special Rapporteur on Extrajudicial, Summary, or Arbitrary Executions," April 9, 2013. www.ohchr.org/Documents/HRBodies/HRCouncil/RegularSession/Session23/A-HRC-23-47_en.pdf.

U.S. Air Force. "United States Air Force Unmanned Aircraft Systems Flight Plan, 2009–2047." 2009. www.fas.org/irp/program/collect/uas_2009.pdf.

van de Mieroop, Marc. *A History of the Ancient Near East*. 2nd ed. Oxford: Blackwell, 2007.

———. *A History of Ancient Egypt*. Oxford: Wiley-Blackwell, 2011.

van Krieken, Robert. *Norbert Elias*. London: Routledge, 1998.

van Tol, Jan, et al. *AirSea Battle: A Point-of-Departure Operational Concept*. Washington, D.C.: Center for Strategic and Budget Assessment, 2010. www.csbaonline.org/publications/2010/05/airsea-battle-concept/.

van Valen, Leigh. "A New Evolutionary Law." *Evolutionary Theory* 1 (1973), pp. 1–30.

van Wees, Hans. "Greeks Bearing Arms: The State, the Leisure Class, and the Display of Weapons in Archaic Greece." In Nick Fisher and Hans van Wees, eds., *Archaic Greece*, pp. 333–78. London: Duckworth, 1998.

———. *Greek Warfare*. London: Duckworth, 2004.

Vanzetti, A., et al. "The Iceman as a Burial." *Antiquity* 84 (2010), pp. 681–92.

Verbruggen, J. F. *The Art of Warfare in Western Europe During the Middle Ages*. 2nd ed. Woodbridge, U.K.: Boydell Press, 1997.

———. "The Role of Cavalry in Medieval Warfare." *Journal of Medieval Military History* 3 (2004), pp. 46–71.

Viner, Joseph. "The Implications of the Atomic Bomb for International Relations." *Transactions of the American Philosophical Society* 90 (1946), pp. 1–11.

Vogel, Ezra. *Japan as Number 1: Lessons for America*. New York: HarperCollins, 1980.

von Ludendorff, Erich. *The General Staff and Its Problems: The History of Relations Between the High Command and the German Imperial Government as Revealed by Official Documents*. Trans. F. A. Holt. New York: E. P. Dutton, 1920.

von Neumann, John, and Oskar Morgenstern. *Theory of Games and Economic Behavior*. Princeton, N.J.: Princeton University Press, 1944.

Walker, Philip. "A Bioarchaeological Perspective on the History of Violence." *Annual Review of Anthropology* 30 (2001), pp. 573–96.

Wang, Zhongshu. *Han Civilization*. New Haven, Conn.: Yale University Press, 1982.

Washbrook, Donald. "India, 1818–1860: The Two Faces of Colonialism." In Porter 1999, pp. 395–421.

Watson, Alexander. *Enduring the Great War: Combat, Morale, and Collapse in the British and German Armies, 1914–1918*. Cambridge, U.K.: Cambridge University Press, 2008.

Watson, Burton, trans. *Records of the Grand Historian*, Vol. 3. New York: Columbia University Press, 1993.

Watson, Peter. *The Great Divide: Nature and Human Nature in the Old World and the New*. New York: Harper, 2012.

Watts, Barry, and Williamson Murray. "Military Innovation in Peacetime." In Murray and Millett 1996, pp. 369–415.

Webster, David. "Ancient Maya Warfare." In Raaflaub and Rosenstein, 1999, pp. 333–60.

Wechsler, Howard. "T'ai-tsung (Reign 626–49) the Consolidator." In Twitchett and Fairbank 1979, pp. 188–241.

Weinberg, Gerhard. *A World at Arms: A Global History of World War II*. 2nd ed. Cambridge, U.K.: Cambridge University Press, 2005.

Weiss, H. K. "Stochastic Models for the Duration and Magnitude of a 'Deadly Quarrel.'" *Operations Research* 11 (1961), pp. 101–21.

Wells, Peter. *The Barbarians Speak: How the Conquered Peoples Shaped Roman Europe*. Princeton, N.J.: Princeton University Press, 1999.

———. *The Battle That Stopped Rome: The Emperor Augustus, Arminius, and the Slaughter of the Roman Legions in the Teutoburg Forest*. New York: Norton, 2003.

Wengrow, David. *The Archaeology of Early Egypt*. Cambridge, U.K.: Cambridge University Press, 2006.

Wheeler, Mortimer. *Still Digging: Adventures in Archaeology*. London: Pan, 1958.

White, Matthew. *The Great Big Book of Horrible Things: The Definitive Chronicle of History's 100 Worst Atrocities*. New York: Norton, 2011.

White, Tim, et al. "*Ardipithecus ramidus*." *Science* 326 (2009), pp. 60–105.

Whiten, Andrew. "The Scope of Culture in Chimpanzees, Humans, and Ancestral Apes." *Philosophical Transactions of the Royal Society B* 366 (2011), pp. 997–1007.

Whiten, Andrew, et al. "Culture Evolves." *Philosophical Transactions of the Royal Society B* 366 (2011), pp. 938–48.

Wickham, Chris. *Framing the Early Middle Ages: Europe and the Mediterranean, 400–800*. Oxford: Oxford University Press, 2005.

Wiener, Martin. *An Empire on Trial: Race, Murder, and Justice Under British Rule, 1870–1935*. Cambridge, U.K.: Cambridge University Press, 2008.

Wilkins, Jayne, et al. "Evidence for Early Hafted Hunting Technology." *Science* 338 (2012), p. 942.

Wilkinson, David. *Deadly Quarrels: Lewis F. Richardson and the Statistical Study of War*. Berkeley: University of California Press, 1980.

Willey, Patrick. *Prehistoric Warfare on the Great Plains: Skeletal Analysis of the Crow Creek Massacre Victims*. New York: Garland, 1990.

Willey, Patrick, et al. "The Osteology and Archaeology of the Crow Canyon Massacre." *Plains Anthropologist* 38 (1993), pp. 227–69.

Williams, John. *The Samoan Journals of John Williams, 1830 and 1832*. Ed. Richard Moyle. Canberra: Australian National University Press, 1984.

Wilson, Edward O. *Sociobiology: The New Synthesis*. Cambridge, Mass.: Harvard University Press, 1975.

Wilson, Michael. "Chimpanzees, Warfare, and the Invention of Peace." In Fry 2013, pp. 361–88.

Wilson, Michael, and Richard Wrangham. "Intergroup Relations in Chimpanzees." *Annual Review of Anthropology* 32 (2003), pp. 363–92.

Wilson, Michael, et al. "Ecological and Social Factors Affect the Occurrence and Outcomes of Intergroup Encounters in Chimpanzees." *Animal Behaviour* 83 (2012), pp. 277–91.

Wilson, Peter. *The Thirty Years' War: Europe's Tragedy*. Cambridge, Mass.: Harvard University Press, 2009.

Witschel, C. "Re-evaluating the Roman West in the 3rd C. A.D." *Journal of Roman Archaeology* 17 (2004), pp. 251–81.

Wittner, Lawrence. *Confronting the Bomb: A Short History of the World Nuclear Disarmament Movement*. Stanford, Calif.: Stanford University Press, 2009.

Wood, Gordon. *The Radicalism of the American Revolution*. New York: Vintage, 1991.

———. *Empire of Liberty: A History of the Early Republic, 1789–1815*. New York: Oxford University Press, 2009.

Woods, John. *The Aqquyunlu: Clan, Confederation, Empire*. 2nd ed. Salt Lake City: University of Utah Press, 1999.

Woodward, Bob. *Bush at War*. New York: Simon & Schuster, 2003.

———. *State of Denial*. New York: Simon & Schuster, 2006.

Woolf, Greg. "Roman Peace." In Rich and Shipley 1993, pp. 171–94.

———. *Tales of the Barbarians: Ethnography and Empire in the Roman West*. Oxford: Wiley-Blackwell, 2011.

———. *Rome: An Empire's Story*. New York: Oxford University Press, 2012.

Wrangham, Richard. "Artificial Feeding of Chimpanzees and Baboons in Their Natural Habitat." *Animal Behaviour* 22 (1974), pp. 83–93.

———. *Catching Fire: How Cooking Made Us Human*. New York: Basic Books, 2009.

———. "Chimpanzee Violence Is a Serious Topic." *Global Nonkilling Working Papers* 1 (2010), pp. 29–47.

———, ed. *Chimpanzee Cultures*. Cambridge, Mass.: Harvard University Press, 2006.

Wrangham, Richard, and Luke Glowacki. "Intergroup Aggression in Chimpanzees and War in Nomadic Hunter-Gatherers." *Human Nature* 53 (2012), pp. 5–29.

Wrangham, Richard, and Dale Peterson. *Demonic Males: Apes and the Origins of Human Violence*. Boston: Houghton Mifflin, 1996.

Wrangham, Richard, and Michael Wilson. "Collective Violence: Comparisons Between Youths and Chimpanzees." *Annals of the New York Academy of Sciences* 1036 (2004), pp. 233–56.

Wright, Lawrence. *The Looming Tower: Al-Qaeda and the Road to 9/11*. New York: Knopf, 2006.

Wright, Quincy. *A Study of War*. 3 vols. Chicago: University of Chicago Press, 1942.

Wright, Rita. *The Ancient Indus*. Cambridge, U.K.: Cambridge University Press, 2009.

Wright, Robert. *Nonzero: The Logic of Human Destiny*. New York: Pantheon, 2000.

Wrigley, E. A. *Energy and the English Industrial Revolution*. Cambridge, U.K.: Cambridge University Press, 2010.

Wu, Xiu-Jie, et al. "Antemortem Trauma and Survival in the Late Middle Pleistocene Human Cranium from Maba, South China." *Proceedings of the National Academy of Sciences* 108 (2011), pp. 19558–62.

Yadin, Yigael. *The Art of Warfare in Biblical Lands*. 2 vols. New York: McGraw-Hill, 1963.

Yalom, Marilyn. *A History of the Breast*. New York: Ballantine, 1998.

Yan, Xuetong. *Ancient Chinese Thought, Modern Chinese Power*. Trans. Edmund Ryden. Princeton, N.J.: Princeton University Press, 2011.

Yang, Anand, ed. *Crime and Criminality in British India*. Tucson: University of Arizona Press, 1985.

Yasuba, Yasukichi. "Did Japan Ever Suffer from a Shortage of Natural Resources Before World War II?" *Journal of Economic History* 56 (1996), pp. 543–60.

Ye, Zicheng. *Inside China's Grand Strategy: The Perspective from the People's Republic*. Trans. Guoli Liu and Steven Levine. Lexington: University Press of Kentucky, 2010.

Yergin, Daniel. *The Prize: The Epic Quest for Oil, Money & Power*. New York: Free Press, 1991.

Yerkes, Robert. *Almost Human*. London: Jonathan Cape, 1925.

Yun-Castalilla, Bartolomé, et al., eds. *The Rise of Fiscal States: A Global History, 1500–1914*. Cambridge, U.K.: Cambridge University Press, 2012.

Zabecki, David. *The German 1918 Offensives: A Case Study in the Operational Level of War*. London: Routledge, 2006.

Zakheim, Dov. "The Military Buildup." In Eric Schmertz et al., eds., *President Reagan and the World*, pp. 205–16. Westport, Conn.: Greenwood Press, 1997.

Zheng, Bijian. "China's 'Peaceful Rise' to Great-Power Status." *Foreign Affairs* 84.5 (2005), pp. 18–24.

Zias, J., and E. Sekeles. "The Crucified Man from Giv'at ha-Mivtar." *Israel Exploration Journal* 35 (1985), pp. 22–27.

Zimmerman, Larry, and Lawrence Bradley. "The Crow Canyon Massacre." *Plains Anthropologist* 38 (1993), pp. 215–26.

Zuber, Terence. "The Schlieffen Plan Reconsidered." *War in History* 6 (1999), pp. 262–305.

———. *The Real German War Plan, 1904–14*. London: History Press, 2011.

ACKNOWLEDGMENTS

In writing this book, I received generous help and support from many, many people. I could not have written the book without the support of Stanford University's School of Humanities and Sciences and Hoover Institution or the encouragement, patience, and good cheer of my wife, Kathy St. John.

Daron Acemoglu, David Berkey, Laura Betzig, Mat Burrows, Eric Chinski, Daniel Crewe, Banning Garrett, Azar Gat, Deborah Gordon, Steve Haber, David Holloway, Parag Khanna, Phil Kleinheinz, Steve LeBlanc, Ramez Naam, Josh Ober, Steve Pinker, Jim Robinson, Walter Scheidel, Kathy St. John, Peter Turchin, Richard Wrangham, and Amy Zegart read and commented on the book as I was writing it. I thank them again for their advice and support and apologize for the places where I was too stubborn to take it or too obtuse to understand it.

Peter Abigail, Daron Acemoglu, David Armitage, Al Bergesen, Mat Burrows, Banning Garrett, Elhanan Helpman, Mike McCormick, Dick O'Neill, Jim Robinson, Peter Turchin, and Norman Vasu invited me to highly informative meetings and conferences, and Karl Eikenberry included me on trips to the National Training Center at Fort Irwin, California, and Nellis and Creech Air Force Bases in Nevada. I thank all of them, as well as Viet Luong, Mark Pye, and the personnel at Fort Irwin, Nellis, and Creech for making the visits so valuable.

Laura Betzig, George Cowgill, Azar Gat, Steve Haber, David Laitin, Peter Turchin, and Richard Wrangham allowed me to read unpublished work, and, in addition to all the above, Jost Crouwel, Jared Diamond, Niall Ferguson, Victor Hanson, Bob Horn, Paul Kennedy, Karla Kierkegaard, Adrienne Mayor, Josh Ober, Richard Saller, Larry Smith, Mike Smith, Hew Strachan, Barry Strauss, Rob Tempio, and Barry Weingast allowed me to engage them in long conversations, more or less related to the book, that I found fascinating.

Finally, this book would never have seen the light of day without the encouragement of my agents, Sandy Dijkstra and Arabella Stein, or my editors, Eric Chinski at Farrar, Straus and Giroux and Daniel Crewe at Profile. They and their teams have been wonderful to work with in every way.

INDEX

Page numbers in *italics* refer to illustrations.